W9-AOR-931

TOUCHSTONE

*Books by David Caute*

POLITICAL STUDIES

Communism and the French Intellectuals, 1914–60
The Left in Europe Since 1789
Essential Writings of Karl Marx (*Editor*)
Frantz Fanon
The Fellow-Travellers: a Postscript to the Enlightenment
The Great Fear: The Anti-Communist Purge under Truman and
    Eisenhower

NOVELS

At Fever Pitch
Comrade Jacob
The Decline of the West
The Occupation

OTHERS

The Illusion: An Essay on Politics, Theatre and the Novel
The Demonstration, *a play*
Collisions. Essays and Reviews
Cuba, Yes?

# The

## *The Anti-Communist Purge*

A Touchstone Book
Published by Simon and Schuster

# Great Fear

*Under Truman and Eisenhower*

**David Caute**

Copyright © 1978 by David Caute
All rights reserved
including the right of reproduction
in whole or in part in any form

First Touchstone Edition, 1979
Published by SIMON and SCHUSTER
A Division of Gulf & Western Corporation
Simon & Schuster Building
Rockefeller Center
1230 Avenue of the Americas
New York, New York 10020

Manufactured in the United States of America

1   2   3   4   5   6   7   8   9   10

Library of Congress Cataloging in Publication Data

Caute, David.
    The great fear.

    (A Touchstone book)
    Bibliography: p.
    Includes index.
    1. Anti-communist movements—United States.  2. United States—Politics
and government—1945-1953.  3. United States—Politics and government—
1953-1961.  4. Right and left (Political science)  5. Eisenhower, Dwight David,
Pres. U.S., 1890-1969.  6. Truman, Harry S., Pres. U.S., 1884-1972.  I. Title
E743.5.C35  1979    322.4'2    78-26755

ISBN 0-671-22682-7
ISBN 0-671-24848-0 Pbk.

*To Martha*

# Contents

# Preface

On May 15, 1954, in the high summer of the great fear, the Emergency Civil Liberties Committee warned that "the threat to civil liberties in the United States today is the most serious in the history of our country." It was indeed a desperate time, a time when the words "democracy" and "freedom" resembled gaudy advertising slogans suspended above an intersection where panic, prejudice, suspicion, cowardice and demagogic ambition constantly collided in a bedlam of recriminations. The wealthiest, most secure nation in the world was sweat-drenched in fear.

From New York to San Diego, from Seattle to Miami, federal, state and municipal employees worried about their pasts, their student indiscretions, their slenderest associations, and hoped that the letter from the loyalty board would never come. Some hastened to save their own skin by denouncing a colleague. Young men inducted into the armed forces were suddenly confronted with political allegations and the threat of a dishonorable discharge. On Capitol Hill the running was now made by professional scalp-hunters; the statute books groaned under several seasons of legislation designed to outlaw dissent. Under harsh klieg lights Congressional inquisitors roasted civil servants, film stars, industrial workers, lawyers, teachers, writers and trade unionists, while reporters jostled in the corridors, panting for another allegation—*any* allegation—from the Senator whose manure was publicity. "NEW PROBE!"

In schools, universities, town halls and local professional associations, a continuous, pious mumbling of oaths was heard—the liturgy of fear. "I do swear, I do affirm . . ." What? "That I am not, was not,

never have been . . . do not intend . . ." To think for myself; or to
join any organization of which the Attorney General might happen to
disapprove. In Russia, students reported dissident parents to their
teachers; to protect America against such deformities, American students now reported unorthodox teachers to their parents.

Resident aliens, many of them elderly people who had lived in
the United States for the greater part of their adult lives, were pulled
from their homes by Immigration officers. To wrench a man from his
American wife and children, to expel him to some distant part of the
world whose language was often foreign to him, was apparently democracy's price for survival. While many American citizens who criticized American foreign policy were deprived of passports, of the right
to travel, aliens who were deemed too subversive to enter were held
on Ellis Island. So few foreign scientists were admitted to the land of
the free that one international conference after another had to be
canceled.

Stalking their prey across the land, two-by-two, prowled the FBI,
J. Edgar Hoover's G-men, hunters of radicalism, whose dreary war of
shadows was occasionally rewarded with real red meat: the arrest, in
the early hours of the morning, of Communist Party leaders. Oozing
from the Bureau into the bloodstream of the nation's working life, the
informers (the bent, the broken, the bought) masqueraded as radicals, drew up lists, took photographs, provoked events, mingled fiction with fact in their reports. Their fantasies filled millions of pages.

A new breed bestrode the land: the security officer. Fordham
men now decided whether Harvard men were fit to work. The long
shadow of the security officer fell across factories, dockyards, ships,
offices. A generation of workers learned to conform or to move on.
Those who moved on learned how to change their identities, to mi-
grate, to lose their trackers, to resurface as immaculate Americans.
But in the process careers were ruined beyond retrieve, marriages
broke up, children were alienated and abused, fathers sat for hours,
stunned, staring blankly at the wall.

The great professional associations collapsed before the tidal
wave, sacrificing their own black sheep to the wolves. While blacklists
flourished, mean, cynical opportunists capitalized on the insecurities,
the missing center of gravity, of a nation of immigrants. Familiar
faces disappeared from film and television screens, radio lost some of
its richest voices.

While the columnists of the witch-hunting press uttered a daily
screech of hatred, innuendo and calumny, the great liberal newspapers trembled and wavered; the purge emerged in their pages as a
mistake, an injustice, an outrage, only when it pricked people who
weren't really witches at all. McCarthy's crime was to add Cold War

liberals to their own Attorney General's list, to give them a dose of their own medicine. McCarthy was giving a good cause a bad name.

When I came to this subject some twenty years post-McCarthy, conditions for research were increasingly favorable; the ice cap which still froze the victims into postures of silence in the middle sixties had now lifted. In the summer of Nixon's disgrace the surviving radicals of the Old Left came out to bask and tell their stories and waggle their tails a bit. This made my task both easier and more congenial. Even so, I am aware that some of those who are named in these pages will not be pleased, and may even feel that whatever havoc history may inflict, historians have no license to repeat.

I am much indebted: first, to that (almost universal) trait in the American psyche that values openness, accessibility, communication, the right to know. Secondly, to those many Americans who made time, rapidly and generously, for the inquiring stranger come among them. More particularly, I am grateful to the following for their kind assistance: the staff of the ACLU Library, Los Angeles; the ACLU Library, New York; the Bodleian Library, Oxford; the British Library, London; Mr. Joseph Oldenburg of the Burton Historical Collection, Detroit Public Library; the staff of the Harvard Law School Library; the Institute for Advanced Legal Studies, London; the Institute of Education, London; the Institute for United States Studies, London; the London Library; the New York Public Library; Nuffield College Library, Oxford; the Press Library, Royal Institute of International Affairs, London; Princeton University Library; Rhodes House Library, Oxford; the Senate House Library of the University of London; Mr. J. Burt and the staff of the Department of Documents and Manuscripts, Sussex University Library; the staff of the University of California Library, Irvine, Los Angeles and Berkeley; Mr. Philip Mason and the staff of the Walter Reuther Library of Labor History and Urban Affairs, Detroit; the staff of the Widener Library, Harvard.

The following kindly allowed me to study private collections of documents in their possession or custody: Mr. Ernest Besig, of San Francisco; Mr. Frank J. Donner, of Norwalk, Connecticut; the National Lawyers Guild, New York; Mrs. Bonté Duran, of Cambridge, England, and her family; Mr. Geoffrey Ryan, of New York; the late Professor H. H. Wilson, of Princeton University; Mr. Robert Z. Lewis and Mr. James Mauro, of United Electrical, Radio and Machine Workers of America, New York; Mr. Tristram Powell, of London, who kindly showed me primary sources he had gathered to make his BBC television documentary "Hollywood On Trial," as well as the transcript of the program.

I owe a great debt to the many Americans (and un-Americans)

who found the time and the energy to grant me an interview. Some wished to remain anonymous; it is a pleasure to acknowledge those who did not: Mr. Ernest Besig, Mr. Leonard Boudin, Professor Ralph S. Brown, Jr., Mr. Harold I. Cammer, Professor John Caughey, Mrs. Rose Chernin, Professor Vern Countryman, Mr. Frank J. Donner, Mrs. Lillian Doran, Professor Thomas I. Emerson, Mr. David Englestein, Mrs. Mary Englestein, Professor Wendell Furry, Mr. Simon Gerson, Mr. Aubrey Grossman, Mr. Alger Hiss, Mr. Abraham Isserman, Mr. Murray Kempton, Mr. Sam Kushner, Mr. Robert Z. Lewis, Mr. James Mauro, Mr. Carey McWilliams, Mr. Edmund H. North, Mr. William Pomeroy, Professor Telford Taylor, Mrs. Edith Tiger, Mr. Robert E. Treuhaft, Mr. Rowland Watts, Mr. Alden Whitman, the late Professor H. H. Wilson, Mr. Nathan Witt.

For helpful critical comments on sections of the text, I am grateful to Professor Ralph S. Brown, Jr., Mr. Harold I. Cammer, Mr. Frank J. Donner, Mrs. Bonté Duran, Mr. Edmund H. North, Mr. Geoffrey Ryan, Mr. Alden Whitman, the late Professor H. H. Wilson.

For many kindnesses and introductions I wish also to thank: Professor H. C. Allen, Ms. Judy Baston, Mr. Jerome Bakst, Mr. Adam Bennion, Mrs. Connie Bessie, Mr. Sam Bottone, Professor Marcus Cunliffe, Professor John P. Diggins, Professor Richard Frank, Professor and Mrs. Charles Fried, Ms. Angeline Goreau, Ms. Berenice Hoffman, Mr. Anthony Lewis, Mr. Arthur Loubou, Professor Arthur Marder, Mr. James Peck, Professor Gerry Rabkin, Professor and Mrs. Neil Rudenstine, Ms. Yaffa Schlesinger, Professor Hugh Thomas, Mr. Oliver Walston, Professor and Mrs. Robert Wohl, Professor Gerry White.

My son Edward contributed unpaid toil at moments of crisis. For my wife's unwavering support during four years of hard labor, and for her expert help in all phases of production, I am profoundly grateful.

Last but not least, I am grateful to the Arts Council of Great Britain for its generous financial assistance.

"Those who do not believe in the ideology of the United States, shall not be allowed to stay in the United States."

—Attorney General Tom Clark,
addressing the Cathedral Club
of Brooklyn, January 15, 1948

# Introduction

The great fear, like the threat of upheaval and expropriation that inspires it, has been a recurrent phenomenon in the history of the bourgeoisie since the French Revolution. It has occurred in France, Britain, Germany, Italy, Spain and the United States, but not in exactly the same form. Indeed its recurrent modes of thought, feeling, rhetoric and delusion are more consistent than its style of action. Much depends on the strength of the bourgeois-democratic tradition, the resilience of liberal values, and the ability of a particular social order to stage therapeutic rituals of repression that fall short of a genuine head-bashing and blood-letting. In France, Italy and Germany, the blood flowed; in Britain and America, mainly tears.

This point is worth emphasizing at the outset. Dark and discreditable an episode in American history as was the one we are about to describe, the purge of the Truman-Eisenhower era was not on the whole a killer. Although its victims on the pro-Communist Left began to scream "Fascism!" at the first subpoena, the repression never reached the frontiers of fascism. The concentration camps established by the McCarran Act remained empty. Nor are the American Legion and the Veterans of Foreign Wars, even in their most xenophobic, bigoted and physically belligerent moods, to be compared to the German SS or SA. If the FBI tortured the radicals it pursued, it has escaped our attention. Shamefully as the American judiciary bowed and bent to the *Realpolitik* of the "American Century," it never completely abdicated its independence and was soon able to stage an admirable recovery of nerve, restoring sap to the Bill of Rights, vitality to the Constitution.

The storms of indignation that America's domestic repressions and imperialist adventures abroad provoke do indeed reflect the genuine adherence of the United States to the liberal-democratic tradition. Thus, when official America sins, she sins doubly; against her victims, and against her own traditions, ideals and rhetoric. Hypocrisy—the gap between professed behavior and actual behavior—gets under our skin as unashamed brutality or flamboyant imperialism do not, partly because it touches a guilty nerve in all of us, partly because it makes a mockery of the idea of progress. For this reason, Stalin's crimes inspire rage and frustration, whereas Hitler's lead to disgust.

Within the framework of modern Anglo-American history, the great fear has repeated itself with chilling mimicry on three occasions: in the 1790s (in England and America), during Woodrow Wilson's second term as President, and in the age of Truman and Eisenhower. In Pitt's England, reformers were identified with revolutionary Jacobins; in McCarthy's America, liberals were called Communists. Heresy was hunted, oaths of loyalty were imposed, professors were ousted, and police spies abounded in all three eras. Pitt's Home Secretary, Henry Dundas, infiltrated his agents into the radical clubs just as J. Edgar Hoover's FBI honeycombed the American CP. And, since it was always difficult to prove that liberals or radicals had actually *done* anything seditious or subversive, it was necessary in both epochs to prosecute them for advocacy, or conspiracy to advocate; for mere words, or even thoughts. Tom Paine was indicted for seditious libel after he published *Rights of Man* (150 years later, Howard Fast's biography of Paine was purged from school libraries), and Thomas Muir was tried for sedition even though he, like the eleven Communist leaders indicted in 1948, denied that he had ever recommended "any means which the Constitution did not sanction." In May 1794, as in the summer of 1951, waves of searches and arrests took place; Pitt, supported by Edmund Burke, had the Commons suspend *habeas corpus* in the same spirit that the Justice Department tried to set prohibitively high bail for Communists indicted under the Smith Act.

In both eras, the great fear was a fear not only of overt acts but also of a contagion, a pestilence of the mind. All contacts with unsterilized outside bodies, whether they be men, printed materials or ideas, excited suspicion. The key notion was guilt by association. Even so, there was a difference between the two eras: in the absence of specific and provable deeds, British juries were not impressed and tended to acquit the radicals, whereas American juries of the Truman-Eisenhower era resembled a rubber stamp with twelve heads.

A few years after the upper classes of England were seized by fear of Jacobinism, the same anxiety gripped the American bourgeoisie.

Across the Atlantic no less than in the Old Country, the contagious power of the French Revolution agitated defenders of the social and religious *ordre établi*. The myth of the secret order of Illuminati sprang up, fanned by John Robison's *Proofs of a Conspiracy*, a conspiracy apparently dedicated to the overthrow not only of all government but also of Christianity itself. In a style all too familiar to students of McCarthy, the New England Congregationalist minister Jedidiah Morse thundered in 1799: "I have now in my possession complete and indubitable proof . . . an official, authenticated list of names, ages, places of nativity, professions, etc., of the officers and members of a Society of *Illuminati* . . . instituted in Virginia, by the *Grand Orient* of FRANCE."

Exploiting the prevailing fear and the concomitant weakening of liberal inhibitions, the Federalists in July 1798 passed the notorious Alien and Sedition Acts (Harry S. Truman recommended that all Americans read them as an example of repression), which, like most of the legislation and much of the administrative action of the Truman era, concussed the First Amendment:

> . . . if any person shall write, print, utter or publish, or shall knowingly and willingly assist in [the same] . . . any false, scandalous and malicious writing . . . against this government . . . or either house of the Congress . . . or the President . . . or to stir up sedition . . . or to excite any unlawful combinations . . . or to aid any hostile designs of any foreign nation . . .

Pointing an accusing finger at Jefferson's Republican Party, the Federalists warned that the Illuminati planned "to worm its votaries into all offices of trust . . . that the weapon of government, upon signal given, may be turned against itself."

During the Red Scare that followed the First World War, the *Wall Street Journal* declared on December 23, 1919: "We talk of parlor Bolshevists, but what of those other Bolshevists, in the Cabinet, or at any rate near the throne?" Twenty-five years later, in 1944, Representative Clare Boothe Luce announced that the Communist Party "has gone underground, after the fashion of termites, into the Democratic Party."

It may well be that an acute student of human affairs will detect these parallels, these repeated motifs, these recurring structures of thought and expression, not merely within the conservative or bourgeois property-defending camp, but even in more broadly defined situations. Frequently it was the Left that accused the Right of serving a foreign power or an international Force of Evil, Capital. The axioms of guilt by association are by no means foreign to the Left: in the late sixties American radicals pursued the "vital center" by much the same logic, if inverted, as McCarthy had pursued it in the early fifties. The power of subversive words, thoughts even, is nowhere more deeply feared than in the Soviet Union; and those who went on trial in Czechoslovakia after the Red Army had restored "socialism" there, in August 1968, were accused not of having raised rifles, merely pens. Such cases, common as they are, point to a universal grammar of political conflict that transcends the division between Left and Right, much as in conjugal quarrels couples tend to employ precisely the same arguments they only yesterday condemned in their partners.

The repression that began in 1917, when America entered the war, was more intense and physically more violent than the patient, bureaucratic, legalistic repression that endured for about fifteen years after the Second World War. In New York City, spectacular raids staged in June and November 1919 resulted in the arrest of several thousand radicals, while Attorney General A. Mitchell Palmer's deportation drive (he referred to "thousands of aliens . . . direct allies of Trotsky") culminated in mass deportations (249 on a single ship in December 1919) far in excess of anything the Justice Department achieved in the time of Truman and Eisenhower. About 1,400 people were arrested under state sedition laws in 1919–20; of them some 300 were convicted and imprisoned. But in the 1940s and 1950s defense organizations were better financed, and judges generally were more inclined to accord even radicals the benefits of due process.

Nevertheless, one suspects that the second repression was the more profoundly corrupting, the more corrosive of habits of tolerance and fair play. It was now that American liberalism failed to sustain the authentically liberal values and standards of tolerance that persisted in Britain despite that country's commitment to NATO, the Korean war, the Berlin airlift, and a general posture of confrontation with Russia (to whose power Britain is obviously more vulnerable than the United States). The British of the Attlee era, unlike the British of the Pitt era or of the sixteenth-century confrontation with Catholic Spain, kept their heads: teachers and professors were not purged; dismissals in the civil service were few and confined mainly to genuinely sensitive jobs; Parliament did not go witch hunting; there was no Un-British Activities Committee to whip up enmity toward radicals or fellow travelers; no rash of loyalty oaths brought disgrace to the professions; welfare benefits were not denied to Communist veterans or their widows; union officials were not required by law to sign non-Communist affidavits; panels of military officers did not hound industrial workers from their jobs or question them as to how they had voted; seamen were not swept off ships by waves of prejudice; CP leaders were not sent to prison for being Communists; there was no government list of proscribed organizations . . . Need one go on? Having stumbled through the Cold War with this myopic attitude, Britain emerged with just as few Communists as before.

In America there was an artificial straining and striving for social cohesion and national unity. In 1951, for example, the American Heritage Foundation summoned delegates from the forty-eight states to gather and draft a Re-Declaration of Faith in the American Dream. Bells were to peal not only as a symbol of high morale, but also as a "gesture of defiance to the Enemy"—the Alien, the Nonconformist, the Critical Force. Here, then, was a palpable lack of trust in the Other, who he was, where he came from, what dark gods he might worship in his strange language, and whether he qualified as a good American or a dangerous "un-American." If, as was clearly the case, American capitalism, business, free enterprise, prosperity and liberty had little to fear from domestic Communism, we must, even granting the force of collective delusion, look elsewhere for the real sources of the "anti-Communist" hysteria; look toward the unassimilated alien, the hyphenated American still carrying the contagion of Old-World Socialism, that creeping, gradualist, Fabian New Dealism, which posed so insidious a threat to unbridled Business, big or small.

Not widely noticed has been the fact that McCarthy (as distinct from many of his supporters) was the first right-wing demagogue in American history who denounced no specific racial, ethnic or religious group (unless it were Harvard professors and Ivy League diplomats!). After the Know-Nothings and other nativist movements had persecuted Catholics for more than a century, Father Charles E. Coughlin aroused Catholic prejudices by branding Jews as Communists and Communists as Jews. Yet McCarthy treated Communism as a perversion to which no man was condemned by birth, only by choice. The reason for this may lie in the fact that the nature of Nazism and the fate of the Jews during the Second World War had made overt racial prejudice (blacks apart), or simply overt prejudice, profoundly unrespectable. Although prejudice against Jews and blacks played its part in the purge (as we shall see), one of the appeals of McCarthyism was that it offered every American, however precarious his ancestry, the chance of being taken for a good American, simply by demonstrating a gut hatred for Commies. In this respect, as an umbrella movement, McCarthyism did closely resemble fascism—but in no other respect.

American liberalism had itself taken on the coloring of latent hysteria. By 1945 America's patriotic imperative had acquired a truly imperialistic and even messianic image of its own mission in the world. This kind of imperialism, particularly rooted in the liberal intelligentsia, is not essentially economic, but rather cultural, idealistic, self-righteous, moral. To this new metaphysical or missionary imperialism it suddenly seemed intolerable that any enemy should challenge the superiority, supremacy and universal relevance of the American way of life. As Professor Robert E. Cushman (a strong civil libertarian, incidentally) put it in 1948: "It has been given to us, as the world's greatest democracy, a post of leadership in the all-important task of establishing our doctrines of civil liberty throughout the world as working principles by which the lives of free nations are to be governed."

What can this "given to us" mean? By God? Of course, by God, by Destiny, by History. And what does "greatest democracy" mean? Most democratic democracy? Or democracy with most money, industrial resources and atomic bombs? It is worth asking these questions because the ideology of the period tended conveniently to blur them, to proceed in a haze of rhetoric and self-congratulation toward frankly repressive postures. In 1954 another liberal professor, Thomas I. Cook, of Princeton, claimed that the American social order had a "universal validity"; it was the liberals rather than the reactionary Right or the heirs of Teddy Roosevelt's Rough Riders, who set the United States on the disastrously interventionist and egotistical course that culminated in the horror of the Vietnam war.

The great fear was not, of course, without its amusing or bizarre episodes. In the District of Columbia a man was refused a license to sell secondhand furniture because he had invoked the Fifth Amendment about Communism. In Indiana professional wrestlers were obliged to take a loyalty oath. When the House Committee on Un-American Activities visited Seattle in 1954, it was greeted not only by the Women's Christian Temperance Union, the Faithful Navigator, the Fourth Degree Knights of Columbus of Tacoma, the Russian All-Cossack Association, and the Gig Harbor Sportsmen's Council, but also by the Little Men's Marching and Chowder Association. A country in which an Official Referee (Frank J. Gregg) could in 1950 grant a woman (Mrs. Maria Careccia, of Utica, New York) an annulment of her marriage solely on the ground that her husband was a Communist, and then boast to reporters that it had never been done before, was surely a country with a claim to a leading role in the human comedy as well as the human tragedy.

# PART ONE

## The Politics
## of Hysteria

# 1

## The Truman Doctrine: Pax Americana

When Harry S. Truman became President of the United States on April 12, 1945, the federal and state statute books were already bristling with anti-Communist legislation. All that was required—and conspicuously lacking under Franklin D. Roosevelt—was the will to enforce it. Two years after the passage of the Foreign Agents Registration Act in 1938, the government had roused itself to prosecute the *Daily Worker*, International Publishers, and World Tourists, Inc., for failure to register with the Justice Department as agents of the Soviet Union. A year later the administration invoked the Alien Registration Act, universally known as the Smith Act, against eighteen Trotskyists of the Socialist Workers Party. (The Smith Act parted company with the honored tradition that only *actions* should be punished. Henceforward words, even thoughts, could cost a man his liberty.) But after the United States and Russia entered the war side by side in 1941, the Democratic administration was understandably reluctant—despite the palpable eagerness of J. Edgar Hoover and the FBI—to persecute American Communists. Indeed, Earl Browder, general secretary of the Communist Party, was amnestied and released from prison.

Such inhibitions were not long to endure under that peppery little bustler, Harry Truman. As the exonerating glow of the wartime alliance evaporated, Truman came under increasing attack from the anti-Communist coalition of embittered Southern Democrats and anti-New Deal Republicans who had been growling and snarling in the wings since the Congressional elections of 1938. On July 2, 1946, the House Civil Service Committee noisily appointed a subcommittee to investigate the loyalty of federal civil servants, which prompted Truman, after the Republican mid-term election victory in November, to noisily appoint his own Temporary Commission on Employee Loyalty. Meanwhile, on July 6, 1946, the passage of the McCarran Rider to the State Department Appropriations Bill had endowed the Secretary of State with powers of summary dismissal "in his absolute discretion" (the Secretaries of the Navy and War Departments had already acquired such powers during the war). The McCarran Rider, renewed annually until 1953, gave Congress a convenient lever for alleging that the Secretary's sense of discretion was more or less Moscow's: on June 10, 1947, the Senate Appropriations Committee wrote George C. Marshall complaining that in the State Department "there is a deliberate, calculated program being carried out not only to protect Communist personnel in high places but to reduce security and intelligence protection to a nullity." The Committee then named nine employees who had been retained although "a hazard to national security," and spoke of "a protégé of Acheson" as "the chief instrument in the subverting of the over-all security program."

The 80th Congress of 1946–47 was a bitterly reactionary one.[1] Representative Clare E. Hoffman (R., Michigan) explained that "from the day that Mrs. Roosevelt appeared with a group of Communists before the Dies Committee, the New Deal, and more recently, the Truman administration, has been coddling and encouraging Communists, who, in federal positions, thrive on the taxpayers' dollars." [2] No feud between the White House and Congress had raged for so long. A coalition of Republicans and Dixiecrats blocked Truman's legislation, overrode his vetoes, abused him personally, investigated his administrative personnel, and continuously screamed about Communist infiltration.

The coming election, declared Republican National Committee chairman B. Carroll Reece in June 1946, would offer a stark choice between "Communism and Republicanism," since the "policy-making force of the Democratic Party" was now committed to the Soviet Union: was not the Political Action Committee (PAC) of the CIO loudly backing the Democratic Party? House Republican leader Joseph W. Martin declared: "The people will vote tomorrow between chaos, confusion, bankruptcy, state socialism or communism, and the preservation of our American life . . ." In the Wisconsin Senatorial campaign Joseph R. McCarthy accused his Democratic opponent, Professor Howard McMurray, of being "Communistically inclined," and offered a taste of things to come three years later by fabricating a *Daily Worker* reference to McMurray as a sympathizer. McCarthy also accused him of "being used by the Communist-controlled PAC." Meanwhile, in California Richard M. Nixon, also fighting for election as a freshman, put it out that "A vote for Nixon is a vote against the Communist-dominated PAC with its gigantic slush fund." Three days before the election the Nixon campaign headquarters accused the Democratic incumbent, Jerry Voorhis, of consistently voting "the Moscow-PAC-Henry Wallace line." There is of course no way of measuring the impact of such propaganda on voting figures: in the event, just as McCarthy red-baited his way into the Senate, so Nixon did into the House, winning by 65,586 votes to 49,994.

In the State of Washington charges of Communist connections were raised even in the Democratic primaries, before the Republicans handed out the same medicine to the official Democratic candidates. These tactics evidently paid off; the reactionary Harry Cain became a U.S. Senator, and Homer Jones, former State commander of the American Legion, swept out Congressman Hugh De Lacy, the candidate of the extreme Left. Republicans won five of the six seats in the House, and two thirds of the State Assembly. Shortly after the election defeat, the right-wing Democratic leaders began a witch hunt within the party.[3]

The 1946 election, a disaster for the Democrats, only reinforced faith in the efficacy of red-baiting. The Democratic share of the House fell from 242 seats in 1944 to 188 in 1946 (and from a peak of 331 in 1936). Candidates supported by the PAC-CIO won in only 75 of the 318 races they entered. Owing to public apathy or cynicism, only three eighths of the eligible electorate actually voted, and the Democratic vote plummeted from 25 to 15 million.

The battle won, the Republican legislators girded themselves for a new attack on the White House. As a result, the loyalty program became a shuttlecock in party politics;[4] it was largely to steal the Republicans' thunder that Truman signed Executive Order 9835, which launched a purge of the federal civil service and inspired imitative purges at every level of American working life. The President himself later confided to Clifford J. Durr that the loyalty order and its accompanying heresy index, the Attorney General's list, was designed mainly to take the ball away from the House Committee on Un-American Activities (HCUA) under its pugnaciously reactionary chairman, J. Parnell Thomas (R., New Jersey).

With this end in view, the administration strove to demonstrate its Americanism. In March 1947, Secretary of Labor Lewis B. Schwellenbach publicly demanded that the CP be outlawed: "Why should they be able to elect people to public office?" In November Commissioner of Education John W. Studebaker embarked on an anti-Communist speaking tour, and the government organized a series of mass demonstrations at which its employees took a "freedom pledge" and sang "God Bless America." From September 1947 until December of the following year, a red-white-and-blue Freedom Train sponsored by Attorney General Tom Clark and the American Heritage Foundation toured the country. The ACLU report for 1946–47 referred to "an atmosphere increasingly hostile to the liberties of organized labor, the political left and many minorities. . . . Excitement, bordering on hysteria, characterized the public approach to any issue related to Communism." [5]

Clark deserves our particular attention. A Texas lawyer who had joined the Justice Department in 1937 and then risen through the Criminal Division to the rank of Assistant Attorney General, he was appointed Attorney General by Truman in 1945 and brought to the post a conservatism verging on bigotry. Constantly he urged Truman to repatriate "alien enemies" and to expand the investigating authority of the FBI. The Communists, he informed the Chicago Bar Association in June 1946, "are driving law enforcement in this country to the end of its tether," citing as an example the previously uncodified crime of "conspiracy to divide our people, to discredit our institutions and to bring about disrespect for our government." When Clark had Gerhart Eisler arrested on February 4, 1947, two days before Eisler was due to appear before HCUA, the Attorney General again revealed his personal conception of law enforcement: "I ordered Mr. Eisler picked up because he had been making speeches round the country that were derogatory to our way of life." Clark's department used the deportation weapon against a large number of pro-Communist militants and trade unionists who were embarrassing the administration by making speeches derogatory to *its* way of life; yet Truman later denounced the deportation powers of the Walter-McCarran Act of 1952 as "thought control."

With Truman [6] it was not so much a matter of what was done, as who was doing it to whom, and who was making capital out of it. When Republicans did it to him it was red-baiting reminiscent of the Alien and Sedition Acts; when he did it to left-wing critics of his own policies, he was putting "Uncle Joe" in his place. Though J. Parnell Thomas irritated Truman by exploiting the Communist issue at the expense of the administration, Clark pledged his full cooperation to HCUA in bringing Communists to book.[7] It was Truman and Clark who produced the loyalty program, who codified the association of dissent with disloyalty and legitimized guilt by association. It was the Truman administration that manured the soil from which the prickly cactus called McCarthy suddenly and awkwardly shot up. The manure was called the Attorney General's list.

To understand Truman's approach to domestic Communism, or "Communism," one must look further than his acutely partisan spirit, his determination not to be outgunned by the Republicans. The generalization—albeit a simplification too—from which we need to advance is this: that whereas the conservatives in both parties loathed domestic radicalism and the New Deal, and merely offered token gestures of defiance toward distant Russia, the Fair Deal Democrats increasingly loathed Soviet policies and offered token gestures of hostility toward domestic Communism. Of course, the two issues were by no means unconnected, particularly when Henry Wallace began to forge a cohesive political force out of left-wing opposition to the Truman Doctrine. Clearly the progressives who favorably portrayed EAM and ELAS in Greece, called for disarmament and characterized Soviet actions in Eastern Europe as peaceful and democratic, angered the President and enraged Clark. This is how Truman wrote of Wallace in his private diary (1946):

> He wants us to disband our armed forces, give Russia our atomic secrets and trust a bunch of adventurers in the Kremlin Politbureau. I do not understand a "dreamer" like that. The German-American Bund under phonies and the "parlor pinks" seem to be banded together and are becoming a national danger. I am afraid they are a sabotage for Uncle Joe. They can see no wrong in Russia's four-and-one-half million armed force, in Russia's loot of Poland, Austria, Hungary, Rumania, Manchuria. They can see no wrong in Russia's living off the occupied countries to support the military occupation.[8]

## THE TRUMAN DOCTRINE

American leaders of internationalist outlook now defined the policy of the United States in global terms: stability, peace and prosperity were America's requirements. Soviet policy challenged America's claim to offer itself, or impose itself, as the model on which the future of world civilization would be based. If prosperity could be guaranteed only by the long-term dominance of the free-enterprise system, then peace and stability could be purchased only in terms of that dominance, which in turn involved the massive presence of the world's "strongest democracy" as guarantor of "the Free World." It also involved checking Russia. About this the Truman generation, Byrnes, Forrestal, Clark, Marshall, Acheson, Kennan, Clay, Clifford, Snyder, Leahy and Harriman were agreed, whatever their differences of emphasis. Anticipating the contours of confrontation, Truman pressed for peacetime military conscription in 1945; Congress inevitably refused. But as Europe slid deeper into economic chaos in 1946–47, and the Communist parties of France and Italy flexed their muscles, the Truman administration braced itself for massive economic intervention: the Pax Americana. The French writer Simone de Beauvoir, visiting America during the first quarter of 1947, commented: "They speak of Europe as of a vassal to be pitied yet far from docile: France in particular is a most undisciplined child."

Recently Professor Alonzo L. Hamby challenged the position adopted by historians of the New Left that the Truman government—and by implication anti-Communist liberalism—was caught in a trap of its own making when it confronted McCarthy. Such a view, argues Hamby, naïvely assumes that the Truman administration "caused the Cold War and that it could have prevented the McCarthy upsurge by refraining from anti-Communist policies and rhetoric." [9] In point of fact we do not have to enter the intractable debate about who "caused" the Cold War; we need only glance momentarily outside the borders of the United States to notice that Britain also committed itself to a political and military alliance against the Soviet Union, *but without the corollary of domestic red-baiting and witch hunting*. The style—tactical and rhetorical—of Truman's immersion in the Cold War therefore emerges as crucial; it was here that the seeds of McCarthyism were sown.

Following careful planning by Dean G. Acheson, Truman came before a joint session of Congress on March 12, 1947, and unfurled the Truman Doctrine—the "turning point," as he later described it, "in America's foreign policy." Wherever "aggression" threatened peace or "freedom," he said, America's security was involved, and it would be necessary to "support free peoples who are resisting attempted subjugation by armed minorities or outside pressures." The speech was greeted with rapture by the legislators, of whom only Representative Vito Marcantonio (ALP, New York) remained seated. Senator Arthur H. Vandenberg had advised the President to "scare hell out of the country" in order to sell intervention in Greece, and this he now did. Equally seriously, he inflamed the natural missionary piety of Americans, the identification of self-interest and self-assertion with the will of God: "For the earth is deeply divided between free and captive peoples . . . And much as we trust in God, while He is rejected by so many in the world, we must trust in ourselves." (Shades of Cromwell; Bernard Baruch described it as "tantamount to a declaration of an ideological or religious war.") Truman was in fact digging deep roots for the double standards that have obscured the motives of American foreign policy for the last thirty years. While committing American money and troops to the support of bitterly reactionary elements in Greece, and while ensuring that the Communists were squeezed out of the French and Italian coalition governments, Truman on April 5 sanctimoniously deplored "the atrocious violations of the rights of nations by the interference of anyone in the internal affairs of another." [10]

## HENRY A. WALLACE: CHALLENGE FROM THE LEFT

On March 31, 1947, the London *Times* commented: "There would . . . be greater opposition to President Truman's Greco-Turkish program from the isolationists if that program were not so bitterly criticized on the Left." Conversely, by focusing hostility on the dissenting Left, the Truman administration hoped to disarm the isolationists. The postwar popular-front spirit, associated with the Independent Citizens Committee for the Arts, Sciences and Professions, soon disintegrated, with the Progressive Citizens of America strongly critical of the Truman Doctrine and the rival Americans for Democratic Action rallying to the anti-Communist cause. The majority of New Dealers, notably Mrs. Roosevelt and Harold L. Ickes, opted for Truman rather than for Wallace as soon as the CP had decided, in the fall of 1947, that the Progressive Party should challenge Truman in the forthcoming presidential election.

A former Secretary of Agriculture (1933–40) and a former Vice-President (1940–44), Wallace had been forced to resign as Secretary of Commerce following his contentious speech, sponsored by the ICCASP, at Madison Square Garden on September 12, 1946.[11] Essentially, the Wallace doctrine in foreign affairs was one of *laisser-faire*, of peaceful coexistence between the Soviet and Western spheres of influence in Europe. By no means a socialist but rather a proponent of "people's capitalism," Wallace edged himself into the classic fellow-traveling position—"I'm an idealist; the Communists are materialists . . . I wouldn't want Communism over here, but it makes more sense in Russia." Increasingly, he interpreted events as the Soviet Union publicly interpreted them, explaining, for example, that the Communist coup in Czechoslovakia was a justifiable prophylactic measure to thwart an imminent rightist coup engineered by American Ambassador Laurence A. Steinhardt. On May 11, 1948, he delivered a speech containing an open letter to Stalin; a week later Stalin described Wallace's proposals as a "good and fruitful" basis for peaceful coexistence.

Wallace also denounced the mounting persecution of radicals at home. "The men who speak of reigns of terror in Europe," he told a radio audience in March, "are fast introducing a reign of terror here at home." In May he testified before HCUA that the Progressive Party would defy the Mundt-Nixon Bill if it became law and if the Attorney General ruled that it applied to the PP. Three days earlier, on June 2, "thousands had marched on Washington to protest the bill." [12]

Had the Communists taken over Wallace, as Truman and the ADA claimed? Certainly the PP's convention held in Philadelphia in July 1948 was so smoothly rehearsed under the platform chairmanship of Lee Pressman that Communist organizational expertise (and cynicism about the value of genuinely open debate) alone could have achieved it. But in reality Wallace's alliance with the CP was strained and fragile. Shortly before the Philadelphia convention he had told a New Jersey audience: "If the Communists would run a ticket of their own this year we might lose 10,000 votes, but we would gain three million." According to Joseph Starobin, "the great untold story of the 1948 campaign was Wallace's antagonism toward the Communists and their own total inability to overcome it." Consequently, the Wallace movement was inwardly beset with "disharmony, suspicion, recrimination, and a conflict of conceptions." On August 24, Wallace announced: "I solemnly pledge that when I am elected President neither the Communists nor the Fascists nor any other group will control my policies." [13] He meant it, but the promise was academic; Wallace was not going to be elected President. [14]

The purpose of the Truman administration's campaign against the Left (the loyalty program, the deportation arrests, the Attorney General's list, the Freedom Train, the indictment of Communist leaders under the Smith Act) was not merely to placate the Republican opposition in Congress and the press, or simply to take the wind out of its sails, but also to harass, isolate and excommunicate from the company of patriotic Americans left-wing critics of Truman's foreign policy. To crush Wallace, a dual strategy was required: to redbait him mercilessly, and at the same time steal some of his leftist thunder. By unsuccessfully vetoing the antiunion Taft-Hartley Act in June 1947, the President had assured that even a soured, alienated labor movement, AFL and CIO, would prefer him to Dewey, even though it was only the CIO that formally endorsed him. (The CIO minority backed Wallace.) Truman's aide Clark Clifford noted in a memo to his chief that the administration was vulnerable to the charge that too many of its members had Wall Street connections. Clifford proposed liberal appointments: "Under their impact, Wallace will fade away." Clifford also proposed that Wallace be red-baited. The chairman of the Democratic National Committee, Senator J. Howard McGrath of Rhode Island, set the tone when he remarked in January 1948, that "a vote for Wallace . . . is a vote for the things for which Stalin, Molotov and Vishinsky stand." On St. Patrick's Day, speaking in New York City, Truman referred to "Henry Wallace and his Communists."

## THE 1948 CAMPAIGN

In late May, Alistair Cooke noted that "the Democrats and the Republicans are now racing each other for the anti-Communist stakes." [15] On the last day of July, preoccupied almost exclusively by electoral strategy, HCUA's Republican majority launched the Chambers-Bentley espionage hearings. On August 8, Truman denounced these hearings as designed to distract attention from the Republican tactic of blocking his anti-inflation program; the only spy ring he knew of was in Representative Karl Mundt's mind. [16]

By September, the vituperation was reaching formidable proportions. On the twenty-seventh, Truman, speaking in Boston, said: "All this talk about Communism . . . is in the same pattern with their appeals to religious prejudice against Al Smith in 1928 . . . I want you to get this straight now. I hate Communism." On the following day he accused the Republicans of "having recklessly cast a cloud of suspicion over the most loyal civil service in the world . . ." This was the essential Truman: to impose on his federal civil service the most stringent and damaging loyalty program in the "Free World," and then to defend it against Republican critics as "the most loyal" in the world; to exploit Catholic anti-Communist passions while at the same time hinting that Republican anti-Communism was a threat to Catholics. The double-edged sword was wielded by Clark in a speech on October 19: as long as he remained Attorney General, "no occasion for hysteria or alarm exists"—even though there were 2,100 alien Communists from the Iron Curtain states at liberty in the country, of whom no fewer than 2,027 (Clark emphasized) had come to America in the 1920's, *when the Republicans had been in power!* Clark also complained that he had asked Congress for a law to take all 2,100 alien Communists into custody, but he had been denied "this simple little law" by a Republican Congress. For good measure, he added that Dewey and Warren, the Republican ticket, had, as Governors of New York State and California, more Communists in their files than anyone else—and precious little they had done about it! Under Clark the Justice Department constantly pressed for its own Internal Security Act, which other departments rejected as excessively damaging to civil liberties. [17] The Senator who advised Truman during the campaign to stress the Communist danger more and the civil liberties issue less, J. Howard McGrath, an easygoing Irish politician, was the man whom Truman appointed to succeed Tom Clark in 1949.

"I suspect there never has been a President who could move in two different directions with less time intervening than Truman. He feels completely sincere and earnest at all times . . ." Admittedly, the source of this comment, Henry Wallace, was not without his bias— but the arrow was not wide of the mark. Deriding those who were "much wrought up about the Communist bugaboo," Truman allowed the Justice Department to indict twelve Party leaders under the Smith Act four months before the election, then went on to trounce not only Wallace but also Dewey. (According to the official count, Wallace received only 1,156,103 votes, of which 501,167 were accounted for by New York and 101,085 by Los Angeles County.) Victory only encouraged Truman to pursue his dual war with greater intensity. The Communist leaders were tried and convicted. The loyalty purge gathered pace. But, once again beating off Republican attacks in June 1949, Truman likened the hunt for spies and subversives to the hysteria of 1798; he urged citizens to read the history of the Alien and Sedition Acts.[18]

In May of the following year, the President, who had given his blessing to the Attorney General's list, wrote the national commander of the Veterans of Foreign Wars: "All this howl about organizations a fellow belongs to gives me a pain in the neck." Having read the manuscript of his friend and adviser Max Lowenthal's highly critical study of the FBI, he wrote him in June 1950: "You certainly are doing a wonderful service to the country by writing a book of this sort." But Truman made no move to correct the procedural abuses that Lowenthal documented.[19] He did, however, as in 1948, oppose legislation to force Communists to register. On September 21, Attorney General McGrath urged that legislation to control Communism must not be influenced by "public hysteria" and the drive for "orthodoxy of opinion"; besides, registration would be ineffective. In vetoing the McCarran Act on September 22, Truman complained that, "It would give Government officials vast powers to harass all of our citizens in the exercise of their right of free speech." Addressing the Legion on August 14, 1951, he defined "real" or "100 percent" Americanism as including support for freedom of speech, fair play, and the assumption that men were innocent until proved guilty. This sentiment shifted reality, as experienced by many victims, as little as did McGrath's pious sentiment of January 13, 1951: "But Mr. J. Edgar Hoover and I are determined that there will be no Gestapo witch hunts . . ."[20]

It would be a mistake to assume that Truman controlled his federal bureaucracy with anything like "the buck-stops-here," tough-little-fighter resolution that he projected in his interviews. "They," he later remarked to Merle Miller, never did produce "the goods" on Hiss; yet it was Truman's Justice Department that prosecuted Hiss. When he appointed McGrath as Attorney General, he was virtually assuring that the Justice Department and the FBI would make their own laws. Although Truman indicated his opposition to the Hobbs Bill, which would have permitted administrative internment of aliens under a deportation order, the Justice Department continued to support the bill. When the Ellen Knauff immigration case [21] came to Truman's attention in June 1950, he ordered his aide Stephen Spingarn to investigate; yet the Justice Department refused to hand over the files to the President's administrative assistant! Nor did he fully control the Attorneys General he appointed. On July 5, 1952, he wrote to McGrath's successor, James P. McGranery, that Owen Lattimore had been "shamefully persecuted," indicating that perjury charges against the China expert, desired by Senator Pat McCarran and the Senate Subcommittee on Internal Security, should not be presented to a grand jury without the President's prior approval.[22] Alas, McGranery owed his Senate confirmation to a deal with McCarran specifically promising that Lattimore would be indicted. And he was.

"All my life," wrote Truman, "I have fought against prejudice and intolerance." And yet, as he said himself, he had been raised in an atmosphere of bitter racial bigotry—a small-town hick from Independence, Missouri, who adopted the values of the New Deal and of the liberal intelligentsia he met in Washington without ever fully absorbing them. No doubt he was sincere when he wrote: "Self-appointed guardians of the country and bigots have even carried on attacks against our schools and colleges and churches . . . the epidemic of investigation has infected school boards and town councils." Had his administration done more to check such corrosions of the democratic ethos, and not in some cases positively encouraged them, it would be less tempting to condemn him as a hypocrite. To take another example of the Jekyll-and-Hyde in the man, in April 1959 he lectured at UCLA on the subject of "Mass Hysteria and Witch-Hunting in American History." He was introduced by Chancellor Raymond B. Allen who, in 1949, as President of the University of Washington, purged three Communist professors of long standing from the faculty. Exactly a year after the UCLA lecture Truman turned up at Cornell to inform the students there that Communists were engineering the student sit-downs at lunch counters in the South. Challenged by Martin Luther King and Roy Wilkins of the NAACP to prove it, Truman replied that he had no proof, "But I know that usually when trouble hits the country the Kremlin is behind it." [23] Even the admiring New York Times had to notice that he was employing the very McCarthyite tactics he had always complained of. But had he ever done otherwise?

In 1949 Truman and Acheson carried the nation into NATO—

the first peacetime alliance America had ever concluded with European nations. Although Robert A. Taft, Kenneth S. Wherry and Arthur V. Watkins opposed the Treaty in the Senate, only thirteen Senators, eleven of them Republicans, voted against it; eighty-three voted in favor. Dedicated now to the global crusade, the administration launched early in 1950 a "Campaign of Truth" on the Voice of America, using an expanded range of shortwave transmitters to pump anti-Communist propaganda into every reachable corner of the globe.

## ELECTIONS OF 1950: THE McCARRAN ACT

As the Congressional election of 1950 approached, a new Republican assault mounted in intensity. Joseph McCarthy was now noisily onstage, carrying the attack to the Truman administration and effectively short-circuiting any hope of alleviating abuses and excesses in the loyalty program. With Senator Kenneth S. Wherry (Nebraska) installed as Republican minority floor leader, Robert A. Taft (Ohio) as chairman of the Republican policy committee in the Senate, and the equally conservative Hugh Butler (Nebraska) as chairman of the Republican Committee on Committees, McCarthy could be sure that even his wildest rampages would be treated with indulgence by his Republican colleagues. Whereas Scott W. Lucas led the Senate Democrats from a center position, Wherry led the Republicans from the far right. [24]

But it was the Republicans who now made the running. When a subcommittee of the Senate Foreign Relations Committee, chaired by Millard E. Tydings (D., Maryland), having examined McCarthy's charges against State Department personnel, called them "a hoax and a fraud . . . an effort to inflame the American people with a wave of hysteria and fear on an unbelievable scale," the Senate split along party lines, with forty-five Democrats voting in support of the Tydings report and thirty-seven Republicans voting against it. Even the seven Republicans who had earlier signed a "Declaration of Conscience" dissociating themselves from McCarthyism—"I don't want to see the Republican Party ride to political victory on the four horsemen of Calumny, fear, ignorance, bigotry and smear," said Margaret Chase Smith, of Maine—felt obliged to vote with their party colleagues against the Tydings report. Occasionally principled voices howled lonely protests: Governor J. Bracken Lee of Utah, Alexander Wiley, senior Senator from McCarthy's own state, and the veteran Senator Ralph E. Flanders of Vermont, who launched his blistering attack in March 1954. But the typical voice was that of Wherry: "Get rid of the alien-minded radicals and moral perverts in this administration."

The attack on Dean Acheson achieved frenetic proportions, particularly when the Secretary of State announced four days after Alger Hiss's conviction for perjury in January 1950: "I will not turn my back on Alger Hiss." Senator Homer E. Capehart remarked that there would be spies in government so long as "we have . . . a Secretary of State who refuses to turn his back on the Alger Hisses." By December the Senate Republican Conference was calling for Acheson's dismissal. In September, Senator Andrew F. Schoppel (R., Kansas) accused Secretary of the Interior Oscar S. Chapman of having had "a personal alliance" with the Soviet cause. The newsletter sent to seven thousand party workers by Republican National Committee chairman Guy G. Gabrielson, accused the government of covering up for traitors, subversives and sexual perverts.

Candidates in the Congressional elections exploited the Communist issue to an unprecedented extent, and not only candidates for national office but also candidates for secretary of state of Indiana, attorney general of California, lieutenant governor of Pennsylvania, and in numerous other local contests. In Illinois, Congressman Everett M. Dirksen defeated Scott W. Lucas for the U.S. Senate, promising a "house-cleaning . . . of sympathizers and party-liners such as this country has never seen before." John Foster Dulles, challenging the liberal Herbert H. Lehman for the Senate in New York, said of his opponent: "I know he is no Communist, but I know also that the Communists are in his corner and that he and not I will get the 500,000 Communist votes that last year went to Henry Wallace in this state." In Florida, Congressman George A. Smathers ran successfully in the Democratic primary against the liberal Senator Claude D. Pepper, by referring to "the spiraling spider web of the Red network" and calling "Red Pepper" an "apologist for Stalin" (Pepper had met Stalin in 1945). In North Carolina, Willis Smith played on Senator Frank P. Graham's association with the Southern Conference for Human Welfare to defeat him in the Democratic primary.[25] (The red-baiters also played on white segregationist sentiment in both Florida and North Carolina.) Charges of Communist proclivities contributed to the defeat of Senator Glen H. Taylor of Idaho (Henry Wallace's running mate in 1948) and of Senator Elbert D. Thomas of Utah.

In California, Richard M. Nixon, having red-baited the New Dealer and former Socialist Jerry Voorhis out of the House in 1946, now employed the same tactics to defeat Democratic Congresswoman Helen Gahagan Douglas for the Senate in 1950. He issued a pink sheet showing how Mrs. Douglas's voting record paralleled that of New York's Vito Marcantonio (who invariably voted the CP line) on 354 occasions. Nixon won by nearly 500,000 votes.

But a most notable feature of the 1950 campaign was the extent to which Democrats themselves resorted to red-baiting. In the California Democratic primary, Mrs. Douglas's conservative opponents painted her every shade of red despite the fact that she had fought the Progressive Party in 1948. Late in July, Helen Douglas herself delivered a speech accusing Nixon of voting with Marcantonio against aid to Korea and of cutting aid to Europe by half.

The Pennsylvania Democratic State Central Committee issued a pamphlet entitled "Fellow-Traveling Pa. GOP Congressmen Follow Red Party Line." In Ohio, the Democratic national committee employed red-baiting tactics against the ultra conservative Senator Robert A. Taft, arguing that his isolationist opposition to Truman's containment program in 1947–48 had helped the Kremlin. Even Taft was found to have voted on the same side as the notorious Marcantonio on several occasions. [26]

One major feature of the legislative session running up to the election was the collapse of the liberal Democrats when faced with the emerging Internal Security (McCarran) Act. Here, at last, the (at least) thirty-eight anti-Communist bills introduced into the 81st Congress bore fruit. The Act principally treated of four subjects: the registration of "Communist organizations"; [27] the strengthening of the espionage laws; the amendment of immigration and naturalization laws; and the detention of potential spies and saboteurs in times of emergency.

All this was justified by a preamble containing the legislative conclusion that world Communism had as its one purpose the establishment of a totalitarian dictatorship in America to be brought about by treachery, infiltration, sabotage and terrorism. American Communists were stated to have transferred their allegiance to a foreign power. This of course meant that if any organization registered it would stamp itself a conspiracy to overthrow the United States government on behalf of a foreign power. Since the CP was scarcely likely to do this out of sheer love of truth, the Act established a procedure whereby the Attorney General would petition a new, five-member Subversive Activities Control Board for an order that an organization be required to register as Communist-action, Communist-front, or Communist-infiltrated. The SACB's decision would be binding. Even so, might the obligation to register not conflict with the Fifth Amendment protection against self-incrimination? So indeed, the Supreme Court finally decided in 1965. [28] No organization ever registered under the McCarran Act and so the penalties for membership were never invoked, just as Section 4(a), which made it illegal knowingly to conspire to perform acts that contributed to the establishment in the United States of a totalitarian dictatorship under foreign control, was never enforced.

Even so, the Act had an immediate, draconian impact on potential immigrants and visitors. Excluded from entry was anyone ever affiliated with an organization advocating any form of totalitarianism, unless he or she had demonstrated positive rejection of that creed, or unless—so it turned out in practice—the form of totalitarianism happened to be Nazi or Fascist.

One clause of the Act emerged out of a liberal maneuver to divert the cannibal's appetite by promising him a feast of blood at some later date. Sponsored by Harley M. Kilgore of West Virginia, Paul H. Douglas of Illinois, Frank P. Graham of North Carolina, Herbert H. Lehman of New York, and Estes Kefauver of Tennessee, S. 4130 was designed as a substitute bill providing for camps in times of national emergency, invasion or insurrection to detain without trial anyone who had been a member of the Communist Party since January 1, 1949. But this measure was merely incorporated into the omnibus McCarran bill by grateful and delighted conservatives. The bill was passed in the House on September 20, 1950, by 312 votes to 20 and in the Senate by 51 to 7. Herbert Lehman later recalled: "I remember a tense scene in the anteroom of the Vice-President . . . A number of my liberal colleagues . . . said that if I voted against the measure it would mean my defeat for reelection that fall. They were wrong. But the fever of fear was on my colleagues . . ." The six Democrats who voted with Lehman against the bill were Graham, Kefauver, Edward L. Leahy and Theodore F. Green, both of Rhode Island, James E. Murray of Montana and Glen H. Taylor of Idaho. Truman vetoed the whole package as asking thieves to register with the sheriff, as unworkable, as authoritarian, and as putting the government in "the thought control business." The presidential veto flushed a little courage out of a handful of liberals; the veto was voted down by 286 to 48 in the House, 57 to 10 in the Senate. The seven Senate liberals who had originally opposed the bill were now joined by Hubert Humphrey of Minnesota, Dennis M. Chavez of New Mexico and Douglas. As Joseph C. Harsch noted, "political expediency" in an election year was the decisive factor. The New York Times referred to "hysteria and frantic, unthinking fear . . . ," while the Christian Science Monitor's headline of September 25 was as sardonic as it was cryptic: "Solons Play it Safe." Hubert Humphrey later wrote to Kefauver that he was "very proud" of Kefauver's original negative vote: "I wish I could say the same for myself."

Despite the furious red-baiting and calumny, the Republicans failed to take control of either chamber in the elections of 1950. In the Senate the Democrats suffered a net loss of five seats, and in the House their majority was reduced by twenty-seven. Herbert Lehman now became McCarthy's most vigorous critic in a Senate where few dared to burn their political fingers by flushing fire from his nostrils. Caution was reinforced by McCarthy's imposing, if exaggerated, reputation for electorally destroying those who crossed him, notably Millard E. Tydings in Maryland in 1950 and William Benton (who moved a resolution to expel McCarthy in August 1951) in Connecticut in 1952. In reality, Benton's percentage of the vote was no lower than that of other Democratic candidates in Connecticut, and McCarthy himself emerged as the weakest vote-getter on the Wisconsin Republican ticket, running far behind Eisenhower.[29] But the *ex post facto* rationalizations of psephologists tell us little about the mood of a time. Ahead lay the age of Korea and McCarthy, the age of the loyalty oath, the Fifth Amendment, the age of suspension and dismissal, of censorship and deportation: the great fear.

# 2

## The Republican Catharsis

### ISOLATIONISM AND ANTI-COMMUNISM

When we come to consider the "isolationist" sentiment that fueled the fires of domestic anti-Communism in the late forties and the fifties, we must distinguish between two types of isolationism. The first (Fortress America) turned its back on Europe, on the corrupt Old World, out of disgust or disinterest; it spurned involvement. The second was the product of an ultrasensitivity about European politics among those sections of the American population—most notably the German-Americans—who recognized in 1940 that the United States must either go to war with Germany or stay neutral. Roosevelt had dragged America into the wrong war: wrong allies, wrong enemies, wrong outcome. It was this breed of isolationism (although the two types often merged in hybrid combinations) that became a vengeful force in postwar America: the isolationism of regret, bitterness, betrayal, revenge. In 1940, there were twenty counties in which Roosevelt lost over 35 percent of the vote he achieved in 1936; nineteen of them were predominantly German-speaking in background. Samuel Lubell concluded that attitudes toward American involvement in the Second World War largely governed attitudes toward McCarthy. A study of Pierce County, Wisconsin, showed that McCarthy received disproportionate support from people of German extraction. "In not one of the German-American counties I visited did I find a single person who believed a settlement with Russia was possible."

Republicans from Midwestern areas recorded a 76 percent opposition to foreign-aid bills in 1952, and 65 percent in 1955, whereas among East Coast and Pacific Coast Republicans only 19 percent opposed the foreign-aid bill of 1955. Senators from the Midwest solidly opposed the censure of McCarthy in 1954.[1] On the other hand, we cannot reduce domestic anti-Communism and red-baiting, the force that unleashed a purge across the face of America, to isolationism, pro-German feeling, or the Republican Party. Many Slavic Americans who had supported Roosevelt and the war against Germany were outraged by the Soviet take-over of Eastern Europe. The indignation of Catholics of Slavic and Irish descent, when blended with the smoldering resentments of German-Americans, matured into a new, high-proof superpatriotism.

In 1945 isolationism was at its lowest ebb; or dared not show its grimace in the face of general euphoria. The nascent United Nations received bipartisan support in the 1944 campaign and remarkable public approval. Several isolationist Congressmen and Senators lost their seats. The Senate consented to the UN Charter by 89 to 2. Eisenhower returned late in 1945 from a trip to Moscow to announce that both the United States and the Soviet Union were anticolonialist, and each wanted friendship with the other. Only gradually did the fear spread that liberal internationalism would involve higher taxes and government control of the economy; that aid would go straight into the pockets of Socialists and ungrateful foreigners to create a global welfare state for the indigent and envious. Such attitudes flourished particularly among older people, country people, people of low education, who were easy prey to anti-Communist rhetoric.[2]

Colonel Robert R. McCormick, proprietor of the *Chicago Tribune*, backed American Action, Inc., heir to America First. Supported by Lammot du Pont, Upton Close and others, this organization acted as a lightning rod for anti-British, anti-democratic, and sometimes anti-Semitic sentiment. The British Labour government's rapid introduction of nationalization measures and a welfare state exacerbated fears of Socialism as a halfway house to Communism. But the irrational or symbolic elements in the new anti-Communist mythology outweighed rational ones. Resentments about style and privilege, about aloof East Coast, Ivy League intellectuals, whose allegiances resided in mid-Atlantic or further east and who aped the manners of British aristocrats while pouring American taxes into the pockets of British Socialists—these passions also fueled the new domestic anti-Communism. McCormick's *Chicago Tribune* described Dean Acheson in 1949 as a "striped-pants snob" who "ignores the people of Asia and betrays true Americanism to serve as a lackey of Wall Street bankers, British lords, and Communistic radicals from New York." Senator Hugh Butler of Nebraska said of Acheson: " . . . I watch his smart-aleck manner and his British clothes and that New

Dealism . . . and I want to shout, Get out, Get out. You stand for everything that has been wrong with the United States for years." McCarthy added: ". . . his primary loyalty in international affairs seems to run to the British Labor Government, his secondary allegiance to the Kremlin . . ." The 1946 loan to Britain was opposed by 122 of 183 Republicans voting in the House. McCarthy demanded that all British ships trading with Red China be sunk. The United Nations, he said, was dominated by the Socialist government of Britain and "the racist totalitarian government of India," both of whom were plotting to thrust America out of the Far East. The Reece Committee revealed that thirty-one college presidents, 113 leading civil servants, and seventy prominent commentators of press and radio had been Rhodes scholars.[3] *Ergo!*

And then there was the United Nations-Communist conspiracy. In October 1947 the ultrarightist *Plain Talk* published a piece, "Trygve Lie: Stalin's Tool in the UN?" In it the question mark was quickly abandoned. His election in January 1946 had been Moscow's doing; had not the *Daily Worker* of March 28, 1946, applauded the secretariat's personnel policy? In July 1949 the Senate Judiciary Subcommittee on Immigration under Pat McCarran heard a "mystery witness" testify in closed session that the UN secretariat under Trygve Lie was terrorized by reds. Two days later the subcommittee released a bitter attack against Lie. Despite protests from Lie (in reality, a dependable anti-Communist and friend of Washington), from two senior Americans in the secretariat, Byron Price and Dr. Ralph J. Bunche, as well as from Acheson, McCarran nevertheless continued throughout July and August to fling charges of Communist infiltration at the secretariat.[4] As John S. Wood, chairman of HCUA, put it in October 1951, UNESCO was "The greatest subversive plot in history."

In the eyes of Truman and the Cold War internationalists, Stalin had betrayed the spirit of Yalta and Potsdam. For Truman's Republican and isolationist opponents, Yalta itself was a betrayal of the national interest by pro-Communist New Dealers. Few dared say so at the time; indeed the Yalta agreement received almost unanimous praise in the press in February 1945. But later, as Cold War tensions stiffened, conservatives criticized the agreements about Eastern Europe and Poland's postwar borders, about occupation zones and reparations in Germany, and about the ceding of certain territorial rights to Russia in the Far East. Conservatives were also irritated about the secrecy of the Yalta conference, the refusal to consult or inform Congress and the public; Truman enraged Taft by refusing to publish the agreement. (When in 1955 the full text was released it revealed no further secret agreements.) Much was also made of Alger Hiss's presence at Yalta (which in fact was of a strictly technical character).

After Hiss's conviction for perjury, Nixon declared in the House: ". . . in 1944, before Dumbarton Oaks, Teheran, Yalta, and Potsdam, the odds were 9 to 1 in our favor. Today, since those conferences, the odds are 6 to 3 against us."

The paradox was this: that in practical terms, in terms of willingness to commit funds, material, even men, to the new global policy of "containing" Soviet power, the Fair Deal Democrats of the Truman era easily outstripped their Republican critics. Indeed, by the end of 1952 the administration was carrying between 33 and 50 percent of France's financial burden in the Indochina war, and had so far abandoned Roosevelt's emphasis on decolonization and an end to empire that almost all nationalist movements rebelling against British or French repression were now regarded as Communist-dominated or, at best, subversively neutralist. It was the Truman government that very energetically planted the disastrous harvest of the late 1960s.

The Republicans liked to point out that twenty-eight years of Democratic rule (Wilson, Franklin Roosevelt, Truman) had resulted in 1,628,480 war casualties, whereas twenty-four years of Republican rule (Theodore Roosevelt, Taft, Harding, Coolidge and Hoover) had resulted in none. Theirs was the politics of catharsis, of domestic revenge for "twenty years of treason," of violent gestures directed less at Soviet power than at a mythical fifth column within the United States.

In 1947 and 1948, a Republican Congress had rejected Truman's proposal for peacetime military training. The *Chicago Tribune* even opposed America's intervention in Korea. On December 20, 1950, ex-President Herbert Hoover, a critic of intervention in 1941 and of the Soviet alliance, called for withdrawal of all American troops from Europe and Asia. Fortress America could rely on air and naval power to protect her. The Republican isolationists talked tough but shrank from the fight. After the truce in Korea, Senator William E. Jenner of Indiana demanded that America reestablish an anti-Communist government in China and unify Korea to the Yalu River. How? By arming Japan and Germany and then applying diplomatic pressure on the Russians. And if the Russians were not amenable? Then expel them from the UN. And if the UN vote went against America? Then withdraw from the UN. (One might call this sulking to victory.) Said Jenner:

We want no American forces sent to Southeast Asia . . . We want no carefully contrived emergencies by which we shall be forced to consent in haste to the sending of troops to Vietnam or Thailand.

. . . there is no way to defend the industrial heart of Europe unless we use those two great wells of tough anti-Communist manpower, Western Germany and Spain [said McCarthy].

Now I do not propose to send American troops into China or Poland. But I do propose that we give the anti-Communist forces in those countries necessary aid when the opportunity presents itself [said McCarthy].[5]

## KOREA: CLIMAX TO "TWENTY YEARS OF TREASON"

A number of Senators and Representatives called for varying degrees of atomic warfare in Korea. The myth flourished that General Mac-Arthur had been forced to fight with his hands tied. MacArthur's most attractive quality, for Republicans and isolationists, was his apparent desire to crush the Communists with Chiang's army or the atomic bomb. When Truman dismissed him on April 11, 1951, a Gallup poll showed 69 percent support for the general, 29 percent for the President. By the end of 1952, when more than a million men had been drafted and almost 25,000 killed, the search for a scapegoat, a domestic fifth column, became the stock-in-trade of Republicans. A Knox County, Ohio, farmer's wife put it this way about Truman: "With our boys dying in Korea, he won't kick out the people who are fighting us—it makes me sick!"

McCarthy's voting record was quite typical of his party's. In 1950 and 1951, he voted against the Point Four program to aid underdeveloped countries and he also voted for cuts in foreign military aid. He opposed a budget increase for the Voice of America. Arthur Schlesinger, Jr., claimed in May 1952 that such isolationists were cheered in the Kremlin while they fought a sham battle at home to cover their stealthy desertion of allies abroad. This sham battle was known as "Twenty Years of Treason," to quote the phrase made famous by McCarthy at a Lincoln Day dinner. "The hard fact is that those who wear the label Democrat wear it with the stain of an historic betrayal . . ." He denounced Acheson, "the Great Red Dean," and his "crimson crowd" who betrayed American boys dying in Korea. He castigated "the Acheson-Hiss-Lattimore group . . ." and dragged up the fact that in November 1945 Acheson had shared a platform with Paul Robeson, Corliss Lamont and Joseph E. Davies, at a Madison Square Garden meeting sponsored by the National Council for American-Soviet Friendship. But one could go even further back: "Before Russia was recognized by the United States in 1933 Dean Acheson was paid by the Soviet Union to act as Stalin's lawyer in this country." Alger Hiss's brother Donald worked in Acheson's law firm—had not Acheson refused to turn his back on Hiss? Had not he been responsible in 1946 for granting a $90 million loan to Communist Poland?

It was McCarthy's thesis—typical of the Republican position—that, "the Communists within our borders have been more responsible for the success of Communism abroad than Soviet Russia." Clearly, Acheson was one of these Communists. In his Senate speech of June 14, 1951, McCarthy focused on two principal targets: Acheson and George C. Marshall, Chief of Staff during the war, later Secretary of State, later Secretary of Defense. (The choice was an odd one; Marshall had not been particularly associated with the New Deal, but McCarthy reinterpreted his career to prove that he was a political general, promoted by liberal favoritism.) Marshall, said McCarthy, had called for a second front in 1942, precisely as Moscow had done; at Teheran he had made common cause with Stalin, and again at Yalta, with Hiss at his elbow; he had induced F.D.R. to bring Russia into the war against Japan, signing thereby the death warrant of Chiang's China. The objective of such protracted perfidy had been to render the United States ultimately helpless before Communist intrigue at home and Soviet military power abroad. "What do we find in the summer of 1951? The writs of Moscow run to . . . a good 40 percent of all men living . . . This must be the product of a . . . great conspiracy, a conspiracy on a scale so immense as to dwarf any previous such venture in the history of man." Jenner had greeted MacArthur's dismissal in similar vein: "I charge that this country today is in the hands of a secret inner coterie . . . which is directed by agents of the Soviet Union . . . Our only choice is to impeach President Truman to find out who is the secret invisible government."

In this key, the Republicans pursued the Democrats into the presidential campaign of 1952. The Democratic presidential candidate, Governor Adlai E. Stevenson, had given a deposition testifying to Hiss's good character during their years together in the State Department. So now McCarthy referred by a slip of the tongue to "Alger—I mean Ad-lie." Nixon commented on TV: "If Stevenson were to be taken in by Stalin as he was by Alger Hiss, the Yalta sellout would look like a great American diplomatic triumph by comparison." The same month, October, McCarthy went on television holding in his hand a photostat of the October 19 edition of the *Daily Worker*, and claimed that the paper said that, while it did not like Stevenson, it would be okay for Communists to vote for him. (This was a fabrication.) He blamed Stevenson for "foisting the Communists upon the Italians" and for bringing Palmiro Togliatti back from Moscow.[6]

Vice-presidential candidate Nixon traded heavily on his key role, as a member of HCUA, in bringing Hiss to justice. "I remember in the dark days of the Hiss case some of the same columnists, some of the same radio commentators who are attacking me now . . . were violently opposing me at the time I was after Alger Hiss . . ." On October 2, speaking at Texarkana, Texas, Nixon referred to "the Truman-Acheson-Stevenson gang's toleration and defense of Communism in high places," and used the word "traitors." In a televised address two weeks later, he accused the administration of having covered the Hiss case up "rather than . . . bringing Hiss to book many years sooner as they should have done." Stevenson himself, driven over the edge of his own moral standards into throwing some of the same stuff, pointed out that in December 1946 Hiss had been selected as President of the Carnegie Foundation by a board of which the chairman was none other than John Foster Dulles. A Detroit lawyer, said Stevenson, had offered to provide Dulles with evidence that Hiss had a provable Communist record, but Dulles had declined to see the evidence.

Genuinely liberal liberals took a beating during the election campaign of 1952. In Montana, for example, Senator James E. Murray, a member of the ADA and one of only seven Democratic senators to have voted against the Internal Security Act, was pilloried in an expensive brochure, *Senator Murray and the Red Web over Congress*, published by the Montana for D'Ewart Committee, which claimed that HCUA's files revealed Murray to be identified by membership, sponsorship or association with thirteen red fronts. Professional ex-Communists like Harvey Matusow were hired to assist this campaign.[7]

## McCarthy

The most dramatic figure in the Republican apotheosis was undoubtedly McCarthy. His name has become associated with a style of politics, "McCarthyism," notable for its crude, below-the-belt, eye-gouging, bare-knuckled partisan exploitation of anti-Communism, usually on the basis of half-truths, warmed-over "revelations," and plain lies. McCarthy was also the man with the briefcase full of incriminating documents—this appealed to a country much enamored of factuality, of the cult of hard fact. At the same time, his pugilistic flamboyance, blatant love of money, women and horseflesh, his Falstaff-like war service and mythical *machismo*, caught a cowboy nation by the gut.

As Richard Rovere put it, McCarthy was a political speculator who found his oil gusher in Communism. His hectic anti-Communist crusade was conducted without real feeling, still less passion—he would have been happy had his victims shaken his hand once the cameras were switched off. During his campaign for the Senate in 1946 he had red-baited a bit, but he had also warned that if enough American leaders "keep on cursing Russia we're going to have a war." He scorned those who "pick up votes by attacking Russia" and after the election he even described "Stalin's proposal for world disarmament" as "a great thing, and he must be given credit for being sincere." McCarthy's political speculation in red-baiting did not begin until his November 1949 attack on Cedric Parker, an ex-Communist journalist working for the liberal Madison (Wisconsin) *Capital Times*, a paper severely critical of McCarthy. On November 15, he made Communist infiltration of the State Department a major theme in a speech delivered to a Young Republicans dinner.[8] Egged on by Father Edmund Walsh, vice-president of Georgetown University, McCarthy sprang to national prominence in February 1950 with a speech at Wheeling, West Virginia, during which he claimed to be holding in his hand a list of 205 Communists employed by the State Department.[9]

Gallup surveys of New London County, Connecticut, and East Stroudsburg, Pennsylvania, showed that McCarthy was admired for being "courageous, sincere, get tough, fearless, and gets a lot done." Increasingly on easy terms with God and man's immortal soul, grooving his style into that of the old patent-medicine pitchmen, playing on popular anxieties and griefs, he toured the country receiving medals, citations and gifts of money from Legion posts, the Order of the Purple Heart, the Veterans of Foreign Wars, and the Marine Corps. "Well," he would begin, "it's good to get away from Washington and back here in the United States." As each of his charges was exposed as fraudulent, he produced a new one—the press was insatiable. As for those who dared to criticize him: "Let me assure you that regardless of how high-pitched becomes the squeaking and screaming of left-wing, bleeding-heart, phony liberals, this battle is going to go on." So he told the Fifth Marine Division's 1951 convention, in a characteristic posture of embattled insurgency. Above all, he appealed to the plebeian appetite for rough justice:

> When I was a boy on the farm, my mother used to raise chickens. The greatest enemy the chickens had were skunks . . . my three brothers and I had to dig out and destroy these skunks. It was a dirty, foul, unpleasant, smelly job. And sometimes after it was done, people did not like us to sit next to them in church.[10]

So brightly did McCarthy's star shine during the 1952 election campaign that Eisenhower, on his way to the White House, prudently deleted at the last minute a section of a speech defending his former superior officer, patron and friend, George C. Marshall, whom McCarthy had denounced as a traitor. Yet, no sooner had the new Republican administration been installed than the ultra-anti-Communists, McCarthy, Jenner and Bridges to the fore, resumed their attack, holding up Senate approval of Eisenhower's nominee as ambassador to Moscow, Charles E. Bohlen, whom McCarthy described as "part and parcel of the Acheson-Vincent-Lattimore-Service clique." Within the Republican Party a rift opened up as deep as the one separating the moderate Fair Dealers from the Eisenhower Republicans—possibly deeper. In November 1953, McCarthy indicted the administration on television for failing to fight Communism effectively and for sending "perfumed notes" to allies who traded with Red China. The Bricker Amendment, which would have made executive agreements as well as treaties subject to Congressional approval, was only the most passionately debated of the hundred-odd amendments to the Constitution introduced by the enraged and xenophobic ultra-Right. Senator Barry Goldwater (R., Arizona) spoke of "a dime-store New Deal" while McCarthy referred to "twenty-one years of treason."

For its part, the administration was determined, as Sherman Adams put it, to "take away some of the glamour of the McCarthy stage play." Herbert Brownell, Jr., the New York lawyer who served as Ike's campaign manager before being appointed Attorney General, did precisely that in November 1953, when, following a couple of Republican by-election setbacks, he accused Truman of having confirmed Harry Dexter White as executive director of the International Monetary Fund despite FBI reports linking White to a pro-Soviet spy ring. To outmatch McCarthy, Nixon announced: "We're kicking the Communists and fellow travelers and security risks out of the Government . . . by the thousands . . ." In his 1954 State of the Union message, Eisenhower himself went so far as to propose depriving Communists of citizenship.

No doubt the endemic institutional rivalry between legislature and executive exacerbated the climate of political hysteria. But this rivalry should not be regarded as an abstraction: executive privilege was the bastion of the Right in the Johnson-Nixon era. The Congressional riot led by McCarthy represented clearly identifiable social and geographical forces; the Midwesteners of traditionally pro-German sentiment, anti-Communist Catholics, small-businessmen and *nouveaux riches* who distrusted big government, as well as large numbers of people who distrusted the Ivy League, New York, liberals, homosexuals and Britain. The great corporations and Wall Street, by contrast, generally preferred Ike (or Taft) [11] to the uncouth upstart, the

Wisconsin skunk-hunter, for whom so many farmers (except in the anti-Catholic, Fundamentalist South) prayed.

Without doubt, McCarthy's objective historical role was a healthy one. He pumped up the festering sore of the loyalty-security program and the Attorney General's list into a monstrously inflamed boil that, sooner or later, had to be lanced. He demonstrated that guilt by association may ultimately incriminate any association. He reminded the establishment, the "respectable elements" in both major parties, the professional associations, the press, the churches, that liberty is indivisible and that what is sauce for the goose is also sauce for the gander.

The politics of McCarthy were the politics of frustration; Fortress America could no longer prosper oblivious to the outside world. This frustration outlasted McCarthy; it had other professional carriers. In 1956 Jenner accused Dulles of a "planned retreat before the Communist advance." When Soviet farmers visited Iowa in 1955; when about 150 American scholars went to Russia between 1954 and 1957; when the Geneva Conference of the Big Four took place in July 1955; when seventeen Soviet and twenty-two American graduate students embarked on an exchange scheme in 1958–59—when these little signs of thaw occurred, the anti-Communist politicians and Congressional committees screamed in protest. So they did when the Atoms for Peace Plan issued from the White House, when the first nuclear test suspension was announced, and when Khrushchev visited America in 1959.

## THE COMMUNIST CONTROL ACT

To complete our sketch of the political foreground to the great purge of American working life under Truman and Eisenhower, we should mention the Communist Control Act (Public Law 637, "An Act to Outlaw the Communist Party"), which passed into law on August 24, 1954. Inspired not only by Senator Hugh Butler's bill against Communist infiltration of unions but also by Hubert Humphrey's bill to make CP membership a crime, the Act set down fourteen indicia of CP membership and stripped the party itself of "all rights, privileges, and immunities attendant upon legal bodies." The Act also shortcut the ineffective registration provisions of the Internal Security Act of 1950 by legislatively declaring the CP to be a "Communist-action organization." The liberal collapse was now complete. Not only did Hubert Humphrey, a leading light of the ADA, vigorously press this legislation, but only one Senator, Estes Kefauver, dared to vote against it. "I have always been sorry," Herbert H. Lehman later remarked, "that I did not join the one Senator who voted against this bill." Irving Howe wrote disgustedly of "this Congressional stampede to prove that each party was as ready as the other to trample the concept of liberty in the name of destroying its enemy." [12]

## IDEOLOGY OF THE COLD WAR
## LIBERAL INTELLECTUALS

Writing in 1946, Lionel Trilling offered a plausible description of the liberalism that had prevailed (particularly among the educated classes) during the New Deal era: ". . . a ready if mild suspiciousness of the profit motive, a belief in progress, science, social legislation, planning, and international cooperation, perhaps especially where Russia is in question." [13] The onset of the Cold War shattered this liberal consensus—the pro-Truman Americans for Democratic Action was founded in January 1947, within a week of the rival, left-wing Progressive Citizens of America, a schism, a polarization, foreshadowing the Truman-Wallace rivalry of 1948. And just as the President won that duel by an overwhelming margin, so, too, Cold War liberalism emerged head and shoulders above its competitors to the Left and to the Right as the dominant ideology within government, the press and the world of learning. The linchpin of this creed was hostility toward the Soviet Union and American Communism; concomitantly, that "mild suspiciousness" of the profit motive became very much milder. The Cold War liberals embraced the Pax Americana.

Both the achievements of the New Deal and the victory over the Axis Powers reinforced their sense not merely of American power, but also of American rectitude. Insisting as they did that Truman's foreign policy was altruistic, defensive, and reactive to the Soviet threat, they became so preoccupied with containing Russia (and later China) that they forgot all about containing America. In a bipolar universe, they desired and demanded an almost limitless extension of American power and influence round the globe "because," as the ADA explained in its founding statement of principle, "the interests of the United States are the interests of free men everywhere." And by 1951 the ADA was supporting limitless assistance to Chiang Kai-shek.

Some twenty years later, Professor Arthur Schlesinger, Jr., describing himself as an "unrepentant anti-Communist," distinguished—or attempted to—between the "obsessive" and destructive anti-Communist fixations of the Vietnam war era, and the more "rational" anti-Communism—"graduated in mode and substance according to the character of the threat"—which had prevailed under Truman.[14] One may wonder. What is indisputable is the point made by Robert L. Heilbroner: "It is, I think, the fear of losing our place in the sun, of finding ourselves at bay, that motivated a great deal of anti-Communism on which so much of our foreign policy seems to be founded." Here was the impulse that prompted so many liberals to endorse military intervention in Greece on behalf of an undemocratic rightist regime and prompted the *New Leader* to portray Chiang as the very embodiment of freedom. Here was the impulse that drew an impressive phalanx of perfectly honest writers and professors, including Daniel Bell and Sidney Hook, into the arms of the CIA by way of the American Committee for Cultural Freedom.

About this episode Bell, a distinguished and influential author in the development of the anti-Marxist ideology of the fifties (the so-called "End of Ideology"), has written:

> . . . in the 1950's the CIA, as a matter of government policy, decided to support and sustain a host of liberal and socialist international organizations, at a time when such organizations could not find the means to be self-sustaining, in order to strengthen opposition to Communist domination of certain milieus.[15]

Yet the anti-Communism of the CIA was not and never has been a principled, democratic anti-Communism, but rather a brazen and imperialistic war against any movement or party likely to challenge American power, American corporate profits, the Pax Americana—in short that conglomeration which the liberals themselves, or most of them, now recognize as discredited.

Although the Cold War liberals were by no means in the vanguard of the forces pressing for the domestic purge, without doubt their obsessive anti-Sovietism blinded them. "We cannot take chances with the ringleaders of a conspiracy that, if successful, would pervert and destroy our institutions," commented the editor of *The Reporter*, Max Ascoli, when the Supreme Court upheld the conviction of the Communist Party leaders under the Smith Act.[16] Every American Communist, insisted the ex-Communist Granville Hicks, "is actually or potentially a Soviet agent." And Sidney Hook, professor of philosophy at New York University and perhaps the most influential Cold War liberal on questions of liberty, contrived to argue that Communists should be excluded from a wide range of professions:

> So long as the radio and television industries operate under commercial sponsorship, it is both unrealistic and unfair to compel sponsors whose income position is being undermined by popular

boycott of Communist or Fascist performers on their programs to continue their sponsorship. . .[17]

Indeed, Hook concluded in 1957 that the Congressional committees, including HCUA, had done more good than harm by educating the public in the dangers presented by the Soviet fifth column.

Criticisms of the state of American liberties in the McCarthy era by West European writers were vigorously and hotly rejected. According to Diana Trilling, writing in August 1952, "the idea that America is a terror-stricken country in the grip of hysteria is a Communist-inspired idea." Hook himself claimed that "the nightmarish picture often painted in the European press of McCarthy stalking up and down the country intimidating writers, educators, newspapermen and other professional groups suggests the vision of delirium rather than the results of sober reporting." Meanwhile Rebecca West assured her British readers in 1953 that "the investigating committees have dealt but little with college professors," and that the only terror prevailing in American academic life was among professors who dared not leave the CP for fear of brutal reprisals.[18] Two years later, in February 1955, the executive director of the American Committee for Cultural Freedom, Sol Stein, applauded the McCarran Committee's harrowing pursuit of Professor Owen Lattimore and the Institute of Pacific Relations as "a valuable service in furnishing the public with evaluated information concerning the work of apologists and agents of the Soviet Union who have not—or cannot be proven to have—broken existing laws."[19]

The conclusion toward which our commentary leads us, then, is that during the crucial years of the great fear the most influential, opinion-forming faction of the American intelligentsia largely (but not wholly) abandoned the *critical* function that all intellectuals in all countries ought to sustain toward government agencies and government actions. Although such an argument as ours cannot be demonstrated by a few quotations alone, all available evidence confirms that this malaise, this insensitivity, this willingness to defend democracy by means of antidemocratic methods, spread rapidly and widely through the middle-class professions and the labor movement.

# 3

## Espionage Fever:
## Myth of the Vital Secret

Spy fever flowed into the bloodstream of the nation from the twin needles of a single hypodermic: the Cold War and the backlash against the New Deal. The notion of the Vital Secret—the fantasy of the "Haves," whose nuclear monopoly was threatened—hypnotized Congressmen, newspaper editors and radio commentators. Despite the fact, familiar to all informed observers, that Washington is a vessel that leaks from the top (a Cabinet discussion in 1945 about the merits of letting Russia share the secret of the A-bomb had been leaked within half an hour to a prominent journalist), the psychological imperative to equate radicalism with treason, with an anarchic alienation from the cradles of loyalty, soon brought about a most pathetic public gullibility to any tale of conspiracy.

*There is no documentation in the public record of a direct connection between the American Communist Party and espionage during the entire postwar period. Even during the Korean war, no evidence of Communist sabotage or attempted sabotage came to light.* The anti-Soviet, anti-Communist historian Theodore Draper has written:

> It would help in understanding the Communist movement if the terms "conspirator" and "conspiracy" were reserved for actual Soviet agents. Except for a tiny minority, the Communist membership has devoted its efforts to gaining mass influence with means that have been blatantly nonconspiratorial.[1]

One thing, however, must be made clear here. Those who deplore the anti-Communist purge tend to dismiss all allegations of espionage as fabrications of the FBI. This would imply either that the Soviet Union did not attempt to suborn, or succeed in suborning, Americans or that, if it did, the FBI never caught the guilty, only the innocent. Such assumptions are silly; they are not shared by the present writer. It is therefore a very real question whether Alger Hiss, the Rosenbergs and others were in reality guilty or innocent of the crimes of which they were accused and convicted. But it is a question which lies outside the proper province of this book. There is already an abundant and contentious literature on the subject. Hiss and the Rosenbergs make their appearance here as elements in our portrait of the foreground, the front-stage dramatics, which inevitably heightened tension throughout the country and greatly exacerbated the purge.

On February 15, 1946, the Canadian government announced the arrest of twenty-two people charged with illegally passing information to representatives of the Soviet Union. This followed the defection from the Soviet embassy in Ottawa of a cipher clerk, Igor Gouzenko, who brought with him incriminating files that conclusively proved the existence of an espionage ring staffed by trained personnel of the NKVD and military intelligence. Washington also noted proven links between the Canadian network and parallel ones in Britain and the United States, together with a demonstrable Soviet interest in devices relevant to the postwar defense and communications system of the Western powers.[2]

Close to home, the *Amerasia* case kicked off the postwar espionage-hunting season. Early in 1945 agents of the Office of Strategic Services (OSS) raided the magazine *Amerasia* and turned up over one thousand documents purloined from the State, War and Navy Departments. Those involved included Philip Jaffe, the editor, Emanuel Larsen, a specialist in the China Division of the Bureau of Far Eastern Affairs, who was subsequently dismissed from the State Department, John Stewart Service, who was not, and Andrew Roth, of Naval Intelligence. Although the Hearst and Scripps-Howard press built the affair up into a great spy sensation, it was much less than that; at his trial in September 1945, Jaffe was described even by the prosecution as merely an overzealous editor. Larsen later turned his coat and published a piece in the September 1946 issue of *Plain Talk*, a right-wing magazine, in which he complained that the State Department had been infiltrated by Communists, and accused Jaffe of having had dealings with Earl Browder and the Soviet Consulate. This was no doubt true; Jaffe, a Russian-born businessman, had been active in Communist circles since the thirties and had visited Mao in Yenan, besides writing for *China Today* under the name of J. W. Phillips.[3] But neither he nor his sources had in mind to pass information to a foreign power; each was committed to publicizing the folly of American support for Chiang. Nevertheless, the incident revealed how quick-fingered politically committed government servants could be, particularly the talented, idealistic, opinionated generation of young intellectuals who came to Washington under the New Deal.

## ELIZABETH BENTLEY AND WHITTAKER CHAMBERS

From the spring of 1947, a federal grand jury in New York—the same one that indicted twelve Communist leaders under the Smith Act in 1948—subpoenaed scores of past and present government employees accused of belonging to the CP, or to Communist espionage rings, by the two principal informers of the era, Elizabeth (*Out of Bondage*) Bentley and Whittaker (*Witness*) Chambers. Curiously, the grand jury indicted not a single one of them, the result being that in 1948 the theater of accusation was shifted to Congress and, principally, the House Committee on Un-American Activities. There, in an election year, with Truman denouncing the whole palaver as a "red herring," publicity at white heat was generated by those intent on damning the New Deal-Fair Deal as Communist and disloyal.

Chambers, who described himself as a Communist and a Soviet agent until early 1938, claimed that at least seventy-five government officials had been involved in varying degrees of pro-Soviet espionage in the late thirties.[4] Bentley, like Chambers a graduate of Columbia, had joined the CP in 1935 and (so she said) been ordered to "go underground" three years later. Jacob Golos, head of World Tourists, a member of the CP, and reputedly an agent of the Soviet GPU, became her contact and lover until his death in 1943. She had continued with her espionage work until in August 1945 she made contact with the FBI, at whose request she maintained her contacts with the CP underground until 1947, when she finally broke cover by testifying before the federal grand jury. At least, this is what she said happened; her reliability as a witness has often been challenged. There is certainly an overlap between those accused by Chambers and those named by Bentley,[5] who made eight appearances before different Congressional committees. Among her other claims was one that Earl Browder, general secretary of the CPUSA, had received Moscow's orders through her after Golos's death. Long after his expulsion from the Party, Browder insisted that his only dealings with her had concerned the Party's investment in U.S. Service and Shipping, for which she worked.[6] *In toto*, she identified forty-three people as having belonged to the Communist underground within the government service, including Lauchlin Currie, administrative assistant to President Roosevelt.

> . . . we had a steady flow of political reports from the Treasury which included material from the Office of Strategic Services, the State Department, the Navy, the Army, and even a limited amount of data from the Department of Justice. We knew what was going on in the inner chambers of the United States Government up to and including the White House.[7]

Many of those named by the "blond Spy Queen," as the newspapers liked to describe her, resorted to the Fifth Amendment when subpoenaed by HCUA in 1947–48, and again when the Senate Internal Security Subcommittee took up the story in 1952–53,[8] by which time the William Remington and Owen Lattimore cases had demonstrated the dangers of a perjury indictment if an unfriendly witness dared to refute one friendly to a committee of Congress. However, when William Ullman, faced with the choice of testifying or going to prison for contempt under the immunity statute passed in 1954, finally denied ever having belonged to the CP or having committed espionage, no perjury prosecution followed. At about the same time a loyalty board found that another civil servant accused by Bentley, William H. Taylor, was loyal.

Nevertheless, it was mainly on the Bentley evidence that the reactionary SISS based its report, *Interlocking Subversion in Government Departments*, which purported to trace Soviet penetration of the New Deal administration from the economic recovery agencies to the war-making agencies of the Second World War, and then to the agencies concerned with foreign policy and postwar planning.

> Powerful groups and individuals were at work within the executive branch [said the report], obstructing and weakening the effort to eliminate Soviet agents. . . . They colonized key committees of Congress, they helped write laws . . . advised Cabinet members . . . staffed interdepartmental committees which prepared basic American and world policies. . . .[9]

The Republican National Committee paid for the distribution of fifty thousand copies of the report, while the Texas millionaire H. L. Hunt financed the printing of a further fifty thousand.

The most senior government official named by both Bentley and Chambers was Harry Dexter White, Assistant Secretary to the Treasury with responsibility for foreign relations, and later for all relations with the Army and Navy. The most dynamic, imaginative and ambitious personality in the Treasury under Henry Morgenthau, Jr., White's bold schemes included the "Morgenthau Plan" for the pastoralization of postwar Germany. In January 1946 Truman nominated him as executive director of the International Monetary Fund, of which he was a principal architect, even though White's name was listed in memoranda sent by J. Edgar Hoover to the President.[10]

According to Chambers, who produced four documents said to be in White's handwriting, he had threatened to denounce White unless he broke his fellow-traveling ties with the CP. But White denied any knowledge of Chambers. Appearing voluntarily before HCUA in August 1948, he agreed that he knew many of the officials named by Bentley (about ten of them had in fact worked under him), but denied knowing that any of them was a Communist or spy, although he was aware of certain accusations. Suffering from a weak heart, and emotionally outraged by the Committee, he died three days after his appearance.

The White case was largely buried and forgotten with White himself until it sprang into massive national prominence in November 1953, when Attorney General Brownell and J. Edgar Hoover alleged that Truman had been culpable in ignoring FBI warnings about White before appointing him to head the IMF. In a national television and radio broadcast on November 16, Truman called Brownell a liar and explained that he had decided to keep White under surveillance so that proof might be developed of his guilt if guilty he was. We may take that with a pinch of salt.[11] Truman regarded all attacks on the loyalty of specific government servants as partisan in inspiration. This attitude enraged J. Edgar Hoover and provoked him to patronize Bentley, Chambers and other informers whom the anti-New Deal Congressional committees also exploited for partisan purposes. The Justice Department under Tom Clark was caught between its inherent sympathy for the FBI and the Attorney General's need to protect the reputation of his chief.

## The Hiss Case

On July 31, 1948, HCUA launched a sensational preelection espionage investigation by hearing evidence from Elizabeth Bentley and Whittaker Chambers. Out of these hearings was born the *cause célèbre* of the postwar, anti-New Deal espionage fever, the Hiss case. Born in 1904, a distinguished graduate of Johns Hopkins and the Harvard Law School, Alger Hiss was appointed clerk to Justice Oliver Wendell Holmes on the recommendation of Felix Frankfurter, himself later a Supreme Court Justice and a character witness for Hiss at his first trial. Under the New Deal, Hiss moved to Washington and served successively in the Agricultural Adjustment Administration, as counsel to the Nye Committee, in the Solicitor General's office, and finally in the State Department. In 1944, he traveled to the Yalta conference as a member of Roosevelt's delegation, and helped to organize the UN Conference on International Organization at San Francisco. In February 1947 he quit the State Department at the suggestion of John Foster Dulles to assume the presidency of the Carnegie Endowment for International Peace, of whose board Dulles was chairman. Hiss's new salary, $20,000 a year, exceeded that of Cabinet members and Congressmen.

Hiss's background, style and career symbolized the ethos of the self-confident, left-wing, East Coast, Ivy League, New Deal bureaucrat. His accuser, Whittaker Chambers, was by contrast a humped, shambling writer with a record as a confessed Communist and spy. When he first gave evidence before HCUA early in August 1948, Chambers said of Hiss and Harry Dexter White: "I should perhaps make the point that these people were specifically not wanted to act as sources of information . . ." In fact, in 1939 Chambers had first reported Hiss, among others, as a Communist-in-government, to Adolf A. Berle, Jr. Late in 1945 Secretary of State James F. Byrnes had retained Hiss despite an FBI report damaging to him—another example of the administration ignoring or frustrating the FBI's drive against suspected pro-Communists.

As soon as Hiss heard that Chambers had named him as a Communist, he wrote HCUA an indignant denial and demanded to be heard. On August 25, he at last confronted his accuser, keenly observed by the youngest and brightest of the new committee members, Richard M. Nixon. In the course of time, Nixon was to make the Hiss case virtually his own. (Standing by the barn of Chambers's Maryland farm, "Nixie" had said to Chambers: "If the American people understood the real character of Alger Hiss they would boil him in oil.") Hiss sat there, lean, cross, rather harsh in manner, cigarette in hand, drily pedantic in a lawyer-like way, a marked contrast to the shifty, hesitant, podgy, poetic Chambers.[12] Hiss said he had known Chambers as "George Crosley," a journalist who had called on him when he was counsel to the Nye Committee, and to whom he had rented an apartment from September 1934 to July 1935, but who never did pay the rent.

On October 14, Chambers appeared before the New York grand jury and denied any knowledge of espionage. But after Hiss filed a $75,000 libel suit against him Chambers led two HCUA investigators on December 3 to the rear garden of his Maryland home and produced from a scooped-out pumpkin rolls of microfilm and documents that, he said, he had preserved in the dumbwaiter of a relative's apartment in Brooklyn as a lifesaver against potential Communist threats on his life.[13] Yet these "pumpkin papers" eventually had little bearing on the political action against Hiss, though their date, 1938, was significant. Hiss denied having known Chambers after 1936.

Chambers now regarded Fabians and New Dealers as ultimately no less dangerous to democracy than violent Bolsheviks:

> The simple fact is that when I took up my little sling and aimed at Communism, I hit something else. What I hit was the forces of that great socialist revolution, which, in the name of liberalism, spasmodically, incompletely, somewhat formlessly, but always in the same direction, has been inching its ice cap over the nation for two decades.[14]

In December 1948 a grand jury indicted Hiss on two charges of perjury: falsely denying that he had passed State Department documents to Chambers, and falsely denying that he had met Chambers after January 1, 1937. The statute of limitations shielded Hiss from a substantive espionage charge. The essence of Hiss's case was that although he did let an apartment to Chambers and his family, contact between the two families was minimal. Furthermore he himself had never been a Communist and had never committed espionage. On the contrary, his upstanding loyalty to the United States could be (and was) attested to by witnesses of high reputation and integrity.

Chambers, on the other hand, testified that while he was in Washington as a member of the CP underground, he had been introduced to Hiss in 1934 by J. Peters, "head of the whole underground . . ." Hiss was to be "disconnected" from an apparatus led by Harold Ware and was to become "a member of a parallel organization" under Chambers. His first assignment was to obtain Nye Committee documents dealing with the munitions traffic. In 1937 Chambers introduced Hiss to his own superior, Colonel Bykov, who asked Hiss to procure State Department documents to help defend Russia against the fascist powers. Hiss did so: some were photocopied by Chambers, but later others were typed out by Mrs. Hiss at home before Hiss returned them to the State Department. The prosecution had copies of material written by Mrs. Hiss on her Woodstock typewriter. According to an FBI expert called by the prosecution, and not challenged by the defense, the microfilmed typed documents produced by Chambers from the pumpkin had been typed on the same Woodstock. The defense did not challenge this assumption, merely argued that Chambers had somehow got hold of the machine to commit "forgery by typewriter."

The jury split: eight found Hiss guilty, four found his guilt not proven. On July 9, 1949, Nixon publicly accused Judge Samuel H. Kaufman of "prejudice . . . against the prosecution." Two other Republican Congressmen added their voices. HISS JUDGE PROBE DEMANDED, declared the *New York World-Telegram*, while the Hearst *New York Journal-American* published an interview with one of the anti-Hiss jurymen: "The foreman was emotional, two were blockheads, and one was a dope." HISS TRIAL CONDUCT WIDELY PROTESTED, declared this paper, which halfway through the trial had printed an attack on the judge as "a New Dealer." The *Journal-American* even printed the names and addresses of two of the minority jurymen, with a report that they had been threatened.[15]

At the second trial a new witness appeared and gave evidence which might well have benefited Hiss. Julian Wadleigh, a former employee of the Federal Farm Bureau, State Department, Department of Agriculture, and UNRRA, with degrees from the universities of Oxford, London and Chicago, described himself as a fellow traveler who had deliberately disguised his views, and confessed to having engaged in espionage in the late 1930s. Although Wadleigh described Hiss as "a very moderate New Dealer with strongly conservative instincts," and although he emphasized that he had shopped around the State Department for documents to such an extent that he might well have been the person who passed on six or seven of the ones attributed by Chambers to Hiss—despite this testimony apparently favorable to Hiss, the sum total effect may have redounded in favor of Chambers. Why? Because Wadleigh had passed documents to Chambers and had met his boss, Sasha, whom Chambers now called Colonel Bykov; because Wadleigh, so to speak, stood in for Hiss as an almost perfect double in the kind of activity Chambers swore to. Wadleigh banished all doubt that the world Chambers described was a real one.

In 1950 Hiss was convicted by a unanimous jury and sentenced to five years' imprisonment.[16] Two years later his application for a retrial, based mainly on new evidence, was turned down. While he was confined in Lewisburg his name sizzled from the mouths of politicians desperate to smear and incriminate their opponents. He became a totem pole for a deeply divided liberal movement—obviously guilty not only to conservatives but also to Cold War liberals, obviously innocent, the victim of a frame-up, to almost all who deplored the purge.[17]

Before Hiss's conviction, American hysteria about espionage was further inflamed by a demonstrably proven case of it. On March 6, 1949, the FBI arrested Judith Coplon, a Barnard graduate working in the Justice Department, during a rendezvous with an attaché of the

Soviet delegation to the UN, Valentin Gubichev. Coplon had been copying out FBI reports for the Russians since February 1946. Convicted in two successive trials, she was nevertheless reprieved by the Court of Appeals in December 1950 on the ground that she had been arrested without a warrant and that the prosecution case depended on inadmissible wire-tapping evidence.

## The Rosenbergs

On June 19, 1953, a married couple with two sons, Julius and Ethel Rosenberg, were executed in the electric chair at Sing Sing prison. They were the first civilians to be put to death for espionage committed in war time—if they committed espionage at all, which they vehemently denied, and which many people doubt to this day. The timing, the passions aroused, the worldwide appeals for clemency, and the ritual-purgatory nature of the act, all enshrine June 19, 1953, as the midsummer's night of postwar anti-Communist, anti-Soviet hysteria. A New York schoolteacher recalls how, when Justice Douglas briefly stayed the execution at the last minute, her high-school pupils visibly shook with rage, frustration, hate.

Both Julius and Ethel Rosenberg were the children of Jewish immigrant families living on New York's Lower East Side. Although her mother was aggressively illiterate, the young Ethel ardently reached out to art and creativity; leaving school at the age of fifteen, working as a clerk during the Depression, living in a yellow-brick tenement frequented by prostitutes, she saved money to buy a piano. In August 1935, at the age of nineteen, she led 150 women workers in a walkout that shut down National Shipping. A week after the strike was settled she was fired.

Three years younger than Ethel, Julius was also a child of the slums, the youngest of fifteen children born to Polish parents. His father was a tailor. After studying Hebrew at the Downtown Talmud Torah, he latched on to Socialist causes (Tom Mooney) and joined the Young Communist League, in whose debates, parades and rallies he immersed himself at the expense of his studies at City College. When he graduated as a bachelor of science in electrical engineering in February 1939, he ranked only seventy-ninth out of eighty-five.

They were married in June of that year. In September 1940, Julius was hired as a civilian junior engineer at the Brooklyn supply office of the Army Signal Corps, despite the conspicuous commitment of both husband and wife to selling the *Daily Worker* and collecting funds, door-to-door, for the Joint Anti-Fascist Refugee Committee. By the time their son Michael was born, in 1943, Julius was earning $3,500 as an inspector of electronic products, visiting defense plants and military installations for the Signal Corps. Not until March 1945 did the Army fire him as a Communist; he denied it and fought the dismissal: "I am not now, and never have been a Communist member . . ." When, six years later, he was asked at his trial whether he had ever been a Party member, he took the Fifth Amendment. Had he told the truth to the Army in 1945? "I refuse to answer," said Julius.

Following the arrest and confession—undoubtedly genuine—of the German-born British nuclear physicist Klaus Fuchs, nine Americans were arrested during the first half of 1950 and linked by the Justice Department to a "Klaus Fuchs spy ring." Fuchs admitted having passed top-secret information to a courier while he was working at Los Alamos in 1944–45. But to whom? *According to the FBI*, soon after his imprisonment in Britain Fuchs was shown photographs by FBI agents and identified a Philadelphia chemist called Harry Gold as the courier.

Gold was arrested on March 23, 1950, three weeks after Fuchs had been sentenced to fourteen years' imprisonment in London. A Swiss-born naturalized American employed by the Philadelphia General Hospital's heart station, Gold *apparently* confessed that he had indeed funneled information from Fuchs to Anatoli A. Yakovlev, Soviet Vice-Consul in New York, in September 1945.[18]

Soon after his arrest Gold *apparently* implicated another person besides Fuchs in his espionage journeys to New Mexico during the war. This was a very humble person unknown to the top-ranking physicist Fuchs, a young machinist from New York called David Greenglass. Arrested on June 15, Greenglass *apparently* confessed and in turn implicated and blamed two more people, his sister and brother-in-law.

Their names were Ethel and Julius Rosenberg.

Julius was questioned, then released, by the FBI the day after Greenglass's arrest. A month later, on July 17, he was arrested and held. On August 11, Ethel too was arrested, leaving their two young sons almost without care or protection.

The government's case at the Rosenberg trial, which opened in New York on March 6, 1951, was masterminded by Irving H. Saypol, described by *Time* magazine as "the nation's number one legal hunter of top Communists." It was Saypol who had supervised the Justice Department's case in the second Hiss trial, as well as the case against the eleven Communist leaders indicted under the Smith Act in 1948. His assistant was the young attorney, Roy Cohn. Saypol, who chose to prosecute the Rosenbergs for *conspiracy* to commit espionage, because such a charge allowed the introduction as evidence of secondhand conversations normally invalid as hearsay, based his case very largely but not exclusively on the *accomplice* testimony of Gold, David Greenglass and his wife, Ruth. Although Gold had already been sentenced to thirty years' imprisonment in December 1950, the sentencing of the two Greenglasses was shrewdly left in limbo until after they had testified against the Rosenbergs.

The prosecution's story was basically that in 1944 the Rosenbergs had persuaded the Greenglasses to enter a conspiracy to transmit atomic secrets to the Soviet Union. In the following year Rosenberg had arranged with Soviet Vice-Consul Anatoli Yakovlev that Yakovlev would send a courier to Albuquerque, where Greenglass was working as a machinist. Yakovlev sent Harry Gold, bearing $500 as payment for Greenglass. Rosenberg was also accused of having run a wider spy ring to cover nonatomic espionage.

According to Ruth Greenglass on the witness stand, Julius had told her in November 1944 that for two years he had been trying to contact people who could help him to bring assistance to the Russians. He believed that atomic information should be shared with Russia, so that no one nation could use the bomb against another. Greenglass testified that in his workshop at Los Alamos high-explosive lens molds were made, that he himself had obtained information by engaging scientists in conversation, and that he had drawn a sketch, representing a cross section of the atomic bomb, for Julius Rosenberg in 1945. Greenglass reproduced what he claimed was the sketch in court. Claiming that Julius had persisted with his espionage activities into the postwar period, he reported that in January 1945 Julius had told him that he had received a citation from the Russians and that it would involve certain privileges if he ever went to the Soviet Union.

The Saypol team was determined to slot this case into the general anti-Communist fever then running higher than ever with the war in Korea. No opportunity was missed to emphasize Rosenberg's connection with the CP, his IWO insurance policy, and so on. At his trial Julius said:

> I felt that the Soviet government had improved the lot of the underdog there, has made a lot of progress in eliminating illiteracy, has done a lot of reconstruction work . . . contributed a major share in destroying the Hitler beast who killed six million of my co-religionists, and I feel emotional about that thing.

Whatever the truth of the matter, there is general agreement that the Rosenberg defense was not well handled. Leonard Boudin recalls that Julius telephoned him from the FBI office immediately after his arrest, and later came to see him. Boudin explained to him that, with the Coplon case already in his hands, it would not do Rosenberg any good if he represented him. Boudin adds that he has "no clear recollection of having been directly asked to represent Julius Rosenberg." Another lawyer, then representing the Soviet Union, also explained to Julius that it would not help him if he took on his case.[19] In the outcome, the Rosenbergs were represented by the big-hearted, devoted lawyer Emanuel Bloch, who cared for their children with selfless dedication and took them on grueling, sad visits to Sing Sing. But Bloch made the basic tactical mistake of accepting the government's contention that Gold and Greenglass were indeed guilty of the espionage they confessed to. The Bloch position was: "How dreadful! But don't try and implicate my clients!" At no point did he cross-examine Gold or indicate to the jury that he was a self-confessed liar; on the contrary, he assured the jury when summing up that Gold was "telling the truth, the absolute truth" when he described his dealings with Yakovlev and Greenglass. The whole weight of the Rosenberg defense was directed toward proving that the Greenglasses were lying to save their own skins and because of enmities bred of family quarrels.

Here we must introduce a third defendant in the Rosenberg trial, Morton Sobell, who had been handed over to the FBI by Mexican agents on August 18, 1950, nearly two months after he had taken his family to Mexico from New York City. On the face of things, it looked as if this journey had been inspired by the arrest of David Greenglass, a suspicion reinforced by Sobell's use of false names in Mexico after Julius Rosenberg was arrested. (Sobell later described this behavior as foolish, provoked by the political fears of the age rather than by guilt.)

Sobell had known Rosenberg at City College, but his life had been linked even more closely with a certain Max Elitcher—at Stuyvesant High School, at City College, and in Washington, D.C., where they shared an apartment for two years. Several days after Rosenberg's arrest a very frightened Elitcher had been questioned by the FBI. He was frightened because, among other things, he had lied about his past CP membership when signing a federal loyalty oath in 1947—anxiety about this had led him to quit the Navy Department and move to New York, where he bought a house back-to-back with that of the Sobells. Both men now worked for the Reeves Instrument Company. But by 1950 relations between the two families (as between the Rosenbergs and Greenglasses) were strained.

Elitcher's testimony, whether true or not, clearly damaged the Rosenbergs and Sobell. According to Elitcher, it was Sobell who had recruited him into the CP (Sobell's wife later confirmed that Sobell had belonged to the YCL, but never to the CP). Both Sobell and Rosenberg, said Elitcher at their trial, had for four years solicited his participation in espionage, but to no avail. He claimed that in 1948 he and Sobell had driven to a point near the Rosenbergs' home so that Sobell could deliver a can of film to Julius Rosenberg. Was this true? Elitcher himself had a perjury charge hanging over him when he testified; like Greenglass, therefore, he had a motive for providing the kind of evidence the prosecution wanted him to provide. But we cannot take it for granted that his story was a fabrication.

The prosecution case against Sobell was that he had agreed and conspired to supply defense data for the use of the Soviet Union (he was not charged with *atomic* espionage). He declined to take the witness stand and called no defense witnesses; although he pleaded not guilty, he seemed almost traumatized by his predicament. He was not only convicted and sentenced to an incredible thirty years' imprisonment (of which he eventually served nineteen), he was also sent to the notoriously brutal Alcatraz federal penitentiary in San Francisco Bay. Sobell was one of the few Americans whose confinement equaled in rigor and protraction that of the Sovet political prisoners of the era.

The Rosenberg jury found Julius and Ethel guilty of conspiracy to commit espionage, but made no recommendation as to sentence. The onus was on Judge Irving R. Kaufman alone. Although espionage during wartime was a crime punishable, under the Espionage Act of 1917, by death, no American court had ever sentenced a civilian to death for such a crime. And the Rosenbergs, after all, were accused of having passed information to *an ally*. Nevertheless, Judge Kaufman, clearly indoctrinated by the paranoid xenophobia of the time, treated them as if they had committed treason, which means making war against or giving aid to an enemy at war with the United States. The temperature of that historical moment, as Kaufman prepared to pass sentence of death on his fellow Jews, was reflected in *The New York Times* headlines of March 28, the day before the jury met to deliberate its verdict:

Acheson Exhorts Americans to Meet Soviet Peril Now

U.S. Power Must "Frighten" Enemy, Wilson Asserts

Danger of Atom Bomb Attack is Greatest in Period
Up to this Fall, Expert Asserts

Red China Rejects M'Arthur's Offer

Ferrer Denies He Is Red

In his sentence-of-death speech, Kaufman surrendered himself to an outpouring of prejudice:

> Yet, they made a choice of devoting themselves to the Russian ideology of denial of God, denial of the sanctity of the individual . . .
>
> I also assume that the basic Marxist goal of world revolution and the destruction of capitalism was well known to the defendants, if in fact not subscribed to by them . . .
>
> . . . this diabolical conspiracy to destroy a God-fearing nation. . . .

The judge went so far as to insist that the Rosenbergs had put the atomic bomb in the hands of Russia and had thus caused the Communist aggression in Korea, with its cost to America of 50,000 casualties. Yes, Julius Rosenberg, seventy-ninth in his class of eighty-five at City College, his wife, who had left school at the age of fifteen, and her brother, David Greenglass, a simple and by all reports rather incompetent machinist, had among them contrived to give Russia the bomb "years before our best scientists predicted Russia would perfect the bomb." [20] Even allowing for the temper of the time, one can only marvel at the judge's ignorance. Whereas Alan Nunn May and Klaus Fuchs, two British nuclear physicists who had confessed to espionage on behalf of Russia, were highly qualified and informed in the field, Julius Rosenberg was merely a humble New York City electrician husbanding pretentious dreams of doing something useful for the Soviet people and of being acknowledged in their prayers.

Not a word about the case was printed in the Communist press during the twenty-three days of the trial. The Communist dilemma was obvious. The Rosenbergs, as defendants, did not contest the reality of the alleged Soviet espionage; and they might at any moment have confessed to bargain for their lives. Only after Judge Kaufman had passed sentence did the Party protest that they had been made into scapegoats for the Korean war. Yet it was a further four months before any newspaper was bold enough to insist on their innocence; it was the *National Guardian*, published by the American Labor Party in New York, that took the plunge.

The Rosenbergs were incarcerated in Sing Sing while the appeal process was set in motion. On October 13, 1952, the Supreme Court declined to review the case, and in February 1953 Eisenhower, acting on the advice of Attorney General Brownell, refused all appeals for executive clemency. By this time the fate of the Rosenbergs had become an issue across the world. On December 21, 1952, a thousand people came in heavy rain to Ossining, New York, bringing season's greetings, but the police did not allow them to approach the prison; they had to sing their songs at the station. The two Rosenberg boys were held aloft at demonstrations like the bewildered orphans they were soon to become. American embassies abroad were deluged with letters. Forty Labour MPs wrote to Eisenhower, Einstein protested, three thousand American clergymen and many American, French and Israeli rabbis sent petitions, and even Pope Pius XII, anti-Communist zealot though he was, urged the President to "temper justice with mercy." The (anti-Communist) League of the Rights of Man, which had protested the rigged verdicts in the anti-Semitic Slansky trial staged in Communist Czechoslovakia, appealed from Paris for clemency. "Fascism," wrote an outraged Jean Paul Sartre, "is not defined by the number of its victims, but by the way it kills them." He denounced the Rosenbergs' execution as "a legal lynching that has covered a whole nation with blood. . . ."

On May 25, the Supreme Court for a second time refused to review the case. A radical California lawyer, Norman Edelman, then petitioned for a stay of execution on the ground that part of the crime for which the Rosenbergs had been convicted had taken place after the effective date of the Atomic Energy Act (1946), which specified that death or life imprisonment for the disclosure of atomic secrets should be imposed only on the recommendation of the jury. Justice Douglas accepted this as an arguable point and granted a stay on June 17. On the following day a Special Term of the Court convened to hear the arguments. With Black, Douglas and Frankfurter dissenting against the unseemly haste of the majority decision, the Court voted on June 19 to revoke the stay of execution.

Their voices were silenced. Those two voices, as conveyed by the letters they sent one another during their imprisonment, were suffused with a warm, private love, offset by a somewhat strident public attitudinizing, almost as if they saw themselves as "the Rosenbergs." Julius wrote to Ethel in 1951:

Dissemination of scientific knowledge to the mass of the people was set up as the greatest crime, heresy. This is true today, as in our own case . . . our case is being used as a camouflage to paralyze outspoken progressives and stifle criticism of the drive to atomic war.

Ethel wrote:

Together we hunted down the answers to all the seemingly insoluble riddles which a complex and callous society presented . . . It is because we didn't hesitate to blazon forth those answers that we sit within the walls of Sing Sing.[21]

After the British master spy Kim Philby finally fled to Moscow in 1963, he published an autobiography in which the following passage occurs:

> Fuchs not only confessed his own part in the business, he also identified from photographs his contact in the United States, Harry Gold. From Gold, who was in a talkative mood, the chain led inexorably to the Rosenbergs, who were duly electrocuted.

Such evidence, of course, is merely suggestive. Equally suggestive is a passage in E. L. Doctorow's brilliantly evocative and empathetic novel, *The Book of Daniel*, where a fictional reporter, "Jack P. Fein," talks to the son of the executed "Isaacsons":

> Your folks were framed but that doesn't mean they were innocent babes. I don't believe they were a dangerous conspiracy to pass defense secrets, but I don't believe either that the U.S. Attorney, and the Judge, and the Justice Department, and the President of the United States conspired against *them* . . . In this country people don't get picked out of a hat to be put on trial for their lives . . . They were little neighborhood commies probably with some kind of third-rate operation that wasn't of use to anyone except maybe it made them feel important.

The son protests:

> "I thought you said the evidence was phony."
> "That's right. Those guys had to bring in a conviction." [22]

# 4

## The States and Subversion

The attempt to legislate Communists and radicals into submission or silence was even more eagerly taken up by state, county and municipal authorities than by the federal Congress. Between 1917 and 1920, at the height of the Red Scare, a score of states had passed criminal syndicalism statutes. Now, in 1949 alone, fifteen states passed antisubversion laws; by 1953, thirty-nine states had made it a criminal offense to *advocate* violent governmental change or to join an organization so advocating. As of January 1955, forty-four jurisdictions (including Alaska and Hawaii) had legislated to punish either sedition, criminal anarchy, criminal syndicalism, or advocacy of violent overthrow. Eleven states forbade "subversive" organizations to use public schools as meeting places.

In terms of its influence on other states,[1] Maryland's Subversive Activities Act of 1949 deserves primary attention. After a commission created by resolution of the state legislature, and including four graduates of Harvard Law School, had heard testimony from the FBI and Armed Services Intelligence, it concluded that there were 2,700 CP members resident in Maryland and that such a situation dictated drastic measures. (The commission, headed by the vehemently anti-Communist lawyer Frank B. Ober, refused to hear representatives of either the CP or the Progressive Party.) What the resultant Act attempted to do was to define and ban subversive organizations. Special Assistant Attorney General O. Bowie Duckett, assisted by a staff of investigators trained by military intelligence, set about compiling dossiers with a view to bringing suspect subversives before a grand jury. If the grand jury brought an indictment, and a state court subsequently ruled that an organization was subversive, then the Ober Act, as it was known, provided that the organization would be dissolved, its records turned over to the state Attorney General, and its property forfeited to the state. Rank-and-file members who, knowing an organization to have been designated subversive, nevertheless failed to leave it, were liable to be fined $5,000, or imprisoned for five years, or both. Leaders were liable to be fined $20,000, or imprisoned for twenty years, or both, a punishment four times more severe than that prescribed by the Smith Act. The Act—no doubt unconstitutionally— also made it a criminal offense to *advocate* the setting up of a United States government under foreign domination, even if violent methods were not advocated. Although the passage of the Ober Act was opposed by the ADA, the Civil Liberties Union, the CIO, and various teachers' organizations (the state Federation of Labor soft-pedaled its opposition), it was approved in November 1950 by a popular vote of 259,250 to 79,120.

The liberals drew temporary encouragement when in Baltimore Court No. 2 Judge Joseph Sherbow ruled the Act defective on the ground that it dealt with thoughts rather than actions, that it was in conflict with the First and Fourteenth Amendments, and that it was a bill of attainder. But the Court of Appeals reversed this ruling. Even so, not a single prosecution followed. [2]

Connecticut's sedition law made it a crime to print, et cetera, "scurrilous or abusive matter, concerning the form of government in the United States, its military forces, flag or uniforms . . ."or to advocate before ten or more persons (!) any measure "intended to injuriously affect the government of the United States or the State of Connecticut." [3] In Illinois it became illegal to advocate violent overthrow or to join any organization so doing. Michigan introduced life imprisonment in 1950 for writing or speaking subversive words, invalidated bequests to subversive organizations, and in 1952 passed its Communist Control (Trucks) Act. In 1951 Tennessee made death the maximum penalty for unlawful advocacy, while Indiana legislated a maximum three-year prison sentence for those who engaged in "any un-American activities." Louisiana threatened schoolboys advocating violent overthrow with expulsion. In April 1949, Governor Dewey of New York vetoed as unconstitutional a bill banning all parties that advocated violent overthrow. Introduced by State Senator Charles V. Scanlan (R., Bronx), it had been passed by a unanimous State Senate. [4]

Seizing the bull by the horns, a few states decided to outlaw the Communist Party. Massachusetts led the way in 1951, threatening with three years' imprisonment anyone who remained a member of the Party knowing it to be subversive, or who knowingly allowed a meeting place to be used by the CP. The statute was passed by 190 to 19 in the Assembly, and on a voice vote in the Senate, after Representative Edmond J. Donlan (D., Boston) declared: "Massachusetts boys, fighting and dying in Korea, will know that we at home stand solidly behind them." Indiana, Pennsylvania and Georgia also outlawed the Party (the Georgia statute carried with it a maximum penalty of twenty years' imprisonment). In February 1954, Governor Allan Shivers of Texas announced his support for making Party membership punishable by death, and in March such a bill was introduced into the state legislature by Senator Robert Patten. However, the Texas legislators lost their nerve and watered down the maximum penalty for CP membership to twenty years in prison plus a $20,000 fine. In 1955 the Washington legislature outlawed the CP without a single dissenting vote. It is worth noting, however, that until the Communist Control Act of 1954, all such state statutes were presumably invalidated by Section 4 (f) of the Internal Security Act of 1950: "Neither the holding of office nor membership in any Communist organization . . . shall constitute *per se* a violation of . . . this section or of any other criminal statute."

The Federal Internal Security Act of 1950 extended to domestic "Communist-action" and "Communist-front" organizations the principle of *registration* already employed in the 1939 Act with respect to agents of foreign principals. But five states had already jumped Senator McCarran's gun: California, Louisiana, Michigan and New York, and the administered territory of Hawaii. Soon they were joined in the registration stampede by Alabama, Arkansas, Delaware, Montana, New Mexico, South Carolina, Texas and Wyoming. In some of these states the registration provisions applied to all organizations advocating violent overthrow.

Largely on the initiative of State Senator Matthew F. Callahan, and with the support of the Legion and the Veterans of Foreign Wars, the Michigan Communist Control Act became law in 1952, endorsed by a popular referendum. All "foreign agencies," whether or not they advocated violent overthrow as well as all organizations so advocating, were obliged to register with the State Attorney General, and to report both their members and their finances. A three-judge federal district court dissolved a temporary order restraining implementation of the act, mainly on the ground of the *Dennis* ruling, but Judge Theodore Levin, dissenting, argued that the Trucks Act not only invaded a field preempted by the federal Internal Security Act, but also denied the due-process requirement of the Fourteenth Amendment. In point of fact neither State Attorney General Eugene

F. Black nor his successor Stephen J. Roth regarded the Act as constitutional, so no attempt was made to enforce it.[5] Indeed not a single organization registered anywhere in the United States.

## LOCAL ORDINANCES

Local registration ordinances[6] were more frequently enforced than were similar state provisions, notably in the traumatic year 1950. Within four or five months of the outbreak of the Korean war a spate of arrests occurred under local ordinances. In Los Angeles County, Henry Steinberg, local legislative director of the CP, was arrested at home for failure to register. Bail was granted and Steinberg won his point that the ordinance was unconstitutional. In Cumberland, Maryland, the Communists William Boyd Coleman and Arthur M. Schusterman were arrested for failing to register at City Hall. The one and only Communist of Jacksonville, Florida, was sentenced to three months in prison for remaining in town; he was set free with the help of the ACLU. The same treatment was meted out to the chairman of the Alabama CP, Sam Hall, but in October 1950 a federal judge declared the local ordinance to be unconstitutional. In November Jersey City's Director of Public Safety, Charles S. Witewski, ordered the police to start rounding up Communists for not registering. Some arrests followed.

One case of a prosecution under a state registration law was that of a sixty-four-year-old Negro, Matthew Knox, who was arrested in Birmingham, Alabama in August 1954 and sentenced to two years in jail for failing to register with the state Department of Public Safety. Knox did not in fact admit to being a Party member and the main evidence used against him was the discovery of purportedly Communistic literature in his room. He was released from jail on $1,000 bond with the support of the ECLC, but the pastor of the white church where he had worked as a janitor since 1943 dismissed him. Knox's conviction was later reversed. Significantly, this was the first occasion on which the Alabama registration statute had been used.

The majority of state antisubversive measures were prompted by local political pressures and rivalries. They were publicity stunts and little attempt was made to invoke them. William B. Prendergast reported in September 1950 that, having consulted the legislative reference services of the relevant states, he found that "nothing resembling a Communist has turned up anywhere as a result of the operation of these laws."[7] On the other hand, a number of prosecutions were set in motion during the early 1950s: Nelson, Onda and Dolsen were convicted in Pennsylvania, while in Massachusetts indictments were brought first against Professor Dirk Struik and later, in April 1954, against the chairman of the state CP, Otis A. Hood, several times a candidate for governor, and six of his colleagues. In May 1956 these cases, brought under the Massachusetts law of 1951, were dropped in the wake of the Supreme Court's *Nelson* verdict. But in the meantime Carl Braden had been convicted under a Kentucky statute.

A number of states [8] found it an expedient precaution, as well as an emblematic gesture, to impose loyalty or disaffiliation oaths on their public officials. Georgia's officials were constrained to disavow "sympathy" for Communism; Ohio made refusal to answer official inquiries a ground for dismissal; and Michigan equated invocation of the Fifth Amendment by a public employee with *prima facie* membership of the CP.

## TAMPERING WITH ELECTORAL DEMOCRACY

Even more contentious was the attempt to exclude certain categories of "subversives" from *elected* office. Admittedly a general oath of allegiance to the Constitution was common practice at both the federal and state levels, but any attempt to force candidates to repudiate specific doctrines or organizations could be construed only as an undemocratic impairment of the people's freedom to elect the representatives of their choice. However, the principle of democracy was not the governing passion of the age. By the end of 1952 approximately half the states barred from the ballot individuals or organizations advocating violent overthrow or sedition or a foreign-dominated government in the United States. In most cases acceptance or exclusion was based on the simple formula of an affidavit: the State of Washington imposed on elected officials the obligation to make a notarized declaration that they were not members of any organization listed by the U.S. Attorney General. Every candidate for state elective offices in Pennsylvania was required to file with his or her nomination papers an affidavit that he or she was not "a subversive person." But an Indiana statute passed in 1945 went further by insisting that each candidate party must "insert a plank in its platform that it does not advocate any of the doctrines"; each local electoral board was duty bound to "determine the character and nature of the political doctrines" of the candidates.

On at least three occasions the imposition of a nonsubversive oath on candidates for elective office was tested in the courts. The New Jersey law of 1949 was found unconstitutional by the New Jersey Supreme Court in the case of *Imbrie v. Marsh* (1950), on the ground that New Jersey's constitutional oath of office was exclusive of all others.[9] Although this ruling could equally well have applied to Maryland, the state courts decided to the contrary. In 1948 the people of Maryland had voted by 202,910 to 84,132 to amend their state Constitution to bar from public office advocates of violent overthrow. In 1950 the Progressive Party candidates refused on principle to execute any such affidavit and were accordingly denied a place on the ballot. They brought suit. In the case of *Shub v. Simpson*, the State Court of Appeals sustained the disqualification of Louis Shub, the Progressive candidate for governor, but at the same time the court overturned the disqualification of Thelma Gerende, candidate for the U.S. House of Representatives, on the ground that a state cannot prescribe qualifications for the U.S. Congress. Later Miss Gerende sought a seat on the Baltimore City Council and again refused to sign the affidavit, subsequently contesting her disqualification as far as the U.S. Supreme Court. In *Gerende v. Board of Supervisors* (1951) the Court, without discussing any basic constitutional issues, concluded that a state had the right to bar from the ballot anyone aspiring to overthrow the government by force. A year later ten candidates of minor parties, including the Militant Workers Party and the Industrial Government Party, were excluded from the ballot in Pennsylvania's state elections for refusing to take the requisite oath.

Some states were even more explicit: they banned the Communist Party and its candidates by name from the ballot. This had been done in New York in 1938: henceforward Communists campaigned under the American Labor Party label. It had been done in California in 1940, but in 1942 the California Supreme Court ruled that it was unconstitutional. In the same year a federal district court made a similar ruling. Even so, by the fall of 1950 seventeen states explicitly excluded the CP from the ballot.[10] There was no validation for such discrimination in federal law until the Communist Control Act of 1954, which, although it did not explicitly bar the CP from the ballot, did hint in that direction as concomitant with outlawry. In the case of *Salwen v. Rees* (October 1954), the New Jersey Supreme Court referred to the Act in ruling that Salwen was ineligible to stand for county office under the CP label.

## INQUISITION IN NEW HAMPSHIRE

In New Hampshire Attorney General Louis C. Wyman persuaded the state legislature to pass the Subversive Activities Act (1951) although, according to the FBI, there were only forty-three members of the CP in New Hampshire. Modeled largely on Maryland's Ober Act (Wyman, like Ober, was a graduate of Harvard Law School), this statute placed the hunt for subversives in Wyman's own, eager hands. Acting under powers conferred on him by the Act and by a resolution of the General Court in 1953, Wyman summoned Hugh De Gregory, formerly secretary-treasurer of the Boston CP, for questioning. Gregory invoked the Fifth Amendment. So persistent was Wyman's harassment that Gregory appeared fourteen times in the New Hampshire state courts and twice before the U.S. Supreme Court, spent two short periods in jail, and was sentenced to a year's imprisonment in March 1956.[11] Wyman's resolute persecution of the fellow-traveling Methodist layman, Willard Uphaus, is described elsewhere in this book,[12] but his report on Uphaus's World Fellowship deserves quotation:

> . . . based upon what information we have been able to assemble, the following individuals would appear at this time to be the usual contingent of "dupes" and unsuspecting persons that surround almost every venture that is instigated or propelled by the "perennials" and articulate apologists for Communists and Soviet chicanery, but of this we are not certain.

Appended were the names of the thirty-six persons about whom the state's highest law officer was "not certain."

Although the Progressive Party's presidential candidate, Henry A. Wallace, had achieved successes somewhat less than spectacular in New Hampshire (1,970 votes, or 0.0084 percent of the votes cast in 1948), Wyman's devotion to the public safety nevertheless dictated that he should interrogate all available Progressives. In January 1954 he subpoenaed Paul Sweezy, the former Harvard economist and coeditor of the Marxist *Monthly Review*. Sweezy flatly denied ever having belonged to the CP, attended its meetings, known any of its members in New Hampshire, or advocated violent overthrow of the government. But when questioned about the Progressive Party and its members, Sweezy invoked the First Amendment. In June, Wyman subpoenaed him again, specifically to discuss a lecture that Sweezy had delivered in March at the University of New Hampshire:

> "Didn't you tell the class . . . that Socialism was inevitable in this country?"
> "Did you advocate Marxism at that time?"
> "Did you in this last lecture . . . or in any of former lectures espouse the theory of dialectical materialism?"

Also subpoenaed was Dr. Gwynne Harris Daggett, associate professor of English at the University of New Hampshire, who had been responsible for inviting Sweezy to lecture in three successive years. Daggett took the First Amendment. Wyman then arranged for the Superior Court of Merrimack County to put the questions, with the same results, whereupon Justice Robert F. Griffith found Sweezy and Daggett to be in contempt, while Governor Hugh Gregg announced that if Daggett did not yield "I will ask for his resignation." It was then agreed that Daggett should answer the questions while Sweezy continued to fight. The nature of the regime he was fighting was further illuminated when Sweezy's counsel complained that Wyman's special assistant had been taking down the license-plate numbers of people attending the Merrimack court. Wyman did not deny it. Commented Judge Griffith: "Well, the matter is completely immaterial to the particular issue at hand." [13] Sweezy, unlike Wyman's other victim, Uphaus, eventually won his case in the U.S. Supreme Court.

## CALIFORNIA: THE TENNEY COMMITTEE

Foremost among the state "un-American" legislative committees whose inquisitorial methods so closely resembled those of HCUA and the SISS was California's Fact-Finding Committee on Un-American Activities, an agency of misery almost universally known as the Tenney Committee, in honor of its forceful chairman from 1941 to 1949, Jack B. Tenney. Like his friend Mayor Samuel W. Yorty of Los Angeles, Tenney had once belonged to the pro-Communist wing of the Democratic Party and had been named as a subversive before the Dies Committee in Washington. It was after a bitter factional fight within Local 47 of the American Federation of Musicians, culminating in Tenney's failure to win reelection as president, that he turned to red-baiting on a grand scale.

Following his elevation to the state Senate in 1943, Tenney and his committee wrought havoc among California's schoolteachers, film and theater people, trade unionists and state employees who supported the New Deal. Running the committee autocratically—its files were locked in his office, he alone hired the staff, ordered the hearings, issued press releases and authorized the reports—Tenney waged war on the Actors' Laboratory Theater, the American Civil Liberties Union, the American-Russian Institute, the Committee for the First Amendment, the Congress of American Women, the Joint Anti-Fascist Refugee Committee, the Screen Writers Guild and the Progressive Party.

In his report for 1948 he listed several thousand individuals, with their political affiliations. He launched assaults on the People's Educational Center of Los Angeles and the California Labor School of

San Francisco. He hectored the University of California, castigated judges, intimidated lawyers, denouncing them as Communists and periodically physically ejected them from the hearing room. Nor was the Tenney Committee above throwing its weight into local political struggles and vendettas, as in the case of Fairfax, a small town north of San Francisco, where a right-wing clique, ousted in April 1946 from the City Council, red-baited Elsa Gidlow, who was appointed to the Planning Commission after the victory of the liberals.[14]

But few of the many bills Tenney supported became law; in 1949 alone he introduced seventeen antisubversive bills that aborted. Increasingly, frustrated ambition warped his judgment and led him to offend the vested interests on whose support he depended. Following the disappointment of running fourth of nine candidates in an April 1949 primary for mayor of Los Angeles, he dug his own political grave by hiring Ed Gibbons, the muckraking editor of *Alert*, to prove that his rivals were disguised reds. Embittered and increasingly rabid, Tenney ran in 1952 as vice-presidential candidate of the Christian Nationalist Party, whose chief was the notorious fascist and anti-Semite, Gerald L. K. Smith.

Under Tenney's successor, Senator Hugh H. Burns, an undertaker by profession, power passed largely into the hands of the Committee's counsel, Richard E. Combs. Whereas Tenney had sought the headlines by launching wild allegations against famous people, Combs was more interested in grass-roots surveillance, in purging California's teachers, in placing agents on the campuses of the University of California, and in exchanging information with HCUA's staff in Washington. In September 1953 the Committee recommended to private employers the discharge of six utility workers who had pleaded the Fifth Amendment, at the same time offering a general screening of utility employees. The Burns Committee was in business primarily to deprive radicals of their jobs.

## WASHINGTON: THE CANWELL COMMITTEE

In 1947 the State of Washington established a Joint Legislative Fact-Finding Committee on Un-American Activities, composed initially of five Republicans and two Democrats, and chaired by a former sheriff, Albert F. Canwell. The real target of the Committee was the New Deal. In the late 1930s, in the era of the Washington Commonwealth Federation and the Washington Pension Union, the Democratic Party had swung far to the left, and now the knives were out. State Senator Jerry J. O'Connell, a member of the CIO-PAC and vice-president of the WPU, was accused of being a secret Communist. So too was Hugh de Lacy,[15] a U.S. Congressman from 1944 to 1946. Following the Republican victories of that year, the right-wing Democrats set about purging their ranks of radicals, while, simultaneously, Dave Beck of the Teamsters Union, AFL, struggled for local dominance against the fellow-traveling leader of the International Longshoremen's and Warehousemen's Union, Harry Bridges. During the last three months of 1947 the *Seattle Post-Intelligencer* (Hearst) and the *Seattle Times* published on average one story about local Communists every other day.

The Canwell Committee's targets were similar to those of the Tenney Committee in California: Harry Bridges, the WPU, the Seattle Labor School (listed by the U.S. Attorney General in December 1947), the Seattle Repertory Playhouse and left-wing faculty members of the University of Washington. Armed with a mandate to investigate anyone "whose activities are such as to indicate a purpose to foment internal strife, discord and dissension," Canwell hired seven investigators and imported such nationally prominent ex-Communist professional witnesses as Louis Budenz, J. B. Matthews, Manning Johnson, Howard Rushmore, Benjamin Gitlow and George Hewitt, all men who knew a Communist when they saw one, even if they had never seen him before.

Canwell enjoyed a measure of success in having recalcitrant witnesses convicted for contempt, but his legislative proposals—which included fingerprinting all teachers and establishing an American "Devil's Island" in the South Seas for deportable aliens whose native countries refused to receive them—had no more success than did Jack Tenney's in California. The Committee's accounts, which should have been itemized in detail, were heavily weighted with such vague attributions as "confidential investigation expense," and it emerged that certain friendly witnesses had been paid as much as $500 for "research and advice." [16] Canwell himself, whose political career was soon cut short by the electorate, admitted in 1955 that he had destroyed a large portion of his committee's records "to prevent them getting into the wrong hands." Later he established in Spokane the American Intelligence Service, which maintained hundreds of files and dossiers, owned a bookstore stocked with Birchite literature, and issued a newsletter called *Vigilante*.

### ILLINOIS: THE BROYLES COMMISSION

In Illinois, the Seditious Activities Investigating Commission was created in August 1947 with a mandate to investigate any person or organization suspected of advocating violent overthrow. Chaired by Paul

Broyles, a Republican Methodist from Mount Vernon and an ex-commander of a Legion Post, the fifteen-member Commission promptly launched an assault on the University of Chicago and Roosevelt College. Although the Commission recommended sweeping legislation against subversive teachers, public employees and even legislators, and proposed that the CP and its fronts be outlawed, none of these proposals was enacted. Indeed, the Commission itself died with its own bills, many of which had been fed into its wide-open mouth by Legion lobbyists like Ellidore Libonati, and then disgorged without any trace of digestion. Indeed, indigestion characterized the Broyles Commission Report:

> . . . a Liberal in current American society is a political thinker or actor whose feelings, thought and actions are in favor of the Kremlin, not without friendly criticism.

> May we further state that this Commission fearlessly and without any pretence of dealing with the subject matter of its investigation; without docility are anxious to advocate legislation to absolutely curb their operations . . . nihiltory legislation so needed to treat them as the mongrel class of citizenry.

In 1951 Broyles persuaded both houses to pass a bill requiring every state employing agency to ferret out subversives. Vetoing the bill, Governor Adlai Stevenson commented: "We must not burn down the house to kill the rats." Two years later Governor William G. Stratton vetoed yet another Broyles bill.[17]

By 1954 thirteen states [18] had at one time or another set up legislative committees with a general mandate to investigate subversion. The Ohio Un-American Activities Commission, which was partly inspired by a campaign in the *Cincinnati Enquirer* and worked in close collaboration with the "red squads" of the Cleveland, Toledo and Cincinnati police forces, was established in June 1951, with instructions to report to the General Assembly two years later. The Blackburn Commission, as it was known, cited twenty-odd witnesses for contempt. One of them, Oscar Smilack, allegedly the "angel" of the Franklin County CP, was committed to Lima State Mental Hospital by the Commission before the Court of Appeals came to his rescue. Headline hunting, the Commission released to the press the names of several people whom Cecil Scott, a former FBI agent with a record of felony and mental disturbance, had named as Communists in closed session. Four of the victims who demanded a hearing got one, nine months later.

The life of the Commission was extended for a further year by 123 votes to 4. Expressing admiration for its work, U.S. Congressman

Frank T. Bow of Ohio warned that with 1,300 Communists in Ohio, about half of them in Cleveland, "there can be no real peace or security for our people, for Communism is the devil's own instrument of hatred, war, chaos and ruin." But Governor Frank J. Lausche took a different view. The Commission, he complained in July 1953, "has not brought to the bar of justice a single person guilty of sedition, treason, or acts contemplating the overthrow of our government." In vetoing the Devine Bill, which nevertheless became Ohio's Anti-Subversion Law, the Governor foresaw "the reputations of innocent persons actually ruined by rumors, doubts, innuendos." [19]

# PART TWO

---

# The Machinery
# of Repression

# 5

# The Congressional Inquisition

## AMERICAN AND BRITISH SYSTEMS—SOME COMPARISONS

"The Grand Inquest of the Nation" was how Pitt the Elder described Parliament in 1742; ". . . as such it is our duty to inquire into every step of publick management, either Abroad or at Home, in order to see that nothing has been done amiss." Although the American Constitution is silent on the subject, from the first days of the Republic, Congress asserted the right to investigate, to subpoena witnesses, and to punish obstructionists. (Since 1857 this has been done through the courts, although Congress, like the British Parliament, holds the power to punish contempt.)

Indeed, while the practice of Parliamentary investigation fell into semiabeyance in Britain, it became a dominant feature of American political life, at no time more so than the one we are considering. Thus, whereas Congress authorized 285 investigations between 1789 and 1925, it authorized no less than 225 investigations between 1950 and 1952. There were four investigations into Communism in the 79th Congress (1945–46); twenty-two in the 80th Congress (1947–48); twenty-four in the 81st Congress (1949–50); thirty-four in the 82nd Congress (1951–52); and fifty-one, an all-time high, in the 83rd Congress (1953–54).[1] During the same period in Britain there were no legislative inquiries investigating Communism, subversion or disloyalty, nor any tribunals of inquiry or royal commissions. In April 1954 Churchill specifically declined to set up a Royal Commission to investigate Communist activities and propaganda in Great Britain.

One of the reasons for the divergence of American and British practice in the matter of legislative inquest lies in the fact that, whereas Parliament has become by virtue of the party system both the master and the servant of the executive, in America executive and legislature, even during periods when the same party has dominated both, have displayed outright rivalry. Time and again Congress has probed, and the White House has balked, pleading executive privilege. At this provocation, Congress probes, prods, pushes and pummels all the more furiously.

The American Congress also suffers from other frustrations not shared by the Westminster Parliament, frustrations stemming largely from the written Constitution and the role of the judiciary. In Britain the legislative power of the Crown-in-Parliament (which today effectively means the House of Commons) is unlimited, is ultimate; whereas in America statute law must conform to constitutional law or, more accurately, to the way the Supreme Court interprets it. Congressmen whose dearest wish is to pass laws sending every "pinko" to Alcatraz or back to Russia, yet gloomily aware that pseudo-liberal justices will mince and moan about the Bill of Rights, have naturally taken refuge in "government by exposure," the rough-and-tumble of the Congressional inquiry.

In fact, British Parliamentary select committees enjoy certain powers unavailable on Capitol Hill: they can, for example, not only subpoena witnesses and their records, but also punish the plea of self-incrimination as contempt; and contempt, like perjury, is directly punishable by the House. Nor does a witness before a Parliamentary committee take with him a lawyer, as in Washington. Nevertheless Parliamentary committees do not attempt to inflict on the executive, the bureaucracy or the armed forces the kind of sharp grilling that is characteristic of Congressional inquiries. The discretions and silences endemic to a relatively unified establishment generally prevail; and although radical MP's may regard the Treasury with suspicion, in general MP's have not treated civil servants with anything approaching the hostility that developed between Congressmen and New Deal bureaucrats in the age of Roosevelt. The fact that MP's can put fifty or a hundred questions to ministers across the floor of the House, four days a week, undoubtedly serves as an immediate and effective outlet for animosities, whereas the Congressional committee wishing, in Pitt's phrase, "to inquire into every step of publick management," must set a full-scale investigation in motion, for which it tends to prepare with elaborate staff work, and a noisy girding of armor.

## CONGRESSIONAL COMPLEXES

The individual Congressman often makes his name as a member of a committee operating in full publicity, whereas even the politically educated and aware in Britain (apart from lobbyists) take little interest in Parliamentary committees or their membership. The Congressman feels more exposed to the passions and whims of his constituents; at election time his fate will be determined by the general state of his party to some extent, but much less so than in the geographically small and homogeneous Britain. The Congressman tends to share with some of his constituents populist resentments toward the intellectuals, the State Department, the liberal judges. Both an excessive desire to please and alternating outbursts of aggression are fed by the Congressman's precarious and not very flattering status.[2]

Ever since federal bureaucrats were appointed on the "merit" system, rather than by political patronage, these assured, educated, sometimes supercilious career men have tended to rub Congressmen the wrong way. Under Roosevelt the federal establishment expanded by 50 percent in five years. Observing the influx of progressive intellectuals into the New Deal agencies and then, during the war, into the OSS, the Office of Scientific Research, the President's Council of Economic Advisers, and the Atomic Energy Commission (AEC)— agencies that tended to become secretive islands of power, eluding legislative scrutiny—the small-town lawyers and businessmen in Congress resorted to the war cry of Communism in government. This slogan condensed a complex of resentments about the advance of organized labor, interfering welfare legislation, and the new laws and agencies designed to keep the human consequences of the profit motive in check.[3]

In 1943 the House created a Special Committee to Investigate Executive Agencies under the Chairmanship of the conservative Howard W. Smith (D., Virginia), its aim being to discredit New Deal policies across the board. In January 1947 a Congressional attack on the Tennessee Valley Authority as Communist-infiltrated was led by Senator Kenneth McKellar (D., Tennessee), who evidently resented the Authority's exemption from the patronage system. (The AEC's general counsel, Herbert S. Marks, was one of those TVA employees alleged to have been Communists during a Congressional probe in 1940.)[4] The knives were out.

To sharpen its knives Congress in 1946 passed the Legislative Reorganization Act, which reduced the number of committees and endowed the survivors with more efficient staffs and a legislative reference service. The Act also gave every Senate standing committee the power to subpoena on any matter within its jurisdiction, without the Senate's adoption of a special enabling resolution, as had up till then been necessary. HCUA acquired the same statutory subpoena power, independent of specific authorization by the House.

The 80th Congress set no less than four committees to work examining the personnel files of the State Department. To the House Appropriations Committee the Department in January 1948 handed over confidential personnel files containing rumor and gossip, with the result that an abstract of the files was placed into public record, with symbols substituted for names. Truman was furious (indeed, he frequently complained of Congressional leaks) and ordered an end to it. In response, the House Committee on Expenditures in the Executive Departments submitted a resolution on March 28 requiring any government department to yield any information to any Congressional committee requiring it. In March 1948 Truman forbade the departments to furnish personnel loyalty data to Congress. In February 1950 he refused to hand over State Department loyalty files to a Senate subcommittee. In January 1952 the Secretary of State refused to give to the SISS reports submitted by foreign-service officers. Three months later Truman instructed that loyalty and agency investigatory files be withheld from a Senate Appropriations subcommittee. Partisan though the spirit of this struggle was, the point should be made that in May 1954 the Eisenhower government released a "memorandum on Separation of Powers," addressed to the President by his Attorney General, which quoted a long line of precedents from Washington to Truman in defense of executive privilege—"Courts have uniformly held that the President and the heads of departments have an uncontrolled discretion to withhold the information and papers in the public interest." [5]

## HCUA

The House Committee on Un-American Activities had its forerunners. The Fish Committee, which in January 1931 issued a report drawing familiar connections between Communism, aliens, blacks and free love, took up the work of the Overman Committee thirteen years earlier and was in turn succeeded in 1938 by the Special Committee on Un-American Activities, whose chairman, Martin Dies (D., Texas), complained that the federal bureaucracy was saturated with "hundreds of left-wingers and radicals who do not believe in our system of private enterprise." Dies's book *The Trojan Horse* devoted 303 pages to the menace of Communism and only 41 to American fascism, even though it was published in 1940. According to Dies, high taxes could produce only poverty and unemployment—"But the cure for the ills of private enterprise is more private enterprise." On November 25, 1938, he listed as "purveyors of class hatred" Stalin, Frances Perkins, Harold Ickes, Harry Hopkins and other New Dealers, "who range in political insanity from Socialism to Communism" and whose resignations he called for, along with their "satellites." According to Dies, who subpoenaed the records of the American League for Peace and Democracy before publishing the names of members employed by the government, "there are not less than two thousand outright Communists and Party-liners still holding jobs in the government in Washington." [6] In 1941 he referred to 1,200 subversive officials.

The Special Committee was almost defunct when it was rescued, refurbished and permanently set up in business in January 1945 by the parliamentary legerdemain of Representative John E. Rankin (D., Mississippi). On his motion the House voted by 207 to 186 to make it a standing committee and the only permanent investigating committee in the House, enjoying unique subpoena powers, with its members free to sit on other standing committees. The narrow majority that carried this motion consisted of 137 Republicans and 70 Democrats, of whom 63 were Southerners. Under Public Law 601, 79th Congress, HCUA was authorized to investigate:

(1) the extent, character and objects of un-American propaganda activities in the United States, (2) the diffusion within the United States of subversive and un-American propaganda that is instigated from foreign countries or of a domestic origin and attacks the principle of the form of government as guaranteed by our Constitution, and (3) all other questions in relation thereto that would aid Congress in any remedial legislation.

Obviously, these terms of reference did not impose upon any single HCUA investigation the necessity of having a legislative purpose, although this was often to be disputed by the Committee's critics and victims, the Supreme Court having previously insisted, in its extremely rare rulings on Congressional investigations, that only a clear legislative purpose could validate them.

As the Cold War intensified, fewer and fewer Representatives dared to oppose publicly HCUA's attitudes, actions, contempt citations or annual bids for renewal. In April 1946 the House accepted HCUA's motion to cite the executive board and secretary of the Joint Anti-Fascist Refugee Committee, by a vote of 292 to 56. Early in 1947, when the witnesses in contempt were two brashly defiant Communists, Gerhart Eisler and Leon Josephson, the contempt citations were voted by 370 to 1 and 357 to 2 respectively, only Vito Marcantonio and Adam Clayton Powell daring to resist. Later in the year, when the House considered the Hollywood Ten's reliance on the First Amendment, Albert Maltz (a test case) was cited for contempt by 346 to 17. On this vote the ultraradicals Marcantonio and Powell were joined by a handful of brave liberals including Emanuel Celler, John A. Carroll, Helen G. Douglas, Chet Holifield and Andy Biemiller. HCUA itself was renewed in 1946 by 240 to 81 and thereafter by even more irresistible majorities.[7] It is said that HCUA became so popular among Congressmen that when the 83rd Congress met in January 1953, 185 of 221 Republicans applied for membership of it. In February 1953, the House, by 315 to 2, voted HCUA a record appropriation of $300,000. In 1959 the appropriation was the highest ever, $327,000, more than double the amount allocated to Education and Labor and to Foreign Affairs.

During the six years of the 79th, 80th, and 81st Congresses, twenty-two Representatives sat on the Committee at one time or another, among them some of the most politically, economically and racially conservative members of the House. In 1945–46, when the Committee contained a Democratic majority and was chaired by John S. Wood of Georgia, the dominant figure was the man who had saved the Committee from extinction, John E. Rankin of Mississippi. A dedicated enemy of the New Deal who had held his heavily poll-taxed seat since 1921, and who periodically reaffirmed his sympathy for the Ku Klux Klan, Rankin described the Fair Employment Practices Commission as "the beginning of a Communistic dictatorship the like of which America never dreamed." Communism had "hounded and persecuted the Saviour during his earthly ministry, inspired his crucifixion, derided him in his dying agony, then gambled for his garments at the foot of the cross." Proposing the investigation of Hollywood that took place in 1947, he referred to "the loathsome, filthy, insinuating, un-American undercurrents that are running through various pictures," and proposed a bill that would render schoolteachers liable to ten years' imprisonment and a $10,000 fine if they "convey the impression of sympathy with . . . Communist ideology."

The guns in Europe had scarcely been silenced when the Rankin-Thomas Committee joyfully resumed the battle with the eternal enemy. Summoning the black CP leader, Benjamin Davis, Jr., HCUA began to rake over the coals of the Nazi-Soviet Pact while representatives of Tass took notes.[8] Within a year the Committee had cited Eugene Dennis, general secretary of the CP, for contempt. From October 1946 until March 1947, J. Parnell Thomas bombarded Attorney General Tom Clark with letters urging him to prosecute the CP for failing to register as a foreign agent and for seeking the violent overthrow of the government. On April 23, 1947, Thomas wrote Truman: "The immunity which this foreign-directed conspiracy has been enjoying for the past fifteen years must cease." The Hollywood investigation of 1947 was obviously aimed at both the New Deal and the wartime alliance with Russia. The Committee's sensational espionage hearings in the summer of 1948 (Bentley, Chambers, Hiss) had the same targets and were timed, as Thomas recalled in February 1954, "to keep the heat on Harry Truman" during the run-up to the election.

But Thomas (born John Feeny) was about to fall. After his secretary spilled the beans to the columnist Drew Pearson, it came out that since becoming chairman he had received about $4,000 for expense vouchers and roughly $7,000 in staff kickbacks.[9] Convicted in November 1949, Thomas was sent to Danbury prison, where his path crossed that of one of the Hollywood Ten, Ring Lardner, Jr.

Also prominent on the Committee at this time were the authors of the Mundt-Nixon Bill, Karl E. Mundt and Richard M. Nixon. First elected in 1938, and with interests in farming, real estate and insurance, Mundt's hostility to the New Deal, the State Department and the UN helped cement his alliance with McCarthy after he moved from the House to the Senate in January 1949. Richard Nixon, who entered Congress in 1946, and who made his career out of the Hiss case, was in some respects a cut above his colleagues—less rabid and venomous than Rankin or Thomas, less obtuse than John McDowell of Pennsylvania, an obscure former newspaperman who called Karl Marx "a bum." Nixon from the outset displayed a good, clear, lawyer's brain. Although he played the standard Republican refrain about Teheran, Yalta and Potsdam, he avoided the rhetorical excesses of the older reactionaries and was consistently polite even to hostile witnesses. "But there is a great difference between the Socialists and the Communists, is there not?" he asked a witness in 1948; and he praised the criticisms of his own bill leveled by Arthur Garfield Hays of the ACLU as "very healthy." [10] A Congressman's conscience belongs to God, only his behavior concerns the historian.

The impression is inescapable, that many members of this Committee fell short both on knowledge and intelligence. Here, for example, Rankin questioned Committee counsel Ernie Adamson about the chairman of the British Labour Party, Harold Laski:

MR. RANKIN: Who is Mr. Laski?
MR. ADAMSON: Mr. Laski is, I believe, one of the leaders in England of the Communist movement.

MR. RANKIN: Is he an American?

It was in 1948 that Robert Miller, a former State Department employee mentioned by Elizabeth Bentley, was called to testify, and faced Representative F. Edward Hebert (D., Louisiana):

> MR. HEBERT: How did [your wife] get to Russia? Why did she go there?
> MR. MILLER: She went there during the depression because she was interested in dancing. She considered the Russians had the best ballet in the world.
> MR. HEBERT: Would that be associated with the Academy of— Mr. Stripling, what is the name of that science academy?
> MR. STRIPLING: Academy of Science.
> MR. HEBERT: The Academy of Science. What is that in Russia?
> MR. MILLER: I frankly know very little about it . . .
> MR. HEBERT: Was she a member of that academy?
> MR. MILLER: Lord, no. The ballet had nothing to do with that. . . .
> MR. HEBERT: Did she have any connection at all with the Academy of Science?
> MR. MILLER: No, sir.
> MR. HEBERT: Do you know what the Academy of Science in Russia is? [11]

In January 1949, John S. Wood of Georgia, a gentle but conservative anti-New Dealer, became chairman of HCUA for the second time. Only he and Nixon had survived from the 80th Congress, and the style of the Committee for the next few years was calmer, more courteous, than under the frenetic J. Parnell Thomas. But the underlying viciousness was sustained by new recruits, notably Francis E. Walter (D., Pennsylvania), the racist co-author of the Walter-McCarran Act, who joined HCUA in 1949 and became chairman in 1954; Harold H. Velde (R., Illinois), a former FBI agent who became chairman in 1953 and led HCUA in a series of hectic publicity stunts; and three primitive bigots, Gordon H. Scherer (R., Ohio), Kit Clardy (R., Michigan) and Donald L. Jackson (D., California). Both Scherer and Clardy later joined the John Birch Society.

Although not an elected representative of the people, the Committee's general counsel was better placed to impose his personality and prejudices on the proceedings—and on unfriendly witnesses— than was any member of the Committee other than the chairman himself. During the 79th Congress (1945–46), the role was filled by a fifty-two-year-old lawyer from Georgia, Ernie Adamson, described by the *Christian Science Monitor* as "suave, bulky, slow-moving . . ." Dedicated to hounding left-wing radio commentators off the air, an enterprise in which he was largely successful, Adamson exceeded himself in December 1946 when he released a report, written by himself and not yet approved by HCUA, in which he described the Library of Congress as "a haven for aliens and foreign-minded Americans." Thomas and Rankin were both exasperated by this act of usurpation,[12] and when Thomas became chairman a month later he promptly fired Adamson, replacing him with Robert Stripling. A tall character with dark rings under his eyes in the style of a Charles Addams cartoon, Stripling had been brought from Texas by Martin Dies and given a patronage job in the folding room of the Old House Office Building at $120 a month. When Dies assumed the chairmanship of the new Special Committee in 1938, he appointed Stripling chief investigator, a post he held for nine years. It was he who publicly interrogated the Hollywood Ten and Bertolt Brecht.[13]

Frank S. Tavenner's [14] run as Committee counsel lasted from 1949 to 1956. He approached his witnesses, wrote Murray Kempton, "like an undertaker welcoming the prodigal son back to the funeral; his wheedling, gentle voice cries out for a little give, for just the semblance of remorse." His successor as counsel and staff director, Richard Arens, was without peer in the intensity of his hatred for reds and aliens. As aide to Senator Chapman Revercomb in 1947–48, he had worked for the exclusion of displaced persons; as counsel to Pat McCarran's Subcommittee on Immigration in 1949, he had helped to defeat Emmanuel Celler's proposal to admit 25,000 displaced Jews from Germany. As an example of his oratorical-inquisitorial style, this hectoring of a member of the Southern California Peace Crusade was not untypical: "Kindly tell us, while you are under oath now, and in the aura of patriotism which you have surrounded yourself [with] in your opening statement, whether or not you betrayed your country by being executive secretary of this organization designed to subvert the security of this great nation." [15] Obsessively he employed the phrase, "Stand up like a red-blooded American . . ." when berating reluctant witnesses at New Haven in 1956, at Baltimore in 1957, at Newark and Boston in 1958, and at Washington, D.C. in 1960.

A passionate Christian who later joined Benjamin Schwartz's Anti-Communist Christian Crusade, Arens received merit citations from the Legion, the Daughters of the American Revolution and many other patriotic organizations, and indeed he had at one time worked for the antisubversion section of the Legion's Americanism Commission. In 1960 House Speaker Sam Rayburn ruled that he should not be receiving payment from an outside source while counsel to the Committee, and he accordingly resigned to become, in September 1960, a Commissioner of the U.S. Court of Claims. By that time the Committee's permanent staff had swollen to forty-nine.[16]

What were the main characteristics of the Committee in operation? Geographical inertia was not one of HCUA's vices. The Committee and its subcommittees customarily rode into town like a sheriff's posse. In 1954 alone it was high noon in Albany, New York; Washington, D.C.; Maryland; California; Michigan; the Pacific Northwest; Philadelphia; Dayton; and Florida. In 1955 the subcommittees visited Fort Wayne, Seattle, Milwaukee, Newark (New Jersey), Ohio, Los Angeles and San Diego. On other occasions law and order came to New York City, Portland, Charlotte, Denver, St. Louis, New Haven, New Orleans, Atlanta and San Juan (Puerto Rico). Sometimes the rough riders focused on Communist infiltration of a geographical area, but usually the area dimension was linked to a professional one: defense industries, longshoremen, lawyers, the press, radio and television, the film industry, teachers, social workers.

Wherever they traveled, HCUA's members basked in the limelight that politicians love. Nor were working conditions exactly Spartan. In 1960 Knight newspapers put in hand a study of HCUA's expense vouchers and discovered that in May 1958 Representative Morgan M. Moulder ran up a bill of $282.17 during a four-day stay at the Plaza Hotel, New York. Later he, Francis Walter and three staff members ran up a bill of $900.22 in Los Angeles. In February 1959 the same team spent $1,187 in a period of four or five days. Motivating it all, apart from mundane political ambition, was a personal striving for status, for recognition, by mediocre men for whom politics was the only escape from obscurity. As J. Parnell Thomas put it, "Those Hollywood bigshots were pretty high and mighty at first, but they got off their high horse all right." [17]

The Committee's lust for publicity was unquenchable. Despite rulings in 1952 and 1955 by Speaker Sam Rayburn that hearings should not be televised, despite the fact that HCUA's own rules, as revised in 1953, specifically included a witness's right to refuse to be televised, and despite resolutions in opposition to televised Congressional hearings by the Federal, New York State, and District of Columbia Bar Associations—all this notwithstanding, HCUA generally worked under the glare of klieg lights. Rights were treated as privileges dependent on good behavior: Chairman Velde asked the actor Lionel Stander, "If we do turn off the cameras, will you answer the questions that are put to you by counsel?" Witnesses faced storms of exploding flashbulbs, sudden sunrises and sunsets from the klieg lights, a stifling atmosphere as reporters pushed for places at the overcrowded long tables. Bishop G. Bromley Oxnam recalled his unfriendly confrontation with the Committee in July 1953: "There were, I think, seven microphones or recording devices in front of me, so placed that it was impossible to have my papers before me in any way that gave easy access . . . when I lifted my eyes to look toward Committee members, I was almost blinded."

But this was merely a preliminary to more painful forms of intimidation inflicted on recalcitrant witnesses. Rankin was only being himself when in 1946 he warned Dr. Jacob Auslander, of the Joint Anti-Fascist Refugee Committee, who emigrated from Austria in 1924 and became an American citizen in 1929: "Do you realize that you are violating your oath of citizenship when you show contempt for this Committee, and are likely to have that citizenship canceled?" To Manuel Magana, also of the JAFRC, he snarled: "You are rubbing your nose right up against the gates of the penitentiary here." When Professor Lyman Bradley of New York University, another member of the JAFRC executive, was testifying, Rankin abruptly exploded— "Now, the next question he refuses, just call up the marshal and send him to jail." Much the same spirit was in evidence when HCUA's Gordon Scherer and Donald Jackson threatened a naturalized English-American, Hugh Hardyman, during hearings in Los Angeles in 1955. Said Scherer: "If it's within my power, you're going back to where you came from." [18]

The Committee often refused to accept the Fifth Amendment; or persisted with the same line of questioning even after the witness had invoked it; or insisted that to take it was tantamount to confessing guilt. Said Kit Clardy in Lansing, Michigan, in 1954,"I don't know of any innocent man that has ever appeared before this Committee and invoked the Fifth Amendment . . ." When the actor Morris Carnovsky was on the stand, Francis Walter tried to argue him out of invoking the Fifth by asking him how a truthful answer to the question could possibly incriminate him. Walter tried this again with Willard Uphaus in 1956: "I must warn you that you are in a serious situation by refusing to answer a question which in no wise could jeopardize you in the criminal courts." Yet Uphaus had not been asked the name of his grandmother; he had been asked to provide the names of Americans who accompanied him when he called on the American ambassador in Moscow with a petition. Later:

> MR. ARENS: Do you honestly apprehend that if you told this Committee who participated with you in the formation of an organization to send people to peace conferences against the orders of the Department of State in violation of passport regulations you would be supplying information which might be used against you in a criminal proceeding?

MR. UPHAUS: Positively, yes. I don't trust the Committee.
MR. SCHERER: Just a minute. I ask that the Chair direct him to answer the question . . .
THE CHAIRMAN: Yes. You are directed to answer the question.[19]

But Uphaus did not.

Of course, the aggression was not all and always in one direction, and the Committee was capable of responding to courtesy with courtesy, particularly when confronted by calm witnesses of high intellectual reputation such as Lillian Hellman and Arthur Miller. Some witnesses were rough, notably Gerhart Eisler and Leon Josephson, who refused to be sworn until they were allowed to read a statement, and the general secretary of the CP, Eugene Dennis, who first demanded to be heard and then, when HCUA subpoenaed him to suit itself, refused to appear on the ground that Rankin's presence violated the Fourteenth Amendment, which stipulates that a state's representation in Congress shall be lowered in proportion to its abridgment of the right to vote. "In the name of the American people," declared Dennis, "I hold this Committee in contempt."

Characteristic of the rougher breed of witnesses was George Tony Starkovich, a Seattle trade unionist—"I do have contempt for this Committee . . . a phony question from a phony Congressman . . . I think some of you guys ought to be investigated by psychiatrists." Occasionally Committee members developed paranoiac symptoms: Kit Clardy moaned during the Bishop Oxnam hearing—"We have sat here and taken abuse day after day and week after week and month after month and if you had gone through the fire and the furnace that we have you would understand what we have gone through." [20]

## CONTEMPT OF CONGRESS

Contempt, cousin of confrontation, was in the air: whereas Congress cited only 113 witnesses for contempt from 1857 to 1949, it cited 117 from 1950 to 1952. Between 1945 and 1957, Congress endorsed every one of the 226 contempt citations voted by fourteen of its committees. The quickest off the mark was HCUA, which cited twenty-one people for failing to produce subpoenaed documents in 1945–46, and a further thirteen in 1947–48 for challenging the Committee's entitlement to inquire into political beliefs and affiliations. Between 1945 and 1957 over 3,000 witnesses testified at 230 public hearings of HCUA; of these 135 were cited for contempt. [21]

Taking the period January 3, 1945, to April 1971, of 187 contempt citations voted by the House, no fewer than 174 emanated from HCUA and its successor HISC. Of these, 142 failed in court.[22] Of course, the contempt of Congress frequently occurred some years before the witness actually went to prison, and the convergence of imprisonments around the years 1959–61 [23] has less to do with a sudden outbreak of testimonial contemptuousness at that time than with the swing of judicial opinion on appeal.

## INTIMIDATION OF DEFENSE COUNSEL AND WITNESSES

"The rights you have are the rights given you by this Committee. We will determine what rights you have and what rights you have not got before the Committee." Thus J. Parnell Thomas, hectoring an unfriendly witness's counsel. When the CP leader Jacob A. Stachel appeared as a witness in 1945, his lawyer made a simple request:

> MR. BRODSKY: May I move my chair up closer to Mr. Stachel, so I can advise with him?
> MR. THOMAS: No.

The Committee normally insisted that counsel could advise a witness only as to his constitutional rights, and not as to what evidence he should give. Counsel was frequently rebuked for whispering in his client's ear, and those witnesses who turned up without a lawyer were sometimes congratulated by the Committee. It was particularly galling to the Committee that some of the most aggressive middle-class Communists still operating—the lawyers—could walk into the hearing room as of right and intervene in the proceedings. Consequently, *ad hominem* attacks on individual lawyers were not infrequent, just as attempts were made to obtain some implicative purchase out of the witness's relationship to his lawyer. During the Hollywood Ten hearings, the lawyer Robert W. Kenny was suddenly called, sworn, and asked whether he was advising witnesses to refuse to say whether they were CP members. Kenny accused Thomas of invading the "sacred province" of the counsel-client relationship, whereupon Thomas menacingly read out the federal conspiracy act. In 1948 Julian Wadleigh, who had just parted from his counsel, Herman Greenberg of Forer and Rein, was asked by acting chairman Mundt at whose initiative the parting had come about. Wadleigh refused to answer. During the Alger Hiss hearings, Thomas, annoyed by a key witness's resort to the Fifth Amendment, ordered William Rosen's counsel, Maurice Braverman, to raise his right hand and be sworn. Braverman refused to do so until he had been properly subpoenaed and was represented by counsel of his own.[24]

In 1953 a committee of the District of Columbia Bar Association recommended that a witness's counsel should have the right to object to questions and procedures, and to submit legal memoranda in support of his arguments. But if HCUA was unlikely to agree to such a reform it was even less likely to tolerate the Bar Association's more audacious proposal, that counsel should have the right where relevant to cross-examine witnesses. In practice, harassment of radical lawyers intensified. When HCUA subpoenaed Robert Treuhaft, general counsel of Local 6, ILWU, during a hearing held in San Francisco in 1953, Treuhaft claimed that seven lawyers he admired had not dared to represent him before the Committee, so damaging was the publicity. In Charlotte eight witnesses represented by Rhoda Laks of New York were asked how they came to retain her and whether they knew she served the Communist cause. This approach was characteristic of Committee counsel Richard Arens, who repeatedly referred to a Los Angeles witness's counsel, John Porter, as "Comrade Porter." After witnesses had been asked whether they knew Porter was a Communist, an FBI agent named Anita Schneider was called in to identify him as one. Things got so rough in Los Angeles that A. L. Wirin, a non-Communist radical lawyer with a notable record in the Southern California ACLU, and Maynard Omerberg were ejected from the hearings. In the spring of 1957 the California State Bar Board of Governors registered a strong protest against HCUA's treatment of counsel representing unfriendly witnesses. But HCUA was unrepentant. In 1957 it subpoenaed Bertram Edises, the California lawyer who represented the Stanford University biochemist William Sherwood, as well as several teachers. Meanwhile in Philadelphia the lawyer J. Harry Levitan was hauled onto the witness stand while representing several witnesses in November 1956, and a former FBI agent, Herman Thomas, was called to identify him as a Party member. When Willard Uphaus appeared accompanied by the distinguished lawyer Victor Rabinowitz, Arens asked:

> MR. ARENS: To get it straight, do you know whether your counsel is a Communist?
> MR. UPHAUS: I certainly do not.
> MR. ARENS: Have you made any inquiry to ascertain whether or not he is a Communist?
> MR. UPHAUS: I have not.[25]

But HCUA did not stand alone in its aggressive approach toward radical "defense" counsel. When George Pirinsky, executive secretary of the American Slav Congress, was testifying in June 1949 before the Senate Subcommittee on Immigration, whose chairman was Pat McCarran and whose counsel at that time was Richard Arens, the latter suddenly turned on Pirinsky's counsel, the Washington lawyer Joseph Forer:

> MR. ARENS: Have you been the counsel for Mr. Gerhart Eisler?
> MR. FORER: Yes, but what does that have to do with this?
> MR. ARENS: Have you been the counsel for Emil Costello?
> MR. FORER: Yes.
> MR. ARENS: Have you been the counsel for Claudia Jones?
> MR. FORER: Just a minute . . .

Forer also represented another witness, Alfred A. Neuwald, who, on taking the witness stand soon afterward, was promptly asked by Senator James O. Eastland the name of whoever had put him in contact with Forer:

> MR. NEUWALD: Do I have to answer that?
> SENATOR EASTLAND: Yes, you have to answer that.
> MR. FORER: Mr. Chairman—
> SENATOR EASTLAND: You keep quiet . . .

The Subcommittee later inserted in the record a passage called "The Record of Joseph Forer," including an item to the effect that he had written an article criticizing the FBI.[26]

Not only did HCUA intimidate its witnesses, it harried its critics whenever possible, equating criticism of itself with subversion. When the actor José Ferrer appeared before the Committee in 1951, he was accused of having once sponsored a mass meeting to abolish the Wood-Rankin Committee of 1945–46. Wood, now chairman, asked Ferrer whether "the abolition of this Committee [was] ever mentioned to you by any person." Ferrer pleaded: ". . . I felt a certain amount of disapproval of the way Mr. Thomas conducted the [Hollywood] hearings." Committee counsel Tavenner then asked him whether he had spoken at a meeting of about one hundred writers and actors who gathered at the Hotel Astor in March 1948 to protest the activities of HCUA and the Tenney Committee:

> MR. TAVENNER: I did not ask you that question with the idea of indicating that you did not have the right to oppose this Committee.
> MR. FERRER: I know you didn't, Mr. Tavenner. I know you didn't.

Later:

> MR. KEARNEY: Do you still believe in the abolishment of the
> House Un-American Activities Committee?
> MR. FERRER: No, I do not. I do think the . . . Committee today
> is not only fulfilling an extremely important function . . .

In 1952 Tavenner asked the writer Michael Blankfort: "Why did you
permit the use of your name as a sponsor of a committee which was
organized to try to destroy the work of this Committee?" Item 17 in
HCUA's file on Bishop Bromley Oxnam quoted him as having criticized the Committee in December 1948 for trying to pin the Communist label on churchmen. When Arthur Miller, author of *The Crucible*, the major dramatic statement of the time on the witch hunts, was
subpoenaed in 1956, the rage that the Committee felt toward its
critics soon surfaced:

> MR. ARENS: Was it likewise just a little farce, your play, *You're
> Next*, by Arthur Miller, attacking the House Committee on Un-
> American Activities?
> MR. MILLER: No, that would have been quite serious.
> MR. ARENS: Did you know that the play . . . was reproduced by
> the Communist Party?
> . . . . . . . . . . . . . . . . . . . . . . . . . . . . . . . . . . . . . . . . . . . . . . . . . . . . . .
> MR. ARENS: Are you cognizant of the fact that your play, *The
> Crucible*, with respect to witch hunts in 1692, was the case his-
> tory [sic] of a series of articles in the Communist press drawing
> parallels to the investigations of Communists and other subver-
> sives by Congressional committees?
> MR. MILLER: The comparison is inevitable, sir.

Arens, who was acutely hostile to citizens who dared to investigate an
investigating committee, asked a witness during a hearing in Pittsburgh in 1959: "Who gave you the information . . . about the voting
records of the members of this Committee?" [27] In July 1958 HCUA
was holding hearings in Atlanta. Learning that Frank Wilkinson was
in town to monitor the hearings, it promptly subpoenaed him and
accused him of inciting hostility toward its work. [28] Wilkinson was
cited for contempt and actually went to jail for it.

The working principle of the Committee was repentance, confession, betrayal. Only he who named names could truly be said to have
purged himself. What the Committee wanted, in the old witch-hunt
tradition, was public denunciation, public purgation, a purification of
the convert by means of his public humiliation as he betrayed his old
friends and comrades. Martin Dies of Texas had called exposure "the

most effective weapon . . . we can trust public sentiment to do the rest." The virtues of exposure for its own sake were constantly reiterated by members of the Committee.

The aim of exposure finds its dichotomy in the aim of legislation. From 1941 to 1960, HCUA made 129 legislative recommendations (of which thirty-three were repetitions); only thirty-five became law. Between 1951 and 1960, of 181 antisubversive bills referred to House committees in general, only thirty-one were referred to HCUA; and of these, HCUA chose to hold hearings on only twelve.[29] Legislative hearings were too dull; besides, one was obliged to hear both sides.

To popularize its philosophy, HCUA published in 1948–49 the six pamphlets of 100 *Things You Should Know About Communism—in the U.S.A.; in the Soviet Union; and Religion; and Education; and Labor; and Government*. Apparently 850,000 copies were distributed free and a further 320,000 copies were sold by the Government Printing Office. The style adopted was that of the question-and-answer catechism. Thus: "What is the difference in fact between a Communist and a Fascist? Answer: None worth noticing." But HCUA was less interested in such dialectics than in exposing, pillorying and crippling radical organizations and individuals, particularly the "teachers, preachers, actors, writers, union officials, doctors, lawyers, editors, businessmen . . ." who, according to the Committee,[30] constituted "the real center of power in Communism . . ." [31]

## HCUA's Filing System

The essential weapon was the filing system. In principle, HCUA maintained two filing systems, one of them "investigative" and based on confidential reports, FBI contacts and so forth, the other "public" and consisting of information obtained from the press, letterheads and other easily accessible sources. Truman's loyalty order of March 1947 directed that federal loyalty checks should be made against HCUA's files, and it is known that from January 1947 to December 1948 accredited representatives of government agencies made 5,975 visits to the Committee's files. During the thirty months preceding December 1948, HCUA's staff reported on no fewer than 25,591 individuals and 780 organizations at the request of members of Congress.[32]

Clearly HCUA's filing system owed a greater debt to prejudice and vindictiveness than to scrupulously impartial research. As a case in point one may cite the file of the Methodist Bishop Bromley Oxnam, who claimed that he had never belonged to five of the twelve organizations he was alleged to have joined. Item 1 in the Oxnam file referred to a speech he had made in February 1930 denouncing secret treaties and urging that "America First" must mean first in world service, not "to be the first to go into Mexico to steal oil lands." Item 18 quoted a speech the Bishop had delivered in February 1949 to the effect that the U.S. should not flirt with Franco in order to thwart Stalin. Item 19 referred to his criticism of HCUA itself—always a deadly sin. Oxnam complained that for seven years the Committee had been deliberately releasing false information about him, and that in response to his protests Chairman Wood had replied that HCUA did not vouch for the accuracy of the material it issued.[33]

## LOSING RADICALS THEIR JOBS

But HCUA's ultimate mission and highest delight was to hound radicals out of their jobs. The pages of this book are strewn with the Committee's economic corpses. Frequently witnesses were fired as soon as they were subpoenaed—the potential publicity alone sufficed to deter employers. It happened to Mildred Bowen and other California teachers in 1954, the year in which Kit Clardy expressed satisfaction at the dismissal of two Flint workers who appeared before his subcommittee as hostile witnesses, the year in which Donald Jackson threatened Captain Strom of the Seattle Fire Department: "There may well be in the balance a very long and faithful service to the city of Seattle." (Strom was subsequently fired a few days before he was due to retire, losing his pension rights.) The Stanford University biochemist, William Sherwood, fearing that his subpoena to attend HCUA's hearings in San Francisco in 1957 would ruin him, took poison and killed himself. The Committee's trail, he wrote in a suicide note, "is strewn with blasted lives, the wreckage of useful careers . . . Scientific workers especially . . . the scientific mind cannot flourish in an atmosphere of fear, timidity and imposed conformity." In 1958 an Atlanta woman who worked for two doctors was fired by both after a HCUA subpoena to her was publicized in the press. When the Committee canceled its California hearings in 1959 it nevertheless played the scorpion by sending the names of over 100 teachers to the Boards of Education, as well as the files on more than ninety to the State Superintendent of Public Instruction. When it emerged that a large proportion of them would keep their jobs—the tide was now turning—Chairman Walter commented petulantly: "It simply proves that the school authorities were derelict in their duty or they did not make use of the furnished information." [34]

Between 1949 and 1959 the Committee furnished data on 60,000 people to inquiring employers. The threat of disemployment was one that HCUA's investigators in the field regularly wielded against reticent witnesses. A witness at a hearing in 1959 recalled a visit on November 3 from two HCUA staff investigators, Williams and Gerhard, who warned him that his promising scientific career would be ruined if he did not provide information. Even those who were self-employed, or owners of small businesses, could be ruined by HCUA. After Mrs. Rose Edelmann Anderson, who owned a prosperous drugstore in Washington, D.C., took the Fifth Amendment before the Committee, the business she had built up over twenty-two years was so effectively boycotted that within a month she was forced to sell out at a low price and quit the area.[35] Another unfriendly HCUA witness, the Florida contractor Max Schlafrock, had to leave town after an ordinance was passed to revoke his license.

## OLD LEFT AND NEW

It became increasingly apparent that the privilege against self-incrimination was a blessing for the Committee. Witness after witness fenced, dodged, hid, and looked furtive; being a Communist, or a radical, was *apparently* something to be ashamed of, something to conceal, something that, in Richard Arens' words, prevented a man from standing up for himself and being counted "like a red-blooded American." The extent to which the inquisition traded on the reticence of its victims of the old Left soon became apparent in the early 1960s when a new generation of young radicals scorned to conceal their commitments. On August 17, 1966, the following colloquy took place between HCUA's counsel, Alfred M. Nittle, and Richard M. Rhoads:

> MR. NITTLE: Were you a member of the Progressive Labor Movement between the period [sic] July 1964 and January 1965?
> MR. RHOADS: I am very proud to state that, right now as I sit here before this Committee, I am a member of the Progressive Labor Party.

And later:

> MR. RHOADS: Are you trying to ask me whether I am a Communist or not?
> . . .
> MR. POOL (chairman): You can answer that if you want to.
> MR. RHOADS: I certainly am.[36]

## THE SENATE INTERNAL SECURITY SUBCOMMITTEE

The Congressional committees investigating Communism and radicalism developed a rivalry so intense that in 1955 an agreement to avoid overlapping was announced. In January 1951 the Senate, by Resolution 336, established a subcommittee of the Judiciary Committee that was intended to rival HCUA; this was the Senate Internal Security Subcommittee (SISS), whose chairman in 1951 and 1952 was Pat McCarran (D., Nevada). Under McCarran the SISS stole the limelight from HCUA by engaging in a spectacular variety of investigations: of career officers in the Foreign Service who had warned that the Chiang Kai-shek government was weak and corrupt; of Owen Lattimore and the Institute of Pacific Relations; of subversive aliens; of Communism in youth organizations; of subversive infiltration of radio, television, and the telegraph industry; of passport policy; of subversive control of five unions; of espionage by Soviet-bloc diplomats; of Communist teachers; and of the political records of American employees of the UN.

The leading figures in the SISS were all diehard reactionaries: Herbert R. O'Connor (D., Maryland), William E. Jenner (R., Indiana), Homer Ferguson (R., Michigan), James O. Eastland (D., Mississippi), Willis Smith (D., North Carolina), Arthur V. Watkins (R., Utah), and Karl E. Mundt, a graduate of HCUA. (The SISS also succeeded in luring from HCUA its celebrated director of research, Benjamin Mandel.) During the last years of the Truman administration, Pat McCarran, an inspirational figure behind both the Internal Security Act and the Immigration and Nationality Act, became one of the most feared and powerful politicians in Washington.

Red-faced and silver-haired, McCarran had first been elected in 1932 on F.D.R.'s coattails, as a New Dealer. During a debate in June 1939 he had denounced those who were "forever and always . . . using the bugbear of Communism to scare someone in order that they themselves might rise up and thus be held as the champions against the so-called dangers of Communism." By 1950 McCarran had emerged as not only an enemy of Communism, but also of the New Deal, subversive aliens, further immigration, and the unions. Putting himself at the service of oil interests, he introduced in 1952 a Senate resolution allocating to the states the right to exploit offshore oil. As a staunch supporter of Franco's regime in Spain, he summoned officials of the State Department and of the Export-Import Bank in May 1951, with the Spanish Ambassador in attendance, to ask them why American aid to Spain was not flowing more swiftly.[37]

McCarran's successor as chairman of the SISS, William E. Jenner, called for the dismissal of teachers whose connection with Communism was "not easily provable" because "Our purpose is to protect and safeguard academic freedom . . . There can be no academic freedom until this Soviet conspiracy hidden in our schools and colleges is exposed . . ." [38] The kind of testimony that the SISS under Jenner encouraged, sponsored and publicized was the kind that reactivated the long, bitter partisan polemics against the Roosevelt and Truman administrations. It was the SISS that in November 1953 invited Brownell and Hoover to testify about Truman's negligence in the Harry Dexter White affair, and it was the SISS that in March 1954 welcomed the testimony of Spruille Braden, former Ambassador to Cuba and Argentina, and former Assistant Secretary of State in charge of Latin-American affairs, who insisted that even under the Eisenhower administration the State Department remained in the hands of "state interventionists, collectivists, 'do-gooders,' misinformed idealists and whatnot . . ."

As for James Eastland of Mississippi, who assumed the chairmanship in 1955, his white supremacism and hatred of radicals found expression in venomous and violent outbursts. When Myles Horton, head of the Highlander Folk School, offered a polite statement in 1954 to a subcommittee that Eastland was chairing in New Orleans— Eastland was always accorded a free run in the South—Horton was bodily ejected by marshals on the Senator's orders. During hearings held in New Orleans in April 1956, Eastland had the lawyer Philip Wittenberg thrown out of the room so violently that he needed hospital treatment. Noticeable, therefore, was the change of atmosphere in November 1960 when the new chairman, Thomas J. Dodd (D., Connecticut), permitted Professor Linus C. Pauling and his counsel to argue, object, and even to criticize the Committee. [39]

In 1953 Robert Morris became counsel to the SISS, having served as counsel to its Republican minority in 1951 and 1952. (Not that there was any deep divergence of diagnosis between Democrats and Republicans in the McCarran-Jenner-Eastland era.) An officer in the Naval Reserve and from a well-heeled social background, a self-taught vigilante, Morris exploited the procedure by which chairmen signed batches of blank subpoenas and entrusted them to counsel to issue at will. From 1954 to 1958 he and J. G. Sourwine, of Nevada, played a game of leap-frog. First Morris withdrew to serve as a judge of the New York municipal court while Sourwine masterminded Eastland's raid on the New York press in 1955. Then Sourwine withdrew to run for a Nevada senate seat (he ran fourth out of four) while Morris returned as SISS counsel. In 1958 Morris ran for a New Jersey senate seat (he finished third out of three) and Sourwine came back! [40]

Having published *No Wonder We Are Losing*, a book obsessed by paranoid visions of conspiracy, Morris was appointed president of the University of Dallas.

## McCarthy and the Subcommittee on Investigations

And there was McCarthy. Following the Republican election victory of 1952, Senate Majority Leader Robert A. Taft rewarded McCarthy for services rendered by appointing him chairman of the Senate Committee on Government Operations. McCarthy promptly appointed himself chairman of its Subcommittee on Investigations—the famous "McCarthy Committee." In the course of a whirlwind assault on the "vital center," the liberal establishment, he succeeded in melodramatizing the American inquisition across the world. In rapid succession he carved up the State Department, the Voice of America, the International Information Agency, the Government Printing Office, the UN, and, finally, the U.S. Army itself. He brought trouble to Harvard, and he ran amok among defense industries. All this was accomplished in less than two years, for by 1954 the subcommittee was almost totally absorbed by its chairman's struggle with the Army.

To fight subversion, McCarthy practiced it. In various executive departments he set up what he called the "loyal American underground," a network of spies whose names he refused to divulge even when under oath to tell the whole truth. Justice Department and FBI men sympathetic to his crusade kept him well supplied with pickings from confidential files. His source of information within the Loyalty Review Board itself was revealed in November 1952, when the Civil Service Commission accepted the resignation of the board's legal examiner, Miriam de Haas. It was in the course of the Senator's war against the Army that he declared, "I have instructed a vast number of federal employees that they are duty-bound to give me information even though some little bureaucrat has stamped it 'secret' to defend himself." As Telford Taylor pointed out, McCarthy's sources within the Army were liable to ten years' imprisonment and a $10,000 fine if discovered.

Not only did McCarthy control his subcommittee's staff and agenda, he also monopolized the headlines. Alert as he was to the potential of the new medium of television, his greatest asset was his uncanny ability to hypnotize and ravish the press by means of sensational charges based on secret evidence given in closed session. The Republican members of the subcommittee could see no political divi-

dend in trying to tame this irresistible force, although three Democrats temporarily boycotted the proceedings.[41]

The immediate cause of their withdrawal was the star of the subcommittee's staff, McCarthy's twenty-five-year-old, shrewd and ambitious chief counsel, Roy Cohn. The son of a judge, but an undistin-
guished student at Columbia, Cohn rapidly climbed into the
headlines as assistant to successive U.S. Attorneys for the Southern
District of New York, Myles J. Lane and Irving H. Saypol, political
prosecutor extraordinary. Involved in the Remington, Rosenberg and
Lattimore cases, Cohn rose so rapidly within the Justice Department's Internal Security Division that he was able to manipulate
the grand jury investigating UN personnel against the wishes of his
superiors.

No sooner had McCarthy appointed him chief counsel than
Cohn in turn appointed his wealthy but dim young friend, G. David
Schine, as "chief consultant." It was now that the Democratic minor-
ity withdrew in protest. Although the Cohn-Schine quick tour of
United States overseas libraries made America the laughingstock of
Europe, McCarthy bestowed on these two spoiled children such
power that generals and heads of departments jumped to attention
when either one of them called on the phone.

While serving as chief counsel, Cohn also drew $25,000 from the
New York law firm of which he was a partner. A cold-blooded operator who embodied the consciencelessness of his era, capable of subpoenaing a victim at 6 P.M. to attend an 8 P.M. hearing, he customarily sat at McCarthy's right hand, whispering in his ear, while his cool,
suspicious eyes gazed banefully at the Hobbesian world he inhabited—"rather like a cherub gone to seed . . ." Nevertheless the Army-
McCarthy hearings subdued Cohn; where once he had shouted
threats when denied instant admission to classified radar laboratories,
or when preferential treatment for Private Schine was hesitantly contested, he now wore a modest, respectful countenance, using the
word "sir" often. Whereas McCarthy became increasingly bull-like
when taunted by the Army's adroit, Dickensian Boston counsel, Joseph N. Welch, Cohn arched his back in catlike alertness—poised,
polite, shifty.[42]

All this came about because McCarthy's hungers were unappeas-
able—this baron of bastard feudalism was capable of subpoenaing
God Almighty. The final act of *hubris* was to take on the Army,
charging that in the highest reaches of the Pentagon Communist
sympathizers were shielding Soviet spies, and that in order to protect
them Secretary of the Army Robert T. Stevens had attempted to
blackmail and smear McCarthy and his loyal staff. In a crowded cau-

cus room the subcommittee convened to adjudicate between its chairman and the Army. His face caked in cream-colored makeup, constantly interrupting with "points of order" in his strong, low voice and generally disregarding acting chairman Karl Mundt's attempts to exercise authority, McCarthy conveyed the impression of a lord commanding retainers whom neither Church nor Crown could any longer control. The upshot was indecisive: on November 11, 1954, the Senate voted by 67 to 22 to *condemn* McCarthy, a sanction less serious than the *censure* recommended by the bipartisan Watkins Committee appointed to examine his record of anarchy. But, although he remained a Senator, McCarthy's wings were clipped.[43]

## THE ROMAN CATHOLIC FACTOR

Our discussion of McCarthy raises the Roman Catholic factor. (The U.S. Census Bureau Survey of 1957 estimated that 26 percent of American households were Catholic.) Catholic anti-Communism has tended to assume particularly virulent forms in the United States, where the pro-Fascist, anti-Semitic, anti-Communist and anti-New Deal "radio priest," Father Charles E. Coughlin, enjoyed considerable support in the 1930s. Although the war inevitably tended to discredit Fascism among American Catholics, the rapid spread of Communist hegemony in Eastern Europe only intensified the traditional fear and loathing of atheistic Communism. The diocesan papers were full of the sufferings of the East European Catholics; Yalta had been denounced by the bishops. Tension increased following the arrests of Archbishop Stepinac in Yugoslavia and Joseph Cardinal Mindszenty in Hungary.

A strong admirer of Mindszenty was the man who stood at the head of the American Catholic hierarchy (four cardinals, twenty-four archbishops, 183 bishops, and over 50,000 priests), Francis Cardinal Spellman. Frequently warning his flock that the nation was already infected with the germs of Communist slavery, he taxed the Truman administration with "appeasement" of the CPUSA. Appropriately, it was from the hands of Spellman that J. Edgar Hoover received the Club of Champions Medal. At Spellman's shoulder stood the leading anti-Communist ideologue of the hierarchy, Monsignor Fulton J. Sheen, Director of the Pontifical Society for the Propagation of the Faith, who fulminated against the "colossal wastage of taxes to pay professors who would destroy America by teaching Russian Bolshevism." It was Sheen who played the leading role in courting ex-Communist informers into the Church: Louis Budenz, Bella Dodd and Elizabeth Bentley (who in 1955 was teaching at the Sacred Heart College, Grand Coteau, Louisiana) were the most conspicuous of those publicity-conscious converts. Sheen revealed how a suspicious character had tried to infiltrate his office, but the FBI had "within half an hour traced the man through China and Mongolia and said he was an international Communist agent." Meanwhile, Archbishop (later Cardinal) Richard Cushing of Boston, a friend of McCarthy's millionaire supporter Joseph P. Kennedy, issued constant imprecations against Communism and went so far as to appoint Louis Budenz as his adviser on the subject.

The American Catholic Church remained, at that time, under Irish domination; it produced not so much poets, scholars, scientists and artists as security officers, immigration officers, policemen, customs officers and prison wardens. According to the Office of Public Opinion Research at Princeton, 56 percent of the nation was "lower class," whereas 66.6 percent of Catholics fell into that bottom category. In defense of the faith (law and order), many of the four million children in church elementary schools aspired to wear a blue uniform, or to marry one. Higher up the scale, Fordham graduates were clearing (or not clearing) Harvard men. Who now carried the flag? Thomas Murphy, prosecutor in both trials of Alger Hiss, remarked during a St. Patrick's Day parade, "I can't even recall one Irish name among the many thousands called upon before the House Committee on Un-American Activities." [44] In fact, the Communist victims of the Smith Act included at least four women and one man of Irish descent, but the real run of Irish-American activity was more accurately reflected by the McCarthys and McCarrans among politicians, the McGoheys and Murphys among political prosecutors, the Shaughnessys and Boyds among leading immigration officials, the Monaghans among commissioners of police. The Irish-Catholic composition of the influential blacklisting magazine, Counterattack, in 1952 tells the story.*

The Irish-Catholic passion for law and order was fully in evidence at a New York City Communion breakfast held in April 1954. Six thousand members of the city's police force and of the Holy Name Society of the Police Department gathered to hear Joe McCarthy, with Cardinal Spellman in attendance. According to a Gallup poll taken a month earlier, McCarthy was supported by 56 percent of Catholics compared to 45 percent of Protestants and 12 percent of Jews.

---

* Including T. C. Kirkpatrick, John G. Keenan, Herman Creary, Hugh P. Dennedy, Patricia Kelly, John F. X. McKenna, Francis J. McNamara, Gertrude E. O'Connor, Thomas A. Brady.

Not surprisingly, the outpouring of Catholic anathemas against domestic Communism was torrential. The News Service of the National Catholic Welfare Conference kept diocesan papers supplied with commentaries concerning every FBI arrest, Congressional investigation and Smith Act trial. The Catechetical Guild of St. Paul distributed in 1948 a comic book, *Is This Tomorrow?*, depicting a Commie mob storming St. Patrick's Cathedral and nailing Spellman to the door. Periodicals such as the Brooklyn *Tablet* and the Los Angeles *Tidings* perpetuated the Coughlinite tradition of brawling, anti-Semitic, anti-liberal red-baiting that so alarmed American Jews. The Catholic War Veterans and the Holy Name societies rallied behind McCarthy as the true defender of "our Western Christian World."

That Catholics in general were highly intolerant of Communists is indicated by several opinion studies. For example, a poll taken at a large Eastern state university during the Foley Square trial of the CP leaders in 1949 found that 22 percent of Catholic students favored *executing* the defendants, compared with 4 percent of Protestant students and 2 percent of Jews. When Berkeley students were asked in March-April 1950 whether Communists should be allowed to teach, 63 percent of Catholic students and 53 percent of Protestants said no, while 75 percent of Jews answered yes.[45]

The Catholic War Veterans (200,000 members) and the Knights of Columbus (600,000) spearheaded the campaign for a weeding out of American radicals. In March 1947 the CWV's national commander demanded the deportation of all Communists, including citizens, failing which a colony or penal island should be established for the American-born variety. The CWV pressured Mayor William O'Dwyer to purge the New York City payroll, and with considerable success. As for the Knights, in 1947 they launched a series of broadcasts over 226 radio stations, "Safeguards for America," and subsequently played a prominent pressure-group role in the blacklisting of radio and television artists.

The relatively liberal dimension of American Catholicism did, it is true, attempt to make its voice heard amid the trumpet calls of the Church Militant. The general drift of liberal Catholicism—notably represented by Bishop Bernard J. Sheil, of Chicago, the *Catholic Worker* and *Commonweal*—was that McCarthy was spoiling by excess the fundamentally sound anti-Communism embodied in the Truman Doctrine. "A shameless, ruthless, exploitation of innuendo . . . may yet rip apart the fabric of our foreign policy," complained *Commonweal* on February 1, 1951. But a priest radical enough to protest Roy Brewer's red-baiting, strike-breaking tactics in Hollywood, George H. Dunne, was rewarded by expulsion from the faculties of St. Louis University and Loyola University in rapid succession.[46]

# 6

## The FBI and the Informers

When Harlan F. Stone became Attorney General in 1924, he put an end to the Bureau of Investigation's antiradical division, its propaganda about the "red menace," its undercover activities within left-wing groups, its unlawful searches and seizures. But the old files remained intact; in 1939 they were dusted off and reactivated with the creation of the General Intelligence (antiradical) division of the FBI by a presidential directive of September 6. It was from this document that the FBI subsequently claimed its power to investigate radical organizations without a specific law-enforcement purpose, to be, in effect, a political police force. But Frank Donner and others have challenged the assumption that the presidential directives of September 1939, January 1943, July 1950 and December 1953 legitimized investigations of political groups suspected of neither war-connected offenses nor conventional violations of the law.[1]

Nevertheless, well-founded legally or not, the FBI's *de facto* theater of political operations constantly expanded. In 1940 there were raids in Detroit, Milwaukee and New York directed against Veterans of the Abraham Lincoln Brigade, on the pretext that a foreign army was being, or had been, raised on American soil. But when the raids aroused a storm of criticism, Attorney General Robert H. Jackson had the indictments quashed. A year later Congress passed a Dies-inspired rider to the Department of Justice's Appropriations Act, authorizing the FBI to investigate every government employee who belonged to a "subversive" organization. Between July 1942 and June 1946, some 6,193 such cases were referred to the FBI, of whom only 101 were discharged by the employing agency and twenty-one resigned while under investigation. Consequently, the Bureau felt deeply frustrated, embittered, during the wartime alliance with the Soviet Union. In January 1947 the FBI's assistant director, D. M. Ladd, advised the President's Temporary Commission that *all* applicants for government jobs should be fully investigated, and not just screened or checked against the files. Although this demand was not granted, the terms of the Truman Loyalty Order enabled the Bureau to vastly expand its political surveillance, supported by the conservative 80th Congress, which allocated to the Bureau $7.4 million of the $11 million it appropriated for the entire loyalty program. By May 27, 1953, some six years after the program was announced, the FBI had processed 4,666,122 sets of fingerprints, checked 4,756,705 loyalty forms (99.4 percent of which were returned "No Disloyal Data"), and conducted 26,236 full field investigations of federal employees or applicants.[2] And these figures do not include the screening operations carried on simultaneously by the Postal Inspection Service, the Secret Service, and the Intelligence Divisions of the Armed Forces.

The Bureau's budget (which, of course, covered all phases of its activity, and not merely the political one) expanded from two or three million dollars during the period 1924–34, to about seven million in 1940, thirty-five million in 1947, fifty-three million in 1950, and 130 million dollars in 1962, by which date the FBI was absorbing almost half of the entire budget of the Department of Justice. (In 1924 the Bureau had 411 special agents; in 1939, 785; in 1951, 4,602. With fifty-two field divisions operating, as many as 263 agents could be assigned to a big political case like the Hiss-Chambers one.) In 1950 Congress also raised the salary of the Bureau's director, J. Edgar Hoover, to $20,000 a year, more than a Congressman or Cabinet member then received. Only a few members of Congress dared to speak out against the extraordinary and extravagant growth of the Bureau's political power. The columnist Drew Pearson reported in July 1957 that the FBI had "a complete rundown on every Congressman, his private life and his family. Furthermore, no Congressman, if defeated or desirous of another government job, can become a judge or hold government office without clearance from the FBI."[3] On November 18, 1974, Attorney General William B. Saxbe announced that the FBI had for years subjected civil rights and political organizations to "improper" counterintelligence harassment, for which he largely blamed J. Edgar Hoover.

## DIRECTOR J. EDGAR HOOVER

In February 1975 Attorney General Edward H. Levi revealed that Hoover had kept some 164 files on leading political figures in his private office, outside of the Bureau's over-all filing system.[4] Hoover became a state within the state; politically sacrosanct, he made the FBI his own private army, modeled according to his own passions and prejudices, dedicated to the cult of his personality. Jack Levine, a lawyer who became an FBI agent in 1960 and later resigned, recalled that agents were expected not only to buy Hoover's book about Communism, *Masters of Deceit*, but also to believe, like Hoover, that the Warren Court should be impeached and that the Justice Department under Roosevelt and Truman had been infiltrated by Communists. Time was on Hoover's side. He served (if that is the word) ten presidents. Who else in Washington could claim to have worked under both Woodrow Wilson and Richard Nixon?

Hoover equated any criticism of the FBI's political role with un-Americanism. Journalists who annoyed him soon had their own dossiers in the FBI files (like Congressmen). Replying to criticisms of FBI behavior set forth in the *Yale Law Journal* in 1948 by Professor Thomas I. Emerson and David M. Helfeld, Hoover impugned the integrity, sincerity and competence of the two authors and commented that opinions such as theirs were most frequently found in the *Daily Worker*. To the Washington journalist Bert Andrews he wrote at this time: "The so-called 'witch hunts,' so far as I can ascertain, exist only in the minds of those who oppose the loyalty program either through ignorance or for more sinister motives." (Indeed, the loyalty program was as much Hoover's work as it was Harry Truman's.) When Professor Max Lowenthal published in 1950 a scholarly but highly civil-libertarian critique of the Bureau's political record, both the author and his publisher, William Sloane Associates, found themselves described in newspapers and over the air as pro-Communist. Lowenthal was promptly subpoenaed by HCUA and questioned about his past membership in the National Lawyers Guild. J. Parnell Thomas observed: "The closest relation exists between this Committee and the FBI. I cannot say as much between this Committee and the Attorney General's office . . ." The FBI also maintained a relationship of reciprocal favors with leading anti-Communist Congressmen.[5]

Hoover's friends in the press were legion, but certain right-wing journalists like Ralph de Toledano, Walter Trohan of the *Chicago Tribune*, Ed Montgomery of the *San Francisco Bulletin*, Karl Hess and George Sokolsky were granted particularly privileged access to Hoover's assistant Cartha de Loach and to the Bureau's files. When they wrote stories about card-carrying Communists, they knew the number of the card.[6]

In April 1940 Hoover told the 49th Congress of the DAR that foreign "isms" were "seeking to engulf Americanism." On other occasions he referred to "the poison of foreign isms"; to the " 'ism' scum"; and to "a cowardly, slithering mass of humanity, too evil and too slinking to assume their true identities." In May 1950 he claimed that "behind this force of traitorous Communists constantly gnawing at the very foundations of American society, stand a half million fellow travelers and sympathizers ready to do the Communist bidding." [7] In May 1947 he warned that America's 74,000 Communists, the "masters of deceit," the ultimate threat to Western civilization and its "Judaic-Christian heritage," represented a larger percentage of the population than Lenin's Bolsheviks had mobilized in 1917. When Party membership fell to 54,000 in February 1950 (as he estimated it), 486,000 fellow travelers emerged in the background: "Each is regarded as a potential spy." The existence of these evil doctors, lawyers, educators and radio-script writers in such large numbers did not have to be proven, just as Hoover in his ghost-written books and articles did not attempt to prove that Communists had actually led riots, or blown up industrial installations: it was enough for him to insist that they "would not hesitate" to do so "if so instructed," and to conclude, deductively, from these hypothetical crimes, "Here is the true Communist at work . . ."

Hoover was the idol of the Legion, the DAR, the patriots. He in turn paid tribute to other idols. Of one he commented in 1952: "McCarthy is a former Marine. He was an amateur boxer. He's Irish. Combine those, and you're going to have a vigorous individual, who is not going to be pushed around . . . I view him as a friend and believe he so views me." He made sure that the small-town lawyers whom he trained at the FBI's National Academy at Quantico, Virginia, learned that "Basic Security" was incompatible not only with socialism but also with "pseudo liberalism"—that is, liberalism—and with materialism of any sort that denied the existence of God, soul and immortality. As he put it in November 1960, "this rejection of God gives Communism a demonic aspect—transforming it into a fanatical, Satanic, brutal phenomenon." [8]

But, as the Cleveland industrialist Cyrus Eaton remarked on television in May 1958, "the FBI is just one of scores of agencies . . . engaged in investigating, in snooping, in informing, in creeping up on people." Indeed, the Bureau was only the most powerful and influential of the government agencies that made it their business to ferret out subversives: the Coast Guard, the CIA, the Post Office Intelligence Division, the Secret Service, the Customs Bureau of the Treasury, the Civil Service Commission, the Immigration and Naturalization Service of the Justice Department, the Passport Division of the State Department were all creeping up on people. The armed forces, too, were by 1945 heavily committed to the pursuit of radicals. In January 1947 Lieutenant Colonel Randolph of Military Intelligence (G-2) told the President's Commission, "A liberal is only a hop, skip, and a jump from a Communist. A Communist starts as a liberal."

## BIAS OF THE FBI FILES

"The 'philosophical Communist' who advocates Marxism-Leninism," Hoover explained in August 1948, "might just as well be working as an agent of a foreign power because he is aiding its cause." He denied that his agents asked questions about the newspapers and books that people read, yet this is precisely what they asked on almost every recorded occasion. How otherwise detect the "philosophical Communist"? An FBI file usually contained reports about a radical's reading habits, his membership in unions and societies, his insurance policies (during raids, the agents were on the lookout for insurance policies of the International Workers Order) and letterheads found in his possession. The files also contained a mire of gossip and hearsay—for example a statement by a landlady that a federal employee had kept books about Russia next to his easy chair, and a statement by his doctor that he believed in socialized medicine.

Despite Hoover's claim that his agents were trained to detect false information, bias and ulterior motive, and to indicate all relevant facts about this in their reports, agent Jack Levine recalled being told by one informant that all Jews are Communists, but he was not allowed to record this remark, or anything indicating racist bias in any informant, in his report. Yet it was the testimony of such informants that the FBI fed to the loyalty boards. It is significant that Hoover opposed the disclosure of the files in court on the ground that they contained unevaluated material, hearsay, and the names of innocent people. "I would not want to be a party to any action which would 'smear' innocent individuals for the rest of their lives." What he really feared—a fear well justified by the Judith Coplon trial in 1949—was that the Bureau's investigatory mentality would be exposed to ridicule and shame by disclosure of its files.

Presidential assistant Stephen Spingarn urged Truman to appoint a task force to evaluate the FBI's records and sources of information, but Truman always ducked a confrontation with Hoover and refused to comment about the files during a press conference held on June 16, 1949.[9] In 1950 the Democratic National Committee published a series of interviews with Hoover and Attorney General McGrath, extolling the Truman administration's record in combating Communism.

Information was gathered through paid informers, work-mates, neighbors, gossip. Surveillance of working-class radicals was facilitated by a War Department directive issued in 1942 that all workers employed on war contracts be fingerprinted. Within two years the Bureau had built up a fingerprint dossier on some 37 million workers, prints which were freely provided to employers engaged in detecting or busting strike leaders. Parades, meetings, benefit concerts, rallies— they were all covered, observed, photographed and sometimes bugged by FBI agents. Even funerals—after the funeral in 1962 of Mrs. Geraldine Lightfoot, the Communist wife of the black Chicago CP leader Claude Lightfoot, some 696 visitors signed their names in the funeral parlor of the Mount Hebron Missionary Baptist Society. Agents both of the FBI and of the Chicago police took notes and copied down car license numbers before seizing the visitor-registration books.[10]

Normally working in pairs (one apparently soft-mannered and considerate, the other tough and aggressive) and rarely informing suspects of their right not to answer questions, the agents' ultimate weapon against those they could not arrest was to deprive them of a livelihood. A mere inquiry, the mention of the man's name, was usually enough to scare the employer into firing the radical; the agents had no need to request anything.

## THE INFORMER NETWORK

According to Hoover, the trial of the eleven national CP leaders at Foley Square had taken ten years to prepare. By January 1950 the Bureau had 12,000 Party members named and docketed for possible future prosecution under the Smith Act's membership clause. Undercover agents operating within the Party were the primary source of information and—when trials were staged—evidence. According to one estimate, by 1962 one Party member out of six was an FBI agent. This may be an exaggeration and in any case it cannot have applied in the late 1940s, when Party membership was between 50,000 and 80,000. Frank Donner comments that there were few active informers in the upper echelons of the Party, but many in the lower ranks. The San Francisco lawyer Aubrey Grossman, long associated with the CP, believes that at any one time not more than 250 or 500 informers were operating within the Party, but he agrees that the Bureau was successful in disguising its agents as genuine militants and surmises that the renegade CP leader Jay Lovestone played a key consultative role in developing FBI strategy. Sam Kushner, a Communist who went "underground" in the early fifties, recalls that although it was difficult to ferret the agents out, they were not all that effective; after all, the Party had managed to hide half a dozen fugitive leaders for several years while they published pseudonymous articles in *Political Affairs*. Simon Gerson, who remains a leading CP official, also believes that FBI penetration was less than successful, mainly because members with roots in a local community rarely became informers and it was therefore possible to keep watch on members who remained single and had no known family connections or political antecedents.

Nevertheless the Foley Square trial in 1949 produced a series of coups for Hoover. As the former Communist leader George Blake Charney put it, "the few stoolpigeons that appeared in the trials stirred up widespread fear that the leadership at all levels was infested with undercover agents and informers. Nobody was beyond suspicion." Frank Donner confirms that an excessive fear prevailed within the Party about the demoralizing effects of FBI infiltration.[11] This pervasive suspicion was mirrored in a secret report, "expulsion of H.," issued by the Michigan CP State Committee after the prosecution produced eight informers at the Detroit Smith Act trial:

> Most of the stoolpigeons "revealed" at the "trial" had been strongly suspected for a long time but not uprooted . . . a lack of vigilance in protection of the working class . . . too much hesitancy in reaching conclusions. . .[12]

Undercover agents and informers provided the authorities with valuable witnesses not only at Smith Act and sedition trials, but also before the Subversive Activities Control Board and Congressional committees,[13] at Taft-Hartley affidavit hearings or trials, and in deportation proceedings. The informers infiltrated not only the Party and its fronts, but also trade unions with a record of radical agitation. Sometimes the informers also acted as provocateurs before they broke cover, intending either to ingratiate themselves with their FBI paymasters or, alternatively, to rise higher in the councils of the Party.

The first bombshell at the Foley Square trial of the eleven CP leaders in 1949 was the unmasking of a certain Herbert Philbrick,[14] who had joined the Party on behalf of the FBI in 1944 and—completely unsuspected—typed out reports and developed photographs for the next five years in a secret room hidden behind a furnace in his Melrose, Boston, home. As the government's case against the Party leaders came to the boil, Philbrick, who earned his living as advertising manager of the M & P Theaters, was several times brought secretly to New York, under heavy guard, to confer with prosecuting attorneys John F. X. McGohey and Frank Gordon. His appearance in the witness box stunned the defense.

Another shock witness at the Foley Square trial was little Angela Calomiris, a lonely daughter of the Lower East Side, who had been picked up by two FBI agents in 1942 and warned that Russia might not always prove to be a loyal ally. Accepting expenses but no wages, Calomiris was able to exploit her reputation as a photographer to provide the Bureau with shots of CP and IWO meetings. Perhaps she was not interested in money; or perhaps she was naïve; in any case, her lack of remuneration was exceptional among undercover agents.[15] Mary Stalcup Markward, who was recruited by the FBI in 1943 at the age of twenty-two, while working in a Washington beauty shop, and who later became a member of the central committee of CP District 4, was paid no less than $24,026 over a ten-year period. In return she testified at the Baltimore Smith Act trial and on other occasions, naming 318 people in all. By the time the Detroit housewife Berenice Baldwin emerged in February 1952 after nine years as an FBI undercover agent in the Michigan headquarters of the CP, she had received $16,717 from the Bureau. Evidently the money was well spent, since she was able to name more than one hundred Michigan Communists before HCUA and to testify for the prosecution at the Detroit Smith Act trial.*

Some undercover agents ran considerable risks; whether inspired by patriotism or venality one can only conjecture. Thus, Lloyd N. Hamlin, a photographer who joined the Party in 1945 on behalf of Naval Intelligence and later reported to the FBI, managed to maintain his cover at the price of being sentenced for contempt by a California investigating committee. (The U.S. Attorney's office managed to keep him out of jail.) By the time Hamlin appeared as a witness in 1952 at the California Smith Act trial, he had been paid $13,182. Not least of the risks endured by these perseverant moles was head-on collisions with other FBI moles in labyrinthine underground tunnels, where genuine identities could only be guessed at. No doubt the genuine comrades looked on with a certain amusement when one agent

---

* For further biographical information about undercover agents, see Appendix A.

denounced the other,[16] as Matt Cvetic did George Dietz and Joseph Mazzei in Pittsburgh.

But how reliable were these informers, how trustworthy in their naming of names, how effective in rendering the Party vulnerable to the assaults of the various government agencies? The obvious point to be made is that the information they passed on while masquerading as Communists, and perhaps on the first occasion when, having revealed their true identities, they testified in public, was more reliable than the information provided by those who became addicted to the role of professional ex-Communist. Knowing less and less about the current state of the Party and its personnel, no longer serving the Bureau, but catering instead to publicity-hungry committees or conviction-hungry prosecutors, they tended increasingly to say what their masters wanted them to say. An agent still operating within the Party might be tempted to color his accounts somewhat, or even to provoke the incidents he reported; on the other hand he would be aware that his accounts could be cross-checked against those of other agents whose identities were unknown to him.

There is no doubt that a considerable number of these agents who served the FBI were unscrupulous and mendacious. William G. Cummings, of Toledo, Ohio, a witness in the Foley Square trial, who was paid $11,023.25 by the Bureau during eight years' service, was actually arrested for perjury during the Federal Communications Commission "trial" of Edward Lamb, at which he gave clearly bogus evidence. It emerged that in taking out a second marriage license, Cummings had denied on oath being married before. Daniel Scarlatto, of Canton, Ohio, an FBI agent in the Los Angeles CP from 1947 to February 1952 at $75 a month, testified at the California Smith Act trial and also before the SACB. Having stated on the witness stand that he had been married in Arizona in 1948, he was forced by the defense to admit that this was untrue and that the girl with whom he had been living was not in fact his wife. The defense claimed that he had in fact violated the Mann Act. The point to be made here is not simply that perjury often becomes a habit; more important was the eagerness of such men to avoid indictment by faithfully serving those with the power to indict them.[17]

Ever since the California syndicalism law of the pre-First World War era, under which a couple of former Wobblies would testify against their erstwhile IWW comrades in almost every prosecution, sending dozens of migratory workers to prison, disillusioned or frightened radicals had learned to save their own skins by hanging out the hides of comrades. Many of these "stoolpigeons" and "fingermen" ended up with the Immigration Service of the Department of Justice, which had eighty-three "informants" under contract in the early

1950s, thirty-five of them regular witnesses performing in all manner of anti-Communist trials and hearings, the remainder part-timers.[18] (The Internal Revenue Service set the pace by paying $499,995 to 290 informers during the fiscal year ending June 30, 1952.)

At the Denver Smith Act trial a former FBI agent called Warren Fortson testified that violence and force had been advocated at six Party meetings he had attended. The court granted the defense's demand that the FBI should produce the written reports that Fortson had submitted after each of the meetings: not one of them mentioned a single instance of such advocacy. The evidence provided by Ralph Clayton Clontz, a black North Carolina attorney, who served as an FBI agent in the CP at $450 a month from August 1948 until February 1953, having written to the FBI offering his services while a student at Duke University, was, to say the least, highly suspect. Clontz, who testified before the SACB against the National Council for American-Soviet Friendship (NCASF) and the Jefferson School, claimed at the Smith Act trial of the Carolina Communist leader Junius Scales that Scales, having invited him home, had told him that Russia would land troops in America if the United States government "declared war on the Communists in their revolution." Another agent, Childs, a student at the University of North Carolina who had all his expenses paid plus $100 a month from the FBI, and whose six years as an undercover agent won him draft deferment, claimed at the Scales trial that an instructor at a Party school had demonstrated how to kill a person with a sharpened pencil.[19]

The case of David Brown was a peculiar one. For seventeen years he had been a Communist trade unionist in the East. Disenchanted, he made his way to California in 1948. The FBI approached him in 1950. Faced with money difficulties and fearing for his job as a warehouseman if the FBI spoke to his employer, he decided to collaborate, receiving $5 for each report on a meeting advertised in the *Daily People's World*, up to a maximum of $50 a month. He infiltrated the Labor League for Peace and managed to become executive secretary of the Rosenberg Defense Committee at $75 a week. His contact in the FBI, Romney Stewart, offered him more money if he could get back into the CP. Brown failed, but pretended to Stewart that he had succeeded. From 1954 on he was sending in phony reports of Communist meetings, for which he was receiving $250 a month. Brown then pretended that he had been kidnapped and murdered; yet when he gave himself up to the FBI in Portland, Oregon, the Bureau, far from abandoning him as a neurotic perjurer, tried to persuade him to start again, but without success. In January 1955 he testified as a defense witness for the Civil Rights Congress before the

SACB, admitting that for four years he had been turning in to the FBI the names of people he did not know.

Most remarkable of all was James V. Blanc, the sixth FBI undercover agent to testify in May 1949 at the Foley Square trial. On the witness stand Blanc proudly related how he had ingratiated himself with the Party by recruiting new members who didn't in fact exist and whose dues he himself paid from funds provided for this purpose by the Bureau. But he had also recruited thirty-five to fifty real people, including his own brother-in-law, and then promptly turned their names over to the Bureau.[20] This was a man whom the FBI and the Department of Justice were proud to offer at the bar of justice as a patriotic American who would tell the truth, the whole truth, and nothing but the truth.

The FBI, of course, did not depend for its information on its own planted agents alone. In 1947 Hoover explained to the Loyalty Review Board that the Bureau relied on three types of informant: the agent operating under top-secret conditions within the Party; the contact who, although not employed by the Bureau, had proven reliable; and casual, once-only informants among neighbors and colleagues. It was therefore in the Bureau's interest for Hoover to stimulate the broadest possible enthusiasm for informing as a way of life. He urged the public to report any indication of subversive activities by friends or neighbors, and in November 1950 he invited doctors to convey to the FBI any information that would help to wipe out the "Communist germs" that "infect the bloodstream of American life." The results, in terms of public attitudes, were evidently highly satisfactory. Asked in 1954 whether people should report to the FBI those neighbors or acquaintances they suspected of being Communists, 72 percent of a national cross section replied in the affirmative.[21]

## THE RED SQUADS

The local police "red squads" also achieved some spectacular *coups* in penetrating the ranks of the Party. Red squads were notably active in New York City, Los Angeles, Detroit and such cities of Ohio as Dayton, Cincinnati, Toledo and Cleveland.

In July 1948 the New York State Association of Chiefs of Police directed that a resolution be drafted recommending legislation "to drive the pinks out of this country." Two New York City policewomen who infiltrated the Party wrought more havoc among city teachers and municipal employees than did any agent of the FBI. Stephanie Horvath, a native of Austria, who became a policewoman in 1942, joined the Party the following year on behalf of the New York Bureau of Special Services. Using the cover name of Stephanie Riedel, she furnished mailing lists and dues statements to the Police Department until, in February 1944, she was expelled as a Trotskyist. Perseverant, she worked her way back into the Party's Yorkville Club under the name of Louise Rader and stayed there until she was unmasked and expelled in 1950. She subsequently testified against certain teachers and employees of the Department of Welfare, and then before the SISS in 1953, the year in which she received a Police Department citation.

Mrs. Mildred Blauvelt joined the New York City police in December 1942 and penetrated the CP within four months, under the name of Mildred Brandt. Ousted in September, she rejoined in April 1944 as Sylvia Vogel and was not uncovered and expelled until November 1951. She provided HCUA with no fewer than 450 names, mostly with addresses attached. There is also evidence that the New York Police Department provided information to professional blacklisters and clearance experts like the notorious Vincent Hartnett.[22]

Despite protests from Governor G. Mennen Williams, the Michigan legislature voted broad powers to the State Police Commissioner to create a secret, antisubversive police squad responsible only to himself. Under Police Chief Harry S. Toy, who described members of the Progressive Party as "un-Americans [who] ought either to be shot, thrown out of the country, or put in jail," and who warned on the radio that "Soviet agents are coming into the United States disguised as Jewish rabbis," Detroit's Police Department employed labor spies like Jacob Spolansky and William Guernay (used by Chrysler) as well as undercover labor detectives such as Harry Makuliak (Harry Mack) and Leo Maciosek (Michaels). Toy set the tone by claiming that he had uncovered a CP plot to blow up the Briggs plant. City loyalty hearings revealed how members of the Subversive Bureau attended and photographed a wide range of radical meetings and picket lines.[23]

## THE EX-COMMUNIST WITNESSES

Here we must distinguish between the FBI undercover agent, the inside informer, and the genuine ex-Communist whose testimony begins only after he leaves the Party. Accorded reverential respect were the confessions of those witnesses who, having renounced the Communist faith in a moment of traumatic apostasy, dedicated the rest of their lives to renewing the Manichaean struggle between good and evil, but in reverse form, insisting that they understood the virtues of democracy and the evils of Communism to a degree that no lifelong democrat and non-Communist could equal. Isaac Deutscher remarked that, "as a rule the intellectual ex-Communist . . . is an inverted Stalinist. As a Communist he saw no difference between Fascists and Social Democrats. As an anti-Communist he sees no difference between Nazism and Communism." [24]

The most famous and successful ex-Communist informer of the postwar period was Louis Francis Budenz. Born in Indianapolis in 1891 and raised a Catholic, he entered the labor movement via the Indianapolis Labor School, edited *Labor Age* during the 1920s, and was arrested some twenty-one times on picket lines. In August 1935 he joined the CP. A member of the Party's New York State committee, and then of its national committee, he became in 1941 managing editor (a technical rather than a political post) of the *Daily Worker*. Although never a member of the Politburo, he attended its meetings irregularly. On October 11, 1945, he left both the *Daily Worker* and the Party. The action was evidently carefully premeditated, for within forty-eight hours he had been appointed a professor at the University of Notre Dame; he soon moved to another Catholic university, Fordham, in New York, where he taught from 1946 to 1956.

It was exactly one year between Budenz's resignation from the CP and his first public appearance as a professional ex-Communist. He named Gerhart Eisler as the Kremlin's top agent in the United States and told HCUA that all Communists were "a part of the Russian fifth column." These and similar utterances attracted major press coverage. Once launched, he never looked back: from October 1946 until his "retirement" in 1957, he testified thirty-three times, wrote four books and numerous articles, and established a reputation not merely as an *informer* whose role might be confined to the perpetual reiteration of his own experiences, but also as an *expert* capable of generalizing about the nature of Communism, its aims and philosophy. Certainly these generalizations were shallow, secondhand, and mainly misleading; nevertheless they brought him gross earnings of $70,000 in his role as an ex-Communist between 1946 and 1953. Money certainly attracted him, including the $899.94 which, as he had to admit during the Foley Square trial in April 1949, he still owed to the CP from personal loans made to him while he was managing editor of the *Daily Worker*.[25]

White-haired, pale-faced, dressed in dark, expensive suits, Budenz was received back into the faith on October 10, 1945, by Monsignor Fulton J. Sheen, in St. Patrick's Cathedral, New York. Insisting that Almighty God is the prime mover in history, and quoting Pope Pius XI's 1937 Encylical on atheistic Communism, "Satanic Scourge," Budenz claimed modestly that "the most truthful people in the world are the ex-Communists . . . they certainly have a resurrection within themselves, on the whole." Thus the author of *Red Baiting: Enemy of Labor* (Workers Library, 1937) became the author of "The Red Web in U.S. Labor" (*Collier's*, October 23, 1948).

Solemnly, almost impassively, Budenz gave evidence at the Foley Square trial, at the Board of Education trial of eight New York teachers in September 1950 (when he explained that American Communists expected the Red Army to bring socialism to America), before the SACB, at the Smith Act trial of "second-string" Communist leaders held in New York in 1952 (when the defense made a strenuous attempt to prove him a perjurer), and on many other occasions. In his wake he left a trail of destruction—people ruined in reputation, people fired from their jobs, people jailed. Increasingly he associated himself with the most reactionary views, denouncing British trade with China and advocates of peace in Korea, and quoting *Counterattack* as a reliable source.

Did he know as much as he claimed to know? Certain other ex-Communists doubted it. Browder pointed out that Budenz's work for the *Daily Worker* had been concerned with copy and production, not with policy. Bella Dodd described him as "an ineffective man" and derided two of Budenz's stories: that the leading Communist Jacob Stachel had given him one thousand names of secret Communists to memorize, and that Owen Lattimore's name had appeared as L or XL on secret onionskin Party documents which were issued on a "read-and-destroy basis," with an instruction that they be flushed down the toilet—"we did not fall into the habit of taking our methods from dime detective stories," Dodd commented.[26]

There were those who came to believe that Louis Francis Budenz was a brazen liar. In May 1950 Senator Dennis Chavez of New Mexico, himself a Roman Catholic, remarked in the Senate that "this man has impeached and exposed himself as a devious, conspiratorial, warped personality . . . I do not think he knows truth from falsehood any more." In December 1952 the commentator Elmer Davis, not similarly blessed with Congressional immunity, referred to Budenz as "the man so gifted at remembering what he forgot to mention last year or the year before." [27]

By 1952–53 Budenz had become both emboldened and careless; he now spun history out of his head as a worm spins silk. During the Cox Committee hearings on charitable Foundations in December 1952, Budenz excelled himself, identifying as CP members twenty-three beneficiaries of Foundation grants as well as four Foundation officials, including Professor Linus Pauling. Among the recipients of Guggenheim grants whom Budenz falsely accused of CP membership were Professor Thomas I. Emerson, of Yale, the Harvard scholar John K. Fairbank, and the editor of *The Nation*, Carey McWilliams.

Among Rockefeller beneficiaries whom Budenz falsely named as Communists were Professor Walter Gellhorn (a liberal academic lawyer teaching at Columbia), Corliss Lamont (a philosophy instructor at Columbia who, though a most zealous fellow traveler of the Soviet Union, was never a CP member), and Dr. Ira De A. Reid, of Haverford College, Pennsylvania. Pauling responded by calling Budenz a "professional liar," while Emerson pointed out that in one of his books Budenz had already called him "a dupe of the Communists," a description hardly applicable to a Communist; McWilliams, in making his denial, pointed out that he was not, as Budenz had described him, "the Reverend." Gellhorn and Reid made their denials under oath, Gellhorn adding that the only organization he had ever belonged to was the ACLU.[28]

In view of Budenz's record was it surprising that he should have been invited to serve, from 1959 to 1963, as adviser on Communist research to Cardinal Cushing of Boston?

John Lautner was a different kind of man; his rage against the Party was, at least in the first instance, genuine, and his behavior that of a wounded bull.

Born in Hungary in 1902, Lautner had served in the Red Army during the revolutionary civil war of 1919. Expelled from the country in the same year, following the defeat of the Bela Kun regime, he arrived in the United States in 1920 and became an American citizen six years later. As a Party member he was generally assigned work among nationality groups, although in the late forties he was appointed head of the Party's New York State cadre and review commission, with the sensitive task of supervising security organization, at a time when the CP was striving to detect infiltrators and bracing itself to go "underground." His sudden and melodramatically staged expulsion from the Party in January 1950 followed obviously false allegations of Titoism and being an FBI agent leveled against him by the Hungarian leaders at the time of the Rajk trial. The effect on the solemn and faithful Party hack Lautner was all the more traumatic in that his wife chose to believe the accusation against him and departed with their child.

On the basis of charges which Louis Weinstock brought back to America after a visit to Hungary, the Party leadership decided to behave in a manner fully worthy of any one of the anti-Communist movies then pouring from Hollywood studios. Lautner was interrogated daily and urged to confess that he was an FBI agent. "He was in a state of shock and could only mumble incoherent answers to the questions shot at him." Lured to a cloak-and-dagger interrogation in a Cleveland cellar, Lautner was confronted by the Party's top security officers armed with guns, knives, and a lie detector. In January 1950 he was expelled and vilified in the Communist press.[29]

Lautner was paraded across the country as the chief prosecution witness in every Smith Act trial after 1950, and in numerous Congressional and SACB hearings. Impassive and workmanlike in his manner, an automaton of the accepted clichés about Party behavior, he was between 1952 and 1956 principal witness in twenty-five proceedings concerning Communist penetration. What was, however, somewhat suspect about his testimony was the fact that in several Smith Act trials, including those in New York, Baltimore, California, and Connecticut, the questions and Lautner's responses to them had been written out beforehand by the prosecuting attorney. On one occasion Lautner denied this, only to admit soon afterward that it had been so. The same appearance of "tutoring" persisted in his testimony before the New York Board of Regents and the SACB. During the California trial Lautner reiterated on six occasions that he had seen one of the defendants, Al Richmond, at the 1945 national Communist convention. In fact in July 1945 Richmond was serving with the U.S. Army in Dorset, England. In 1956 Lautner revealed that he had been paid $22,000 by the Department of Justice during the previous five years.[30] In 1958 he was put on the HCUA payroll as a consultant.

For the payroll pickings (and the limelight, the sore spot in the national psyche), a number of aging defectors of doubtful credibility were in competition. There was Benjamin Gitlow, expelled from the Party in 1930 as a result of a high-level faction fight, a ghost from the past privy to obsolete information. There was Maurice Malkin, born in Minsk, a charter member of the American CP, a renegade since 1937, a person twice convicted for felonious assault. (Another ex-Communist witness, William H. Teto, was periodically jailed for larceny.) Malkin, who sold himself as an expert on Communist infiltration of trade unions by specializing in extravagant allegations, was nevertheless eclipsed as an entertainer by another charter member of the CP, Joseph Zack Kornfeder.[31] In 1950 Kornfeder admitted having persistently and falsely testified under oath that he was born in Scranton, Pennsylvania (instead of Slovakia), and he also staged a mock Communist putsch, with the help of the local Legion post, in Mosinee, Wisconsin. Such was the excitement that the mayor and a Catholic priest both died of heart attack.[32]

Paul Crouch, who claimed to have left the CP in 1942 after seventeen years, but to have been issued a membership book as late as 1947, must rank as one of the most brazen and colorful liars in the business. Having been Party organizer in Alameda County, California, in 1941, he assured the Burns Committee in 1950 that J. Robert Oppenheimer had at that time been a secret Party member. From sunny California Crouch moved to sunny Florida, which provided him with a pretext for fabricating the involvement of two left-wing Florida lawyers, Leo Sheiner and Paul Newman, in a "secret plot" to go underground and stage an uprising after the Red Army landed. Crouch was a political vampire. He threatened the career of Truman's economic adviser, Dr. Leon Keyserling, and damaged that of his wife, Mary Keyserling, who was suspended by the Department of Commerce for eighteen months until cleared in January 1953 by a loyalty board. Crouch also claimed to have met at Party central committee meetings Jacob Burck, Pulitzer Prize-winning cartoonist of the *Chicago Sun-Times* and a former Communist, who underwent protracted deportation proceedings despite his recent record of outspoken anti-Communism.[33]

Crouch and his wife Sylvia, also an expert witness, approached their careers as informers in a thoroughly professional manner. Engaged in August 1951 as a special consultant to the Immigration Service at $4,840 a year, Crouch traveled regularly from his home in Hawaii (where he testified at the Smith Act trial) to Washington (where he was accommodated, rent free, in the establishment of the Most Rev. Pane Yu-pin, Nationalist Archbishop of Nanking.) As acting executive secretary of the "Federation of Former Communists, Inc.," Mrs. Crouch wrote to other informers soliciting their collaboration with a view to achieving higher status, recognition and fees.[34] But what kind of man was Paul Crouch?

In 1925 he had joined the Army and was promptly court-martialed for offenses aginst the military code so serious that he was sentenced to forty years' hard labor on Alcatraz island. To the court martial he explained: "I am in the habit of writing letters to my friends and imaginary persons, sometimes to kings and other foreign persons, in which I place myself in an imaginary position." This, roughly, is what he was still doing when he told Pat McCarran's Senate Subcommittee on Immigration in May 1949 that, "I was in charge for several years of sending Communists into the armed forces of the country."

> MR. CROUCH: In talking with the generals over there [Moscow] I got directives for concentration points in Panama, which I carried through.
> MR. CHAIRMAN: What did you carry through?
> MR. CROUCH: I carried through the plans, sending the first soldier into Panama and giving directives for reports . . . on his progress in building a Communist organization inside the Army in Panama. I never received from him and I was not—I was

never personally; I would like to make this clear—I was never personally in a position to carry out other parts of these directives . . .

Later Crouch filed with the McCarthy Subcommittee a memo describing how he and Marshal Tukhachevsky had hatched a plot to subvert the entire American military establishment thirty years earlier. According to Roy Cohn, it was this amazing relevation that set off the Fort Monmouth investigation.

Crouch's testimony was riddled with inconsistencies. Among the Soviet leaders whom he claimed to have met in Moscow, Georgi M. Malenkov was never mentioned—until, that is, he became Premier in March 1953. Whereupon Crouch immediately filed a statement with the McCarthy Subcommittee to the effect that he had conferred with Malenkov in 1927. In May 1949 he told HCUA that he knew Armand Scala of Local 500, the Transport Workers Union, but had no idea whether he was a Communist. Five days later Crouch described Scala as the chief Communist courier to Latin America. When he repeated this charge in (nonprivileged) newspaper statements, Scala brought suit for libel and was awarded $5,000. Crouch was also one of the many perjurers who claimed to have personally "seen" Harry Bridges elected to the CP's national committee in New York in 1936.[35] In court in Pittsburgh, Steve Nelson addressed him as "Mr. Stoolpigeon" and sometimes as "Mr. Stoolie." Crouch didn't mind.

What he did mind was the campaign to discredit him conducted by the influential conservative journalists, Stewart and Joseph Alsop, whose renewed aspersions in May-June 1954 forced Attorney General Brownell to promise an investigation. Crouch reacted hysterically, calling on J. Edgar Hoover to investigate the loyalty of Brownell's aides, and later petitioning McCarthy to investigate the Attorney General himself. On August 25, Crouch filed a libel suit for half a million dollars against the Alsops and the *New York Herald Tribune*. Nothing came of it, and his career was effectively over, as Brownell indicated in February 1955. Crouch retired to Hawaii, where he died in November of lung cancer, at the age of fifty-two.

The leading black informers, originally recruited by the Party because they were black, sent to Moscow, and then hastily elevated, comprised a sad crew of Uncle Toms, and none sadder than William O. Nowell, son of a poor farming family from Georgia. Converted to Communism during the Depression, Nowell spent a month in the Soviet Union in 1929 and later returned to the USSR to attend the Lenin School. Active as a trade unionist in the Detroit region, he was expelled from the CP in 1936 and was soon afterward recruited into the Ford Motor Company employment office by the notorious Harry

Bennett, to spy on the militants of the UAW at the River Rouge plant. Testifying at the Foley Square trial in 1949, an angry Nowell claimed that he had been dismissed from the Ford "labor service" in 1945 (when Henry Ford II had fired Bennett) because "the Ford Motor Company entered into a conspiracy with the Communist Party to dismiss those of us who were opposing Communism." Appointed a "consultant" by the Immigration Service in December 1948, Nowell had by June 1954 testified in about forty deportation and denaturalization cases. He specialized in flourishes of brazenly invented but marvelously detailed information, particularly at Smith Act trials.

Manning Johnson, also black, joined the CP in 1930 at the age of twenty-two, rose to membership on the national committee, then quit in 1940. Having promptly turned informer, he testified before the Coudert Committee of the New York State legislature in 1942, at Harry Bridges's perjury trial in 1949 (Johnson swore he had seen Bridges elected to the CP's national committee in 1936), and at many Immigration Service cases. The Justice Department went on paying him $4,548 a year even after he admitted, during the Nelson sedition trial in Pittsburgh, that he had perjured himself in a deportation case. "I think the security of the government has priority over . . . any other consideration." Indeed, he confessed before the SACB that he would lie "a thousand times" if it were in the interests of the government and the FBI for him to do so. (It was.) Yet the Justice Department did not flinch until Johnson swore before a loyalty board that Dr. Ralph Bunche, a black American occupying a senior position in the UN Secretariat, was a Party member. After the loyalty board cleared Bunche by 6 to 0, the Justice Department announced that it was investigating Johnson for perjury. Johnson promptly became an insurance salesman. He died in July 1959, an early recruit to the John Birch Society.

Leonard Patterson, another black informer, also swore that Bunche was a Communist. A child of the rural South like Nowell and Johnson, Young Communist League district organizer for several Eastern states before he went to study in Moscow, and a Party member from 1930 to 1937, Patterson later testified in a number of deportation cases. In 1952 he gave evidence at the California Smith Act trial against Al Richmond, whom he had not met for twenty years; a year later he obliged HCUA by "identifying" two fellow-traveling Methodists, the Reverend Harry F. Ward and the Reverend Jack McMichael, as Party members (which they were not). Although he never earned as much as Manning Johnson (only $3,775 in two years—he had to drive a hack in New York in his spare time), he fell into disgrace as a perjurer at the same time as Johnson.[36]

The lengths to which the authorities would go in order to protect their paid perjurers was most vividly illustrated in the case of another black, George Hewitt, who joined the YCL in 1926 and the Party a year later, and remained a member until 1944. He claimed to have attended the Lenin School in Moscow from 1929 until 1933. Like two other Negro ex-Communists, George Peters and Charles H. White, he constantly testified about the revolutionary activities of the Party at deportation hearings in the late forties. He was a witness at Carl Marzani's perjury trial in 1947 and in the deportation proceedings against John Santo, Charles A. Doyle, Claudia Jones and Ferdinand Smith, all of them Communist trade unionists, and the latter two both black.

In July 1948 the Canwell Committee convened in Seattle to investigate Communist infiltration of the University of Washington. On July 22, Hewitt testified against a member of the English faculty, Melvin Rader, and against Ralph Gundlach of the psychology department, swearing that both of them had attended a Communist school near Kingston, New York, for six-week periods in 1938 and 1939. Before he could be nailed down on this, Hewitt was swiftly spirited away to New York. Washington's State Prosecutor then pressed perjury charges against him, requesting the New York police to hold him for extradition. Hewitt, meanwhile, was extremely active. In September he testified at the deportation hearing of August Cohn, a thirty-six-year-old carpenter living in Queens, who had arrived in America in 1946 after twelve years in Buchenwald concentration camp, and on December 22 Hewitt appeared before the federal grand jury considering Chambers's allegations against Hiss. Despite this trail of conspicuous activity, the New York police somehow could not locate him, even though the *Daily Worker* helped them along by printing his address.

Back in the State of Washington considerable pressure was being exerted on District Attorney Charles O. Carroll to drop the perjury charge against Hewitt, notably by a local U.S. Immigration inspector, John P. Boyd, and by the editor of the Hearst *Post-Intelligencer*, Edward T. Stone. Boyd said the Immigration Service had asked the New York police to protect Hewitt from Communist harassment. However, on February 10, 1949, Hewitt surrendered to the police. When his lawyer contested the extradition request and filed a petition for *habeas corpus*, Justice Aron J. Levy released Hewitt by an extraordinarily biased and unjudicial ruling in which he virtually condemned Melvin Rader *in absentia*. In the fall of 1949 President Raymond Allen of the University of Washington, a devout anti-Communist, announced that he was satisfied that Hewitt's allegations had been disproved.[37]

Apart from Elizabeth Bentley, there were two other notable

women defectors from Communism who ultimately turned informer. Both had been deeply committed to the radical movement and both were persons of education, dedication and substance. Bella Dodd, small, dark and born in Italy, had degrees from Hunter, Columbia and New York University. Legislative representative of the New York Teachers Union since 1936, and an active, fellow-traveling member of the ALP, she joined the CP in 1943, was appointed to its New York State board under Gilbert Green, and served on the national committee until her expulsion from the Party in 1949. At first she flinched from the role of professional informer, withdrawing into her small law practice and mourning the lost syndrome of energy and comradeship in which she had busily thrived as a New York radical. When the Tydings Subcommittee subpoenaed her in 1950, she conducted herself with restraint. But by the time of the SISS's hearings on education in 1952, Bella Dodd had been rebaptized in St. Patrick's Cathedral by Bishop Fulton J. Sheen, and was ready to place her unrivaled knowledge of the political histories of New York teachers at the service of the nation. By January 1953 she was denouncing progressive education as a tool of subversion in the hands of the Party.

The defection of Barbara Hartle draws our attention to the remarkable fact that, despite the saturation attack launched against the Party by almost every agency of government, not one Communist of the first rank other than Budenz (Lautner had been expelled against his will) turned informer in the postwar period until Barbara Hartle walked into the Seattle office of the FBI on March 12, 1954. Born in Oregon in 1908, a graduate of Washington State University, married to a railroad worker, she had served as organizer of the King County and Washington State CP from 1942 to 1950. In October 1953 she was sentenced to five years' imprisonment under the Smith Act. She began naming names publicly in June 1954, soon after beginning to serve her sentence, and eventually she named 470 people, including her former husband and her former common-law husband. Predictably, she was granted parole in January 1956 and released on February 1, while her colleagues remained in prison. She was still naming names in 1963, by which time there was at least one piece of evidence to suggest that she had begun to invent Communists.

Invention was in any case the specialty of renegades, who traded heavily on mounting American popular fears of Soviet military aggression. Crouch was full of detailed Soviet invasion plans. During the Foley Square trial Charles W. Nicodemus, who had left the CP three years earlier, testified that the Party planned to coordinate its revolutionary putsch with a Red Army invasion through Alaska and Canada.[38] Soviet émigrés like Victor Kravchenko, Alexander Barmine and Igor Bogolepov (a Soviet colonel who had defected to the

Nazis in 1941 and operated a radio transmitter on their behalf) were always ready to delight Congressional committees with the wildest "inside stories" of diabolical Kremlin plots.

## THE INFORMER RACKET EXPOSED

In 1954 the informer racket began to attract public criticism even from conservatives, so blatantly opportunistic and inconsistent was the testimony of the professionals. (Ultimately the testimony of Johnson, Crouch and Harvey Matusow before the SACB was stricken from the record by direction of the Supreme Court.) In July the Department of Justice announced it was considering perjury charges against Crouch, Johnson and Patterson, but nothing came of it. In fact the Department now launched a determined rearguard action to defend the credibility of its expensive stable. On July 23, Assistant Attorney General Warren Olney III delivered a speech decrying "the unprecedented barrage of abuse, emanating mostly from certain newspaper columnists" against the Department. The "informants" had helped to secure seventy-two Smith Act convictions—surely this was proof of their reliability. Assistant Attorney General William F. Tompkins told a Senate committee that the current attack on the witnesses "has its roots in a Communist effort." [39]

The Justice Department now resolved to make a punitive example of M. L. Edwards, a Miami aviation mechanic whose evidence had helped Armand Scala win his libel suit against Paul Crouch. On June 1, 1954, the Department moved in New York to have Edwards indicted 1,500 miles from his home in Miami. Bail was fixed at $10,000. Bondsmen's fees, lawyers' fees, witnesses' fees, travel expenses and loss of work cost Edwards nearly $10,000. (The Emergency Civil Liberties Committee gave him what help it could.) When the New York jury audaciously acquitted Edwards, refusing to believe the string of ex-Communist informants whom the Justice Department paraded against him, a new age dawned.

If this was a blow to Brownell and the unscrupulous clients of the Internal Security Division, worse was to follow. Within a few months a number of informers openly confessed to perjury, some of them "prosecution" witnesses at the hearings by which the Federal Communications Commission was theoretically determining whether Edward Lamb, a wealthy businessman, should be granted a broadcasting license—but in practice striving to prove that he had been a Communist. The tale originally told by Mrs. Marie Natvig, of Miami Beach, who claimed to have been a Party member from 1925 to 1937, was that in 1936 Lamb had spoken to her of future plans to seize communications and stimulate insurrection in the armed forces. Assuring the FCC that it was her infidelity with Lamb that had led to her divorce, she swore that he had recently tried to bribe her not to testify. Early in 1955 Mrs. Natvig recanted, claiming that her perjurious evidence had been coached by FCC prosecutor Walter Powell. Her affair with Lamb, like her Communist past, was fictitious. She was convicted of perjury and given a sentence of eight months to two years.

Two other witnesses who also retracted, Clark Wideman and Lowell Watson, likewise pleaded that FCC lawyers had coached them. Watson, a Kansas farmer with a criminal record and an Immigration Service informer since 1952, had testified in nine deportation and denaturalization cases.[40] Some time after his recantation, the Department of Justice ordered the deportation of Doris and Alan Shifrin against whom Watson had been one of only two direct witnesses.

### THE STRANGE CASE OF HARVEY MATUSOW

The major scandal of the time was the spectacular recantation of one of the most energetic informers on the Justice Department's payroll (he had named 216 names), Harvey Matusow.

Matusow had returned to New York from military service in Europe in 1946, joined the CP in 1947, and quickly dropped out of college. An unscrupulous adventurer with a taste for publicity, he contacted the FBI in 1950 and found it already had a dossier on him. Henceforward the Bureau paid him about $70 a month to attend CP meetings as an informer. Exposure was inevitable and on January 19, 1951, the Daily Worker reported that he had been expelled from the Tompkins Square section of the CP as an "enemy agent." Matusow then took himself off to New Mexico, where he joined the Air Force (henceforward he would describe himself as a "veteran of the Korean war") and—out of ambition, apparently—wrote an angry letter to HCUA denouncing his own presence in the armed forces. By November he was testifying before the Committee as an ex-Communist expert, and the following month he left a bewildered and relieved Air Force.

Moving to Dayton, Ohio, he fell under the influence of two older professional informers, John J. and Martha Edmiston, and of HCUA's investigator Donald T. Appell. (Edmiston, the financial editor of the Dayton Journal, had testified before HCUA about Communist strikes and infiltration of the armed forces.) Thanks to such connections Matusow was soon taken on the payroll of the Ohio Un-American Activities Commission at $300 a month plus expenses, to spy on radical meetings, to "finger" labor leaders, and to collect old nominating petitions for county elections bearing the names of sponsors of left-wing candidates.

Early in 1952 the Edmistons, who taught him how to temper his testimony and play his cards one at a time, brought him to Washington and introduced him to Jack Clements, director of public relations for Hearst publications. Out of this came a big Howard Rushmore story about Matusow, the proceeds of which Matusow split with the Edmistons. But Matusow was now launched; a meeting with T. C. Kirkpatrick brought him the chance to sell *Counterattack* on a commission basis and to serve as a consultant to the New York City Board of Education, at that time busily purging left-wing teachers.

Soon Matusow was exceeding himself in mendacity and rubbing shoulders with Joe McCarthy and his assistant Don Surine. In June 1952 he was paid $600 for writing "Reds in Khaki" for the *American Legion Magazine*. HCUA, the SISS and the SACB all required his services as a witness. It was in 1952 that Matusow delivered a speech in Great Falls High School claiming that the Sunday section of *The New York Times* was currently employing 126 dues-paying Communists, and that the staffs of *Time* and *Life* contained seventy-six "hard-core Reds." His association with McCarthy was such that he smuggled out of the country Mrs. Arvilla Bentley, a financial contributor to the Senator's career, who had been served with a subpoena that the Senator was anxious she should not honor. As a further gesture of loyalty Matusow married this wealthy lady.

Herbert Brownell's law firm of Lord, Day and Lord paid him to testify on behalf of one of their clients that the New York school strike of 1947 was Communist-led and to identify photographs of the strike leaders.[41] He acknowledged no debts now; on May 16, 1952, Martha Edmiston wrote him complaining that he owed them money, and although he did reply apologetically two years later they never forgave him—testifying before the SISS in February 1955, Martha Edmiston called him "a cheap and petty chiseler."

One incident demonstrates how a Justice Department informer was virtually endowed with a license to ruin careers and lives. In July 1950, while still an undercover FBI agent, and on the surface a Communist militant, Matusow had visited the San Cristobal Valley Ranch near Taos, in New Mexico. Run by Craig and Jenny Vincent, who were either Communists or friendly to the CP, the Ranch was evidently a haven for left-wingers. Subsequently Matusow reported to the world the names of the people he had met there, or claimed to have met there, including a certain Helen Barteline, wife of Leo J. Barteline. The repercussions of this story for the Barteline family were grim.

On June 23, 1953, Barteline, a Chicago lawyer, wrote to assure

Matusow that he himself had never visited the San Cristobal ranch, nor heard of it, nor heard of the Vincents; and that *if* his wife had accompanied Matusow to the ranch in 1950 or 1951, she had been completely innocent of any Communist connection. As Special Commissioner of the Illinois Supreme Court and soon to become chairman of the Public Relations Committee of the state bar association, Barteline pleaded that he would never be able to qualify for any federal post while so scandalous a charge hung over his head. It was true that he had once belonged to the National Lawyers Guild, but in all innocence. He virtually begged Matusow to sign an affidavit that Barteline wished to submit on behalf of his son-in-law, Oscar Cassada, who had been informed by the AEC in New Mexico that his eligibility for classified work was being reconsidered. Nor was Cassada the only other indirect casualty of Matusow's allegation; Barteline's stepson, Sergeant William Whalen, had been interrogated at Selfridge Air Base, Michigan, and was now regarded as a security risk.[42]

Early in 1954 Matusow began to have second thoughts. The leading informers patronized by the Justice Department were rapidly becoming discredited; Matusow began to put out feelers with a view to becoming an ex-ex-Communist. In private he confessed his perjuries to the Methodist Bishop G. Bromley Oxnam, but when the bishop made public his *mea culpa*, Matusow panicked and told HCUA he had never said any such things. Nevertheless, on March 24 he signed an affidavit that, contrary to his testimony before the SISS in October 1952, he did not know the name of any present or past CP member working for *Time* magazine. On the same day he wrote a six-page, rambling letter to Henry R. Luce, expressing sorrow for his own past lies, which had been prompted by selfishness and hate. The Justice Department showed no signs of being agitated by the affidavit; on the contrary, two Assistant Attorneys General of the Internal Security Division, Warren Olney III and William F. Tompkins, merely wrote Matusow urging him to pay the $59.30 he owed the Department for transcripts of his own testimony specially run off to convenience him.[43]

By the fall, Matusow's conversion was no longer in doubt. After he spoke with representatives of *The Nation*, notably its general counsel R. Lawrence Siegel, for whom the affair was to end disastrously, he was approached by the Communist lawyers Nathan Witt and John T. McTernan, whose interest in Matusow's conversion was understandable: on February 5, Charles F. Herring, U.S. Attorney in Austin, Texas, had written Matusow [44] thanking him for testimony essential to the conviction of the left-wing Mine, Mill and Smelter Workers union leader Clinton E. Jencks under the Taft-Hartley Act. (Matusow had sworn in April 1953 that three years earlier Jencks had confided to him that he was secretly a Party member, even though he had signed the Taft-Hartley non-Communist affidavit.) Witt, representing Jencks, shrewdly recognized that Matusow could not be expected, either realistically or effectively, to provide an immediate recantation with regard to Jencks alone. Not only would such a recantation gain credibility within the wider context of a general confession, but it was also the case that Matusow was down on his luck and in urgent need of money; every songbird has his price. Witt now approached the stridently pro-Soviet propagandist Albert E. Kahn, of the new publishing firm of Cameron and Kahn. Out of this approach Matusow's book, *False Witness*, was born. A contract was signed on October 24.

A Communist plot? Witt himself agreed that Mine, Mill put up $1,000 to subsidize the book and its impoverished author, while Kahn also mentioned financial support from the Fur Workers and the United Electrical, Radio and Machine Workers of America, both leading pro-Communist unions. The *Mine-Mill Union* gave *False Witness*, published in February 1955, a big boost in its March issues, providing mail order forms for the book at one dollar a copy. Proponents of the "Communist plot" outlook, notably the SISS, were also able to capitalize on certain passages of twelve tape-recorded conversations between Kahn and Matusow which preceded the writing of the book, and which the SISS subsequently subpoenaed. The Kahn tapes contained no word from Matusow about having testified falsely at the Smith Act trial of twelve Communists in 1952, nor of the allegations against Roy Cohn he was to make in his forthcoming affidavit of January 1955.

The SISS also made much of apparent discrepancies in Matusow's crucial testimony about Clinton Jencks. In a District Court affidavit, he now claimed that in October 1952 he had presented the SISS with a fabricated yarn about a conversation with Jencks during which the Mine, Mill leader outlined a plot to strike the copper mines in order to sabotage the Korean war effort. (Matusow had repeated this charge at Jencks's Taft-Hartley trial.) In his recantation affidavit, Matusow asserted that there had been no basis for his having stated in court that Clinton Jencks was a member of the Communist Party. But in the course of a tape-recorded conversation with Kahn, held on December 14, Matusow had said: "I knew Jencks was a Party member and I said so . . . But I shouldn't have testified, that's the important thing." This would seem damning. However, when Kahn asked him *how* he knew that Jencks was a Party member, Matusow replied that it was merely his *opinion*, and that for all he knew Jencks might have left the CP for tactical reasons.[45]

This goes to the heart of the matter. The informers as a group made a living out of pretending to an encylopedic knowledge of the

Communist movement across the face of a vast country. On a nod from prosecutors, they sold hunches or guesses as inside knowledge, supporting their claims with bogus reports of conversations and encounters.

Matusow's confession generated an immense press; reports and comments filled the columns for months afterward. Fellow informers were quick to react. Philbrick, writing in the *New York Herald Tribune*, described Matusow as a publicity hound greedy for gain, while Bella V. Dodd insisted that he was "acting the part of a Communist plant." [46] More serious for Matusow was a three-pronged official attack. Down in Texas federal Judge Robert E. Thomason angrily rejected his affidavit in the Jencks case, spoke of a Communist plot, and sentenced Matusow to three years' imprisonment for contempt of court. (The sentence was later reversed on appeal.) Meanwhile, Attorney General Herbert Brownell described the Matusow case as "part of a concerted drive to discredit government witnesses, the security program, and ultimately our sense of justice." He told the Greater Boston Chamber of Commerce that Matusow was the focal point in the Communist campaign to destroy the informant system. Insisting that Matusow was lying *now*, but had not lied earlier, he put a grand jury to work in February to dig up evidence of the plot. Not only Matusow and his publishers, with their manuscripts and tapes, were subpoenaed, but also the printers and production staff who physically produced the book. [47]

The grand jury also indicted Matusow himself for perjury. Rashly, Matusow had sworn an affidavit that that favorite son of the Internal Security Division, former Assistant Attorney General Roy Cohn, had in 1952 tutored him to testify, falsely, that a Smith Act defendant, Alexander Trachtenberg, head of International Publishers, had expressed approval of a revolutionary passage in a book written by Andrei Vishinsky. Cohn denied it in the Federal District Court, producing two U.S. Assistant Attorneys as witnesses, and on July 13 the grand jury indicted Matusow on six counts of perjury. On the other hand, Judge Edward J. Dimock was sufficiently impressed by Matusow's recantation to rule in April that two of the defendants in the 1952 Smith Act trial, one of them Trachtenberg, should be granted new trials. "The internal evidence," commented Dimock, "all points to the original story as the lie." (But the two Communists were again convicted on retrial.) In September 1956 Matusow was convicted of perjury, that is to say, of lying under oath when he claimed that he had earlier lied under oath. In June 1957 he began a five-year sentence handed down by Judge John F. X. McGohey, prosecutor in the Foley Square Smith Act trial of 1949.

The third prong of the official attack came from the SISS (of

whose members only Senator Thomas Hennings was not strongly
hostile to the reformed Matusow), which grilled Matusow, Witt, Angus Cameron, and Kahn, all three of whom invoked the Fifth with
regard to CP membership. SISS counsel J. G. Sourwine's principal
line was to suggest that Matusow had fallen into debt and had sold
himself for a mess of pottage. (Senator Price Daniel developed a line
of his own, persistently asking Matusow whether he had spent last
Friday night in bed with a woman other than his wife.) Matusow
himself resorted to the Fifth Amendment on a number of occasions,
having answered directly on others, and the Committee, deciding
that he had thereby waived the privilege, cited him on three counts of
contempt. For his part, Matusow assured the SISS that Elizabeth
Bentley, Paul Crouch, Louis Budenz, Manning Johnson, Matt Cvetic
and Herbert Philbrick were all persistent perjurers.[48] Under Counsel
Sourwine's guidance, the Committee produced a 120-page report,
supported by 1,300 pages of testimony, tearing Matusow and his sponsors into red shreds.

Meanwhile, the Justice Department continued its rear-guard action; in October 1955 Tompkins attacked Richard Rovere's objective
account, "The Kept Witnesses," while Brownell, supported by J. Edgar Hoover, insisted that national security depended on keeping informers secret in loyalty cases.

This new and different issue blew up in June 1957, when the
Supreme Court ruled in the case of the same Clinton E. Jencks, by 7
to 1, that the defense had the right to examine a witness's earlier
statements on the subject about which he testified. In practice this
meant access to the reports made by FBI agents and other informers.
Dissenting, Justice Tom Clark spoke darkly of possible fishing expedi-
tions in FBI files. Hoover's sulky response was a threat that the FBI
would drop out of certain espionage and subversion cases in order to
protect its informers. In August he demanded new legislation to protect the FBI files. Eisenhower obliged by speaking of the "incalculable damage" that would follow an opening up of the files. Lobbying
through Louis B. Nichols and the Congressional liaison branch of his
office, and mobilizing the 3,500 voices of the National Society of Former Special Agents of the FBI, Hoover pushed through Congress a
law protecting FBI files, which the Supreme Court upheld in 1959.

Murray Kempton described Harvey Matusow as

a parody on all that part of the fifties which has jerrybuilt façades
to hide its empty interiors—the spiritualism of nonbelievers, the
patriotism of those who hate their country . . . his every ism has
been an affectation born of a morbid love of admiration and the
vision of what everyone would say as he walked his garish way.[49]

# 7

## The Constitution
## Concussed in the Courts

During the Truman-Eisenhower era grand jurors and jurors reflected a general popular attitude of respect for "the government," or, in a phrase used with significant frequency, "*our* government." Not only was it widely accepted that "our government knows" or "knows best," but it was virtually inconceivable to the average juror that the FBI or the Justice Department could deliberately fabricate evidence or frame a victim. Many political cases, moreover, were brought to trial within the District of Columbia, wherein a high proportion of jurors were themselves government employees and therefore—it could be argued—biased in the government's favor. Such a situation would violate the Sixth Amendment, which guarantees a fair trial, but the Court of Appeals and the Supreme Court rejected the contention of bias in the Josephson and Dennis cases, thus opening the door to one of the Justice Department's golden decades.

Disqualification for jury service because of suspected CP membership became increasingly common. From July 1955, prospective jurors in New York City were obliged to fill out a questionnaire disavowing violent overthrow of the government; the following year a New York statute barred Communists from jury service. There was also much truth in the defense's contention, argued vigorously before the Foley Square trial began in 1949, that the social and ethnic composition of juries was rigged to ensure a general attitude respectful of the *status quo*, of established authority.

## BIASED JUDGES

That some federal judges were politically biased in favor of the government cannot be doubted. Judge Alexander Holtzoff, formerly an Assistant Attorney General and personal counsel to J. Edgar Hoover, delivered himself of one prejudiced judgment after another. In December 1956, upholding the conviction of the physicist Bernhard Deutsch for contempt of Congress, Holtzoff commented: "This court has gleaned the inference that the younger generation of scientists, particularly in the field of physics, has succumbed to Communist propaganda." Judge Irving R. Kaufman, who passed sentence of death on the Rosenbergs, was persistently an "establishment" judge.

In California, U.S. District Court Judge William C. Mathes, a Texas graduate of Harvard Law School and a devoted member of the American Legion, gave the Smith Act defendants a rough time; he set "reasonable" bail at $50,000 for an offense involving a maximum jail sentence of only five years. When, 104 days later, on November 5, 1951, the Supreme Court ruled that $50,000 was not reasonable bail, Mathes claimed to be so baffled by the ruling that he needed at least six days to meditate on it. Not until twenty-three days after the Supreme Court's decision (twenty-three more days of imprisonment for the defendants, on top of 104 they had already suffered), did Mathes finally rule—that $50,000 was indeed reasonable bail! "In his flamboyant homage to the flag, in many comments and asides from the bench he signified to us that he was the avenging defender of his social order. . . ." [1] The Circuit Court of Appeals then interpreted the Supreme Court's ruling and set bail at $10,000 for some, $5,000 for others. Later, Mathes treated Oleta O'Connor Yates savagely when she refused to answer certain questions under cross-examination, imposing a three-year sentence where other judges were content with thirty days. Finally, in 1957, the Supreme Court found that Mathes had failed to instruct the jury correctly and threw the case out.

Meanwhile, in Detroit, Judge Frank A. Picard, who presided in 1953 over the Smith Act trial of six Michigan Communist leaders, sent two of the defendants, Saul Wellman and Philip Schatz, to jail for contempt (they had refused to name others), but declined to cite for contempt two government witnesses, Milton J. Santwire and Stephen Schemanske, undercover operatives both for the FBI and the Ford Motor Company, after they admitted the most blatant perjury before the court. To cite them, argued Judge Picard, might prejudice the jury. Picard warned the Rotary Club of Traverse City in September 1954 that Communists might well be planning to sabotage heavy industry in the area—scarcely indicative of judicial restraint.

Federal Judge Robert E. Thomason, of Texas, kindly and humane in most respects, displayed psychotic behavior when Communism was the issue. When Harvey Matusow recanted his perjured evidence in the Jencks case early in 1955, Thomason sensed a plot and a personal insult to himself, put the defense lawyer Nathan Witt, who had filed a motion for a retrial, on the witness stand and then ejected him from the court.[2] More than one judge in those years gratuitously advised defendants, including native Americans, to "go back to Russia."

Yet the federal judiciary was a model of impartiality when contrasted with the performance of certain state judges. In Chapter 10 we shall describe how in the Pittsburgh area Judges Musmanno, Montgomery and Gunther, all activists of a pressure group called Americans Battling Communism, flouted the law and the principles protected by the Sixth Amendment with grotesque abandon. In New York, Justice Aaron Levy completely disregarded the law, as interpreted by the Supreme Court, when in May 1948 he ignored the only question relevant in an extradition case—whether the defendant was present in the extraditing state when the alleged offense took place— and rejected the State of Washington's bid to extradite the perjurious ex-Communist professional informer, George Hewitt. Another New York Supreme Court Justice, Ernest E. L. Hammer, delivered in May 1950 the first decision in any court upholding the right of labor unions to take disciplinary action against their members solely on the ground of Party membership. Emphasizing that the Attorney General had listed the CP as subversive (although this listing had no status in law), he quoted Truman on the desirability of ridding labor organizations of Communist officers; he quoted J. Edgar Hoover's claim that American Communists belonged "body and soul" to the "Red Hitler" in Moscow; and he quoted General Douglas MacArthur on the necessity of curbing Communism. In what amounted to judgment by quotation, Judge Hammer then quoted such anti-Communist labor leaders as William Green, Walter Reuther and David Dubinsky. He complained:

> The evidence . . . was that as . . . party members the plaintiffs at union meetings preached the superiority of the Soviet Union to the United States . . . they predicted the fall of China to Communism . . . they prophesied a depression in this land . . .

> Such conduct on the part of plaintiffs was anticountry and anti-union and completely political . . .

foreshadowing, Hammer warned, "a resort to violence."

In Ohio, a leading Communist, Frank Hashmall, was given a ten-year prison sentence for a minor motoring offense. The Ohio Supreme Court reduced the sentence and reprimanded the trial judge with the reminder that "even Communists are entitled to even-handed justice." Nevertheless Hashmall served two years in prison before he was granted parole.[3] In Florida, when the lawyer Leo Sheiner refused to disclose whether he had ever been a Party member, Judge Vincent Giblin promptly disbarred him with an opinion that deserved to be quoted in all its protracted intemperence:

> Of those apathetic and unaroused Americans who remain oblivious to the danger of Communist machinations, it is those who regard themselves as "intellectuals" and advanced libertarians who, perhaps, give the greatest aid and comfort to the enemy. These pygmies on stilts who parade as giants . . . waving their masters' [sic] degrees . . . they protest of "witch-hunts" . . . no need to depend on the advice of college professors . . . in devising effective ways and means of exterminating the vermin gnawing at the foundations of our governmental structure. . . . What, it may well be asked, is the bench and bar of America doing to rid the legal profession of the adherents of Communism . . .

Giblin's colleague, Senior Circuit Judge George E. Holt, also abused his position by imposing the maximum penalty of one year in jail—simultaneously refusing bail—on a series of witnesses whom the State Attorney of Dade County, George A. Brautigam, had summoned before a grand jury under Florida's "Little Smith Act." These witnesses had invoked the Fifth Amendment and Article 12 of the state Constitution, whereupon Brautigam introduced the novel theory that he was not investigating *a crime*, because all his questions referred to a period of time immunized by the statute of limitations. (Yet the sole purpose of a grand jury is to determine whether a crime has been committed.) Even when the Florida Supreme Court ruled in over a dozen such cases that bail should have been allowed, Judge Holt continued to deny bail in similar cases. Thirty-six people of radical background spent up to a month in prison.[4]

The judiciary was constantly reminded of the rewards not merely of political orthodoxy, as interpreted by the government, but of crusading zeal in the anti-Communist cause. One successful prosecuting attorney after another secured personal advancement. Thomas Murphy, prosecutor in the Hiss trial, became Commissioner of Police in

New York City before his appointment as a federal judge in 1951. John F. X. McGohey, in 1949 prosecutor in the trial of the eleven Communist leaders, was appointed a federal judge by Truman the day after the trial ended. Irving Saypol, prosecutor in the Remington and Rosenberg cases, became in 1952 a judge in the New York Supreme Court. Myles J. Lane, prosecutor in the trial of the "second-string" Communist leaders in 1952, also became a judge. (One Sunday in the middle of the trial, Lane informed a communion breakfast that the Rosenbergs had given the Soviet Union information about a "sky platform" intended to set the course of guided missiles.) Judicial dignity was conferred also on successful counsel for Congressional investigating committees, notably Richard Arens, counsel for HCUA and the SISS, who became a Commissioner of the Court of Claims, and Robert Morris, counsel for the SISS. In New York, the Board of Education's counsel, Saul Moskoff, who was instrumental in bringing radical teachers to trial, was duly rewarded with an appointment as a judge of the Family Court; Michael Castaldi, who performed a similar function for the Board of Higher Education, became a justice of the New York Supreme Court.

Judges who stuck their necks out in a liberal direction, or showed themselves to be unduly solicitous about the legal rights of radicals, were often the targets of political attack. Leon R. Yankwich, a federal judge in California, who ruled in favor of the dismissed Communist screenwriter Lester Cole after he brought suit against MGM, was sharply criticized by the Tenney Committee for having opposed the state's criminal-syndicalism law twenty years earlier, and also for having participated in forums of the ACLU: "Yankwich is not qualified, because of his obvious bias and sympathy for pro-Communist, pro-Soviet causes, to sit on the federal bench." In 1952 Representative Richard B. Vail R., California), a member of HCUA, called for a Congressional investigation of Yankwich's fitness to be a judge. When Judge Delbert Metzger reduced the bail of the Hawaii Smith Act defendants from $75,000 to $7,500, Senator Joseph C. O'Mahoney warned that Metzger would not be reappointed when his term expired three months later. And he was not. Metzger subsequently came out in support of the view that the Smith Act prosecutions endangered the First Amendment.

## COURTS OF APPEALS

In political and constitutional cases, the Court of Appeals for the District of Columbia exercised an influence second only to that of the Supreme Court. Indeed, four out of every five of its decisions were not reviewed by the Supreme Court. It was this Court of Appeals that ruled on cases arising out of the loyalty and security programs, the Attorney General's list, contempt of Congress, and denials of passports. Its nine judges normally sat in divisions of three, to keep pace with the volume of work, only occasionally sitting together "in banc."

In a series of 2-to-1 decisions, the appellate courts of the District of Columbia and of the Second Circuit (in essence, New York) found in favor of the government and against the rights of the "individual." Whenever the Supreme Court refused to review, district courts were bound by these decisions. Judge Prettyman set the tone of the Court of Appeals for the District of Columbia [5] in 1948: "The remedy for unseemly conduct, if any, by committees of Congress is for Congress, or for the people; it is political and not judicial." [6]

## THE VINSON SUPREME COURT

The most important factor in enabling and consolidating the purge, the great cleansing of American working life, was the performance of the Supreme Court under Chief Justice Fred Vinson. This was the Truman Court, a compliant instrument of administrative persecution and Congressional inquisition. From 1949 to 1954 the Constitution was concussed in the courts. But when the Warren Court handed down a batch of liberal rulings, the back of the purge was quickly broken. [7]

During the Truman-Eisenhower era radicals and genuinely liberal liberals urged the Court to intervene and strike down executive policies and Congressional legislation. Conservatives, by contrast, generally reverted to a doctrine of judicial restraint. But fifteen years earlier, when the Supreme Court had struck down a series of New Deal statutes, radicals and liberals had loudly argued that the Founding Fathers did not intend to endow the Court with powers to thwart "the will of the people" as expressed by their elected representatives. It all depended, in short, on whose ox was being gored. In America, both Left and Right tend to regard their opponents as *groups* subversive of the general will, and their allies as *individuals* whose liberties it is the proper task of the courts to defend. Bedrock principle is conspicuously absent; where Europeans may regard politics as a striving toward the permanent supremacy of a specific Principle, Americans tend to treat politics like the market place—an arena for lobbying, wheeling and dealing, with each vested interest invoking any temporarily expedient argument.

In 1946 Fred M. Vinson was appointed by Truman to replace Harlan Fiske Stone as Chief Justice. It was a disastrous choice, but symptomatic of worse to come. The President's first appointment to the Supreme Court, Harold H. Burton, was a Republican Senator from Ohio of conservative outlook; four years later, in 1949, the deaths of two liberal justices, Frank Murphy and Wiley Rutledge, enabled Truman to appoint two more of his conservative cronies, Sherman Minton, a federal judge and formerly a Senator from Ohio, and Attorney General Tom Clark of Texas. Thus was terminated the liberal decade during which, under Hughes and Stone, the Court had staunchly defended the Bill of Rights.

Vinson was a distinguished administrator—director of the Office of War Mobilization, then Secretary of the Treasury. But first and last he was a politician, a party man, foreign to the ideal of an independent judiciary. Willingly would Vinson have lent his high office to an opportunist electoral maneuver had not Truman entertained second thoughts about sending him to see Stalin in 1948. The columnist Drew Pearson, who knew Vinson well and invited him to dinner often—"a square-shooting loyal friend"—recorded in his diary for September 12, 1950: ". . . the Chief Justice came to dinner last month and asked me whether [Louis A.] Johnson was knifing Acheson . . . I gathered that both Truman and Vinson were strong for Acheson . . . Vinson mentioned the difficulty of finding a successor for Johnson and wanted to know who I thought could do the job well." There, in essence, was Vinson and the *locus* of his interests— so close to Truman and party political intrigue, it is hardly surprising that he rubber-stamped the administration's position on almost every occasion, virtually eroding a tripartite system of government into a bipartite one.

Tom Clark's career as Attorney General had already stamped him as a red-hunting vigilante in the A. Mitchell Palmer mold; nor did his years on the Supreme Court mellow his almost primitive reverence for the power of the state. In retrospect, Truman had this to say: "Tom Clark was my biggest mistake . . . I don't know what got into me. He was no damn good as Attorney General, and in the Supreme Court . . . he's been even worse." But the truth is that not one of Truman's three Attorneys General, and hardly any of his judicial appointees at any federal level, displayed a lively regard for the Bill of Rights.

Within the Supreme Court, Vinson, Reed, Burton, Minton and Clark were dependable in their support for the executive or the legislative committees in virtually any conflict with individual rights. Felix Frankfurter and Robert H. Jackson, appointed in 1939 and 1941 respectively, the one a former academic lawyer and the other a former Attorney General who served as chief war crimes prosecutor at Nuremberg, both had liberal reputations, but in the event they normally fell into line with the majority and the *Weltanschauung* of the Pax Americana after a decent display of qualms of conscience. Both relied on a theory of judicial limitation. Said Jackson in 1949: "I should . . . lean the responsibility for the behavior of its committees squarely on the shoulders of Congress." [8]

The only occasion in which the Vinson Court embarrassed a loyalty-security measure was when it instructed the Attorney General to remove three organizations from his subversive list. Otherwise the Court sanctioned the use of undisclosed evidence in loyalty proceedings, and the deportation of aliens for conduct that had been legal when it was committed. [9]

## METAMORPHOSIS OF THE WARREN COURT

When Vinson died in 1953, Eisenhower appointed as his successor Earl Warren, a respected Republican Governor of California with local support as a presidential candidate both in 1948 and 1952. When Jackson died a year later and was replaced by John Marshall Harlan, the conservative composition of the Court seemed to be more secure than ever. Yet now came an astonishing and unpredictable metamorphosis: like a man who had seen the light, Warren turned to the Bill of Rights in 1955, voting with Black and Douglas in eighty-three out of ninety-one full-opinion cases. As yet the three remained on most occasions a minority; Frankfurter, a conservative liberal, and Harlan, a liberal conservative, still tended to see things as the government saw them. The balance was tipped in October 1956 when William J. Brennan, a fifty-year-old Catholic from the New Jersey Supreme Court, replaced the conservative Minton. With Brownell still at the head of the Justice Department, it is difficult to account for Brennan's appointment; such was his reputation for liberalism that the Senate Judiciary Committee gave him a rough ride. The replacement of Reed by Charles E. Whittaker in 1957, and of Burton by Potter Stewart in October 1958, certainly carried the Court no further to the right.

It was in 1954 that Warren and the Court alienated the South with its historic ruling on segregated schools in *Brown v. Board of Education*. Within two years the Warren Court had aroused to fury not only the white-supremacists but all those who wished to perpetuate the anti-Communist campaign by means of legislative harassment, executive fiat, and judicial exoneration. In 1956, a year in which about 40 percent of the cases in the list issued by the Court concerned Communism or subversion, the Court rejected civil-liberties claims in only 26 percent of the cases it decided by full opinion. The corresponding figures for 1957 and 1958 were 41 percent and 48.8

percent respectively. In general the Court preferred not to meet the constitutional issues head-on, relying instead on a "strict" statutory interpretation. This raised only a low barrier to protect civil liberties from the new, corrective legislation and shifts in administrative procedure that inevitably came into operation in reaction to the Court's liberalism. Yet a low barrier was a barrier; it served. The Court itself was now subjected to a barrage of threats and criticism. In August 1958 the Conference of State Chief Justices voted by 36 to 8 to rebuke the Supreme Court for adopting the role of policy-maker and for lack of judicial self-restraint. Consequently the Court began to retreat, although Warren, along with Black and Douglas, dissented on almost every occasion; during the period 1957–59, he cast seventy-nine dissenting votes in full-opinion cases. Brennan tended to vote with the liberal minority, while Harlan and Frankfurter oscillated in the center, producing a series of apparently contradictory decisions. Warren, whose day of supreme achievement was June 17, 1957, when the momentous Watkins, Yates and Sweezy decisions were handed down, could not forgive Frankfurter for his subsequent retreat. Such was the antagonism between them that in 1957 Warren did not assign to Frankfurter the formulation of opinion of the Court in any of the fourteen civil-liberties cases in which they voted together in the majority.[10]

## CONTEMPT OF CONGRESS AND THE FIRST AMENDMENT

A witness wishing not to answer questions put to him by a Congressional committee might object on five possible grounds: (1) the Fifth Amendment; (2) the First Amendment; (3) Congress has not authorized the committee to ask *that* question; (4) the question is not pertinent to the matter under investigation; (5) the inquiry is not in aid of a legislative purpose.

Traditionally the Supreme Court had been extremely reluctant to interfere with the operation of Congressional committees and until 1953 never ruled on the procedure adopted by any committee of the legislature. The precedent it then set in the Rumely case (which was not political in nature) greatly strengthened objection three above, the result being that the courts threw out a number of contempt cases brought by McCarthy on the ground that the particular line of inquiry had not been authorized by Congress.

However, a witness would have been ill-advised to base his refusal on this technical and contentious objection alone. In the initial flush of postwar Communist confidence, leaders like Eugene Dennis, Gerhart Eisler and Leon Josephson were inclined to challenge

HCUA's right to exist to the point of refusing to be sworn; for this they were sentenced and jailed for contempt. The next wave of objectors, notably the Joint Anti-Fascist Refugee Committee and the Hollywood Ten, opted for the First Amendment which, they felt, had more dignity than the Fifth, with its implication of criminal activity. By 1950, however, it was obvious that the First Amendment cut no ice with the Vinson Supreme Court, and it was then that the Fifth Amendment began to be invoked on a massive scale. Generally, defense lawyers were not inclined to advise their clients to base their refusal on the hazardous objections four and five above, unless as supplementary objections. On the other hand the Supreme Court, when it began to draw a line in 1956, often chose to reach a decision on a technicality rather than on the issue of constitutional privilege raised by those who invoked the First or Fifth Amendments.

In the time of the Stone Court (1941–46) it was established that First Amendment rights enjoyed a "preferred position" and were not subject to "reasonable regulation." But after the deaths of Justices Murphy and Rutledge in 1949, the preferred status of the First Amendment went into mothballs. Judges in general, assuming that legislators were acting in the national interest, now tended to give them the benefit of every doubt—as did Vinson, Reed, Burton, Minton and Clark invariably in the post-1949 Supreme Court, with Frankfurter and Jackson tending to be acquiescent. Some judges even denied that the First conferred any right of silence or privacy in speaking, since its original purpose was to protect the individual against prosecution for sedition. Learned Hand, the most admired legal brain among the senior judges of the time, argued that the extent to which the government could restrict freedom of speech depended on ". . . whether the gravity of the 'evil,' discounted by its improbability, justifies such invasion of free speech as is necessary to avoid the danger." [11]

In 1948 and 1949 two important Courts of Appeals (for the District of Columbia and for the Second Circuit) ruled on several occasions that the First Amendment did not limit the power of Congressional committees to investigate political beliefs or associations, or to punish witnesses who refused to cooperate. In the famous case of the Hollywood Ten, *Lawson v. United States* (1949), the Court of Appeals for the District of Columbia ruled that, films being a potential medium of propaganda reaching millions, those who made them were obligated to reveal their political affiliations—in view of the world situation. After Clark and Minton had replaced Murphy and Rutledge, the Supreme Court denied *certiorari* in April 1950 (Black and Douglas dissenting), and the Ten went to jail.

There was a provocative quality in McCarthy—and also in those he marked out as his victims—which prompted unfriendly witnesses he subpoenaed to resort to the stormy First Amendment rather than the watertight Fifth. Some suffered for it: in November 1954, for example, District Court Judge Joseph C. McGarraghy gave the writer and civil libertarian Harvey O'Connor a suspended sentence of one year in prison and a $500 fine. But by 1955 the courts were beginning to clip the wings of Congressional inquisitors on technical grounds. The cases against Corliss Lamont,[12] the lawyer Abraham Unger and the engineer Albert Shadowitz, all of whom had risked the First Amendment before McCarthy, were thrown out by a District Court on the ground that Congress had not granted McCarthy the right to ask the questions he did ask. In January 1956 Judge Bailey Aldrich, of the Federal District Court in Boston, dismissed a contempt case against the Harvard instructor Leon J. Kamin, who had refused to answer McCarthy's questions about the CP cell Kamin had once belonged to. According to Judge Aldrich, the subcommittee over which McCarthy presided lacked statutory power to inquire into alleged subversion in universities.

In general the courts preferred to defend individual liberties on the basis of such technicalities rather than to confront the constitutional issue head-on. The single occasion on which the Supreme Court unambiguously upheld the First Amendment occurred in 1957, when it reversed the New Hampshire Supreme Court's adverse ruling against the Marxist economist and lecturer, Paul Sweezy. Because the questions Sweezy refused to answer on First Amendment grounds referred to the content of a lecture at the University of New Hampshire, the U.S. Supreme Court ruled that political and academic freedom was threatened by the inquiry, without the balancing justification of a threat to the security of New Hampshire.

But state Attorney General Louis C. Wyman was a scalp-hunter not easily deterred. Most notable of his victims was the old Methodist layman Willard Uphaus, one of those misguided but fundamentally honorable fellow travelers of Communism often found in the more eccentric corridors of Anglo-Saxon Protestantism. On the pretext of protecting the state against possible subversion, Wyman demanded the list of guests at Uphaus's World Fellowship summer camp together with the names of the camp's employees. Uphaus refused and was sentenced to languish in prison until he purged himself, although by that time (1956) he was sixty-six years old. Despite the Sweezy precedent, the Supreme Court performed a dazzling high-wire act in November 1958, arguing that in the Uphaus case "the academic and political freedoms . . . are not present here in the same degree, since

World Fellowship is neither a university nor a political party." Such was the general record of Communist-front activity among Uphaus and his guests, said Justice Tom Clark, that "the governmental interest in self-preservation is sufficiently compelling to subordinate the interest in associational privacy . . ." This was the notion that had hypnotized the American judiciary since the Second World War. Although Brennan, Black and Douglas pointed out that Wyman's objective had clearly been "the impermissible one of exposure for exposure's sake," [13] Frankfurter's crucial vote tipped the balance on June 8, 1959, in favor of Wyman by 5 to 4. In December, Uphaus was incarcerated in Merrimack jail, in a six-by-eight-foot cell furnished with a metal cot and no chair. There he remained for a year, a political prisoner, and stubborn. [14]

As the great purge began to slacken in the middle fifties, a growing number of unfriendly witnesses took courage and resorted once again to the Fifth Amendment. By 1960 as many as thirty-two such cases were passing through one stage or another of the legal treadmill. But after the high point of the Sweezy case the results were not encouraging; the Court was in retreat, the heretics went to jail. [15] It was not until the *Brandenburg v. Ohio* decision in 1969 that the Court took an effective step toward restoring the First Amendment's precedence over political expediency.

## CONTEMPT OF CONGRESS AND THE FIFTH AMENDMENT

The Fifth Amendment guarantees that no person "shall be compelled in any criminal case to be a witness against himself." This privilege or right has its origin in the stand taken by English dissenters like John Udall and John Lilburne in resisting the inquisitorial techniques of the Court of High Commission and of the Star Chamber. Lilburne told the Star Chamber that he would not answer "as to things concerning other men," and Francis Jenks, when called before Charles II in 1676 for having criticized royal policies, declared: "To name any particular person (if there were such) would be a mean and unworthy thing. . . ."

In America the Fifth Amendment became, to some extent from 1948 onward, and to a much larger extent from 1950, the favorite resort of radicals called to account for their beliefs, affiliations and associations by grand juries and Congressional committees. Some five hundred witnesses invoked the privilege between 1950 and 1956. The courts made it quite clear that the Fifth Amendment was not intended to protect a man's sense of honor; it did not extend to testimony about any third party or group unless that testimony might tend to incriminate the witness himself. This point was affirmed by the Supreme Court in *Rogers v. United States* (1951). Jane Rogers admitted that she had been the treasurer of a local Party branch but refused to name the person to whom she had turned over the records. The Court ruled that once she had testified as to her own affiliation, she waived the privilege. Marcus Singer, of Cornell University, answered HCUA's questions about his own activity in Marxist study groups at Harvard in the early 1940s, denied ever having joined the CP, but invoked the Fifth when asked to name other members of the study groups. The Court of Appeals for the District of Columbia ruled that by his early testimony he had waived the privilege.

Anti-Communist observers like Sidney Hook tended to discount the possibility of an "innocent" man invoking the Fifth, although, according to Dean Emeritus Paul Shipman Andrews, of Syracuse University Law School, a professor of mathematics pleaded the Fifth before HCUA when he was erroneously identified as a former Communist, fearing that he would otherwise be accused of perjury. A perjury conviction, after all, could result in five years' imprisonment, whereas a contempt charge carried a maximum sentence of one year plus a $1,000 fine. Perjury charges were brought against Hiss, Remington, Lattimore, Christoffel and others. Sidney Hook claimed that he did not know of a single case where an innocent man "denying Communist connections" had been convicted of perjury.[16] He was clever to say "convicted" rather than "indicted"; Val Lorwin, an "innocent" employee of the State Department, was indicted for perjury and later acquitted; Lattimore was acquitted eventually, but only after a most harrowing ordeal lasting several years; it was this ordeal that a witness might be anxious to avoid.

The phrase "in any criminal case" raised doubts as to whether the Fifth could properly be invoked before a Congressional committee, since committee hearings are not judicial proceedings. But common sense indicates that they can precipitate criminal proceedings and, whether they do or not, that the record of such hearings could be quoted in a court case. By 1960 the Supreme Court had on three occasions affirmed that the privilege did indeed extend to witnesses before committees.

But in what sense is a question about political belief or affiliation linked to possible criminal proceedings? The Communist Party, after all, was not illegal, and not until 1951 did the Supreme Court rule that leaders of the Party, and possibly members too, could be convicted under the Smith Act on charges of conspiracy and association. Consequently some Communists found that their invocation of the

Fifth was not accepted. Five witnesses before the Canwell Committee in the State of Washington, having pleaded the Fifth, were briefly jailed for contempt on the ground that to confess to CP membership involved no imminent threat of a prosecution. In September 1948 Nancy Wertheimer, Jane Rogers and Irving Blau pleaded the First and Fifth Amendments before a federal grand jury in Denver, Colorado, but Judge Foster Symes held them in contempt on the ground that the CP was a legal party. By July 1949 no less than sixteen Communists had been convicted of contempt in California—and many of them jailed—for invoking the Fifth before a grand jury. [17]

Considering that eleven national leaders of the Party had been indicted under the Smith Act fully a year earlier, one can only conclude that the federal judiciary in California was completely lacking in scruple. Furthermore, in November 1948 even the Justice Department had requested Congressional committees to drop contempt cases against witnesses who invoked the Fifth about Communism, in the light of the Smith Act indictments. Yet, as late as September 1950, Judge Ben Harrison, of California, sentenced Dr. Eugene Brunner to six months in prison for invoking the Fifth with regard to past Party membership. [18] Out of these events emerged two Supreme Court rulings, *Blau v. United States* (1950) and *Brunner v. United States* (1952), that established that the admission of being either an official or a member of the CP tended to incriminate.

During the fall and winter of 1953–54 the press became vastly preoccupied by the Fifth Amendment issue. Attorney General Brownell complained to the Law Club of Chicago on November 6 that examples of "almost every heinous crime on the law books" remained uncovered because of the privilege against self-incrimination. True or not, when Congress passed the Compulsory Testimony Act on August 20, 1954, its provisions were confined mainly to "crimes" related to the "Communist conspiracy," as Representative Kenneth B. Keating (R., New York) explained. The essence of the new provision was that henceforward a witness could be compelled to testify on pain of contempt, but that by invoking the Fifth Amendment he could protect himself against prosecution on the basis of the evidence he was compelled to give. Although the National Lawyers Guild submitted a spirited *amicus curiae* brief arguing that legislation could not detract from a constitutional privilege, Frankfurter argued for the majority of the Supreme Court that "once the reason for the privilege ceases, the privilege ceases." (*Ullman v. United States*, March 1956.) Edward J. Fitzgerald, one of those named by Elizabeth Bentley as government officials engaged in espionage, became in October 1956 the first person to go to jail under the Act, following his persistent refusal to testify. [19]

## THE COURT AND THE RIGHT TO WORK

No issue was more sensitive than that of employment, for the central thrust of the great purge was directed against men's right to work regardless of political belief. Had radical workers and professional people been able to retain their jobs they could have proudly defied the committees without resort to the Fifth Amendment. The threat of immediate dismissal was the universal weapon wielded by inquisitors, FBI agents and security officers, and in no respect did the Vinson Supreme Court fail more lamentably than its failure to protect the right to work.

In *Garner v. Board of Public Works*, the Court upheld by 5 to 4 a Los Angeles municipal ordinance of 1948 imposing an oath and non-Communist affidavit as a condition of public employment; thus guilt by association was validated. In *Adler v. Board of Education*, which arose out of a challenge by certain New York teachers to the constitutionality of the Feinberg law,* Minton, for the Court, showed it at its most slavishly subservient to the *Zeitgeist*:

> From time immemorial, one's reputation has been determined by the company he keeps.
>
> . . . one's associates, past and present, as well as one's conduct, may properly be considered in determining fitness and loyalty.
>
> If . . . a person is . . . disqualified from employment in the public-school system because of membership in a listed organization, he is not thereby denied the right of free speech and assembly.

Teachers could either work for the school system on its own terms or retain their beliefs and associations and go elsewhere.[20]

A related punitive weapon was the discharge from their jobs of witnesses who pleaded the Fifth Amendment before Congressional committees. Liberals made some fuss about this on the ground that it presumed a man to be "guilty" as soon as he used his constitutional privilege. Such an argument might be relevant if the witness had pleaded the Fifth on a charge of murder or rape, but the root of the injustice was not the *presumption* of guilt (or guilt by association) but *the particular notion of guilt*, the core of which held Communists ineligible for most types of employment.

---

* See Chapter 23.

This core concept was scandalously affirmed in *Black v. Cutter Laboratories*. The case arose from the discharge in 1949 of Mrs. Doris Brin Walker, a Communist lawyer at that time employed as a manual worker by Cutter (pharmaceutical) Laboratories, Berkeley. In 1955 the California Supreme Court ruled by 4 to 3 that CP membership was of itself cause for dismissal and for the termination of any collective contract, and that a Communist employee could be assumed to be dedicated to the "practice, of sabotage" (although not a single case of Communist sabotage came to light in the postwar years). Dissenting, California Chief Justice Phil Sheridan Gibson pointed out: "Thus can a landlord break his lease with a Communist on the ground that his building may be sabotaged? . . . If contracts with Communists are illegal, cannot Communists themselves violate them with impunity?" [21] In June 1956 the U.S. Supreme Court ruled that the law as so interpreted in California did not violate the United States Constitution. Not until eleven years later did the Supreme Court timidly reverse itself by ruling that mere CP membership was not a legally valid reason for dismissal unless a "specific intention to further the unlawful aims of the Communist Party" could be shown.

Anti-Communist liberals and conservatives were infuriated [22] when, in *Slochower v. Board of Higher Education* (1956), the Supreme Court ruled that the summary dismissal without a hearing of a teacher who invoked the Fifth Amendment violated due process, and that Professor Harry Slochower, of Brooklyn College, had been dismissed on an inference of guilt only. Section 903 of the New York City Charter, which stipulated such summary dismissal, was ruled unconstitutional. Dissenting, Justice Harlan (warmly endorsed by Professor Sidney Hook) argued that Section 903 did not infer guilt, merely that the employee had refused to cooperate and had thereby undermined public confidence. Quibbles of this sort ultimately obscure our view of what was really going on—that a man's political opinions or affiliations had become a legitimate area of inquiry, and that radicals had taken refuge behind constitutional privileges because candor led straight to the bread line. Nevertheless, the Supreme Court backed off and down. When in 1958 it came to consider the case of Max Lerner, a New York City subway conductor fired under the New York Security Risk law after he pleaded the Fifth when questioned by the City Transit System on the subject of Party membership, the Court miraculously managed (*Lerner v. Casey*) to circumnavigate the Slochower precedent by casuistically adopting the Harlan-minority position in the earlier case: Lerner, said the Court, had not been dismissed on an inference of guilt but because his refusal to answer had created doubts about his reliabilty. Warren,

Black, Douglas and Brennan dissented: it was Frankfurter who crossed over to create a conservative majority.

*Beilan v. Board of Education* (1958), a companion case to *Lerner v. Casey*, arose out of the dismissal of Herman A. Beilan after twenty-two years' service in the Philadelphia school system. Having refused to answer the Superintendent of Schools about alleged Communist activities in the past, he had nevertheless been retained and rated "satisfactory" for a further thirteen months until HCUA came to town and subpoenaed him. Five days after he invoked the Fifth he was suspended. The Supreme Court upheld Beilan's dismissal, although Black and Douglas pointed out that a CP member may believe in peaceful, parliamentary change and abhor violence. (Yet beliefs themselves should be irrelevant; only *conduct* inside the classroom, and sometimes outside it, should be relevant.)

In 1954 the United Electrical, Radio and Machine Workers brought suit against the General Electric Company to prevent the discharge by the company of John W. Nelson, who had invoked the Fifth before the SISS. District Court Judge Charles F. McLaughlin ruled that GE had not violated the national agreement between itself and the union, and that the dismissal did not violate due process or deprive Nelson of any of his constitutional rights. The company, said the judge, was entitled as the second-largest defense contractor in the United States to consider the effect on its customers and shareholders when its employees pleaded the Fifth. In March 1956 the Court of Appeals for the District of Columbia ruled that it lacked jurisdiction because such labor disputes were exclusive to the jurisdiction of the National Labor Relations Board. In October 1956 the Supreme Court let stand GE's policy of firing Fifth Amendment workers.

In 1960 the Supreme Court ruled on the case of a different Mr. Nelson who, with Arthur Globe, had been dismissed by the County of Los Angeles after taking the Fifth before HCUA (*Nelson and Globe v. County of Los Angeles*). Warren, Douglas, Black and Brennan could detect no difference in principle between this case and the Slochower one, but Clark for the Court argued that Slochower had been dismissed under a City Charter that treated invocation of the Fifth as a confession of guilt, whereas Globe had been dismissed for insubordination in refusing to give information. *The New York Times* commented that the Court was "cynical" in paying homage to the Slochower decision while robbing it of all meaning.

Indeed, the coy hesitations of the Court on the issue of Fifth Amendment discharges—the engine room of the whole purge—looked in retrospect like no more than liberal froth on the rim of the radical coffin. Across the country, reactionary judges took comfort and courage from the Supreme Court's retreat. It was in 1960 that New York Supreme Court Judge Ferdinand Pecora upheld the dismissal of Alexander Koval, an assistant mechanical engineer employed by the New York Board of Education, who had invoked the Fifth before HCUA.[23]

## THE WARREN COURT VERSUS THE CONGRESS

If the Supreme Court's capacity to hinder or even halt the purge required any demonstration beyond that implicit in the case rulings themselves, then it was dramatically provided by the hysterical reaction of American conservatives to the Court's crucial decisions during the high tide of 1956–58. In seven separate decisions, the Warren Court threatened to dismember the octopus of repression: Fifth Amendment dismissals (Slochower); state sedition laws (Steve Nelson); investigation of beliefs, utterances and affiliations (Sweezy); the power of Congressional investigation (Watkins); the Smith Act (Yates); the power of professional groups to bar admission to radicals (Schware); and the FBI-informer system (Jencks). The Court, in short, had outraged every vested interest.

Prior to the Nelson ruling,* the attorneys general of forty-two states and two territories had, as *amici curiae*, submitted to the Court briefs proving the absolute indispensibility of state sedition laws. Incensed by the Court's refusal to heed them, thirty-five of these attorneys general denounced the Nelson ruling as "dangerous to public safety." Senator Davis (D., Georgia) described the ruling as "a brazen attack on the sovereignty of all the States." The Southerners were now able to make common cause with the Northern anti-Communists under the banner of "states' rights." The Georgia legislature adopted a resolution asking Congress [24] to impeach Warren and five associate justices for bringing aid and comfort to the Communist enemy and for other crimes "too numerous to mention." HCUA's Representative Donald Jackson (D., California) called the Watkins ruling "a victory greater than any achieved by the Soviet on the battlefield since World War II." The SISS, under Senator James O. Eastland, published a report carrying an appendix which claimed that recent Supreme Court decisions "have done more for enemy forces and objectives than might have been accomplished by any other agency or form of paralysis, [sic] short of the actual overthrow of the govern-

---

* The CP leader Steve Nelson. Not to be confused with the GE worker John W. Nelson, or the Los Angeles County employee Nelson.

ment." Eastland told the Senate in July 1958 that since October 1953, when Warren became Chief Justice, the Court had sustained the "Communist" position in thirty out of the thirty-nine cases concerning Communism that it had heard.[25] *Life* Magazine accused the Court of naïveté.

More than seventy bills were introduced into the 84th Congress to curb the powers of the Court. So furious was the backlash that during the first session of the 85th Congress, from January to August 1957, 101 anticivil-liberties bills were introduced, compared with only eight designed to reinforce civil liberties. Senator William Jenner's S.2646 aimed to remove from the Court's jurisdiction precisely those issues that had provoked the uproar: contempt of Congress, the loyalty-security program, state antisubversion statutes, the regulation of employment, subversive activities in schools, and admission to the bar.[26]

Another anti-Court bill, H.R.3, introduced by Representative Howard W. Smith (D., Virginia), after whom the Smith Act was named, proposed that no act of Congress should occupy the field to the exclusion of state laws unless it expressly said so.[27] The climax came during the week of August 19–23, 1958, when several bills that had passed the House were defeated in the Senate, due mainly to the political skills of Majority Leader Lyndon B. Johnson. Smith's H.R.3 went down to defeat in the Senate by 41 votes to 40.[28] Other anti-Court bills died with the 85th Congress; as a result of the elections of 1958, seven anti-Court Republicans were defeated or retired; and although several such bills passed the House in 1959, none negotiated a passage through the Senate. The only legislation which actually materialized out of the furor was one limiting the impact of the Jencks case on FBI files. In June 1959 the Supreme Court, by this time thoroughly alarmed, voted by 5 to 4 to uphold this new statute, and thereby implicitly to emasculate its own ruling in the Jencks case.

Nevertheless, the uproar generated by the Warren Court's short season of liberalism from 1955 to 1958, and the frenzy in Congress demonstrate beyond doubt how crucial was the role played by the courts first in validating the purge and later in curbing it. Upon the men whom Truman appointed (Vinson, Burton, Minton and Clark) and upon the man who appointed them fell a responsibility out of proportion to their numbers and their talents. They failed almost every test. Against Frankfurter and Jackson it can also be charged that they, at least, should have known better, and that their collapse most perfectly illustrated the retreat into *Realpolitik* and purblind patriotism of many of the best minds of American liberalism. Black and Douglas cannot be too highly praised; Warren achieved greatness;

Brennan did well; and Harlan, conservative though he was in outlook, and frequently though he voted with the execrable Tom Clark, did at least display the fine judicial mind and the high judicial independence so sadly lacking in Truman's appointees.

# PART THREE

---

# The Assault
# on the Left

# 8

## Bureaucratic Persecution

Freedom of assembly assumes an ugly grimace when there is nowhere to assemble—from early in 1947 meeting halls began to close their doors to Communists and progressives. Whereas the Shrine Auditorium's 6,700 seats had been sold out when William Z. Foster, chairman of the CP, visited Los Angeles in 1946, a year later both the Shrine and the Olympic auditoriums refused to rent their facilities to the Party. Frequently meeting halls were denied to Henry Wallace's supporters during the 1948 campaign. In October the Book-Cadillac Hotel in Detroit, for example, turned down a request for accommodation from Wallace, Robeson and other CP leaders. In August 1950 Madison Square Garden refused an application to hire the hall by the Council on African Affairs on the ground that the Internal Security Act, then pending in Congress, would make it illegal to rent to a subversive organization.

What the Act did was to invent a new crime: joining with others to perform any act which would substantially contribute to the establishment of a totalitarian dictatorship under foreign domination. Auditoriums, hotels, school boards, printers, retailers, and bail-fund donors had better consult their lawyers before offering their services to radicals! The effect was as intended: almost all doors closed. San Francisco denied the use of the City Auditorium for public meetings organized by the Committee to Save the Rosenbergs; the California Supreme Court refused, by 4 to 3, to order the city to lift the ban.[1]

Even at local, neighborhood level, the doors began to close in

1947. To take three typical examples from the year 1949: in February, Mayor Walter S. Gaspar of Palo Alto, California, refused to allow the Community Center to be used for a meeting that was to be addressed by a Communist professor recently dismissed from the University of Washington; the New York City Board of Education barred a number of left-wing organizations from school buildings; [2] and in September the Santa Barbara, California, Board of Education voted to deny the use of high-school facilities to the Young Progressives. The Attorney General's list was the magic wand waved to exonerate all such assaults on the freedoms that the United States claimed to defend. And the blight had stamina; it persisted.

Here are three equally typical cases from the years 1956–57: the town supervisors of Hempstead and Oyster Bay refused to allow the ALP to hire Levittown Hall, because the scheduled speaker, the black octogenarian scholar Dr. W. E. B. DuBois, had "reputed Communist-front affiliations"; a Puerto Rican Communist indicted under the Smith Act, Pablo M. Garcia, who was trying to raise money for the defense of himself and his comrades, was refused access to the AFL Center in Denver, Colorado, and to all schools controlled by the Denver School Board; and in March 1957 the Martinique Hotel in New York succumbed to Legion pressure and canceled a meeting called by the ACLU to hear John Gates, editor of the *Daily Worker*. [3]

So why not meet in the streets, the parks? The authorities had an answer to that one, too. The Mayor of New York ruled that organizations listed by the Attorney General should be barred from soliciting funds in the streets; in 1948 the Civil Rights Congress and the Joint Anti-Fascist Refugee Committee lost the right to hold tag days. In August 1950 Mayor O'Dwyer dispatched a thousand policemen to suppress a Union Square peace demonstration that he and the State Supreme Court had banned. Fourteen people were arrested and many were "badly beaten by the police." In April 1953 the State Supreme Court obliged Mayor Vincent Impellitteri by banning a May Day parade on Eighth Avenue by the United Labor and People's May Day Committee, because, as Police Commissioner George P. Monaghan put it, the marchers were "puppets of the Soviet government." [4] However, they were allowed to gather in Union Square. On the following day the Veterans of Foreign Wars (VFW) paraded down Fifth Avenue—nobody's puppets.

For the veterans, of course, the best argument one could have with a radical, a pinko, was always a physical argument, and this consideration compels us to enter a long and emphatic parenthesis in our general depiction of political repression under Truman and Eisenhower as primordially nonviolent. In fact, meetings were frequently broken up. In October 1947 five thousand Trenton, New Jersey, veterans prevented the Mercer County CP from meeting to hear Gerhart Eisler. A month later a CP rally at Bridgeport, Connecticut, .was dispersed by veterans, and a PCA rally at Independence Hall Square in Philadelphia was stoned by members of the Legion and the VFW. In Los Angeles, Legionnaires invaded a suburban home and ordered the meeting to scramble within ten minutes, only to discover that they had hit the wrong lot. Representative Chet Holifield, of California, referred to this incident in Congress as part of a wave of "fear, suspicion and hysteria" sweeping the country.[5] When a mob broke into and ransacked the Columbus, Ohio, home of Frank Hashmall, executive secretary of the state CP, in March 1948, no one was arrested. "There wasn't an organized mob," Governor Thomas J. Herbert explained. "I don't intend to interfere unless there is a pattern established." Of Hashmall he added: "He should go back to Russia."

## PHYSICAL ATTACKS ON THE LEFT

The Progressive campaign of 1948 took it on the jaw: gunplay and car chases in West Virginia, kidnappings in Georgia, mob violence in Alabama and North Carolina, stonings in Illinois, where the police refused protection. Wallace rallies met violent receptions in Evansville, Boston, Cleveland, Philadelphia, Detroit, Augusta, Raleigh, Durham, and throughout the South, where mobs greeted Wallace with eggs, tomatoes and obscenities. Meetings were invaded by hostile crowds in New York, Trenton, Newark, New Orleans and Chicago. Even murder went by another name if the victim was a Wallace supporter. In Charleston, South Carolina, an anti-Communist member of the National Maritime Union called Rudolfo Serreo telephoned the police to announce that he intended to murder Robert Now, the twenty-eight-year-old port agent for the NMU and chairman of the local Wallace-for-President committee. This Serreo then did, in cold blood. He was convicted of manslaughter only and sentenced to three years in prison—apparently the victim was known around town as a "nigger lover."[6]

As the campaign approached its climax, election day, a group of thugs knifed one of the leaders of the CP, Robert Thompson, on the street. The New York police made no attempt to investigate. Subsequently a "private detective," Robert J. Burke, broke into Thompson's home while he was out, insulted the black woman who was baby-sitting, and, as he later admitted, indecently exposed himself in front of one of the children. Unaccountably, he was actually convicted in court; more predictably, his conviction was reversed at a second trial. Soon afterward members of a boys' club in Greenwich Village broke up a CP meeting and shattered the windows of the local Party headquarters.[7]

## PEEKSKILL

The most dramatic physical confrontation of the entire period took place on August 27 and September 4, 1949, in the Lakeland area near Peekskill, a small town situated on the Hudson River some forty miles from New York. The inhabitants of this somewhat stagnant, depressingly bigoted town increasingly resented the annual summer influx of 30,000 New York Jews, and the regular arrival of Communists, many of them Jews and blacks, to hold conferences in Camp Beacon. Although Paul Robeson [8] had successfully staged concerts in the area in three successive years, Cold War fever was such that his announced return in August 1949 sparked off a violent riot.

On August 23, the local newspaper, the *Evening Star*, reported that this "avowed disciple of Soviet Russia" would sing under the sponsorship of People's Artists, Inc., in a fund-raising concert for the benefit of the Harlem Chapter of the Civil Rights Congress—cited as subversive by the Attorney General. Roared the *Evening Star*: "The time for tolerant silence that signifies approval is running out." Local veterans saw red. Two Catholics, Herman Schwiter of Cortlandt and Vincent Boyle, Commander of the Verplanck Post of the Legion, were mainly responsible for organizing the counterdemonstration that greeted Robeson's followers.

For liberals living in the Peekskill area now was a time to lie low. After Mrs. Mary Mobile, the wife of a local businessman, wrote to the paper stressing that peaceful assembly is protected by the Constitution, she received a spate of abusive telephone calls addressing her as "you dirty red bitch" and urging her to get out of Peekskill. On the evening of the concert Legionnaires surrounded the Lakeland area, barricaded the approach roads, threw stones at the concertgoers, and burned chairs, platforms and songbooks. This was despite the fact that half the concertgoers were women and children completely unprepared for the attack. Although at least three requests for police protection had been made by the sponsors in advance, only four sheriff's deputies and two uniformed police turned up.

The sponsors decided to hold the same concert a week later—to "slug it out, toe to toe," as the Communist leader Benjamin Davis, Jr., put it, with the aid of some three thousand friendly security guards (fur workers, longshoremen, seamen) armed with baseball bats and tire irons. During the intervening week the tension mounted. When Stephen D. Szezo, owner of the Holland Brook Country Club, rented a meadow for the second concert, a car fired a volley of .22 bullets into his house at 3 A.M., and four separate attempts were made to set it on fire. Meanwhile, racketeers moved into Peekskill persuading businessmen to buy American flags at fourteen dollars each. Governor Dewey ordered State Troopers to guard the grounds. One thousand police were on hand.

The concert itself passed off peacefully, with some 15,000 Robesonites singing under the protection of 3,000 guards and 1,000 police. Robeson sang *Ol' Man River* and *Peat Bog Soldiers*, then Howard Fast appealed for funds and—his remarks amplified for the benefit of the veterans parading outside—denounced them as "un-American filth." The trouble began after the concert. The first contingent of cars to leave was ambushed and at least 150 people were injured. Buses were attacked and cars were stoned as far away as Yonkers, at a distance of twenty miles. All accounts agree that while the State Troopers did their best to curb the violence, the Westchester County police openly fraternized with the stone-throwing veterans.[9]

The ACLU issued a report severely critical of the veterans, the police, and the authorities. (Among the six young Westchester residents indicted for the September 4 riot was the son of the Peekskill chief of police.) Governor Dewey issued a statement which, while admitting that Robeson's guards "behaved with discipline and committed no assaults," argued that these guards, by adopting military formation and by carrying weapons which, *though legal*, could be deadly, kept the police force at the ground and prevented it from deploying along the roads.

In June 1950 a Westchester County grand jury whose foreman was Howard R. Pugh, assistant vice-president of the Empire Trust Company of New York, found the police and local officials to be entirely blameless in connection with both riots. The grand jury also rejected all reports of race prejudice, although the evidence pointed overwhelmingly to the conclusion that what most inflamed the natives and veterans was the fact that the concertgoers were not only reds but also "niggers and kikes." The grand jury's 9,000-word presentment warned communities to be on their guard against Communist "strong-arm" forces because these were "the shock troops of a revolutionary force which is controlled by a foreign power." In June 1952 Robeson and twenty-nine others lost a damages suit brought against Westchester County officials and two veterans' organizations.[10]

## THE RED AND THE BLACK

Paul Robeson, the focal point of the Peekskill riots, symbolized the convergence of two threats to the American Celebration: *le rouge et le noir*. Soon after the war the Congressional committees sank their claws into Robeson. Having informed HCUA in 1946 that he was not a Party member, he never deigned to answer the question again, insistently though it was repeated. Contesting his passport application in the Court of Appeals, the Department of Justice complained that "during his concert tours abroad [he] has repeatedly criticized the conditions of Negroes in the United States." When HCUA subpoenaed him in 1956, the convergence of the red and the black was the flash point of a violent confrontation: "In Russia," Robeson told the Committee, "I felt for the first time like a full human being. No color prejudice like in Washington. . . ." He accused the Committee members of responsibility for one hundred million black people who died in slave ships or on the plantations. He blasted Chairman Francis Walter as the author of bills to keep colored people out of America at the behest of "Teutonic Anglo-Saxon stock." When Representative Scherer asked him, "Why do you not stay in Russia?" Robeson replied: "Because . . . my people died to build this country, and I am going to stay here and have a part of it just like you." [11]

It was, of course, in the South that black aspirations toward civil and economic equality were most vehemently denounced as Moscow-inspired Communism. Many of the leading figures among witch-hunting legislative committees were also Southern racists, most notably Martin Dies, of Texas, John E. Rankin, of Mississippi, and James O. Eastland, of the same state. Said Rankin, whose electoral district carried the highest poll tax in the nation: slavery was "the greatest blessing the Negro people ever had." It was in the South that the white backlash coalesced with anti-Communist hysteria in 1950 to ensure the defeat of two liberal Senators, Frank P. Graham, of North Carolina, and Claude Pepper, of Florida. The Supreme Court's bitterly detested ruling on the desegregation of schools in 1954 generated a new alliance between white supremacists from the South and Northern anti-Communists in Congress. As Representative George W. Andrews, of Alabama, put it: "How much longer will this Congress continue to permit the Supreme Court . . . to destroy States rights and protect the Communist Party?"

The leading exponent of this dual war in the fifties was James O. Eastland, a member of the SISS since 1951 and its chairman from

1956. "What other explanation could there be except that a majority of [the Warren] Court is being influenced by some secret, but very powerful Communist or pro-Communist influence?" [12] Bringing havoc, often physical, to trade unions and liberal groups working for black emancipation, Eastland issued scores of subpoenas, ordered records to be seized, caused Southern radicals to lose their jobs, and instructed his marshals to use physical force on witnesses who irked him.

The Carl Braden affair likewise illustrated the close mesh of the red and black issues in the South. In an attempt to break down the rigid racial barriers between neighborhoods in Louisville, Kentucky, Braden, a copyreader for the liberal *Courier-Journal*, and an avowed Socialist, bought a house in a white area and resold it to Andrew Wade IV, a Negro electrical contractor. All hell broke loose: shots, a fiery cross, a bomb under the house. Not only were Braden and his friends indicted on a charge of seditiously inciting racial conflict, but much was made of the red, "subversive" literature seized from Braden's own home. Ten professional ex-Communist witnesses (including Cvetic and Manning Johnson) were imported to testify how subversive it really was, with the result that Braden and a colleague were convicted of advocating criminal syndicalism and sedition. The Court of Appeals later reversed the verdict, but not before Braden had spent eight months in jail for want of an astronomical $40,000 in bail money. HCUA later got its teeth into Braden on the pretext that it was CP policy to create mass agitation and foment discord among the Negro people. [13]

But it would be misleading to suppose that the equation of the red and the black was confined to the South alone. (Peekskill, after all, is in New York State.) Between 1940 and 1950 the nonwhite population of New York City had increased from 500,000 to 750,000, that of Chicago had doubled to 500,000, that of Detroit had doubled to 300,000. (HCUA described the 1943 race riots in Detroit, which resulted in over forty deaths, as Communist-inspired, even though the CP was at that time playing down all divisive issues in the name of a united war effort.) Tension over housing ran high. When the Broyles Commission convened in Illinois to probe Communist influence within the state, the American Legion's spokesman, Ellidore Libonati, testified:

> . . . the Chicago Housing Authority. I think definitely one or two of their people are Communists. . . . For example they pass it out that 10 percent of the project should be given to colored families . . . They did not want those folks there. There was a riot.

Meanwhile, the chairman of another anti-Communist legislative committee, Albert Canwell, of Washington, announced: "If someone insists there is discrimination against Negroes in this country . . . there is every reason to believe that person is a Communist." [14]

Nor can we dismiss or isolate such sentiments as characteristic of a lunatic fringe of witch-hunters alone. For many middle-of-the-road white Americans, the issue of blood, of color, stood forth as a vital component of national identity; black tissues in the organism subverted the Celebration. The extent of this fixation was revealed in the course of the federal government's loyalty-security program. The somewhat conservative and strongly anti-Communist leader of the National Association for the Advancement of Colored Peoples, Walter White, wrote Truman in 1948 to express his concern about

> an increasing tendency on the part of government agencies to associate activity on interracial matters with disloyalty . . . many colored government employees, who are now being charged with disloyalty . . . have actively opposed segregation and discrimination. [15]

In fact, at the time of White's complaint, twenty-nine Post Office employees were under investigation in Cleveland for suspected disloyalty; four were Jews and twenty-three were blacks. Similar patterns of prejudice surfaced in Philadelphia, Illinois and elsewhere.

In a prominent case, the dismissal of the black civil servant Dorothy Bailey, a member of the loyalty board asked her whether she had ever written a letter to the Red Cross favoring the desegregation of blood banks. The board member later explained in a letter to the *Washington Post* that desegregation was the CP line.

A security officer, Armstrong, asked a Department of the Interior employee facing loyalty charges: "What were your feelings at that time concerning race equality?" The chairman of a departmental loyalty board remarked: "Of course the fact that a person believes in racial equality doesn't *prove* that he's a Communist, but it certainly makes you look twice, doesn't it?" [16]

It was all a fantasy. Of approximately fifteen million black Americans, only some 4,000 were members of the Communist Party in 1950. Despite the strong quota of middle-class blacks among the leadership of the Progressive Party, Henry Wallace picked up only 28,903 votes in Harlem, less even than Dewey (34,076) and far less than Truman (108,643). But fantasies can be both fertile and destructive.

## THE ATTORNEY GENERAL'S LIST AND THE SACB

We return now to the main theme of this chapter, the cold, clinical but deadly bureaucratic repression whose primary instrument was the Attorney General's list.

The practice of officially listing radical organizations as subversive began with the Deportation and Exclusion Laws of 1917–20. Attorney General A. Mitchell Palmer listed twelve organizations membership in which would lead to automatic deportation for aliens. During the Second World War, Attorney General Francis Biddle revived the practice on a minor scale in an attempt to provide government agencies with an informal guide to personnel-security policy. Following Truman's Executive Order 9835, which launched the federal Loyalty Program, the Internal Security Division of the Justice Department compiled a more extensive and up-to-date list during the spring and summer of 1947. This list, which was sent to the Loyalty Review Board in November, but not published until March 20, 1948, named under six categories [17] seventy-eight organizations, forty-seven of which had previously been listed by Biddle.[18] The last revision of the list took place in 1955, after which no additional organizations were included, although some were subsequently removed for lack of what the Justice Department called "strict standards of proof." [19]

What was the purpose of the Attorney General's list? According to Truman and Tom Clark, the list was merely to be regarded as a course of administrative guidance, indicative but not conclusive, for the federal Loyalty Program. Such claims were disingenuous. Very soon the list had become a yardstick for assessing "loyalty" in almost every department of American working life—an instrument of moral terror. It was even used by government prosecutors attempting to impeach the word of defense witnesses; in the case of *U.S. v. Remington*, Judge Swann, of the Court of Appeals, was obliged to point out that "the list is a purely hearsay declaration by the Attorney General, and could have no probative value in the trial of this defendant." As late as 1962, the trial judge in the John Henry Faulk case felt obliged to reiterate that the list had no probative value in law.

From the outset, the list was used to intimidate and morally outlaw the Left, to pillory and ostracize critics of the Truman administration, and to deter potential critics. (As Tocqueville remarked, when some associations are permitted and others are not, people soon fear to join any.) When the Connecticut State Youth Conference presumptuously demonstrated against American intervention in Greece in the spring of 1947, Tom Clark immediately listed it; the

Conference then found that a Hartford Hotel was no longer available for a planned convention.[20] In May 1948 the American Council for a Democratic Greece was listed as subversive because it opposed the government's foreign policy, and the American Committee for the Protection of the Foreign Born was listed because it opposed the government's deportation policy.

Under Executive Order 9835, the Attorney General was not required to hold hearings before listing an organization; nor was there any provision for appeal or judicial review. After the Attorney General refused to grant hearings to the JAFRC, the IWO, and the National Council for American-Soviet Friendship, these bodies joined to bring suit against him. In one of the decisions typical of the time, the Court of Appeals for the District of Columbia ruled that in listing the organizations the Attorney General invaded none of their legally privileged rights; he was merely exercising *his* right to advise the President. Judge Henry W. Edgerton, dissenting, argued that listing involved arbitrary official action that resulted in obloquy, financial loss, and a *de facto* restriction of freedom of speech. When the case reached the Supreme Court (*Joint Anti-Fascist Refugee Committee v. McGrath*) in April 1951, the Court ruled by 5 to 3 that all three cases should be remanded to the District Court, because the lack of a hearing was unconstitutional, and because the organizations had been injured in their common-law right to be free from defamation. The ruling virtually declared the list illegal as constituted at that time. The executive took no notice whatsoever and the Attorney General continued his declamatory riot.

In May 1953, Attorney General Brownell issued new regulations providing listed organizations with a chance to protest *after* they had been listed, but Brownell displayed no eagerness to implement his own procedures; not until July 1955 was the first hearing granted—to Max Schachtman's (anti-Communist) Independent Socialist League. But not until three years after that was the ISL removed from the list for lack of what the Justice Department called "strict standards of proof." [21]

The Internal Security Act of 1950, which was passed over Truman's veto, provided the Attorney General with an additional weapon of intimidation. The new Subversive Activities Control Board [22] could, on a petition from the Attorney General, and after holding due-process hearings, order an organization to register under the Act as "Communist-action," "Communist-front" or "Subversive." Groups ordered to register would be required to file lists of their officers, maintain supervised records, and to label their mail. On November 22, Attorney General McGrath petitioned the Board to order the CP to register as a "Communist-action" organization and thereby to brand itself, to quote the Act, as dedicated to "treachery, deceit . . . espionage, terrorism"; as having the objective of setting up a totalitarian dictatorship subservient to a foreign power; and as consisting of members who "repudiate their allegiance to the United States, and in effect transfer their allegiance" to a foreign power.

The Party filed a suit to enjoin the Board from proceeding. This failed. Hearings began in April 1952 before a two-member SACB panel consisting of Peter Campbell Brown and Dr. Kathryn McHale. The government, which called twenty-two witnesses including Budenz, Lautner and a number of FBI undercover agents, laid great stress on the Party's relations with the Soviet Union. Testifying for the government, Professor Philip Mosely, Director of the Russian Institute of Columbia University, enumerated forty-five international issues that had arisen during a thirty-year period, pointing out that there had been no substantial difference between the Soviet line and the American Party line on any of them. John Gates was brought from prison in chains to testify for the defense on June 9, 1952. Constantly pressed to offer an example of a divergence between the Soviet and CPUSA lines, he insisted that they shared a common philosophy—there was no question of the CPUSA being an agent of the USSR. Both Gates and Elizabeth Gurley Flynn argued in testimony that the CP never received directives or financial aid from any outside body. (In fact the SACB admitted it could discover no recent evidence of Soviet financial support.)

On October 20, the two-member panel ruled that the CP was both foreign-dominated and dedicated to violent overthrow. On April 20, 1953, the full Board issued a 138-page report finding that the Party was a "Communist-action organization" and ordering it to register, with full disclosure of its rolls and finances. In June, the Party petitioned the Court of Appeals for the District of Columbia for a review, claiming that the Internal Security Act was unconstitutional. In December 1954 the Court of Appeals overruled all the Party's objections to the Act and to the Board's orders. But in April 1956 the Supreme Court remanded the case on the ground that the Court of Appeals had erred in not granting the Party's motion to reconsider the case in the light of allegations against the testimony of three perjurers, Crouch, Matusow and Manning Johnson, allegations that the Attorney General did not deny. Consequently the SACB expunged the testimony of these perjurious witnesses from the record, then in December 1956 again ordered the CP to register. Shenanigans continued for a further five years.

In an *amicus curiae* brief to the Supreme Court, the National

Lawyers Guild argued that the Act violated not only the Fifth but also the First Amendment, because it directly curtailed the registrant's practical ability to exercise the rights of free assembly and speech. The Court was bound to reject this contention: had it not done so, every weapon employed by the inquisition would have been fatally blunted. On June 5, 1961, the Supreme Court therefore ruled, by 5 to 4, that the SACB's order to the Party to register was justified; in December the CP was indicted for failing to register. Four years later, however, the Court ruled that the Act violated the Fifth Amendment, and in 1967 the Justice Department gave up the ghost, thus terminating a curious episode in political pathology apparently sustained by a fanatical determination to humiliate a heresy into branding itself as infamous.

From April 1953 until the end of 1956, Herbert Brownell petitioned the SACB to order twenty-three organizations to register (including two labor unions charged with being "Communist-infiltrated" under the Communist-Control Act of 1954). Of the twenty-three, fifteen claimed to have dissolved. For this reason, the cases against five organizations [23] were dismissed. Ten organizations [24] were ordered to register, but none did; the whole legal position depended on the test case of the CP, interminably ploughing its protracted path through the courts. By the end of 1964 the Board had held hearings with regard to thirty-six organizations, and had ordered twenty-six of them to register. In 1965 the Supreme Court finally ruled that to compel an organization to register violated the Fifth Amendment. [25]

The Labor Youth League, founded in May 1949 as the restructured youth section of the Party, was hauled before the Board in 1954 and ordered to register as a Communist front in February 1955. [26] According to its New York State Chairman, Jacob Bucholt, the League had by then only 6,000 members; in February 1957 it announced its intention to dissolve. Orders to register were handed down also to the American Youth Congress, American Youth for Democracy, and the Young Communist League.

## BREAKING THE FRONTS

The SACB, like the Attorney General's list, was directed less at the Party itself, for whom rougher treatment was in store, than at the broad, fellow-traveling spectrum of "progressives," Marxists, popular-fronters and radicals who, according to HCUA and J. Edgar Hoover, served the Party's purposes without holding Party cards. "Today it is not the open Communist . . . who is likely to trip us up," said the CIA's Director, Allen W. Dulles, in January 1954. "It is the neutralist, the soft thinkers about agrarian reforms, those who merely decry the methods but are blind to the aim of international Communism." [27]

The most conspicuously successful Communist front in the United States, and obviously a prime target for the authorities, was the International Workers Order, a fraternal benefit society founded in 1930 and specializing in low-cost insurance. At its peak in 1946 the IWO, which was particularly popular among Slavic and Jewish immigrants from Eastern Europe, had 185,000 policyholders whose sickness, disability, funeral and death-benefit policies were worth $122 million. But the IWO was no ordinary benefit society. According to Max Bedacht, director of the CP's agit-prop branch and president of the IWO from 1933 to 1947, the ultimate purpose of the IWO was to develop the revolutionary consciousness of the workers. Two points about the IWO stand out. First, it was a genuinely efficient and beneficial insurance society; alone among such insurance organizations, it offered identical rates to whites and blacks, and to those engaged in dangerous work. Year after year it was classified by the New York State Insurance Commission as first or second in service to its policyholders. Secondly, it was completely at the Party's service. Not only did its organ, *The Fraternal Worker*, invariably follow the Party line, but in 1946 the IWO spent $37,570 advertising in the Communist press, which, in effect, its policyholders were subsidizing. [28]

The IWO and its sixteen constituent national groups, the largest of which was the Jewish People's Fraternal Order, were among the first organizations to be listed by the Attorney General. However, the assault on so large, wealthy and socially secure a Communist mushroom was inevitably many-sided. In 1949 the New York State Board of Education barred the IWO from holding classes or lectures in city schools. A year later—more serious—the IWO's charter was rescinded when Justice Greenberg of the New York State Supreme Court granted the application of Alfred J. Bohlinger, Superintendent of Insurance, for an order directing him to take over and liquidate the IWO, Inc. The "legal" argument advanced by Bohlinger was that the IWO's present condition rendered its continuation in business hazardous to its policyholders, its creditors, and the public; and that by associating with the CP it had exceeded its corporate powers and practiced a fraud on the state.

The prosecution called eleven witnesses, including Joseph Zack Kornfeder, and persuaded Justice Greenberg to impose an injunction preventing the IWO from holding its annual convention while the trial was in progress. In April 1953 the Court of Appeals in Albany upheld the liquidation; in October the U.S. Supreme Court refused to review. The SACB ordered the IWO to register as a front in January 1954, but the case was dismissed soon afterward when the IWO, thoroughly holed and pirated, finally sank much to the detriment of its policyholders, with the artist Rockwell Kent gallantly manning the bridge as the last president.

An equally grim fate awaited another Party-sponsored welfare organization, the Washington Pension Union, launched in 1937 under the auspices of the Washington Commonwealth Federation and listed as a front, like the Idaho Pension Union, by Attorney General Clark. The WPU's efforts, directed primarily toward increasing the retirement pension and liberalizing social-security benefits, had met with some success. After the war the WPU was furiously attacked by the Canwell Committee at a time when the Washington Democratic Party was purging its popular-front wing. Brought before the SACB by Attorney General Brownell, the WPU was ordered to register as a front. The WPU's thirty-seven-year-old president, William Pennock, committed suicide during the Seattle Smith Act trial, in which he was a defendant. By 1956 the WPU's membership had fallen from forty thousand to fewer than one thousand.[29]

Obvious targets for elimination were the adult-education establishments by which the Party forged its intellectual links with students and the most politically committed elements of the working class. Although nominally autonomous and often endowed with bewitchingly respectable names,[30] these schools, of which the Jefferson School of Social Science in New York was the most famous and influential, were in practice rigorously controlled by the Party. Without exception they were destroyed by the American inquisition. The California Labor School of San Francisco, founded in 1943 and a focus of pro-Communist ideological activity on the West Coast, survived attacks by the Tenney Committee and listing by the Attorney General before being ordered to register by the SACB in 1955. A year later it was dead. The Seattle Labor School forfeited the valuable monthly contributions of the International Association of Machinists local and other unions soon after Clark listed it as "an adjunct of the Communist Party."

Founded in 1944, the Jefferson School of Social Science enrolled more than 45,000 students during its first four years. When Brownell carried the school before the SACB, the Justice Department wheeled out its most celebrated informers, Louis Budenz, John Lautner and Bella Dodd, to document the charge of Communist domination. So destructive was the cumulative pressure on the School that its student enrollment fell from 5,200 in 1946 to 1,900 in 1954—since 1951 the school had deliberately maintained no record of its students' names and addresses. The SACB's order to register in 1955, involving as it did further odium and costly litigation, was the last straw; by October

1956 the faculty was reduced to twenty-five and the student enrollment had fallen below four hundred. In November the school closed.[31]

The Pax Americana now shone above all horizons and those who would not bow and bend the knee and light a candle to it saw their names defamed and their imagined allegiances burned in effigy across the nation. Traitor! For the groups whose *raison d'être* was friendship with the Soviet Union, the fall from grace was particularly rapid and calamitous. Once listed by the Attorney General, the American Russian Institute gave up the ghost, closed its branches in New York, San Francisco and Philadelphia, and sought a buyer for its Slavic library. At least six other friendship societies were listed by the Attorney General, including the American-Russian Fraternal Society, the Friends of the Soviet Union (founded in 1929), and, perhaps most influential, the National Council for American-Soviet Friendship.

Founded in New York in 1938 under the inspiration of the Reverend Thomas L. Harris and Corliss Lamont, the NCASF burgeoned from its modest beginnings after June 1941, setting up branches in many cities and organizing an ambitious series of rallies. In November 1942 the NCASF was responsible for a three-day Congress of American-Soviet Friendship, to celebrate the twenty-fifth anniversary of the Bolshevik Revolution, attended by cabinet members, diplomats, the governors of twelve states, and many mayors; telegrams arrived from leading Allied generals. Those were the days! After the war the "respectable" element among the backers and sponsors hastily withdrew. Harold L. Ickes, Karl T. Compton and others resigned in October 1946, when the NCASF came out in opposition to the American (Baruch) atomic-energy plan. When HCUA subpoenaed the National Council's leaders and its records, the response of its executive secretary, the Reverend Richard Morford, and of its chairman, Corliss Lamont, was less than cooperative. Morford admitted having custody of the records but refused to produce them. Cited for contempt, he was sentenced in March 1948 to three months in prison and a $250 fine by the federal district court.[32] Contempt proceedings against Lamont were dropped by a grand jury on the ground that custody of the records was not his.

After the NCASF was listed by the Attorney General, it reported a catastrophic loss of members, sponsors, public support, and revenue. Schools and colleges no longer exposed themselves to the contamination of NCASF exhibits, books and pamphlets. Meeting halls and radio time were suddenly unobtainable. The NCASF sued for redress along with two other listed organizations. In *Joint Anti-Fascist Refugee Committee v. McGrath* (1951), the Supreme Court remanded the NCASF case to the district court and instructed the government to show cause for listing it. The government never bothered to do so. Instead, the Justice Department launched a new campaign against the National Council in proceedings before the SACB in 1954. The government's perennial witness Louis Budenz insisted that the Reverend William Howard Melish, a former chairman of the NCASF, was a Communist, but Melish denied it. The present chairman, Dr. John Kingsbury, told the Board that the blame for the Korean war was an "unsettled question," and insisted that the NCASF was in no way a front for the CP.[33] In February 1956 the Board ordered the National Council to register as a Communist front; the appeal dragged on for many years until the Supreme Court finally quashed the SACB order in 1964.

If friendship with the Soviet Union had become subversive, so, naturally, was peace with the Soviet Union; or that version of "peace" sponsored by the World Peace Council and embodied in the Stockholm Appeal of 1950. Marked down for suppression was the Peace Information Center, after it had printed and distributed 485,000 petitions for signatures to the Stockholm Appeal. In August 1950 the PIC received a letter from the Department of Justice demanding that it should register as an agent of a foreign power under the 1938 Act. In February 1951 a grand jury in Washington indicted five of the PIC's officers for failing to register, including the black radical scholar W. E. B. DuBois, then aged eighty-three, Abbott Simon, executive secretary, Kyrle Elkin, treasurer, and Sylvia Soloff. The venerated DuBois, who had traveled to peace conferences in Paris and Moscow in 1949, was now handcuffed, fingerprinted, bailed, and remanded for trial. Insisting that guilt must be proven by more than mere quotations and uncorroborated statements, Judge James McGuire refused to put the case to the jury and acquitted the PIC in November 1951. But the damage was done. Although Vito Marcantonio offered his services as counsel free of charge, and although $6,500 was raised at a Harlem meeting addressed by Paul Robeson, the PIC cracked under the strain of litigation costs of $35,150 and public odium. In October 1951, a month before the verdict in its favor, it liquidated itself.[34] The American Peace Mobilization and the American Peace Crusade were likewise listed by the Attorney General, the latter being ordered to register as a Communist front by the SACB in July 1957.

Those who argue that the American government, by persecuting those who called for "peace," thereby betrayed its own preparations for war, capture less than the whole truth. The word "peace" signified in the collective consciousness not merely the absence of war, but also a particular conception of world order, the *Weltanschauung* of the Soviet Union, the Pax Sovietica. In the same way, the word "freedom" symbolized the opposing, rival world order, the Pax Americana: Both Washington and Moscow were now committed not merely to a Manichaean struggle for the allegiance (or subservience) of the world, but also to absolute conformity among their own citizens. This rivalry cannot be understood in terms of the long struggle between capitalism and socialism alone, but must be compared to the fanatical quest for discipline and domination that has possessed other imperial ideologies during periods of xenophobic expansion.

Thus, the Justice Department became praetorian guard for the State Department, publicly pillorying the Council for a Democratic Far Eastern Policy, the Council for Pan-American Democracy, and the Council of Greek Americans—all of whom challenged the Truman Doctrine—and driving out of business the Council on African Affairs, which, under the leadership of DuBois, Robeson, Max Yergan, W. Alphaeus Hunton and Frederick V. Field, encouraged independence movements in the British and French colonies. By the early fifties all such independence movements were officially regarded as tainted by Communist influence; consequently the Council was hauled before the Subversive Activities Control Board.

The Joint Anti-Fascist Refugee Committee had been launched in 1942 to provide relief for refugees of the Spanish Civil War then living in France and North Africa, and to help them escape to Mexico, Canada and the United States. Headed by Dr. Edward K. Barsky, a distinguished New York surgeon who had directed the International Medical Service in Republican Spain, the JAFRC had originally operated under license from President Roosevelt's War Relief Board. After the war, conditions changed rapidly. Those elements in Congress and the Pentagon, encouraged by the Catholic hierarchy, who favored close ties with Franco's regime, were determined that all pro-Republican organizations should walk the plank. According to one of the JAFRC's Communist directors, the novelist Howard Fast, the JAFRC's decision to invite Harold Laski to speak at Madison Square Garden on the role of the Vatican in the Spanish Civil War led the Catholic Church in New York City to urge HCUA to take action against an organization that had disbursed one million dollars in cash, and $217,903 in kind. HCUA did not require much prompting; J. Parnell Thomas had notably close ties with the Franco regime. Accordingly, sixteen members of the JAFRC's executive board were subpoenaed to appear on April 4, 1946, and to bring the organization's records. They refused to bring the records, knowing that the anonymity not only of some 30,000 American donors and sympathizers but, much more crucial, of many Republican activists still working underground in Spain was at stake.[35] As a result, all the

members of the board were found guilty of contempt. Eleven of them
went to prison in June 1950, including Barsky and Fast.

Although the Truman-Acheson administration, under pressure
from liberals within the Democratic Party and from the ADA, maintained its nominally cool attitude toward the Franco regime until 1950
at least, HCUA's droppings were always manure for the Justice Department, which placed the JAFRC on the Attorney General's list,
along with the United Spanish Aid Committee, the Veterans of the
Abraham Lincoln Brigade, and the North American Spanish Democracy.[36] Brownell duly petitioned the SACB to order the JAFRC to
register, and in February 1955 the JAFRC announced that it could no
longer withstand the persecution and had dissolved itself.

## BREAKING THE DEFENSE ORGANIZATIONS

Not only Congressional committees but also the Justice Department
clearly adopted the view that to defend the constitutional or legal
rights of a subversive was in itself a subversive action. Consequently,
Attorney   General   Clark   listed   a   wide   variety   of   defense
organizations,[37] of which the most influential was the Civil Rights
Congress. Founded in 1946 as a successor to the formidable International Labor Defense, and sponsored by such leading fellow travelers
as Robeson, Marcantonio, Pressman and the Reverend Harry F.
Ward, the CRC was administered on a day-to-day basis by two Communists, William L. Patterson and Aubrey Grossman. As Grossman
later put it, whereas ACLU policy was to contest an injustice by filing
a suit, the CRC attempted both to file a suit and mobilize public opinion. There was also one other important distinction between the two
organizations: whereas the ACLU generally defended the civil liberties of all groups, including both Communists and Fascists, the Civil
Rights Congress was exclusively preoccupied with defending the liberties of the pro-Communist Left. Indeed, when it staged a Bill of
Rights Congress in October 1949, to condemn the Smith Act, a resolution calling for the release of the sixteen Socialist Workers Party
leaders jailed in 1942 was "howled down." Trotskyists, commented
Robeson, no more deserve liberty than do Fascists.[38]

The CRC's causes were invariably the Party's causes. When the
twelve Communist leaders were indicted under the Smith Act in July
1948, the CRC put up bail of $35,000 in Treasury Bonds and a further
$5,000 for each defendant. It was in fact the CRC's Bail Fund that
most profoundly exasperated the Justice Department, particularly as
the Fund received $1.5 million in loans or donations between 1946
and 1951. When four of the eleven Communist leaders convicted at

the Foley Square trial jumped bail in 1951, the government seized on the pretext to smash the Bail Fund, which immediately forfeited $60,000. In July Judge Sylvester Ryan revoked the bail of fifteen New York Communists on the ground that it had been posted by the CRC's Bail Fund, which, he claimed, had impeded the Court in its search for the four fugitive Communists. [39]

By this time three of the Bail Fund's trustees, the millionaire Frederick V. Field, the novelist Dashiel Hammett and W. Alphaeus Hunton, had flatly refused to produce the Bail Fund's list of contributors. According to his friend Lillian Hellman, Hammett did not in fact know who the contributors were, but refused to say so; in any event the author of *The Maltese Falcon* served a six-month jail sentence. Field, the Bail Fund's secretary, collected two contempt sentences, each of six months, for refusing to hand over the records to Judges Ryan and McGohey. The story is told how, when Field was carried off to prison and instructed in the routine manner to drop his pants and bend over, he remarked: "You're not going to find four missing Communists up there." When the FBI began a hunt for the Bail Fund's assistant treasurer, Aubrey Grossman, who possessed the list of contributors, he made himself "unavailable." But in August, Field handed over to the New York State Banking Department the CRC's books and records, including the names of four thousand lenders. [40]

Like the International Workers Order, the CRC Bail Fund had been marked down for administrative destruction. In May 1952 New York Attorney General Nathaniel L. Goldstein obtained a temporary court order freezing the Fund's assets of $717,000 and enjoining the trustees from activity. Goldstein argued that the Fund had violated the State Banking Law by soliciting and receiving deposits without proper license, and that it had violated the Martin Act by failing to file with the State Attorney General statements describing the CRC's activities. Finally, it was alleged that the trustees had been unfaithful to their trust in refusing to cooperate in recapturing the fugitive Communists. In June Goldstein announced that he had "broken" the Bail Fund by obtaining a permanent injunction, and that he had handed over to the FBI the names of 6,442 individuals and organizations who had deposited funds or securities. The lesson for other citizens who might be tempted to champion the legal rights of political outcasts was clear.

Attacks on the CRC multiplied from all sides. After a HCUA subcommittee arrived in Detroit in February 1952 and subpoenaed Arthur McPhaul to produce the local records, he was sentenced to nine months in prison and a $500 fine for refusing to do so on Fifth Amendment grounds. The CRC's national executive secretary, William L. Patterson, was jailed for contempt in April 1954 after failing to provide a grand jury with records that he claimed he did not possess, but after fifty days he was released by the Court of Appeals, which had earlier thrown out a contempt of Congress indictment against him. In 1955 the CRC was hit by massive FBI infiltration and job-intimidation of its members. In the East Bay (Oakland) area of California, teams of agents working in pairs toured the places of work of black CRC workers, many of whom had clung to the jobs in government installations that for the first time had been opened to them during the war. A word in the ear of the supervisor was enough to procure dismissal. Meanwhile, Attorney General Brownell petitioned the SACB to order the CRC to register. In advising that it should indeed be so ordered, the Board's Examiner, David Goddaire, described the CRC as "conceived by the Kremlin." The CRC then announced its intention to dissolve,[41] although the final order to register did not come until July 1957.

The Emergency Civil Liberties Committee, an independent left-wing organization founded in 1951, and the most effective and authentically liberal body of its kind, was neither listed by the Attorney General nor brought before the SACB. Its leading members did, however, suffer a certain amount of harassment from Congressional committees, notably Harvey O'Connor and Corliss Lamont, chairman and vice chairman respectively, both of whom took the perilous First Amendment rather than the Fifth. In 1956 HCUA interrogated Clark Foreman, director of the ECLC, and cited him for contempt when he refused to hand over his passport, but on this occasion the full House did not endorse the citation.

## THE TAX WEAPON AND OTHER DIRTY TRICKS

One of the administrative weapons most frequently employed by the federal government against left-wing organizations critical of its policies was that of fiscal discrimination. In January 1948 it was reported that the Internal Revenue Service was checking the charitable status of eighty-one organizations listed by the Attorney General on December 4, 1947. (This, of course, punctured the claim that the purpose of the list was solely to assist the federal Personnel Loyalty Program.) Tax exemption status was later revoked by the Treasury from sixteen listed organizations including the Hollywood Writers Mobilization; the IWO; the NCASF; the Ohio School of Social Science; the Tom Paine School of Social Science, Philadelphia; the Samuel Adams School, Boston; the School of Jewish Studies, New York; and the JAFRC. America now had a government of men, not of laws.

These men made laws to legitimize repression. Section 11 of the Internal Security Act (1950) stipulated that no organization that registered as Communist-action or Communist-front under the Act could receive tax exemption as a religious, charitable or educational institution. But no organization registered. The Treasury nevertheless decided to behave as if many had: Assistant Commissioner Norman A. Sugarman explained in June 1954 that "it is the firm policy of the Revenue Service to deny exemption to any organization which evidence demonstrates is subversive"; every organization listed by the Attorney General had ceased to be tax-exempt.[42] In August 1955 Eisenhower authorized HCUA to examine the tax returns of organizations judged to be Communist fronts by the Attorney General, with a view to exposing the "secret angels" of the CP.

California was exceptionally addicted to the tax-exemption weapon. Although the state constitution accorded veterans a property-tax exemption, from 1954 applicants had to sign an oath disowning violent overthrow of the United States government or support for a foreign government in time of war against the United States. In 1954–55 some veterans refused and were denied their exemption. A few churches too were defiant about taking an oath as the price of tax-exemption, notably the Los Angeles Unitarians and their pastor, Stephen H. Fritchman. Although the California Supreme Court upheld the oath as lawful, the U.S. Supreme Court in *Speiser v. Randall* and *First Unitarian Church v. Los Angeles* (1958) ruled by 7 to 1 that the California law violated free speech and lacked the procedural safeguards required by the due-process clause of the Fourteenth Amendment.

But the armory of dirty tricks assembled by official America in pursuit of Communism was very far from exhausted. In 1952 Congress passed a rider, known as the Gwinn Amendment, to the Housing Administration Act, stipulating that no housing built under the Act was to be occupied by any current member of any organization listed by the Attorney General as subversive. Local housing authorities were instructed to send each tenant a copy of the Attorney General's list, together with a certificate of nonmembership to sign. The Gwinn Amendment in effect endowed the list with the force of an administrative decree.

Local housing authorities reacted with varying degrees of enthusiasm. In California, the San Francisco authority sidestepped the issue by deciding that it applied only to future tenants, but the Richmond authority attempted to enforce the provision in its low-rent housing, culminating in a ruling by a local judge in April 1955 that the Gwinn Amendment was unconstitutional. In March 1953 the director of housing in Contra Costa, California, Sigmund Maller, announced that he had experienced no difficulty at all in obtaining oaths from the five hundred tenants in his low-rental units.

The ACLU, meanwhile, filed suit to enjoin the threatened eviction of thirty-six tenants in thirteen Los Angeles projects who had refused to sign, and also filed a test-case suit in Newark, New Jersey. In September 1953 a New York State court blocked the attempt of New York City's housing authority to put the amendment into practice, and in September 1955 the Brooklyn Municipal Court ruled in favor of sixteen familes living in federally aided housing units and threatened with eviction. Having lost some twenty cases in the courts in two years, and following a ruling by the Wisconsin Supreme Court in June 1955, which the U.S. Supreme Court refused to review, that the amendment was unconstitutional, the government finally announced in August 1956 that it would abandon attempts to enforce the amendment. But in Detroit, Pittsburgh and certain other cities, alleged Communists continued to be threatened with eviction from public housing. [43]

Attempts were also made to starve radicals, *pour encourager les autres*. It was in 1955 that the Department of Health, Education and Welfare ruled that the CP was an agent of a foreign government—an assertion as yet untested in the Supreme Court—and that, *ergo*, CP employees were ineligible for old-age benefits. Not only were payments abruptly stopped, but in some cases refunds were demanded. In April 1956 the Social Security Administration in New York, disregarding the fact that Old Age and Survivors Insurance was supported by compulsory payments, proceeded to terminate monthly benefits payable to nine employees of the Party, including William Z. Foster and Jacob Mindel, both aged seventy-five, Mindel's wife, sixty-five-year-old Alexander Bittelman (who had been paying social security taxes for seventeen years), and Mrs. Sadie Amter, widow of Israel Amter. At the same time the Social Security Board deprived a widow of her benefits because her late husband had worked as a handyman in the CP office. However, a legal referee reversed this ruling in June 1956, and soon afterward Washington abandoned the whole policy.

In June 1947 the House Committee on Veterans Affairs had approved a bill to deny all veterans' benefits to Communist and "sympathizers." Although nothing came of this in terms of legislation, the Veterans Administration took the law into its own hands in 1954 when it ruled that no further disability payments would be granted to veterans convicted under the Smith Act. An obvious target was the much decorated war hero and Party leader Robert Thompson, who had jumped bail in 1951 and who was now accused of "willfully and intentionally conspiring to aid an enemy of the United States . . . in time of armed hostilities." Although Thompson had been charged with no such crime, let alone convicted in a court of law, he lost his appeal in August 1956. Punitive action was likewise launched in May 1954 against the leader of the Michigan CP, Saul Wellman, recently convicted under the Smith Act and a recipient of disability benefits as a result of a near-fatal heart wound suffered during the Battle of the Bulge. It was a further two years before the Veterans Administration withdrew its demand that he repay the $9,581.85 he had received since June 1945, and reinstated retroactively the family allotments due to his wife and two children. But not until he gained a favorable ruling in the Court of Appeals in 1958 did Wellman recover the $70 a month due to him. [44]

Should reds be allowed to eat? was a question that several states answered in the negative. Pennsylvania theoretically refused public assistance to people actively seeking to change the system of government by unconstitutional means. (However, advocacy had to be accompanied by overt acts, so presumably no one was affected.) A similar stipulation was included in the Ohio Unemployment Compensation Law of 1949. When the CP of New York State applied in 1955 to the Health Insurance Plan of Greater New York for medical insurance for thirteen employees, the application was rejected. Following the denial of unemployment insurance benefits to William Albertson, a CP employee, a New York State Appellate Court ruled in June 1959:

> Claimant-appellant Albertson was employed by the Communist Party . . . as an assistant labor secretary . . . On July 16, 1956, being unemployed, he filed a claim for unemployment insurance benefits . . . The Industrial Commissioner denied claimant benefits and suspended the registrations of the national and state Communist parties as contributing employers . . . The reason . . . is that they constituted a criminal conspiracy and had been outlawed by Congress in the Communist Control Act . . . But having permitted the Communist Party to hire and pay the claimant . . . and to file and pay unemployment insurance taxes, the benefits of such payments should be paid in accordance with the law. [45]

Quite arbitrarily, unemployment benefits were frequently denied to people who lost their jobs in private employment as a result of taking the Fifth Amendment. After Matt Cvetic called her "the Red Queen" before HCUA in 1950, Mrs. Toni Nuss (and her two children) were removed from the Pittsburgh welfare rolls. Early in 1952 the Allegheny County Court of Common Pleas ruled that no Communist was eligible for state aid. Unemployment benefits were withheld in Maryland, Pennsylvania and Massachusetts from people discharged after being uncooperative witnesses before Congressional committees. In 1955 a New York woman, Scott, discharged for the same offense, was for seven weeks held ineligible for unemployment compensation. The following year a Multilith operator, Marion Syrek, was discharged by the Arthur Anderson & Company accounting firm in California because he refused to sign the firm's private loyalty oath; the California Department of Employment refused him unemployment pay. A Pennsylvania board refused to compensate a steelworker dismissed in 1958 after taking the Fifth Amendment before a Senate committee.[46]

These bureaucratic attempts to deprive radicals of the financial and welfare benefits to which all eligible citizens were entitled must rank among the meanest harassments of the purge. That the bureaucrats were more often than not thwarted in the long run was, nevertheless, a tribute to the American judiciary.

# 9

## The Communist Party Goes Under

### NATURE AND INFLUENCE OF THE CP

What was this Leviathan, the American Communist Party, against whose revolutionary and subversive designs it was evidently necessary to array not only the law, the FBI and the Congressional inquisition, but also a massive propaganda campaign?

In reality, the CPUSA was a flea on the dog's back, no more. Founded in 1919 in the wake of the Bolshevik Revolution, persecuted and forced underground in the 1920s, it emerged in 1929, dwarflike but aggressive, as the Communist Party of the United States, a strictly orthodox member of the Comintern. But always a flea: even at the height of its popularity, during and immediately after the Second World War, when the warm flush of the American-Soviet alliance still prevailed, the CP could garner only 60,000–80,000 members out of a population of 150 million. By 1950 membership was down to about 43,000; by 1951, to about 31,608; by 1955, to about 22,600 and by the summer of 1957 to about 10,000. Nor was this meager membership socially or geographically distributed in a way to lend credibility to fears of proletarian uprisings, political strikes, or industrial sabotage. The Party itself admitted in April 1946 that only 29 percent of its members were industrial workers, and the FBI estimated in 1951 that just over half of American Communists lived in the New York area, where they occupied white-collar jobs or worked in light industry.

Furthermore, although a hard core of steeled cadres did undoubtedly exist, the cohesion and discipline of the Party was constantly undermined by the high turnover in membership; according to one estimate, *annual* turnover during a thirty-year period was as high as one third of total membership. It was suggested in 1959 that no fewer than a quarter of a million former Communists were living in the United States.

The limits of the Party's influence are clearly reflected in the circulation figures of the *Daily Worker:* fairly constant at between 20,000 and 23,000 between 1945 and 1950, sales fell to 10,433 in 1953. The Sunday *Worker*, which enjoyed a circulation of some 65,000 in the late forties, fell to 28,822 in 1953.[1]

In terms of electoral power or influence, the CP and its close allies never made a scar on the smooth belly of American capitalism. When William Z. Foster impudently ran for President in 1932, he garnered 102,991 votes from a nation deep in Depression and unemployment. Four years later Earl Browder received only 80,195 votes, despite the rising popular-front euphoria, the radical mood that gave Roosevelt an unprecedented majority. In 1940 Browder's vote fell to 46,251; thereafter the Party risked no more presidential candidates of its own, supporting F.D.R. in 1944, Henry Wallace in 1948, and Vincent Hallinan, the last of the Progressive Party candidates, in 1952. The CP never elected a single Congressman on its own ticket, although two Communists were elected to the New York City Council in the middle forties. Only Vito Marcantonio, Congressman for the 16th (East Harlem) District on the American Labor Party ticket, scrupulously followed the Party line until his defeat in 1950.

From June 1941 to early in 1945—that is to say, from Hitler's invasion of the Soviet Union until the collapse of Nazi Germany became inevitable—the CPUSA pursued, under the leadership of General Secretary Earl Browder, a policy of ardent collaboration with the government and of accommodation with American capitalism—most notably dramatized by the no-strike pledge—which culminated in the self-dissolution of the CPUSA and the substitution in May 1944 of the Communist Political Association, apparently committed to a long-term collaboration between capital and labor in anticipation of postwar American-Soviet friendship. This program, closely associated with Browder and subsequently damned as "Browderism," came under sharp attack in an article published in April 1945 by France's second-ranking Communist, Jacques Duclos. The consequent overthrow of Browder and the rebirth of the CPUSA in June under the leadership of William Z. Foster, Eugene Dennis and Robert Thompson certainly marked a sharp turn to the Left and an abrupt end to collaborationism.

But did this turn to the Left also mark, as the United States government later claimed, the moment when the Communist movement in America rededicated itself to the violent overthrow of the government? The Party denied it, and the historian can have no doubt that the new leftist phase did not embrace any unrealistic revolutionary schemes. Much more a moot point was the Party's potential attitude and actions in the event of war with the Soviet Union. On March 2, 1949, Foster and Dennis followed up statements by Communist leaders in Italy, France and Britain with one of their own, pledging the Party to oppose any antidemocratic, antisocialist war against the Soviet Union. Pressed by reporters to state the means by which they would manifest their resistance, Foster and Dennis evaded the question. Yet no plausible evidence ever emerged to prove that the CP drew up contingency plans to sabotage vital industries and lines of communication in the event of war. The government took a sledgehammer to squash a gnat.

## THE FOLEY SQUARE TRIAL OF THE CP LEADERS

On July 28, 1948, a federal grand jury in New York returned two indictments against twelve [2] members of the national board of the Communist Party, excluding from the indictment only the board's one woman member, Elizabeth Gurley Flynn. (Her turn came later.) Those indicted were: William Z. Foster, Eugene Dennis (chairman and general secretary of the Party respectively), Robert Thompson, John Williamson, Benjamin J. Davis, Jr., and Henry Winston (both black), John Gates, Irving Potash, Jacob Stachel, Gilbert Green, Carl Winter and Gus Hall. They were charged, first, with willfully and knowingly conspiring to organize as the CPUSA a group teaching and advocating the violent overthrow of the government, and, secondly, with teaching and advocating the duty of violently overthrowing the government. The indictment charged that Article 2 of the Alien Registration Act of 1940 (the Smith Act) proscribed these actions, and that the alleged conspiracy violated Article 3.

These Communist leaders, it should be noted, were not accused of attempting to overthrow the government or even of teaching the technology of such an overthrow. The gist of the indictment was that, in dissolving the Communist Political Association and resurrecting the CPUSA, they entered into a conspiracy dating from April 1, 1945 until July 20, 1948 (the day of their indictment). The crucial notion here is *conspiracy to advocate*; by introducing the charge of conspiracy, the Justice Department opened the door to drag-net trials based on sympathetic association and obviated the hard task of proving the case against each defendant at the same level of rigor. Now, at last, the Justice Department and the FBI were on the verge of achieving their ambition of imprisoning Communists simply for being

Communists, and not, as during the Roosevelt era, for mere passport and immigration violations. Only one potential stumbling block presented itself: the First Amendment, which protected beliefs, speech, assembly and advocacy.

However, the courts had been searching for a formula to diminish the practical scope of the First Amendment ever since *Schenck v. United States* (1919), when Justice Holmes argued that words spoken or written had to be assessed in the context of whether there existed a "clear and present danger" that they would bring about evils that Congress wished to prevent. Thus the Justice Department could take courage. On the other hand, a comparatively recent case, *Schneiderman v. United States* (1943), had culminated in a Supreme Court ruling that was distinctly discouraging: that it was "a tenable conclusion" that the Party "desired to achieve its purpose by peaceful and democratic means, and as a theoretical matter justified the use of force and violence only as a method of preventing an attempted forcible counteroverthrow once the Party had obtained control in a peaceful manner . . ." The Court had also—most discouragingly—quoted Charles Evans Hughes's view that "guilt is personal and cannot be attributed to the holding of an opinion or to mere intent in the absence of overt acts . . ." But the Schneiderman case did not provide a direct judicial precedent for the simple reason that it was a deportation case and in no sense connected with the Smith Act. When Judge Harold R. Medina summed up for the jury at the conclusion of the trial of the eleven Communist leaders in 1949, he was careful to point this out—as the prosecution had requested.

Following the grand jury's indictment, bench warrants for the arrest of the twelve were signed on the eve of the Progressive Party's convention. Bail was granted. The original date set for the trial was October 15 (the eve of the presidential and Congressional elections), but the defense lawyers introduced a host of delaying motions which resulted in postponement until January 17. The trial, which then began in the Foley Square courthouse in lower Manhattan, lasted until October 21 and was the longest (nine months and four days) criminal trial in American legal history.[3] Five million words were uttered in evidence.

The defendants, whom Bruce Bliven of the *New Republic* described as resembling small businessmen (you could shuffle them with the male members of the jury and never know the difference), sat in leather armchairs, facing Judge Medina, whom Bliven described as "smallish and pink-faced, with a constant expression of mild surprise behind his little grey mustache and steel-bowed spectacles." [4] The defense accused the sixty-year-old Medina of prejudice from the outset and characterized him as a former corporation lawyer and slum landlord.

On the first day of the trial four hundred uniformed policemen and plainclothes detectives ringed the courthouse, while approximately the same number of demonstrators picketed the building in silent protest. The defense lawyers immediately claimed that this show of force was designed to intimidate the jurors, and then launched a massive challenge to the whole jury system, a challenge that lasted until March 1.

The essence of the complaint was that the method of selecting federal juries in the Southern District of New York discriminated against Negroes, workers, and the poor. Medina denied there was any evidence of bias in the selection system. Nevertheless, it was beyond dispute that in 1948–49 no jurors had been called from Harlem or the Lower East Side; John McKenzie, the jury clerk, admitted that he had sent no notices to these districts. Subpoenaed by the defense, Chief Judge John C. Knox agreed that in 1939 he had revamped the jury system to get "a better class of juror," but he denied that this process involved social or economic discrimination. But according to Abraham J. Isserman, one of the defense attorneys, juries were selected from special lists provided by Con Edison and the insurance companies. Robert Bendiner commented in *The Nation* that the Southern District jury system seemed to rely heavily on *Poor's Register of Directors*, *Who's Who in New York*, *The Social Register*, and even on names submitted by a right-wing private group called the Federal Grand Jury Association.[5]

Having failed to impeach the entire system, the defense began to challenge specific jurors. By March 16, a panel of twelve had been chosen, including three Negroes, two manual workers, and at least two names suggesting Jewish lineage. Four of the jurors were men and eight were women. Sociologically and racially the defense had gained a jury that was a fairly representative cross section of American society, but there was one particular thorn in the form of Russell Janney, a best-selling author who is reputed to have declared before the trial, "We must fight Communism to the death," and then, during the trial, to have told friends night after night, "I'm going to hang those Commies." But Medina brushed aside all defense protests concerning Janney's behavior.[6]

The prosecution case was, essentially, that the Party had attempted to mask its conspiracy by engaging in double talk and Aesopian language, resorting to false names and destroying membership books. The Party, the Justice Department's Attorney John F. X. McGohey said, had plans to place militants in key industrial positions to provoke strikes and to commit sabotage at a given signal. It indoctrinated its members and won recruits by playing on minority grievances, by encouraging admiration for the Bolshevik Revolution, by insisting that capitalism was on its last legs, by depicting the army and the police as instruments of Wall Street, and by insisting that any war with Russia would be imperialistic, unjust and a cause for civil war. (During cross-examination, the government did succeed in demonstrating that some of the defendants, most notably Gilbert Green, had used false names and filed false oaths when applying for passports and other documents.)

The first government witness was Louis Budenz, the great exponent of the Aesopian-language theory, who testified that just as the CP had fomented the Allis-Chalmers strike in 1941, so Dennis had instructed the Party to be ready to go underground and prepare for civil war in the event of war with Russia. According to Budenz, the new Party line had been laid down to the Americans by Dmitri Z. Manuilsky when he visited San Francisco in May 1945 as a UN delegate. Budenz also claimed that he himself and some of the defendants had taken a personal oath of loyalty to Stalin.

For eight weeks the court heard the testimony of thirteen FBI undercover agents who had masqueraded as members of the Communist Party. Theirs was an essential part of the case that the FBI had assembled in 1946–47 and that, in the form of a 1,350-page brief supplemented by 546 exhibits, together with two supplemental briefs and a further 300 exhibits, the FBI had deposited on the desk of Attorney General Tom Clark in February 1948. The witness who completely took the Party by surprise and shook its confidence to the core was the FBI undercover agent Herbert A. Philbrick, who claimed he had attended secret Party schools that taught that the right moment for a revolution was during a time of war and depression. He also reported Party plans to "colonize" key industries with a view to developing political strikes into armed insurrection. Thomas A. Younglove, a St. Louis businessman who had operated as an FBI agent within the CP since 1945, also spoke of plans to sabotage a war against Russia, while William Cummings, a Negro automobile worker from Toledo, Ohio, who had been operating in the CP since 1943 on behalf of the FBI, claimed that the Party taught its militants that one day the streets of America would run with blood. Charles W. Nicodemus, a foreman working in the Celanese Corporation plant at Cumberland, Maryland, reported that he had quit the CP in 1946, when the Party began to insist that, in the event of redundancies, white men should be the first to go, regardless of seniority. According to Nicodemus, CP officials had confided to him a plan for Russia to attack from Siberian bases through Alaska and Canada, mainly by air; American Communists were laying their sabotage plans against that day.

Angela Calomiris brought to the trial the traditional romance of the female spy. An undercover agent who joined the Party at the instigation of the FBI, who had been financial secretary of the West Midtown branch of the CP and whom the comrades still trusted as a Party member, she had briefed the prosecuting attorneys during frequent car rides round town. And then, when her moment to testify arrived on April 26, 1949, she made her way to the U.S. Attorney's office in the Foley Square courthouse:

> The agents drove through an underground tunnel to the garage beneath the building. There we made a quick dash for the elevator. We rode a few floors up on the elevator, got off, walked down a flight, took another car up, went through several corridors . . . Sometimes he would lead me behind a pillar . . . One Irish agent always carried a big clean handkerchief into which I could pretend to weep.

Under oath she claimed that "the defendants had personally taught me the need to overthrow the Government." [7]

On May 19, the Government completed its case. Four days later Judge Medina denied defense motions to throw the case out.

The defendants adopted as their basic premise that Marxism-Leninism taught that force and violence are necessary only when the ruling class resists a peaceful transition to socialism. The Party constitutions of 1945 and 1948, dismissed by the prosecution as window dressing, were therefore genuine in their repudiation of force and violence. Acting as his own counsel, Eugene Dennis argued that the conspiracy alleged by the government "limps on only three active verbs"—to organize, to teach, to advocate. Marxism was not a blueprint for all situations, but a philosophy that constantly modified itself in the light of historical circumstances. "You cannot find out what to do in 1949 by reading what Lenin said the Russian workers should do under quite different circumstances in 1917." Dennis appealed to the jury's sense of patriotism by recalling that Marx had not only described Abraham Lincoln as the one truly popular statesman in the world, but had also helped to organize British labor support for the Union cause in the Civil War. Dennis referred glowingly to the war records of fifteen thousand Communists who had served in the armed forces during the Second World War.

The position adopted by John Gates, editor-in-chief of the *Daily Worker*, who occupied the witness stand for three weeks, was that even in the event of an imperialist war against the USSR, the CP did not advocate a civil war, merely the formation of a people's govern-ment to bring about peace. Gates also suggested that socialism was not the immediate issue in America because the majority of the people were not yet convinced of its necessity. And because they were not so convinced, argued the defendants, it was impossible for Communists to secure a fair trial. When one of the eleven, Irving Potash, was injured while traveling home from the second Robeson concert at Peekskill on September 4, the defense lawyers immediately seized upon this incident, and the climate of hatred that sparked it, as ground for a mistrial. Judge Medina was not impressed.

The relationship of the defendants to Judge Medina was no less abrasive than that of the five defense attorneys whom Medina ultimately sent to prison for contempt. Gates was imprisoned for thirty days when he refused in June to provide certain names. When Winston and Hall rose to protest against this treatment the judge imprisoned them for the duration of the trial. Gilbert Green spent four weeks in prison for a chance remark he uttered while replying to a question. Carl Winter was imprisoned after refusing to disclose whether his father-in-law was a Communist. Those found guilty of contempt were confined in high summer to ill-ventilated cells in West Street jail, where relatives could not bring food and where proper consultation with lawyers was impossible. Winston suffered two heart attacks while in jail, but the judge would not allow him to see his family doctor.[8]

For the benefit of the jury Judge Medina summed up what he held to be the main legal issue:

> It is not the abstract doctrine of overthrowing or destroying organized government by unlawful means which is denounced by this law, but the teaching and advocacy of action for the accomplishment of that purpose, by language reasonably and ordinarily calculated to incite persons to such action . . . as speedily as circumstances would permit.

But the distinctions contained in this apparently sober and lucid exposition are spurious. When is any doctrine strictly "abstract," strictly divorced from the "advocacy of action"? Had the government attempted to distinguish between "mere advocacy" on the one hand, and "concrete action" on the other, its logic would have been unassailable, but the government had no hope of pinning concrete revolutionary action on the Communist defendants. Furthermore, Medina's reference to "language reasonably and ordinarily calculated to incite persons to such action" begs a host of vital questions: which persons, where, when? Words which, in time of depression, war or famine, will excite the masses to revolt, may fall on deaf ears in time of peace and prosperity. The word "calculated" as used by Medina was meaningless; if he meant "likely" (to incite), he would have to specify the circumstances.

And this he did. In one of the nimblest and most cynical manipulations of a jury that any judge could undertake, Medina instructed: "I find as a matter of law that there is a sufficient danger of a substantive evil that the Congress has a right to prevent to justify the application of the statute under the First Amendment of the Constitution." And he repeated: "This is a matter of law with which you have no concern." [9] The audacity of this stroke was such that even Sidney Hook later agreed with Justice Douglas that Medina had made a matter of law what was vitally a question for the jury to decide. As soon as Medina informed the jury, *ex cathedra*, that a clear and present danger existed, the jury's own function of determining the innocence or guilt of the defendants was largely expropriated—for how could there be a clear and present danger unless the defendants were guilty? How could there be a clear and present danger of a Communist revolution (perhaps assisted by Russia) if the Communist leaders were not conspiring to advocate such a revolution and to organize for its advocacy? Yet the defendants denied that they were so conspiring or so advocating. Consequently it was properly a matter for the jury, not the judge, to decide. *Yet Medina's charge to the jury on what he claimed was strictly a matter of law in effect left the jury with the alternatives of rejecting the judge's ruling or convicting the defendants.*

The jury delivered its verdict on October 14: guilty. A week later Medina handed down sentences of five years' imprisonment (the maximum) and a $5,000 fine to all the defendants except Thompson, whose heroic war record inspired the judge to reduce his term of imprisonment to three years. After Medina had initially refused to grant bail (the government insisted the eleven might do incalculable harm if set at liberty), bail was granted on appeal. A few days after their release, on November 8, Davis and Gates were barred from voting in the City Council elections by the New York Supreme Court on the ground that they had been convicted of a federal crime. In August 1950 the eleven lost their appeal in the Court of Appeals for the Second Circuit, and early in December the Supreme Court began to review the case.

In his seventy-ninth year, Judge Learned Hand delivered the 20,000-word unanimous judgment of the Court of Appeals. Despite the high esteem in which he was held, Hand, no less than Medina, emerged as deeply biased in favor of the prevailing political assumptions of the day. The "only plausible complaint" of the convicted

Communists, he argued, was that they had been penalized for exercising the freedom of speech "which they would be the first to deny" to others. (But a citizen's legal rights are not determined by his alleged thoughts or intentions.) Turning to the Soviet Union, Hand declared that "no such movement in Europe of East to West has arisen since Islam." The defendants, he went on, maintained close contact with important Communist groups in Western Europe, groups aiding this advance of the infidel. Hand's Spenglerian sense of the "West" as a unique and precious civilization was reinforced by his conception of America as a uniquely virtuous Power: "We had become the object of invective upon invective; we were continuously charged with aggressive designs upon other nations; our efforts to re-establish their economic stability were repeatedly set down as a scheme to enslave them; we had been singled out as the chief enemy of the faith . . ." This "we" boded ill for judicial impartiality; in Hand's Cold-War diatribe the judiciary merely fused its values and its criteria of judgment with those of the President and the Congress, of the aggravated *patria*.

When the case (*Dennis v. United States*) came before the Supreme Court, Jackson expressed the opinion that the courts should not appraise global political situations: "The answers given would reflect our own predilections and nothing more." But the majority of the Court agreed with Hand that the Soviet and Communist threat was of such magnitude that even if the danger of revolution was not exactly "present" it was certainly "probable," and therefore essentially "present" in view of "the inflammable nature of world conditions." Vinson himself wrote the main opinion, which was of poor legal and intellectual quality, with Reed, Burton and Minton concurring (Clark did not participate). Frankfurter (who distinguished between the statement of an idea that may prompt its hearers to take unlawful action, and advocacy that such action be taken) and Jackson (who thought this dividing line difficult to determine) wrote separate concurring opinions. Only Black and Douglas insisted on the elementary point, that Medina should have submitted to the jury the question whether a clear and present danger actually existed. Black hoped that in future and calmer times, the First Amendment liberties would be restored to their preferred position. Douglas, dissenting, described the CPUSA as "the least thriving of any fifth column in history. Only those held by fear or panic could think otherwise." [10]

In 1952 the ACLU pointed out that the Supreme Court's ruling appeared to permit Congress to
   (1) prohibit a number of persons (but not one person)
   (2) from advocating (but not discussing)

(3) under certain circumstances (but not all)
(4) violent overthrow of the government.

The absurdity of this position should have been obvious to the Court.

The leaders of the Communist Party had revealed themselves during this trial to be sadly lacking in imagination, flair, humor, inspiration and charisma. They were solid, steady, earnest, gray men. Frank Donner, who wrote the appellate briefs in four of the Smith Act cases, including the *Dennis* case, now feels that the Party did not know how to mobilize sympathy and support in terms of the available culture.[11] There is no doubt that the Party suffered from its addiction to camouflage and its perverse decision to present Marxism as a kind of quick-tempered Fabianism, rather than rely on the American revolutionary tradition as expressed by Jefferson in a letter to James Madison in 1787:

> . . . a little rebellion, now and then, is a good thing . . . It is a medicine necessary for the sound health of government.

and by Lincoln at his first Inaugural:

> [whenever the people] shall grow weary of the existing Government, they can exercise their *constitutional* right of amending it or their *revolutionary* right to dismember or overthrow it.

No sooner had the Supreme Court upheld the conviction of the Foley Square eleven than four of them—Thompson, Green, Winston and Hall—acting on the collective decision of the leadership, jumped bail and disappeared. Two weeks later, on June 20, the FBI struck. Seventeen second-string Party leaders were arrested in the New York area. Four others fled. In August, six local leaders were picked up in Baltimore and Cleveland. In September, the FBI arrested eighteen Communist leaders in the cities of the Midwest and the Pacific Coast.[12] The average age of these eighteen men and women was forty-two; they belonged to the generation that had reacted with fierce, youthful indignation to its experience of the Depression and the rise of Fascism—this was the only generation whose "pacification" was not yet complete.

In the post-Foley Square trials the battle words constantly ranged over familiar terrain, with the prosecution inevitably quoting Lenin: "The proletarian revolution is impossible without the forcible destruction of the bourgeois state machine"; and Stalin: ". . . the law of violent proletarian revolution, the law of the smashing of the bourgeois state machine as a preliminary condition for such a revolution, is an inevitable law of the revolutionary movement of the imperialist countries." [13] The "overt acts" charged in the various indictments continued, as before, to fall into the category of "actions" normally protected by the First Amendment: "did attend and participate"; "did formulate and cause to be published and circulated"; "did cause to be used . . . a safe-deposit box"; "to conceal his true identity . . . did use the false name . . ." Nine tenths of the testimony, however, was about the conspiratorial nature of the CP, and only one tenth as to whether the individual defendants had conspired. Thus, these conspiracy trials came close to being mere membership trials based on guilt by association alone.

Few of the defendants took the stand on their own behalf. This may have left a poor impression with juries but it was the only alternative to the fate of Carl Winter, of Elizabeth Gurley Flynn, of Oleta O'Connor Yates, of Terry Pettus and John Daschbach—all of whom were jailed for a common refusal to reveal under cross-examination the names of comrades.

The five defense attorneys who represented the Foley Square eleven, Harry Sacher, Richard Gladstein, George Crockett, Jr., Abraham J. Isserman and Louis F. McCabe, were all politically sympathetic to their clients. Flamboyant in style, Sacher and Gladstein— and occasionally Isserman too—carried disruption of the proceedings to lengths unusual at that time, though mild by contemporary standards. But Judge Medina was frequently provocative in his behavior, and the contempt sentences he handed down at the close of the trial were extremely harsh: six months' imprisonment to Sacher, Gladstein and Dennis (who defended himself), four months' to Crockett and Isserman and thirty days' to McCabe.

In subsequent Smith Act trials disruptive defense tactics were not repeated; obviously they were counterproductive. On the contrary, defendants now began a search for "respectable" lawyers who would serve them out of a sense of professional obligation rather than out of political sympathy. The aim was to stir a broader constituency of liberal support. But such lawyers were not easy to obtain. The seventeen defendants in the Flynn case (New York, 1952) submitted an affidavit to the Court of Appeals establishing that they had approached more than twenty-eight law firms, requesting an interview, but had received no reply from twelve and had been refused by sixteen. When Judge Sylvester Ryan took the step of appointing left-wing lawyers on their behalf, these were declined because, as Flynn put it, the defendants wanted to be represented by someone of a stature comparable to that of the late Wendell Willkie. The Baltimore defendants apparently appealed in vain to more than thirty lawyers.

This situation reflected unhealthily not only on the Bar but on the illiberal climate of opinion then prevailing. In 1953 a special committee of the American Bar Association reported that "counsel of outstanding reputations, well known for their anti-Communist views," had been subjected to "severe personal vilification and abuse" when they took on cases "involving Communists or persons accused of being Communists . . . out of a sense of public duty." [14] But it was not merely that many lawyers feared for their careers. Other, liberal lawyers believed that they could successfully defend "the innocent" (i.e., fellow liberals or people who had genuinely renounced Communism) only if they refused to serve "the guilty." Thus, it was said of one well-known and very liberal Washington lawyer that the very fact he represented a client was a signal to judges that the client was really "all right."

## THE SECOND NEW YORK TRIAL

Simon Gerson recalls that June 20, 1951, was a very hot day. The FBI arrived at his Brooklyn home at seven in the morning. By this time he was used to being under constant FBI surveillance and to having his neighbors questioned—most of them, he stresses, were "decent people" and refused to be intimidated. Despite the protests of his wife, the agents had come to arrest him before he had shaved and had breakfast. (He suggests they wanted "mug shots" of unshaven rascals for the papers.) Even so, they were more nervous than he; one agent lit a cigarette for him in the car with an unsteady hand. At Foley Square he met up with his fourteen arrested comrades, including the seventy-five-year-old Israel Amter, who, suffering from advanced Parkinson's disease, was carried in by two agents. (Amter did not stand trial.) They were fingerprinted, then taken to West Street prison and X-rayed for hidden objects (a paper clip was found in Gerson's pocket). The women Communists were taken to the Women's House of Detention in New York's Greenwich Village. [15]

Now that Thompson, Hall, Green and Winston had jumped bail, obtaining bail money that the courts would accept was not easy. Prosecutor Irving Saypol demanded that bail be raised from $185,000 to $875,000. Although this was refused, Judge Ryan did revoke the defendants' Civil Rights Congress bail, with the immediate result that while four were able to raise alternative bail, the eleven others returned to prison. When Alice Citron, one of the radical teachers dismissed in 1950, produced bail money on behalf of her husband, Isidore Begun, Judge Edward Dimock declined to accept it, because she refused to follow the standard practice and identify the five people who had lent her half the money. Friends of Simon Gerson lent bail money to his wife on the assurance of anonymity. When this proved to be of no value, a wealthy woman sympathizer came up with the full $10,000 and Gerson came out of West Street after three weeks' incarceration.[16]

Their trial began on April 15, 1952, in Room 110 of the Foley Square courthouse. On this occasion the jury of six men and six women was appointed without allegations and recriminations. Indeed the whole atmosphere of the trial, and notably the relationship of Judge Edward J. Dimock to the defense counsel, suggested that neither side desired a repeat performance of 1949. Midway the judge threw out the cases against Simon Gerson and Isidore Begun for lack of evidence; he frequently angered the prosecutors by overruling their objections and sustaining others made by the defense.

Budenz testified for fourteen days, Lautner for twenty-nine days. Harvey Matusow described the Party's alleged plan to sabotage basic industries in the event of war with Russia. The government closed its case on September 5. In November the judge sent Flynn to jail for thirty days for refusing to name names or, as she put it, "to degrade or debase myself by becoming an informer." On December 3, the defense rested its case with the complaint that its legal costs were running between three thousand and five thousand dollars a week. On January 15, after a trial lasting 263 days, the case went to the jury. After fourteen hours of deliberation the jury alarmed the prosecution by announcing that it was unable to agree, whereupon it was locked up in the Knickerbocker Hotel, 120 West 45th Street, until, six days later, it found all thirteen guilty.

Before sentence was passed, each defendant had his say. Flynn ridiculed the evidence "of a motley array of bought and paid-for informers, stoolpigeons and renegades . . . " Ideas, she said, cannot be jailed. She quoted Jefferson and also F.D.R.: "We have nothing to fear but fear itself." She also referred to the jury as "poisoned by prejudice, fearful for their futures, incapable of assimilating scientific concepts, hypnotized by legalistic language . . ." It was the speech of a fighting Irishwoman. Pettis Perry saw himself as a victim of a frame-up so enormous as to resemble the Reichstag Fire trial. How could a Negro get justice from a white jury? Claudia Jones, also black, complained that the jury system virtually excluded Negroes, Puerto Ricans and manual workers. (There was in fact one Negro juror who replaced an ill white juror.) She stressed the threat of war to children and delivered a long indictment of America's treatment of black people. Alexander Bittelman warned of the coming police state and called Stalin the greatest leader of men of the epoch. Pointing with pride to the role of Jews in the world progressive movement, he regretted that Jews (Saypol, Roy Cohn) figured among the prosecutors at this trial. Alexander Trachtenberg, head of International Publishers, quoted Milton on liberty. V. J. Jerome, the CPUSA's cultural commissar, warned that the men of Wall Street were pressing gold from the blood of American youths sent to fight the Korean people. He too praised Stalin and denounced thought-control trials. Betty Gannett spoke of her poverty-stricken childhood in Harlem and described her passionate encounter with the Marxist classics in the New York Public Library. George Charney quoted from Mark Twain's *A Connecticut Yankee* on the nature of true patriotism.

Then came a surprise turn. Judge Dimock offered all thirteen the chance to go to Russia as an alternative to prison. It was not exactly a firm offer—he asked Flynn whether she would accept such a plan if it "could be worked out." All the defendants hotly rejected any such proposal. Flynn, with a flash of humor uncharacteristic of Communist leaders, remarked that it was like the Romans asking the early Christians whether they would not prefer to go to Heaven right away. Dimock then passed sentence.

Jailed for three years with a fine of $5,000 were Elizabeth Gurley Flynn, a member of the national committee, and a veteran of the IWW; Alexander Bittelman, who had the distinction of being deported to Siberia by Tsar Nicholas II, before reaching the United States in 1912; V. J. Jerome, born in Poland, naturalized in 1928, and chairman of the Party's cultural commission; Arnold Johnson; Pettis Perry, secretary of the Party's Negro Commission; Alexander Trachtenberg, born in Odessa, naturalized in 1914, and later head of International Publishers; and Louis Weinstock, a native of Hungary and a house painter by profession. Jailed for two years with a fine of $4,000 were George Charney, born in Russia, trade union secretary of the New York State CP; Betty Gannett, a native of Poland, a graduate of the Lenin School in Moscow, and national education director of the CP; Albert Lannon; Jacob Mindel, born in Minsk and naturalized in 1915; and William Weinstone, born in Vilna. Sentenced to one year and one day in prison, with a fine of two thousand dollars, was Claudia Jones, aged thirty-six, a native of the British West Indies.

Two years later Harvey Matusow confessed that he had twisted the evidence and distorted the words of four of the defendants. Dimock ruled in April 1955 that Trachtenberg and Charney should be granted new trials and released forthwith from prison.[17] Both men were again convicted.

## CALIFORNIA, BALTIMORE, HONOLULU, SEATTLE

On July 26, 1951, the FBI arrested Oleta O'Connor Yates and eleven other leaders of the Communist Party in California. Late in August three more were picked up in Los Angeles.[18] According to a Communist account, when Ernest Fox's wife tried to phone her lawyer, the FBI men tore the phone from her hands. Mrs. Loretta Stack was at home giving breakfast to her children, aged three and four, when the FBI arrived at 8 A.M. The agents refused to allow her to finish feeding the children or even to call friends to take care of them; she was forced to dress with an agent looking on. Al Richmond, editor of the *Daily People's World*, was at his typewriter by the time the San Franciso Ferry Building siren wailed its 8 A.M. call. The siren was the signal for at least ten FBI agents to burst into the office; Richmond recalls the trembling hands of the agent who slipped handcuffs on him. U.S. Commissioner Francis St. J. Fox accepted the government's astronomical demand of $75,000 bail for each of the Bay Area men, but chivalrously set $7,500 for the women, Oleta O'Connor Yates, Bernadette Doyle (who was in poor health) and Loretta Stack. The men went to jail and the women went free. The average age of those arrested in California was forty-three; at the height of the Depression their average age had been twenty-three. As Al Richmond puts it: "The 1930s had been a great cadre-molding experience and there had been nothing comparable since." [19]

On the following day U.S. District Judge Louis E. Goodman described the offense with which they were charged as "more serious than treason" and less chivalrously fixed bail at $50,000 for men and women alike. The three women thereupon went to jail. At the direction of Judge William Mathes, the fifteen defendants and their lawyers were granted the use of a prison cage, eighteen by sixteen feet, to prepare their collective defense. The defendants appealed against the $50,000 bail, which was justified by the government on the ground that four Communists in the East had jumped bail. In *Stack v. Boyle* (1951), the U.S. Supreme Court ruled that bail had not been fixed by proper tests, and bail was eventually set at $10,000 for some, $5,000 for others.

At the trial, which began on February 1, 1952, in Los Angeles, the defense position rested on the constitutional right of advocacy, and also on the fundamental probity and rationality of Party policy. When Mrs. Oleta O'Connor Yates, California State Secretary of the CP, was asked in cross-examination whether she knew a certain Harry Glickson as a Communist, she refused to answer and was held by Judge Mathes to be in contempt. She spent the night on a cot in a crowded hallway of the Los Angeles county jail, with a light glaring overhead and people coming and going. She slept not at all. Her lawyer, Ben Margolis, requested that execution of the contempt sentence be stayed until she had finished testifying, but Judge Mathes wasn't having it. After she had been in jail for five very hot weeks (July–August), Mathes sentenced her to one year in prison on eleven counts of criminal contempt, but, not content with this, on September 8 he heaped on her a further three-year sentence, again for contempt. (Each of these sentences was set aside on appeal.)

On August 6, the jury of eight women and four men convicted all fourteen defendants, whereupon Mathes handed down maximum sentences of five years in prison and a $10,000 fine for them all. They appealed. Although the Supreme Court refused to review the contemporaneous New York and Baltimore Smith Act trials, the California Communists were lucky and remained free on bail while their Eastern comrades went to prison. On October 17, 1955, the Supreme Court granted their petition for *certiorari* and in June 1957 handed down its memorable decision, to which we shall refer later in this chapter.

In August 1951, six Communists were arrested in Baltimore and Cleveland, and in March of the following year they were brought to trial. They too were charged with having conspired with one another and with the eleven convicted in New York to knowingly teach the duty of violent overthrow of the government with the intention of bringing it about as speedily as circumstances permitted. Basic to the prosecution's philosophy was the assumption that to become a member or an officer of the CP was of itself an act of conspiracy; likewise to organize groups and clubs, to conduct classes in Marxism-Leninism, and to form plans for the Party to go underground in an emergency, with the use of false names and documents. The defendants were charged, for example, with having attended and participated at the CP convention for Maryland and the District of Columbia, in August 1948; having attended a class on the "History of the Communist Party of the Soviet Union," held in Baltimore on January 28 and February 11, 1949; having written and caused to be published an article entitled "Concentration and Trade Union Work"; and so on. Yet not one of these revolutionaries was accused even of owning a penknife. As the judge summed it up: ". . . it is not alleged in the indictment that the defendants have actually committed violations of the Act but only that they have agreed or conspired to do so . . ." [20]

But the jury, apparently convinced by the testimony of the professional witness Paul Crouch, convicted all six. On April 4, Philip Frankfeld was sentenced to five years in prison and a $1,000 fine,

George A. Meyers to four years and $1,000, Leroy H. Wood, Maurice L. Braverman and Mrs. Dorothy Rose Blumberg to three years and $1,000 and Mrs. Regina Frankfeld to two years and $1,000. They all went to prison, the women to Alderson.

The trial of seven Communists [21] began in Honolulu, Hawaii, in October 1952 to coincide with hearings of the Senate Interior and Insular Affairs Committee which was then examining a bill to grant statehood to Hawaii. Significantly, the professional ex-Communist Paul Crouch testified both to this committee and to the District Court—factions racially opposed to granting Hawaii full statehood were playing up the penetration of the island by the CP and the pro-Communist ILWU. In July 1953 six of the accused were sentenced to five years' imprisonment and a $5,000 fine, while the only woman accused, Eileen Fujimoto, got away with three years' and $2,000. All these convictions were reversed in January 1958 by the Ninth Federal Circuit Court of Appeals.

On April 15, 1953, seven [22] leading Communists from Washington and Oregon went on trial in Seattle. It was an eventful and tragic affair; not only did Judge William J. Lindberg sentence an elderly defense witness, Dr. Herbert J. Philips (dismissed by the University of Washington in 1949 solely because he was a Party member), to three years' imprisonment for contempt, he also handed down similar sentences to two defendants who opted to testify, Terry Pettus and John Daschbach. Most poignant was the suicide during the trial of the youthful and popular president of the WPU, William Pennock—according to Joseph Starobin, the intense pressures from CP national headquarters in the East to conduct the defense on the basis of a broad defense of world Communism may have contributed. [23] On the other hand, the Seattle jury became the first in a Smith Act trial to acquit a defendant, Karly Larsen of the International Wood Workers, CIO, who claimed that he had quit the Party in 1946. The remaining five were convicted and sentenced to five years' imprisonment, one with a $5,000 fine and the others with a fine of $1,000. Later Barbara Hartle turned informer, was granted parole, sang to the FBI, and in February 1956 was released from prison. In January 1958 the Ninth Federal Circuit Court of Appeals reversed the convictions of the remaining four.

## DETROIT, PHILADELPHIA, CLEVELAND AND OTHERS

The trial of six Michigan Communist leaders opened in October 1953 before Judge Frank A. Picard. In the course of a four-month trial the prosecution produced as witnesses eight professional ex-Communists or undercover agents, whose total earnings over the years as informers amounted to $172,650. The jury returned verdicts of guilty against all six,[24] including the thirty-eight-year-old Party leader in Michigan, Saul Wellman, Party coordinator for the automobile industry, a veteran of the Spanish Civil War, and a paratrooper who was severely wounded in the Battle of the Bulge. Like Judge Dimock in New York, Judge Picard in Detroit offered the convicted Communists transportation to Russia as an alternative to imprisonment in the United States. He got the same answer. He then fined all six $10,000 and handed out prison sentences of four to five years.

In May 1954 five-year sentences were imposed in St. Louis on four male leaders of the Missouri CP, and a sentence of three years on the one female defendant.[25] Meanwhile in April, state and local police had prepared the ground for a sedition trial under the Massachusetts Anti-Communism law by raiding the CP headquarters in Park Square, Boston, and seizing such "evidence of great value" as a bust and death mask of Lenin.[26] Soon afterward Otis A. Hood and other Bay State reds went on trial.

In Philadelphia six leading Communists were arrested by the FBI in July 1953. Within a month two more were picked up in Boston and a third in Atlantic City. Having been held in a total bail of $300,000, the nine went on trial before Judge J. Callen Ganey in April 1954. Typical of the "overt acts" with which they were charged (and which the Alien and Sedition Acts of 1798 had likewise proscribed) were these: " . . . did attend . . . a class . . . a convention . . . a meeting . . . a conference . . . a rally . . . an affair . . . a forum; . . . did prepare . . . a press release; . . . circulated copies of a letter." Professor John Somerville, who testified as an expert witness not only at the Philadelphia trial in 1954, but also at the Cleveland trial in 1955 and the second Philadelphia trial in 1956, described the atmosphere peculiar to this series of talmudic inquisitions in which ideological deductionism replaced evidence of concrete action: "The anterooms reserved to counsel and clients . . . became reference and lending libraries, with books indexed and catalogued, instantly available for courtroom quotation or counterquotation . . . Library hand trucks resembling large tea wagons are wheeled in and out of the courtroom for each session. . . ."

A non-Communist scholar who had visited the Soviet Union for two years in the late 1930s and had subsequently published *Soviet Philosophy: A Study of Theory and Practice,* Somerville took the witness stand and insisted, in the most homely fashion, that the Marxist approach to violence was no different from the ordinary man's attitude toward self-defense. Confronted by the prosecution with numerous passages from Stalin's works about the impossibility of ballot-box socialism and the inevitability of revolutionary violence in the United States, he persisted in the view that the CPUSA believed in using force only when there was what he called a "revolutionary situation." [27]

Judge Ganey questioned this witness extensively about *who* would decide whether a revolutionary situation had materialized; the judge rather suspected that it would be the Communist Party alone that would decide. Perhaps the jury did too: in August all nine defendants were found guilty. After an unusual delay of ten months, sentences were handed down: three years' imprisonment for four of the Communists and two years' for five of them. In November 1957 the Court of Appeals for the Third Circuit set aside the convictions of Walter Lowenfels, Sherman Labovitz, Benjamin Weiss and Irvin Katz, and ordered a new trial for Joseph Kuzma, David Dubinsky (Davis), Thomas Nabried, Samuel Gobeloff and Robert Klonsky. [28]

In July and August 1954 the FBI picked up seven leading Communists in Utah and Colorado. They were brought to trial and quickly convicted. As a result of a Supreme Court decision they were all granted a new trial in January 1959, but this trial resulted only in renewed convictions. Arthur Bary was sentenced to five years in prison with a $5,000 fine; Mrs. Patricia Blau to four years and $4,000; Anna Correa, the former wife of Bary, to four years and $3,000; Joseph Scherrer to three years and $2,000; Maia Scherrer to two-and-a-half years and $1,500; and Harold Zepelin to three years and $2,000. [29]

On May 29, 1954, the FBI arrested seven leading members of the Connecticut CP, trailing three of them to a "secret meeting place" in a third-floor art studio at 38 Old Broadway, New York. This case, which was tried in 1955, was notable for the appearance of four non-Communist academic, "expert" defense witnesses, [30] who testified that the statements charged to the defendants did not constitute a clear and present danger to the security of the United States. But neither the jury nor Judge Anderson was convinced, and they were convicted. This case (*United States v. Silverman*) was the first to highlight the possible effects of the Communist Control Act (1954) on the Smith Act prosecutions. Defense lawyers argued that Section 5 of the Act would inhibit defense lawyers and witnesses, who now had reason to fear that, under the Act, any aid or counsel they lent to accused Communists might be interpreted as proof of Party membership, and therefore as self-incriminating. The judge replied that this was merely a new instance of the ancient problem of getting "criminals" to testify as witnesses.

In October 1953 the FBI arrested eleven leading Communists in Ohio. The trial, which took place in Cleveland from October 31, 1955, to February 10, 1956, was marked by an unusual atmosphere of restraint, which extended even to the local press. The fact that the

Communists were represented by court-appointed and highly respected members of the Ohio bar certainly encouraged this atmosphere. After Judge Charles J. McNamee had acquitted David Katz, the jury proceeded to acquit four more; Mrs. Freda Katz, Elvador G. Greenfield, Robert A. Campbell and Joseph M. Dougher. Six were convicted: Joseph Brandt, Mrs. Lucille Bethencourt, George Kwatt, Martin Chancey, Anthony Krchmarek and the much-persecuted secretary of the Ohio CP, Frank Hashmall.[31]

## THE FUGITIVES

What had become of the eight Communists who had fled in June and July 1951, four to evade going to prison and four to evade trial? Gus Hall was picked up in Mexico City in October 1951, after only four months at liberty. He had dyed his normally blond hair and eyebrows, shaved off his mustache, and thinned himself down by forty pounds. He was handed over at the Texas border after the FBI had penetrated the Communist network in Mexico, and his attempt to leave Mexico for Moscow had been bungled. Hall was eventually released from prison in 1958 and elected general secretary of the Party by the seventeenth national convention in December 1959. Robert Thompson, as befitted a war hero, lasted longer. Having grown a mustache, dyed his hair strawberry blond, and assumed the name of John Francis Brennan, Thompson was tracked to a California mountain hideout in August 1953 by a squad of federal agents armed with tommy guns and cameras. He was seized, chained to a tree, and left for three hours in the blazing sun.[32] They never caught Gilbert Green or Henry Winston until, concluding that the underground phase was now over, the Party ordered them to surrender to the police. Green gave himself up on February 27, 1956, Winston on March 4. Whereas Thompson had been sentenced to four years for contempt of court, Green and Winston got only three years (in addition to their five-year sentences for conspiracy to advocate).

As for the four "second-string" New York Communists who (also acting on Party instructions) had evaded arrest and trial in 1951, the FBI found only one of them. Sidney Stein was taken in 1953 and accused, along with Samuel Coleman and Mrs. Patricia Blau, of harboring Thompson. For this he was given a three-year sentence. Fred Fine and James E. Jackson surrendered when the Party told them to, in December 1955, and William Norman followed.

In New York the FBI and the Justice Department still had scores to settle. The grand old man and chairman of the Party, William Z. Foster, had achieved the age of seventy-five when, in March 1956, the government moved yet again to prosecute him, but Foster had been examined six times by court-appointed doctors and on each occasion they had reported arteriosclerosis affecting the heart and cerebral circulation. In April Judge Sylvester Ryan ruled that a trial might result in the death of America's leading Bolshevik.

But in May 1956 New York's third Smith Act trial got under way, involving four Communists who had vanished when indicted in 1951, two who were convicted in 1952 but subsequently awarded a retrial, as well as the writer Marion Bachrach (sister of the lawyer John Abt), who was mortally ill of cancer. With a fine sense of discrimination, Judge Alexander Bicks handed down sentences of five, four, three and two years to William Norman, Fred Fine, Sidney Stein and James E. Jackson, and of one year to George Charney and Alexander Trachtenberg. In April 1958 the Court of Appeals for the Second Circuit reversed these convictions. Meanwhile in New Haven the jury acquitted one Communist, Alfred L. Marder, failed to agree on another and convicted six.[33] Eleven CP leaders were indicted in Puerto Rico early in 1956, some of whom were incarcerated for a considerable time in mainland prisons, far from their families, because of the difficulty of raising a total bail of $149,000.

Nineteen fifty-six was a year of almost hectic activity on the part of the authorities—almost as if they realized that their license for repression was terminal. On March 27, the federal Bureau of Internal Revenue raided and seized Party offices in New York, Chicago, San Francisco and Philadelphia, as well as the *Daily Worker* [34] offices in New York, Detroit and Chicago. The seizure of assets was justified on the ground that the *Daily Worker* owed $46,049 in taxes and penalties for the period 1951–53, and that the Party owed $389,265. The seizure of lists of subscribers was also held to be relevant. The whole operation, which was apparently coordinated by the New York regional revenue chief, Donald R. Moysey, so resembled a police riot that not only the liberal press but even such dedicatedly anti-Communist organizations as the American Committee for Cultural Freedom expressed disquiet. The *Daily Worker* meanwhile managed ingeniously to continue publication. A week later, following a hearing before federal Judge Edmund Palmieri, the premises were returned.[35]

## THE MEMBERSHIP TRIALS

In addition to the "conspiracy to advocate" prosecutions under the Smith Act, the Justice Department also brought eight membership prosecutions. Paradoxically, since 1948 membership carried a heavier maximum penalty—ten years—than did advocacy. When the principal Communist leaders came out of prison they were immediately reindicted for "joining an organization to conspire to advocate." The Justice Department, however, chose not to prosecute a second time any of the Foley Square eleven—perhaps because of the double-jeopardy consideration. The first membership prosecution was brought against the secretary of the Illinois CP, Claude Lightfoot, a forty-five-year-old Negro Communist influential among the blacks of Chicago's South Side during the Depression and an Army veteran of the Second World War. Arrested on June 26, 1954, he spent nearly four months in jail before $30,000 could be raised for bail. Refusing to reduce this bail, federal Judge Samuel Perry remarked: "The government needs to produce very little evidence, if any, in order to establish the defendant is guilty of the charge in the indictment." In January 1955 Lightfoot was convicted of being a member of the CP *knowing* that it advocated the violent overthrow of the government. The sentence of five years in prison and a $5,000 fine was upheld by the Supreme Court in January 1956.

In April 1955 began the trial in Greensboro, North Carolina, of Junius Scales, the thirty-five-year-old white secretary of the North and South Carolina CP. Arrested in November 1954, he too was charged with "knowing membership." Three months after the Lightfoot sentence, Scales was given a six-year prison term, the heaviest punishment in any Smith Act case. The prosecution witnesses included not only the perennials like John Lautner and William Cummings, but also Barbara Hartle, brought from prison to sing her way toward a parole, release and a long career as an anti-Communist witness.

In March 1956 the FBI arrested Emanuel Blum in Chicago on a membership charge, while almost simultaneously the top Communists in Massachusetts, Otis A. Hood, Sidney Lipshires, Mrs. Ann B. Timpson, Daniel B. Schirmer and Michael A. Russo, were arrested in different cities. In April John F. Noto was brought to trial in Buffalo, found guilty of membership and sentenced to five years in prison. (The verdict was overturned by the Supreme Court in 1961.) In the same year there opened in Philadelphia the trial of Albert E. Blumberg, aged fifty, a member of the CP since 1933, at one time the Party's legislative director, and a former professor of philosophy at Johns Hopkins University. Blumberg, arrested in New York City on September 30, 1954, having been "underground" since 1949, was accused by a prosecution witness, a Baltimore teacher, of having advocated violent overthrow of the government during lunch—in 1941. He was convicted. His wife, Dorothy Rose Blumberg, had been jailed for conspiracy to advocate after the Baltimore trial in 1953.[36]

It was in July 1957 that the Warren Court handed down its crucial ruling in *Yates v. United States*, effectively reversing the seminal ruling of the Vinson Court in the Dennis case, which had opened the door to the legal persecution of the Communist Party. The Warren Court ruled that, under the Smith Act, advocacy, to be criminal, must be of some future *action*, rather than of the desirability of believing something. The defendants in the Dennis case, argued the Court, had been found guilty of "indoctrination preparatory to action." In fact the Warren Court was now imposing on any future prosecution an insupportable burden of proof. As Judge Chambers of the Ninth Circuit Court of Appeals put it when setting aside the Hawaii and Seattle convictions: "One may as well recognize that the *Yates* decision leaves the Smith Act, as to any further prosecution under it, a virtual shambles."

The Justice Department agreed. Although the Supreme Court ordered the acquittal of only five of the Yates case defendants in California, in December the government announced that it was dropping the case against the remaining nine. The edifice now crumbled rapidly. In Boston a prosecution against seven Communists was dropped; in Puerto Rico the case against the eleven was dismissed; the Detroit six were granted new trials by the Court of Appeals in March 1957, but the government declined to prosecute. Cases were dropped against the Cleveland six, the Philadelphia nine, the Pittsburgh five and the St. Louis five. The Court of Appeals for the Second Circuit overturned the convictions of the Connecticut seven. Only in the Denver case were the original seven convictions reaffirmed in a second trial. In total, at least seventy Smith Act convictions were reversed or referred back and not pursued further, and at least eighteen pending prosecutions were dropped.

In summary, by the end of 1956 there had been 145 indictments under the Smith Act leading to 108 convictions, five severances and ten acquittals. The other cases were pending. The combined sentences totaled 418 years and one day, while the fines amounted to $435,500. And yet, of the 108 actually sentenced, as of June 1, 1958, only twenty-eight of them actually served time in prison *after* conviction, all of them involved in either the Dennis and Flynn cases (New York, 1949 and 1952) or the Frankfeld case (Baltimore, 1952).

Nevertheless, the Supreme Court was to display a renewed loss of nerve in 1961. As a result of the Jencks decision of June 1957, which implied the defense's right of access to the statements of informers contained in FBI files, the Smith Act membership convictions of Claude Lightfoot and Junius Scales were dismissed on appeal. Scales was brought to trial a second time in North Carolina in February 1958, again convicted, and again sentenced to six years' imprisonment. When the case came before the Supreme Court in 1961, the verdict was astonishingly sustained by 5 to 4 on the ground that Scales's utterances and conduct demonstrated that he was both active within the Party and fully conversant with its illegal activity. Yet no violent action was attributed to Scales himself. Douglas, dissenting alongside Warren, Black and Brennan, commented: "Nothing but beliefs are [sic] on trial in this case." Scales's counsel, Telford Taylor, surmises that the ruling would have been different had Arthur Goldberg already replaced Felix Frankfurter on the bench.[37] A year later Scales was set free by John F. Kennedy.

## COMMUNISTS IN PRISON

The Communists who were indicted under the Smith Act and actually entered prison appear to have suffered less from emotional or psychological problems than from physical ones. The hardest hit, naturally, were the elderly and the sick. In September 1955 the Federal Parole Board refused to parole Jacob Mindel, even though he was seventy-four years of age. Alexander Bittelman, who spent five years in Atlanta Penitentiary, was in his middle sixties. Others found the physical regime in prison almost unendurable after a life spent largely in offices. Betty Gannett, imprisoned in the reformatory for women at Alderson, West Virginia, was twice assigned to such heavy manual labor in the storehouse as lifting hundred-pound sacks, even though she was suffering from arthritis and angina. By November 1955 her weight had fallen from 127 to 111 pounds. Claudia Jones, who suffered from an acute asthmatic-cardiac condition which was to lead to her death at an early age, worked a loom with her feet on cement floors in Alderson. After ten months she was committed to a New York hospital. Born in the West Indies and faced with certain deportation after her release, she left for England with the help of a British consul who had visited her in prison and whom she described as "a good guy." Jack Stachel nursed a weak heart in Danbury.

For some it was worse. Henry Winston, one of the eleven leaders convicted in 1949, and later a fugitive, lost his eyesight in prison as a result of neglect and a too-long-delayed operation by prison doctors.[38] Philip Frankfeld, one of the brightest and most self-assured young Communist leaders before and after the war, had been expelled from the Party by the time he was convicted in the Baltimore Smith Act trial of 1953. Beaten up by his fellow prisoners in Atlanta Penitentiary, and treated harshly by the authorities, he came out of prison shrunken and almost blind. His wife, Regina Frankfeld, was imprisoned in Alderson.

But the most scandalous cases of physical maltreatment were

those of Steve Nelson (described in the next chapter) and of the captured fugitive Robert Thompson, one of the three or four most powerful leaders of the Party. In October 1953 Thompson was attacked in prison by a Yugoslav seaman, Alexander Pavlovich, who faced imminent deportation and, he claimed, execution in his own country for having assassinated Communists. Evidently hoping that assassinating one more would win him favor with the authorities, he cracked Thompson's skull with an iron bar. After three operations Thompson was released from prison but died soon afterward. The government refused him a war hero's customary privilege of burial in Arlington Cemetery.

Another source of friction in prison was the racial segregation still more or less universal in federal penitentiaries. John Williamson recalled that in Lewisburg Negroes were confined to separate cell blocks and dining halls, and even to separate seating during movie shows. George Charney, state chairman of the New York CP, who was sent to Lewisburg with V. J. Jerome in January 1955, recalled that racial tensions were high there. Finding himself the victim of segregation in Terre Haute, Benjamin Davis, Jr., protested and was immediately put to work mopping floors. A lawyer by training, he started a court case from prison. As a result he was placed in round-the-clock administrative segregation. The court case failed. Later, in Pittsburgh county jail, he again encountered segregation and again began a court case. Refusal to collaborate with the authorities brought trouble on the heads of several Communist prisoners. John Gates, for example, spent a week on starvation rations in the "hole," a bare cell in Atlanta Penitentiary, because he refused to pull a lever that locked the cells of his fellow prisoners.[39]

Eugene Dennis went to jail twice: in 1950, for contempt of Congress, and in 1951, hot on the heels of his release, for conspiracy to advocate violent overthrow. As general secretary of the Party, Dennis conducted himself in Atlanta as a militant political prisoner. All his mail, in and out, was censored. The warden informed him in September 1951 that his editorial comments on political affairs were contrary to the Bureau of Prisons regulations; henceforward he must not comment on national or international events. This order was reversed in October, allowing him and Gates to discuss in their letters happenings reported in the press—but not to send any "directives" to the CP. Only two visits per month were allowed. On learning that his nine-year-old son, Gene, was suffering from name-calling at school, Dennis wrote to him, recommending Hemingway's *The Old Man and the Sea*, as good for young and old alike, and enclosing a poem of his own:

*For Gene is a fine young son of the people*
*And as he grows tall and straight as the steeple*
*He will be proud to have the whole world know*
*That he fights for justice and peace, against the people's foe.*

The Party's senior woman leader, Elizabeth Gurley Flynn, already in her sixties, was locked up in the Women's House of Detention, in New York City, five times between 1951 and 1955. "The vile language, the fights, the disgusting lesbian performances, were unbearable." Arriving in Alderson with Betty Gannett and Claudia Jones in January 1955, she found she was allowed only five correspondents, not including her attorneys, each one requiring clearance with the FBI. It took a visit from James Bennett, head of the Federal Bureau of Prisons, before she was allowed paper for writing anything but letters.

To protect the interests and minimum comforts of these political prisoners, the Families Committee of Smith Act Victims was set up, with Mrs. Peggy Dennis as chairman. The families themselves experienced, on the whole, rather less ostracism and hostility from their local communities than might have been expected. George Charney recalled that although a Jewish taxi-driver neighbor stared at him with evident hatred, his children did not experience humiliations in school or on the block. On the other hand, Eugene Dennis's son, as we have seen, did. When the California Communist leader Rose Chernin was arrested, some neighbors would not let her eleven-year-old daughter into their houses. But the partly black community in whose Parent-Teacher Association she was active remained loyal to her and her husband. She recalls that Dorothy Healey and Ben Dobbs were similarly protected. When the Smith Act bail was reduced to $20,000, friends and neighbors lined up to give money.[40]

The shadow of the FBI was a long one. While out on bail, Simon Gerson took his family to the beach; the FBI followed. Gerson recalls that Alexander Trachtenberg enjoyed making his trackers sit through his favorite Soviet films two or three times. On one occasion, when Louis Weinstock was changing trains, the FBI men, half obligingly and half to save themselves an unnecessary journey, pointed out to him he was about to take the wrong one. In the case of the fugitive James Jackson, the FBI called on his children's teachers at school. Wives of husbands on the run were persistently followed to supermarkets and the houses of friends; Communist wives who had of necessity to support their children found that the FBI constantly harassed their employers.

But the FBI was not the only source of fear. Every government

agency and Congressional committee had its agents, its security officers (often former FBI men), prowling, probing, dropping hints. For
some, it was all too much. Just as blacklisted film stars took wing for
England and Europe, so did those Communists who could afford to
uproot themselves cross into Mexico (no passport was required) and
settle in Mexico City or small, picturesque communities like Cuerna-
vaca and San Miguel de Allende. There they tended to launch successful business enterprises and make a lot of money.[41]

## THE COMMUNIST UNDERGROUND

The life led by those Communist militants who went "underground"
was a thing apart, a B movie. This American Communist "underground" was unusual, perhaps unique, in that the "fugitives," apart
from the eight leaders who jumped bail or evaded arrest, were in no
way acting outside the law. The Party was not strictly illegal, they
were not engaged in sabotage or terrorism, and no warrant had been
issued for their arrest. But, expecting the Reichstag to burn again at
any moment, they played cat and mouse with the FBI.

According to Starobin, the decision to commit a sector of the
Party apparatus to a clandestine existence and to set up a dual leadership was originally taken in 1947. Early in 1949 the CP stopped issuing
membership cards and destroyed its central membership list. A severe
loyalty check of every member followed. In 1950–51 the underground
militants were assigned to units of three to five members, with orders
to destroy all written documents after reading them. The decision to
keep eight leading Communists at liberty was an integral part of this
scheme, heavily supported by Foster, Davis and Thompson, who argued that a long period of fascism lay ahead and that the American
Party must model itself on the successful underground *apparat* developed by Lenin and by the Italian and Japanese CP's. Above all, the
fate of the German Communists must be avoided.

Minor Party leaders now said goodbye to their families and disappeared, assuming new names and appearances in the proverbial spy-
film fashion. George Charney described "Eric Ambler escapades, dis-
guises, and a system of contacts that relied on simple devices like a
red rose or a *Life* Magazine . . ." False driving licenses and social
security cards were forged. J. Edgar Hoover informed a horrified public about the life of the underground Communists with their false
names and changed physical appearances, their dyed hair and, sometimes, surgery to remove identifying marks—"a nightmare of deceit,
fear, and tension . . ." According to Hoover's account, Communist
women entered beauty parlors as blondes and came out as brunettes

at six dollars a time, "and two dollars extra for eyebrow dye." These masters of deceit hopped yellow lights, turned corners at high speeds, jumped out of their cars and walked up one-way streets against the traffic, leapt out of subway trains at the last minute, and cunningly used store windows as reflectors. During a "scramble" after a meeting they would enter one car, abruptly get out of it and leap into another car and away.[42] Yet similar behavior, when practiced by FBI agents, was nightly admired by millions of American television viewers.

Early in July 1951 the Party's organizational department publicly announced that all members who had not reregistered would be dropped, and that henceforth the CP would operate as a "cadre organization," a skeletal force. (In fact, the CP "overground" continued to operate quite openly and almost normally.) The underground itself was, according to Starobin, divided into three categories of cadres: (a) the "deep freeze," which included those who had evaded jail or trial, as well as several hundred not yet indicted but liable to be; (b) the "deep, deep freeze," consisting of those trusted cadres who were instructed to change their lives completely (many of them moved to Mexico, Canada or Europe) and to be ready to take over if all other levels of the leadership were arrested; (c) the OBU, "operative but unavailable" militants who moved about the country, often in disguise, and acted as liaison between the open Party and the "deep freeze" leadership.

The cost, financial and emotional, was high. "Vast sums of money, probably running into millions of dollars, were expended for the lodging, the transportation, and the conclaves of different cadres." Several thousand left their families, there were scores of nervous and mental breakdowns, and many broken homes. When Martha Stone, the forty-four-year-old underground leader of the New Jersey CP, was arrested by the FBI in the Bronx in November 1954, it was learned that she had left her husband and six-year-old son in 1951 and had not emerged from hiding even when her son went into hospital after an automobile accident, or when her father died. The California Party, much to the anger of Foster, regarded the whole strategy as dangerous and futile, but was not able to dispense with it entirely.

To what extent was it futile? Although the militants of the underground made elaborate studies of FBI techniques and often carried about with them long lists of FBI car license plates (forcing the FBI in turn to rent cars commercially), in the majority of cases the FBI agents were able periodically to demonstrate that they knew all about it. David Englestein, an Illinois Communist who left his family, was tracked to work at regular intervals by agents who wished only to prove that they were there. Englestein recalls a comrade in the underground who one day sat down for a cup of coffee in a drugstore and was joined by two FBI agents who informed him—with corroborating detail—that they had been shadowing him for four years. They then offered him $50,000 if he would reveal the hiding places of Gilbert Green and Henry Winston.[43]

A colorful anecdotalist of the underground experience is the journalist Sam Kushner, now a resident of Los Angeles. Having joined the CP in 1933, Kushner worked as a lathe operator and business agent of the militant Local 111, UE, in Chicago, before committing himself to full-time Party work in 1949. In the early fifties he wrote for the Chicago edition of the *Daily Worker* while leading a semiclandestine existence as leader of the Party's trade-union wing in the city. Separated for five years from his family, whom he met only occasionally with the help of an elaborate system of couriers and weekend picnics, he lived with a worker whose main Party assignment was to protect Kushner's anonymity. To bluff or shake off the inevitable pursuit squad became the obsessive central thread of the human condition; a journey to New York, for example, involved a complicated mesh of nighttime diversionary subjourneys, together with fatigue, loneliness and, on one occasion, being informed by a friendly baggage man that the box he was sitting on contained a "stiff."

In Chicago, says Kushner, you could buy anything: all the driving licenses, social-security cards and other documents he carried were false. Even so, the agents were never far away. One night he kept a date to meet a comrade in a restaurant. The comrade warned him that he had been followed; Kushner was angry—the comrade should not have kept the rendezvous. Stepping outside, he spotted several FBI cars from the list of license plates he carried in his pocket. He headed for a movie; they followed; he took a subway train, then another, still they followed. Finally he began to run, hailed a cab, and shouted at the black driver, "I'm in trouble with my wife, put your meter down, I'll give you five dollars for five blocks."

He emerged from the underground phase in 1955–56, when it was generally liquidated. But the FBI continued the B-movie game with him for years afterward; what better had they to do?

Although some Party leaders now agree that the danger of fascism was overestimated and that far too much emphasis was laid on keeping members "unavailable"—that a more open and direct approach would have been preferable—there are still those, like the San Francisco lawyer Aubrey Grossman, who argue that the underground was both necessary and effective and succeeded in preventing the FBI from arresting a further three hundred leaders, which would have smashed the Party.[44]

## Public Opinion—A Pattern of Intolerance

If opinion polls in any measure reflect the spread of public opinion, then neither the harassment of left-wing groups nor the hounding of the Communist Party prompted any appreciable opposition among the American people at large. On the contrary, one can assume at least tacit approval. The Cold War—leaving aside the question of responsibility for it—aggravated a tradition of intolerance. Whereas in June 1946 outlawing the CP and legally prohibiting membership in it was favored by 44 percent of respondents to a Gallup poll, by 1949 the figure was 68 percent.[45]

An extensive survey conducted under the direction of Professor Samuel A. Stouffer, of Harvard, and published in 1954, showed 52 percent of a national cross section in favor of imprisoning *all* Communists (other polls yielded an even higher percentage). Eighty percent wanted to strip all Communists of their citizenship. A poll taken in 1952 showed 77 percent of respondents agreeing that Communists should be banned from the radio. But this massive intolerance was not focused on Communists alone: 45 percent would not allow Socialists to publish their own newspapers, and 42 percent wanted to deny to the press the right to criticize the "American form of government."

Yet only 3 percent of Stouffer's national cross section claimed ever to have met an avowed Communist, although a further 10 percent harbored suspicions about a certain person. And why?

He was always talking about world peace. (Housewife, Oregon.)

I saw a map of Russia on the wall in his home. (Locomotive engineer, Michigan.)

Just his slant on community life and church work. He was not like us. (Bank vice-president, Texas.)

He brought a lot of foreign-looking people into his home. (Housewife, Kansas.)

And so on.[46]

# 10

## Hell in Pittsburgh

The violent epicenter of the anti-Communist eruption in postwar America was the steel city of Pittsburgh, in western Pennsylvania. Here, among the Polish, Croatian and Hungarian proletarian communities, the American Slav Congress and kindred nationality groups of the Left had by 1945 built up a considerable reservoir of sympathy for the Communist-Soviet position. Russia's postwar actions in Eastern Europe rapidly reversed the current of sentiment, provoking a violent backlash, a strident assertion of Americanism and a wave of indignation in response to the martyrdom of Cardinal Mindszenty and Archbishop Stepinac.

From 1947 onward the press was pumping anti-Communism into every artery of Pittsburgh. From April 11 until April 30, 1948, the Scripps-Howard *Pittsburgh Press* published the names, addresses and places of employment of about one thousand citizens who had signed Wallace nominating petitions. At the great Westinghouse plant a campaign conducted by Father Charles Owen Rice and the Association of Catholic Trade Unionists, vigorously supported by the priests from their pulpits, culminated in a victory for the anti-Communist IUE-CIO, led by James B. Carey, over the pro-Communist United Electrical Workers.

In 1950 J. Edgar Hoover announced that there were 2,876 Communists in Pennsylvania. Presumably this figure included Hoover's numerous undercover agents within the Party, the most celebrated of whom, Matt Cvetic, emerged from his disguise in February 1950 and named about three hundred alleged Communists from western Pennsylvania and thirty-five from eastern Ohio during highly publicized hearings before HCUA. Cvetic, who had a background in military intelligence, had joined the Party in 1943 on behalf of the FBI. Destined to appear as a witness at least sixty-three times and to name at least five hundred people, he claimed that he had been privy to Wallace's back-room caucuses on strategy and that he had tried to "trap" Wallace by offering to secure him the votes of the American Slav Congress. (A meaningless boast.)

No sooner had Cvetic begun to name his victims than the *Pittsburgh Press*, Hearst's *Pittsburgh Sun-Telegraph*, the *Pittsburgh Post-Gazette* and other local papers joined in the witch hunt by blazoning the names, addresses and employers of the red termites across their pages. Nearly one hundred people lost their jobs in short time,[1] notably at U.S. Steel, Etna Steel, and the Crucible Steel Company. In March 1950, for example, Alice C. Roth was fired by the American Coin-A-Matic Machine Company and then dismissed as a grand juror after the *Pittsburgh Press* and the *Post-Gazette* had publicized Cvetic's indictment of her. More or less simultaneously, Paul H. Morrison was fired by the Hanan Corporation after the *Sun-Telegraph* performed the same service for him. Many workers were ostracized, were refused credit at local stores, saw their kids abused or attacked at school, were denied state welfare benefits, or were threatened with denaturalization or deportation. As this steel city began to boom with the Korean war orders, the fever rose: perhaps two hundred people had to leave town.

A number of men whom Cvetic "fingered" were expelled from their unions. Nick Lazari and George Nichols were instructed by Local 237 of the Hotel and Restaurant Alliance (AFL) to deny the charges or resign. They resigned. A young veteran was forced to resign his position with the AFL after Cvetic named his father as a Communist; indeed, a few unions even asked Cvetic to inspect their membership lists.

## NELSON, MUSMANNO AND CVETIC

The red bogeyman of the Pittsburgh area was a carpenter called Stephen Mesarosh. Under the internationally famous name of Steve Nelson he had attended the Lenin School in Moscow, served as a Party leader in the anthracite coal district, been wounded while fighting for Loyalist Spain and then, in the early forties, moved to the Bay Area of California. It was from this latter period that many rumors stemmed—mainly his supposed contacts with Soviet agents like a cer-

tain Vassili Zubilin and with two or three young physicists working at
the Berkeley Radiation Laboratory. By 1950 he was chairman of the
Western Pennsylvania Communist Party, a remarkable and charis-
matic leader admired by militants who knew him as kind, open and
compassionate. And he was tough.

In June 1950, the month of the outbreak of the Korean war, a
leading Pittsburgh radical lawyer called Hymen Schlesinger was arrested at a bus station in the city, handcuffed, taken to jail, denied an
attorney, and assaulted by a guard in the presence of a state judge
called Michael Angelo Musmanno, who had supervised his arrest and
of whom we shall hear more. Schlesinger happened to be Nelson's
lawyer, and the campaign against him involved disbarment charges
brought by the local bar association. A year later, when Schlesinger
was in court to try a trespass case, Musmanno, as presiding judge,
abruptly demanded that the attorney answer questions concerning
CP membership. Schlesinger refused, Musmanno ruled that he was
"morally unfit to try a case in this courtroom" and held him in contempt—whereupon the Supreme Court of Pennsylvania granted a
writ of prohibition against Musmanno. It was Judge Michael Angelo
Musmanno who had barred Mrs. Alice Roth from serving on a grand
jury after Cvetic had accused her of being a Communist and she had
taken the Fifth Amendment; [2] here again Musmanno's action was
later condemned as illegal by the Pennsylvania Supreme Court.

As a young man, Musmanno had studied law in Mussolini's Italy,
whence he had written a letter to the *Pittsburgh Press* referring to
"the heroic work of the Fascisti in driving Bolshevism from the country when the Fascisti began their purification of Italian soil . . ." On
the other hand, he had championed the cause of Sacco and Vanzetti,
declared himself a friend of organized labor, embraced the New
Deal, and been regarded as sufficiently free of Fascist taint to sit as a
judge at Nuremberg. Nevertheless, Musmanno who, with two of his
fellow Pennsylvania judges, Blair F. Gunther and Harry M. Montgomery, belonged to a vigilante organization called Americans Battling Communism—closely allied to the powerful Alesandroni of the
Legion's Americanism Commission—was not only a registered Democrat but also an unregistered demogogue. Nelson recalled him
"strutting up Liberty Avenue at the head of the St. Patrick's Day parade, raising his knees in majorette fashion . . ." [3]

On August 31, 1950, Musmanno shed his judge's robes, donned
his sheriff's hat and led a posse in a raid on Steve Nelson's office at
Party headquarters. Having seized a heap of papers and documents,
some of which he later dispatched to HCUA, he marched to the office of another Allegheny County judge and requested him to issue a
warrant for Nelson's arrest under the state's sedition law, which dated

back to 1919 and had been unused for almost twenty years. The trial
of Nelson, Andrew Onda and James Dolsen began in 1951, but Nelson was severed from the case following a serious car accident. During the trial the local press lampooned the defense and published
hearsay accusations linking Nelson to wartime atomic espionage. To
encourage the jury a bit, and perhaps to dramatize the judicial culture
then prevailing, United States marshals chose the moment that Onda
was making his final statement to the jury to arrest him and Dolsen
under the Smith Act. How could a jury acquit in the face of such
theater? It couldn't. On August 31, 1951, Dolsen, the sixty-eight-year-
old Pittsburgh correspondent of the *Daily Worker*, and Onda were
sentenced to twenty years' imprisonment and a fine of $10,000 for a
crime—in fact, neither man had done anything at all—that Judge
Henry X. O'Brien characterized as "worse than murder" and comparable to that of the Rosenbergs. So low did the American judiciary
then sink.

Now it was Nelson's turn. While convalescing, he and five other
Pennsylvania Communists, including, as we have seen, Onda and
Dolsen, were arrested under the Smith Act, but Musmanno and
Montgomery were determined to get the first bite at the cake. In December 1951 Nelson's postponed state sedition trial opened, following
a terrific but fruitless battle before Judge Montgomery for delay on
the ground that Nelson had approached twenty-five lawyers in the
area and written to a further fifty in several cities, but without avail.
Somewhat unethically, Nelson later not only quoted but also named
the lawyers who had at least honored him with a reply. One of them
wrote, "I am not in a position to make the sacrifice that would be
required." A second explained, "I am sympathetic in your present
circumstances, and particularly I regret that my commitments which
are many . . . I am the nominee of the Democratic Party of Philadelphia for our City Council." Nelson, in fact, was making hay; he was
ideally cut out to play the role of Dimitrov at his own trial, and he did
receive help from two left-wing lawyers, Bertram Edises of California
and Victor Rabinowitz of New York.

Nevertheless, the defendant's chances in *Pennsylvania v. Nelson*
became slender to the point of invisibility when Musmanno appeared
as a witness with a pile of books, maps and magazines he had seized
from Nelson's office, including a copy of *Masses and Mainstream* that
contained a cartoon depicting the devastation of Korea by United
States forces. Declared Musmanno, "I regard those books as more
dangerous than any firearms." Another factor militating against Nelson was the extraordinary hysteria surrounding Matt Cvetic, whom
Nelson described in court as "a degenerate, shifty-eyed barfly." On
April 19, 1951, the Stanley Theater, Pittsburgh, had witnessed the

world premiere of the film, *I Was a Communist for the FBI*, attended by Mayor Lawrence, who declared April 19 to be Matt Cvetic Day at a special luncheon held in his honor at the William Penn Hotel. (After lunch a parade formed in front of the Allegheny County Courthouse, where the Dolsen-Onda sedition trial happened to be in progress.)

In the Pittsburgh area, however, the concept of a mistrial because of a climate of prejudice was unknown; not even the fact that the Cvetic film depicted Nelson, by name, committing a fictitious murder was considered relevant. In court Cvetic justified the inclusion of this incident by claiming that Nelson had once confided to him that "there would be a liquidation of one third of the United States population." Cross-examined by Nelson, Cvetic revealed that he had been paid $18,000 for serial and motion-picture rights (it was also a successful radio serial), of which he himself had retained 40 percent, the rest being shared by his ghost writer and his agent-manager Harry Sherman, local vice-president of Americans Battling Communism, the organization to which trial judge Montgomery belonged.[4]

In Pittsburgh there was no way out. On the eve of the trial verdict a juror named Roman, drinking in a bar, proclaimed his belief in Nelson's innocence. After a thorough beating, he was brought into court painted in iodine, accompanied by detectives, and no longer convinced of Nelson's innocence. Montgomery then handed down not only the maximum sentence of twenty years' imprisonment and a $10,000 fine, which was predictable, but also ordered that Nelson should pay the court costs of $13,291, which covered the expenses of Matt Cvetic and his fellow prosecution witnesses. Later this conviction was affirmed by the Pennsylvania Superior Court, but was reversed, 5 to 2, by the State Supreme Court on the ground that the state's Sedition Act had been superseded by the Smith Act. Musmanno and State Attorney General Truscott lodged an appeal to the U.S. Supreme Court, which upheld the Pennsylvania Supreme Court in April 1956.

However, this is to jump ahead, and time did not move so fast for Nelson. Sentenced to twenty years in prison and awaiting his trial under the Smith Act, he was sent to Blawnox Workhouse, where, as the saying goes, they were waiting for him. As Nelson described it, "The administration followed medieval practices in handling prisoners, who were treated as subhuman, beaten at will by the guards, thrown in the hole and kept on bread and water for nine days at a time. The food was very bad; the medical set-up was frighteningly bad . . . Negro prisoners were discriminated against in the bathhouse, kitchen, hospital and bakery." Nelson's wife was allowed to visit him only once a month, for thirty minutes. At one stage he was put in "the hole," a cell completely empty except for a seatless commode which was flushed once every twenty-four hours: no bed, no chair, no water. He left the hole "starved, dirty, unshaven, sore-footed, naked." The local press ran stories in January 1953 charging him with responsibility for prison riots at Blawnox, whose Superintendent, Lawrence P. Keenan, was quoted as saying, "Nelson is pretty clever. He never does anything himself and stays in the background." When a fire broke out at the workhouse, the press naturally linked him to that.[5] In preparation for the Smith Act trial he was transferred to the city jail, then back to Blawnox and the hole, where he was kept during a course of penicillin injections for an infected ear. His main comfort was the letters he received from Spanish Civil War veterans in many countries.

When the Smith Act trial opened, Nelson's was not the only familiar face. William A. Cercone, a nephew of Musmanno and the prosecutor in the sedition trial, now appeared as a special assistant to the U.S. Attorney General. The defendants, Onda, Nelson, L. Careathers, Dolsen, William Albertson[6] and Irving Weissman, all of whom had been arrested in August 1951 (Weissman in the main reading room of the New York Public Library), made strenuous efforts to prove that the prejudice in the area was so intense that the trial should be moved. To no avail. Prosecution witnesses included Cvetic, on whose chest the Pennsylvania Legion's Americanism Award had now been pinned by Governor John S. Fine and Miss America, but also the FBI undercover agent Joseph Mazzei, whom Cvetic had in ignorance denounced as a Communist in 1950.

## ENTER MAZZEI

Mazzei, no less than Cvetic, was a flamboyant character, a plump movie-theater manager now making his debut as a professional informer. Like Cvetic's, his sex life seemed to be murky; in November 1952 he pleaded guilty to adultery and bastardy in Allegheny County Criminal Court; the following year he was arrested for molesting a young boy in the movie theater he ran. Claiming that he had served as an FBI agent in the Pittsburgh CP from 1941 to March 26, 1953, he boasted that he had been trained by the CP to blow up bridges and poison water reservoirs "and how to—in other words, how to eliminate people. We even done that, sir." From the FBI, said Mazzei, he had received "a salary plus expenses. My expenses sometimes would go almost a thousand dollars a month." [7] (But the FBI's records showed that he had been paid only $172.05 as expense money from 1942 to 1952.)

Now the Immigration Service of the Justice Department had assumed the burden of supporting him. Final condemnation of Mazzei came from the mouth of the Solicitor General of the United States, who in October 1956 argued that the testimony Mazzei gave against Steve Nelson was probably true, but that he had become "a psychiatric case" thereafter and had perjured himself so often that the Nelson case should be remanded to a lower court. But the Supreme Court did not accept the Solicitor General's convenient distinction between the truthful Mazzei and the fantasist Mazzei; said Chief Justice Warren, "Mazzei, by his testimony, has poisoned the water in this reservoir and the reservoir cannot be cleansed without draining it of all impurity." In October 1956 the Supreme Court ordered that the five Communists convicted in the Nelson case (*Mesarosh v. United States*) must be tried afresh. Eleven months later the government dropped the case for good, following the recantation of yet another prosecution witness, seventy-three-year-old Alexander Wright.

In Pittsburgh the witch hunt persisted for years. In November 1953 the SISS sent a task force under Senator John M. Butler into the city to hear Cvetic, Mazzei, Cvetic's manager Harry Alan Sherman, and William Harris of the Legion denounce Communist influence within the United Electrical Workers locals in Pittsburgh and Erie. The subpoena of John W. Nelson, an official of UE's Local 506 at the Erie plant of General Electric, was the bugle call for a new wave of mass firings. Pittsburgh was the worst area for "run-outs." On March 30, 1954, Westinghouse dismissed Thomas J. Fitzpatrick, former president of UE Local 601, and Frank Pazio, former UE business agent in East Pittsburgh. In January 1955 Westinghouse Electric in Pittsburgh dismissed five workers named as Communists before McCarthy's Permanent Subcommittee on Investigations. It was two months later when the black Communist leader Benjamin Davis, Jr., was taken straight to Pittsburgh county jail on his release from a federal penitentiary, to serve a sixty-day sentence for contempt handed down to him when he testified as a defense witness for Nelson.

The year 1955 was a bad one for the master informer Matt Cvetic. Having been committed in a Pittsburgh psychiatric ward for chronic alcoholism, he complained of the hard, thankless life that befell a patriot. (His victims had accumulated prison sentences totaling eighty-five years.) In July the Court of Appeals unanimously described Cvetic's testimony in the deportation case of Matthew Brzovich as "unbelievable and incredible," and dismissed the case. [8]

In 1956 the disbarment action against the lawyer Hymen Schlesinger came before the Pennsylvania Supreme Court. The National Lawyers Guild argued, as *amicus curiae*, that there was no record either of revolutionary activity on his behalf or of advocacy of it, or even of approval. To the chagrin of Supreme Court Justice Musmanno, who was obliged to stand down, Schlesinger's disbarment was reversed in 1961. Yet Musmanno rode into action again, supported by HCUA, the SISS, the Legion, the VFW, and other interested parties, when it was revealed that the University of Pittsburgh was employing a professor, Robert Colodny, who had fought in Spain on the Republican side.[9]

# 11

## The Deportation Terror

A nation of immigrants developed a great fear of the immigrant; hyphenated Americans strove to become hyper-Americans. The quest for "Americanism," the hunting-down of "Un-Americans," reflected the insecurities, the historic fragmentation of the national culture. But it was a class question too, firmly embedded in an economic system that taught the survival of the fittest, which for the majority implied middle-class and petit bourgeois conformism: the standard portfolio—a house of one's own in the suburbs, a car, insurance policies, a bank account, a few shares even—that distinguished Mr. Citizen from the tenement proletarian. Each generation, climbing desperately away and upward from the port of entry, turned its back on the scum of Europe following in the next wave. The cry "enough" translated itself finally into the immigration acts of the early twenties.

But even after the doors were closed, strains persisted, mirrored in the patriotic parades, the ostentatious flag-waving, the bombastic rhetoric. By 1950 there were still 10.3 million foreign-born citizens, and a further two or three million aliens, residing in the United States. As a representative of the Daughters of the American Revolution put it to the Dickstein Committee in 1945, Communists could so easily infiltrate and subvert the southwestern part of Chicago: "Slavish nationalities, Italians, Jewish section . . . this group of not-desirables."

Before a Senate subcommittee chaired by Pat McCarran, a succession of anti-Communist witnesses paraded to testify about the links between Communism and the Slavs, the Finns, the Puerto Ricans, the Jews. In the proletarian 10th Congressional District (New York City), red teachers were said to be doubling voter registration lists by helping hundreds of immigrants to pass their literacy tests—apparently a subversive enterprise. A Russian émigré, J. Anthony Marcus, vividly expressed the composite nightmare lurking in the shadows of the American Celebration:

> Prior to the First World War, countless thousands of immigrants came here without any intention of becoming full-fledged members of this democracy . . . Since the conclusion of the First World War a new type has made his way here . . . stirring up political and labor troubles among their compatriots, promising paradise on earth à la Stalin . . . Crowding into our congested cities they formed islands within this country . . . a little Poland, Russia, Hungary, Romania . . . all over the continent.

How easily the Communists could blackmail those with relatives still living in Eastern Europe!

> It is such an innocent little thing to filch a blueprint or a ship drawing or a chemical process and send it over to one's native country.[1]

This diabolical link between Communism and the alien was one that greatly preoccupied Attorney General Tom Clark, who commissioned a socio-ethnic study of 4,984 leading Party members. Of these (so he reported in 1947) 78 percent of the whites were of "foreign stock" compared to only 30 percent of all white Americans; 56 percent were born in Russia or its neighbors or had at least one parent born there or were married to a person of that derivation. Only 9 percent had the stars and stripes tattooed on their umbilical cords—native-born of native stock and married to the same.

The connection was real enough: the CP leadership was teeming with Jews from Eastern Europe. Probably no aspect of the great purge met with such universal approval as the deportation drive—send 'em back to Russia. The Internal Security Act of 1950 and the Immigration and Nationality Act of 1952 set the Congressional seal on widespread xenophobia. People were afraid, and also ashamed; a survey taken in 1954 found that 20 percent of white people would not say where their ancestors came from. McCarthyism was the umbrella held out to all Americans, a repudiation of the Other (the alien), even when the Other was the Self.

Attorney General Clark automatically listed as Communist fronts the organizations and associations that fostered pro-Soviet sentiment among Americans of East European origin.[2] At the same time a range of Congressional committees sought to ostracize and pillory these bodies by subpoenaing their officers, linking them to East European embassies, and hinting at dark plots. In the summer of 1949 the Senate Judiciary Subcommittee on Immigration and Naturalization, directed by Senator Pat McCarran and the ever-vigilant staff director Richard Arens, paraded a number of anti-Communist defectors from Poland, Slovakia, Rumania, Hungary and Yugoslavia, who related sinister plots to subvert the hyphenated fifth column. The chief target of the subcommittee was the influential American Slav Congress, whose executive secretary, George Pirinsky, was simultaneously subpoenaed and proceeded against for deportation. (By 1951 the Slav Congress had been driven to dissolve itself.) The harassment continued into the middle fifties. In October 1955, for example, an SISS subcommittee visited Chicago to probe Communist influence in the foreign-language press, and in June of the following year the Rumanian-American Publishing Association of Detroit was indicted by a grand jury for failing to register under the Foreign Agents Registration Act.

## DENATURALIZATION: LOSS OF CITIZENSHIP

But the cutting edge of the terror was intensely personal—the threat to deprive radicals of their citizenship, to deprive aliens of their residence permits, and physically to deport them. The Immigration and Nationality Act[3] of 1952 provided the Immigration Service with a powerful weapon, and both Democratic and Republican Attorneys General rejoiced in their new powers. In October 1952 McGranery announced a drive to denaturalize racketeers and Communists, and in March of the following year Brownell informed the Friendly Sons of St. Patrick that about 10,000 naturalized citizens suspected of subversive affiliations were under investigation. At that time the American Committee for the Protection of the Foreign Born was defending over thirty cases that had come to the boil, but many more foreign-born radicals were in touch with the ACPFB following frightening interviews with FBI agents and officials of the Immigration Service.

Leading Communists indicted under the Smith Act were prime targets. In California denaturalization proceedings were launched against such notable leaders as William Schneiderman, Al Richmond (editor of the *Daily People's World*) and Rose Chernin, but all these cases were defended successfully. On the East Coast, Smith Act victims who were accorded the additional excitement of denaturalization actions included Louis·Weinstock, V. J. Jerome, Isidore Begun, Sidney Steinberg (or Stein) and Simon Gerson. Not that Gerson himself was eligible for such victimization, but the Justice Department was sufficiently piqued by his acquittal in the *Flynn* trial to make an example of his Ukrainian-born wife, Sophie Gerson. That the Department's primary preoccupation was publicity was suggested by a preparatory leak to the witch-hunting, ex-Communist, Hearst columnist Howard Rushmore: "Simon W. Gerson . . . is still sounding off. His tirade against American justice probably will be broadened to include the Immigration Service in the near future when a close relative is seized for deportation to her native Poland" (sic). Finally the government dropped its case against Sophie Gerson and twenty-three other naturalized Americans, but not before a federal judge had reminded her that if she didn't like America she should go back to Russia.[4]

Left-wing trade-union leaders were also prime targets. Leonard Costa, president of an Amalgamated Clothing Workers, CIO, local claimed that he was American-born, but the Immigration Service thought otherwise and tried to send him back to Sicily. Louis J. Braverman, a waterfront official of Russian origin, was accused of having been a Communist prior to his naturalization in 1931. Of the leaders of the militantly pro-Communist United Electrical Workers, James Lustig was subjected to denaturalization proceedings twenty-eight years after he became a citizen, while James J. Matles, director of organization in the union, had his citizenship revoked in March 1957 by federal Judge Walter Bruchhausen on the ground that he had lied in denying Communist affiliations when naturalized in 1934. But Matles hailed from Rumania, a country that refused to accept American deportees, and he has continued until this day to lead UE's affairs.

Because denaturalization is a judicial procedure accompanied by due-process safeguards, it is relatively hard to achieve. It has been estimated that only thirteen *political* denaturalization actions succeeded between 1945 and 1956 (the victims had, on average, lived for thirty-eight years in the United States). But the word "succeeded" is deceptive. The Justice Department's aim, after all, was to harass and frighten radicals to the point where the light was no longer worth the candle. A classic case of such tactics in action, and of the hookup between local vested interests and the Justice Department was that of Stanley Nowak, a Polish-born radical who had lived in America since 1913, when he was ten. Having made his mark in the thirties as an organizer in the UAW-CIO, in the front line of the industrial working-class wars, Nowak was elected state Senator for Michigan's 21st Senatorial District in 1938. Reelected four times, he held the post as a registered Democrat for ten years, the only radical in the state Sen-

ate. Nowak made powerful enemies. Not only was he active in the
American Slav Congress and obviously very close to the CP, but he
also denounced conditions in the automobile industry and the job-
selling racket which prevailed at nonunion Ford. In December 1942
U.S. District Attorney John C. Lehr made himself the spokesman of
local pressure groups by arresting Nowak on a charge of having falsely
sworn that he did not belong to any organization "teaching disbelief"
in organized government when he became a citizen in 1937. Attorney
General Francis Biddle intervened despite Lehr's furious opposition,
and the charge was dropped.

In 1952, however, they tried again under the Walter-McCarran
Act, and on this occasion the Attorney General was not sympathetic.
During the intervening years Nowak had run for the Detroit Com-
mon Council and in the Democratic primary for the 16th U.S.
Congressional District, red-baited by the *Detroit News* and campaign
rivals but spurred on by John Abt, general counsel of the Progressive
Party and a leading CP lawyer. Nowak called for withdrawal from
Korea and a renewal of FDR's policy of Soviet-American friendship.
He didn't get elected.

In a denaturalization trial that began in July 1954, the government relied on professional informers with curiously erratic memories
to swear that Nowak had been a Communist in 1937. Nowak's citizenship was canceled in July 1955, and the Court of Appeals sustained this ruling. In an *amicus curiae* brief, the National Lawyers
Guild argued before the Supreme Court that the current assumptions
that naturalized citizens were less privileged than the native born was
unconstitutional, as was the habit of treating them as wards of investigators and judges. The Court reversed the ruling against Nowak.[5]

## STATISTICAL SURVEY

The two and a half million aliens who resided in the United States in
1950 were, of course, far more vulnerable to deportation than were
naturalized citizens. In the pages that follow, over 130 cases of attempted deportation will be alluded to. Some of these cases resulted
in the actual physical ejection of the alien from American territory
(this was true of at least twenty-six of the cases mentioned below, and
probably more) but most of them did not. Many of those whose appeals failed with the Board of Immigration Appeals nevertheless could
not be deported, because no foreign country would accept them.
Alien Communists from Britain or the British West Indies were far
more vulnerable to actual deportation than those from the USSR and
Eastern Europe.

The statistics demonstrate that the outbreak of xenophobia during and immediately after the First World War was more drastic, direct and brutal in its consequences than was the slow, patient, persistent battle of attrition waged by the Truman and Eisenhower administrations against resident alien Communists. From February 1917 until November 1919, sixty aliens were deported for political reasons. On December 21, 1919, 249 "anarchists" and "subversives" were shipped out of New York on the *Buford*,[6] and in 1920–21 a further 591 aliens were deported. From 1945 to 1954, by contrast, only 163 "subversives" were actually deported.

Nevertheless if we are correct in assuming that what the Justice Department had in mind was to intimidate radicals of foreign birth, the number of actions instituted is almost as significant as the number of actual deportations. By the end of 1949, the Truman administration had arrested 140 "political" aliens for deportation in nineteen states; by December 1951, 205 (only six of whom had been living in America for less than twenty years); by 1953, some 300 had been arrested for deportation. In California alone, 190 "subversive" aliens were arrested for deportation from 1948 to 1956. Although only three of the latter were actually deported, forty-six of the others did not have the charges against them dropped until 1964. Protracted anxiety, periods of imprisonment, and possible loss of employment extended over a period of ten or fifteen years—this was not a fate widely envied.

A study of 307 political deportation cases up to 1956 revealed that 60 percent had lived in America for more than forty years, and 81 percent for more than thirty years. Slightly over half had children who were American citizens, and 92 had grandchildren who were American citizens. Of these 307, at least 173 had attempted without success to become citizens and a further seventy-eight had applications pending. As many as sixty-two could not read or speak the language of their country of birth.[7]

## DEPORTATION LEGISLATION

In 1940 the Immigration Act of 1918 was amended to enable deportation on the basis of *past* membership in organizations advocating violent overthrow of the government. Any alien who, after his entry, belonged to such an organization was henceforward theoretically subject to deportation. But was the Communist Party such an organization? The Schneiderman ruling (1943) suggested that, in the eyes of the Supreme Court, it was not necessarily so. Thus until the passage of the McCarran Act in 1950 the obvious intention of the 1940 Alien

Registration Act was largely frustrated, and the government was unable to deport more than approximately ten radicals.

Then came the Internal Security Act, which for the first time specifically identified in legislation the CP as advocating violent overthrow, and permitted the deportation of aliens who at any time after their entry into the country had been anarchists, or members of organizations advocating violent overthrow, or members of any group required to register under the Act of 1950. Immediately after the act came into force in October, McGrath ordered a nationwide roundup of eighty-six Communist aliens. By October 24, thirty-one had been brought in. Meanwhile, with the Korean war going badly, the Immigration Service dragnet swept through the homes, offices and places of work of Chinese residents in San Francisco and New York. The strategy was to expel those Chinese who wished and expected to stay, but to manacle those—students and scholars, mostly—who desired to leave. In September, nine Chinese students were taken off the liner *Cleveland* at Honolulu and seven of them were sent back to America.

Two years later, on June 25, 1952, the racist Immigration and Nationality (Walter-McCarran) Act was passed, by 278 to 113 in the House, and by 57 to 26 in the Senate. As Averell Harriman, Director of Mutual Security, put it to Truman when urging the President to veto the bill, it "looks upon immigrants and aliens with suspicion and hostility . . . It transforms naturalized citizens into an inferior class . . . The bill is . . . shortsighted, fearful and bigoted." [8] Under the act an alien could be arrested without a warrant, held without bail, and deported for an action that was legal when committed, to any country willing to accept him. He could be jailed for ten years for failing to deport himself. No hearing need be granted to deportees if the disclosure of evidence entailed by a hearing was deemed incompatible with national security. In what was effectively a bill of attainder, the act rendered deportable any alien who at the time of his entry would have been inadmissible if the 1952 Act had then been in force. Although the Supreme Court softened the impact of the act by establishing that the Attorney General's "final" decision was subject to judicial review, the Court also turned a blind eye to the fact that a bill of attainder is unconstitutional. Quite so, said the Court, but this prohibition applies only to laws relating to the punishment of crimes—deportation is not strictly a punishment, merely an administrative adjustment! [9] While bemoaning the violation of "the sense of fair play, which is the essence of due process," the Court nevertheless sanctioned the deportation of ex-Communists who had ceased to be Party members before the relevant legislation was passed.

## THE IMMIGRATION SERVICE MENTALITY

The human instruments of the government's deportation policy were the officers of the Immigration and Naturalization Service of the Department of Justice. Rose Chernin, herself the victim of a denaturalization case, describes these officers as bigoted, biased, low-grade hacks—their lawyers were the worst. A perhaps less prejudiced view was offered by former Congressman Maury Maverick of Texas: "Our Immigration Service is the greatest bureaucracy on earth. Stricken by the McCarthy terror of Communism, it looks upon all aliens as wicked people and constantly fights them." The editor of the *New York Post*, James A. Wechsler, wrote: "In some brighter day there will be a compilation of the inane injustices and inhumanities committed by the U.S. Immigration and Naturalization Service . . . an agency that seems to specialize in the muddled application of quiet, prolonged, mental torture." [10]

In 1954, some ninety special inquiry officers of the Service conducted deportation hearings. Only twenty-four of them had "some legal education," and only nineteen were attorneys. Their salaries were much lower than those paid to hearing officers in other government agencies. [11] Almost all the Immigration Service's hearing officers had been promoted from within the Service, thus encouraging inbreeding and a narrow, bureaucratic approach to acute human dilemmas. They were also overworked; each officer averaged about 1.8 deportation hearings and 0.7 exclusion hearings a day.

The regional directors were often bigoted, destructive and arrogant; this was certainly true of New York's Edward Shaughnessy and San Francisco's Bruce Barber. It was Barber who principally pursued the unfortunate Soviet refugee Alexander Lobanov and, when the ACLU began to publicize the case, telephoned local editors to urge them, in Lobanov's own interest, not to print the story. As regards the Immigration Commissioners themselves, outstandingly reactionary was Eisenhower's tough, brash appointee and West Point contemporary, General Raymond Swing. It was he who, defending in April 1958 the extraordinary hustling of William Heikkila aboard a plane bound for Finland, commented: "This man is just as much an enemy as the Japs I fought in the Pacific. When a Jap was captured, did we say 'Go home and kiss your wife goodbye?' " [12] Just as the poet Terence wrote, "Nothing human is alien to me," so General Swing and his subordinates could have written, "Nothing alien is human to me."

## THE BAIL ISSUE

The first "right" the alien demanded after his arrest for deportation was release on bail. The Eighth Amendment stipulates that bail should be "reasonable," but did it apply to aliens? On March 1, 1948, five leading Communists who were detained on Ellis Island began a hunger strike that resulted in their release on bail six days later. In August the Court of Appeals ruled that the Attorney General's refusal to release aliens on bail was subject to judicial review. In practice, Justice Department policy under the alien-hunting Clark and his successors was to grant bail whenever adverse publicity dictated it and to revoke it again as soon as the story fell off the back page. The idiosyncracies of particular judges heightened the uncertainties; for example, George Pirinsky and Mrs. Beatrice Johnson were held on Ellis Island for ninety-one days after Judge Alexander Holtzoff, an ally of the administration at all times, ruled that the demand for $25,000 bail was reasonable. But when the Court of Appeals ruled that $5,000 would be a great deal more reasonable, Pirinsky, Mrs. Johnson, Rose Nelson Lightcap and fourteen other alleged Communists were released on bail. Many of them were married to American citizens and had American children.

But the Internal Security Act turned the bail screw exceedingly tight, and in March 1952 the Supreme Court voted, 6 to 2, to uphold the Attorney General's authority to hold alien Communists without bail if their liberty might "endanger national security." By that time bail had been revoked in the cases of thirty-nine potential deportees whose bonds had been posted by the blacklisted Civil Rights Congress, and a wave of arrests followed. In October 1952 Attorney General McGranery ordered eight alleged Communists who had been placed under final deportation orders during the previous two years, yet were undeportable because they were born in countries now under Communist rule, to surrender immediately or face forfeiture of bond.[13] Bail was denied to seventy-two-year-old Herman Nixon, who had been a resident of the United States for fifty-two years, and to Mrs. Antonia Sentner, who had lived in America since she arrived from Croatia in 1914, at the age of eight. She was jailed even though her affidavit showed that she alone in the household could look after her two young children and her invalid mother.[14]

This brutal regime was considerably softened after Ellis Island and Terminal Island, Los Angeles, were closed down in November 1954. Two months later Brownell announced that henceforward deportable aliens would be released on parole, excepting those deemed dangerous to national security. As of January 21, 1955, only seventy-three deportable aliens of *all* categories, excluding Mexican "wet-backs," were held in detention.

## DEPORTING COMMUNISTS

Having surveyed the legal and administrative framework within which the deportation policy operated, we have to examine in more detail the political manipulation of this machinery by the Truman and Eisenhower administrations. Despite what he regarded as onerous restraints on his freedom of action, Attorney General Tom Clark was determined to act on the axiom he forcefully expressed on January 15, 1948, to the Cathedral Club of Brooklyn, "Those who do not believe in the ideology of the United States shall not be allowed to stay in the United States." By April he had arrested over thirty politically suspect aliens, his principal targets being Communist leaders and trade unionists who were supporting the Wallace campaign and opposing Truman's foreign policy. In October he asked why the Republican-dominated 80th Congress had denied him the "simple little law" he had requested to take all 2,100 Communists of Russian and East European extraction into custody.[15] In July of the following year he complained to a Senate subcommittee that 4,000 alien Communists were freely "walking the streets."

This *cri de coeur* followed by only two months a highly publicized incident that symbolized rising official hysteria. No resident alien acquired a more demonic character in the imagination of American officials than Gerhart Eisler, a leading operative of the Comintern who, having fled from the Nazi invasion of France, reached New York in June 1941 and managed to convince a special board that he had never belonged to any Communist organization and was just, as he invariably described himself, "an anti-Fascist." Having spent the war years quietly, contributing to the American Communist press under the pseudonym Hans Berger, Eisler was on the verge of returning to East Germany in 1946 when he was arrested for deportation. A violent confrontation with HCUA in February 1947 resulted in a one-year prison sentence for contempt. Meanwhile Ruth Fischer, the ex-Communist sister of Gerhart and Hanns Eisler (the composer), warned HCUA that Gerhart was now "head of a network of agents of the secret Russian state police" and "the perfect terrorist type." [16]

In May 1949, facing the prospect of five years in prison (for illegal entry) before being deported, Eisler decided to take matters into his own hands, walked out of his 12th Street apartment, eluded the FBI, purchased a 25-cent visitor's ticket for the Polish ship *Batory*, and brazenly boarded it. When the *Batory* docked off Southampton, the British police on dubious legal grounds boarded the ship and arrested Eisler at the request of the United States, and on May 22 the State Department requested his extradition. Unfortunately for the prosecution, the Chief Metropolitan Magistrate, giving legal technicalities priority over the safety of the Free World, ruled that Eisler could not be extradited. Four days later Eisler arrived in Prague and was promptly "elected" a member of the People's Council of the Soviet Zone of Germany, as well as professor of political science at Leipzig University. On June 4, when the *Batory* returned to New York, armed police and Immigration Department officers swarmed aboard, sealed the ship, grilled the passengers and detained 111 of them on Ellis Island. The city's two leading newspapers called this behavior "blustering intimidation . . . petty, undignified and unworthy."

Among CP leaders who served prison sentences under the Smith Act, the Scottish-born John Williamson, spokesman on labor affairs and one of the top four in the Party, recognized that his case was hopeless and set sail for Britain in May 1955, soon after his release from prison. Irving Potash, a member of the national board of the CP, a former manager of the New York Furriers' joint council and one of the Foley Square eleven, departed for Poland under a final deportation order in March 1955, but turned up again in Bronxville in January 1957, where he was arrested and charged with illegal entry. He told the judge he had come back to see his family, but was nonetheless sentenced to two years' imprisonment and a $1,000 fine. Potash had been imprisoned as long ago as 1920, during the Palmer raids.[17]

Jacob Stachel, one of the Foley Square eleven, and Alexander Bittelman, convicted in the second New York Smith Act trial in 1952, both faced deportation actions. Bittelman, who had the distinction of having been deported to Siberia by the Tsar as a dangerous radical, was arrested for deportation in 1948, charged with having possessed false passports, with having made secret trips to the Soviet Union, and with illegal entry. Although both Stachel and Bittelman proved undeportable for geographical reasons, both spent four to five years in prison under the Smith Act.[18]

Nor were women spared. Claudia Jones, a native of the British West Indies and secretary of the CP's national women's commission, as well as Negro-affairs editor of the *Daily Worker*, was arrested for deportation in the big sweep of January 1948, jailed under the Smith Act in 1952, and finally forced to leave for England in December 1955. (Her coprisoner in Alderson, Betty Gannett, ultimately proved undeportable because she had been born in Russia or Poland.) Even mothers of small children were fair game for the Immigration Service. Forty-two-year-old Mrs. Beatrice Johnson, described as one of the top women Communists in the United States, was arrested on February 18, 1948, a few minutes after she had dropped off her four-year-old daughter at nursery school. She was actually deported on November 10, 1950, along with the Danish-born Communist Andrew Overgaard.[19] The wives of Smith Act defendants were clearly singled out for attack. We have already seen how denaturalization proceedings were brought against Simon Gerson's wife, Sophie. Antonia Sentner, wife of William Sentner, the Missouri CP leader, was put through the mill, as was Peggy Wellman, the Russian-born wife of Michigan's CP leader Saul Wellman, and Anna Ganley, wife of Nat Ganley and mother of a thirteen-year-old daughter. Arrested in June 1949 and charged with having entered the country illegally in 1925 and 1931, Anna Ganley was jailed when she failed to produce an acceptable bond of $5,000.

## DEPORTING RADICAL LABOR LEADERS

By 1948 the CIO had fallen into line with the administration's foreign policy while its pro-Communist faction had committed itself to the third party and the presidential candidacy of Henry Wallace. During his major offensive against left-wing aliens [20] Clark wielded the deportation weapon against every pro-Communist labor leader who was not a citizen.[21] Charles A. Doyle, a native of Britain and international vice-president of the United Gas, Coke and Chemical Workers, CIO, visited Canada in January 1948, when his union's Niagara Falls local went on strike. The government promptly canceled his reentry permit. Doyle, who had lived in America for twenty-three years, came back anyway and was arrested. After several internments on Ellis Island he was finally deported to Britain in November 1953.

John Santo, the Communist organization director of the New York Transport Workers Union, was charged in September 1947 with having entered the country illegally twenty years earlier. Although he had served in the Army for three years during the war, Santo abandoned his appeal and departed in June 1949 for Hungary, where he joined the government bureaucracy. By January 1957, however, he was a refugee in Vienna, having renounced Communism. He later returned to the United States and became a government witness. Another Transport Workers official, Gordon A. Barrager, president of Local 252, was in the process of negotiating a strike settlement on behalf of Long Island drivers, when he was seized for deportation to Canada.

Ferdinand Smith, the black secretary of the National Maritime

Union and a member of the CIO executive board, was arrested in February 1948 as part of what the *Christian Science Monitor* candidly described as "the latest federal move to help American labor purge itself of obstructive left-wingers . . ." Smith, who was in dispute with the NMU's anti-Communist president, Joe Curran, over Wallace and the Marshall Plan, was summoned to what he called a "kangaroo court" at the Immigration Service offices on Columbus Avenue, and there denounced as a Party member by ex-Communist witnesses. In August 1951 he left the country for his native British West Indies.[22] The pressure on radical trade unionists was now unremitting. Michael J. Obermeier, president of Local 6, Hotel and Club Employees Union, AFL, was charged in October 1947 with having falsely denied CP membership when applying for citizenship in 1945–46. In July 1950 Obermeier began a two-year sentence in Lewisburg penitentiary and in December 1950 he left the country. Soon afterward the Internal Security Act was invoked against Harry Yaris, secretary of the Diamond Workers Protection Union and a brother of Betty Gannett; two officials of the Fur and Leather Workers, Myer Klig and Jack Schneider; the secretary of the Federation of Greek Maritime Unions, Nicholas Kaloudis; and Frank Borich, a labor organizer for the NMU, who had been resident in the United States since 1913.

Anthony Cattonar, the Italian born son-in-law of the veteran Communist Israel Amter, and a resident of Brooklyn, was arrested in August 1950. Vice-president of Local 1125, UE, from 1939 to 1945, Cattonar was said by the government to have been a Party member before his last entry into the country in 1939. As soon as charges were brought, he was dismissed from his job as a production machinist at the Bommer Spring Hinge Plant, Brooklyn, after a wildcat strike demanding his dismissal. Pete Nelson of Everett, Washington, an agent of an International Woodworkers local and a native of Sweden, had been living in the United States for twenty-five years when his reentry permit was canceled during a visit to Canada. He returned *incognito*, was arrested and faced deportation charges. Arduilio Susi, secretary-treasurer of Local 89, Chefs, Cooks, AFL, was arrested by the Immigration Service in June 1948 for deportation to Italy.

A determined effort was made to exploit the deportation weapon against the Alaska Cannery Workers Union, affiliated to Local 7 (Seattle) of the ILWU. This union, which had raised wages tenfold between 1934 and 1949, was bitterly opposed by the Associated Farmers of California and the Alaska salmon industry. In September 1949 the union's president, business agent, and three members of the executive board, as well as four rank-and-file workers, were arrested in Seattle for deportation. Of these, Ernesto Mangaoang, Chris Mensalvos and Pouce Torres were all Filipinos. Mangaoang was held for many weeks in King County jail where neither books nor papers were allowed. In 1953, the federal Court of Appeals ruled that he was not deportable.[23]

Frank Ibanez, a baker and a left-wing trade unionist, had arrived from Cuba more than thirty years earlier. Although he denied he had ever been a member of the Party, Manning Johnson and Leonard Patterson, both notoriously untrustworthy professional ex-Communists, swore that he had. In April 1955 the Board of Immigration Appeals ordered him deported. Mrs. Eulalia Figueiredo, an organizer in the textile, shoe and garment industries of New Bedford who had been a resident since childhood, was arrested in 1950 and charged with former CP membership. In January 1953 she was deported to Portugal.

The most celebrated or notorious pro-Communist trade unionist in America was the Australian-born Harry Bridges, chairman of the San Francisco longshoremen's strike committee during the famous shut-down of the port in 1934, and since 1936 president of the ILWU. The battle to deport Bridges lasted twenty years and can be interpreted either as a tribute to American due process and rule of law, or as a saga of manic political persecution. Or both. Two things are certain: Bridges was both a highly able trade-union leader (the average earnings of the ILWU's members had risen to $5,000 a year by 1951) and a dedicated supporter of the Soviet cause.

The campaign to deport him began at the time of the 1934 strike and reached its first climax when his case was heard in 1939 by Dean James M. Landis, the trial examiner appointed by the Department of Labor. The Landis report accepted evidence submitted by the defense demonstrating crude collusion between West Coast employers, the local police and the Legion, and advised that evidence was lacking to prove that Bridges had been a member of the CP at the time the warrant against him was issued in March 1938.[24]

In 1940 a bill to deport Bridges passed in the House but died in the Senate. By now Congress had amended the Immigration Act to cover *past* membership, and in February 1941 it ruled that Bridges was deportable; the Board of Immigration Appeals reversed this ruling; yet in May 1942 Attorney General Francis Biddle nevertheless ordered Bridges to be deported. Administrative remedies thus exhausted, Bridges carried his case to the courts, with the result that in June 1945 the liberal Supreme Court found in his favor by 5 to 3, on the ground that the evidence showed "little more than a course of conduct which reveals cooperation with Communist groups for the attainment of wholly lawful objectives." Said Justice Frank Murphy:

The record of this case will stand forever as a monument to man's intolerance to man . . . Industrial and farming organizations, veterans' groups, city police departments, and private undercover agents, all joined in an unremitting effort to deport him . . . Wire-tapping, searches and seizures without warrant . . . have been widely employed in this deportation drive.

Although Bridges was granted his citizenship papers three months later after swearing he had never been a Party member, the "unremitting effort" was not yet remitted. Clark's Justice Department persuaded a federal grand jury to indict him for perjury in May 1949, and in the trial that followed the informers were once again wheeled out: Crouch, Johnson, John H. Schomaker (who swore he recruited Bridges into the CP) and eleven ex-Communists who swore they had attended CP meetings in Bridges's company. According to one source, two agents from the Justice Department approached Herman Mann of the ILWU during the trial and promised special facilities for his critically ill wife at a cancer institute if he would only testify that Bridges was a Communist. Mann refused. At the end of the trial lasting eighty-one days Bridges was found guilty of perjury and sentenced to five years' imprisonment. The inevitable order that he should be denaturalized followed from a District Court in June 1950.

Hysteria concerning the opposition of the ILWU to the Korean war, and the possibilities of political strikes or sabotage at West Coast ports, now ran rampant, although no such action materialized. When the Supreme Court set aside Bridges's conviction on technical grounds in June 1954, the Eisenhower administration became the third to enter the fray by bringing a civil suit to deprive him of his citizenship. But an adverse ruling by federal court Judge Louis E. Goodman in San Francisco in July 1955 persuaded the government finally to abandon the fight. By now shipping employers had come to terms with him.

## DEPORTING RADICAL JOURNALISTS

Another prime target for deportation proceedings were journalists and editors working for the pro-Communist press, whether English- or foreign-language. Knut Heikkinenen, of the Finnish-American daily *Tyomies-Eteenpain*, was arrested in November 1949, released on $5,000 bail, rearrested in October 1950 under the McCarran Act, held in jail, and ordered deported in April 1952 on a charge of past CP membership. Although neither Finland nor Canada would accept him, he was arrested again in October 1953 for failing to apply for travel documents to deport himself. Six months later he was sentenced to ten years' imprisonment. The Supreme Court reversed this verdict in January 1956 on the ground that the charge against him was unproven.

Michael Salerno, editor of the New York paper L'Unità del Popolo, was arrested in 1948 and deported on November 23, 1950. Paul Juditz, the sixty-three-year-old labor editor of the Morning Freiheit and a native of Russia, was held on Ellis Island in 1951. Sang Rhup Park, editor of a Los Angeles weekly Korean Independence, who denied that he was a Communist, was nevertheless arrested in 1952 on a charge of having intended to stay in the United States permanently when he was admitted as a student. After Judge Goodman enjoined his deportation on the humane ground that, as a sharp critic of President Syngman Rhee, he would suffer physical persecution if sent back to South Korea, the Immigration Service in its wisdom "found" that he would not. But in December the case against him was dropped. [25]

A prominent and bitterly contested case was that of Peter Harisiades, a Greek-American newspaper reporter resident in the United States for thirty-six years. Harisiades had been a member of the CP from 1925 to 1939 (when most aliens were dropped from the Party rolls as a matter of policy). When he applied for second citizenship papers in 1944 he encountered resistance, which developed into a decision to deport him. In May 1949 the BIA upheld his deportation and in January 1951 so did the Court of Appeals, although it ordered the Attorney General to investigate whether he would be physically persecuted in Greece, where the power of the extreme Right had been secured by American military and financial intervention. When the case Harisiades v. Shaughnessy, which also concerned two other ex-Communist Party members, [26] came before the Supreme Court in 1952, the Court upheld the retroactive provision of the 1940 Act. In November Harisiades left for Poland (not Greece) accompanied by his American wife and children.

The installation in power of the Eisenhower-Brownell regime (as we may define it from our perspective) occasioned a new deportation drive against editors and journalists critical of the American Celebration. In the course of 1953 at least fifteen editors [27] of pro-Communist papers were arrested for deportation or denaturalization, including Al Richmond, editor of the West Coast Daily People's World, who had recently been convicted under the Smith Act. But the case which most forcefully demonstrated the government's refusal to tolerate criticism from the far Left was that of Cedric Belfrage, cofounder of the ALP's National Guardian, a resident alien of British nationality who had served briefly as an Allied press officer in Germany and had been named by Elizabeth Bentley as a wartime Soviet "courier." In 1950 Belfrage had been summoned to Immigration Service headquarters, where he refused to answer questions concerning his writings, views and associations. For a time he heard no more and was able to concentrate his energies on creating a fellow-traveling newspaper, which did, however, deviate from the Party line on a certain number of topics: Earl Browder, Tito and Anna Louise Strong were the most conspicuous.

Trouble resumed for Belfrage in 1953, when he (in reality not a Party member) took the Fifth Amendment before HCUA and McCarthy in rapid succession. The day after his appearance before McCarthy he was arrested on a deportation warrant and taken to Ellis Island. Fourteen months later, in August 1954, the informer Martin Berkeley told the BIA that Belfrage had been a Party member in 1937–38; in May 1955 Belfrage was arrested yet again and held in West Street prison—because, as District Director of Immigration Shaughnessy informed the press, he was an agitator of the most dangerous breed who belonged with the "rough, tough, criminal types" in jail. Meanwhile Immigration Commissioner Swing announced that Belfrage was in prison because his "political beliefs are allied to a world-wide conspiracy to destroy the free world . . ." At this point Belfrage gave up and left America. [28]

Leading members of front organizations listed by the Attorney General or brought before the Subversive Activities Control Board were invariably selected for attack if born outside the United States. Among the most influential victims in this category were the executive secretary of the American Slav Congress, George Pirinsky, who was finally forced to leave for Czechoslovakia in August 1951, and Andrew Dmytryshyn, organizer for the Ukrainian-American Fraternal Union, one of the national groups affiliated to the much-persecuted International Workers Order. District Director Shaughnessy staged a show-trial of Dmytryshyn at Immigration headquarters on Columbus Avenue, a trial at which anti-Communist liberal witnesses like Simon Weber, city editor of the *Jewish Daily Forward* and a former member of the IWO, testified for the prosecution. [29]

## THE UNDEPORTABLE ALIEN

The great thorn in the Immigration Service's flesh was the unsporting refusal of the Soviet Union and the People's Democracies to receive back those of their friends who were forcibly expelled from the United States. [30] A second ground for nondeportability emerged whenever the alien could justifiably claim that he would suffer physical persecution or death if compelled to return to his country of origin. But the Walter-McCarran Act merely authorized, and did not require, the Attorney General to act mercifully in such circumstances, the result being (such were the quotas of mercy then available) that in 1954 only 53 of 258 such applications were granted. The staff of the House Judiciary Committee found that in "many cases" well-justified claims of persecution "have been flatly rejected without the presentation of anything even remotely resembling a factual rebuttal of the claims made by the deportees," by immigration officers lacking the historical or intellectual background to evaluate such claims.[31]

For the "undeportable deportee" the Walter-McCarran Act introduced a vindictive system of supervisory parole by which such Communists as Bittelman and Betty Gannett were required to report weekly to Ellis Island, to report on their associations, and to abandon all political activity. In October 1955 fourteen persons [32] ordered deported as CP members, pleaded to the Supreme Court that such supervisory parole was unconstitutional. In May 1957 the Court ruled in the Sentner case that Mrs. Antonia Sentner could not be ordered by the Attorney General to discontinue her membership of or association with the CP while under supervisory parole.

## NOTHING ALIEN IS HUMAN

The prospect of breaking up families was not one that inhibited the Immigration Service. Time and again deportation proceedings were launched against long-term residents married to American citizens and against parents of American citizens. A Communist who had been living in the United States since 1929 was deported to his native Cuba in 1953 despite the protests of his American wife. Mrs. Goldie Davidoff was arrested on April 23, 1953, soon after her American husband had left for work; she had no alternative but to take her two-year-old child with her to Ellis Island. Accused of having been in the Canadian CP, she was deported after Harvey Matusow had testified for the government. Mrs. Stella Petrowitz, of Philadelphia, a native of Poland and a mother of eight, was ordered deported in August 1953. Giacomo Quattrone, of Boston, an Italian who had lived in America for forty-five of his sixty-five years, and who had eight American-born children, was deported to Italy not for Party membership but for having attended meetings and given money. Hamish McKay was deported to Canada in November 1960 after thirty-two years' residence in the United States. Charged with CP membership in the thirties (Paul Crouch was the principal government witness), McKay left behind him a wife, two sons, and a grandchild, all American citizens.

A Finnish-born American, William Mackie, had arrived in the United States as an eight-month-old baby. Having served in the Army during the war, he was deported to Finland in 1960 under the Walter-McCarran Act on a charge that he denied—that of having been a CP member from 1937 to 1939. He left behind him his wife, children, two sisters, and eighty-year-old father.[33] In the case of yet another Finn, William Heikkila, who had arrived in America at the age of three months, and who had quit the CP in Minnesota in 1939, the Immigration Service finally grew so exasperated by the cumbersome machinery of justice that one day in April 1958 they simply seized him as he left work and, without any notice to his American wife or his lawyer, bundled him aboard a plane bound for Finland. Heikkila found himself in Helsinki with thirty cents in his pocket and no overcoat. Protests brought him back a week later.

Gus Polites came to America from a Greek family farm when he was sixteen. During the Depression he joined the CP and led hunger marches. In 1942, four years after he left the Party, he became a citizen. During the war he sold $50,000 worth of war bonds. After the Supreme Court, by 5 to 4, upheld the cancellation of his citizenship, he began a fight against deportation that brought on so severe a heart attack that he was not able to work after 1959, becoming dependent on social security and 100 percent disability payments, which he stood to lose if deported, though he had paid contributions for years. In a pamphlet put out by the ACPFB, his daughter Bernice Polites (or some ghostwriter on her behalf) recalled:

> The FBI went to our neighbors! Our phone was tapped! We would go to a picnic and they'd follow us. The FBI followed my mother to work and talked to her boss about my father. My father sold meat to restaurants. They went to his customers, and many stopped buying from him, which made it impossible for Dad to make a living. Then—my Dad became sick. He got heart trouble. He could no longer work.

In 1963 Polites was finally deported. He chose to go to Poland, where, ignorant of the language, he died utterly alone.[34]

The Immigration Service had no mercy for the old. In November 1953 they arrested Mrs. Baumert, of Elsinore, California; she was seventy-six. In Los Angeles they arrested Mr. and Mrs. Lars Berg, aged sixty-nine and sixty-seven respectively. Residents in the United States since 1904, they were confined to Terminal Island for deportation to Sweden. Tom Dutton, a seventy-year-old Detroit carpenter, was threatened with deportation to Britain because he had allegedly attended Communist meetings in the 1930s. Francesco Costa, of Rochester, New York, was arrested for deportation at the age of eighty-three, because he refused to provide deportation testimony against his own son Leonard. Israel Blankenstein, Russian-born and a charter member of the CP, had been convicted under the Pennsylvania Sedition Act in 1922 and ordered deported two years later. He then disappeared. In May 1953, at the age of sixty-six, he was arrested for deportation. Cecil R. Jay, a sixty-five-year-old resident alien who had emigrated from England in 1914, was ordered deported in 1952 because he had belonged to the CP from 1935 to 1940. He applied for a suspension on the ground of hardship, but the Supreme Court ruled against him, by 5 to 4, in 1956. Indeed nearly one third of those arrested for deportation for political reasons were over sixty years of age and had lived in America for more than forty years. Not surprisingly, some found the physical and nervous strain too much for them. Norman Tallentire, a cardiac patient, died while fighting a case after thirty-three years' residence in America. Lewis Corey, an anti-Communist economist and writer, died in 1953 at the age of sixty-one while fighting deportation proceedings brought against him because he had been in the Party thirty years earlier.[35]

## Assault on the ACPFB

The main, if not the only, hope of Communists or sympathizers threatened with deportation was the American Committee for the Protection of the Foreign Born and its attorneys. The ACPFB, successor to the National Council for the Protection of the Foreign Born (1926), advertised to the foreign-born their rights: to be accompanied by a lawyer during interviews; to refuse to answer questions and to terminate an interview; to deny an immigration officer entry into the home unless he held a warrant. In fact, the ACPFB aided most of the leading Communists and sympathizers who faced deportation or denaturalization proceedings. In 1953 the ACPFB was defending more than 275 aliens and more than thirty naturalized citizens who faced political charges. Honorary positions at the head of the ACPFB tended to be held by fellow-traveling Protestant clergymen of Anglo-Saxon derivation like the Reverend John Darr and Bishop Arthur W. Moulton, but the organizational dynamo was Abner Green, executive secretary since 1941 and the inspiration behind many of the area committees. The most effective of these was the Los Angeles Committee for the Protection of the Foreign Born, founded in 1950 under

the leadership of Mrs. Rose Chernin. This Committee and its journal, *Defense*, intervened in almost two hundred West Coast political
denaturalization and deportation cases; it also succeeded in getting
the cases of twenty-seven Mexican-born and twelve Japanese-born
"subversive" aliens transferred to Washington, D.C., on account of
West Coast prejudice. All these cases were won. The ACPFB was in
fact able to pitch itself into the struggle over the release of aliens on
bail by establishing its own bail fund of one million dollars.

The Department of Justice sought to crush the ACPFB by the
usual methods; it was listed as a Communist front by Attorney General Tom Clark in May 1948. Following his refusal to hand over the
records to a federal grand jury in July 1951, Abner Green served six
months in prison. In April 1952 Saul Grossman, secretary of the
Michigan ACPFB, took the Fifth Amendment before HCUA and
managed to evade producing his files without specifically refusing to
do so. (Grossman was later convicted of contempt, but the verdict
was reversed by the Court of Appeals.) In April 1953 Attorney General Brownell petitioned the SACB to order the ACPFB to register as
a front. The government complained of "strong efforts to undermine
public trust in the Department of Justice, to relate the deportation of
Communists to attacks upon the constitutional rights of all Americans
. . ." Hearings began in June 1955. In August of that year New York
State Attorney General Jacob Javits charged that the ACPFB was violating the law applicable to charitable organizations; but the ACPFB
argued that it was a political organization, not a charity. When Louis
Lefkowitz succeeded Javits he intensified the attack and a serious situation arose when, following Justice Steiner's ruling in June 1957 that
the ACPFB was indeed a charity, Lefkowitz promptly obtained an *ex
parte* injunction restraining it from all activity. In March 1958 the
New York County Supreme Court ordered the ACPFB not to solicit
funds unless it registered as a charity.

Meanwhile, Chairman Francis E. Walter of HCUA, defending
the Walter-McCarran Act against its critics, subpoenaed the files and
correspondence of the ACPFB. Assisted by an FBI agent who had
lifted documents from the Los Angeles files, HCUA was able to publish a 1,300-page appendix detailing the ACPFB's un-American activities. The SACB too had decided that the ACPFB must register as a
Communist front, following testimony from Mary Markward, John
Lautner, Barbara Hartle and a number of FBI agents. Lautner testified that he had seen Green at CP meetings and at the 1948 Party
national convention. (Green himself took the Fifth Amendment on
Party membership.) The SACB concluded from Green's opinions
that he was a Communist.[36]

# 12

## The Golden Curtain:
## Passports and Immigration

The right to hold a passport was, generally speaking, denied to American Communists, sympathizers, unrepentant former Communists, and strong critics of the Pax Americana. It is not possible to estimate how many radicals were effectively denied a passport after 1947, because many of them, recognizing the inevitable, did not bother to apply.

The Internal Security Act made it illegal for members of organizations designated and registered as Communist-action groups to apply for a passport. But no organization ever registered; and when a test case, *Aptheker v. Secretary of State*, eventually came before the Supreme Court fourteen years later, in 1964, the Court ruled that in this respect the Act violated the Fifth Amendment. Nevertheless the executive had developed considerable discretionary power, and in May 1952 Secretary of State Dean Acheson explained that it was his policy to withhold a passport from anyone about whom there was "reason to believe" that he was in the CP, from anyone whose "conduct abroad is likely to be contrary to the best interest of the United States," or from anyone who might reasonably be believed to be "going abroad to engage in activities which will advance the Communist movement . . ." [1] This policy, it should not be forgotten, was formulated by the "leaders of the Free World" and the liberal champions of the open society.

A Board of Passport Appeals was set up in 1952, affording an applicant the right to a hearing, and to counsel, but only on condition that he signed an affidavit denying present *and past* membership in the CP. Confidential information was rigorously concealed despite the Administrative Procedure Act's provision for "such cross-examination as may be required for a full and true disclosure of the facts." Normally the State Department did not explain its adverse rulings but relied on the bland formula, "contrary to the best interests . . ."

Directing the State Department's Passport Office was a crusading anti-Communist, Mrs. Ruth Shipley. From May 1951 to May 1952, she barred some three hundred Americans from going abroad. After January 1953 she worked in close collaboration with the newly appointed McCarthyite administrator of the State Department Bureau of Security and Consular Affairs, R. W. Scott McLeod, to ensure, she reportedly put it to Professor Thomas I. Emerson, that no one who had criticized American foreign policy would leave the country. It was also reported in 1954 that before issuing passports to ex-Communists, Mrs. Shipley demanded evidence of their willingness to collaborate with government agencies. Her successor, nominated by Dulles in April 1955, was a protégé of McLeod and a member of McCarthy's "loyal American underground" who had channeled information about her colleagues in the International Information Agency to the Senator. Indeed Miss Frances Knight was a no less dedicated anti-red than her predecessor. Although the Passport Office's policy, as described by the generally conservative Commission on Government Security, resulted in delays in issuing passports "ranging from several months to more than a year" as being "the rule rather than the exception," [2] attempts by the federal courts after 1955 to erode these arbitrary powers were fiercely resisted not merely by the Office but also by HCUA, which entered the fray in 1956 with hearings to investigate how Americans heading for foreign conferences designed to "discredit" the United States had obtained passports.

An example of the Shipley regime in action was the case of Dr. Walter G. Bergman, director of instructional research in the Detroit public-school system, and a member of Norman Thomas's Socialist Party. Years earlier Bergman had been accused of attending a "Communist meeting" by two Dies Committee witnesses and by the red squad of the Detroit police. He was lecturing in Denmark in April 1953, when his passport and his wife's were suddenly revoked. Mrs. Shipley hastened to inform the press that she had evidence that Bergman was a Communist. On June 3, Bergman visited the U.S. vice-consul in Copenhagen, heard a paraphrased version of the charges, but was not allowed to see them or even to take verbatim notes. One of them related to attendance at a Moscow summer school nineteen years earlier, and all but one of them referred to events more than ten years before. (Bergman had recently called for the repeal of the

Michigan Trucks Act, which, in fact, was opposed by virtually all trade unionists.) None of the charges, despite Mrs. Shipley's public accusation, had anything to do with Party membership. Only after expensive litigation was his passport returned unconditionally in October.[3]

Communists had no hope of obtaining passports after 1947 (the novelist Howard Fast was refused) unless they were accredited members of the press, and even here the entitlement was eroded. In March 1948 a second application by the *Daily Worker* correspondent A. B. Magil, who wanted to travel to Geneva to attend a UN conference, was turned down; after adverse publicity the decision was reversed. In August 1953 the passport of the *Daily Worker's* European editor, Joseph Starobin, was revoked. Passports were refused to the paper's correspondents again in 1957.

Politicians thought to be too friendly to the CP also suffered. Representative Leo Isaacson of the American Labor Party was not allowed to attend a Paris conference in 1948, because it supported the Greek Communist guerrillas. And if a Congressman could not travel abroad, why should a Supreme Court justice? Justice William O. Douglas was refused a passport for travel to China. A number of film and theater personalities discovered that the Passport Office did not favor their evading the blacklist by finding work abroad. Edward G. Robinson was refused a passport from the late forties until he made his peace with HCUA in 1952; Ring Lardner, Jr., was denied one from 1953 to 1958. Donald Ogden Stewart, who had been living in London since 1950, began a five-year fight for a passport renewal which culminated in a favorable Court of Appeals decision in November 1957. In 1954 Arthur Miller's hopes of traveling to Brussels to see a production of *The Crucible* were dashed, but he did obtain a passport a year later. The film director and writer Carl Foreman, also living in England, was refused in 1954 after he filed an affidavit that he had not been in the Party for many years, but declined to name names. He brought a lawsuit, but Judge David A. Pine denied a motion for a preliminary injunction. However, in 1956 a passport was forthcoming after Foreman made his private peace with HCUA's Chairman Francis E. Walter.

Perhaps the most celebrated case affecting a public entertainer was that of Paul Robeson. The passport he had held since 1922 was revoked in August 1950. In February 1952 United States officials prevented him from entering Canada, where he was to attend the Canadian convention of Mine, Mill and Smelter Workers—even though no passport was required to enter Canada. (Dr. Vincent Hallinan, Progressive Party candidate for president in 1952, was also prevented from addressing a Vancouver labor union.) With the aid of loudspeakers and ingenuity, Robeson was able to give the concert from one side of the border to the other, at Peace Arch Park, on May 18; according to Robeson, 30,000 Canadians came to hear him. (For the next three years this became an annual event.) When he brought a lawsuit, the Department submitted a brief to the Court of Appeals in February 1952 containing a revealing observation:

> Furthermore, even if the complaint had alleged, which it does not, that the passport was canceled solely because of the applicant's recognized status as spokesman for large sections of Negro Americans, we submit that this would not amount to an abuse of discretion in view of the appellant's frank admission that he has for years been extremely active politically in behalf of the independence of the colonial people of Africa.[4]

Robeson refused to submit a non-Communist affidavit, and in *Robeson v. Dulles* (August 1955), Judge Burnita S. Matthews dismissed his complaint on the ground that he had failed to exhaust administrative remedies. Not until after the Kent decision in 1958 (see below) did he get his passport back.

Those penalized included liberal lawyers conspicuous in civil-liberties cases, like A. L. Wirin of the California ACLU, and Leonard Boudin, who himself represented many passport litigants. Not only intellectuals prominent in front organizations, like Corliss Lamont and W. E. B. Du Bois, were denied passports, but also independent Marxists or critics of American foreign policy such as the economist Paul Baran, the Far East expert Owen Lattimore, and Judge William L. Clark, who was refused a passport to visit Germany where he had been Chief Justice of the Allied Control Commission courts, but who had subsequently criticized American policy in Germany. Academics who lost their teaching posts after confrontations with Congressional committees usually forfeited their right to travel.[5]

As Judge Charles E. Wyzanski pointed out, if an American was not allowed to travel because of what he had said in the United States, not only was his freedom of speech curtailed geographically but also his freedom of speech at home was punished and therefore threatened; hence a violation of the First Amendment.

## THE COURTS INTERVENE

The Federal court decisions which virtually dismantled the Passport Office's discriminatory policy were a long time in coming. They occurred in two waves, in 1955 and 1958.

Dr. Otto Nathan, professor of economics and executor of Einstein's will, had lived in America since 1939 and supported a number of front organizations. In December 1952 he filed for a passport, without success, so in August 1954 he filed a complaint for an injunction to direct the Secretary of State to issue him one. Under protest, he finally agreed to swear the non-Communist affidavit. In March 1955 Judge Schweinhaut directed the Secretary of State to afford Nathan a prompt hearing; when the Secretary did not comply, the judge directed him on June 1 to issue Nathan a passport without delay. These were unprecedented orders. The State Department appealed and the Court of Appeals ordered that a quasi-judicial hearing be granted to Nathan; on June 6, Nathan was issued a passport without a hearing. As a result of this decision, the ACLU sponsored several lawsuits demanding a quasi-judicial hearing; in each instance the State Department preferred to issue the passport.[6]

*Schachtman v. Dulles* was also decided in 1955. For six years Max Schachtman fought for a hearing to contest the Attorney General's listing of the Independent Socialist League as "Communist" and "subversive." The persistent refusal of a passport to Schachtman brought him into the courts, with the result that the Court of Appeals for the District of Columbia for the first time challenged the nature and sufficiency of the State Department's criteria for refusing a passport. Judge Henry Edgerton pointed out that the purpose of the Attorney General's list was to screen government employees, not to determine the fate of passport applications.

In *Boudin v. Dulles*, also decided in 1955, the State Department justified its denial of a passport to the prominent civil-liberties attorney Leonard Boudin in terms of confidential, undisclosed information. The District Court held that it was a denial of due process to use information *dehors* the record of the actual passport hearing. Judge Luther W. Youngdahl ordered the Department to give Boudin a hearing within twenty days, and to make known the evidence against him so that it could be challenged directly. The Department appealed, but later issued a passport after he had testified before HCUA that he had never been in the CP or YCL.[7]

The second wave of crucial judicial decisions came in 1958. *Dayton v. Dulles* was an action brought by the nuclear physicist Weldon B. Dayton, who swore the non-Communist affidavit but was nevertheless denied a passport to work in an Indian research institute on the basis of undisclosed, confidential information that he had been closely associated with Communist agents. The Supreme Court, basing its decision on statutory rather than constitutional grounds, voted by 5 to 4 that a citizen could be denied a passport only if he engaged in criminal or unlawful conduct. Dayton got his passport.

The most influential decision of 1958 was that in *Kent v. Dulles*. The artist Rockwell Kent had written in 1940: ". . . I am not a Communist. It is, however, not true that I feel the least abhorrence of those socialist principles for the promotion of which the Communist Party is organized." He also wrote: "Is Stalin backing us? God bless you, Stalin!—as once our fathers prayed that God should bless the King of France. God bless our fellow-travelers." [8] In 1953, when the artist was seventy years old, the State Department refused him a passport to visit friends in Ireland, where he wanted to paint; he was told by the Department he would not be granted a passport "to travel anywhere for any purpose." He refused on principle to swear the non-Communist affidavit, arguing that only citizenship was relevant. In 1957 the Court of Appeals for the District of Columbia ordered the Department to grant Kent a quasi-judicial hearing and to explain to him the reasons for denial, but the Court did not insist on the disclosure of confidential informants. The State Department complied and then again refused to issue Kent a passport. In a companion case, *Briehl v. Dulles*, the Court of Appeals argued that since the days of the English kings the executive had possessed the right to restrict travel. It being now a period of official national emergency, the Secretary of State had not exceeded his powers. Judges Bazelon and Edgerton, dissenting, found that Congress had delegated to the President only the power to delimit certain geographical areas for travel, not categories of people. "We have temporized too long with the passport practices of the State Department," said Edgerton.

> The Secretary proposes to continue restricting the personal liberty of a citizen because statements by informants whom the Secretary does not identify have led him to think that if the citizen goes abroad he will do something, the nature of which the Secretary does not suggest, which the Secretary thinks, for reasons known only to him, will be contrary to what, for reasons known only to him, he conceives to be the "national interest." [9]

A year later the Supreme Court broke the State Department's stranglehold by ruling in *Kent v. Dulles* that the right to travel can be removed only with due process under the Fifth Amendment, including the right to know and cross-examine hostile informants. Although the Nationality Act of 1952 did accord discretion to the Secretary of State, it did not, the Court ruled, give him authority to withhold passports because of people's beliefs or associations. The Court also ruled, 5 to 4, in favor of Walter Briehl.

The Supreme Court decisions of 1958 inspired a passionate countercampaign by the State Department. In July Eisenhower urged

Congress to authorize the Secretary of State to refuse passports for any reason of national security. "Each day and week that passes without it," said the President, "exposes us to great danger." [10] The lobbying was intensive. In a November speech to the Veterans of Foreign Wars, whom he urged to support new legislation, Roderic L. O'Connor, of the Bureau of Security and Consular Affairs, announced gloomily that since the Supreme Court's ruling in June the State Department had received passport applications from 596 people with pro-Communist records, like William L. Patterson, general manager of the *Daily Worker*, who wished to travel to the USSR. Passports had been issued to such "hardened Communists" as Hugh Hardyman, Anita and Henry Willcox, Earl Browder, and Anna Louise Strong.[11] But, despite such appeals, and although several bills were introduced, Congress declined to legislate and to provide the State Department with blanket authority to deny passports for any reason of foreign policy. But in an act of petulance, the loyalty oath declared illegal in 1958 was retained on passport application forms by the State Department on the pretext that it would be expensive to junk all the old forms.

And yet, even after the Kent decision, the right to travel remained restricted. The passport of the black journalist William Worthy had been withdrawn after he returned from China in 1956. In July 1959 a three-man panel of the Court of Appeals of the District of Columbia ruled that geographical restrictions lay beyond judicial intervention. The Court took the same view with regard to the complaint of the noted writer Waldo Frank, who had been refused permission to travel to China although forty other newsmen had recently been allowed to do so, the implication being that the discrimination was personal. Surprisingly, the Supreme Court declined to review these decisions.

## STATE DEPARTMENT VISA POLICY

Even before the passage of the Subversive Activities Control Act in 1950, the Voorhis Act of 1940 endowed the government with broad powers to exclude political radicals. After 1947 it was the policy of the Truman administration to close the door to almost all foreign Communists, apart from those traveling on diplomatic passports.[12] The British Communist MP Philip Piratin was refused a visa in July 1948, as were the British CP leaders Harry Pollitt and R. Palme Dutt, together with the chairman of the Swedish Party, Hilding Hagberg, when they applied for permission to attend the December 1950 convention of the CPUSA. Foreigners wishing to attend Communist-front meetings or conferences normally got the cold shoulder: for example, Professor J. D. Bernal, Carlo Levi and the Abbé Boulier were not allowed to attend the Waldorf Conference in 1949. When the Dean of Canterbury, the Right Reverend Hewlett Johnson, was refused even a transit visa in April 1950, he referred tellingly to the "Golden Curtain." Later twelve distinguished foreign members of the peace movement, including Picasso, were refused entry.

Foreign labor leaders too were frequently excluded by Attorney General Clark and his successors. The CIO's president, Philip Murray, arranged with Léon Jouhaux, Socialist leader of the French General Confederation of Labor, to hold a conference of the two organizations in New York on October 28, 1947. The American consulate in Paris then turned down the visa applications of two Communist delegates, Henri Reynaud and Pierre Lebrun, though Attorney General Clark subsequently granted them three-day visas restricted to New York. They rejected this offer as an insult and the whole meeting was canceled.[13]

James B. Carey's attempt to arrange a World Federation of Trade Unions conference in Chicago foundered on the visa problem. In June 1948 a visa was refused to the secretary of the Latin-American Federation of Labor, Salvador Ocampo, on the ground that he was also a Communist senator in Chile. In September a visa was refused to the president of the same organization, Vicente Lombardo Toledano. In the same month seven Ontario trade unionists belonging to Mine, Mill and Smelter Workers were barred at the border while on their way to a meeting of the union in San Francisco. Several British Communist trade unionists failed to obtain visas. In 1952 the American government invited the Norwegian labor movement to send a delegation of trade-union leaders to study the life of American workers. The Norwegians nominated nine, but the State Department ruled that four of them could not be granted visas under the 1950 Act without an intensive investigation of their life histories. The Norwegians called it off.

Scholars, artists and journalists were also excluded even before the passage of the 1950 Act. In January 1948 a visa was refused to Brazil's leading architect, Oscar Niemeyer, who had been invited to lecture by the Yale School of Fine Arts, because he was an open Communist. In October Dr. Ian Cameron, a young Edinburgh University graduate, was refused a visa as being "politically undesirable," although no reason was apparent except that his sister was secretary of the Socialist Medical Association. Even avowed anti-Communist intellectuals were suspect if they had come to anti-Communism by way of Communism. In 1949 the British poet and critic Stephen

Spender, who had been a member of the British Party for about three weeks some twelve years earlier, and who had recently contributed to *The God That Failed*, ran into visa difficulties when he was invited by Harvard and other universities to lecture. The American Embassy in London recommended a "waiver" in his case, and the visa was finally granted; Spender wrote indignantly to *The New York Times* about the whole episode.[14]

The Subversive Activities Control Act came into effect in October 1950. It barred those who advocated "the economic, international and governmental doctrines of world communism or . . . of any other form of totalitarianism." Past and present members of any totalitarian party were barred, and for the first time the Communist Party was specified by name. The only loopholes applied to those who had ceased to be members before the age of sixteen; to those who had been compelled to join by law, or to obtain employment or food; and to those who not only had defected five years previously but also had demonstrated active opposition.

Truman vetoed the bill, but after Congress overrode his veto, Attorney General McGrath implemented it with such vigor that Senator Ferguson accused the government of deliberately causing chaos to subvert the act. In October it was announced that all visas already issued were suspended until new rules could be drafted to conform to the legislation. Ellis Island became the scene of wholesale detentions of impeccably respectable visitors; a bewildered group of German civil libertarians, for example, went straight to a confinement on the island even though they had been invited to visit America by the State Department. Ellen Knauff recalled:

> The large detention hall, which offers more or less comfortable accommodations to a maximum of 300 people, harbored close to 700 at times. The majority had no place to sit down. The noise became unbearable, and the establishment was a complete madhouse.[15]

So painstaking was the scrutiny into individual biographies imposed by the McCarran Act that by December 31, 1951, there was a backlog of 9,197 visa applications. In December twelve Congressmen, including McCarran and Walter, wrote McGrath protesting that the term "totalitarian" as used in the act was not meant to apply to former Nazis and Fascists. In fact the State Department itself had already adopted this general point of view; in 1948 the Department's visa chief, Hervé L'Heureux, remarked during a press conference on the Displaced Persons program: "Under normal immigration laws there is nothing that would exclude a Nazi or a Fascist . . . I don't think we have ever concluded that the Nazi Party agreed that it is for [sic] the overthrow of government by force." In 1953 it was finally established in the courts that the Nazi and Fascist parties did not fall within the act's definition of "totalitarian" parties.[16]

For would-be temporary visitors, the prospects were now much worse. Of all those excluded at the port of entry in 1950, only 3 percent were branded as subversives or anarchists; by 1957 the proportion had risen to 33 percent. In 1947 nine were excluded; in 1948 three; in 1949 thirty-nine; in 1950, 157; in 1951, 165. Detentions of temporary visitors who had been issued valid visas became increasingly common. In March 1952 a senior official of Trans-Australia Airlines, Herbert Maley, was held for thirteen days in Honolulu, because he refused to answer questions about his political beliefs, except to deny that he was a Communist.[17] In July 1952 the State Department apologized for having detained Grantley Adams, leader of the Barbados Assembly.

But the great majority of those who were excluded on political grounds never reached an American port of entry. Section 221 (g) of the McCarran Act specified that no visa should be issued if it appeared to the consular officer abroad that the applicant was ineligible. No appeal was allowed; thus a minor official was vested with considerable power, and all the evidence indicates that American consular officials at this time tended to be frightened, ignorant, prejudiced, arrogant and naïve. Two novelists of international reputation encountered visa difficulties in 1952. Alberto Moravia, whose visit had been suggested by State Department educational-exchange officials, was refused a visa in July despite his denial of ever having been associated with Communists or Fascists. Graham Greene, who had been a member of the CP for four weeks in 1923, while an Oxford undergraduate, finally got his visa in February after a long delay, provoking a *New York Times* editorial to lament: ". . . to what depths of puerility our immigration laws have been allowed to sink." Greene himself commented during his visit: "People came here not to win television sets or refrigerators, but to gain freedom from house spies, informers and a military regime. But there are a lot of informers working here now."[18]

Evidently perturbed by the failure of several noted foreign anti-Communist intellectuals to obtain visas, the American Committee for Cultural Freedom issued a memorandum in December 1952 complaining that American consular officials were more often than not novices who understood neither the language nor the political history of the country in which they found themselves.

## FOREIGN SCHOLARS AND ARTISTS BARRED

Scholarly and scientific exchanges were now seriously damaged, so much so that the American Psychological Association waived the chance to be host of the International Congress of Psychology in 1954, because the Association did not wish to subject six hundred foreign psychologists to visa humiliations. Visas were refused to the Polish poet Czeslaw Milosz, author of *The Captive Mind*, and to Joseph Krips, conductor of the Vienna State Opera, who was not permitted to fulfill an engagement with the Chicago Symphony Orchestra because he had conducted in Moscow and Leningrad. Maurice Chevalier, the sixty-three-year-old French actor, was barred because he had signed the Stockholm Petition and, according to Secretary of State Acheson, had taken part in pro-Communist entertainments. The French sociologist Georges Friedmann discovered that permission to enter prior to the McCarran Act did not guarantee the same privilege after it. Following a visit in 1948, Friedmann published his highly regarded *Où va le travail humain* and was invited by the American Council of Learned Societies to participate in the Corning International Conference in May 1951. Although he had broken with the French Communist Party in 1938, a visa was now refused despite the intervention of the French Minister of National Education, who offered himself as Friedmann's guarantor.[19]

More remarkable was the denial of a visa to Dr. Michael Polanyi, the distinguished British political scientist, author of *The Logic of Liberty* (1951), and a lifelong critic of Soviet Communism. Having been elected to the chair of social philosophy at the University of Chicago, he applied in January 1951 for an immigrant visa. The two American consuls in Liverpool who questioned him were particularly interested in his erstwhile membership in the League of Free German Culture and, during the year 1946–47, of the Society for Cultural Relations with the USSR. The two consuls had read none of his writings, nor did they perceive the significance of the fact that Arthur Koestler had dedicated *The Yogi and the Commissar* to Polanyi. Although he desperately changed his application from an immigrant to a visitor's visa, the answer was no.[20]

The sphere of learning and research most critically affected by America's version of the Iron Curtain was that of the natural sciences. On August 8, 1952, Assistant Secretary of State John D. Hickerson addressed the International Geographical Union's Assembly in Washington:

With a feeling of humility, I say: We Americans recognize how directly our own progress and well-being are related to the scientific achievements of other nations, and we are ever ready to give others the understanding and the respect which we ourselves seek to merit.

However, this "understanding" and this "respect" often stopped short of allowing them to enter the United States on temporary visits.

Edward Shils estimated that by 1955 at least one hundred, and probably several hundred, foreign scientists had been refused visas. Another authority, referring to sixty specific cases where visas were either refused or indefinitely delayed, added, "And the indications are that the actual number is at least three times as large." Every foreign scientist applying for a visa was obliged to list all the organizations to which he had belonged or subscribed during the previous fifteen years. Frequently American consuls also subjected him to a verbal interrogation: "What do you think of the United States' policy in Korea?" or "What's your stand toward the NATO?" According to a report in the *Bulletin of Atomic Scientists* (October 1952), at least 50 percent of foreign scientists who applied for visas experienced some difficulty and, in the case of the French, 70 to 80 percent. Almost any member of the Association des Travailleurs Scientifiques was automatically refused, largely because Frédéric Joliot-Curie had been president after the war.[21]

The astonomer Daniel Chalonge, a member of the Institut d'Astrophysique in Paris, was invited in 1948 to work at the McDonald Observatory and to visit observatories at Climax, McMath and Yale. Chalonge, however, was a member of both the left-wing friendship society France-URSS and the editorial board of the pro-Communist cultural journal *La Pensée*. Arriving at the American consulate in Paris on October 27, he found testimonials on his behalf spread out on the desk of the Consul, Cecil W. Gray, who remarked contemptuously, "Scientists will invite anybody." Gray asked him whether he was active in politics; whether he had met Russian diplomats in France-URSS; whether he had considered what might happen to him in the event of war. A visa was finally granted him on January 26, 1949, five days before he was due to *complete* his visit to McDonald Observatory. Two months later he called at the consulate again to apply for a new visa, and was reprimanded for having signed a letter in *La Pensée* that criticized *Le Monde* for an attack on the USSR. His application was now denied.[22]

Invited to America by the American Chemical and Harvey Societies, Jacques Monod, of the Institut Pasteur, was informed that he was an "inadmissible alien" under the McCarran Act because he had been in the CP from 1943 to 1945. Questions such as "Have you signed a petition against the Atlantic Alliance or against the atomic bomb?" were frequently encountered by French scientists. In 1952 the physicist Louis Leprince Ringuet, a member of the French Academy of Sciences, wrote to the Federation of American Scientists that many of his fellow countrymen "are no longer willing to make the request . . . The applicant has the real feeling of being a suspect who is put off from week to week, the more so because he receives a long interrogation as if before a police magistrate . . . I have even seen the expression 'Iron Curtain of the West' applied to the United States . . ." [23]

Professor E. B. Chain, a British Nobel laureate, was refused a visa, probably because he had made several trips to Eastern Europe as an official of the UN Health Commission to promote penicillin production. A visa was refused outright to Professor Jean Wyart of the Sorbonne, a member of France-URSS and of the editorial board of *La Pensée*, who was due to represent France at an international minerology conference in New York.

V. R. E. Davies, a biochemist from Sheffield University, was invited to spend the academic year 1950–51 in the department of physiology of the University of Utah. In May 1950 he received his contract, and July 14 he visited the American consulate in Manchester to fill in the requisite forms. The Consul immediately told Davies and his wife that their application was rejected, would provide no reasons, but indicated they might understand if they looked at Section 3 of the 1917 Immigration Act. Davies had in fact been a Party member from 1942 to 1944, when he was in his early twenties, but in 1945 he had campaigned publicly against the Communist candidates during the Parliamentary election: "By this time . . . considerable expense had been incurred. Seventy letters had been written; I had resigned my position at the University, and my wife her teaching appointment at the Technical College, and we had arranged for others to live in our home for a year."

In June 1951 a visa was denied to Professor Mogens Westergaard, a Danish geneticist and former Communist who had broken with the CP over Soviet censorship of Ivan Michurin's theories. He had been invited to attend an international conference of geneticists on Long Island. Professor Bruno Ferretti, of the Marconi Institute of Physics, Rome, was invited by J. Robert Oppenheimer to spend the year 1951–52 at the Princeton Institute. Although he belonged to no political party, Ferretti had not received a definite answer to his application after fourteen months. He decided to cancel his travel reservations at a personal cost of $100. [24]

Conferences suffered. The 12th International Congress of Pure and Applied Chemistry was held in New York in September 1951, but many of the most distinguished foreign delegates were, through no choice of their own, absent. Marguerite Perey, discoverer of element 87, francium, had offended the State Department by once inviting Professor Irène Joliot-Curie, a Nobel Prize winner, a fellow traveler and the wife of a Communist, to the dedication of her laboratory. She got her visa too late. So did Professor Leopold Ruzicka, of Switzerland, dean of steroid chemists and a Nobel Prize winner who, more than a dozen years earlier, had been made an honorable member of an academy of science behind the Iron Curtain. Ruzicka did not receive his visa until two or three days before the Congress opened and therefore did not bother to come. Professors Marotta (of Italy), George Harvey and Steig Viebel (of Denmark) encountered difficulties and called off their trips. Dr. Francesco Giordano, head of the Italian delegation, and two of its members were turned down, as was Dr. Michel Magat of France, who was scheduled to chair a symposium. The British physical chemist E. A. Guggenheim visited the American consulate in London, surveyed the onerous and odious questionnaire, and concluded he might as well stay at home.

In the same month the University of Chicago held an International Congress on Nuclear Physics. Ten of the twenty-four extremely distinguished foreign scientists invited had visa difficulties. Neither Professor S. Devons, of Imperial College, London, nor Dr. Lew Kowarski, the French physicist, was able to attend. Professor Rudolph E. Peierls, a German-born British physicist who had played a leading role in the development of the A-bomb, and who was both head of the mathematical physics department of Birmingham University and a fellow of the Royal Society, received his invitation to the congress in March, six months ahead of time. At the American consulate he was asked whether the Atomic Scientists' Association, to which he belonged, was Communist. While waiting for a visa he actually traveled as a member of a British government delegation to Washington to take part in a declassification conference, the most super-top-secret activity of all. While in America, he was able to call in on the Chicago congress. As for his visitor's visa, it did not arrive until November, two months after the congress.[25]

Also invited to the congress was Professor M. L. Oliphant, a fellow of the Royal Society, then working in Australia as director of the Research School of Physical Science. Apparently he had given offense by criticizing American government policy on the international control of atomic energy. An expert on microwave radar, Oliphant had been the first British scientist to make official contact with the United States atomic-energy project in 1941. In 1943 he had led the British team that worked with Edward O. Lawrence on the electromagnetic-separation project at Berkeley. But none of this was material to his visa application in 1951.

> Late in the evening of September 11, when we were packed and ready to leave next morning, I received a telephone message from the embassy saying that it was regretted that permission to issue the visas had not been received from Washington . . . Since my wife was to accompany me, and we were going on to Great Britain, I had to arrange for the letting of my house, accommodation for my children, and so on.

No reason was ever provided; a year later the ban remained in force.

In January 1951 M. Minnaert, professor of astronomy at the University of Utrecht, was invited to lecture at the Observatory of Michigan's summer school and also to give a course at California Institute of Technology. Although he received a visa a mere two weeks after applying for one, a fortnight later the U.S. consulate in Amsterdam asked him to call in with his passport, and then informed him that his visa was not yet granted. It was now so late in the day that Minnaert canceled the trip—"I leave it to the reader to picture the mental strain . . . I had also to prepare the lecture which I had intended to give, to plan the work at my institute for the months of my absence . . ." His own explanation for the State Department's attitude was that after the International Astronomical Union had agreed to meet in Leningrad in 1951, the executive council had then changed its mind; he was one of those who protested the change.

Charles Sadron, professor of physics at the University of Strasbourg and a former inmate of a German concentration camp, was invited to the International Union of Pure and Applied Chemistry, held in New York and Washington in September 1951. He was a member of the Peace Movement and his visa application went completely unanswered. In May 1952 the American Consul in Strasbourg commented to him that if he had signed the Stockholm Appeal he must be violently anti-American.

Professor E. A. Pringsheim, of Cambridge University, a botanist and an outstanding authority on algae, had been a Czechoslovak citizen before emigrating to Britain in 1939. During the war he participated in an all-party organization connected with Beneš's government-in-exile, but he left it before the end of the war because he considered it to be too left-wing. In 1947 he became a British citizen. By 1952 his plate was heaped with invitations from Yale; the Oceanographic Institution, Woods Hole, Massachusetts; Harvard; Indiana; the University of California and the New York Academy of Science. At the consulate he was humiliated, fingerprinted, made to fill in from memory forms he had previously completed and finally informed by letter—without reasons—that "your entry is deemed prejudicial to the interests of the United States." [26]

In November 1951 the Mexican delegation refused to attend the American Physical Society conference in Houston, after two of its four members, Juan de Oyarzabal and Marios Moshinsky, had been denied visas. Oyarzabal was apparently suspect because he had served in the Republican Navy during the Spanish Civil War; his aunt had been the Republic's ambassador to Sweden. The International Congress of Genetics passed a resolution in August 1953 not to meet in any country where delegates were liable to be refused entry. The International Union of Crystallography and the International Botanical Congress decided to hold their next meetings in Canada rather than in the United States. In October 1954 the International Astronomical Union resolved to meet in the Soviet Union in 1958, rather than in the United States, and to return to America in 1961 if, and only if, the government admitted all the delegates. When the fourth annual High Energy Physics Conference was held in Rochester, New York, in February 1954, five of the twenty foreign scientists invited had visa difficulties; for the fifth conference, ten out of forty foreign physicists encountered problems, including Nobel Prize winners. This latter conference was sponsored by the AEC, the Office of Naval Research and similar organizations, but the Passport Division of the State Department was not impressed. [27]

## THE CASE OF DR. TSIEN

Lastly, we come to the anomaly of "visa denial in reverse"—cases where the U.S. government attempted to prevent a foreign scientist from leaving America and returning to his own country. One such case, which went to the courts, was *Han-Lee Mao v. Brownell* (1953), in which the Attorney General brought an action to prevent Han-Lee Mao from returning to China whence he had come to take an MA in oceanography. It was feared that he would place his newly acquired understanding of sea-beds at the disposal of another Mao.

Much the most celebrated case [28] of this kind concerned Tsien Hsue-shen, referred to henceforward as Dr. Tsien, the genius behind Chinese missile development in the 1960s. Born in Shanghai, he first arrived in America in 1935, at the age of twenty-six, and played a key role in American rocket development during the Second World War. Appointed Goddard professor of jet propulsion at Caltech, with ample funds, a generous staff and enough prestige to warrant a *Time* story in 1949, Dr. Tsien seemed in every way to be a happily integrated American when he applied to become a citizen in that year. The FBI now began to investigate his prewar friends and political associates. In June 1950 his security clearance was revoked—a traumatic shock to Tsien. Uncertain about his long-term future, he decided to spend a year in China, where his father was still alive. The Assistant Secretary of the Navy gave orders that Dr. Tsien must not be allowed to leave the country, and from now on he was shadowed by the FBI continually. On August 23, 1950, he was detained, and eight boxes of documents that he was shipping to China were confiscated by Customs. In fact Tsien, who said he intended to return after visiting Shanghai, had scrupulously returned all the classified material in his care; not one classified document was found in the cases. But on September 7 he was arrested by the FBI on a charge of concealing CP membership and thus entering illegally when he last returned to America from China in 1947. Two weeks later he was freed on bail on condition that he did not leave Los Angeles County.

Now deportation proceedings were launched against the man whose departure had been forcibly prevented. During hearings in November witnesses came forward to testify that Dr. Tsien had been in the CP in 1939—that the discussion group in which he had taken part had been a Party chapter. In December 1952 his appeal against a deportation order was denied; yet the government had no intention of allowing him to leave the country; for both sides the real issue was his freedom of movement. All along Tsien enjoyed the support and help of Dr. Lee A. DuBridge, president of Caltech, enabling him to work there in a kind of legal limbo, separated from all classified material, until 1955. Then a quiet exchange deal was negotiated with China; Tsien departed voluntarily in September of that year and was warmly received in China, where the Academy of Sciences appointed him chief of research in applied mechanics. In the course of a press interview he announced that he never had been a Communist; but in 1958 he joined the Chinese Communist Party. The moral of this story need hardly be labored.

Whereas aliens already residing inside the United States were entitled to at least a curtailed version of due process when the Immigration Service sought to expel them, the alien knocking at the gate had, according to the Supreme Court ruling in *Knauff v. Shaughnessy* (1950), no rights of access or procedure beyond those that Congress, exercising its plenary powers on behalf of the sovereign nation, might allow. Although we cannot catalogue here all the cases of severe hardship [29] that arose, one highly publicized case exemplified the Kafkaesque dimensions of the system. Ellen Knauff, Jewish and born in Germany in 1915, had emigrated to Czechoslovakia under Hitler then escaped to England, where she served "efficiently and honorably" with the RAF. After the war she found civilian employment in Germany with the U.S. War Department, which rated her work "very good" and "excellent." In 1948 she married Kurt Knauff, a naturalized American war veteran, and in August she arrived in New York harbor hoping to enter the country and be naturalized under the War Brides Act. Instead she was detained on Ellis Island, where she was informed by an interrogator that if she asked to see a lawyer she must be guilty.

Her husband flew home, went from office to office in Washington, but could get nothing firm. Every time she and her lawyer, Gunther Jacobson, went to a lower court in Manhattan on a writ of *habeas corpus* the Immigration Department asked for a postponement, and back she went to Ellis Island. The District Court and the Court of Appeals upheld the Attorney General's right to exclude an alien without any hearing at all on the basis of confidential information. Finally the Supreme Court granted *certiorari*, and Justice Jackson released her on $1,000 bond (the government asked that it should be $20,000). At long last she could tread the streets of Manhattan on her own! But the Supreme Court later sustained the judgment of the District Court and the Court of Appeals, rejecting her plea for a hearing and due process: she was without rights. Despite press agitation on her behalf, Commissioner of Immigration Watson B. Miller announced on February 2, 1950 that he planned to deport her immediately. Congressman Walter subpoenaed her before the House Subcommittee on Immigration; when the Immigration Department, which was threatening to send her back to Europe any hour, refused to honor the subpoena, Walter threatened it with contempt. She arrived in Washington, was treated in a friendly way by the subcommittee, then whisked back to Ellis Island. On May 17, 1950, she was taken to Idlewild Airport and her luggage was put aboard a plane bound for Germany. But, with a bill on her behalf already passed by the House, Celler had warned Attorney General McGrath that the House would regard deportation as an act of contempt—this gained her a last-minute reprieve. The plane took off with her luggage still on board.

In January 1951 McGrath granted her parole. In March she came to an Immigration Service hearing in Washington and discovered at last something of the nature and source of the allegations against her. A Czech female witness testified that in 1947 Ellen Knauff had been in touch with the espionage section of the Czech mission in Germany. The Immigration Board reaffirmed her exclusion without allowing her counsel to cross-examine the hostile witness in any meaningful way. Now she was back on Ellis Island for the third time. In June the case came before the Board of Immigration

Appeals, which unanimously decided that, since the government's witnesses based their story on hearsay alone, she should be admitted to the country. On November 2, 1951—almost three and a half years after her arrival—the Attorney General finally exercised his discretion in her favor. Ellen Knauff concluded her vivid account of these harrowing trials: "We have accepted fear as our supreme master." [30] This was a charitable view of politicians, bureaucrats and petty officials whose behavior was arbitrary and corrupt. The essential corruption was to protect and conceal flimsy, hearsay rumors, the tittle-tattle of paid or otherwise interested informers, by which the Immigration Service was manured, and to do so under the bogus mask of national security.

# PART FOUR

## Purge of
## the Civil Service

# 13

## The Federal Civil Service

### POLITICAL TESTS IN THE CIVIL SERVICE

Since 1884 Civil Service Rule I had forbidden the government to inquire into the "political or religious opinions or affiliations of any applicant" for the federal civil service. During America's brief participation in the First World War, however, the Civil Service Commission (CSC) conducted 3,672 loyalty investigations in addition to thousands of investigations launched by separate agencies. The procedure was informal, and most of the subjects were not aware they were being investigated. In 1918, there were 660 applicants who were barred from federal employment because of questionable loyalty.[1]

The Hatch Act of 1939 stipulated that no person was to be employed by the federal government if he had "membership in any political party or organization which advocates the overthrow of our constitutional form of government." The Justice Department Appropriations Act of June 28, 1941, made $100,000 available to the FBI for investigating federal employees who were "members of subversive organizations." On October 17 of that year, Representative Martin Dies sent the Attorney General the names of 1,121 government employees whom he regarded as "Communists or affiliates of subversive organizations." After investigation, only two of the 1,121 were discharged. Attorney General Francis Biddle reported to Congress, "It is now clear that the objective test of membership in a 'front' organization is thoroughly unsatisfactory." This attitude was what mainly distinguished the Roosevelt administration from the Truman one.

Although the Civil Service Commission argued in 1942 that a CP member or "follower" was primarily loyal to a foreign government, so that there was "a strong presumption in favor of his willingness to take steps designed to overthrow our constitutional form of government if directed so to do," [2] nevertheless the CSC in the Roosevelt era forbade its investigators to inquire into the trade-union affiliations of employees, and into sympathy for Loyalist Spain, the Abraham Lincoln Brigade, the Washington Bookshop, the National Lawyers Guild, the ACLU, the Socialist Party, the League of Women Shoppers, et cetera, and into any question of reading matter. Roosevelt made a few discriminatory gestures, partly out of concern, but mainly to placate Congress.

There is no doubt that during the war the government actually favored Communists for certain agencies and phases of military intelligence work. Professor H. Stuart Hughes later recalled that a "few hundred" Communists entered federal service, mostly clustered in the new war agencies, but with only three or four of them occupying senior positions. His own experience in the State Department was that Communists generally strove to do their job well, seriously and zealously, and were only occasionally deflected by ideology. Nearly all of them resigned in 1945–46. The process of easing them out was fairly quietly performed, at least until 1947. [3]

It is worth emphasizing, before we turn to the Truman loyalty program, that the war years saw *little over one hundred dismissals and some thirty-odd "political resignations."* These figures make a striking contrast with what was to follow. [4]

## The Truman Loyalty Program

In July 1946 a subcommittee of the House Civil Service Committee published a report to the effect that existing federal security was inadequate. Attorney General Tom Clark and Civil Service Commissioner Arthur S. Flemming urged Truman to tighten the screws. From July to November the President temporized, but, following the Republican Congressional election victory, he issued on November 25 Executive Order 9806, establishing the President's Temporary Commission on Employee Loyalty. Membership of the Commission was confined to senior representatives of the Justice, State, Treasury, War and Navy Departments, and of the CSC. Its chairman was A. Devitt Vanech, Special Assistant to Attorney General Clark, who told the Commission on January 23 that "the serious threat which *even one* disloyal person constitutes to the security of the United States Government" was insupportable. Equally ominous, most of the witnesses summoned by the Commission were representatives of the investigating agencies (the FBI, Military and Naval Intelligence) who, by profession and cast of mind, were obsessed not only by the need for total vigilance but also possessed by hatred for the New Deal. It was here that Lieutenant Colonel Randolph, of Military Intelligence (G-2), pointed out that, "A liberal is only a hop, skip, and a jump from a Communist. A Communist starts as a liberal." [5]

Most of the Commission's recommendations were implemented by Truman. A few deserve special attention. The Commission granted the right of double appeal for incumbent employees; to the head of the agency, then to a Loyalty Review Board within the CSC. But for applicants there would be no appeal. The Commission advised that charges should normally be specific, and that the sources of information should be revealed, *except* when the investigating agency certified in writing that concealment was necessary to protect its sources. In such an (rare?) event, the FBI must furnish "sufficient information about such informants on the basis of which the requesting department can make an adequate evaluation of the information furnished." [6] But the FBI concealed its sources in nine cases out of ten from the accused and in the vast majority of cases even from the assessing agency.

On March 25, 1947, Truman launched the new loyalty program with Executive Order 9835, to take effect from October 1. It contained the most sinister and destructive departure in postwar domestic politics, one which was to ramify far beyond the federal service and poison wide areas of American working, educational and cultural life. Truman authorized the Attorney General to list those organizations that he considered to be "totalitarian, Fascist, Communist, or subversive, or as having adopted a policy of approving the commission of acts of force or violence to deny others their constitutional rights."

In the Truman loyalty program not only membership but also "sympathetic association" with such groups was to be taken into account. The notion of sympathetic association was novel in American law, but the loyalty program put itself beyond the principles of law on the assumption that no man has a constitutional right to a job in government. Although E.O. 9835 did not define disloyalty and did stipulate that membership in a listed organization was not to be regarded as conclusive proof of disloyalty, "only one piece of evidence which may or may not be helpful in arriving at a conclusion", in practice, the very precision of the list (an organization was either on it or not, in clear, hard print) was to make *present* membership almost automatic grounds for dismissal; in cases of past and regretted membership, the employee retained some hope.

The President announced that he was determined to defend not only national security but also democracy. He later conceded that the loyalty program had its flaws, notably that every time a man was promoted or transferred he had to undergo the whole loyalty investigation all over again.[7]

Professor Ralph S. Brown estimated in 1958 that about 13.5 million Americans came within the scope of the loyalty program. Of these, 2.3 million were in the federal civil service, 3 million in the military departments (including civilians), 4.5 million in industry and transport. Another 2 million in state and local employment were covered by regional loyalty-security programs that drew inspiration from the federal one; 1.6 million in the professions (about 1 million of whom worked in public employment) were affected by either federal or state laws, or both. In 1955 about 3 million men and women were working in private industrial concerns whose defense contracts required clearance for access to top secret, secret and confidential information. About 1.5 million others worked in industries that by the middle 1950s had their own security programs inspired either by the employer or by the union. Estimating the total labor force at 65 million, this meant that one out of every five working people had to take an oath or receive clearance as a condition of employment. But these figures merely measured the work force at any given moment; taking into account the normally high American turnover in employment— in the federal civil service it was annually 500,000—the actual number of people affected at one time or another must have been considerably higher.[8]

The civil-service unions surrendered to the rising patriotism of the day and virtually abandoned their members to the purge. Said James B. Burns, president of the American Federation of Government Employees, AFL: "The AFGE is confident that the loyalty program will be carried out by the Civil Service Commission and the FBI in a truly American fashion. Certainly there is no reason for hysteria or the notion that this is a witch hunt." Luther Steward, president of the National Federation of Federal Employees (independent), remarked, "Federal employees who have nothing to conceal—and they are the overwhelming majority—are not those who are crying out most passionately against the loyalty program and raising the bogey of persecution." The single thorn in the flesh was the pro-Communist United Public Workers (at that time in the CIO), whose president, Abram Flaxer, took a different view: "Every member of every trade union is in grave peril as long as this type of union-busting witch hunt is allowed to continue."[9] Fairly soon membership of the UPWA became virtually incompatible with federal employment.

## SECURITY OFFICERS AND SECURITY FILES

The security officers now came into their own. Their number increased sharply, and they wielded enormous power, responsible as they were for scrutinizing the behavior patterns, associations and sex lives of employees in their department, and for making preliminary assessments that, if damaging, could ultimately ruin careers and lives. S. A. Goudsmit, chairman of the physics department of Brookhaven National Laboratory, wrote of certain security officers: "They relish the collection of derogatory information; their job is an outlet for their frustrated hatred of men. They are biased against intellectuals and anyone who reads a book." The journalist and broadcaster Elmer Davis recalled that, having given a reference for a girl who wanted to rejoin the Navy Department as a civilian employee, he was visited by a security officer from Naval Intelligence. When Davis spoke highly of the girl's mental capability, the officer commented, "These intelligent people are very likely to be attracted to Communism." [10] The lawyer Joseph Borkin, who acted as an intermediary for many federal employees with clearance problems, observed that the worst security officers proposed deals by which the employee would be allowed to resign on condition that he not defend himself or attempt to return to government service—thus vindicating their own power and judgment while demonstrating their "magnanimity."

More powerful than mere men, however, were the files that men compiled. Feeding one upon the other, passed from hand to hand, the files maintained by the FBI, the military intelligence agencies and the CSC were only the start of a process by which a man's name might ultimately be checked against HCUA's files, local law-enforcement files, the records of schools, colleges and former employers and, as E.O. 9835 permitted, of "any other appropriate source" (it specifically directed that the HCUA files should be consulted in federal loyalty checks). The scale of this political data-gathering, and the elastic criteria upon which it was based, were demonstrated when Philip Young, chairman of the CSC, announced in November 1955 that the Commission maintained a card index of two million people affiliated with subversive organizations.

Whatever went into a file stayed there. If someone called a man a vegetarian, and this information was filed, and if subsequently the man proved to the loyalty board that he ate meat every day, and thus was "cleared," his file would continue to record the allegation of vegetarianism. When Charles E. Bohlen was having trouble winning Senate confirmation as Eisenhower's ambassador to the Soviet Union, it came to light that a principal derogatory document in his file was a statement by a State Department stenographer who claimed that she could detect immorality in men by her delicate attunement to their unseen emanations. After a half hour of taking dictation from Bohlen, she had concluded that his emanations were not pure.[11]

## THE LOYALTY BOARDS

The inquisitorial mesh established by E.O. 9835 to sift the orthodox from the eccentric comprised some two hundred agency loyalty boards subordinate to the heads of agencies, who appointed the members, laid down rules of procedure and made final decisions. Fourteen regional loyalty boards were appointed by the regional directors of the CSC, composed largely of conservatives and Republicans, which was Truman's tactic for taking the wind out of the Congressional sails. Seth Richardson, the first chairman of the Loyalty Review Board, established the style that was to prevail when he announced that in the majority of cases identification of allegatory informants and information "probably will not be practical." [12] Yet the Republican opposition and the right-wing Democrats continued to berate the LRB as being soft on Communism, the hard evidence being that although the LRB under Richardson never overruled the State Department on a dismissal, it had by May 1950 reversed findings of suspect loyalty in 143 out of 451 cases. Following McCarthy's attacks on Richardson's successor, the Republican former Senator and Governor of Connecticut, Hiram Bingham, the LRB panicked and urged Truman to tighten the criteria for dismissal.

This the President obligingly did by issuing E.O. 10241 on April 28, 1951, only three months after he publicly voiced fears that the program was infringing civil liberties. Whereas under E.O. 9835 the criterion was to *retain* a man if there was reasonable doubt about his disloyalty, the amendment stipulated that he should be *dismissed* if there was reasonable doubt about his loyalty. The burden of proof was reversed at a stroke; henceforward every civil servant would have to prove his innocence—and who, in such a time, is wholly innocent? In May the LRB ordered that the new standard be applied to 565 cases under consideration, and called for a review of 846 cases where the employee had been cleared under the old criterion only on appeal. By March 1952, of the 9,300 employees who had been cleared 2,756 were again under review in the light of the new criterion.[13]

## THE SECURITY-RISK CONCEPT

Two further developments intensified the repressive nature of the program. In 1950 Congress passed Public Law 733, which permitted the suspension of an employee, without procedural protections, in eleven specified government agencies, including State, Justice and Commerce, for reasons of "national security." (P.L. 733 accorded the employee the right to inquire of the CSC his eligibility for other government agencies.) The loyalty program was now supplemented, and to some extent supplanted, by a security-risk program. A security risk is not necessarily a disloyal person; he or she may be a loyal person whose character, habits and associations make him or her potentially liable to disclose classified information, or vulnerable to blackmail. Homosexuals were regarded in this light. The most important practical effect of introducing the security-risk criterion was that even where left-wing political associations could not be construed to indicate more than innocence, naïveté or stupidity—and therefore not disloyalty—they could be interpreted as security risks. The Attorney General's list loomed even larger. R. W. Scott McLeod, who became Administrator of the State Department's Bureau of Security in 1953, remarked that the security system is preventive—"There can be no proof, since future events are not susceptible to proof."

We have seen, then, a succession of ever stiffer measures—E. O. 9835, P.L. 733, the shift in "reasonable doubt," the introduction of summary dismissal on security grounds in certain agencies—the cumulative effect of which is reflected in the fact that of employees eventually dismissed about 40 percent had suffered previous loyalty-security proceedings before the fatal one. The situation that had developed by the middle fifties was well described by Henry Mayer:

> The great jeopardy of the average employee stems from the enormous flexibility of the measuring rod applied by the government, the lack of specificity in ultimate charges, the star-chamber hearing including nonconfrontation and deprivation of cross-examination, the wide discretion of the security boards, the absence of findings and the utter hopelessness of review, because even the reviewing courts . . . may not see the basic material if the government feels that it is not in the national interest to reveal it.

After "twenty years of treason" the Republicans were set to clean house. All eggheads, planners and innovators in the federal service were suspect. The new Under Secretary of the Interior would presently boast how many Harvard and Columbia Ph.D.'s he had sent packing. What lingering traces of the New Deal spirit had survived the Truman era were to be snuffed out. E.O. 10450 of April 1953 extended the "security risk" criterion of P.L. 733 (1950) to every agency and every type of job.

The loyalty program was now scrapped; henceforward security would be the only yardstick; employment had to be "clearly consistent" with national security. While seven categories of offense were listed as incompatible with this yardstick, Section 8 (I) (i) of E.O. 10450 provided a scattershot solution in the event of doubt: "any behavior, activities or associations which tend to show that the individual is not reliable or trustworthy." Previously, denial of access to classified material had to be preceded by charges; this was no longer necessary. Worse, under the new system, charges involved automatic suspension *without pay*. (This was a form of pressure intended to cause quick resignations, and it did.) As regards hearings, Eisenhower's E.O. 10450 made no provision for them, leaving it to the discretion of agency and department heads, subject to the requirements of P.L. 733. No hearings were permitted for applicants and probationary employees.

On October 13, 1953, the President amended E.O. 10450 to add a new criterion for automatic dismissal: reliance on the Fifth Amendment before a Congressional committee regarding alleged disloyalty or other misconduct.

With the abolition of the loyalty program, the regional loyalty boards and the LRB, which Republicans regarded as deplorably soft on Communism, were scrapped. According to one source, of 8,026 cases adjudicated by regional and agency loyalty boards up to May 1950, 94 percent resulted in clearance. Of the remainder, nearly one third were cleared by the LRB.[14] Despite the pressures of the *Zeitgeist*, even the narrowly conservative *nongovernmental* loyalty-board members enjoyed an independent status that afforded at least a possibility of objectivity. The Eisenhower regime eradicated this independence; henceforward employees fortunate enough to be accorded a hearing would be judged by three government servants from another agency.

## STATISTICS OF THE PURGE

A statistical assessment of the havoc wrought in the federal civil service by the loyalty and security programs indicates that under Truman 1,210 were dismissed and about 6,000 resigned, compared with a little over 100 dismissals during the war years under the Roosevelt administration. Figures for dismissals and resignations during the first three years of the Eisenhower administration are more difficult to disentangle, partly because the Republicans played an inaccurate and misleading numbers game, partly because the statistics were often issued in a form that blurred the line between dismissals of "subversives" and dismissals of others. R. W. Scott McLeod put it this way: "I don't think the people are concerned with any breakdown. They don't care if they are drunks, perverts or Communists—they just want to get rid of them." The best estimate is 1,500 security dismissals from 1953 to 1956, and at least 6,000 resignations.

*Taking the 1947–56 period as a whole, then, we find there were about 2,700 civilian dismissals and 12,000 resignations as a result of investigations into subversive activities and associations within the federal civil service.*[15]

## THE GREAT FEAR IN WASHINGTON

Great was the fear prevailing in Washington. Suspicion was universal, and caution also. The Washington lawyer Joseph Fanelli recalled how people employed in government would cross a street to avoid a lawyer known to be handling loyalty cases, and how they would shun political discussion at dinner parties. "Loyalty Issue Keeps U.S. Employees Jittery," announced the *New York Herald Tribune* on June 4, 1950. "Charges, Dismissals and Demands for Investigations Upset Departments." John Lord O'Brian commented, "In such an atmosphere of fear, key government employees tend to become mentally paralyzed. They are afraid to express honest judgments, as it is their duty to do, because later, under a changed atmosphere and different circumstances, they may be charged with disloyalty by those who disagree with them." Psychoanalysts working in areas with a heavy concentration of government workers reported a rise in mental illness combined with a penalization of civil servants receiving psychiatric treatment.

Two psychologists, Marie Jahoda and Stuart W. Cook, interviewed seventy federal employees of professional rank from more than a dozen agencies in October 1951.[16] Most of those interviewed regarded the loyalty-security program as part of a much larger interrelated complex of formal and informal pressures: "Official loyalty checks are not so bad," said one man, "the real danger comes from the Hill." Some spoke of "Gestapo methods" or "just like Germany," and a few of those whom they approached were worried that Jahoda and Cook really worked for the FBI, or, alternatively, that talking to these outsiders might incur departmental censure. The universal aim was to avoid the process of investigation, even if the outcome might be final clearance, for the process itself was a punishment and, in view of legal fees on top of suspension without pay, a fine.

Caution was intense. As one employee put it, "Why lead with your chin? If things are definitely labeled I see no point in getting involved with them. If Communists like apple pie and I do, I see no reason why I should stop eating it. But I would." Most of those interviewed were conscious of having prudently limited their reading of periodicals to *Collier's* and the *Saturday Evening Post*; several bought *The Nation* on a newsstand rather than appear on a subscriber's list. One man found a pile of the *New Masses* when he moved into a house—"I didn't know what to do with it; it seemed dangerous. So in the end I burned it." As for organizations, it was safer not to join them, however respectable or innocuous—the Attorney General's list was always on the move. Anyone active in an organization concerned with social reform or the spread of ideas was automatically suspect.[17] The topics that had become taboo for discussion proliferated rapidly: admitting Red China to the UN, atomic energy, religion, equal rights for Negroes. Many felt that their superiors would not support them if their loyalty were challenged.[18]

## LOYALTY-SECURITY PROCEDURES

The first major case to reach the courts and raise the whole issue of due process in federal loyalty procedures was that of a black woman, Dorothy Bailey, who, having pursued graduate work at Bryn Mawr College, served in the U.S. Employment Service from 1933 until 1947 and rose to the rank of Supervisor of the Training Section, at a salary of $7,911. In June 1947 she was separated as a result of a reduction in force. When she was reemployed in March 1948 she was obliged to undergo a new loyalty check and was charged with having been in the CP or the Communist Political Association, with having attended *un-identified* Communist meetings, and with having associated with Communists. She was also accused of having joined two organizations on the Attorney's General's list, the American League for Peace and Democracy and the Washington Committee for. Democratic Action.

Dorothy Bailey categorically denied Party membership at any time. She also denied attendance at any CP meeting except as part of a graduate seminar in social economy at Bryn Mawr in 1932. She admitted she had been in the ALPD. The Regional Board also questioned her about organizations not on the Attorney General's list, including the Southern Conference for Human Welfare and the League of Women Shoppers, as well as her activities as president of Local 10, United Public Workers, a left-wing union expelled by the CIO in 1950.

Dorothy Bailey believed that her denouncers might well be those who had opposed her reelection to the presidency of her local. But she never learned the evidence against her, or its sources, nor did the LRB ever explain its final adverse judgment. In the case *Bailey v. Richardson*, she asked the court to reinstate her because the loyalty boards had failed to provide due process. The U.S. Court of Appeals for the District of Columbia agreed about the lack of due process, yet justified it as one of the "harsh rules which run counter to every known precept of fairness to the private individual," but which the present world situation imposed. Government employment, argued the Court, is not property and involves no rights. Dissenting, Judge Edgerton pointed out that Dorothy Bailey had submitted seventy affidavits on her behalf to the LRB, and had proven that she had publicly adopted such anti-Communist positions as supporting the Marshall Plan. The government had introduced no evidence at all. In April 1951 the Supreme Court split 4 to 4 on the case, allowing the Appeals verdict and Dorothy Bailey's dismissal to stand.[19]

In his self-congratulatory *Memoirs*, Harry S. Truman wrote: "In many instances the accused was confronted with the accuser or was told who had made the charges, providing the accusers agreed to appear." And Eisenhower, too, professed to dislike the whisperers, telling a Washington dinner in November 1953 of the code on which he was raised as a boy in Abilene, Kansas, the code of Wild Bill Hickok: "In this country, if someone dislikes you, or accuses you, he must come up in front. He cannot hide behind the shadow. He cannot assassinate you or your character from behind . . ." *Yet of 326 sample cases of dismissed employees tabulated by Robert T. Bower, only 6 percent were confronted by prosecution witnesses.*

The loyalty boards themselves had no power to subpoena witnesses; they could question the FBI about the reliability of informants, but they could not demand to know who they were—and in how many instances would the FBI cheerfully confess that it gathered information from unreliable people? During the Dorothy Bailey case, LRB Chairman Seth Richardson mentioned five or six reports from people certified as reliable by the FBI, but, he confessed, "I haven't the slightest knowledge as to who they were or how active they have been in anything." (If a witness did choose to appear, he could elect to testify without the accused employee being present.)[20] When William V. Vitarelli appeared before a security board in June 1954, the government introduced no evidence or witnesses in support of the charges. Though Vitarelli presented four witnesses, the Secretary of the Interior dismissed him in September.

Cases wherein the prosecution witnesses either appeared or their identity was correctly guessed at reinforced the conviction that all informants should have been made available for cross-examination. In three cases the employee correctly guessed who the accuser was— all three accusers were of unbalanced mind. Abraham Chassanow, a senior official of the Navy's Hydrographic Office, was dismissed by a Navy Security Appeal Board even though a Security Board had found him to be a moderate and even conservative citizen whose employment was clearly consistent with national security. In August 1954 the Navy Department reinstated him, condemning the unidentified informants who, apparently out of anti-Semitic bias, had accused him of left-wing associations but failed to corroborate the charges when requestioned.

Milton Mandel, a special assistant in the Labor-Management Bureau of the Department of Labor, was suspended on April 6, 1954, and was not restored to duty until October 18. He was charged with CP membership (false), his wife's membership (false), and his wife's father's membership (also false, apart from the fact that his father-in-law had been dead for six years). Luckily the witness against him appeared at his hearing and was forced to admit that his motive had been Mandel's refusal to recommend his promotion.[21]

During a San Francisco hearing before a Regional Loyalty Board in 1951, a federal employee was confronted by three of his accusers. The lady who admitted she had "turned in" the employee testified:

> . . . he would never wear his tie home or his coat home. He would hang them up in our locker and go home with his shirt open; for a while he wore one of those great big mustaches and I have heard people say according to party lines those are indications that he is not a capitalist . . . Well, I forgot to mention, too, that he used to cut things out of the *Chronicle* and they were always about our Government or about Russia . . . I would say it was perhaps to send them over to Russia to have them see what our paper said; that is just my idea . . .

In another case resulting in final clearance, a hostile witness was cross-examined. He replied: "Well, my impression was that he thought the colored should be entitled to as much as anybody else, and naturally I differed on that." Asked what sort of things a person might say if he were pro-Russian, and what sort of things he might approve of, the witness answered: "Naturally, strong in labor—well, I mean, more or less what it says, that the party line would be that labor should have the upper hand."

"Upper hand over who[sic]?

"Over your, well, so to speak, white-collar man." [22]

A stenographer working in the Public Housing Administration in northern California was accused in 1949 of talking against the government and praising Russia. Suspecting that her accusers were the former manager of her apartment block and his wife, who were gossips, she confronted them. The case against her was then dismissed without a hearing.

These employees, then, were either shrewd or fortunate; the twisted voices of calumny whispering against them were flushed into the daylight and exposed. Dissenting in a 1953 case, Justice William O. Douglas commented: "A hearing at which these faceless informers are allowed to present their whispered rumors and yet escape the test and torture of cross-examination is not a hearing in the Anglo-American sense. We should have done with this practice." A year earlier Justice Hugo Black had quoted the Emperor Trajan's injunction to Pliny the Younger that "Anonymous informations might not be received in any sort of prosecution." The ACLU urged a reform of the system, and in 1957 the American Jewish Congress reported:

> Experience in actual security cases shows that, when it can be exposed or challenged, the so-called information supplied by casual informers rarely results in an adverse decision . . . On the other hand, the anonymity given to such informers is an open invitation to scandalmongers, crackpots and personal enemies. [23]

## GUILT BY ASSOCIATION AND THOUGHT CONTROL

The perils of the system were reflected in the charges, often vague, often crudely prejudiced, often both, that many accused employees had to face. While the vagueness resulted from tittle-tattle and gossip, the prejudice emanated not only from the informants but also from the members of the hearing boards. Quite typical was the allegation: "You have sympathetically associated with members of an organization known to be subversive." But who, which, what, where, when?

In 1949 a postal employee in northern California was accused of having attended CP-sponsored meetings, and having engaged in sympathetic association with Communists or fellow travelers. But no instances were cited. A young civil servant, also from northern California, was charged with being "unduly critical of the United States Government and unduly praiseful of the Communist Government of

Russia." In his five-thousand-word reply he listed every book that he and his wife owned but he could think of nothing to justify the allegation other than having signed a Progressive Party petition in 1948. Suspended for two years, he never had a hearing. In 1955 John Blann, Chairman of the Board of Appeals of the CSC, wrote to him acknowledging that it had all been a mistake—but he was not offered the pay he had lost or a new job.[24]

When four civilians working in the tailor shop at West Point were dismissed in 1951 and 1953, two at a time, the charges included fundraising for the defense of Harry Bridges and soliciting contributions to Russian War Relief during the war. An applicant for a civil-service job in northern California was accused of having favored the freeing of Tom Mooney and of sympathizing with Harry Bridges's fight against deportation. Another employee was accused of having protested against the Regents' loyalty oath at the University of California in 1950. A typist for the Army Recruiting Service was charged under P.L. 808, not with membership of any organization, or even of associating with members, but simply of having expressed Communistic opinions: "You do not favor the Marshall Plan"; "You believe the United States should get out of Germany"; "You said you were glad that Cardinal Mindszenty got what was coming to him in Czechoslovakia [sic]."

A federal employee was charged thus: "You maintained in your library books on Communism, Socialism and Marxism." A northern-California surgical secretary was accused of having criticized monopolies and big business, and with having praised the Soviet system; he was said to have attended a "Communist meeting" at an interracial church in Berkeley. A civilian employee of an armed-services department was charged: "That about 1937–38 in or around (city, state) you actively participated in collecting funds for the use of the Loyalist Army in the Spanish Civil War." When it was "discovered" that a bootblack in the Pentagon had given ten dollars *before he was born* to the Scottsboro Defense Fund, it required seventy FBI interviews to clear him as safe to shine the shoes of Army officers.[25]

A professional-rank employee of a defense agency with access to secret material was charged under E.O. 10450:

> In connection with your study at the University of ——— in the pursuit of a Ph.D. degree in 1950–51, you wrote a thesis which was based mainly on material obtained from the Institute of Pacific Relations which has been cited as a Communistic Front organization by the [HCUA] . . . furthermore it is believed that your thesis definitely sympathized with the aims and ambitions of Soviet Russia.

On the principle of a nursery rhyme he was also accused of (1) having a close association with a man (2) who wrote a book (3) which was advertised in a publication run by Louis Adamic (4) who had been listed in 1948 as an official of the Progressive Party (5) which was cited as a Communist front (6) by the Tenney Committee in California. The employee was cleared.

"We have a confidential informant," another employee was told, "who says he visited your house and listened in your apartment for three hours to a recorded opera entitled *The Cradle Will Rock*." The informer explained that this opera "followed along the lines of a downtrodden laboring man and the evils of the capitalist system." [26]

While formal charges normally reflected the prejudices or mean ambitions of anonymous informers and of the FBI agents themselves, the questions posed at loyalty hearings dramatized the prevalent assumption that major disagreements with government policy were un-American and subversive. Loyalty boards even asked employees what they thought of loyalty boards. The secretary of the Regional Loyalty Board of Northern California asked a witness, "Would you be willing to extend the Marshall Plan to Spain?" Security Officer Armstrong asked William V. Vitarelli:

How many times did you vote for Henry Wallace? How about Norman Thomas? Did his platform coincide more nearly with your ideas of democracy? At one time, or two, were you a strong advocate of the United Nations? Are you still?

Questions of social philosophy, supposedly protected by the First Amendment, were grist to the mill. A geographer employed by the government was asked:

Have you provided any sort of religious training for your children?
Do you believe in government ownership of public utilities as a general proposition?
Have you indicated that you favor redistribution of wealth?
What do you consider a "reactionary" to be?
Do you think that workers in the capitalist system get a relatively fair deal?
In your opinion should Guatemala be both legal and Communistic [sic]?

A State Department employee was asked by Board member Arch Jean whether some of the people he had known had expressed "an ideology that differs from American philosophy." Other defendants or witnesses were asked:

Have you at any time condemned the totalitarian nature of the USSR and deplored the absence of civil liberties in that country? Does he [the employee] believe in the internationalization of patents?
Which would you choose, freedom or security?
Do you think that an outspoken philosophy favoring race equality is an index of Communism?
Have you ever discussed the subject of the dance in Russia with ———?

One employee was hard pressed at her hearing because, *prior* to the grand jury's indictment of Alger Hiss for perjury, she had expressed a belief in his innocence.

What were your feelings at the time concerning racial equality? How about civil rights?
The file indicates . . . that you were critical . . . of the . . . large property owners.

Reading habits obsessed security officers and Loyalty Board members. Ten out of seventy-five cases studied by Eleanor Bontecou involved the allegation of having read Communist literature, which apparently included Edgar Snow's *The Pattern of Soviet Power*, the Webbs' *Soviet Communism*, and E. H. Carr's *The Soviet Impact on the Western World*. The government geographer was asked:

Do you have any favorite newspaper columnists of the day? Do you have any favorite radio or TV news commentators or news analysts? Were you a regular purchaser of the *New York Times*?

Others were asked why they read *Consumer Reports* or belonged to the Book Find Club. Boards also asked about tastes in foreign films, Howard Fast novels, and Paul Robeson records.

Nor were sexual questions inevitably out of bounds. A Navy Department employee was asked numerous questions about sex, although sex did not figure in the charges: "What do you think of female chastity?" A man was asked: "When did you become engaged to your wife? You were married, I think, in May—when did you reach some sort of understanding?"

The hard core of serious charges and questions was directed toward membership in organizations designated by the Attorney General as subversive, mainly the CP and its "fronts." But this "hard core" by no means accounted for the majority of cases; out of seventy-five loyalty cases studied in depth by Eleanor Bontecou, only twenty involved alleged past or present membership of the CP or

Young Communist League. Of these twenty, sixteen denied it, and all but three were believed. Actual membership of fronts was alleged in only twenty of the seventy-five cases—the remainder all concerned some form of sympathetic association.[27]

The fact is that after about 1948 virtually no Communists were uncovered in the federal civil service.[28] But for most agencies, past membership created a presumption of continuing membership, and the burden was on the employee to disprove this. Even if he did, it was often assumed that his withdrawal was purely tactical, an expedient. For example, a clerical worker who had been employed by a government department since 1925 in a fairly humble capacity, was charged under E.O. 10450 with Communist affiliations in 1931–32, 1934–38, and 1943–44. He denied the last one completely, admitted the others, but insisted he was never a Party member. He lost his job. In 1948 a northern-California employee of the U.S. Bureau of Reclamation admitted he had been in the CP for eight months in the early 1940s, and also admitted having purchased the *People's Daily World* in 1940. This employee, who was supporting his mother on a salary of $3,025, failed to request a hearing and was dismissed. A civilian employed by the Navy in California admitted that he had belonged to the CP for two months in 1945. After six months of delay, he was dismissed. The case went to the LRB in Washington, which asked the FBI to investigate further. After sixteen months no decision had been reached.

Tom Clark listed the Trotskyist Socialist Workers Party as "Communist," "subversive" and aiming to change the government by unconstitutional means. In several cases membership in the SWP was imputed to federal employees, most notably James Kutcher, a clerk in the Newark branch of the Veterans Administration who had lost both legs in 1943 during the battle of San Pietro. He denied that either he or the SWP advocated violent overthrow, but the country for which he had given his legs took away his job. In June 1956 the Veterans Administration ordered him restored with full seniority after the Court of Appeals ruled that he had been denied due process, and that membership in the SWP was not of itself cause for dismissal.

"Guilt by association" was a notion written deeply into the Truman loyalty program, and it was during the years 1948 to 1950 that the decisive criterion for judging a man ceased to be his actions or outspoken attitudes, but rather his affiliations and associations. Although loyalty boards were forbidden to take into consideration affiliation with any organizations other than those listed by the Attorney General, frequently in loyalty cases the organizations referred to did not appear on the Attorney General's list but on HCUA's list, published in December 1948, of 564 organizations and 190 publications "which have been declared to be outright Communist or Communist-front enterprises." But "declared" by whom?

The Tenney Committee in California was also quoted; the government geographer was charged with membership in the American Association of Scientific Workers, which the Tenney Committee alone had thought fit to label Communist. Bernice Levine, a Fort Monmouth clerk-typist, was charged: "You were employed from October through December 1951 and during August 1952 by the Egg Local No. 1, Farmers Union, Second Street, Lakewood, New Jersey, a subsidiary of the Eastern Division of the Farmers Union, which reportedly has been used by the Communist Party to publicize and carry out Communist Party farm policies."

Eleanor Bontecou found that the charges of "sympathetic association," which applied in the majority of her seventy-five sample cases, could mean small donations, sponsorship or attendance at meetings, a name on a mailing list, participation in a May Day parade. In two thirds of the seventy-five cases, the charge referred to association with other individuals said to be subversive or connected with organizations on the Attorney General's list.[29] A Mare Island (California) federal employee was charged with having associated with a Permanente Hospital physician who was "known" to be a Communist. William V. Vitarelli, a Ph.D. from Columbia, was in 1952 appointed by the Department of the Interior to the Education Department of the Pacific Islands, where he taught handicrafts. In 1954 he was suspended without pay, charged with "sympathetic association" with two named persons alleged to have been members or sympathetic associates of the CP, and also accused of having registered as a supporter of the ALP in New York City in 1945, of having subscribed to the USSR Information Bulletin, and of having purchased the *Daily Worker* and the *New Masses*. In June 1959 the Supreme Court ruled that Vitarelli had been dismissed illegally in 1954 by the Department of the Interior.

Luigi Mario Laurenti was not charged with membership in any organization listed by the Attorney General, but the record shows that he was precisely the kind of articulate, pushy, letter-writing liberal whom the establishment did not favor and would, given half a chance, suppress. In December 1953 he discovered that the security officer of the Berkeley campus of the University of California, William W. Waldman, had filed five of his actions. What were they? Laurenti had written to the Berkeley Board of Education in May 1952 to congratulate it on making a high school available for a speech by Paul Robeson; he had attended a lecture given by Jerome Davis at Epworth Memorial Church, Berkeley; he had served on the Quakers' Social-Industrial Committee, which exhibited the film *Steps to Peace;*

and, having already shown a sympathetic interest in the Rosenberg case, he had upheld the right of the Committee to Secure Justice for the Rosenbergs to be heard. These charges all came up at his security hearing. He was cleared. [30]

A common variant of guilt by association was guilt by kinship. Time and again federal employees were confronted with the real or imaginary activities and beliefs of members of their families. In August–September 1955 the press was full of such cases; on August 31 *The New York Times* solemnly denounced the practice. A typewriter operator for the Signal Corps faced allegations relating solely to her parents. She was asked: "Have you been closely associated with your father?" In August 1955 the Coast Guard refused a reserve commission to N. Pierre Gaston on the ground of his mother's alleged former ties with allegedly subversive organizations. After the press raised protests, Gaston got his commission. But two years later, in June 1957, the government denied clearance to a twenty-six-year-old engineer of the Radio Corporation of America on the ground that he corresponded with his mother, then living in California.

The harrowing nature of such charges can be seen in the cases of two women employees. Adele Warren, a thirty-year-old divorced mother of two, and the sole support of her children on a salary of $3,200 a year, was handling classified material for the Signal Corps. In October 1953 she was charged with "a close and continuing association with your brother," whose allegedly sympathetic acts toward Communism were listed. Mrs. Warren lived with her children in a separate apartment in the same building as her mother, her brother, and their three younger siblings. She denied all knowledge of her brother's political sympathies. A Board member then asked her whether she would inform her supervisor if she discovered that her brother was, in fact, connected with organizations on the Attorney General's list. Astounded, she asked: "Would that be part of my duties?" The Board cleared her but the government resisted; in July 1953, three and a half months after the hearing, she learned from the Security Review Board that her continued employment *would be clearly consistent* with national security, but that the Board intended to recommend her discharge *"in the interests of national security."* (Italics supplied.)

When Bernice Levine was suspended in March 1954 as a Fort Monmouth clerk-typist, kinship charges figured prominently in the indictment:

Your father, Samuel Levine, was Treasurer of IWO Lodge 228 . . . in January 1949.
The names of S. Levine and E. Levine . . . appeared on a peti-

tion to Judge Medina protesting the jailing of the twelve [sic]
Communist leaders . . .
The names of S. Levine and E. Levine . . . appeared on a peace
petition issued by the Campaign Committee for the World Peace
Appeal . . . cited by the . . . Committee on Un-American Activi-
ties as having "received the official endorsement of the Supreme
Soviet of the USSR."

Bernice Levine stood no chance.[31]

## ONCE ACCUSED, ALWAYS ACCUSED

Neither the loyalty nor the security program ensured that, once investigated and cleared, a man would stay cleared. For this there were
two parallel reasons. First, every new promotion or transfer entailed a
new check; secondly, as laws and executive orders succeeded one another, imposing increasingly stringent criteria, old cases had to be
reconsidered in the light of new standards. A Negro meat inspector
working for a federal agency in a western state, with thirty-eight
years' service, was shown a photostatic copy of the cover of a CP
membership book bearing his name. Twelve defense witnesses testified that he had never been a Communist and was a man of strong
Christian convictions. Cleared in October 1949, he returned to his
job. Later, under Eisenhower's E.O. 10450, he was suspended without pay and charged with perjuring himself in his original denial of
Party membership. In April 1955 he was reinstated with back pay,
eleven months after his suspension.

A geographer, expert in the preparation of climatological mono-
graphs, had been cleared four times: during the war, when he worked
for the OSS and the State Department; at his own request by the
CSC Regional Loyalty Board; by a Senate subcommittee considering
charges leveled by a Senator; and early in 1951 by the Department of
the Army's Loyalty-Security Board. All this notwithstanding, he was
suspended under E.O. 10450 in March 1954 and confronted with a
stupendous list of left-wing and Communist front affiliations, but
none more recent than the middle 1940s. The Security Board found
against him, but the Security Review Board reversed and he was reinstated nine months after his suspension. Such cases were numerous.[32]

Civil servants from the suspect professions of social sciences and
economics were particularly vulnerable to perpetual reaccusation, just
as those who had crossed their paths, however casually, were also
incriminated. Many of them were named by Elizabeth Bentley or

Whittaker Chambers as having operated as reds or spies within the Agricultural Adjustment Administration, the Foreign Economic Administration, the OSS, and the La Follette Committee on Civil Liberties. Peveril Meigs had been in the clear when he moved in 1948 from the State Department to the Department of the Army, just as Hans Landsberg had transferred from State to the Department of Commerce with a clean slate, but both men were given short shrift after McCarthy named them. Solomon Adler, named by Bentley, had been cleared both by the Treasury Loyalty Board and the LRB when he found the relentless pressure insupportable and, in 1950, threw in the towel.

Possibly the most dramatic of the Bentley cases concerned a forceful young man whose social background and early political orientation bore resemblances to those of Alger Hiss. William Remington, a graduate of Dartmouth and Columbia (1940), worked for the Tennessee Valley Authority and the War Production Board, served in Navy Intelligence, the European Recovery Program, and the President's Council of Economic Advisers, before joining the Commerce Department in 1948.[33] In April 1947, as a result of Elizabeth Bentley's confessions to the FBI, Remington was questioned by a federal grand jury. No indictment followed. A year later Bentley testified to a Senate subcommittee that she had been introduced to Remington by her lover, the GPU agent Jacob Golos, and that in the following two years she had visited Remington up to thirty times, bringing him Communist literature from New York and, in return, taking from him not only classified War Production Board material, including figures on aircraft production, but also his Party dues.

The Commerce Department suspended Remington. Despite affidavits from his superiors that he was strongly anti-Russian, the Fourth Regional Loyalty Board found a reasonable doubt as to his loyalty. According to his own account, he had been introduced to Golos and Bentley by the Communist journalist Joseph North, and had subsequently been pursued by Bentley, whom he knew as Helen Johnson of the newspaper PM. The information he had given her had been of the declassified type he normally offered to newsmen. These admissions alone were enough to put his career in jeopardy. Nevertheless, Bentley failed to appear three times to give evidence to the LRB (which enjoyed no subpoena power), and finally the Board cleared Remington, leaving him free to return to his desk in the Commerce Department. Meanwhile, Bentley had repeated her charges over the radio. After Remington brought a libel action against her, NBC and the program sponsor, General Foods, the two companies settled out of court for $10,000

There the matter rested. But the Congressional committees that fed on the testimony of ex-Communists would not allow anyone named by a star witness like Bentley to rest for long. In May 1950 two self-confessed former Communists testified before a secret session of HCUA that they had known Remington as a Communist when he worked for the TVA in Knoxville in 1936–37. Remington appeared before HCUA and denied it. Under pressure from the Committee, the Justice Department assigned the case to two prosecuting attorneys building careers out of anti-Communism, Irving H. Saypol and his assistant, Roy M. Cohn.

A federal grand jury in New York whose foreman, John Brunini, had contracted to help prepare Elizabeth Bentley's autobiography for the publisher Devin-Adair, and therefore had a financial stake in sustaining her credibility, heard evidence from Remington and his former wife, Ann Moos Remington. At first Ann Moos Remington substantiated her ex-husband's story. Brunini, who lectured his fellow jurors on the need to protect ex-Communists from those who smeared them, snarled and snapped at Mrs. Remington: "We haven't raised our voices and shown our teeth . . . I don't want them to bite you." He informed her, falsely, that she was not privileged to refuse to answer any question, and would not let her take a break for food until she changed her testimony. Yet Remington's attorney was not permitted to see the transcript of these astonishing hearings in preparation for the trial that followed the grand jury's indictment of Remington for perjury (i.e., for denying that he had ever been in the CP).

The trial opened in December 1950 in a New York District Court. Mrs. Remington now corroborated Bentley's account, going so far as to say that she had personally witnessed Remington giving Bentley a formula for making explosives out of garbage. (Bentley had always maintained that she met Remington alone—she now explained away the discrepancy in her evidence as a result of her nerve-wracked condition when appearing before Congressional committees.) On February 7, 1951, he was convicted of perjury. The Court of Appeals unanimously threw out the verdict but did not quash the indictment: the government was free to try again. At the second trial, which began in January 1953, Remington was convicted on two perjury counts out of five: having lied at his trial about giving Elizabeth Bentley classified information, and having lied in denying knowledge of the YCL while a student at Dartmouth. In November the Court of Appeals upheld the verdict by 2 to 1, with a strong dissent by Learned Hand, who scathingly drew attention to Brunini's illicit intimidation tactics at the original grand jury hearing.[34] Remington began a three-year prison sentence in Lewisburg Penitentiary (where Alger Hiss was also held), but he was murdered by a fellow prisoner on November 22, 1954.

The only one of Elizabeth Bentley's victims who managed to salvage his public career despite a merciless hounding was William Henry Taylor. Having served as a monetary expert under Harry Dexter White during the war, Taylor had been named by Bentley as a member of the so-called Silvermaster spy ring. When the *Washington Daily News* repeated the allegation, Taylor sued for libel and the paper settled out of court. During his celebrated attack on the memory of White, Attorney General Brownell publicly denounced Taylor, then employed by the International Monetary Fund, as a spy, and in 1955 his case came before the International Organizations Employees Loyalty Board. When the IOELB concluded, in its wisdom, that Taylor "has engaged in espionage and subversive activity against the United States . . . and that he was and possibly still is an adherent of the Communist ideology," Taylor filed a brief describing his experiences:

> For a period of at least eight years, to my knowledge, I have been subjected to suspicion, unfavorable publicity, derision and a form of persecution. I have been questioned by FBI agents and Congressional investigators. I have been forced to appear repeatedly, always in secret, before Federal Grand Juries, Congressional Committees, and now several sessions of the Loyalty Board . . . I have been interrogated, or called for interrogation, on nineteen occasions and sometimes in a manner reminiscent of the Inquisition. Not once have I been confronted with accuser or informer; not once have I been allowed to cross-examine.

Taylor noted that at the time of writing he was under subpoena to HCUA, the SISS, the Senate Subcommittee on Government Operations, a federal grand jury in New York, and a federal grand jury in Washington.

On January 5, 1956, the IOELB reversed itself, evidently impressed by the detailed refutation and exposure of Elizabeth Bentley's testimony on all subjects, and concluded: "There is not a reasonable doubt as to your loyalty to the Government of the United States." If that was true, then Elizabeth Bentley was a liar.

Clearance by a loyalty or security board by no means ensured that a civil servant would keep his job. Congress had invested the heads of certain agencies with the power of arbitrary dismissal, and this was used. Michael Lee, born in Manchuria of Russian parents, was head of the Commerce Department's Far Eastern Division when Senator George W. Malone of Nevada accused him of deliberately delaying shipments to Chiang's forces. In 1949 Lee was cleared by the Department's Loyalty Board, but in June 1950 the Secretary of Commerce, Charles Sawyer, responded to Congressional pressure by dismissing him as a security risk. Ralph Russell, of the Department of the Interior's Fish and Wildlife Service, but a member of the branded United Public Workers, was suspended in October 1953. Eighteen months later he was cleared. But Secretary of the Interior Douglas McKay reversed the decision and dismissed him. In July 1958, following the Supreme Court decisions in *Cole v. Green* and *Peters v. Hobby*, Russell gained reinstatement with $20,000 in back pay.[35]

## LEGAL COSTS

Any employee who decided to contest the charges leveled against him had to find an attorney. The lawyer Joseph Borkin claimed he could always spot loyalty-security cases, because they never telephoned in advance and invariably showed up during the lunch hour looking shrunken and shriveled.

Adam Yarmolinsky, a Washington lawyer who handled many such cases, concluded that whereas normally it was the lawyer's job to keep his client from chattering irrelevantly and to get to the root of the matter, in loyalty-security cases his task was akin to the psychiatrist's, the first step being to get his client to sit down and tell the story of his life, leaving out nothing however remotely relevant—a reflection of the imprecise nature of the charges and the obscurity of their source. Yarmolinsky found that the boards increasingly believed that the content of the charges was less important than the fact that charges had been made (no smoke without fire), so it was necessary to submit an affidavit portraying a broad view of the employee as a person, to build up a favorable picture.

To Joseph Fanelli, who handled about two hundred loyalty-security cases, about 95 percent of which resulted in clearance, there was something degrading in this necessary exposure of a man's whole life, his tastes in books, music, clothes and friends. Fanelli noted that every defense of a client involved a distortion of his life so as to present a more orthodox and less intellectual impression than the reality, thus continually reinforcing the prevailing climate of conformity and anti-intellectualism.[36]

The prospect of heavy legal expenses must have persuaded many government employees on low salaries to abandon their defense. The LRB soon put a stop to the habit of some agencies of providing government counsel to represent accused employees, and so onerous became the burden of legal costs that in January 1955 the District of

Columbia Bar Association launched a scheme to provide free legal assistance to security cases who could not afford to pay.[37]

The most expensive cases were normally the most protracted, though a complex defense involving a large number of supporting affidavits might also prove costly. Milton I. Sacks, technically an employee of the government but in practice working in the academic field, spent about $5,000 in fighting for clearance and a passport validated for the countries to which he needed to travel.

But it should not be imagined that the legal profession made hay out of loyalty-security cases. On the contrary, the attorney who was willing to take on such cases and risk opprobrium and possible loss of income was normally an idealist who charged less than he would in the normal course of business. Fanelli's normal rate, for example, was $50 an hour, but he never charged loyalty-security defendants more than $20 an hour and he sometimes let them set their own fee at the conclusion of the case.[38]

It is worth noting that in 16 percent of the 326 cases published by Brown, the lawyer gave his services free or sustained a net loss.[39]

Before concluding that this record sheds glory on the legal profession as a whole, we must remember that there were instances where dishonest lawyers took loyalty-security clients for a ride, quickly collecting fees from desperate men and then ignoring their affairs or pronouncing the case hopeless. It is also true that only a minority of those lawyers qualified to do so were willing to take such clients once the fever of guilt-by-association had penetrated the bar associations and professional classes. Yet the record stands: the American bar contained its fair share of courageous liberals, men prepared to put principle before profit.

A man or woman dismissed from federal employment as a loyalty or security risk faced the grim prospect of finding a suitable job in private employment. Most employers would not touch such people—it was like a sentence for embezzlement. The LRB made certain that adverse decisions pursued the employee into private life, directing that prospective employers should be notified when a job had been terminated under E.O. 9835. In December 1947 LRB Chairman Seth Richardson claimed that "this loyalty program applies only to government employees and of course not to citizens in general," but in July 1950 he conceded that after federal dismissal for disloyalty "a man is ruined everywhere and forever. No reputable employer would be likely to take a chance in giving him a job."

The case of "Mr. Blank" provides a classic example of this ruination. It was eight months after his dismissal from the State Department in June 1947 before he could get any sort of job, even though the Department magnanimously recast his dismissal as resignation five months later. Nor was Mr. Blank without support. Not only was a press campaign being waged on behalf of him and six fellow victims, but he received letters of commendation from influential friends as well as generous testimonials from his erstwhile superiors. He tried colleges, municipalities, advertising agencies and private corporations, but without luck. His savings and his retirement money soon ran out; he mortgaged his house; he spent every weekday away from home, desperately searching for a job. But the problem for the historian is to discover what did become of the majority of dismissed government employees.[40] Professor Paul Tillett attempted without success to locate some three hundred who had been dismissed between 1947 and 1950.

## THE LIBERAL REACTION

By the summer of 1955 there was loud agitation in the liberal press about "abuses" in the security program, and this concern extended to the more liberal elements in Congress. In May 1955 Senator Olin D. Johnston (D., South Carolina) charged the Post Office and CSC with flouting the laws protecting employees' job security. The Senate voted $75,000 to investigate his allegations, and on May 27 Johnston, as subcommittee chairman, launched an investigation that culminated in a report severely critical of employee-security procedure. Even more effective in bringing abuses to light and in pressuring government departments to revise their more arbitrary practices were the hearings held in the fall of 1955 by the Senate Judiciary Committee's Subcommittee on Constitutional Rights, chaired by the liberal Democrat Thomas C. Hennings, Jr., of Missouri. With Hennings the tide began to turn, and the rights of the individual resurfaced.

Yet there were few concrete achievements in terms of legislation; the conservative coalition in Congress remained too powerful. A notably disappointing venture was the bipartisan commission to review the fairness and effectiveness of the security program; the Senate approved it in 1955, and Eisenhower set it up under the chairmanship of the conservative lawyer Loyd Wright. When the commission published its report in 1957 it actually proposed an extension of the scope of the security program to the legislative and judicial branches and even to employees of civil air-transport companies, along with the creation of a Central Security Office. The commission rejected the growing demand for a distinction between sensitive and nonsensitive jobs.

The most effective challenge to the excesses of the security program came, in the late 1950s, from the courts, and specifically the

Supreme Court. By 1952 eight cases involving thirty litigants arising out of the loyalty program had come to trial. Four of them reached the Supreme Court. The Bailey case, in which the Court upheld the government's right to deny accused employees due process, was clearly the most momentous and influential decision. In *Washington v. McGrath*, an action brought by black and Jewish postal employees, the Court of Appeals adopted the same position as in the Bailey case.

The turning point came in 1955, with the Supreme Court's decision in *Peters v. Hobby*. John P. Peters, senior professor of medicine at Yale and a Special Consultant to the U.S. Public Health Service, had been cleared by the agency's Loyalty Board, but the LRB decided to review the case "post audit" and found reasonable doubt as to his loyalty. After Peters was discharged as a security risk by Eisenhower's Secretary of Health, Education and Welfare, Mrs. Oveta Culp Hobby, he contested his dismissal on the ground that the evidence against him had not been disclosed and that he had been accused by informers some of whom were not known even to the Board. The Supreme Court evaded the issue, but ruled that P.L. 733 distinguished between sensitive and nonsensitive jobs, and that Peters's consultancy had been nonsensitive. The Court also ruled that the LRB could not on its own motion review a case that had been decided favorably by an agency loyalty board. This decision restored some nineteen other individuals to their jobs.

Kenneth M. Cole, a federal food and drug inspector in New York, had also been dismissed by the Department of Health, Education and Welfare. In November 1953 he was suspended without pay after being accused of sympathetic association with Communists and with the Nature Friends of America (listed by the Attorney General). Cole refused to answer the charges or to request a hearing, claiming that his rights of association were being violated. In *Cole v. Young* (June 1956), the Supreme Court again ruled that P.L. 733 applied only to positions sensitive in terms of national security. As a result, 109 employees were restored to their jobs, and proceedings were dropped against seventy-four others.

Three years later, in June 1959, the Supreme Court knocked the stuffing out of the Truman-Eisenhower loyalty-security inquisition when, in *Greene v. McElroy*, it ruled that neither the President nor Congress had authorized that employees should be deprived of the right to cross-examine hostile witnesses in security cases. Eisenhower then issued an Executive Order in February 1960 considerably enlarging the scope of confrontation, and under Kennedy the right of confrontation became general. In *Vitarelli v. Seaton* (also decided in 1959), the Court appeared to proscribe wide-ranging inquisitions. [41]

# 14

## The Armed Forces:
## A Code of Dishonor

It is not surprising that, in the immediate post-World War II period, confronted by the gargantuan task of de-Nazifying Germany, the Army incorporated into the occupation force a number of civilian professionals with liberal or radical backgrounds. To this a Congressional reaction was inevitable. In July 1947 Representative George Dondero (R., Michigan) accused Secretary of the Army Robert P. Patterson of failing to get rid of Communist sympathizers working for the War Department.[1] Dondero's attack had its effect. George Shaw Wheeler, former chief of the de-Nazification branch of the Army manpower division, was not retained by the U.S. Military Government, despite General Lucius D. Clay's assurance that a loyalty board had cleared him. Heinz Norden, editor of the German-language magazine *Heute*, was also accused by Dondero of being pro-Communist. His contract was allowed to expire on October 1. According to Norden, Clay told him that as an "avowed liberal" he would expose the Military Government's "middle of the road" policies to criticism. These and other such cases were eagerly picked up by the *Tägliche Rundschau*, the organ of the Soviet Military Government in Berlin, on October 7.

In January 1949 Samuel L. Wahrhaftig, a thirty-three-year-old immigrant from Poland, who served as a political analyst for the U.S. Military Government in Berlin, was suspended, then dismissed for disloyalty. Denying that he was a Communist and pointing out that no real charges had been brought against him, Wahrhaftig cited in his defense an anti-Communist testimonial from Mayor Ernst Reuter of Berlin. He was lucky; in August he was completely exonerated and, on the unanimous recommendation of the Army Security Board, reinstated with back pay.

In June 1949 the Army's embarrassment became apparent when Gordon R. Clapp, chairman of the Tennessee Valley Authority, was declared ineligible for a special job with the Military Government in Germany. It emerged that at least ten other civilians of distinction had been declared "unemployable" by the Army.[2] Following a protest by Senator Estes Kefauver, Secretary of the Army Gordon Gray apologized for these errors and promised to purge from the Army's files stigmas on "a very considerable number of civilians."[3]

A plethora of laws endowed the Defense Department with almost unlimited powers to discharge its civilian employees. P.L. 713 provided for dismissal for "conduct inimical to the public interest in the defense program"; but the military agencies normally operated under P.L. 808, the summary-dismissal statute, until the enactment of P.L. 733 in 1950.

In March of that year the Defense Department announced that 375 civilians had been discharged, with 216 cases pending, since 1942. The rate of dismissal was stepped up under Eisenhower, the Department reporting 1,311 dismissals and 1,877 resignations "with security information" from May 1953 until October 1954. The mood of the time was reflected in a Navy statement distributed in 1955 to all domestic and foreign installations, advising civilian employees to guard against "an indiscreet remark."[4]

## SCREENING MILITARY PERSONNEL

We turn now to military personnel. The relatively liberal policy prevailing under Roosevelt was reflected in an Army policy instruction issued on January 31, 1945:

> No action will be taken that is predicated on membership or adherence to the doctrines of the Communist Party unless there is a specific finding that the individual has a loyalty to the Communist Party . . . which overrides his loyalty to the United States . . . No such findings should be based on the mere fact that an individual's views on various social questions have been the same as the views which the Communist Party has advanced.[5]

This statement brought protests from John Rankin and others on the Congressional extreme Right, causing Chairman Andrew J. May of the House Military Affairs Committee to order an investigation. In March 1946, following criticism from HCUA, the Army barred "subversive or disaffected" persons from sensitive jobs, from officer-candidate schools and flight training, from cryptographic work, education and information programs.

The effect of this backlash can be illustrated statistically: whereas only eighty Army men were discharged for disloyalty from 1941 to June 1946, ten times more were discharged for disloyalty between July 1946 and April 1947. Ralph S. Brown estimated a total of 750 *loyalty* discharges from all the services during the years 1948–56. However, these figures apparently do not tell the whole story, since the Army reported 726 soldiers dismissed for *security* reasons from 1948 to 1955. There were also about fifty instances, from 1950 to 1954, of doctors and dentists being refused a commission on account of their political record prior to induction.[6]

The Army's six-page pamphlet, *How to Spot a Communist*, issued in June 1955, advised that a Communist could be "spotted" by his predisposition to discuss civil rights, racial and religious discrimination, the immigration laws, antisubversive legislation, curbs on unions, and peace. Good Americans were advised to keep their ears stretched for such give-away terms as "chauvinism," "book-burning," "colonialism," "demagogy," "witch hunt," "reactionary," "progressive," and "exploitation." The pamphlet generated such an outcry that it was withdrawn within a week.[7]

In December 1957 the Army announced that 776 *conscript* soldiers had been discharged as security risks from 1948 to 1955.

## The Dishonorable-Discharge Policy

In postwar America a military conscript was normally "separated" from active duty after two years and "discharged" after six years' service in the reserve. The great majority of conscripts received "honorable" discharges, but less favorable alternatives were available: the "general discharge under honorable conditions," and, worse, the "undesirable" discharge. A man with a general discharge forfeited some of his veteran's benefits, his federal civil-service priority, his mustering-out pay, his New York civil-service priority, and his veteran's educational scholarship in New York and certain other states. His general job prospects were gloomy. A less-than-honorable discharge for security reasons became part of his permanent FBI file. The effect of an undesirable discharge was more radical: universal opprobrium; immediate reduction to the lowest rank in the Army, Private E-1; deprivation of mustering-out pay; loss of monetary credit for unused leaves;

immediate loss of uniform; detention until released from the camp; loss of reemployment benefits; and a delay in receiving G.I. benefits, such as the school subsidy, while awaiting the opinion of the Adjutant General, which was usually not forthcoming for a year or more. Such a man had little hope of getting a job in industry.

Before or immediately after entry into the service, the inductee was instructed to execute the loyalty form DD 98, which contained the Attorney General's list. The inductee was entitled either to sign it, thus indicating that he had not been a member of any of the proscribed organizations, or to list those of which he had been a member, or to take the Fifth Amendment. According to regulations, a man should not be inducted if the authorities already possessed sufficient derogatory information to suggest that his induction was not in the national interest. But, in political cases, this procedure was rarely followed.[8] Admiral Arthur W. Radford, Chairman of the Joint Chiefs of Staff, remarked that the armed forces did not want people evading military service by refusing to execute the loyalty form or by taking the Fifth Amendment. In practice the armed forces, and most notably the Army, pursued a vindictive policy totally lacking in soldierly standards of honor. It is difficult to think of a civilized country wherein senior officers have ever stooped so low to discredit the men serving under them.

The initial tactic, frequently pursued, was to present the loyalty form to the inductee under conditions of harrowing (hurry, hurry, hurry) discipline. One conscript recalled: "I know I am a lawyer, I have a BA, an MA and an LLB, and I signed this DD Form 98 without looking at it . . . the fear of God was put in me by these noncoms, and I signed." The Army's strategy was to allow the inductee to serve all or most of his active duty, and then to "get" him for his *preinduction* political affiliations with a "dishonorable" or "general" discharge. This was done under Army Regulations SR 600-220-1, of December 6, 1950, superseded by a similarly designated Regulation of June 18, 1954.

In the course of time, either shortly before or shortly after "separation" from active duty, the inductee would receive a letter of allegations (only seven days were allowed to file an answer, even when the soldier was on active duty in Korea)[9] which offered four alternatives: (1) to request within five days a hearing before a Field Board of Inquiry; (2) to rebut the charges in writing within fifteen days; (3) to do nothing; (4) to agree to an undesirable discharge by signing the (conveniently) enclosed form.

In November 1955, after taking a beating before the Hennings Subcommittee on Constitutional Rights, the Defense Department promised that future investigations would be made *before* induction, and the type of discharge issued would be based solely on the conscript's service record. Although this promise was made by Secretary of the Army Wilbur M. Brucker, a spokesman for the legal division of the Army wrote to Representative Adam Clayton Powell early in 1956 that "allegations may include preservice activities. No restriction as to the use of such activities has been imposed on the Army." In November 1955 the Army stopped informing inductees under charge what the Field Board of Inquiry had recommended—a move designed to stifle the adverse publicity that attended the Adjutant General's habit of reversing favorable recommendations made by the Field Boards. The attorney Stanley Faulkner noted that not one of the approximately hundred conscripts he had represented in such cases had a less than "excellent" or "superior" rating for character and efficiency during active service. In December 1957 the Army announced that about 220 conscripts previously discharged as security risks *might* be granted fully honorable discharges.[10]

The Army's Field Boards of Inquiry—three officers of field rank—were subject to all the biases of procedure and prejudice that vitiated the loyalty-security boards of the federal civil service. Not untypical was the question put to a draftee in August 1954: "Did you believe at one time that the Government of the United States and the Communist Government of Russia could coexist in a peaceful manner?" Reporting on forty-nine cases of "less than honorable" discharges, the Workers' Defense League counsel Rowland Watts listed charges of CP membership in only eleven cases. Other charges were of the nebulous, associational type already familiar: [11] writing an examination paper critical of capitalism; writing to a radio station to protest the dismissal of a left-wing commentator; and working on a collective farm in Israel.

The Army's capacity for premeditated malice is illustrated by the case of a young man who forewarned his local draft board that the Coast Guard had screened him off merchant ships as a poor security risk. Nevertheless, he was not only inducted but was appointed an instructor in an indoctrination course on world events provided for American troops stationed in Berlin! But four months after his separation from active service he received a Letter of Allegations almost identical to the one he had received from the Coast Guard. Another case concerned an admitted member of the Socialist League who became an instructor at the Fort Monmouth Signal School and was handed an undesirable discharge eleven days before his separation from active service. Yet only a month earlier his superior at the Signal School had written him: "You have displayed and exercised such qualities and abilities as loyalty, leadership, dependability, earnestness, and other attributes of an exemplary soldier and conscientious worker." After protests by Norman Thomas and others, he was awarded a "general discharge under honorable conditions"—that is, still less than an honorable discharge.[12]

The troubles of James M. Staebler began when he protested against the resegregation of a mixed company that had been temporarily integrated. The Army then gave him a dishonorable discharge on the ground that he and his wife had been members of the SWP. The Emergency Civil Liberties Committee took up his case, and in April 1955 he was awarded the general discharge under honorable conditions. In May 1955 Robert Martinson, of Monterey, received an undesirable discharge but, after Senator Hennings applied pressure on the Pentagon, this was changed eighteen months later to honorable. Martinson wrote to the ACLU, which had supported him, "The Army has spent thousands of dollars giving me a 'hearing.' Dozens of witnesses were called, hundreds of documents inserted, thousands of words inscribed into the record. Yet I knew that the real decision would be made by some phantom in the Pentagon."

## GUILT BY KINSHIP

The kinship charges usually contained an element of absurdity, though perhaps not so absurd as the accusation against one soldier of having retained in an automobile liability case a lawyer who represented the ACPFB. One soldier was thus accused: "You have a father who is reported to have said if Communism offered anything good he would accept it." Another faced a charge relating to his mother-in-law, even though she had died when he was ten, and ten years before he met his wife. Of the forty-nine cases reported by Rowland Watts, mothers cropped up in eleven, fathers in eleven, wives in eight, brothers in five, stepmothers in three, sisters in two, parents-in-law in two, and siblings-in-law in two.[13]

Such charges were also brought against members of the armed forces reserve, generating something of a popular sentimental backlash. A Negro reserve officer, Captain Charles A. Hill, had been decorated three times during the Second World War. In January 1951 he was instructed by the Continental Air Command to resign his reserve commission or face disloyalty charges, which were, principally, that he had been seen reading the *Daily Worker;* that his father, a Baptist minister, had taken part in 1949 in the National Conference Against Deportation Hysteria; that in 1945 his father had run for the Detroit City Council with Communist support; and that Hill's sister was interested in Communist principles. A month later the Air Force regretted and dropped its charges. Victor Harvis, of Detroit, an Air Force master sergeant with fourteen years' service, was stationed in Europe when he was declared a security risk in 1952. The sole charge against him was that his father, now dead, had taken him to some CP meetings when he was twelve years old. A Democratic Congressman from Michigan prevailed on the Air Force to reconsider the case, and a special board cleared Harvis.

But the Armed Forces persevered. Midshipman Eugene Landy, second in his class of ninety-six at the Merchant Marine Academy, was denied a reserve commission in 1955 because of his continued association with his mother. HCUA quickly got into the act by subpoenaing his mother. Following adverse publicity, the Secretary of the Navy awarded Landy his commission in September. Milo J. Radulovich, a twenty-six-year-old student at the University of Michigan and a meteorologist in the Air Force Reserve, was asked to resign his commission on account of the alleged radical beliefs of his father and sister. When he refused he was discharged as a security risk. Once again adverse comment in the media reversed the decision. [14]

## THE LEGAL DEFENSE CAMPAIGN

There is no doubt that the soldiers who stood the best chance of reprieve were those whose cases were taken up by civil-liberties organizations and by dedicated lawyers who could generate the publicity that the Army, in its murky conscience, so much feared. A case illustrative of this also introduces perhaps the most unseemly phase of Army discharge policy. It is astonishing to recall that the U.S. Army originally protested benefit payments to some five hundred soldiers who had been prisoners-of-war in Korea, on the ground that they had collaborated with the enemy. Sixty percent of these five hundred already had honorable discharges. Half the allegations of collaboration were later withdrawn by the Army—perhaps it occurred to the Pentagon that five hundred collaborators did not reflect too shiningly on American society or on the Army itself. Robert I. Simpson, a twenty-four-year-old Korean-war veteran from Sacramento, California, had been a prisoner for thirty-three months. The Army, basing its case on a secret file, denied him the $2,500 in benefits due to him on the ground that he had collaborated in captivity with the Chinese. But, with the support of the ACLU's persevering counsel Ernest Besig, and of Senator Thomas C. Hennings, Jr., Simpson eventually got his full war benefits. [15]

The Army's policy of treating preinduction activities and associations as a basis for decision as to the type of final discharge issued was finally cut down in the Supreme Court, but not without a long struggle. Three major cases deserve attention.

In the summer of 1955 Theodore Bernstein and seven other draftees [16] stationed at Fort Dix, New Jersey, were confronted with a variety of allegations relating to membership, associations, kinship and reading habits. They faced dishonorable discharges. Defense lawyers specializing in this field, like Rowland Watts and Stanley Faulkner, had argued all along that a regulation providing for punishment for preinduction activities constituted a Bill of Attainder or its equivalent. Supported by the ECLC, Bernstein and his comrades brought suit against the Army, citing the First, Fifth, Sixth and Ninth Amendments, and contending that there existed no statutory authority for the powers that the Army accorded itself in Regulation 604-10.

In November 1955 federal Judge David N. Edelstein ruled that the Army violated their civil rights if it awarded draftees less-than-honorable discharges for preinduction associations. But the Court of Appeals found for the Army and in October 1956 the Supreme Court refused to grant *certiorari*. By this time seven of the eight draftees had been discharged, five of them with undesirable discharges, although two, Bertram Lassuck and Rudolph Thomas, were granted honorable discharges on the ground that the Army no longer regarded taking the Fifth Amendment as a mandatory reason for a less-than-honorable discharge. In short, this case was lost. [17]

Howard D. Abramowitz, formerly a private in the Army and a veteran of the Korean war with the bronze star, had been given an honorable separation from active service on June 30, 1953. Subsequently he was discharged from the Enlisted Reserve with an undesirable discharge, the allegations against him being CP membership in 1948–49, membership in the Labor Youth League in 1949–51 and in the AYD in 1946–48. Abramowitz declined a hearing and contended that the allegations were not a lawful ground for a less-than-honorable discharge. The Army Discharge Review Board turned down his appeal. The District Court dismissed his complaint on the ground that the courts possessed no jurisdiction. Carrying his case to the Court of Appeals for the District of Columbia, and supported by the ECLC, Abramowitz argued that Congress had not vested the Secretary of the Army with sole discretion in this matter, and that the courts had jurisdiction. In 1958 he won his case in the Supreme Court.

A further victory for the draftees came in the case of *Harmon v. Brucker*—John H. Harmon, of New York, was accused of Communist activities prior to his induction—which came before the Supreme Court in January 1958. The Justices listened skeptically as Donald B.

MacGuiness, attorney for the Justice Department, while conceding that the Army's policy was without legal foundation, yet claimed that the courts could not interfere. In March the Court ruled by 8 to 1 that preinduction activities could not be taken into account when awarding a discharge. But this ruling, like many comparable ones, came many years too late.[18]

# 15

## The State Department
## and the China Experts

The enemies of the New Deal depicted the State Department of the late Roosevelt era as a veritable nest of Communists, fellow travelers, homosexuals, effete Ivy League intellectuals and traitors. Those elements of the Right who had never reconciled themselves either to the war against Germany or to the alliance with Russia that it entailed, who distrusted the UN as formerly they had rejected the League of Nations, and for whom the "fall" of China to Mao Tse-tung's Communist armies threatened American hegemony in the Pacific, focused their resentments on the State Department. In *McCarthy and His Enemies*, William F. Buckley, Jr., and Brent Bozell complained that, after Truman took office and Acheson achieved influence, senior officials within the Department who favored "a pretty clean-cut showdown" with the USSR, like Assistant Secretary Adolf Berle, Under Secretary Joseph C. Grew and Deputy Assistant Secretary for Administration J. Anthony Panuck, were shown the door.[1]

The Buckley-Bozell thesis, however, loses some of its force when the statistics are considered. Under James F. Byrnes (1945–46), screening resulted in 341 "disapprovals," of whom two were discharged and 281 were "removed through various types of personnel action" as the Department expressed it. Thus, even before the Truman loyalty order came into operation, 283 State Department personnel had to pack their bags. The Right—McCarthy, Buckley, Bozell— complained that of the 341, fifty-six were retained and left free to pursue their insidious subversion of American interests. This, in short, was the issue that was to explode in 1950, making McCarthy the best-known Senator in the nation.

The first employee to be dismissed under the McCarran rider to the Appropriations Bill of July 1946 was Carl Marzani. Transferred from the OSS to the State Department during the war, and highly praised by his superiors, Marzani, the son of an Italian anti-Fascist immigrant and himself an Oxford graduate, was discharged on December 20, 1946. Although he subsequently denied in court that he had ever been a Communist or used fictitious names (such as Tony Whales), he was convicted in May 1947 on eleven counts of perjury, including concealing his Communist Party membership to keep his job. The Supreme Court upheld his conviction [2] on a split vote of 4 to 4 in December 1948 and again in March 1949, Justice Douglas on both occasions disqualifying himself. Marzani spent three years in jail. In 1952 he published a book on the origins of the Cold War, We Can Be Friends, and in June 1953 he took the Fifth Amendment on past and present membership of the CP before a Congressional committee. He later set up as a radical publisher. [3]

On January 31, 1947, the State Department disclosed that forty employees had been dismissed for "close connections or involvement" with foreign powers. On June 23, ten more were dismissed as "potential security risks" without formal charges, Secretary Marshall contenting himself with a tantalizing allusion to "indirect association" with representatives of foreign powers. (Three of the ten were subsequently permitted to resign without prejudice.) Although no formal hearings were provided, "Mr. B" was granted an informal one on July 2 with a four-man panel composed of Hamilton Robinson, Director of the Office of Controls, his subordinate Arch K. Jean, Saxton Bradford and Thomas E. Hoffman. Robinson began by explaining that while they would listen to anything Mr. B. chose to say, they would ask no questions and answer none. And so, confronted by four silent interlocutors, scavenging his own conscience, Mr. B. mentioned that an FBI agent had showed his wife a photo of him crossing a street in the company of another woman. The four wise men received this information impassively; perhaps it was not news to them. "The only way I can suggest helping you," Hamilton Robinson finally ventured, "is that you just go ahead and spill your feelings about all the things that you might think have been involved."

On November 17, two weeks after Bert Andrews published this story in the New York Herald Tribune, the Department announced that the seven would be allowed to resign without prejudice, "in order to avoid a possible injustice to them." Not long afterward a possible injustice befell Hamilton Robinson himself, alumnus of Taft School, Princeton, Oxford and Yale Law School, and a distinguished member

of the New York Republican Club, when he was accused by Repré-
sentative Fred E. Busby (R., Illinois) of being too cautious in cleaning
out the Department. And didn't Robinson have a "leftist" cousin
somewhere? At this Secretary Marshall called for "fairness and de-
cency," Assistant Secretary of State John Puerifoy denounced "character assassination," and Robinson demanded a full hearing. He got
one. His opening words were truly memorable: "Let us start out with
what the charge is. What is the charge?" But in the end he had to
resign. [4]

## McCarthy and the Tydings Subcommittee

Armageddon came to the State Department early in 1950 in the
shape of Senator Joseph R. McCarthy. On February 7, speaking at
Wheeling, West Virginia, he claimed to be holding in his hand a list
of 205 people known to Secretary of State Dean Acheson to be Communists, yet still employed in the State Department. When the Department asked for the names of the 205, McCarthy said he had been
misquoted and had spoken only of "bad security risks." He then
claimed that fifty-seven Communists were still working in the Department. Six weeks later he put the figure at eighty-one. But under oath
he told the Tydings Subcommittee, "At this particular moment I
could not give you the names of half of these persons." In the open
Senate he mumbled his way through a list (which he refused to let
Senator Herbert H. Lehman look at) and confessed that certain
names did not involve Communist activities. In March Senator Robert A. Taft advised him "if one case didn't work, to bring up another." [5] In his book, *McCarthyism, the Fight for America* (1952),
McCarthy conceded that his original figure of 205 was based on a
letter sent by Byrnes in July 1946 to Congressman Adolph J. Sabath,
about *dubious cases under review*. But he omitted to mention that of
these 205, only fifty-six, all thoroughly screened, remained in the Department.

After much wrangling Truman finally authorized the members of
a Senate Foreign Relations subcommittee chaired by Senator Millard
Tydings to scrutinize the State Department's files. McCarthy immediately answered that this would prove nothing since the files would
have been "raped." Attorney General McGrath then informed Tydings that the FBI confirmed that the files still contained all the relevant FBI reports. This piece of news should have deflated McCarthy
but it made little impact. On July 17, 1950, the Tydings Subcommittee reported that McCarthy's allegations constituted "the most nefar-
ious campaign of half-truths and untruths in the history of this repub-

lic," and Tydings himself expressed confidence in the public servants who ran the State Department's loyalty program. But for most of the Department's employees whose names had now been publicized, the future was to be a dark one.

In the fall of 1951 Conrad E. Snow, chairman of the State Department's LRB, declared: "This is McCarthyism—the making of baseless accusations regarding the loyalty and integrity of public officers and employees . . . The purpose of it all is, of course, not the public interest, but political advancement in a period of public tension and excitement." On February 11, 1952, Snow returned to the attack: "The dust in the present case is created by one man, tramping about the nation and making, over and over again, the same baseless and disproved accusations." But the State Department resisted McCarthy's demand for a purge more in word than in deed; by January 1, 1953, eighteen of those named by McCarthy to the Tydings Subcommittee had left the State Department.[6]

William T. Stone had been assistant to McCarthy's political enemy, Assistant Secretary of State (later Senator) William Benton. McCarthy claimed that Benton had failed to remove Stone after an adverse security ruling on him. Stone resigned finally on February 2, 1952, as the Loyalty Review Board of the Civil Service Commission prepared to hear his case.

Edward Posniak, born in Russia, came to America in 1935 and was naturalized four years later. He served in the Department of Justice, the Public Housing Administration, the OSS, the Army (1943–45), and joined the State Department in October 1945. At the time that McCarthy pointed the finger at him, Posniak was working as an economist in the State Department's West European Division. The FBI had reported that Posniak had continued to associate with Communists until 1948, and a fellow employee in the State Department had accused him of bias in favor of Czechoslovak interests and Czech-Soviet friendship. Even so, the Loyalty Board had cleared him in 1948. According to an account hostile to McCarthy, McCarthy forged a document purporting to be a secret FBI report demonstrating that Posniak was a red agent. When J. Edgar Hoover sent two of his men to talk with McCarthy, the Senator made himself unavailable and instructed his staff not to discuss the matter. Posniak resigned in November 1950 rather than accept suspension pending a new investigation.

Esther Brunauer, Case No. 47 in McCarthy's Senate speech of February 20, 1950, was assistant director of policy liaison of the State Department's UNESCO relations staff. She agreed that her Hungarian-born husband had been in the (Communist) Young Workers League until 1927, she admitted having presided at a Washington meeting of the Friends of the Soviet Union in 1936, and she agreed that she had signed the call to the annual meeting of the American Youth Congress two years later, describing herself as a lifelong liberal. She was cleared by the Department's Loyalty Board and by the Tydings Subcommittee, but when her husband was suspended as a security risk by the Navy, the State Department invoked P.L. 733 and dismissed her in April 1951.[7]

The case of Val Lorwin was among the most scandalous in terms of the State Department's capitulation to McCarthy. Lorwin, who had entered government service in 1935 and transferred to the State Department from the OSS after the war, was denounced to McCarthy by a certain Harold Metz. Suspended in February 1951, he was found to be a security risk, but was granted a new hearing in March 1952 and was reinstated with back pay. He then resigned to become an assistant professor at the University of Chicago. Lorwin had once been an anti-Communist socialist and, until 1938, active in Norman Thomas's Socialist Party. Thomas led a parade of ninety-one witnesses who testified on his behalf at the loyalty hearings. Nevertheless, and despite the fact that he had left the government service nearly two years before, the State Department and the Justice Department, stampeded by McCarthy's snarls of admonition at Lorwin's clearance, had him indicted in December 1953 for denying under oath that he had ever been a Communist. Having no case, the government acted in a desperate manner. In order to persuade the grand jury to indict Lorwin, the Justice Department's attorney, as was later admitted, falsely told the jury that two FBI agents would corroborate Metz's story. He also assured the jury that Lorwin, if called before it, would take the Fifth Amendment and decline to testify; he thus excluded Lorwin from the jury's own investigations. On May 25, 1954, Assistant Attorney General Warren Olney III asked the federal district court to dismiss the case, which he conceded had been deliberately misrepresented. And yet, typical of the Justice Department ethics prevailing under Brownell, while the case was withdrawn, the indictment was not.[8]

## THE DULLES-SCOTT MCLEOD REGIME

The Eisenhower administration brought McCarthyism into the bowels of the State Department out of deference to McCarthy, Bridges and the Republican forces of vendetta. The most ominous appointment was that of the former FBI agent R. W. Scott McLeod as administrator, Bureau of Security and Consular Affairs. With his arrival in the Department began an era of almost incredible confusion, harassment, fear and petty bureaucratic sniping. On the face of it, the Department's security procedure, as outlined by McLeod in a speech to the American Political Science Association [9] in September 1955, looked impressive—indeed, it afforded far more due process than did comparable procedures in the British civil service. But the ritual masked the reality. While the staff of the Security Division doubled in a couple of years, the leading lights of McCarthy's "loyal American underground" rose to power in the State Department.[10] The State Department reported that during the period May 1953 to June 1955, there were only ten *dismissals* under Section 8(a) of E.O. 10450, but 273 *resignations*.

Symptomatic of the hysteria prevailing was the case of a Russian-born Jewish expert in Asian land reform, Wolf Ladejinsky. Although he was acknowledged as the architect of the postwar Japanese land reform sponsored by the American occupation, and although his reputation as an anti-Communist was confirmed by his colleagues and superiors, he had, in this age of suspicion, two black spots on his record: three of his sisters were still living in the Soviet Union; and in 1931, after graduating from Columbia, he had been employed by the Soviet trading company, Amtorg. While awaiting transfer from the State Department to the Department of Agriculture, he learned in December 1954 that Secretary of Agriculture Ezra T. Benson would not reappoint him agricultural attaché of the U.S. Embassy in Tokyo because he was "a security risk." Benson's actual motivation was exposed when he remarked that he would not want to see such a program of land reform as the Japanese one implemented in the United States; some of his aides described Ladejinsky's ideas as "socialistic." Early in July 1955, after the Foreign Operations Administration had slapped Benson in the face by appointing Ladejinsky to direct land reform in South Vietnam, Benson admitted that he was not a security risk.[11]

At the best of political times, the Foreign Service did not provide the most financially attractive of careers for a man of education and initiative. In 1954, a Class I officer serving in the United States might earn $12,500 a year, with a pension on retirement. But since 1945 the Foreign Service had been accorded little support or respect, with its members the favorite whipping boys in public debate, depicted as homosexuals, bunglers and Communists. In 1955 Hans Morgenthau commented that Europeans now regarded American diplomats they met with contempt and condescension. Even before the rise of McCarthy, the loyalty-security program subverted morale in the Service. Thirty-two men had turned down the job of assistant secretary of state before the thirty-third accepted it on February 1, 1950. Every promotion incurred a new security investigation; every incident already explained had to be explained again. College graduates now shunned the Service, which by 1954 had declined from its postwar peak of 1,429 officers to only 1,285.[12]

In January 1954 a letter appeared in *The New York Times* signed by five distinguished former diplomats, Norman Armour, Robert Woods Bliss, Joseph C. Grew, William Phillips and G. Howland Shaw, in which they warned that

> a Foreign Service officer who reports . . . to the very best of his ability and who makes recommendations which at the time he conscientiously believes to be for the best interests of the United States may subsequently find his loyalty challenged and may even be forced out of the Service and discredited forever as a private citizen after years of distinguished service.

Of forty-three chiefs of mission who by May had replied to a letter of inquiry from Henry M. Wriston, president of Brown University and chairman of the bipartisan committee appointed in 1954 to study the Foreign Service, thirty-three reported low or very low morale, owing to the style of the security program, attacks by public figures, and the lack of support from the top. Theodore H. White observed that "to the native caution of Foreign Service officers had now deepened "to a level of timidity that gives the American people a Foreign Service of eunuchs." Personnel overseas, fearing that what they now wrote in their reports, however orthodox, might be held against them ten years hence, even staged mock Congressional hearings to anticipate harsh questions and to forestall "mistakes." Nor did matters improve rapidly. It was in 1960 that a State Department official confided to Professor Paul Tillett that it was eight years since any chief of mission abroad had sent in a report with which the chief personally disagreed but which he regarded as worthy of study.[13]

## THE CHINA TRAUMA

Unlike his policy toward Europe, Truman's China policy was not securely anchored in bipartisan consultation. In February 1949 Senator Pat McCarran introduced a bill to provide greater military aid to Chiang; Acheson opposed it, saying it could only prolong the hostilities, the suffering. McCarran, Bridges, Wherry and Knowland hit back by describing the government's White Paper of August—drafted by the State Department, it washed America's hands of the outcome of the Chinese civil war—as a whitewash. When China finally "fell" and Chiang Kai-shek fled to Formosa, the Republican Party in general and the "China Lobby" in particular bitterly denounced the "betrayal" and began a hunt for scapegoats. In January 1950 Taft alleged in the Senate that the State Department had been guided by a leftist group determined to dump Chiang and willing to turn China over to the Communists.[14] McCarthy claimed that Acheson and Marshall had ensured that the Kremlin gained a friendly government in China and that America gained a bloody and pointless war in Korea. Had not Marshall imposed an arms embargo and a truce when Chiang's forces were at the height of their power? The villains of the plot, according to McCarthy, included John Paton Davies, John Stewart Service, Raymond P. Ludden and John M. Emerson of the State Department, as well as General Joseph Stilwell, Brigadier General Evans Carlson, Agnes Smedley (a journalist who befriended the Red Army during the Long March) and an academic expert, Owen Lattimore.

The State Department officials and academic experts who had influenced policy and had for years foreseen that the corruption of Chiang's regime could lead only to its eventual collapse, were now exposed to merciless attack. Prompter and promoter number one of the purge was an archconservative businessman, Alfred Kohlberg, who first visited China in 1916 and organized a profitable business importing Chinese embroideries. As a director of the American Bureau for Medical Aid to China, he returned from an investigatory trip to China in 1943 convinced that the ABMAC had been maligned with unfounded charges of graft originated by Communists within the Institute of Pacific Relations, of which he was also a member. Falling in with such anti-Communist zealots as Isaac Don Levine and Louis Budenz, Kohlberg established the periodical *Plain Talk* and whipped up such a campaign against the IPR that the Institute held a special meeting in April 1947 to discuss his allegations. Defeated by 1,163 votes to 66, Kohlberg angrily resigned. Thereafter he formed an alliance with witch-hunting Senators like McCarran and McCarthy, supplied them with material, and generally stimulated an atmosphere of hysteria about Communist spies and saboteurs lurking in the State Department.

As the Second World War progressed, the basic drift of the reporting of the Foreign Service's China experts had been that Chiang's eventual defeat was inevitable—not necessarily desirable, just inevitable. When they were proven right in 1949 they had to be punished for their prescience—and accused of having willed the event, ensured the outcome. Such was the impact of the purge that followed, that of twenty-two Foreign Service officers who had joined the China service before the war, only two remained at State Department desks in Washington in 1954. The others had either been dismissed or scattered round the globe: one with twenty-five years' experience of

China was posted to Vancouver; another with twenty-two years' experience found himself in Athens; yet another, with eighteen years', was assigned to Guayaquil. Wherever they were they sheltered gratefully in their obscurity, hoping not to be flushed out by an alert Congressman.[15]

One to whom shelter and obscurity were denied was O. Edmund Clubb, Jr., a Foreign Service officer with twenty-two years' service involving long periods of separation from his family as well as eight months' internment by the Japanese in 1942. Since 1944 Clubb had served as Consul General in Vladivostok, Mukden, Changchun and finally Peking, where he defended his country's interests with force and dignity until the flag was finally hauled down. In July 1950 he returned to Washington to take up the top-ranking post of Director of the Office of Chinese Affairs in the State Department.

On December 28, 1950, he was confronted with an interrogatory containing eight allegations, including association with Communists in Hankow in 1931–34, and having displayed "pink" tendencies in Peking in 1934–35. It was also alleged—this proved to be the crucial charge—that in 1932, when home on leave, he had delivered a sealed envelope to the office of the *New Masses* in New York, for transmittal to a certain Grace Hutchins, a reported Communist. On June 27, 1951, Clubb was suspended.

The *New Masses* incident had occurred nearly twenty years previously, and Clubb remembered very little about it. To refresh his memory, he managed to obtain his diary for that year from Peking, with the help of a British diplomat. He turned this diary over to the Loyalty Security Board and soon learned that distorted versions of it were being leaked around Washington. Both HCUA and the SISS subpoenaed him, together with his diary.

In point of fact Clubb's difficulties originated with that archinformer and walking memory bank, Whittaker Chambers, who had been sitting in the *New Masses* office on the day in 1932 when Clubb had called in—a fact that Chambers had divulged to the FBI and HCUA, and repeated in May 1950 to the State Department's Loyalty Security Board, hinting at the same time that he connected Clubb with the CP underground. But on August 16, 1951, Chambers told the SISS that he had "no knowledge whatsoever" whether Clubb had ever belonged to a Communist organization. On December 21, 1951, Clubb learned that the Loyalty Security Board (consisting of Brigadier General Conrad Snow, Lieutenant Colonel Francis Murphy and Ambassador Fletcher Warren) had ruled that there existed "no reasonable doubt" as to his loyalty, but nevertheless recommended separation on the ground that Clubb constituted a security risk. It became clear that the 1932 incident—which now enmeshed Clubb in a nightmare of trivial and circumstantial hair-splitting—was the sole basis for the verdict. In February 1952 his appeal was heard by Ambassador Nathaniel P. Davis, who ruled that his removal was not necessary. Thereupon Clubb was relegated to the Division of Historical Research. By this time McCarthy was chewing over the case on a loud, guilt-by-association basis (Clubb had known or encountered such suspect characters as Agnes Smedley, Philip Jaffe and Owen Lattimore). In disgust Clubb decided to quit the State Department, where desks were searched, private correspondence opened, telephones tapped and secretaries required to inform by a corps of several hundred security men.[16]

Haldore Hanson, chief of the Technical Cooperation Projects staff, one of three groups responsible for administering the Point Four program, was denounced by McCarthy as a security risk because Hanson had spent time with the Chinese Communist armies as an AP correspondent in the late thirties and had reported on them favorably in his book, *Humane Endeavor* (1939). Hanson explained before the Tydings subcommittee that his book had been influenced by the spirit of the united front, when Chiang and Mao made common cause against the Japanese invaders. But these early views did not reflect his opinions eleven years later "in the midst of a cold war between the democracies and world Communism." Budenz put in an appearance to announce that Hanson had been a Party member: "I carried his name with me." The Tydings Subcommittee completely exonerated Hanson, who kept his job until 1953, when Harold Stassen, Eisenhower's appointee as head of the Foreign Operations Administration, demanded his resignation because of a "reduction in force."[17]

John Carter Vincent had been a Foreign Service officer since 1924. In 1942 he was serving as Counselor to the U.S. Embassy at Chungking. He talked with Chou En-lai, accepted some of his criticisms of the Kuomintang, but nevertheless reserved some friendly thoughts for Chiang. In 1944 Vincent was appointed chief of the State Department's Division of Chinese Affairs. Following his (later notorious) visit to Soviet Asia as adviser to Vice-President Wallace, he was appointed Director of Far Eastern Affairs. By the time McCarthy denounced him as part of the clique that had betrayed China, Vincent was on the way down: Minister to Switzerland. Trouble piled up when Budenz came before the McCarran SISS and declared that to his certain knowledge Vincent and Lattimore had been assigned by the CP to guide Wallace along pro-Communist lines during the 1944 tour. But a former member of Major General Claire Chennault's staff at Kunming, the noted journalist Joseph Alsop, now interceded to report that he had personally witnessed Vincent urging Wallace to telegraph Roosevelt to dismiss the left-wing General Joseph W. Stilwell, and to replace him with the anti-Communist General Albert C. Wedemeyer. This was then done. Alsop suggested that Budenz be prosecuted for perjury.

The State Department LRB voted by 3 to 2 that Vincent's conduct of Chinese affairs raised a reasonable doubt as to his loyalty, but Acheson, with Truman's approval, referred the case to an *ad hoc* board headed by Judge Learned Hand. Vincent was retained. When Dulles became Secretary he condemned Vincent's reporting as inadequate and demanded his resignation. The scores were now being settled.

A Foreign Service officer who served as political adviser to Stilwell in 1943–44 and who, recognizing the corruption endemic to Chiang's regime, urged Washington to keep an open door to Mao rather than drive him into the arms of Russia, was John Paton Davies. The son of American missionaries, born in China in 1908, Davies had studied at Yenching University as well as the Universities of Michigan and Harvard. Consul in Kunming, Hankow, Peking and Shenyang, he had in fact spent the greater part of his life in China. Toward the end of the war he regularly informed Washington that the American observer team at Yenan were convinced that Mao desired a friendly relationship with the United States. Denounced by McCarthy, Davies had been cleared four times by the State Department and the LRB when, in April 1953, he was transferred to an obscure post in Peru. Pressured by McCarthy, Dulles submitted the case to a five-member Security Board, which found no evidence of disloyalty but concluded that Davies lacked "judgment, discretion and reliability." Refusing to retire discreetly, Davies was fired by Dulles on November 5, 1954.

China, again, was the cradle and the grave of John Stewart Service's career. As Third Secretary of the Embassy, he had dispatched Report No. 40, dated October 10, 1944:

> We need not fear the collapse of the Kuomintang Government . . . Any new government . . . will be more cooperative and better able to mobilize the country . . . The example of a democratic, non-imperialistic China will be much better counter-propaganda in Asia . . .

After the war the overzealous Service made an error he was lucky to survive—he gave "eight or ten" personal copies of classified memoranda he had drafted while attached to the military mission in Yenan to Philip Jaffe, the pro-Communist editor of the journal *Amerasia*.[18] The motive was, however, innocent; it was standard strategy to try to influence policy by means of a leak. A grand jury concluded that he had not known that Jaffe and his colleagues were Communists, and decided not to indict him.

After McCarthy launched his attack on Service, the State Department's Loyalty Board cleared him four times, until finally the LRB found against him. Acheson thereupon (December 13, 1951) fired Service. Six years later, following the Supreme Court's ruling in *Service v. Dulles*, he was reinstated on the ground that the manner of his dismissal had violated the procedural rules that Acheson himself had laid down. Now aged forty-eight, he was appointed to supervise overseas shipments at a salary of $12,900; but his legal costs had been $70,000.[19]

The "China Tangle" also enmeshed the most distinguished of the career diplomats whom McCarthy brought down, Philip Jessup. Descended from seventeenth-century English immigrants (his grandfather had chaired the committee that drafted Lincoln's reelection platform), a member of the Legion and a pillar of the Presbyterian Church, Jessup embodied all the qualities that brought blood to McCarthy's eyes. He had even appeared as a character witness on behalf of Alger Hiss at both his trials and refused to repudiate Hiss even after his conviction for perjury. Scarcely less incriminating, Jessup had, during the early forties, been a prominent member of the IPR, serving as chairman of its American Council, its Pacific Council, and its Research Advisory Committee.

Writing in *China Monthly* in August 1949, the obsessive Alfred Kohlberg assailed Jessup as "the originator of the myth of the democratic Chinese Communists." Speaking from the Senate floor in March and again in June 1950, McCarthy echoed Kohlberg's words. Defying Republican pressure, Truman nominated Jessup in October 1951 to serve on the American delegation to the UN, a job he undertook with the benefit of tributes from Marshall, Eisenhower and General Lucius Clay, who advised a subcommittee of the Senate Foreign Relations Committee that Jessup had taken a firm and realistic approach to the Russians during the Berlin blockade. At the UN Jessup was soon exchanging words with Vishinsky. But McCarthy renewed his attacks while his orchestrated followers deluged the subcommittee with protest mail, stampeding it into a 3 to 2 rejection of Jessup's appointment. One of the majority, Senator Alexander H. Smith (R., New Jersey), had only recently assured the victim: "I have known you too long to have any doubts about your loyalty and integrity." [20] Jessup left the State Department to take up a chair of international law at Columbia. The sclerosis that now gripped American policy toward China rapidly extended to all thinking about Asia.[21]

As fiercely partisan as his President, Acheson was no less inclined than Truman to discover the evils of the inquisition only when they were magnified by his Republican opponents. Although he himself, on becoming Secretary of State in January 1949, had appointed Carlisle H. Humesline, a former colonel who had joined the State Department after the war, as Deputy Under Secretary in charge of loyalty-security investigations, he strongly upheld the view, once out of office, that Foreign Service officers should have judgment passed on them only by their colleagues in the Foreign Service. Quoting such liberal intellectual critics of the program as Shils, Chafee and Ralph S. Brown, Jr., Acheson declared in 1955: "The trial of Foreign Service officers . . . because their views ten years ago are now regarded as heretical by a politically powerful and obstreperous group, is a purge no different from the Moscow type . . ." Acheson did, however, have the good grace to acknowledge that after both world wars Democratic administrations had departed from principle and overlooked the dangers of secret evidence provided by anonymous informers: "These practices had their root in the President's Executive Order 9835, of March 21, 1947 . . . and the Act of August 26, 1950, . . . I . . . share . . . the responsibility for what I am now convinced was a grave mistake and a failure to foresee consequences which were inevitable." [22] Acheson regarded Dulles's dismissal of John P. Davies as disgraceful; he said nothing about his own dismissal of Service or about the 600-plus loyalty-security cases which had brought terror to the Department in the Truman era and laid the basis for the twenty years of timid conformism that the Department itself lamented in December 1970 (Publication 8551).

## ATTACK ON THE IPR

We return now to the attack on the IPR, in whose ranks McCarthy (coached by Kohlberg) detected such "Soviet agents" as Jessup, Owen Lattimore, Michael Greenberg, Chao Ting Chi and Frederick V. Field. Of these, Field was certainly a Communist—donor, trustee, executive secretary of the American IPR from 1938 to 1940, he was also a sponsor of the Wallace movement, a contributor to the CP's *Political Affairs* between 1945 and 1950 and a consistent advocate of the Chinese Communists. He took the Fifth Amendment before the Tydings and McCarran Subcommittees. Michael Greenberg, who succeeded Lattimore as editor of *Pacific Affairs* in 1941, and who had worked for the Board of Economic Warfare, was one of those whom Elizabeth Bentley claimed to have recruited into her spy ring; William Buckley called him a "British-born Communist." As for Lattimore, as editor of *Pacific Affairs* from 1934 to 1941 he had published both pro-

and anti-Communist articles, but Kohlberg and his friends counted up only the pro-Communist ones and seized on the fact that in *Far Eastern Survey*, organ of the American IPR, Thomas A. Bisson had in July 1943 described the Chinese Communists as democrats and agrarian radicals, not real Communists. Nor could it be denied that several IPR staff members, including Field, had helped to create the magazine *Amerasia* (Bisson and Lattimore served on the editorial board). In 1945 *Amerasia*'s editor, Philip Jaffe, was convicted of receiving confidential documents relating to China from John Stewart Service of the State Department. By the time that such witnesses as Dr. Karl Wittfogel, Bentley, Budenz, Alexander Barmine and Hede Massing had finished testifying before the McCarran Subcommittee, at least sixty officials and writers connected with the IPR had been "named under oath as Communists," including Lattimore, Greenberg, Bisson, Lawrence K. Rosinger and Maxwell S. Stewart. Bentley claimed that Jacob Golos told her that the IPR was "the center of all Communist activity in the Far Eastern field." [23]

The McCarran Subcommittee of the SISS met from July 1951 to June 1952. The hearings began five months after the SISS had dramatically and illegally seized the IPR's files from a barn in Massachusetts belonging to Edward C. Carter, former secretary of the American Council of the IPR. On July 2, 1952, the subcommittee reported to the Senate that, "but for the machinations of the small group that controlled [the IPR], China would be free." This sweeping conclusion was accepted by *Time*, the *Saturday Evening Post*, the *Los Angeles Times*, the *Chicago Tribune* and other papers; so, too, was the implicit evaluation of what "free" meant.

Individual China experts now suffered. Professor John K. Fairbank, of Harvard, who—like Joseph Barnes, T. A. Bisson and Maxwell Stewart—denied before the McCarran Subcommittee that he had ever been in the CP (Louis Budenz claimed that he had been), retreated from political involvement and was dropped as a consultant by the State Department. In 1951 the Army forbade him to enter Japan; mass-circulation magazines no longer wanted his articles. The case of Fairbank demonstrates how the purge affected liberal attitudes and tightened the parameters of permissible dissent. In 1947 he had described America's fear of Communism as an expression of a general fear of the future; he regarded American aid to rightist regimes in Indochina, China and Indonesia with grave misgivings:

This American fascism will come, if it comes, because American liberals have joined the American public in a fear of Communism abroad rather than fascism at home as the chief totalitarian menace . . .

But his posture toward the McCarran Subcommittee was somewhat different:

> I am grateful to know that the Russians fear my activities as a threat to their success. But I cannot be of help in this fight if I am discredited and repudiated by own people.[24]

In other words, I am a more effective anti-Communist than thou, if thou wilt only allow me to be.

The IPR itself suffered grievously. Companies long faithful to it, like Standard-Vacuum, severed relations in the face of protests from stockholders. Grants were reduced by half during the 1951–52 period, then dried up. Income fell from $77,000 in 1951 to about $18,000 in 1956. Membership dropped from 933 to 341. The establishment had taken fright; during the Cox Committee investigation into foundations in 1952, Dean Rusk, president of the Rockefeller Foundation, said he was "concerned" about allegations of bias on the part of IPR staff, and that the chances of further grants were "remote." This meant that research, thought, initiative, controversy about the Far East was stifled; a long and sterile orthodoxy had taken root. A new blow fell in May 1955, when Commissioner of Internal Revenue T. Coleman Andrews, a friend of McCarthy, wrote IPR that its tax exemption was being revoked retroactive to January 1, on the ground that it had disseminated "controversial and partisan propaganda." Two months later the American branch of the IPR suffered the same fate. In July 1956 the IPR filed suit, and in March 1960 District Judge David N. Edelstein held that not a "scintilla of evidence" existed to show that the IPR had in 1955 been behaving in the way described (the government's sole exhibit was the McCarran Report, describing events only up to 1952). Nevertheless, both the IPR and the AIPR were about to expire. The death had been protracted but inevitable.[25]

## THE TRIAL OF OWEN LATTIMORE

Of all those scholars and writers who suffered in their careers as a result of the China witch hunt—including notably Lawrence Rosinger, Bisson and William Marx Mandel—none was hounded so furiously as Owen Lattimore, Director of the Walter Hines Page School of International Relations at Johns Hopkins University. Born in Washington, Lattimore had been taken to China as an infant. In 1926–27 he explored little-known parts of Central Asia, for which he won a Royal Geographical Society Award. After graduate work in anthropology at Harvard, Lattimore traveled in Manchuria and Inner

Mongolia. He learned Russian, studied Russia's Asian frontier, visited the Soviet Union, and served as editor of the IPR's *Pacific Affairs* from 1934 to 1941. In 1938 he joined Johns Hopkins, and in 1941 he was chosen by Roosevelt to serve as Chiang's personal political adviser. From 1942 to 1944 Lattimore headed the Pacific operations of the Office of War Information, and in 1944 he accompanied Vice-President Wallace on his tour of Soviet Asia. The following year Lattimore served as a member of the Pauley Reparations Mission to Japan. Early in 1950 McCarthy denounced him as "the chief architect of our Far Eastern policy" and "an extremely bad security risk," and followed this up with the even more sensational accusation that he had been "Alger Hiss's boss in the espionage ring in the State Department" and was now the top Soviet espionage agent operating in the United States. Lattimore flew back to America and engaged Abe Fortas as his counsel. Lattimore had then published at least nine books; [26] it was to be a further eighteen years before any American firm agreed to publish another.

An important witness against Lattimore before the Tydings Subcommittee was Louis Budenz, who testified on April 20 that CP policies were dispatched from Moscow to the CPUSA via Field and Lattimore and that in 1941 Jacob Stachel, a CP leader, had instructed him to regard Lattimore as a Communist and to treat his advice and writings as authoritative. Why, he was asked, had Lattimore so radically departed from CP policy by championing Finland in her war against the Soviet Union in 1939, and by supporting the Marshall Plan? Budenz replied that Lattimore might have been granted an "exemption"—perhaps modeled on the Papal indulgences of the church that Budenz himself had now embraced? It was also the case that Lattimore's recent book, *The Situation in Asia* (1949), had been criticized by the *Daily Worker* as "completely off the beam" for its espousal of the "third force" of nonaligned nations and for its prediction that these emerging states would steer clear of both Moscow and Washington. Budenz, again, had an answer: "They are pushing a certain line; I mean the Communists beyond the Party." So Lattimore was a Communist "beyond the Party"?

Freda Utley, who bore a personal grudge against Lattimore, testified that his function had been "to lead us all unknowingly to destruction." But Bella Dodd, who had recently quit the CP, testified that she had never heard of Lattimore and derided Budenz's story of Lattimore's name appearing as L or XL on onionskin secret documents which had to be flushed down the toilet after reading. Earl Browder, former general secretary of the CPUSA, described Lattimore as "a person of anti-Communist views, of a very decided and profound character," and completely denied Budenz's story that in 1937 Browder and Field had discussed Lattimore's work for the CP. Indeed Budenz's testimony was scarcely credible in any respect. At one point Senator Green asked him how many of Lattimore's published writings he had read:

MR. BUDENZ: Very few indeed.
SENATOR GREEN: How many?
MR. BUDENZ: Well, that I cannot say, offhand . . . I have read hurriedly *Situation in Asia*.
SENATOR GREEN: Just looked it through?
MR. BUDENZ: Yes, sir.

It came out during the hearings that in September 1947 Budenz had told a State Department official on the telephone that he could not recall any incident that definitely would indicate that Lattimore was a member of the Party.

Four members of the Subcommittee, having heard a summary of Lattimore's FBI file read to them in the presence of J. Edgar Hoover and the Attorney General, concluded that there was nothing to indicate that Lattimore, whose connection with the State Department had in any case been both "peripheral" and "sporadic," had been a Communist or had engaged in espionage.[27]

It was certainly true, as anti-Communist liberals like Sidney Hook and David Dallin angrily stressed, that in 1938 Lattimore had written that the discovery of the "conspiracies" in Russia amounted to a "triumph for democracy." And later Lattimore had described the Soviet labor camp of Kolyma somewhat lyrically in an American magazine. Among the IPR files seized from the Carter barn was found a letter from Lattimore to Carter, dated July 10, 1938, suggesting that the IPR should keep behind the official Chinese CP position, "far enough not to be covered by the same label—but enough ahead of the active Chinese liberals to be noticeable." In 1949 he had advised: "The thing to do, therefore, is to let South Korea fall—but not to let it look as though we pushed it."

Whatever one may think of such attitudes and stratagems, a private citizen is surely entitled to recommend them without suffering a protracted official inquisition. Lattimore's real crime was to have challenged the guardian-angel concept of America's role in the American Century: "We must chasten the feeling of unlimited power with which we came out of the war." An indigenist who admired Ho Chi Minh and believed that local forces were primary, he argued that China would not fall into Russia's embrace unless America drove her to it.[28] "The present American policy in China should be changed," he wrote in June 1948, "not because it is anti-Communist, but because it is unsuccessfully anti-Communist."

Lattimore appeared before the McCarran Subcommittee on February 28 and began to read from a harshly worded statement. So frequently was he interrupted that he got through only eight sentences in three hours. The battle continued for twelve days—all the familiar anti-Communist academics and professional witnesses were wheeled out, including Igor Bogolepov, a Russian colonel who had defected to the Nazis in August 1941. Then came a further turn of the screw: on the basis of the evidence he had given, a District of Columbia grand jury indicted Lattimore on seven counts of perjury in December 1952. Now he was on trial, in the exact sense of the word, for his opinions.

Lattimore's indictment charged him with having lied when he denied he had been "a sympathizer or any other kind of promoter of Communism or Communist interests"; when he said he had no reason to believe that a certain Chinese had been a Communist; when he said he did not know that a contributor to *Political Affairs* called "Asiaticus" was a Communist; when he denied he had as editor published articles by persons (other than Russians) whom he knew to be Communists; when he said that his lunch conference with Soviet Ambassador Oumansky had taken place after Hitler invaded Russia; when he said he did not take care of Lauchlin Currie's mail at the White House while Currie was out of the country; when he said it was not necessary to get permission from the Communist authorities to cross a demarcation line to go to Yenan; and when he said he had not prearranged with the Chinese Communists to make such a trip. In May 1953 Judge Luther W. Youngdahl of the U.S. District Court for the District of Columbia dismissed four of the seven counts. Youngdahl pointed out that perjury occurred not merely when a man said something false, but when he knew it to be false. Where general beliefs and political labels were in question, a man's state of mind could not be accurately penetrated. But the Justice Department argued to the Court of Appeals that a state of mind is a fact even when hard to prove, and that misrepresenting a state of mind is perjury. The term "Communist sympathizer" had, said U.S. Attorney Lee A. Rover, acquired a definite legal connotation. In July 1954 the Court of Appeals restored two of the four counts dismissed by Youngdahl.

The Justice Department decided to start again. On October 7, 1954, it secured a new grand-jury indictment on two counts only, by listing twenty-five topics about which Lattimore's views paralleled "the Communist line." After Rover had attempted in vain to bludgeon Judge Youngdahl into disqualifying himself, the judge threw out the two-count indictment on January 18, 1955. On June 28, the Justice Department finally dropped all charges—five and a half years after McCarthy had hurled Lattimore's name, career and reputation into the headlines.

One honorable aspect of this baleful story was the behavior of Johns Hopkins University. When Lattimore was indicted in December 1952, the university suspended him on full pay, and when the government dropped the case two-and-a-half years later, he was restored. But his international-relations program had disintegrated and few students dared study under him.[29] At the age of sixty-three, Lattimore took up the chair of Chinese studies at Leeds University in England. He returned to China in 1972 and was accorded a friendly reception, but two years later, during the anti-Confucius campaign, the Peking press recalled that he had once been an adviser to Chiang, and referred to him as an "international spy." Evidently Joe McCarthy was alive and well in Peking.

## McCARTHY AND THE VOICE OF AMERICA

The first target of the Permanent Subcommittee on Investigations under McCarthy's chairmanship was the Voice of America. Founded in 1942 and latterly the shortwave propaganda arm of the State Department's International Information Agency, the Voice had recently benefited from a fifty-million-dollar Congressional appropriation for a worldwide ring of shortwave transmitters designed to penetrate the Iron Curtain and reach every corner of the globe. In bringing havoc to the IIA, with its staff of 10,000 and its annual budget of one hundred million dollars, McCarthy was certainly sabotaging the voice of the Pax Americana at its most strident and assertive. After McCarthy made a fuss about a shortwave transmitter—which, he wrongly claimed, had been mislocated as part of a red plot—one of the engineers who had worked on the transmitter, Raymond Kaplan, killed himself. As he blasted the Voice's programs and roasted leading officials of the IIA, the Democratic members of the subcommittee, McClellan, Jackson and Symington, watched in glum silence. It was now that the Cold War liberals associated with the American Committee for Cultural Freedom, Commentary and the New Leader, who had hitherto applauded the purge of Communists, fellow travelers and Progressives, began to complain.

The McCarthy hearings were fueled and fired by rivalries and intrigues within the IIA, many of whose staff had been inherited from the liberal Office of War Information. McCarthy and his aides found a "loyal American underground" within the Voice willing to advance themselves on the broken necks of their colleagues.

During the first week of the hearings, Secretary Dulles promised full cooperation. The new Republican State Department leadership showed its mettle with Information Guide 272 (February 19, 1953), issued by Assistant Secretary of State for Public Affairs Carl McCardle, forbidding the Voice to use or quote from the works "of any Communists, fellow travelers, etc. . . ." When Alfred H. Morton, chief of the Voice in New York, wired Washington that he would continue to quote Stalin, Vishinsky and Gromyko "to the extent that the use of such material advances our cause," he was told not to. On March 17, McCardle sent the IIA Dulles's modified directive: to employ material from Communist or sympathetic sources only with great care and when uniquely effective in confounding international Communism; and not to identify by name any international Communist leader except when absolutely necessary. On June 15, Dulles washed his hands of this directive, claiming it had been issued by the head of the IIA, Robert L. Johnson.

In February, Dulles had invited Dr. Johnson, president of Temple University, to head the IIA. A beaten man from the start, he began on the defensive. When asked about McCarthy's charges, he told reporters on February 26: "I think he is trying to be helpful, and maybe he'll dig up stuff that will help us." Sworn in on March 3, he immediately called for a security check on the IIA's top twenty staff members. To Scott McLeod he wrote: "Send me information on anybody you think is a risk and I'll fire him." But the situation was beyond McLeod's control, as also beyond Johnson's. Visits and telephone calls from Cohn and Schine were frequent; having promised his informers within the IIA that they would be protected and promoted, Schine exerted relentless pressure on Johnson and his assistant Martin Merson to spare his men from the consequence of the drastic budget cutback that early in April resulted in 633 dismissals.[30] Among Cohn and Schine's allies within the IIA, the key informer was Paul Deac of the French desk. Born in Rumania, Deac had come to America in the 1930s and evidently began reporting on his colleagues from the moment he arrived at the Voice in January 1951. Operating from Schine's suite in the Waldorf Towers, Deac prowled around the offices of the Voice with his pocket full of blank subpoenas which, as Philip Horton put it, fluttered on desks like raffle tickets. Fear spread, gossip gathered momentum, and few division or branch chiefs were prepared to defend their subordinates under fire.

On April 29 Martin Merson asked C. D. Jackson, a friend of Eisenhower, whether the President would support the IIA's leadership in the event of a showdown with McCarthy's espionage system within it. Jackson told him that Eisenhower did not wish to offend anyone in Congress. When the IIA defended its overseas libraries against the testimony of McCarthy's "expert," Karl Baarslag, Mc-Carthy released to the press a letter he had written Johnson, warning that his conduct had harmed the IIA's chances of getting adequate funds. From the White House, Sherman Adams instructed Johnson not to reply to McCarthy and not to give out any statements until further notice.

In August Johnson resigned, having discharged six employees as "security risks." The McCarthy investigation revealed, as usual, no Communists, but it did lead to the dismissal or resignation of about thirty people, including some of the most dedicated and able. The injustice and absurdity of these dismissals, even by the standards of the time, were conspicuous. In March 1954 a key officer resigned because he had fathered a child out of wedlock during the war and, even though he remained on good terms with the mother, was there-fore considered a security risk. Joseph M. Franckenstein, head of Amerika Dienst, was dismissed as a security risk because he associated with his wife, the novelist Kay Boyle, who, despite her denials, was said to be pro-Communist. Four years later, in April 1957, the State Department found these charges to be baseless and cleared Franck-enstein.[31]

Herbert T. Edwards, head of the IIA's film division and a man of conservative leanings, resigned in April 1953 after McCarthy had roasted him at a hearing for the "widespread waste and Communist propaganda" in the film division. Dr. William C. Johnstone, director of the Voice's field officers round the world, W. Bradley Connors and Raymond Gram Swing all quit. Swing, a veteran radio commentator and expert on foreign affairs, jeopardized his career by criticizing *Red Channels*, the witch-hunting magazine of radio and television. Sub-poenaed by McCarthy, he resigned in protest against the State De-partment's abject failure to protect the Voice.

The case of Marcelle Henry, a Frenchwoman naturalized in 1943 as an American, who had joined the Voice after working for the United States propaganda services overseas, deserves some attention. On October 2, 1952, she was summoned to the State Department's Security Division and grilled for eighty minutes by three security men, mainly about her sex life: "When did you last buy contracep-tives?" In January 1953 she received a letter from the personnel de-partment accusing her of uncouth behavior in the office, whereupon thirty-nine colleagues signed an affidavit refuting all the charges against her. On February 20, at the McCarthy hearings, two wit-nesses leveled allegations against her, one being that on the French program she had favorably reviewed Edna Ferber's novel *Giant*, de-spite its caustic view of Texan *mores*. Then, during a televised hear-ing, McCarthy and Cohn alleged that she was pro-Communist, un-

American, and that she had already been dismissed. Two weeks later this premature discharge became a reality, though the pretext given said nothing about Communism or un-Americanism, only about a "disregard for the generally accepted standards of conventional behavior." She went back to France.

But McCarthy's most histrionic displays were reserved for two senior members of the IIA, both of whom carried the odor of authentic New Deal liberalism. After nineteen years' government service, Reed Harris headed the IIA during the brief interregnum between Truman and Eisenhower, then stepped down to become Robert Johnson's deputy. But the McCarthy staff unearthed skeletons in Harris's political closet: he had been expelled from Columbia in April 1932 on account of radical editorials he had written in the *Spectator*, and a strike in support of his claim to reinstatement had been led by the Communist-influenced National Student League. Five years later his name had figured among the sponsors of a dinner of the Communist-dominated American Students Union. Harris explained that he had long since put all that behind him. McCarthy, however, wanted him to put his career behind him, and on April 10 Harris was forced to resign from the IIA. (When Edward R. Murrow became director of the USIA under Kennedy, he appointed Harris to a top post.)

McCarthy's second prize-scalp within the IIA was Theodore Kaghan. As acting director of the Office of Public Affairs of the U.S. High Commission in Germany, Kaghan had been rash enough to publicly describe Cohn and Schine, during their spellbinding tour of the IIA libraries in Europe, as "junketeering gumshoes." He was whipped back to Washington to face the Senator; Schine telephoned Johnson to demand his instant dismissal. Unfortunately for Kaghan, while never in the CP he had attended Communist meetings during the period 1935–40, signed a nominating petition for a Communist candidate for New York City council, and written left-wing plays. Explaining that he had become anti-Communist after 1945 when dealing with the Russians in Vienna, Kaghan produced a letter from the Austrian Chancellor Leopold Figl in praise of his anti-Communism. McCarthy was not impressed. While his hearing was still in progress, Kaghan received a letter from Scott McLeod threatening him with security charges if he did not resign. He resigned.

After Johnson's own resignation in August 1953, Theodore C. Streibert was appointed Director of the IIA's successor, the U.S. Information Agency. But the atmosphere scarcely improved while McCarthy remained a power; by June 1955 seventy-four members of the staff had resigned under political pressure.[32]

# 16

## *The UN, Brief Refuge*

The United Nations had been from its inception a prime target of the American Right. Not only was its internationalism offensive to the isolationist forces that had rejected the League of Nations, but its creation was associated with Roosevelt, Alger Hiss, and the spirit of Yalta. The American Right increasingly depicted the UN's skyscraper Secretariat, located on Manhattan's East River, as a tower of immunity for foreign Communist "spies and saboteurs," disguised as diplomats. The mounting hysteria concerning school textbooks praising, or even dispassionately explaining, the aims of the UN, its Charter and its Declaration of Human Rights, reflected the fears of a rich people encircled by an encroaching forest of poverty.

Article 100 of the UN Charter stipulates that the Secretary General and his staff "shall not seek or receive instructions from any government." But, under the anti-Communist Norwegian Social Democrat Trygve Lie, this principle was honored more in the breach than in the observance. Initially inclined to accommodate the sensitivities of the budget-supporting host nation (American citizens and those who had applied for permanent residence in the United States accounted for about two thirds of the headquarters staff), Lie eventually found himself surrendering abjectly to America's escalating politics of purge. It was in July–August 1949 that McCarran's Senate Judiciary Committee launched widely publicized allegations that the UN was infiltrated by Communists.

Ostensibly, the UN Secretariat hit back; there were indignant protests from Lie, Byron Price, the American administrative chief of the UN, and from Dr. Ralph J. Bunche, who denounced the "witch hunt." Behind the scenes, however, Lie capitulated. Already in June he had authorized Price to approach the FBI for derogatory information on American applicants for positions in the Secretariat, and in September–October he made a secret agreement with the State Department to cover the screening of all American personnel, both incumbents and applicants. Price testified to the General Assembly in 1953 that adverse evaluations from the State Department were not accompanied by evidence. Despite this, the Secretariat even deferred to State Department wishes with regard to promotions.[1] When Acheson appeared before the House Committee on the Judiciary in December 1952, he refused to provide the names of the State Department personnel responsible for the vetting of UN employees, explicitly admitting the practice in the face of Congressional accusations that it was not performed ruthlessly enough.[2]

Lie's policy on personnel questions had become increasingly partisan and autocratic. Insisting that the Secretary General need not provide reasons for terminating contracts (specific clauses of the Charter notwithstanding), he and Byron Price made the issue one of loyalty to Lie personally. For example, when in 1951 a group of dismissed staff personnel took their case to the UN Administrative Tribunal, and the elected representatives of the Staff Association supported them, six of the seven elected members of the Staff Association's committee were dismissed, Price accusing them of "disloyalty and self-seeking." Lie's attitude was blatantly partisan: all demands from Russia, Czechoslovakia and other Communist countries for the dismissal of White Russians or émigrés he resisted. The United States, of course, provided approximately 40 percent of the UN's budget.

## THE NEW YORK GRAND JURY AND THE SISS

In 1952, a presidential-election year, the anti-Stevenson forces judged it opportune to launch a violent attack on the loyalty of American citizens working for the UN. Senator McCarran's SISS led the attack, subpoenaing thirty American employees of the UN, twenty-two of whom obliged by taking the Fifth Amendment. But the scent of so much blood never brings just a single shark. Inspired and directed by Roy Cohn, Special Assistant to the Attorney General, a grand jury of the Southern District of New York had launched its own investigation in 1951. Between the grand jury and the SISS there was not only close collaboration but also the customary competition for the headlines—sharks of this breed need not only to eat but also to be seen to be eating. The grand jury summoned forty-seven American employees of the UN, past and present. Although the State Department, according to one source, had transmitted to the UN adverse judgments on thirty-five of the forty-seven in a detailed "presentation" issued in December 1952, the grand jury accused the State Department of laxity in regard to Soviet espionage in the UN, and reported that "over a score" of employees called to testify had taken the Fifth Amendment with regard to past or present membership of the CP and, in some cases, with regard to espionage.

According to the grand jury, some witnesses admitted to past membership of the CP, while others revealed a continuing sympathy—"many other disloyal United States citizens are occupying high positions of trust in the United Nations," all of them a menace to America.[3] The grand jury saluted Senator Pat McCarran and thanked J. Edgar Hoover and Roy Cohn, who had served it "with unremitting zeal." Indeed, Cohn had skillfully whipped the grand jurors into a high fever of indignation over a ten-month period, hinting at a conspiracy to stifle its findings while the SISS was stealing the headlines. On December 29, 1952, the foreman, Joseph P. Kelly, complained before a House committee that the State and Justice Departments had pressured the jurors to "postpone" and "tone down" their discovery that "an overwhelmingly large group of disloyal" Americans had penetrated the UN.

## TRYGVE LIE WIELDS THE AXE

Intimidated by repeated Congressional threats to slash the appropriation, Lie surrendered. He conferred with young Roy Cohn and SISS counsel Robert Morris, as a prelude to a massive purge. *The New York Times* reckoned that Lie dismissed a minimum of forty-five staff members in 1952, the majority of them Americans in the UN professional category. Some were permitted to resign with extra indemnities in return for their silence, but compensation was due only to holders of permanent contracts, and the majority of those purged held "Temporary-Indefinite" contracts and were thus ineligible. Determined to dismiss all twenty-two Americans who had taken the Fifth Amendment before the SISS, and insisting that a pro-Communist American was an unrepresentative American, Lie submitted the issue to a Special Commission of Jurists. On November 30, 1952, the Commission advised Lie that such dismissals would conform to the Charter, since American Communists and members of organizations designated subversive by the U.S. Attorney General (or those unwilling to deny such membership) might reasonably be suspected of disloyalty to the United Nations. Lie then wielded the axe.[4]

This crisis precipitated the suicide of Abraham Feller, the American general legal counsel of the UN, and Lie's close friend and collaborator. On November 13, he jumped from a window, evidently deeply distressed about the propriety of dismissing employees who had merely invoked a constitutional right. Lie then lashed out at the hysterical, reactionary assault on the UN, protested that Feller was a victim of the witch hunt, declined an impudent, retaliatory summons to appear before the New York grand jury—and proceeded to implement the witch hunt. The French newspaper *Le Monde* called for the removal of the UN from American soil.

Not all of the victims of this purge had invoked the Fifth Amendment. Ruth Elizabeth Crawford, who had worked for the U.S. government for eleven years and for the UN for five years as public-information officer for the International Children's Emergency Fund, had joined the Communist Party in New York some seventeen years earlier out of sympathy, as she put it, for the unemployed. After a year or so her membership had lapsed. But as a current member of the Progressive Party who was not prepared to offer the SISS the required anti-Communist genuflections, she stood no chance. Asked to resign, she refused. On January 7, 1953, Lie dismissed her "in the best interests of the United Nations." She expressed despair.[5]

Mary Jane Keeney and her husband, Philip, were veterans of an academic-freedom battle of the late thirties at Montana University. Like so many other radicals of the New Deal era, both wife and husband had had a "good war"—she under Henry Wallace at the Board of Economic Warfare, he as assistant to Archibald MacLeish at the Library of Congress. After the war both were granted diplomatic passports—the Radical Hour was not quite spent. But when Mary Jane returned from economic work in Germany carrying a book written by the French Resistance martyr, Gabriel Péri, a Communist, which she intended to deliver to Alexander Trachtenberg at International Publishers, the world of the Keeneys began to collapse. Philip was sent home from Tokyo; both lost their passports. Even so, by one of those lapses still possible in 1947, she found a job as documents editor at the UN. But when the UN assigned her to the General Assembly in Paris, the State Department continued to deny her a passport.

During the trial of Judith Coplon in 1949, the FBI's dossier on the Keeneys came to light. Grim reading it made! To know Earl Browder was bad enough, but to have entertained in one's home Gerhart Eisler and Nathan Gregory Silvermaster (a master spy, according to Elizabeth Bentley) was suicidal for any public servant. When the Keeneys were subpoenaed by HCUA in June 1949, Mary Jane answered all questions, denying CP membership and Communist activity, but refusing, on account of UN regulations, to divulge by whose intervention she had obtained her job at the UN. On January 27, 1951, she was dismissed. Subpoenaed by the SISS in February of the following year, she now resorted to the Fifth Amendment. Persistent in her belief that UN regulations bound even a former member not to divulge who had secured her appointment, she was cited for contempt, found guilty in August 1954, awarded a new trial by the Court of Appeals, and found not guilty on retrial in April 1955.

This woman's biography, of course, illuminates the whole radical predicament; not merely her fate, but the succession of impulses that led a person of progressive outlook to invest New Deal idealism in the war against Nazi Germany until, encountering and evading the mud barriers of the Cold War, this same idealism flowed outward into the new international agencies, where peaceful coexistence and the war against poverty might still be fought. This little historical subplot of the American Left explains why the fishermen collected so rich a haul when they turned their attention to the East River.

Following the dismissals, the Staff Council of the UN Secretariat approved a statement that amounted to a polite but unmistakable censure of Lie's actions. The Staff Council pointed out that,

> whatever advice or information the Secretary General may receive from an outside authority concerning a candidate for a post in the Secretariat or concerning a staff member, the Secretary General's decisions in engaging and terminating his staff are to be governed only by the Charter, the Staff Regulations and the directives of the General Assembly.

Turning to the opinion of the Commission of Jurists, that those invoking the privilege against self-incrimination could be dismissed under Article 1.4 or Article 1.8, the Staff Council insisted that "no new power of discharge can be added by interpretation"; the use of a constitutional privilege before a national authority must not be considered automatic ground for dismissal.[6] Dag Hammarskjold later modified Lie's position, making invocation of the Fifth Amendment by an American open to explanation rather than a basis for automatic dismissal.

The victims, meanwhile, banded together in a common refusal to take their fate lying down. An appeal was lodged with the Administrative Tribunal constituted by the General Assembly. A brief on behalf of nineteen dismissed American employees argued that "the issue is whether the Secretariat remains an international body within the

United Nations or becomes an appendage of the Federal Bureau of Investigation and the State Department . . ." In August 1953 the Tribunal sustained the dismissal of nine temporary employees, but reversed the dismissal of twelve, all but one of whom were permanent employees. Substantial compensation awards included one of $40,000, plus $300 costs, to Jack S. Harris, and one of $27,000, plus $300 costs, to Julia Older Bazer, both of whom had invoked the Fifth Amendment.[7] The Tribunal's adjudications provoked an uproar in the Capitol: Congressmen threatened to cut off appropriations, while Henry Cabot Lodge, the American delegate to the UN, and American ambassadors throughout Latin America drummed up opposition.[8] The strategy was partly successful; Lie's successor, Dag Hammarskjold, judged it wiser to ignore the Tribunal's findings and not to reinstate any of the dismissed employees.

Having blocked the reinstatement of the eleven Americans whose dismissals had been countermanded by the Tribunal, the United States government filed a statement with the International Court of Justice in March 1954 challenging the indemnity awards to the eleven. So vindictive and unconstitutional was the American position that even Britain opposed it. Meanwhile, the Congressional committees continued their vendetta. In April 1954 the SISS described the UN Secretariat as a "cover shop" for Communist spy operations, citing the case of the American David Weintraub, appointed division head in the UN Department of Economic Affairs in 1949, three of whose subordinates had been dismissed.[9] Weintraub resigned.

In July the International Court of Justice upheld the legality of the compensation awards.

## THE IOELB RENEWS THE PURGE

The lapses of the Truman administration were soon to be made good by the incoming Eisenhower government. Executive Order 10244 stipulated that Americans serving in international organizations must be screened formally by an International Organizations Employees Loyalty Board (IOELB), which would conduct hearings, make advisory determinations and transmit derogatory information to the Secretary General. The IOELB, set up in January 1953, no more satisfied the criteria of judicial due process than did any other loyalty board; allegations were unstated or unspecific, informants remained anonymous and hostile witnesses could not be cross-examined.

But Washington's challenge to the independence of the United Nations did not stop here. With Lie's approval, a branch office of the

FBI was established on the third floor of the UN Secretariat to interrogate the staff. Despite outraged protests by European staff members, fingerprinting facilities were installed in the basement. Although
Hammarskjold coaxed the FBI out of the building after a year in office, even a decade later an American scholar discovered that UN
staff selections remained largely the preserve of the State Department.[10]

In July 1953 the IOELB set out for Europe to investigate American employees working for specialized agencies of the United Nations. When fifteen Americans employed by UNESCO in Paris were
ordered to appear before the Board, seven refused. The American
Director General of UNESCO, Dr. Luther Evans, formerly Librarian
of Congress, promptly informed four of the seven that their contracts
would not be renewed at the end of the year. One of these, David
Leff, had already refused to answer subpoenas from the SISS and the
New York grand jury, though ordered to comply by Evans. Suspended, Leff was reinstated by the UNESCO Appeals Board and upheld by the UN Administrative Tribunal in September. When in November the UNESCO Appeals Board reinstated all four American
employees, Evans refused to heed the ruling and to reinstate them.
Evans himself had been publicly attacked a month earlier by Henry
Cabot Lodge for retaining at UNESCO eight Americans whose loyalty (to the United States, of course) was in doubt.

Meanwhile, in Rome, another American employee, Gordon
McIntyre, had been dismissed from the UN Food and Agriculture
Organization in August, following a letter from the State Department. In September the FAO decided to pay him $11,000 for wrong-
ful dismissal rather than reinstate him. Aggrieved, the State Department promptly withdrew his passport.

After a hearing before the IOELB in May 1954 during which the
Immigration Department's prize informers perjured themselves once
again, the black American Dr. Ralph Bunche was cleared and
promptly promoted by Hammarskjold to be Under Secretary General.

In December 1954 the chairman of the IOELB, Pierce J. Gerety,
boasted that the Board had in sixteen months investigated 3,939
Americans working in international organizations, and had had great
success in weeding out an unspecified number of "undesirables." [11]

## THE STORY OF GUSTAVO DURAN

We can now study in greater detail [12] the experiences of a naturalized
American whose grueling struggle to clear himself, first as a State

Department officer and later as an employee of the UN, was haunted by the curse of Sisyphus.

Born in Barcelona in 1906, Gustavo Duran attended Madrid University, the School of Commerce and the Madrid Conservatory of Music before undertaking his military service. From 1928 to 1934 he lived in Paris, working as a musician and composer, moving in artistic circles (Lorca, Buñuel) and dubbing films for Paramount Pictures. He later testified that, prior to his return to Spain in 1934, "I had never been involved in any manner or degree in political activities of any sort."

Duran's involvement in the Spanish Civil War, and particularly one episode, later became the *fons et origo* of the allegations leveled against him under the United States loyalty-security program. At the outbreak of the Civil War in July 1936 he joined the Republican army. His first politically significant appointment was in November—"I was appointed liaison officer between the Chief of Staff of the Army of Madrid, Colonel Vicente Rojo, and the Commander of the XI (International) Brigade, General Emile Kléber. In this capacity I accompanied General Kléber to Communist Party Headquarters on occasion." In January 1937 Duran was promoted to Brigade Commander, and in July, on Rojo's initiative, Division Commander. "I had many reasons to believe," he later insisted, "that the political commissars assigned to the military units under my command had as one of their principal functions that of watching me and of informing on me to the Communist Party." [13]

If so, their reports can hardly have been adverse, for in October—this is the crucial episode—Duran was appointed head of the Madrid Zone of the Military Intelligence Service (SIM). But: "My tenure in this position was of approximately two or three weeks' duration . . ." Duran subsequently went back to the front, rising to the rank of lieutenant colonel in command of the XX Army Corps. His reputation as a fighting commander in the battles of Brunete, Teruel and Valencia, where he was wounded, was of the highest. In the light of the allegations later brought against him, his account of the last phase of the armed conflict is worth quoting:

> Toward the end of the Civil War, the Communists in Spain were interested in keeping the war going, possibly in the belief that its continuation would inevitably result in the outbreak of a war between Germany and the Western European countries. I actively sided with General Miaja, Julian Besteiro and Colonel Segismundo Casado when they arose against the Communists on this issue . . . [14]

As Republican resistance collapsed, Duran was taken aboard British and American ships and transported to England via France. On May 28, 1940, he and his new American wife, Bonté Romilly Crompton, arrived in the United States.

After taking several jobs connected with music, ballet, modern art and film, he was naturalized on December 3, 1942. His unusually rapid acquisition of American citizenship, which was later to become the subject of dark speculations by anti-Communist newspaper columnists like Howard Rushmore and George Sokolsky, apparently followed from the belief of his friend Ernest Hemingway and Selden Chapin of the State Department that his expertise was urgently needed by the American Ambassador to Cuba, Spruille Braden, possibly in connection with Spanish Falangist activities there. It was Chapin who hurried up Duran's naturalization.

From February 1943 until September 1945, Duran served in the U.S. Auxiliary Foreign Service as adviser to Braden on political relations, first in Havana and later in Buenos Aires, where he arrived in May 1945, when Braden became ambassador there. However, he later insisted that he never exercised his influence in a pro-Communist direction and cited as proof of this having advised Nelson A. Rockefeller in July or August 1943 that the best hope for the future of Spain would be "the restoration of the monarchy with Prince Don Juan as king and with, among others, the support of Mr. Indalecio Prieto and the right wing of the Spanish Socialist Party . . ." [15]

If Duran's short period as boss of the SIM in Madrid in October 1937 was the source of his later troubles, his service in Argentina acted as the catalyst. In September 1944, Roosevelt castigated the Perón regime's collaboration with Germany, and Ambassador Braden constantly clashed with the dictator. When indirect approaches were made to Duran to meet Perón outside normal diplomatic channels, he declined and reported the overtures to Braden. The bitter harvest of this rectitude he was soon to reap, following the publication in February 1946 of the United States government's "Blue Book," which documented the extent of German-Argentine wartime collaboration and named the Spanish Ambassador to Argentina as a vital intermediary.

In both Madrid and Buenos Aires the government-controlled press now hit back. It was alleged in the Madrid papers A.B.C. and Diario de la Noche that the sections of the Blue Book that referred to Spain had been written by Gustavo Duran. (Duran denied it and Braden confirmed his denial in 1954.) The Falangist paper Arriba, echoed by the Argentine press, charged that during the Civil War Duran had been the liaison between the Soviet Ambassador and the

"Reds"; indeed Duran was now accused of having returned to Spain in 1931 as a GPU agent disguised as a representative of Paramount Pictures.[16] These attacks were repeated on March 3 by Radio Nacional de Madrid.

None of this need have troubled Duran had not the charges been eagerly taken up by American politicians friendly to Franco and engaged in witch-hunting among Loyalist groups in the United States. During the course of the spring, Duran was publicly attacked by Representative Alvin E. O'Konski (R., Wisconsin), Senator Kenneth S. Wherry (R., Nebraska), and, most serious, by the future chairman of HCUA, J. Parnell Thomas, who announced that Duran had been known to the Republican Minister of Defense, Indalecio Prieto, as a Communist, as a member of the Comintern and as an agent of the NKVD. Thomas also charged that Duran was the guiding genius of the JAFRC, whose directors had recently been cited for contempt by HCUA. Duran denied membership in the JAFRC and any knowledge of its leader, Dr. Edward K. Barsky.

A State Department investigation was now inevitable. Copies of all the memoranda and dispatches prepared by Duran from February 1943 to January 1945 were sent from Havana. He was interviewed by an FBI agent; he also provided correspondence for transmission to J. Edgar Hoover. But here Duran had a stroke of good fortune: Prieto cabled him on April 3, 1946: "I affirm that the statements of Mr. John Parnell Thomas are not founded on any words said by me . . . I have never accused you of being [an] agent of the Russian police nor [a] member of the Comintern." In a second cable from Mexico, dated April 12, Prieto filled in certain vital details that Duran said he had hitherto known nothing about:

> Dear friend: . . . in the report I made in Barcelona on August 9, 1938 . . . to explain my reasons for resignation as Minister of National Defense . . . you are alluded to when I refer to the brief period when you acted as chief of the [SIM] . . . this [sic] allusions however do not imply the charge (imputation) that you were an agent of the Russian Secret Police nor [sic] a member of the Comintern.

Yet Duran can scarcely have been pleased by a letter dated April 26 in which Prieto reported a visit from two American diplomats who wished to discuss Duran. Prieto had told them that he had appointed Duran head of the SIM at the suggestion of General José Miaja, who "was undoubtedly acting under the influence of the Communist Party . . ." [17]

Nevertheless, Duran was told informally on August 7 that he had been cleared. The following day he applied for a job with the United

Nations. In October he became head of the Survey, Research and Development Branch, situated in New York. During the following two or three years he traveled widely on official business, and the press and radio attacks that had dogged him through the spring of 1947, greatly distressing his wife, gradually died away. He could relax now, enjoy his family, his house in New Hampshire, and find time to record and conserve Latin-American music. This peace was shattered in February 1950, when McCarthy delivered his celebrated attacks on reds in the State Department. On March 14, he called Duran a "rabid Communist" before the Tydings Subcommittee, quoting a 1946 report from Colonel Wendell G. Johnson, military attaché in Madrid, who had repeated unquestioningly Falangist accusations.[18] Echoing *Arriba*, the Senator claimed that it was to Moscow that Duran had repaired at the end of the Civil War, throwing in for good measure imputations of a dissolute youth and homosexuality.

Henceforward Duran had two full-time careers: at the UN and as his own archivist, updating his file, clipping foreign newspapers, inscribing his innocence in a mass of neatly typed, clearly ordered, biographical detail—the file, in short, from which we now draw. He issued statements, made explanations: he had never been a Communist; had never been to Russia; had never been in trouble with the police anywhere, except when ignoring a stop sign in Mineola, Long Island. He demonstrated how the U.S. Army intelligence reports on which McCarthy relied were cut out of whole cloth from the Falangist press. Mrs. Duran wrote to Senator Styles Bridges of New Hampshire (in fact a staunch McCarthyite), describing "a nightmare for me, and for my mother and for our whole family. We have . . . three children whose lives can be affected by these terrible lies . . . You told me that if there should by chance be another attack in the Senate you would defend Gustavo . . ."[19]

To the Tydings Subcommittee (before which Article 100 of the UN Charter prevented him from appearing) and to J. Edgar Hoover, Duran sent a memorandum in which he referred to Prieto's statement about having appointed Duran head of the SIM at the instigation of General Miaja, but omitted—it cannot have been inadvertent, Duran was meticulously accurate—to quote Prieto's account of Miaja as "undoubtedly acting under the influence of the Communist Party, a membership card of which he had accepted . . ." Duran claimed to have objected to the assignment because of "a deeply rooted aversion to the proposed type of activity." He added: "Mr. Prieto has asserted that he was subjected to various pressures to keep me in Madrid. I was completely unaware of such pressures . . . General Vicente Rojo y Lluch, Chief of the General Staff (and now living in Bolivia) can verify the above account."[20]

The Tydings Subcommittee put aside the Duran case on the ground that he was no longer employed by the State Department. But on August 30, 1951, McCarthy renewed his attack during a speech to the Veterans of Foreign Wars. Holding aloft a photograph of Duran wearing a uniform which he claimed was that of the SIM, an organ of "the Russian secret police," McCarthy said that Duran was presently in charge of screening displaced persons and deciding which of them should be admitted to America. (This was not so.) On October 22, *Time* magazine blasted "Demagogue McCarthy," describing Duran as "never a Red" and "definitely and clearly anti-Communist."

Unlike many of his subpoenaed UN colleagues, Duran did not resort to the Fifth Amendment when he appeared before the SISS and the New York grand jury in October 1952. (Such a course, as we have seen, incurred automatic dismissal by Trygve Lie.) Despite his diplomatic status, however, he had been denied a passport since 1951; apparently his application for renewal was under permanent investigation by the State Department's Security Division. [21]

With the creation of the International Organizations Employees Loyalty Board, Duran entered the final and decisive confrontation. Members of the American embassy in London questioned his British friends, including the military historian Captain Basil Henry Liddell Hart, and Henry Walston, whose wife was a sister of Duran's wife. (So, too, was Michael Straight's wife—McCarthy did not let pass the opportunity to smear the proprietor and editor of the *New Republic*.) In February 1954, DeWitt Marshall of the American embassy in Mexico twice visited Prieto to discuss Duran. Prieto revealed to him that in his 1938 report he had stated that the fact that Duran "was a Communist was not concealed from me." But Prieto now added: "I do not have nor did I have any evidence whatsoever that that was so, and I based what I said on rumors which then reached me." Since talking with Duran in Havana in 1944 he had been increasingly convinced that Duran "has never sincerely adhered to Communist ideas." [22] Prieto passed a copy of this statement to Duran, who forwarded it to his lawyer, Hiram C. Todd.

Duran's hearings before the U.S. Civil Service Commission's IOELB began in May 1954 and, with long intervals, were not terminated until January 1955. What was at stake was not only the job of chief of the UN's Social Policy and Development Section, grade P-5, salary $14,144, but also the man's whole future and, with it, the principle of justice.

At the first hearing, on May 14, Duran's former boss, Spruille Braden, testified. Braden had become prey to paranoiac fears of Communist infiltration and influence in Washington, fears that he had fully exposed to Congressional committees in December 1953 and March 1954. However, asked whether he now had a "reasonable doubt as to Duran's loyalty to the U.S.," Braden replied, "I would say no. I don't know. I don't think so." Had Duran behaved like a homosexual? Absolutely not. Braden recalled that many of the dispatches and memoranda that Duran had helped him to draft had been "strongly anti-Communist." Braden did complain, however, that his butler had overheard Duran criticizing his policy toward Perón, and Duran's aloof attitude toward certain social invitations had engendered doubts exacerbated by "my experience with the other State Department officer whom I discovered was a Communist."

Inevitably the interrogation focused on the vital three weeks during which Duran had headed the Madrid zone of the SIM. Now Duran provided new information about the nature of that organization:

> I was instructed to absorb a police unit in Madrid run by Pedrero [Angel Pedrero Gārcia] . . . Peculiar things were happening in this police unit. People were vanishing so that one of the first things I did was to tell Pedrero that no one was to enter without my knowledge and no one was to leave without my knowing where he was going . . . [Pedrero] went to see Prieto and told him stories about me . . .

He added that he had not previously wished to commit this aspect of things to paper "out of respect for Spain." On November 24, after Duran and his lawyer had unsuccessfully attempted to persuade the Board to clarify the essential issues, Duran submitted a fifty-six-page "Trial Memorandum" in which he admitted: "It is possible that I may have naïvely repeated in conversations some of the superficialities and false illusions about Russia that were then generally accepted . . ." Asked why two leading Cuban Communists, Juan Marinello and Nicolás Guillén, had in 1938 reported him as having said to them: "I went to my party, the Communist, to receive orders," Duran replied that he had been indignant about this and "the many asinine remarks that were attributed to me by the writers." Likewise, he could not be held responsible for friendly mentions in the Spanish Communist press—had not Eisenhower and other American generals been praised in the Soviet press during the war?

The Loyalty Board now fired a scattershot of allegations at him, the most serious linking him to the NKVD. Firmly he denied it all. The crucial charge echoed the one originally made by Prieto in 1938—that he had been appointed chief of the SIM by the Communists and had been removed from the post for making "numerous unauthorized appointments of Communists." He now added one further detail: on taking up his duties, he had reported to the chief of the National Intelligence Service, who had informed him of which experts' advice he should follow. During his brief tenure of office a few temporary appointments were made at the recommendation of these experts. Here Duran was elusive; who were these experts? Part of the answer emerged when he was asked to comment on his personal knowledge of twenty-five named persons, including Alexander Orlov, who at that time was one of the leading Soviet NKVD agents operating the purge in Spain:

> I was introduced to a member of the Russian embassy whose name was Orlov by the then head of the Servicio Investigacion Militar, Mr. Sayagues. I never knew what Orlov's first name was. I spoke with Orlov once or twice, I remember that he told me how necessary it was to organize an effective counter-espionage system in the Republican army . . .

After his fifth and final hearing in January 1955, Duran was cleared of all charges and finally was left free to continue his career in the UN until his death in March 1969, at the age of sixty-two. In view of what the Loyalty Board had revealed—the technique of firing a wide range of charges, some of them even more severe than the Board's private information warranted, was designed to unnerve the suspect by convincing him that the Board knew more than it actually did—Duran's final clearance can be regarded only as astonishing. In making this point we do not pass judgment on him, or set ourselves up in the murky business of assessing loyalty; we merely set what was finally known of his past against the guilt-by-association standards prevalent in McCarthy's America. Two of the mildest charges brought by the Board—charges that astonished and outraged Duran himself—remind us what those standards were: "That in April 1951, you attended a meeting to celebrate the 20th anniversary of the Spanish Republic"; and "That on at least one occasion you said you were sorry you had become an American citizen." [23]

# 17

## State and City Employees

The petitioner may have a constitutional right to talk politics; but he has no constititional right to be a policeman.

—JUSTICE HOLMES, 1892

By the fall of 1950 thirty-two states had barred "subversives" from public employment. Even so, there was generally more bark than bite in the local loyalty-security programs; the passage of the legislation was an end in itself, a war dance with no war to follow.[1] The most common pretext for dismissal was refusal to answer questions posed by legislative committees—Fifth Amendment discharges. A particularly sad case was that of the Seattle Fire Department captain who denied current CP membership but refused to discuss his past. As a consequence he was suspended only forty days short of the twenty-five years' service that would have entitled him to retirement benefits, then dismissed.[2]

### DETROIT AND LOS ANGELES

In December 1949, Detroit launched a full-scale investigation of the beliefs and associations of its public employees, a step first requiring an amendment to the City Charter of 1918, which specifically forbade any such inquisition. Supported by Mayor Eugene Van Antwerp, Police Commissioner Harry S. Toy, and Civil Service Commission Secretary Donald Subletto, not to mention the *Detroit News*, the campaign to amend the City Charter culminated in victory on September 13, 1949; 263,989 voted in favor, with only 78,160 against.

The principal target of the Mayor and Common Council was the United Public Workers, a pro-Communist union about to be expelled from the CIO and long since at war with Subletto. It was to the UPWA's thirty locals in the city that he pointed accusingly when he announced in July that the city was employing at least 150 Communists or sympathizers. The *Detroit News* announced that "150 Reds Work for City." The *Detroit Times* prophesied, "Mayor Set to Fire 149 Cited as Reds." The UPWA's local president, Yale Stuart, who had lost an arm while fighting in Spain, had for years been a thorn in the side of the city administration, which he accused of attempting to divert attention from its policy of wage cuts and discrimination against Jewish and Negro employees of the city. Subpoenaed by the Council, he swore, under protest, that he was not a Party member.[3] Even so, things got so hot for Stuart that he later had to take himself and his family away from Detroit.

The Common Council followed up the Charter-amendment victory by appointing a Loyalty Commission and an advisory Loyalty Committee, which consisted of seven dependable citizens. Evidence of subversive association was to be based on the Attorney General's list.[4] When fifty militants of the UPWA obtained an injunction to temporarily halt the probe, Police Commissioner Harry S. Toy promptly had them investigated. But the first employee to lose his job, a junior mechanical engineer called George Shenkar, was fired in January 1950 on an insubordination charge, without reference to the loyalty program. Apparently he had been distributing CRC literature among his colleagues and declined to tell the Civil Service Commission whether, when chairman of Wayne University's Marxist Club, he had also been a CP member.

The first case referred to the Loyalty Commission by the Loyalty Committee was that of a fifty-year-old Negro, Thomas J. Coleman, who had come to work for the Detroit City Garbage Department in 1925. A 32nd-degree Mason, an activist in the NAACP, an admitted member of the pro-Communist National Negro Congress and president of Local 285 of the UPWA, Coleman flatly denied membership in the CP at any time. FBI and local police spies alleged that Coleman had campaigned for the Progressive Party in 1948, had participated in a 1949 rally to raise bail money for the Communist leaders convicted under the Smith Act, had been present at Paul Robeson and CRC meetings and so on. The fact that Coleman had a son serving in Korea and that he had helped to organize one of the first Negro Legion posts in Michigan, the Charles Jones Post 77, was not enough to save him his job.

On February 25, 1955, Alfred A. May, chairman of the Committee, wrote Mayor Albert E. Cobo a summary of recent activity. During 1953, 6,888 names had been checked; in ninety-six cases there had been preliminary investigations. For 1954 the corresponding figures had been 3,198 and 161, of whom sixty-two had been fully investigated. As a result, "certain city employees resigned . . . rather than appear at a hearing." (May explicitly refused to be more specific.) A further report to Mayor Cobo, dated December 26, 1956, revealed that during the year 1955, seventy-one employees were subjected to a full investigation, as a result of which four resigned rather than undergo hearings. In 1956 twenty-nine were fully investigated, and two resigned on the same grounds. A report by Auditor General David V. Addy to the Common Council, dated September 14, 1955, revealed that the Investigating Committee had, during 1953 and 1954, paid $1,174 through its imprest cash fund, plus $3,318 through its contractual pay roll, to confidential informers.[5]

In October 1950, Governor Earl Warren of California signed the Levering Act, which transformed all public employees into "civil defense workers" and allowed them thirty days in which to swear that for the previous five years they had neither advocated violent overthrow nor belonged to any organization that did. From 1953, state employees were required also to answer all questions put by state agencies and legislative committees on pain of dismissal.

In the meantime, the Los Angeles County Board of Supervisors had in August 1947 established its own loyalty program, which required employees to attest that they did not belong to any of 142 organizations regarded with disfavor by Jack B. Tenney. Of the county's 22,000 employees, sixteen refused to take the oath and sign the affidavit (they were discharged), while eighty-eight others balked at the affidavit alone. Of these, fifty-nine later changed their minds; at the close of 1952, litigation concerning the other twenty-nine was still in progress. Interestingly enough, none of the "considerable number" who confessed to membership in the proscribed organizations was dismissed, so the county's relatively generous procedure for hearings and cross-examination of hostile witnesses was not tested.

The City of Los Angeles introduced a similar program in the shape of Ordinance No. 94,004 in 1948, the difference being that, whereas the county listed 142 organizations, the city listed none, leaving it to the individual to decide which organizations advocated violent overthrow of the government. Of the city's 28,000 employees, sixteen refused to execute the oath and affidavit, while two others rejected the affidavit alone. After an administrative hearing, all were discharged as of January 6, 1949, although their occupations[6] scarcely suggested any capacity, individual or collective, to make Los

Angeles a suburb of Leningrad. Fewer than ten employees admitted to having been members of the CP during the previous five years; of these, current members were dismissed, while no action had been taken by late 1952 with regard to the former members. Some of the seventeen then brought suit, claiming that the ordinance was an *ex post facto* law forbidden by Article I, Clause 10 of the federal Constitution, and that it violated the First Amendment. In *Garner v. Board of Public Works* (1951), the U.S. Supreme Court once again laid the First Amendment low and ruled that the ordinance was by no means *ex post facto*, since the law of California had barred subversives from public employment since 1941.

## THE NEW YORK PURGE

It was in New York City that a local loyalty-security program assumed really serious dimensions and rivaled its federal exemplar in the scale of its repercussions. The witch hunt among public employees in New York during the fifties was both unrestrained and vicious, although the famous Feinberg Law, signed by Governor Thomas E. Dewey in April 1949, which empowered the State Board of Regents to list organizations as subversive and to regard membership in them as *prima facie* evidence of disqualification for employment, ultimately played no more than a morally supportive role. It proved to be too slow and cumbersome to satisfy the quick-kill hunger of the city's administrators. Nor was the City Charter manure enough for their crop of vengeance; in 1951 the state passed its Security-Risk Law, which included public-lavatory attendants in the roster of sensitive, dismissible jobs. By the end of 1957 no fewer than 179,059 state employees had been screened under its provisions; twenty-four had been removed, disqualified, or had resigned.

In New York City the purge got under way in 1948, when Mayor O'Dwyer and the Borough President of Manhattan ousted over 150 supporters of the ALP from the city administration. In November 1950 it was announced that all civil-defense workers—400,000 were potentially involved—would sign a loyalty oath, be fingerprinted and be asked whether they belonged to any organization listed by the U.S. Attorney General.

At first the purge was concentrated in the Department of Welfare, whose roughly 5,800 employees fed, clothed and housed more than 4 percent of the city's 7.8 million people. Of these 5,800 employees, approximately 1,500 were members of the pro-Communist UPWA, led by Abram Flaxer and expelled from the CIO in 1950. A succession of Welfare Commissioners, Benjamin Fielding, Edward E. Rhatigan and Raymond M. Hilliard, denounced the subversive influence of the UPWA in the Department. But the fur really began to fly when O'Dwyer brought in from Chicago Raymond Hilliard, a Catholic graduate of Notre Dame, whose vision of America was identical with that of the *Saturday Evening Post*.

Hilliard was no doubt correct in claiming that Communists controlled Local 1, UPWA, the Department of Welfare. He also alleged that the UPWA was exploiting relief for political purposes, and that it was offering favored treatment to jobless people who were willing to sign up with the Tenants' Council or the Workers' Alliance. He ordered photographs to be taken of UPWA members participating in demonstrations. ("We had to fire or shelve the lefties.") Finding that the lefties were "inefficient" in their work, he fired them. ("Most of them were Party-liners.") In March 1950, after the UPWA had been expelled from the CIO, he simply withdrew recognition from the union. The UPWA didn't care for the Welfare Commissioner; according to his own account they picketed his apartment building on Riverside Drive and forced their way in to terrorize his stranded wife.

But Hilliard was not to be intimidated. When an anonymous informant told him that a UPWA official, Eleanor L. Goldner, had during office hours written the draft of a pamphlet hostile to himself, he fired her. Her dismissal was upheld by a review board in September 1950. Hilliard now set the spies to work. "To root them out, I asked for, and received from Police Commissioner William P. O'Brien, twenty-four rookies who could pose as new employees and go into our district offices." They reported the names of those who had been overheard criticizing Commissioner Hilliard, whereupon Hilliard fired them on technical charges. Max Gaber, for example, was said to have failed to investigate the private resources of 157 relief recipients; Morris Sipser was said to have worked short time. As for the hard-working ones who could not be proven to be Communists, they were mostly dispatched to the Brownsville office in a poor section of Brooklyn.[7]

According to Hilliard, he fired 191 of his employees between July 1948 and March 1951. According to another source, 217 were "separated." By May 1951 Hilliard's successor, Henry L. McCarthy, had launched a new purge. Two stenographers and two assistant supervisors resigned at the Brownsville Welfare Center, then two social investigators, Christian J. Lewis and Murray Stein, were suspended for refusing to answer questions. Stein was dismissed. In July two further resignations followed, an assistant supervisor with eleven years' service, and a telephone operator with twelve years' service. In February 1953 it was reported that Henry L. McCarthy and his two top deputies had taken the anti-Communist oath as a symbolic prelude to questioning all 1,200 supervisory employees of the Department of Welfare about their political affiliations.[8]

The purge now reached in many directions. In November 1953 two New York firemen, brothers, Daniel M. Stern and Milton C. Stern, resigned after being questioned by the Chief Fire Marshal following a "tip" that they belonged to left-wing groups. The brothers denied it. In May 1953 a major purge of the Police Department got under way. Patrolman Meyer E. Rubinstein was discharged for falsely denying former CP membership. Police Lieutenant Arthur Miller, of Brooklyn, was tried by the Department and found guilty of being a Party member, a conclusion assisted by the testimony of John Lautner; the Assistant Corporation Counsel described Miller as "a robot without a soul." Then Detective John D. Jones of Brooklyn was accused of lying about Communist affiliations.

In March 1954 Mayor Robert F. Wagner appointed Peter Campbell Brown, former chairman of the federal Subversive Activities Control Board, as City Commissioner of Investigation, a move that heralded a purge of the city's more humble jobs. Two Transit Authority employees, Gabriel J. Skrokov (who had worked in the transit system since 1927) and Max Lerner (who had worked in the system since 1935), were dismissed for refusing to answer certain questions. (Lerner's appeal was later lost in the U.S. Supreme Court—*Lerner v. Casey*.) A city inspector in the Department of Water Supply, Gas and Electricity, Samuel Frankel, was dismissed from his $4,200-a-year job for refusing to answer questions arising out of a report by Commissioner Peter Campbell Brown. Still in the water area, but at lower depth, Bonaventura Pingerra, a fifty-seven-year-old city washroom attendant and part-time artist's model, lost his job because he had been in the CP from 1936 to 1939. But the New York Supreme Court reinstated him.

In February 1956 it was announced that 62,000 employees of the Transit Authority and Welfare Department had been checked, twenty suspects had resigned, and eleven had been suspended. Investigation Commissioner Charles Tenney reported that of the fifty-three employees dismissed since January 1, 1955, twenty-one were employed by the Welfare Department, seventeen by the Transit Authority, and seven by the Housing Authority. One of these, the subway towerman Patrick Hehir was ousted after twenty-nine years' service, because he claimed that the questions put to him were illegal. Although he had received a formal commendation for saving a fellow employee from serious injury, he was nevertheless fired, two years before he would have become eligible for a retirement pension.[9]

If the Russians intended to overthrow the government of the

United States by way of New York's public lavatories and subways, then these men did indeed hold sensitive positions. But common sense might have indicated otherwise. A study commission appointed by Governor Averell Harriman in 1956 reported that the Security-Risk Law of 1951 (under which the Civil Service Commission's discretion was absolute—there was no appeal to the courts) had been so interpreted as to place 81 percent of the city's public jobs under the title of security positions. Nevertheless, in 1956 the state legislature reenacted the law with only eight dissenters in the Senate and one in the Assembly (Bentley Kassal, Liberal-Democrat). The *New York Post* asked, "But where were all the other flaming fellows who so valorously affirm their liberalism when campaigns are in progress and the legislature is in recess?" Even amendments calling for the right to confront and cross-examine hostile witnesses were swept aside. The purge of the state and city slackened somewhat in the late fifties, but it did not die: in July 1960 the State Power Authority discharged deputy chief systems operator Orville E. Linton on a charge of having been an active Communist in the 1950s.

Professor Ralph S. Brown, Jr., estimated that, *excluding teachers*, about five hundred employees of state, municipal and local governments were dismissed for political reasons during the period 1948 to 1956.[10] If this figure is correct, then well over half of the dismissals occurred in New York City.

# PART FIVE

Pacification of
the Working Class

# 18

# *How to Break a Union*

Neither "Wall Street" nor big business launched and masterminded the purge. Certain politicians made the running, supported by patriotic and vigilante pressure groups. These politicians and these groups, however, cannot be regarded simply as crackpots and hate-mongers; they represented the fears and aspirations of clearly discernible strata within the prevailing economic system and social structure.

There is no denying that within the business community were elements that could never come to terms with the New Deal and saw in anti-Communism a convenient weapon with which to smear progressive legislation and to weaken the effectiveness of organized labor. The National Association of Manufacturers, representing some 17,000 affiliated companies (of which about sixty were dominant), spent several million dollars each year on stimulating the belief that the Wagner Act, the union shop and the repeal of "right to work" laws were all products of Moscow's machinations. Indeed, the NAM did not shrink from harnessing to this propaganda the most virulently reactionary of Hearst journalists, like Westbrook Pegler and George Sokolsky, as well as the notorious radio commentator Fulton Lewis, Jr.

Of like mind was the U.S. Chamber of Commerce, whose commitment to postwar European democracy was perhaps best expressed in the lament, "We have lost virtually all oil wells and refineries in the Balkans, as well as giant industrial plants in Germany and Hungary." As early as December 1945 the Chamber commissioned a report on "the menace of Socialism to Europe and its effect upon this country." The Chamber followed up with two influential booklets (each sold about half a million copies) on *Communist Infiltration of the United States* (1946) and *Communists Within the Labor Movement* (1947). In 1948 the Chamber's Permanent Committee on Socialism and Communism (a very active body) published a *Program for Community Anti-Communist Action*, which included hints on how to compile a filing system on local suspects. That the Chamber's real fears were directed less at oncoming totalitarianism than at the curtailment of unbridled free enterprise implied by the New Deal was writ large in a statement issued in December 1949:

> In spite of a partial house-cleaning, the CIO has never rid itself of its Marxist economics. Virtually every important speech and publication . . . is replete with class consciousness, hatred for employers . . .

Three years later the Chamber's president, D. A. Hulcy, remarked:

> The trend toward Socialism in America has been the theme of more than sixty of my speeches during the last year . . . Socialism is junior-grade Communism looking for promotion.[1]

No doubt a majority of the Chamber's affiliated companies would have agreed with that. One must, however, resist the temptation so frequently indulged in by left-wing historians to conclude, *Ergo!* Pressure groups tend by their composition to form opinion as much as reflect it. The dynamic of the Chamber's campaign was provided more by the professional red-baiters it hired, like Emerson Schmidt and Francis P. Matthews, than by businessmen calculating future profits.

The core of the matter is that businessmen in general, and particularly self-made entrepreneurs, were highly susceptible to alarm calls of collective paranoia. Here one must emphasize the crucial, opinion-setting role of the veterans' organizations, notably the American Veterans of Foreign Wars and—monarch of the species with its 3.2 million members and 1 million auxiliaries (in 1947)—the American Legion. Backed by the weight of 17,000 Legion posts and property holdings worth a hundred million dollars, the Legion and its Americanism Commission molded opinion within the heartland of Middle America, among those who believed the free-enterprise system, whereby a small man could run a small business in his own way, to be inseparable from red-blooded Americanism. The fears and antipathies that these men directed toward organized labor at home, British Labour nationalization abroad and the claims of the UN to ad-

vance the hungry hordes of Asia formed the flashpoint of the purge,
the emotional constituency of the politicians. The world they sought
to defend was portrayed, time and again, on the cover of the *American Legion Magazine*, in the bright, clean, cheery, Norman Rockwell
style of the *Saturday Evening Post*: the smiling, pink-skinned family,
one son, one daughter, a house, a garden, a car, a flag. No blacks in
sight. The pages of the magazine, which went out to 2,817,750 subscribers, reeked of prejudice and barely sublimated aggression; it was
a home away from home for the red-baiters of the Hearst press.

The staple guest at Legion conventions was J. Edgar Hoover. In
1950 the national convention resolved that all CP members should be
interned and tried for treason. A year later the Legion's Medal of
Merit was awarded to General Franco. Incessant was the clamor for
harsher deportation measures. In 1952 the convention urged the government to investigate the ACLU and to prosecute it under the Smith
and McCarran Acts if the findings so warranted. At a local level, Legion posts for years harassed colleges that, like Sarah Lawrence, declined to dismiss the professors of whom the Legion disapproved. Legionnaires itched for the final showdown at home: in the course of
"Freedom Fortnight" during February 1953, eleven upstate New York
cities were liberated following "Communist uprisings." And throughout it all those skulking, cowardly American Commies lay low,
brooding over their plans for sabotage and never showing their red
hands.

Behind these surface dramatics lay the genuine social anxieties
we have alluded to, anxieties reflected in a series of nine programs
broadcast by the Legion over station WHBC, Canton, Ohio, from
February to April 1951—to mention only one instance. A speaker
named Crowe claimed that the new United States budget contained
an appropriation of twenty-five million dollars "for the furtherance of
socialist ideas" such as those that had brought the "broken nation of
Great Britain" to bankruptcy. In Socialist England, according to a
speaker named Krause, workers were compelled to change their jobs
at a nod from the government. "Americanism," explained a certain
Jack Sengler, "offers God as the material force from which our products are made." God was a staple totem pole in the free-enterprise
ceremony; others included the Founding Fathers, unique freedom,
and resistance to the UN, the masses of Asia, taxation, government
spending on welfare and world government. In short, Communism.

Remember Sinclair Lewis's immortal Babbitt—real-estate agent,
Elk, Rotarian and advocate of "business English"; fearful of labor,
envious of the East Coast magnates, sweating to hold the middle
ground, to inch upward, to hold back the envious masses pressing in
on his terrain, his Zenith.

## American Labor Embraces the Pax Americana

The creation of the Congress of Industrial Organizations in 1936, at the height of the New Deal, signaled a new radical militancy within an important segment of American labor. By the time the CIO threw in the towel and merged with the American Federation of Labor in 1955, the American trade-union movement had become the most conservative and ideologically acquiescent among the capitalist democracies. The most important phase in this regressive process was the anti-Communist purge of the CIO between 1946 and 1950. It was a further twenty years before the most dynamic and brilliant of the CIO anti-Communists, Walter Reuther, president of the United Automobile Workers, recognized the full consequences of his own actions. These consequences can be encapsulated in two names: Vietnam and George Meany. Reuther then took the UAW out of the AFL-CIO.

The purge of the CIO took place at two levels. Reuther and Joe Curran of the National Maritime Union waged a successful struggle to wrest control of their unions from elements friendly to the CP. Mike Quill turned his coat and achieved the same coup within the Transport Workers. James B. Carey, failing to take over the United Electrical Workers, set up a rival union with CIO support. At the same time the CIO itself, under the presidency of the Catholic Philip Murray, inexorably imposed on its member unions the orthodoxy of the Truman doctrine and the Marshall Plan. It was quite true that about a dozen pro-Communist unions would, if they could, have imposed a Stalinist orthodoxy with equal zeal; nevertheless, Maurice Travis, of Mine, Mill and Smelter Workers, complained very justly that "I would like to know where in . . . the constitution of the CIO it says that we have to support the Marshall Plan or . . . conform to the foreign policy of the Democratic Administration."

It was in November 1946 that the CIO's executive board launched its campaign for uniformity, authorizing Murray to take over the funds and property of any local or state council that refused to conform. Collaboration with certain organizations of the Left like the National Negro Congress and Civil Rights Congress was proscribed. After a number of pro-Communist unions stubbornly endorsed the presidential candidacy of Henry Wallace, the CIO's executive council met in January 1948 and voted, 33 to 13, against Wallace and in favor of the Marshall Plan. During the election campaign that followed, the CIO's Political Action Committee spent $513,000 in support of Truman.

Bitterness on both sides deepened. Murray removed Harry Bridges as regional director of the Northern California CIO, and a number of local CIO councils had their charters removed. Pro-Communists within the CIO's national headquarters, notably general counsel Lee Pressman and the editor of CIO-News, Len De Caux, were forced out by Murray. The overwhelming defeat suffered by Wallace strengthened the resolve and the nerve of the anti-Communists within the CIO; by the time of the Cleveland convention in 1949 the die was cast for a purge of all recalcitrant unions. By this time the influence of Father Charles Owen Rice and the Association of Catholic Trade Unionists was such that, according to radical witnesses, the convention hall and the hotel lobbies were swarming with priests.

At Cleveland a five-day orgy of attacks on the Left was interspersed with speeches from distinguished guests: Secretary of State Acheson; Chairman of the Joint Chiefs Omar Bradley; and Federal Security Administrator Oscar Ewing. Truman sent a two-page letter to his CIO. Murray himself fulminated against "skulking cowards . . . apostles of hate . . . lying out of the pits of their dirty bellies." The executive board was empowered by the convention to expel unions for nonconformity in nonunion affairs. The United Electrical Workers were expelled on the pretext of nonpayment of dues, and during the months that followed ten other unions were subjected to a bizarre inquisitorial grilling by three-man committees representing the CIO's executive board. One got the message and ousted its left-wing leaders, but nine others, representing about 900,000 workers, were expelled, most notably Harry Bridges's ILWU. Determined to win back these workers, the CIO rapidly set up rival unions; the enterprise was generally successful. Very little attempt was made to demonstrate that the expelled unions had, in following the CP line, deserted the economic interests of their members.

Pockets of Communist influence were similarly chased out of unions belonging to the AFL. By 1954, according to the U.S. Bureau of Labor Statistics, fifty-nine of a hundred unions had amended their constitutions to bar Communists from holding office. Forty-one of them discriminated not only against Party members but also against advocates and supporters. Forty unions barred Communists not only from office but also from membership.[2] Nor were such provisions mere window dressing; expulsions were numerous and almost always upheld by the courts.

We need not endorse or sympathize with the aims of the Communist Party in order to condemn this sweeping internal purification of the ranks of labor. The impact of such a purge, of course, cannot be confined to the individuals directly victimized, nor was it intended to be. The American worker took note and retreated into either orthodoxy or disinterest or both. (When in 1956 every member of the new AFL-CIO was invited to contribute one dollar to its political arm, COPE, only one member out of twenty-four did so.) Henceforward the government could embark on virtually any foreign adventure without fear of a murmur of dissent from organized labor.

## THE TAFT-HARTLEY ACT: RADICAL UNIONS UNDER FIRE

The anti-Communist campaign in the field of industry and labor was conducted on three interrelated fronts: by the government (the industrial-personnel security program); by Congress (the Taft-Hartley Act, the Communist Control Act, and the committee investigations); and by the trade unions themselves. But the terrain on which these three fronts converged was, of course, that of industry itself, of business, of capital, of the large corporations. Neither the government, nor Congress, nor the anti-Communist trade unions could *directly* fire a radical worker or trade unionist; the government could remove his access to classified material, the Congress could harass and expose him to public obloquy, the anti-Communist union could expel him, inform on him or refuse to defend him: but only his employer could dismiss him.

In exerting pressure to ensure that the employer did precisely that, Congress and its committees made most of the running; the federal government hustled to keep pace with Congress; finally the labor unions, under overwhelming pressures to conform, enacted rituals and vendettas of their own to pulverize the radical, dissenting spirit that had characterized the CIO in its formative years. During or after a hotly contested union election, the anti-Communist faction, particularly if disappointed, would talk to the FBI; the FBI would talk to the company's security men; word would reach the staff of HCUA, the SISS or the McCarthy Subcommittee; the government Screening Panel, having consulted the FBI files, would deny the radicals access to classified material; the rival anti-Communist union or a friendly company would demand an NLRB election; the Justice Department would attempt an indictment under the Taft-Hartley Act's non-Communist affidavit; Congressional committees, armed with subpoenas, would swoop down on the area; the press would publicize the latest exposures in lurid headlines; there would be much talk of potential sabotage; and finally the company would fire a bunch of tight-lipped, amendment-invoking radicals.

Does this therefore imply, as a matter of analysis, that Wall Street, monopoly capitalism, the great cartels, did not primarily instigate this purge? That, in other words, anti-Communism was not at base an expedient, culturally validated weapon for union-bashing and labor-bashing? Can we afford to ignore the strident anti-Communist propaganda of the U.S. Chamber of Commerce and the National Association of Manufacturers? The evidence of the time suggests that capitalist corporations were most likely to take the *initiative* in anti-Communist propaganda and purges in those parts of the country (notably the South) where the legitimacy of trade unionism, collective bargaining and the union shop was still fiercely contested. But relatively sophisticated and pragmatic corporations of the North, the Middle West and the Pacific Coast, the corporations most deeply involved in government defense contracts, and therefore subject to the government's personnel-security program, normally preferred business as usual; government defense contracts as usual; a low profile. It was the politicians, the committee counsel, the anti-Communist trade unionists, who had a vested interest in raising the specter of the Red Menace, of incessantly warning the public that vital defense installations were vulnerable to Kremlin-inspired sabotage.

When the French writer Simone de Beauvoir visited the United States during the first months of 1947, she was astounded by the virulence of antiunion propaganda in the press. During the first two months of the year, following the election of the right-wing 80th Congress, more than sixty bills and amendments to curb the powers of unions were introduced in Congress. Out of these emerged the Labor-Management Relations Act, known as the Taft-Hartley Act. On June 18, supported by both the AFL and the CIO, Truman vetoed the bill; the Senate promptly overrode his veto. The section of the Act that particularly concerns us here is 9(h), by which, on pain of certain disabilities in law, every responsible union official was required to sign on oath an affidavit that

> he is not a member of the Communist Party nor affiliated with such party, and that he does not believe in, and is not a member of or supports any organization that believes in or teaches, the overthrow of the United States Government by force or by any illegal or unconstitutional means.

A union whose officers did not comply could not be certified as a bargaining agent with the National Labor Relations Board, could not insert a union-shop clause in any subsequent or renewed collective-bargaining agreement and could not apply to the NLRB for redress against an employer for unfair labor practices. A false affidavit was punishable under section 35A of the Criminal Code by a penalty of $10,000, of ten years' imprisonment, or both, for perjury.

In two similar cases, *American Communications Association v.*

*Douds*, and *Osman v. Douds*, the Supreme Court in 1950 sustained the constitutionality of the Act. Despite the incompatibility of the "does not believe in" clause of Section 9(h) with the First Amendment, the Vinson Court once again subordinated the Bill of Rights to *raison d'état* with the contention that

> it is sufficient to say that Congress had a great mass of material before it which tended to show that Communists . . . had infiltrated labor organizations not to support and further trade union objectives . . . but to make them a device by which commerce and industry might be disrupted when the dictates of political policy required such action.

The Court also ruled that the privilege of being an exclusive bargaining agent, which Section 9(h) threatened to withdraw, was not a constitutional right but a statutory privilege. Yet obviously nonaccess to the NLRB and its elections put a union in a worse position than if the NLRB and its powers had not been legislated into existence.

The pro-Communist unions declined at first to sign the affidavit, as indeed did certain anti-Communist leaders within the CIO who were outraged by other provisions of the Act. By September 1949, however, the unions had learned their lesson—loss of bargaining rights to noncomplying unions—and decided to comply. In July 1957 the NLRB announced that about 250 international unions were in compliance (involving about 2,750 affidavits) and about 21,500 locals (involving some 193,500 affidavits). These figures reveal the vast scale on which conformity was imposed—at shop-floor level nearly 200,000 trade-union leaders had formally sworn that they did not belong to the CP or believe in its doctrines. Only two major unions stubbornly held out: the (non-Communist) United Mine Workers and the International Typographical Union.

Even if they signed the affidavits, trade-union leaders suspected of being Party members or of supporting CP objectives could still be hounded on perjury charges. Although the Supreme Court frustrated the NLRB's attempts to cancel the exclusive bargaining rights of the Fur and Leather Workers and of the Mine, Mill and Smelter Workers on the ground that president Ben Gold of the Fur Workers and secretary-treasurer Maurice Travis of Mine, Mill had been convicted of falsely signing Taft-Hartley affidavits, these judicial decisions came only in 1954, after radical unions had suffered a great deal of harassment and a devastating depletion of strength. For example, while the leaders of the United Electrical Workers were hesitating whether to sign the non-Communist affidavit, the union lost contracts, recognition rights and strikes in rapid succession; some locals were so worried that they seceded to rival unions. A further draining-away of membership followed events such as the arrest and conviction of E. Melvin Hupman, a UE local leader at the General Motors Frigidaire plant at Dayton, Ohio. In January 1954 Hupman was sentenced to five years in prison and a $5,000 fine after being convicted of falsely signing the Taft-Hartley affidavit in 1949.

Perjury charges of this sort were brought by the government as instruments in the ultimate smashing of the Fur Workers and of the West Coast Marine Cooks and Stewards, both of which had been expelled from the CIO in 1950. President Hugh Bryson of the MCS went to prison after a Taft-Hartley perjury conviction. Although Ben Gold, president of the Fur Workers and a veteran Communist, never actually entered the prison gates after his similar conviction, the punitive effect of it on his union was soon apparent. In May 1954 the Fur Workers were negotiating on behalf of 1,500 skilled workers at the A. C. Lawrence plant at Peabody, Massachusetts, when the Amalgamated Meat Cutters, AFL, capitalized on Gold's conviction by petitioning the NLRB for an election to determine which union should represent the workers at A. C. Lawrence. Not only did the company promptly suspend negotiations with the Fur Workers but the Massachusetts Special Commission got into the act, inviting Professor W. W. Rostow of MIT to testify how the Fur Workers had donated funds to Communist unions in Europe and to at least eighteen organizations listed by the Attorney General. After interrogation by the Commission, the local's business manager could take no more and denounced the Fur Workers to the CIO Convention in December as the "hard core of Communism in this country." Two months later the Fur Workers gave up the ghost and merged with the Meat Cutters. By August, fifteen Fur officials had been expelled in the United States and Canada; by October more than a hundred reds had been purged.[3]

Also greatly harassed and weakened was Mine, Mill (headquarters, Denver, Colorado), a union whose militant Marxist philosophy of class struggle was reflected in the blacklisted film, *Salt of the Earth*. At the second attempt the government won its case against Maurice Travis, secretary-treasurer of the union, who was sentenced to a brutal eight years' imprisonment plus an $8,000 fine for having falsely signed the Taft-Hartley affidavit in 1948. Meanwhile, the Justice Department imported Harvey Matusow to testify before a grand jury that Clinton Jencks, a leading Mine, Mill official who appeared in *Salt of the Earth*, had been a Party member when he first signed the affidavit. Matusow later recanted his testimony and Jencks's conviction was thrown out by the Supreme Court. Enraged by this decision, the Justice Department struck again in November 1956, obtaining indictments in Denver against fourteen Mine, Mill leaders on charges of conspiring to file false affidavits. Eleven of them were brought to trial in November 1959, and nine were subsequently jailed for perjury.

The Justice Department had first resorted to this conspiracy charge under the Taft-Hartley Act in January 1957, when a federal grand jury indicted two UE leaders, Fred and Marie Haug, for falsely signing the affidavit, and six Cleveland, Ohio, Communists for conspiring with them. Marie Haug was the quintessential target of the great fear: a graduate of Vassar (1935, the radical hour), she had served as a delegate to the Women's International Democratic Federation and on the national committee of the Progressive Party. She had invoked the Fifth before the SISS in 1952, when she was president of UE Local 735. During her trial she claimed that she had resigned from the CP in 1949, but the jury chose to believe eight professional informers, with the result that seven of the eight defendants were sentenced to eighteen months' imprisonment and fined $2,500.[4]

In 1954 Congress passed the Communist Control Act, which imposed drastic disabilities on any union found to be "Communist-infiltrated": denial of access to the NLRB's services and elections, and ineligibility to complain about unfair labor practices or to sue in federal court to enforce collective-bargaining agreements.[5] In July and December 1955, Brownell, thus armored, petitioned the SACB to declare UE and Mine, Mill "Communist-infiltrated." Although in the long run the action against both unions withered on the legal vine, the cumulative impact of this harassment, combined with raids by the United Steelworkers (CIO), had by 1956 reduced Mine, Mill's membership to about one third of its postwar peak of 100,000.

## CONGRESSIONAL HARASSMENT OF RADICAL UNIONS

The notion of effective harassment must be extended to include not merely legal actions and administrative attacks, but also the constant exacerbation of a climate of hysteria and hostility by Congressional committees. After the war the lead in the red-baiting of unions was taken by the House Committee on Education and Labor under its chairman Fred Hartley, coauthor of the Taft-Hartley Act. This Committee, hostile to the New Deal and graced by such freshman stars as Nixon of California and John F. Kennedy of Massachusetts, fastened its claws into the Communist militant who had led highly publicized strikes in 1941 and 1947 at the Allis-Chalmers Company in Wisconsin. What happened to Harold Christoffel could well serve—and was intended to serve—as an example to any other union leader tempted to adhere to the Marxist principles he had absorbed in the thirties.

Cordially detested by Walter Reuther and the new anti-Communist leadership within the UAW, removed from his post in Local 248 and subpoenaed by the Hartley Committee, Christoffel denied he was a Communist. A grand jury indicted him for perjury, and in March 1948 he was convicted. After the Supreme Court had thrown out the verdict on a technicality, he was tried and convicted again. In May 1953, though he was relentlessly pursued by John F. Kennedy, Christoffel's sentence was reduced from four years to sixteen months.

To the harassment of red unions HCUA, too, was irresistibly drawn. In July 1947 Committee Counsel Tavenner congratulated friendly UE witnesses for having ousted twenty-six alleged Communists from their local. If only other locals would follow their example, said Tavenner, "We wouldn't have to pass some of the labor laws we are passing today." In July 1948 the Committee intervened to influence a struggle between pro- and anti-Communists at UE's Local 203 (the Bridgeport plant of General Electric), and in August 1949 HCUA interrogated the UE's three top officials, Fitzpatrick, Emspak and Matles, at the moment when delegates to the forthcoming UE national convention were being elected. (Not to be outdone, Pat McCarran's SISS waded into the fray, snapping at the heels of several left-wing pariah unions, notably UE and Mine, Mill, the latter a special target in his home state of Nevada.) Having cited thirty-nine officials of Harry Bridges's International Longshoremen and Warehousemen's Union for contempt in 1950, HCUA turned its attention to the sensitive automobile industry in the Detroit area, where the UAW's huge, 55,000-strong Local 600 (Ford) remained stubbornly anti-Reuther and anti-anti-Communist.

This raid was a classic of its kind. After the Committee had demonstrated that a handful of Communists within the UAW had attempted to colonize the Buick plant at Flint, Michigan, with Eastern, college-trained militants masquerading as proletarians, General Motors immediately fired the impostors, and a purge of the assembly lines, accompanied by violence, was set in motion. Wherever capital was in dispute with organized labor, the Committee was ready to invoke the specter of Communism on behalf of capital. In June 1954, for example, HCUA arrived in Seattle at the moment when tense negotiation between the International Woodworkers and the lumber companies was leading toward a big strike. In later years both HCUA and the SISS sustained their marauding, fire-raising forays into those radical unions that, with the exception of the impregnable ILWU, clung to the ledge of existence with ever-weakening fingers.[6]

Out of the fire and ashes of these experiences Communists within the labor movement developed an amusing semantic quirk: they learned to refer to themselves as "alleged Communists."

# 19

## How to Fire a Worker

### THE "EXPOSURE" WEAPON

The persecution of the radical minority within the American working class has gone largely neglected by all except the most specialized historians. Industrial workers apparently lack the glamour of film stars, the symbolic importance of scientists and the kinship status that academics and teachers have for historians. And since workers tend not to record their own experiences in writing, they seem to lack the biographical "flesh" that brings human contours to bare statistics. We must nevertheless recognize that all the big guns of the great purge subjected the proletariat to a heavy bombardment:

> The way to get results, sir, is to hold our hearings, get these peo-ple in public session, have them claim the Fifth Amendment, have the witnesses name them as Communists, have them fired from the defense plants . . . The employers have adopted an ar-rangement that they *will not act against these people unless and until we hold these hearings* . . . [Emphasis added.]

These words, spoken by Roy Cohn on June 2, 1954, at a session of McCarthy's Subcommittee on Investigations, indicate the extent to which, in matters of anti-Communist dramatics, the great corpora-tions were compelled to run to keep up with the politicians. Not only General Electric and the International Telephone and Telegraph Company, but also Westinghouse, the Radio Corporation of Amer-ica, Bethlehem Steel, U.S. Steel and others found themselves obliged by *political* pressure to announce that they would discharge any employee who invoked the Fifth. So acute was the fear of commercially damaging publicity, that some employers fired workers who had merely been mentioned unfavorably before committees, without any opportunity to defend themselves. For example, when HCUA visited Seattle in 1955, a nineteen-year-old potwasher in a hospital kitchen was dismissed because her husband and her father had been named before HCUA. The husband, a draftsman working for a truck-body builder, was fired when he refused the personnel manager's request to deliver himself to HCUA and tell all. Another Seattle worker, who had belonged to the Molders Union for thirty years and who was "identified" before HCUA, was dismissed by his company after a woman had phoned every day for several weeks demanding "Fire him." His union did not protest.[1]

The worst year for dismissals of left-wing workers was probably 1954. Bethlehem Steel fired about a dozen under pressure from Congressional committees, with arbitrators upholding the company on the ground that such men must constitute security risks whether or not their work was classified. (It wasn't.)[2] Among a number of workers fired at Flint, Michigan, during 1954 were half a dozen accused by HCUA of being professional CP agitators;[3] indeed the Committee claimed to have unmasked the Party's plan to "colonize America's basic industries" and to have exposed twenty-seven such "colonizers" in Flint alone, including several disguised college graduates. One of these, Howard I. Falk, apparently had concealed the fact that he had a degree of Bachelor of Electrical Engineering, and he admitted that on his application he had falsified his employment record. In the same vein, Mervin I. Engle, employed by the Chevrolet division, had withheld mention of his CCNY bachelor's degree from his application form and had falsified his record. Both men were fired by GM.[4]

In October 1956 the Singer Manufacturing Company fired Bert D. Gilden, who was said to have omitted reference to his degree from Brown and his previous employment with GE, when he applied for work at Singer's Bridgeport, Connecticut, plant. Like Engle and Falk, he was described by FBI agents as an activist Communist. Gilden invoked the First and Fifth Amendments before HCUA, whose subcommittee chairman, Edward E. Willis, expressed eloquent outrage: "It is to get these smart boys, these smart college intellectuals after their [sic] get their college education, to plant them in these plants and to try and colonize them plants." Although Local 227 of the IUE-CIO refused to honor Gilden's grievance (just as the UAW had abandoned Falk and Engle to their fate), the State Supreme Court of Errors ordered Singer to go to arbitration. Gilden was lucky: Arbitrator

Sidney L. Kahn ordered his reinstatement on the ground that he was not engaged in sensitive work and that Singer had fastened on to his falsification of his record "merely as a pretext" to fire a radical.

But the standard discharge was, of course, the "Fifth Amendment" discharge,[5] following swiftly on a worker's refusal to testify. These occurred on a considerable scale in a climate of hysteria that apparently eroded normal loyalties and restraints. In 1956, for example, Westinghouse Airbrake decided to fire two members of UE who had served the company for a combined total of sixty-five years! Both were admitted to be excellent, conscientious workers, but as soon as they resorted to the Fifth the Senate committee exerted pressure and the Air Force stalled on a contract award. In such cases, arbitrators differed. On this occasion Arbitrator Harry Abrahams upheld the company; but a year earlier Arbitrator Joseph D. McGoldrick ordered the Worthington Pump Corporation to reinstate a couple of Fifth Amendment workers. In seventeen "refusal to testify" cases that went to arbitration between 1945 and 1951, eight decisions went against the dismissed grievant. This was a more favorable proportion than in federal security program cases, where 75 percent of arbitration decisions went against the grievant.[6]

When HCUA hit Baltimore in 1957, fifteen of twenty-two witnesses who resorted to the Fifth lost their jobs, including seven Bethlehem Steel workers with seniority ranging from ten to twenty years.[7] Their union, the anti-Communist United Steelworkers, refused to support them. In December the Committee moved on to Bethlehem's plant at Buffalo, where five were dismissed, with the same union again declining to intervene.[8]

## KOREA AND THE "RUN-OUTS"

The American Century complex and the Korean war were driving factory workers to a high pitch of intolerance that, from time to time, exploded in violence. These "run-outs," as they were called, occurred very largely in the automobile industry, particularly in the three or four years following the outbreak of the Korean war. The summer of 1950 was the epicenter of the emotional storm, an ugly, vicious time, shaped out of the convergence of Korea, the Smith Act verdict, the Rosenberg indictment, and the inflammatory speeches of McCarthy. Radical workers were thrown out bodily from the Allis-Chalmers plant in South Milwaukee; a UE organizer in an automobile plant was physically attacked, while another UE organizer and his wife were arrested as they were taking the Stockholm petition from door to door. Three workers who had been distributing pamphlets attacking

American intervention in Korea were chased out and injured by fellow workers at the GM plant at Linden, New Jersey. At the Chrysler plant at Maywood, near Los Angeles, Frank W. Zaffina led a posse of veterans in an attack on workers who were thought to be reds. A photograph appeared in *Fortune* magazine, showing a bloodstained auto worker on the verge of collapse as he attempted to leave the plant. The vigilantes had taken care to alert the press in advance: although the police were on hand they arrested no one, not even the victims. There were also fights within the San Francisco Longshoremen's Union. In Detroit patriotic workers physically ejected colleagues who had invoked the Fifth before HCUA.[9]

In 1952 the mood remained ugly. In February John Cherveny, formerly chairman of American Youth for Democracy at Wayne University, was hustled out of the American Metal Products Company factory by co-workers after invoking the Fifth before HCUA. In the same month Paul Henley, a shop steward at Chrysler's Dodge plant, was run out of the engine plant there by fellow workers—same offense. In November 1953 a tense situation arose when McCarthy descended on General Electric and subpoenaed a certain Henry Archdeacon who worked at the Lynn, Massachusetts, plant. McCarthy knew how to play the game to the full:

> McCARTHY: Were you engaged in espionage over the past few weeks?
> ARCHDEACON: I decline to answer that question on the basis of the Fifth Amendment . . .
> McCARTHY: As a matter of fact, you have been giving to the Communist Party complete detailed information on everything going on in the GE plants?
> ARCHDEACON: I decline to answer on the basis of the Fifth . . .
> McCARTHY: Just one further question. If we were to have war with Communist Russia, and if the Communist Party ordered you to sabotage the facilities at GE, would you disobey that order of the Communist Party?
> ARCHDEACON: I decline to answer that question.

It was a game, a legal gambit, but not one that most workers either understood or appreciated. On the following morning, November 20, Archdeacon came to work at the usual time, seven o'clock. Soon afterward the workers in Building 66 began "milling around and refusing to work while Archdeacon was on the premises."

When Kit Clardy decided to boost his campaign for reelection by taking a subcommittee of HCUA into his native Michigan on a strident, red-baiting spree, Mervin I. Engle was roughed up and tossed out of the Chevrolet Manufacturing plant, Flint; Sherwood Baumkel was threatened by co-workers at Buick, Flint; and Murray Borod was not only fired from Chevrolet, Flint, but had his house stoned and daubed with red paint. William Van de Does, fired from the Fisher Body plant, Flint, had his car stoned, while Howard Foster was attacked in the Chevrolet plant. Clardy commented, "This is the best kind of reaction there could have been to our hearings." [10]

## THE INDUSTRIAL PERSONNEL SECURITY PROGRAM

Under the federal Industrial Personnel Security Program, some four million Americans working for private employers in about 21,000 different facilities had to be cleared for access to confidential, secret or top-secret information during the period 1947 to 1956. The industries affected were those with contracts from the Atomic Energy Commission and the Defense Department, as well as the maritime workers covered by the Port Security Program. The "confidential" information category accounted for about two thirds of all clearances, and here the government delegated responsibility for investigation and clearance of the employee to the company itself, or the agencies it might hire. How many of the four million of them were denied clearance?

> Under the Industrial Personnel Security Program, from July 1949 to July 1956, about 1,035.
> Under the Atomic Energy Commission Program, from January 1947 to March 1955, about 494.
> Under the Port Security Program, about 3,783.

As regards the Industrial Personnel Security and AEC programs, it is not possible to state exactly what proportion of those denied clearance were dismissed by their employers, and what proportion were transferred to other, nonclassified work. But the majority lost their jobs.

The regulations provided twenty-two criteria for deciding whether clearance of a company or of an individual worker was "consistent with the interests of national security." In "secret" cases the FBI and similar files would be scanned for derogatory information; in "top-secret" cases, the FBI would be asked to conduct a field investigation. All this took time—from six to twelve months in secret cases, often over a year in top-secret. Delay of itself, let alone an adverse decision, could cost a man his job.

The decision whether or not to grant an employee clearance was vested in the military department's regional industrial security office.

If one or more members of the screening panel regarded clearance as being unwarranted, the employee became entitled to a hearing before the Industrial Employment Review Board, which operated by delegation of authority from the Secretaries of the Army, Navy and Air Force to hear appeals on their behalf. Until 1949 the IERB was entirely military in composition and entirely crude in procedure. Not until the middle of 1948 did the IERB yield to the requests of defense lawyers that the charges be stated; not until 1949 were workers allowed to receive transcripts of their own hearings; and it was only when the IERB came under a civilian chairman in that year that due process was adopted and that it began to reverse about half the denials of clearance that were appealed to it from the normally all-military screening panels. (This proportion of clearances on appeal continued to hold true in 1955.) [11]

Guilt by association or kinship was a no less ubiquitous charge in the Industrial Personnel Security Program than in its federal civil-service counterpart. A plumber-foreman job supervisor working on the West Coast ran into trouble when his employer got a contract for plumbing work at an Air Force base. The Air Force Board ruled that he was a security risk, and in July 1952 he was discharged. It was not until fourteen months after his dismissal that, with the help of his Congressman, he obtained the charges against him—his wife was said to be associated with the CP. This turned out to be more false than true; twenty months after his discharge the plumber was cleared by the Appeal Division of the Western Industrial Security Board. Even so, his original employer refused to take him back, and he received no compensation for the period of his suspension, which had involved him in considerable legal fees.

The charges against Dr. Wilbur A. Hanes, a physicist suspended by the Boeing Aircraft Company in 1952, were all of associating with other people; not until May 1957 was he finally cleared.

A woman inspector in an electrical plant was discharged because her sister had signed a Communist petition against the Taft-Hartley Act and because at her hearing the inspector said she intended to go on seeing her sister.

Arthur Manning, a Philadelphia Navy Yard employee, was suspended when it was discovered that his wife's grandmother, in whose house he was temporarily living, had once been a Party member and a friend of Mother Ella Bloor, the veteran Communist. With the help of the ACLU, he got his job back eighteen months later. [12]

Many companies almost automatically dispensed with the services of employees who were denied access to classified material, even when they could usefully be employed in nonclassified work. Douglas Aircraft and Republic Aircraft made it a practice to dismiss any worker who was denied clearance. For a while Bell Aircraft stig-matized employees denied clearance by pinning a label to their cloth-ing, but from 1954 it was Bell's policy to fire the man and see if he fought. A study based on a three-month survey of the electronics in-dustry on the San Francisco peninsula and of the Los Angeles aircraft plants found that when regional screening boards denied employees clearance for secret or top-secret material, just over half the firms automatically fired them. In June 1954 Sperry Gyroscope, at Lake Success, dismissed fourteen workers who had been denied security clearance, although two were not engaged in classified work and at least eleven had led the fight against the Communists in UE. After long and expensive litigation, most of them were reinstated by 1957. The lawyer Henry Mayer commented in 1955: "Many employers, tired of waiting for an employee's clearance to come through, will discharge him because the security board has not acted." [13]

The case of "Dr. X," a thirty-one-year-old political scientist, illus-trates the tendency of mere delay to terminate a man's employment. In August 1959, Dr. X began work at the New Jersey installation of System Development Corporation, in connection with classified work for the Strategic Air Command. Dr. X therefore needed clearance for access to secret and top-secret material. Ten months later, when nothing had been heard in response to the application, the Corpora-tion put him on involuntary leave without pay; he then discovered that so long as his security status remained in limbo he could not hope to get a job in any government agency or defense-related indus-try.[14]

Charles Allen Taylor worked for the Bell Aircraft Corporation in Buffalo, New York, from 1941 to 1956 as a skilled toolmaker latterly earning about $5,000 a year. In September 1956 he was informed by the Defense Department's Office of Industrial Security Review that he was no longer cleared for access to classified material. Two days later Bell fired him. He then received a "Statement of Reasons"—it was alleged that he had been a CP member in 1942–43 and might still be one. When he came before the Board in New York in November, they refused to show him the evidence against him. Although eleven witnesses testified that during the war he had supported Walter Reuther against the Communist demand for a speed-up and a no-strike pledge, this board nevertheless ruled in April 1957 that the gov-ernment's charges were true.

Taylor's attorney, Joseph L. Rauh, Jr., appealed to the Secretary of Defense, pointing out that there had been another Taylor in the same UAW local with the reputation of being pro-Communist. Five months passed without reply, so Rauh filed suit in the federal District

Court. In the meantime, Taylor earned only $1,718 throughout 1957 and only $497 during the first eight months of 1958. After further complications and new charges from the Defense Department, the Supreme Court granted review—the Defense Department then abruptly reversed itself and declared that "clearance of Charles Taylor is in the national interest." But the moment he reported for work at Bell Aircraft the whole security process was set in motion again; Rauh went back to the Supreme Court. In March 1959 Solicitor General James Lee Rankin conceded before the Court that five of the six informants against Taylor were of the "casual" type, but contended that citizens would not feel free to inform unless guaranteed anonymity. Having said this, the government then agreed to expunge the whole record.[15]

Yet the IERB and its successor, the Industrial Personnel and Facility Security Clearance Board, continued to flout the principles of due process until in 1959 the Supreme Court, in *Greene v. McElroy*, ruled that the Defense Department had received authority from neither Congress nor the President to deprive a worker in private industry of his job without due process. The Supreme Court's belated acknowledgment that the personnel-security apparatus had for years been perpetrating a fraud led the lower courts to reappraise cases like that of Rachel Brawner, a civilian cook employed by M & M Restaurants, Inc., in a naval installation until the Navy Department excluded her from the base on the ground that she did not satisfy security requirements—yet denied her, her union, and her employer a hearing. Naturally she lost her job. The *Greene v. McElroy* ruling set in motion a slow reversal of the attitude, endemic both to courts and arbitrators, that government security regulations superseded collective-bargaining contracts.[16]

It should not, of course, be assumed that employers dismissed radicals only when they had been named before committees, invoked the Fifth, or been denied clearance under the Industrial Personnel Security Program. Any red who stuck his neck out was lucky to earn a living. For example, Flo Hall was dismissed by the Stewart-Warner Company, Chicago, as soon as she testified for the defense in the Foley Square Smith Act trial. Paul Kuznitz, an MIT graduate engineer specializing in steel construction, who had participated in the building of the Moscow subway, was working for Flour, a large construction firm, when it was awarded a government contract. Simultaneously (1948), the FBI arrived to demand his summary dismissal, and got it. Kuznitz was able to get a new job, and all went well until his wife, Rose Chernin, was indicted in 1950 under the Smith Act. His new employer, a Republican businessman, at first suggested to

Kuznitz that he divorce her. But (so Rose Chernin recalls) he not only retained Kuznitz, he also came to his funeral many years later to say a few words.[17]

## RED-BAITING, INC.

It was a common practice among certain firms to dismiss workers who made their radicalism too obvious, either by action or by association. At common law, and in the absence of a contract, employers were entitled to dismiss without cause. But this power was already restricted by federal and state statutes, and also by collective-bargaining agreements with the unions. About half the states had adopted laws prohibiting interference with the worker's right to free political activity; it was also a criminal offense for employers to maintain a political blacklist. But so compelling was the anti-red obsession that during the 1950s the courts in nine cases out of ten subordinated such basic protections to that predatory god, "national security."

In 1946 the Lockheed Aircraft Corporation discharged eighteen workers on the ground that it lacked sufficient proof as to their loyalty. The Supreme Court of California ruled that although a California statute forbade dismissal "because of political opinions or the exercise of political rights and privileges granted to every citizen of the United States by the Constitution," when it was a question of loyalty to the United States every other consideration took second place. In 1947 the Curtiss-Wright Corporation (which later signed a contract with the Navy Department obliging the Corporation to report and discharge all subversives) fired a UAW member on the ground that he had violated the plant rule by distributing Communist pamphlets. But the arbitrator ruled that since the worker had done this in his lunch time, and therefore within his rights, he must be reinstated. A year later Jackson Industries dismissed a black worker who had been attacked in the *Birmingham* (Alabama) *Post* as a leading Communist masquerading under an alias. Arbitrator Whitley P. McCoy ruled that to lose one's job was a natural consequence of being a Communist. The local CIO Industrial Union Council seemed to agree; it expelled the man.

In 1951 the Firestone Tire and Rubber Company discharged a worker for making provocative statements about the relative merits of the United States and the Soviet Union. A year later Henry Willcox, professional engineer and president of the Willcox Construction Company, New York, went with his wife on a two-month visit to China. When they returned they found that Willcox had been hastily voted out of the company without a hearing by a board of directors that feared the loss of a six-million-dollar contract with the New York Housing Authority.[18]

Of course, red-baiting had long been a favorite tactic among employers who wished merely to gain a tactical advantage over workers or unions. In 1950 the Grand Central Airport Company of Tucson, Arizona, distributed literature to its employees accusing the UAW and CIO (at the time engaged in an election drive to organize the plant) with being Communistic. The company circulated a pamphlet written by the fascist Joseph P. Kamp, "Vote CIO and Build a Soviet America," and also quoted from a *Chicago Tribune* editorial of August 6, 1944: "The people who support the New Deal ticket this November are supporting the Communists and building up the day when they plan the Red Terror sweeping down upon America. A New Deal vote is an invitation to murder." Warning of the danger of "strike terror," the company quoted the 1948 report of the Tenney Committee that nineteen CIO unions were Communist-dominated—a claim that not only was exaggerated but was now rendered obsolete by the expulsion of eleven such unions from the CIO in 1949–50: "Our own labor bosses spend millions for socialized medicine, which means the enslavement of your family doctor and dentist. Isn't this Communism? They spend millions to put out rent controls which means the confiscation of property. Isn't this Communism?" This saturation propaganda paid off; in the election that took place on April 20, 1951, the union was defeated by nearly 3 to 1.

In October 1952, the National Industrial Conference Board issued a document:

> . . . industrial security can . . . help you rid your plant of agitators who create labor unrest . . . The spies, traitors, and the misguided fools who promote Communism constitute our number one industrial security problem today. But . . . any and all who . . . destroy our peacetime source of wealth . . . must be looked upon as bad security risks . . .

The following year, the owner of Hearn's two department stores in Manhattan and the Bronx, Albert Greenfield, entered into a conflict with the Distributive Processing and Office Workers Union because he had laid off workers without regard to seniority. Out of this came a strike, a court injunction, a mass firing by Greenfield, and a full-scale strike. Greenfield ran ads in the press stressing the old CP-line records of the DPOWU leaders Arthur Osman, David Livingston and William Michelson, and called the union "Red," even though Osman had broken with the CP in 1951. The NLRB found that some of the Stewart-Warner Corporation's dismissals of so-called Communists were in fact motivated by hostility to the UE as a trade union. Although the Taft-Hartley Act, revising the Wagner Act in this respect, permitted employers to express "views, argument or opinion" about interunion rivalries, so long as there was "no threat of reprisal or force or promise of benefit," this proviso was constantly flouted in practice, often with the assistance of Congressional committees.

Another case involving the DPOWU occurred in Boston, where its Local 1282, representing 375 agents of the Boston Mutual Life Insurance Company, was in 1953 threatening to strike over new contract terms. At this juncture Everett H. Lane, president of Mutual, suggested to the Massachusetts Special Commission that it should investigate the local. A public hearing was held on February 2, 1954; the local's president, Frank Siegel, took the Fifth; and the strike, which had originally been voted by 7 to 1, was hastily canceled. Mutual felt strong enough to withdraw recognition of the local, and the agents suffered an average weekly pay cut of $15.[19]

An anti-Communist historian of the labor movement, David Saposs, has written:

> Employers . . . were influenced primarily in their attitude toward Communists by immediate, practical considerations of plant harmony, advantageous labor relations, and effect on business prospects, rather than by the principle or ethics of having dealings with Communists.

Yet such pragmatic calculations might work in unexpected directions. In March 1955 Vice-President Christophal of the Sanotone Corporation circulated a "read and destroy" memo to all production supervisors at the Elmsford and White Plains plants, in which he pointed out that although the company was ideologically out of sympathy with the pro-Communist UE, the union had nevertheless promised to get behind a new incentive scheme and raise production by 30 percent:

> I believe that in the present weakened position of the UE it is advantageous for the Company to deal with them . . . we feel we again have a way to lay off and discharge employees with a minimum of risk . . . we urge our supervisors NOT TO DISCOURAGE *any* employee from voting for the UE in the next election.

(The UE duly won the election against the Teamsters and the IUE, but the election was invalidated after the discovery of the memo. Nevertheless in July UE again won with a majority of 358 votes.)

Professor Ralph S. Brown, Jr., has calculated that at a conservative estimate one-and-a-half million employees in private industry were subjected to private security programs and checks at the initiative of the employer or the union. The Bell Telegraph System alone accounted for 780,000, and General Electric for some 280,000. New company security departments came into being to sift information about what workers read, joined and thought. In 1949 Consolidated Edison signed a contract with the Utility Workers, CIO, that all workers must take a loyalty oath and all job applicants must state whether they belonged to any Communist organization. Stewart-Warner's 1950 contract with the International Brotherhood of Electrical Workers, AFL, provided for a non-Communist oath for all employees. In the Southern Counties Gas Company of California's contract with the Chemical Workers, AFL, it was agreed that advocacy of violent overthrow would be a cause for dismissal. The Bell Telephone Company introduced its loyalty oath in 1954, while AT&T's subsidiary, Western Electric, imposed a non-Communist (past and present) statement that also involved disavowal of violent overthrow and dissociation from any organization listed by the Attorney General. Arthur Anderson & Company, a large public-accountant firm, required a loyalty statement of its employees.

In October 1954 the Director of Security of Republic Aviation, Farmingdale, Long Island, wrote in *Factory Management and Maintenance* that his company had fired 250 workers as security risks. As for methods:

> We may get information on a man through anonymous letters, phone calls or personal visits. Several years ago we encouraged employees up and down the line to report suspicious activities of fellow workers . . . We're alert to which men are becoming prominent in plant organizations, ranging from hobby and sport to religious and political grounds.[20]

Some companies gained access to HCUA's files or those of state investigating committees and police red squads—a process of interchange and intercourse greatly facilitated by the movement of inquiry agents, usually light-fingered and corrupt, from public to private employment. In Michigan a particularly cordial rapport grew up between the great automobile companies, Ford, General Motors and Chrysler, and the local police departments of Dearborn, Detroit and Flint, whose armories they sometimes stockpiled in the 1930s. Before the Second World War, red-baiting was the most familiar tactic employed, apart from head-cracking, to resist the claim of the UAW for recognition and collective bargaining.

Although Ford's tactics became more sophisticated and less physical after Henry Ford II fired the notorious Harry Bennett and his Service Department thugs in 1945, the rise to influence within the company of John Bugas, previously head of the FBI's Detroit Bureau, ensured that the Investigation Section continued to employ professional anti-Communists like Stephen Schemanske, originally hired by Bennett in 1936, and Milton J. Santwire, who in the early fifties were receiving money from both Ford and the FBI. Schemanske was paying Santwire $75 a month to spy on fellow workers at the River Rouge plant.[21]

Some firms relied on private detective agencies. The Dun and Bradstreet Corporation offered a loyalty-investigation service on a subscription-contract basis. Among the private investigatory agencies used by employers on the West Coast were the Better America Federation, Los Angeles, and the Western Research Foundation, San Francisco; about one third of the electronics and aircraft companies interviewed in the two metropolitan areas used them. But such agencies did not evaluate the relevance of their information to the job, and—like the FBI itself—sometimes did not even evaluate the reliability of the information. Clearly the American political blacklist has to be understood as an outgrowth of a commercial habit that was practiced on a prodigious scale. According to one authority, the Dunhill International List Company by 1964 had 12,500 separate lists containing 40 million names; if Americans could be listed according to age, sex, religion, means, hobbies, causes, activities, purchases, pregnancies, medical operations, subscriptions and stockholdings—because such information could be sold—then why not catalog political information, if it could be sold? [22] The habit of spying and of bribing sources of information to supply names (county-court clerks, high-school seniors, hospital nurses, etc.) was developed through the commercial values of the society and extended to its political values. A radical now meant someone with a low political credit rating.

The Church League of America, of Wheaton, Illinois, had been compiling files on radicals since 1937; its agents sat in on left-wing meetings, equipped with miniature tape recorders and cameras. By 1961 the League claimed to possess over 850,000 cross-referenced index cards, information from which was sold to commercial concerns. But pride of place among organizations specializing in the listing, monitoring and surveillance of radicals went to the American Security Council, which was set up in 1955 on the basis of the Mid-American Research Library and Harry Jung's Vigilante Intelligence Foundation. The clients of the ASC (staffed mainly by ex-FBI agents) included such major defense contractors as GE, Honeywell, Stewart-Warner, Motorola, Lockheed Aircraft Corporation, U.S. Steel and the Emerson Electric Company. By 1961 the ASC's files covered a million Americans.

Once the file check proved to be positive and the dirt had been dug, the company could either dismiss the radical worker within the twelve-week probationary period during which unions customarily did not protest, or catch him on some technical irregularity, or accuse him of having falsified his employment application.

Brown calculated about 700 dismissals under private industrial-security programs through 1956.

## Arbitration and the Courts

Up to the time of the Korean war the NLRB generally regarded private loyalty measures as being both superfluous and spurious. Before the summer of 1950, in 66 percent of cases, arbitrators and the NLRB refused to tolerate the discharge of workers for suspected disloyalty where government screening was not involved. But the pattern changed early in 1951, when the NLRB's general counsel upheld the discharge of a worker expelled from his union after signing a Stockholm Peace Pledge petition, thereby causing unrest among fellow workers.[23] In 80 percent of cases arbitrated during the Korean war, the employers were upheld, including one of a Firestone worker who had merely expressed provocative comparisons of the United States and the Soviet Union during company time to "a captive audience." It was at this period, following a ruling in 1949 in the Consolidated Western Steel Corporation case, that dismissals on the ground of potentially adverse publicity or potential loss of business were accepted almost automatically, notably in the film and newspaper industries. The only rulings that went the other way on this issue were: Chrysler Corporation (1952), J. H. Day Company (1952) and Republic Steel Corporation (1957).

In cases involving general Communist or fellow-traveling activity, 40 percent of cases went against the grievant.[24] Thus the prospects for the dismissed worker were by no means hopeless, unless he had been denied federal security clearance; but much depended on the attitude of the union to which he belonged. Among the unions most willing to support such grievants were the UAW, United Steelworkers, the American Newspaper Guild (all anti-Communist) and the UE.

The men and women who were dismissed found it extremely difficult to secure alternative employment. Or they suffered a catastrophic loss of earning power. William L. Greene, the vice-president of an electronics firm who was denied clearance until the Supreme Court ruling in his favor (*Greene v. McElroy*) in 1959, sank from $18,000 to $4,000 a year during the six years he worked as an architectural draftsman. Stephen Kreznar, former president of Local 5501,

Communications Workers of America, was fired as a PBX installer by the Wisconsin Telephone Company in 1954, following denial of security clearance—although he was not working in classified material. In the following eighteen months he was able to obtain only one week's unskilled labor. Such experiences were typical.

Nor did local unemployment compensation boards look kindly on the victims of political dismissals; they tended to agree with the Pennsylvania Unemployment Compensation Board of Review, which ruled in 1958 that a steelworker dismissed for invoking the Fifth had thereby been guilty of "willful misconduct," and was accordingly not entitled to benefits. By this doctrine a man availing himself of his constitutional right is thereby condemned to starve; an observer of hypersensitive imagination may detect in such a situation at least a minimal erosion of the constitutional right. ("You have free speech," the Queen might have said to Alice, "at the cost of your life.")

In 1956 a California Appeals Board denied unemployment compensation to Marion Syrek, dismissed as a Multilith operator by Arthur Anderson & Company, public accountants and auditors, for refusing to sign the company's private loyalty oath. Bert D. Gilden was turned down by the district unemployment commissioner after his dismissal by the Singer Manufacturing Company for having falsified his application form. The eight Bethlehem steelworkers dismissed in 1957 for taking the Fifth before HCUA were refused unemployment pay by the Maryland Employment Security Board; two years later this Board reached the same uncharitable conclusion with regard to Jeanette K. Fino, who had been fired as a waitress following an unfriendly appearance before HCUA in Baltimore.

As for those cases wherein workers suspended under the federal Industrial Security Program were later cleared and reinstated, until 1954 the onus was on the employer to make up the lost wages. But there was no guarantee that the employer would do so—Bell Aircraft Corporation's refusal to provide back pay was sustained in a 1951 arbitration case—unless a clause to that effect had been inserted in a collective-bargaining agreement. After mid-1954, the government provided what was known as restitution money (not the same as back pay) in such cases, but normally the unfortunate employee would forfeit one third of it to his lawyer.[25]

Defending a job in industry threatened by the security program could be an expensive enterprise. A cataloguing technician earning $4,600 a year spent $500 on lawyer's fees but failed to regain his job; a foreman in a large plant earning $8,400 a year paid his lawyer $500 after he had been denied clearance. A top executive in two major business organizations who was subjected to a Navy security check finally won clearance, but at a cost of $1,750 for seventy hours of his attorney's time. A draftsman earning $4,000 a year who lost his job late in 1952 received $900 in restitution money in February 1955, but legal fees had cost him $590. Some unions supported their members with free legal aid whenever they could, thanks largely to the idealism of radical lawyers. The attorneys who acted for workers belonging to the United Electrical Workers, for example, did so for scratch rates; Allan R. Rosenberg, a Massachusetts lawyer, charged UE only $125 for acting on behalf of a UE member who had been denied access to classified material in 1950, even though he had also retained a second lawyer to work on the case for a day and a half.[26]

# 20

## United Electrical Workers on the Rack

The United Electrical, Radio and Machine Workers of America, with its half-million members, emerged from the war as the most important Communist-led industrial union in the United States. Founded in 1936, UE had been the first to break the hold of the company unions at General Electric and Westinghouse; in a trial of strength, UE took on these two giants in 1946, forcing GE to settle for 18½ cents on March 13, and Westinghouse for 19 cents on May 12. The long red shadow of UE now lay across the national defense industry, haunting the Defense Department and enraging Congress.

UE prided itself on being a "rank-and-file" union (only 5 percent of its convention delegates were full-time officials) which represented all shades of opinion; perhaps half of its members were Catholics. Nevertheless in 1947 (when Henry Wallace and Carl Marzani, the latter already convicted of perjury, were guests at the convention), UE passed a resolution that Wall Street controlled the Truman administration.

Even before its expulsion from the CIO in 1949, UE was coming under severe attack from a variety of quarters—from the government, from Congress, from employers, from rival unions and from within its own ranks. The split within the union's leadership went back to 1941, when Julius Emspak and James B. Matles engineered the defeat of UE's first president, James B. Carey, and his replacement by Albert Fitzgerald. Emspak, a thirty-year-old skilled tool and die maker who was also a university graduate, became in 1936 UE's first secretary-treasurer, while the even younger Matles moved from a machine shop to become the union's first director of organization. These two dynamic figures, Communists by belief whether Party members or not, ran the union until Emspak's death in 1962, when Matles succeeded him as general secretary. Fitzgerald, whose campaign for president they successfully supported in 1941, was by no means a Marxist ("as a citizen of the United States I despise the Communist philosophy," he said), but he has been described with some justice as "a man willing to spout anti-Communist epithets while actually submitting to the Party line." To the CIO's Portland convention in November 1948 he declared: "I tell you frankly I do not give a damn for Russia . . . If President Truman makes a sincere effort to carry out his promises . . . I will tell the Progressive Party to go to hell." [1] But Truman never did and Fitzgerald never did.

The spearhead of the antileadership forces within UE was the embittered and ousted James B. Carey, secretary-treasurer of the CIO. Launching a campaign to regain control early in 1947, he formed the Members for Democratic Action and accused the leadership of making the union "a transmission belt for the American Communist Party." His MDA faction published its own paper, *The Real UE*. The leadership retaliated by threatening to expel the dissidents. Meanwhile, the Association of Catholic Trade Unionists under the leadership of Father Charles Owen Rice was propagandizing Catholic members of UE in the Pittsburgh area on a house-to-house visitation, urging them to quit the union or vote out its Communist leaders. Rice and the ACTU masterminded the crucial victory of the Carey opposition in the elections at Local 601, Westinghouse, in 1948. The priest's close friend, Congressman Francis E. Walter, persuaded HCUA to subpoena the local's left-wing leaders at the critical moment.

In the same year about 25,000 UE members seceded to join the UAW. The Atomic Energy Commission instructed General Electric to withdraw recognition from UE at the Knolls Atomic Power Laboratory because of the Communist associations of the UE's officers and their refusal (up to that time) to file Taft-Hartley affidavits. The AEC sent similar instructions to the University of Chicago as regards the Argonne National Laboratory. UE protested bitterly.

The union was now thrown out of the small-arms industries of Connecticut and Massachusetts, and was replaced mainly by the UAW. The CIO sponsored the new International Union of Electrical Workers (IUE) led by James Carey, and by June 1950 UE had been wiped out of big industry with the exception of two plants, GE at Erie, and Westinghouse at Philadelphia. UE was now the tail not the dog, and generally had to settle for whatever IUE negotiated elsewhere; the old "walk-out" response to a dispute had to be abandoned.

Interunion rivalry was bitter; before the February 1950 NLRB election at the Delco, Michigan, plant, Local 755 of the IUE-CIO prepared for the struggle with the following advice: "If you are pestered [by UE representatives] trying to force themselves into your homes, call the police . . . The American home is not even [sic] sacred to Moscow's agents." IUE also printed photostatic reproductions of what apparently were UE checks made out to the *Daily Worker* ($250), the JAFRC ($50 and $10), the NCASF ($50), the National Negro Council ($50) and the ACPFB ($50).[2] IUE employed "scabs" to cross UE's picket lines at Sharon, Pennsylvania, where, despite the general deportation terror, many foreign-born UE members stood their ground and passed out leaflets in the face of verbal abuse, physical intimidation, FBI harassment and organized ostracism within the community.

Desperately UE tried to prevent locals from seceding with their funds and property; litigation tied up the funds of the new IUE locals never certified as such by the NLRB. But it was not only the IUE and the UAW that UE had to contend with; plunging into the raiding game were United Steelworkers, CIO, as well as the International Brotherhood of Electrical Workers, AFL, and the AFL craft unions like the Machinists, the Sheet Metal Workers, the Pattern Makers.[3] In the meantime, Truman's Secretary of Labor behaved like a CIO staff organizer campaigning to exterminate UE, frequently appearing at factory gates to appeal to members to switch allegiance. Truman himself sent a message of blessing to the IUE.

Carey's star was now in the ascendant. He lauded the AEC's discriminatory policy and advised the Humphrey Committee that the Defense Department should investigate suspected Communist unions and force prospective defense contractors to withdraw recognition from them. He even accused General Electric of pandering to UE, because, he said, it preferred to deal with a weak union, without regard for national security. To the best of his ability Carey followed the advice contained in his *American Magazine* article, "We've Got the Reds on the Run" (September 1948), to build a machine in every local, as Reuther had done within the UAW, and then to purge, purge, purge. In the 1950 elections IUE gained control of fifty-six General Electric units (including Lynn and Everett) with 53,000 members, but UE still dominated forty-six units with 36,000 members, including Erie and Local 301 at Schenectady, the largest in the electrical industry, where the Communist Leo Jandreau was business agent.

In December 1953 Carey retained control of Lynn and Everett by the narrow margin of 5,546 to 4,806 after a month of bitter campaigning involving collusion among the IUE, GE, McCarthy and the Massachusetts Special Commission on Communism, to whom Carey presented the names of some 200 alleged Communists or sympathizers within UE.[4] General Electric chose the day before the vote to announce that it would suspend any worker who invoked the Fifth Amendment. By 1955 UE's membership had fallen to 90,000 (compared with IUE's 300,000 and IBEW's 500,000), the deterioration accelerated by the Attorney General's move under the Communist Control Act to have the union declared "Communist-infiltrated" by the Subversive Activities Control Board. Four district presidents plus about thirty members of UE's international staff and local business agents decided the game was up; about 50,000 members deserted, mainly to IUE or the UAW. For UE it was thereafter a long, slow haul to climb back to a membership of 165,000 in 1966.

Despite all the dire prognostications, neither UE nor any other radical union made a discernible move to sabotage or hinder war production. UE's workers continued to service the "capitalist war machine" while circulating peace petitions. Such restraint was not rewarded. Among the union's outstanding leaders, Emspak was indicted for contempt of Congress, William Sentner was convicted under the Smith Act, John T. Gojak was convicted of contempt and James T. Matles was almost denaturalized. In March 1957 federal Judge Walter Bruchhausen upheld the revocation of his citizenship on the ground that when applying for naturalization in 1934—Matles was born in Rumania—he had lied about Communist affiliations. However, this ruling was reversed on appeal.

## IUE AND BIG BUSINESS

From a strictly business point of view—profits—General Electric didn't give a damn whether the union with which it negotiated was Communist-dominated or not. What it did want to do was to weaken UE's postwar hold on 96 percent of the company's 230,000 workers, to divide and rule. The Communist issue provided the ideal pretext in terms of public and political relations. Once again patriotism could be reconciled with the pursuit of profit. In April 1949, W. B. Merihue, the company's manager of employee and community relations, told the Pittsburgh Personnel Association: "Our fight to get out from under the domination of the left-wing UE, we expect to consummate this year." What complicated this consummation was GE's deep aversion to *all* effective trade unionism and to the New Deal. Thus only seven months before Merihue's remarks, the company had issued a statement denouncing both left- and right-wing collectivists as "believers in government being big and in people being little." As late as 1952, GE's most influential executive, Lemuel R. Boulware, vice-president in charge of employee relations, complained to the Humphrey Committee that some of the anti-Communist unions he had to deal with were "just as much help to Joe [Stalin] as if these union officials were, in fact, Communist agents." The Humphrey Committee sharply reprimanded him for this failure to comprehend the legitimate boundaries of red-baiting.

The guts of the matter was that both GE and Westinghouse were now dealing mainly with a malleable union, IUE, which they had helped to put on its feet and for whose president, James B. Carey, they entertained nothing but contempt. "We took Mr. Carey off the hook by filing our own petitions for an NLRB election. This, under the NLRB rules, made it unnecessary for the IUE-CIO to show any membership at all." Here, in 1960, Carey negotiates with GE attorney Hilbert:

> CAREY: . . . You know it's hard for me to hold my head up when I meet with Reuther and McDonald. Reuther has been able to get things we haven't been able to get in our industry . . .
> HILBERT: Mr. Carey, what does that have to do with what we are here for today?
> CAREY: . . . Who is GE to shut me off? You know Mrs. Roosevelt called me last night?
> HILBERT: Was it a sympathy call?

In effect, Boulware could produce his annual wage, holiday and pension package on a take-it-or-leave-it basis; IUE took it, and UE had to follow; not until 1969 were they able to bury the hatchet sufficiently to make a concerted stand.[5]

## IMPACT OF THE LOYALTY-SECURITY PROGRAM

We turn now to the impact, devastating as it was, of the Truman loyalty-security program on members and officials of UE—here the systematic purge of the radical worker, the worker of suspect orthodoxy, is seen at its most relentless.*

On July 1, 1948, a Westinghouse official, accompanied by a Navy representative, informed the design engineer Frank Carner that he was "a poor security risk." Carner was immediately suspended without

---

* Owing to the courtesy of Frank J. Donner, Robert Z. Lewis and James B. Mauro, Jr., I was granted access to UE's personnel security files. According to their ruling, some UE members are referred to by their names in the text, and some by initials only, to protect those who may have avoided publicity at the time.

pay and escorted from the Gas Turbine Plant at Lester. The leaders of UE's Local 107, to which Carner belonged, quickly orchestrated a sit-down protest by 6,000 workers, with the result that Carner and another suspended employee, the sheet-metal worker Herb Lewin, were both taken back on nonclassified work while they appealed. On September 9, Carner arrived at the Pentagon for his hearing. According to his lawyer, he was asked:

> Who do you think is right in the Berlin crisis, us or the Russians?
> Who should back down, us or the Russians?
> What do you think of the Marshall Plan?

And so on. The lawyer also reported: "The Army officer quizzed Carner on why he had not been in the service . . . On learning that Carner's employer had requested a deferment . . . the Army officer snapped nastily, 'Nobody stopped you from enlisting, did they!' " In fact, the answers Carner (a self-confessed sympathizer of the Workers Party) gave were those of an intellectual Socialist generally critical of the CP, the USSR and the use of political violence. Yet, neither Carner nor UE's lawyers were permitted to take away from the hearing notes on what had transpired; Colonel Farr, the presiding officer, tore up the lawyer's notes under their noses, even though the Board was in reality deciding whether a civilian should be allowed to retain his job with a civilian company. The final decision was adverse to both Carner and Lewin.[6]

Or take the case of J.M., of Local 130, Westinghouse, Baltimore, who assured the Industrial Employment Review Board that he had resigned from the CP ten years earlier, in 1937, after only two years as a member. On this occasion Colonel Farr would neither allow notes to be taken during the hearing nor provide a statement of the charges, a summary of the information on which they were based, or a transcript of the hearing. Albert J. Fitzgerald, president of UE, wrote Truman with some justification: "These 'hearings' are a travesty of justice and fair play. They are conducted as Star Chamber proceedings . . ." (But Truman was hardly likely to respond favorably to criticisms from the chairman of the Progressive Party, and a leading supporter of Henry Wallace—two caps that fitted Fitzgerald.) The IERB upheld the denial of access to J.M., who was then fired by Westinghouse.

E.L., also of UE's Local 130, worked at the Westinghouse Gas Turbine Division at Essington, Pennsylvania, having served as a machine-gunner during the Battle of the Bulge. Yet such a record rarely if ever attracted the sympathy of military officers when set against discernible signs of radicalism—and E.L. admitted having joined the

CP in November 1947, although he claimed to have paid only one month's dues and attended only half-a-dozen meetings before losing interest. When he appeared before the IERB, having been suspended by Westinghouse in 1949, he was asked: "Have you ever advocated repeal of the Taft-Hartley Act?" UE's counsel reported that:

> They first stated that things like a man's religion, political views and associations had no bearing on whether he was a poor security risk; and in the next breath they defended their inquiry into those fields on the ground that it was necessary to know the man's background . . .

The Board informed Westinghouse that E.L.'s suspension was "with sufficient cause."

If war service for his country could not save a man his job, neither could long and loyal service for his company. F.P. had been working "on motor generator sets, on standard lines of motors" at GE for twenty-nine years, when in April 1950 he was suddenly denied access to classified material and suspended by GE. He was accused of having joined the Party in 1943. He denied it, but admitted he had subscribed to the *Worker* and had been active in UE's fight against the anti-Communist IUE. What the Board called "the derogatory evidence contained in the case file" was enough to damn him, but his refusal to answer the Board's oral questions about *The Communist Manifesto* and "the Soviet Union's taking border countries by force and deceit," not to mention "Malik's stand in the UN," no doubt counted heavily against him.[7]

Though the Board improved its procedures somewhat during the late forties, its style can be described only as crude and bullying. Here is a description of Colonel Farr's successor, Lieutenant Colonel Francis M. Wray, in action: "At this point Col. Wray blew up and shouted that he would not stand for any further cross-examination of the Board. He stated that the Board was not required to divulge any of its procedures . . ."[8] When Wray informed a Westinghouse worker, N.S., in August 1949 that denial of his access to classified material was affirmed, the letter was stamped in the margin: "Its transmission or the revelation of its contents in any manner to an unauthorized person is prohibited by law." Taken literally, this meant that N.S. could be prosecuted for telling his wife why he no longer went to work in the morning. The purpose of all such official bully-bluster and purple ink, of course, is to bemuse the individual into an eroded awareness of his own rights.

The Board now provided a transcript of the hearing, but it con-

tinued to frame its charges in the most vague and Kafkaesque manner—"currently maintaining a close continuous association with persons who are engaged in activities which would indicate they may be
members of or sympathetic to subversive movements" was quite typical. So too was the following allegation against a research engineer
requiring top-secret clearance: "Your statements over an extended period of time show your dissatisfaction with the U.S. form of government . . ." [9]

Few Americans were more aggressively and openly chauvinistic
than the military officers who grilled workers belonging to UE and
other unions when they were summoned before the IERB or the
Army, Navy and Air Force Personnel Security Board. In December
1947, M.T., a UE shop steward, was asked: "If this country went to
war, would you support it, whether it was right or wrong?" Workers
who had attended tenants' protest meetings against higher rents several years earlier were taken to task for it. "Where were your parents
born? Do you have any relatives in Europe?" a young UE activist was
asked in November 1949. Nor were the members of the Board conspicuously well informed: the periodical *In Fact* was wrongly described as "a paper published by the Communist Party" just as the
*National Guardian* was erroneously said to be "put out by the Communist Party," when suspended workers were accused of having read
these publications. Workers were also asked whether they had taken
active part in certain strikes and why they had supported the present
leadership of UE against Carey and the anti-Communists. [10]

## BREAKING THE LOCAL LEADERSHIP

Indeed this conflict surfaced very frequently when security charges
were brought against leaders of the various UE locals; without doubt
the IERB was in the union-busting business. For example, Leonard
Mollett, chief steward and a vice-president of UE Local 608, Syl-
vania, and Betty Jean Watson, a very young steward in the same local, were denied access to classified material and suspended in September 1949 after they had waged a successful campaign to oust
Mildred Turner, the anti-Communist president and business agent of
the local. Access to classified material was denied in April 1947 to
J.L., who was vice-president of District No. 1, UE, and an official in
Local 103, at the Radio Corporation of America plant at Camden,
New Jersey, largely because he was a member of the IWO and the
CRC. At the same time the Army, Navy and Air Force took con-
certed action to bar UE shop stewards and local officials from per-

forming their normal functions in restricted areas of factories, even though contracts between the union and the companies guaranteed such plant visitations to check on grievances.[11]

"I am married, have three children and am the sole support of myself and two of my children who are still going to school. My oldest son was in the Army." This was written by Mrs. Opal Cline, a shop steward at UE Local 1102, Emerson Electric, St. Louis, who had antagonized the company by fighting a cut in piece-work rates and by protesting the constant use of intimidating and abusive language toward women workers by department foremen. Having worked for Emerson since 1935, Opal Cline was denied access to classified material in April 1948, charged with "associating" with Communists, and offered a choice between a transfer and a layoff. She chose the transfer even though it involved a wage cut of 45 cents an hour. "Prior to my transfer . . . I was considered one of the faster operators and constantly produced at a rate of 150 percent or more, and earned $1.40 or more an hour." In September she was again suspended, this time on the ground that she had voiced too many complaints about piece-work rates and that she was making the other women dissatisfied with their 88 cents an hour. Unfortunately for Mrs. Cline, the executive board of Local 1102 took the view that workers removed for security reasons had no grievance, but the District and International unions came to her assistance. As William Sentner, the militant Communist president of UE District 8, put it when writing to the chairman of the IERB, Lieutenant Colonel Farr:

> Don't you think that you people have some obligation to workers like her who are trying to earn enough to keep themselves and their children in food and clothing. I think she is getting the dirtiest deal I have ever seen . . . This is a fine way to treat the mother of a boy who spent five years in the Army . . . have the American decency to give her a prompt hearing . . . It is about time that your Commander-in-Chief, Harry S. Truman, starts practicing some of the civil rights that he keeps yapping about.

Although the Board reversed Opal Cline's denial of clearance and affirmed her entitlement to back pay, Emerson Electric refused to reinstate her, and once again Local 1102 did nothing on her behalf. In rapid succession she was hired and fired at four St. Louis plants.[12]

Mrs. Cline's original suspension by Emerson had coincided with that of two other active trade unionists, Helen A. Sage and Matt Randle, a Negro militant known to be critical of management policies and of the restriction of black workers to jobs as laborers and porters. Helen Sage had worked at Emerson since 1941 and had frequently been at loggerheads with the management; in 1947 she had been threatened with dismissal for circulating a petition against the Taft-Hartley Act, and in January 1948 she had twice been questioned about her union and political activities. On April 14, she circulated a statement to all members of Local 1102: "It is because the Communist Party understands this greed for profits and knows how to help working people fight against it that I, as a Communist, am among the first to be hit." Even in 1948 such statements were rare. Sage, of course, was now doomed, and although she appeared before the IERB on the same day as Cline, the verdict against her was upheld. To the Board she had this to say: "[My work] was merely a spot check of the wire . . . used by the company . . . security could not have been the reason for my transfer . . . My fight against rate-cutting and speed-up concerning demands on the company to settle the grievances of the workers and the bad conditions in the department is the real reason the company has been trying to get rid of me." [13]

A UE memo written in April 1950 listed thirty-two members of the union hitherto involved in security cases; significantly, only three of them had been relatively inactive in the union: "Virtually all the others were active as shop stewards or local officers." Furthermore: "Factional charges of the Carey or similar groups appear to be the basis of instigating the denial in the cases of [seven persons named]. There are good grounds for believing that this is true in most cases." By the time (1956) that the secretary-treasurer of the AFL-CIO issued a warning that the security program must not become the private preserve of employers bent on destroying unions, many AFL and CIO unions had developed methods of exploiting the program with a view to destroying left-wing unions. [14]

Without doubt the Magnavox Company at Fort Wayne exploited the loyalty-security program in an attempt to break union solidarity, whether Communist or anti-Communist. UE's Local 910 circulated a memorandum about Magnavox's industrial-relations director, McClaren: "*Remember*: McClaren is the one who boasted of wrecking the 7-week IUE-CIO strike at the Paducah Magnavox plant . . . McClaren is the one who used every union-busting trick in the book to smash the CIO in the election at Greeneville Magnavox." To take a few examples of how this policy affected UE: in November 1951 UE District 9's recording secretary, Mrs. R.K., was denied clearance at Magnavox. Leroy Williams complained three years later that the company would no longer allow him to function as UE plant chairman in the processing of grievances after his clearance was revoked by the Central Industrial Personnel Security Board in Chicago. William Arthur Ives, a Magnavox employee for twenty years, was not allowed to function as president of UE Local 910 after his clearance was revoked.[15] Other cases confirmed the pattern and the evidence of collusion between the company and the government.

## THE COMMITTEES PRECIPITATE A PURGE

Among Congressional committees, a favorite pretext for intervention against UE was the imminence of an NLRB election in which the union was challenging, or being challenged by, an anti-Communist rival. The company, GE or Westinghouse, would petition for an NLRB election under the Taft-Hartley Act, then permit IUE free run of the plant for its campaign, and, when a Congressional committee appeared over the horizon, fire those UE militants who took the Fifth—*pour encourager les autres*. Even the President himself was not above the fray: "Please send my cordial greetings to the officers and members of the IUE-CIO," Truman wrote in 1949. "They will always oppose subversive activities in and out of the labor movement."

HCUA repeatedly subpoenaed national and local UE leaders and scheduled hearings to coincide with NLRB elections, as well as negotiations and strikes. It was done at Emporium, Mine Hall and Warren, in Pennsylvania, and at Cincinnati, Ohio; it was done in August 1951 at Lynn, Massachusetts, and at Schenectady, New York, a month later. It was done at Baltimore in July 1951, and at Fort Wayne, Indiana, in February 1955, to coincide with an NLRB election involving the UE at the Magnavox plant. The main target was UE's District 9 president, John T. Gojak; Francis E. Walter of HCUA told the press that the aim was to put UE out of business, and indeed UE duly lost the election.[16]

The impact of McCarthy on General Electric was generally electric. In October 1953 an article in the widely read *Saturday Evening Post*, bolstered by an indignant editorial, alerted the nation to the menace posed by Commies and subversives working in GE's plants at Schenectady and Lynn. This theme was quickly taken up by the local press and the wire services. Worried shareholders began to call GE's president, Ralph J. Cordiner; customers cabled their concern. As the nation's second-largest defense contractor, with contracts worth a billion dollars accounting for about 30 percent of the company's business, GE had to do something. Cordiner began immediately to formulate a new policy to improve the company's image, a policy which, he later testified under oath, he did not discuss "with anyone in government" or with any Congressional committee. Meanwhile, G. A. Price, president of Westinghouse, not only kept pace with GE's red-baiting but even outstripped it with a germ-theory suggestion that any worker who had participated in a Communist-dominated union should be presumed to have tainted any other labor organization with which he had associated.

On November 12, 1953, two employees of the Erie plant, Alexander Staber and John W. Nelson, appeared before the SISS in that Mecca of the inquisition, Pittsburgh. General Electric had suspended both men the day *before* their appearance. A devout Catholic who sent his children to Erie parochial schools, the thirty-six-year-old Nelson had served as president of UE's Local 506 since his honorable discharge from the Army in 1946, and in that capacity he had signed five Taft-Hartley non-Communist affidavits.

> MR. NELSON: I resent being called a saboteur.
> MR. ARENS: Would you resent being called a Communist?
> MR. NELSON: I have been called that many times.
> MR. ARENS: Well, is it true?
> MR. NELSON: I invoke the privilege of the Fifth Amendment.
> MR. ARENS: Now, as a hard-core Communist, what do you think of the Butler bill?
> MR. NELSON: As a loyal citizen of the United States of America, I think the Butler bill is a very infamous frameup to destroy my union and all other labor organizations . . .

Witnesses against him included the perjurious informer Joseph Mazzei, who testified that he knew Nelson to be a Communist, as well as the Pittsburgh attorney Harry Alan Sherman, business manager for Matt Cvetic, who claimed he had actually set eyes on Nelson's Party card.

Six days later McCarthy launched his own hearings in Albany and Boston. On November 17, the *Lynn Item* carried two streamer headlines: NLRB ORDERS GE UNION POLL; McCARTHY DUE TO QUIZ LYNN WORKERS ON RED TIES. Two days later McCarthy staged televised hearings in Boston, hot on the heels of the announcement of the NLRB election between UE and IUE at Lynn and Everett. A witness claiming to be an FBI agent said he knew of thirty Communists who were working in the Lynn plant; two of those he named were immediately suspended by GE; both had been active in UE's campaign to win back its bargaining rights at Lynn. Two other workers who appeared before McCarthy were expelled from the IUE and suspended by GE.[17]

In the course of the suit Nelson later brought against General Electric, UE's counsel David Scribner read from depositions taken from Alfred C. Stevens, an employee of GE, according to whom McCarthy's assistants, Roy Cohn, Frank Carr and George Anastos, met early in November at the Mohawk Club, Schenectady, with Stevens himself, a Mr. LaForge and Russ E. White, all representing GE.

Cohn and his colleagues had talked about their immediate objectives and asked for help in obtaining the addresses of the workers they wished to subpoena. "As I recall, Cohn, I think it was, made the general statement that industry was lax and that he hoped they would be alert to the situation and, in effect, he kind of threw out a general challenge for us to do something about what he proposed to reveal." This evidence tends to confirm that it was the politicians who reached out for the company, forcing it to collaborate or risk public castigation. After McCarthy subpoenaed some radical GE workers and made a fuss about the refusal of one of them, Henry Archdeacon, to say whether he was engaged in espionage, there was frenetic activity on the part of GE's President Cordiner and Vice-President Boulware.

On December 9, Cordiner issued new regulations providing for a ninety-day suspension of those employees who invoked the Fifth as to past or present Communist affiliation. Discharge would follow unless the questions were answered within ninety days. The rule was made retroactively applicable to all cases that had occurred within the previous six months. UE protested that the rule established a new condition of employment and violated the collective-bargaining contract, but the Company insisted that national security overrode any contract. In Cordiner's text, GE was presented as patriotically supervigilant:

> . . . the Company recommended that the Government agencies should also determine and direct when an employee should be excluded from civilian, as well as classified military work. This recommendation . . . was rejected [despite] the danger arising from having any possible subversives working on civilian jobs who might thereby find opportunities to associate and talk with employees doing confidential and secret work in the same or other building.

In an open letter to McCarthy, which in the event was not sent, Boulware went even further:

> . . . we have repeatedly urged and pleaded with Congress that legislation be promptly enacted . . . which would . . . render those unions identified as Communist-dominated wholly illegal and thus prevent their operations entirely . . . The necessity that we be able—practically overnight—to convert any GE plant from civilian to essential war work leads inevitably to the conclusion that neither we nor the country can tolerate at *any* plant . . . employees of doubtful loyalty . . . We will apply to the NLRB for a new representation election at all locations where UE is now the certified bargaining agent . . . We will urge the NLRB that

UE not be permitted on the ballot . . . unless present national and local officers . . . have been removed or cleared of Communist taint to the satisfaction of the FBI or other appropriate Government security agency.[18]

It is perhaps not surprising that GE decided not to release Boulware's panacea in which the workers' right to elect their own representatives was extinguished.

What were the consequences of the new policy? Twenty-eight employees at the Schenectady, Erie, Syracuse, Fitchburg, Louisville and Bridgeport plants were suspended, then dismissed. These men [19] were facing the loss of careers no less important to them than a Hollywood scriptwriter's to him, even though they earned in a year what Dalton Trumbo had once earned in two weeks.[20] Twenty-eight other workers now lost their seniority rights and the pension rights due to them at the age of sixty-five, with little possibility that other companies would take them on and even less that local unemployment-compensation boards would come to their assistance. Family men for the most part, they were condemned to disgrace and poverty, not for anything they had done, or were accused of doing, but for what they believed in—or, were assumed to believe in.

UE decided to bring a test case. John Nelson sued on behalf of himself and his colleagues for a declaratory judgment as to his right to work, for damages and injunctive relief. Resting his claim on the collective-bargaining contract between GE and UE, and on the Civil Rights Act, he contended that the company had conspired with the McCarthy Subcommittee to deprive him of his rights. (Nelson had in fact been subpoenaed by the SISS, but UE believed that GE's policy, as declared on December 9 by president Cordiner, had been inspired by the McCarthy staff. In fact all but four of those dismissed were subpoenaed by McCarthy; two fell to the SISS, and two to HCUA, which staggered in to the feast rather belatedly in April 1954.) The Nelson case dragged on until 1960, when it was dropped following the death of John W. Nelson himself at the early age of forty-three.

## COLLUSION AT WESTINGHOUSE

In the year of Nelson's death, UE lost another battle at the end of a campaign that demonstrated with unprecedented clarity the mechanics of collusion between a rival union, a company, and a Congressional committee. Two documents [21] illuminate the struggle. When Senator James O. Eastland brought the SISS to Baltimore early in 1960 to begin an investigation of Westinghouse's Air Arm Plant, an

NLRB election was due on March 25 to determine whether 1,200 workers should continue to be represented by UE, or should transfer their bargaining powers to the International Brotherhood of Electrical Workers (AFL-CIO). The company made its position clear in a press release: "In this election, our position is simply that we oppose the UE." A day later Westinghouse ran a large advertisement in the *Baltimore Sun*, calling for "defeat for UE," because "*Westinghouse cannot take chances with national defense*." [22]

On Tuesday, March 15, the arrival of two investigators from the SISS was loudly announced by the company's TV station, by the plant intercom system, and by the local press and radio. By 3:30 P.M., the company's television cameras were at the gates taking pictures of any workers who dared to talk with UE organizers; these pictures appeared on the TV news at 7:20 P.M. On the following day the company held a press conference and implied that defense orders would be lost if UE won the election. This supposed fear (many years had passed without such penalization) was also expressed in a letter the company sent to the homes of its employees, vigorously urging them to vote against UE. Meanwhile, radical members of UE were called before the two SISS investigators inside the plant amid rumors that discharges were imminent; many UE supporters now ripped off their UE buttons.

The third party in collusion was the rival union, the IBEW. Clarence E. Wallace, of Baltimore, submitted an extremely illuminating affidavit to the NLRB. Having worked at Air Arm from 1952 to 1956, Wallace had been employed since December 1959 as an assistant to Paul H. Menger at the IBEW's headquarters in Washington. In January 1960 Wallace was present, along with Menger and two other top IBEW officials, at a meeting in Washington with Edward Naumann, assistant to the president of Westinghouse Electric Corporation, at which Naumann complained that the campaign was going badly for the IBEW at Air Arm and that UE was leading in worker allegiance by 2 to 1. In the company's opinion, the IBEW was not using the Communist issue with sufficient vigor against UE: "Westinghouse had enough friends in Washington so as to possibly arrange for a Congressional committee investigation which could be carried out in some form during the election campaign at Air Arm." Menger remarked that more current material on James Matles and Julius Emspak, national officers of UE, and Louis Kaplan and Ed Bloch, UE organizers of the Air Arm campaign, was needed.

Naumann stressed that no one must know of his cooperation with IBEW, not even Mr. Lee, manager of industrial relations at the Air Arm plant—sometimes local management objected to the kind of thing he was doing.

Toward the end of January 1960 Tony Bucella, a national representative from the 4th District of the IBEW, told Menger that it would be necessary to bring into the Air Arm plant IBEW activists from other locations. Three politically experienced girls were called in from Local 1504, Indianapolis, and two "hot shot" machinists from Local 1470, Kearney, New Jersey. By arrangement with Westinghouse's Naumann, the five were taken onto the company's payroll. Their orders were to conceal their identity and affiliation, and merely to win the confidence of UE workers.

UE, having led by 2 to 1 early in January, in the company's estimation (perhaps exaggerated for effect, to stimulate the IBEW), duly lost the election on March 15. In the opinion of UE counsel Frank Donner, it was the most brazen such operation ever undertaken against the union.[23]

# 21

## On the Waterfront

Even before the port-security program was formally inaugurated in 1950, East Coast seamen and longshoremen with radical backgrounds were being picked off one by one, abandoned to their fate by their anti-Communist or racket-ridden unions. When Benjamin Rutter, a shipyard worker and secretary-treasurer of Local 401, the International Sheet Metal Workers Union, AFL, came before a Brooklyn Naval Shipyard Loyalty Board composed exclusively of Navy officers in December 1947, he insisted that he had never been a Communist, but admitted membership of the Jewish People's Fraternal Order, an affiliate of the listed IWO. He was asked:

> Is it true that you were present at a meeting of radicals in Madison Square Garden during the war?
> Do you consider that a member of the Communist Party or its affiliates is guilty of treason against the United States?
> Which newspapers do you read?
> To what publications or book club do you subscribe?
> Does Lion Feuchtwanger write for [the Book Find Club]?
> Would you say that your wife has liberal political viewpoints?

Benjamin Rutter was fired for "disloyalty" after ten years' service.

In February 1948 the Loyalty Board convened to consider the case of Charles Oscar Matson, a fire-control mechanic born in Sweden and *for thirty years* employed in the Brooklyn Naval Shipyard. Matson denied Party membership and said that he disliked Communists and that he had always voted Democrat or for the ALP. Having agreed that he occasionally visited the Workers' Bookshop on 13th Street—such admissions were fatal with these naval officers—he was asked:

> How many books did you buy?
> What kind of books did [the Literary Guild] put out? . . . Did they put out books by Theodore Dreiser? . . . Feuchtwanger? . . . Have you read . . . Howard Fast?
> What do you think of the Truman Doctrine?
> What do you think of the Italian situation?
> Did you ever go to the Stanley Theater?

(The Stanley Theater specialized in Soviet and other foreign films.) Matson was fired in the evening of his working life; what could he do for work now? Also dismissed from the Naval Shipyard was an artisan who evidently failed to provide a reassuring answer to the question "Do you think that Jacques Duclos or De Gaulle would offer France a greater chance of recuperation?" [1]

## THE PORT-SECURITY PROGRAM

In July 1950 the government invited the maritime employers and the non-Communist maritime unions to attend a conference in Washington convened by the Secretaries of Labor and Commerce. The objective was to break Communist influence on the waterfront and to crush the ILWU and the Marine Cooks and Stewards, two West Coast unions recently expelled from the CIO for heresy. (In fact, three anti-Communist locals of the ILWU attended the conference.) All parties involved agreed that the nerve center of the purge should be the Coast Guard served by the files of the FBI and Naval Intelligence, with the anti-Communist unions themselves providing the necessary extra muscle to chase all reds off all ships. A month later Congress endorsed the proposed purge by passing the Magnuson Act, which provided for the screening of all seamen and waterfront men by the Coast Guard. (Covered barges on the Great Lakes and the Western rivers were also included.)

In December the Coast Guard announced that henceforward maritime workers must as a condition of employment apply for security cards, which would be denied where there was reasonable ground to believe that a man was subject to the influence of a foreign government. Dismissal would almost automatically follow denial of clearance. Applications were checked in Washington for derogatory information; those denied clearance were entitled to appear before a

Review Board accompanied by counsel, although they were not entitled to learn more about the charges than the chairman of the Regional Board chose to disclose. What this could mean in practice was well illustrated when an attorney wrote to the Coast Guard in 1952 requesting detailed charges on behalf of a seaman. He was informed in reply that "the rules of evidence do not apply to proceedings of this nature hence specificity of charges are [sic] not necessary." But the role of the Regional Board was advisory only; the final decision rested with the local Coast Guard Commandant. The appeal mechanism was slow; reporting some two hundred appeals on file in April 1951, the Northern California ACLU noted that the average appeal took six months. Those men who were fortunate enough to be cleared on appeal received no compensation at all for the pay they had lost while under suspension.

The purge began with a bang: "The Heat Is On," declared *The New York Times* on August 20, 1950, reporting that about one hundred men had been pulled off ships within only two weeks. On one ship nearly forty men had been forbidden to sign the ship's articles. Early in September, Captain Theodore R. Weitzel arrived on the West Coast at the head of a twenty-eight-member security team to screen stevedores. Later in the month Captain Henry T. Jewell, chief of the Coast Guard's personnel division, admitted that many "loyal Americans" had been barred by mistake, but he refused to say how many, or how many had been reinstated.[2]

Before we turn to individual cases, we should emphasize the role of the anti-Communist unions in the purge that followed. Joe Curran's National Maritime Union, CIO, the West Coast Marine Firemen and the Seafarer's International Union, AFL, were among the keenest in turning in the names of their own radical members to the Coast Guard. Known Communists like Walter Stack of the Firemen's Union were immediately screened out. Indeed, only one month after the passage of the Magnuson Act the NMU went so far as to complain that the crew of the liner *America* had not been screened thoroughly enough. The radical unions, particularly the Marine Cooks and Stewards, with about 4,000 members, the Masters, Mates and Pilots and the Marine Engineers were soon decimated. Each had to contend with its own fifth column: within the MCS, for example, a dissident progovernment faction known as "the Dirty Dozen" and regarded by their colleagues as stoolpigeons, fought secretary Hugh Bryson's opposition to the Korean war and even won a court case over it. In NLRB elections the AFL-CIO rival union with the same name won a series of government-supported victories (Senator Hubert Humphrey's Labor and Labor-Management Relations

Subcommittee got into the act in January 1953) that ultimately deprived the MCS of its bargaining rights and therefore its *raison d'être*. The Justice Department did its bit by indicting Hugh Bryson for perjuriously signing the Taft-Hartley non-Communist affidavit, for which he served a three-year prison sentence. Nor was solidarity on the Left all that it might have been: MCS militants comment bitterly that Harry Bridges's pro-Communist but less vulnerable ILWU turned its back; Joseph Starobin recalls that the much hounded Frederick N. "Blackie" Myers of the NMU had difficulty finding work in San Francisco, where Bridges was king.[3] As for ILWU longshoremen who were denied clearance, they were normally able to find alternative work on nonmilitary piers to which the Security Program did not extend.

"Len Roberts," a seaman who first arrived in San Francisco in 1939 and became an MCS official a year later, remembers how in the late thirties, in the glowing aftermath of the great dock strike of 1934, solidarity was tight enough to ensure that if a man was fired off a ship, everybody walked off. By the fifties rates of pay had vastly improved but the bonds of working-class solidarity had slackened; the anti-Communist inquisition was designed to snap the last ties. Whenever a ship signed on a crew, a Coast Guard officer was on hand carrying a blacklist of names and serial numbers. "Len Roberts" recalls how on the SS *Lurline*, a passenger ship of the Matson Steamship Company, they screened off as many as twenty in a single trip.

The criteria by which the Regional Boards operated followed the familiar channels of conformity. Because his brother was alleged to be a Communist, a member of the engine crew of a Standard Oil tanker was screened from his job in November 1950, although at a hearing in March 1951 it was admitted that the two brothers didn't get along well or agree politically. George B. Rogers, a steward for sixteen years and a member of the MCS, assured an appeal hearing in Seattle in 1951 that he had always been opposed to Communism; apparently the only derogatory information against him was that he had twice rented the basement of his house to Progressive Party members for fund-raising parties, although he did not attend himself. He had also bought a ticket in a raffle sponsored by the Northwest Labor School. Rogers was denied clearance.[4]

James D. Tucker, having been screened off his ship in July 1951, had a hearing in San Francisco a month later before a Security Appeals Board consisting of chairman George S. Franklin and two other members, representing management and labor. Tucker, who had a chief mate's license, admitted membership in the CP from 1934 to 1936. When asked about the 1934 strike, he insisted that the cause of the unions and of the Communists had been identical then; but since that time he had changed his mind about the Party. Franklin asked him:

> How about your boy, has he been going to Sunday school?
> Does your wife go to church regularly?
> What do you read? What papers?

Franklin was a chairman very keen to open a little window into his own almost perfect way of life:

> You have no stable church affiliations and that harmonizes with my understanding of Communist practices. I don't attend church as regularly as I'd like to, but my boy goes to Sunday school . . . a lot of these people we talk to, we go into their church affiliations quite strenuously . . .

Now Ashfield E. Stow, the Board member representing management, began to ventilate his own obsessions:

> All right, I was on the other side of the 1934 strike . . . Mrs. Perkins . . . and the government of the United States gave us very little comfort and no help at all . . . I think you had a whole lot of help from the government in the strike, I really sincerely do.
>
> Now, suppose for the sake of arguing . . . a lot of employers got together and were successful in getting up a union-busting organization . . . would you go to the Communist Party for help?

Tucker, obviously an intelligent man still faithful to his early beliefs, was informed that he was a security risk. Not until January 1956, nearly five years later, was he granted clearance.[5]

This and many similar cases are recorded in the files of Ernest Besig, a lawyer of strong liberal principles who for many years vigorously headed the Northern California ACLU. Among other cases:

James L. Kendall, a merchant seaman and a member of the MCS, was adjudged a security risk by the Coast Guard in January 1951. A Negro who had been at sea for thirty years and a member of the union since 1941, he came before a Security Appeals Board under the chairmanship of Tilden H. Edwards three months later and denied that he had ever been in the CP.

> QUESTION: Have you ever seen [the *Daily People's World*] in the Marine Cooks and Stewards Hall?
> ANSWER: Oh yes, it's always there . . .

Kendall explained that under Hugh Bryson's leadership blacks like himself had for the first time been able to get work on ships:

QUESTION: Is that what sold you on the present leadership of the union?
ANSWER: That is what I'm trying to get at now. I'm leaving it to you. Who would you support if you were in my place? . . . I have supported Communists in our union for pure economic reasons.

Certain things counted against Kendall: Paul Robeson had been a guest in his house in the summer of 1950 (and what could be worse than that?); he also admitted having signed a petition for Wallace, but insisted that he finally voted for Truman. Questioned on the subject, he agreed that the MCS collected money on behalf of screened-off seamen; the union patrolman visited each ship at the payoff and asked members to contribute. He was asked:

You are friendly with Mr. Bryson, aren't you?
Have you ever attended left-wing meetings?

Almost desperately he insisted: "Nothing in the Soviet Union would interest me." He wished—but did he really?—the MCS had taken the opposite line and supported the United States government's intervention in Korea. When Chairman Edwards asked: "What do you believe? That is what we are concerned with," Kendall said:

I don't know if the Communists are dangerous to the security of the United States. I don't think they have ever done anything that I have seen that is against the country . . . The leaders are using us but we are also using them . . . to get decent jobs . . . It's a kind of mutual exploitation.

Having raised the awful specter of Eddie Tangen, one of the Communist leaders of the MCS, Edwards repeatedly hammered at Kendall's beliefs about the CP's purposes and ties with the Soviet Union. Unfortunately for Kendall, being a Mason and a member of the Methodist church in Sacramento did not atone for having signed the Stockholm Peace Pledge; and when he insisted that he had never heard Bryson speak of Russia or war with Russia, no one took any notice. His appeal was turned down.[6]

Thirty-six-year-old Frank C. Drum, a member of Local 10, ILWU, received a letter from the Coast Guard in May 1951: "You are affiliated with or sympathetic to the principles of organizations, associations, groups or combinations of persons, subversive or disloyal to the government of the United States." Therefore no port-security card could be issued to him. In September Drum came before the Security Appeals Board again chaired by George S. Franklin. A member of the ILWU since 1943 and previously a labor representative for the Steel Workers Organizing Committee from 1936 to 1942, Drum was accused of having acted as a pallbearer at Tom Mooney's funeral in 1942, and of having sponsored Russian War Relief. By now Drum was fairly eager to disown the Communists and accused them of throwing sand in the eyes of the workers. But Chairman Franklin wanted to know how a good Catholic could have been so close to the Commies, and Board member Stow, too, reactivated his obsession— Would Drum turn to the Communists for help if "some forces were ruining your union, so you practically didn't have any protection on the waterfront?" Drum said he wouldn't; but his appeal was denied. Nearly five years elapsed before the Coast Guard informed him that he was no longer regarded as a security risk.[7]

What happened to the seamen who were suspended or dismissed? Some found work on foreign-flag vessels (about 730 privately owned vessels transferred to foreign registration between 1939 and 1951 in order to be able to pay lower wages). Others left the sea for good, haunted by the fear that the past would catch up with them. Norval Welch, director of the Seamen's Defense Committee Against Coast Guard Screening, reflected such fears as late as January 1964, when he declined to put his knowledge of such fugitives at the disposal of Professor Paul Tillett. Into whose hands, Welch wondered, would the data fall if the present directors of the project were to leave Rutgers? Of the large number of victimized seamen known to him, many had never recovered psychologically from being deprived of the only work they knew. Nor, Welch stressed, had this kind of persecution ended ten years later; the FBI and other agencies continued to track down former radicals with the aim of obtaining their discharge from whatever work they had found. Out of self-defense some seamen had changed their names, moved to remote areas, and invented fictitious personal histories.[8]

## THE COAST GUARD AND THE COURTS

A major defeat was suffered by the Coast Guard when, in October 1955, the Ninth Circuit Court of Appeals (California) considered the case of some seamen who had been refused clearance without adequate charges or the right to confront hostile witnesses. The Court asked: "Is this system of secret informers, whisperers and talebearers of such vital importance to the public welfare that it must be preserved at the cost of denying to the citizen even a modicum of the protection traditionally associated with due process?" In an important judgment (*Parker v. Lester*), the Court said no and ordered the Coast Guard henceforward to permit the defendant access to the evidence against him as well as confrontation with hostile witnesses.

In April 1956 the Coast Guard amended its regulations accordingly, and after further litigation the Court ordered that the licenses of all those who had lost them must be restored pending the implementation of the new procedures. On August 27 the Ninth Circuit Court of Appeals voted by 2 to 1 to uphold federal Judge Edward P. Murphy's injunction ordering the Coast Guard to issue sailing papers "forthwith." In November the Coast Guard finally complied, but it did so in as vindictive a manner as possible, issuing credentials specially stamped "Order of U.S. District Court" so as to ensure that the seamen remained branded.[9] Furthermore, the Coast Guard continued to reserve the right to conceal its informants where "national security" was involved.

Meanwhile, on the East Coast the forbidden practices continued. In April 1956, attorneys for seven screened-off seamen filed a complaint in the District Court of the District of Columbia, requesting injunctive relief (*Kasik v. Richmond*). In October Judge David Pine ordered the Coast Guard to give hearings to the seven. The Coast Guard's attorney then assured the Emergency Civil Liberties Committee attorney representing the seamen that about five hundred blacklisted seamen on the East Coast would now have their papers restored to them.

Almost half a million seamen were affected by the port-security program; taking into account the turnover among maritime workers, some 800,000 men had been screened by 1958. The toll of lost jobs was extremely high—higher than in any other trade or profession.[10]

By December 31, 1956, there had been 3,783 denials of clearance, of which about 2,500 affected seamen and about 1,300 affected waterfront men. (Roughly one fifth of the total worked in the San Francisco area, focal point of maritime radicalism.) Thus, approximately 0.6 percent of all waterfront men lost their jobs due to the purge. Although in principle *Parker v. Lester* "cleared" them all at a single stroke, it is doubtful whether more than a handful carrying the new, invidiously stamped credentials were able to find work. The right-wing unions simply refused to take them back, particularly the Engineers, the Firemen and the NMU. Typical was the case of Frank Lundquist, of Palo Alto, California: according to the rules of the Marine Engineers Beneficial Association, in order to secure reinstatement he needed only to pay three months' dues in advance, plus $50, and to show that he had not worked as a marine engineer while he held his withdrawal card. After Lundquist's security card was returned to him by the Coast Guard, he paid the union his fees and waited for his papers. None came. In the end he sued.[11]

# PART SIX

---

# Purge
# of the Professions

# 22

## Purge of the "Reducators"

The pressures on the professions to conform were now immense. The Post Office and the Customs Bureau embarked on a massive—and largely illegal—program of censorship. It was in 1948 that the Post Office began a full-scale interception and opening of mail from certain countries. The Customs seized and held huge quantities of printed matter, much of it solicited by American citizens, so that even specialist scholars and university libraries found themselves studying the enemy in a void. As Abe Goff, Post Office Solicitor (and chief censor) put it: "If ignorant people read it, they might begin to believe it." [1]

The record of the professional associations in the face of such pressures was less than admirable—with a few exceptions, notably the American Library Association and certain bar associations. By 1952 the New York State Medical Society had introduced a loyalty oath; by 1954, the state's Association of Architects, the same. The American Bar Association and the American Medical Association (seized by a fear of socialized medicine) were in competition for the Purple Heart of anti-Communism, with the ABA proposing political tests for admission to the bar, suggesting that lawyers who advised clients to invoke the Fifth Amendment on political matters should be driven from the profession, applauding the work of HCUA and the SISS, and so vehemently attacking the liberalism of the Warren Court that the Chief Justice himself resigned from the ABA in 1957 in disgust.

The American teaching profession has almost invariably stood exposed as a target for suspicion and aggression at times of superpatriotic sensitivity. During the First World War quite a few professors suspected of pacifism or pro-German sentiment were shown the door. Between 1917 and 1923, charges of disloyalty were leveled against teachers in thirteen states; teachers were actually fired in eight. Such was the fear during the "Red Scare"—Harding's Commissioner of Education declared his intention of eliminating "Communism, Bolshevism, and Socialism" from schools—that the American Federation of Teachers lost about half of its 10,000 members.

By 1940 twenty-one states had introduced loyalty oaths for teachers. From 1942 to 1946 there was a hiatus in oath incantations (America being temporarily allied to the devil) followed by five or six frantic years during which a further fifteen states plunged into loyalty legislation, even though the conservative National Education Association unanimously condemned oaths designed exclusively for teachers. Indeed, in some areas additional affirmations were required by local school boards. Six states specifically barred teachers who belonged to the CP, but the Kansas oath was more typical:

> I,————, swear [or affirm] that I do not advocate, nor am I a member of any political party or organization that advocates the overthrow of the government of the United States or of the State by force or violence . . .

Thirteen states imposed on teachers oaths explicitly disclaiming membership of a list of organizations usually based on the Attorney General's list, but sometimes garnishing it.

Pressures on colleges and schools tended to be implicit when federal, explicit when locally instigated; although explicit enough was HCUA's letter of June 1949 to eighty-one colleges and high schools, demanding lists of textbooks in use in the fields of literature, economics, government, history, political science, social science and geography. The military authorities demanded the right to scrutinize the curricula of about two hundred colleges engaged in classified work under military contract; in 1953 fourteen of forty-six universities refused to renew their contracts with the U.S. Armed Forces Institute because it added a clause endowing itself with the power to veto faculty members conducting correspondence courses under the scheme.[2]

Schools and colleges were governed very rarely by educators, but more commonly by businessmen, bankers, lawyers and, in the case of state universities, by politicians. By 1950 such people accounted for about 80 percent of university trustees or regents. For example, the trustees of the University of Washington at the time of the 1948–49 purge were seven in number: two attorneys, two major industrialists, an investment broker, the corrupt vice-president of the Teamsters, Dave Beck—and a solitary liberal educator. The Board of Regents of the University of California at the time of the loyalty-oath calamity included an osteopath who specialized in property deals, a lawyer who sold his interest in a gold mine for $325,000, two prominent members of Associated Farmers employing sweated Mexican labor and the president of the largest bank in the world, the Bank of America, who declared, "I feel sincerely that if we rescind this oath flags will fly in the Kremlin."

Whereas in Britain the universities have been carefully shielded from transitory public pressures, the heads of American colleges have had to face the rude winds of populist intolerance. A statement put out in March 1953 by the Association of American Universities indicated acquiescence: "The state university is supported by public funds. The endowed university is benefited by tax exemptions. Such benefits are conferred upon universities not as favors but in furtherance of the public interest." While most heads of colleges paid pious lip service to "free, untrammeled research and intellectual speculation," almost all were agreed, like President James B. Conant of Harvard, that CP members were "out of bounds as members of the teaching profession." A distinguished liberal, Mrs. Millicent McIntosh, president of Barnard, explained: "If the colleges take the responsibility to do their own house cleaning, Congress would not feel it has to investigate." [3]

Across the country universities barred controversial speakers; in 1955 the University of Washington distinguished itself by banning an address by J. Robert Oppenheimer. Under Superintendent Hobart M. Corning the District of Columbia school system made a practice of embargoing speakers listed by HCUA, and of submitting names to the Committee for clearance.

The professors and teachers themselves suffered from lack of tenure, low salaries, low status. More than half of American teachers lacked any kind of tenure protection, and only 60,000 out of one million were bold enough to join the American Federation of Teachers. In 1954–55 the average secondary-school teacher was earning $4,194, compared to the automobile worker's wage of $4,947. Indeed the average of assistant professors was also lower than that of automobile workers. Nothing wrong with that; but, whereas in Europe low-paid professionals can enjoy a high status and the self-confidence that goes with it, in America money has tended to operate as the indicator of public esteem. In short, here was a profession it was all too easy to bully and browbeat.

Not surprisingly, the profession bent its knee to the *Zeitgeist*. The National Education Association, with 425,000 members and 800,000 affiliates, declared in June 1949 that CP members had surrendered the right to think for themselves and therefore the right to teach. Professor Sidney Hook's influential discourses on this subject—he was short of evidence that Communist teachers actually indoctrinated their pupils, but argued deductively from a few dated Party texts—were thus accepted. It was in 1952 that the AFT resolved not to defend any teacher proven to be a Communist, or who refused to deny that he was one. Only the American Association of University Professors attempted to combat political discrimination in education.

The political purges that hit American colleges and schools during the Truman-Eisenhower era cost at least six hundred, and probably more, teachers and professors their jobs, about 380 of them in New York City. The scale of intimidation was partly reflected in a survey conducted in 1955 of 2,451 social-science teachers, in 165 colleges and universities, who reported 386 incidents involving allegations of Communism, subversion or fellow-traveling, 10 percent of which resulted in dismissal or forced resignation. In a further 108 cases involving charges of "leftist" political sympathies or activities (almost invariably sympathies), no fewer than 16 percent culminated in dismissal or forced resignation.[4]

## COMMUNIST INFLUENCE IN THE TEACHING PROFESSION

How strong was authentic Communist commitment in the teaching and academic professions when the postwar purge was launched? In 1935 the Party reported that 425 teachers were members; three years later, at the height of the CP's popularity, as many as 440 teachers joined it in a single year. Bella Dodd claimed that about 1,500 school teachers had been Party members or—a large or—"sympathetic" to the CP at one time or another, and she listed a number of colleges where Communist units had flourished, notably the city colleges of New York, NYU, Columbia, Long Island University, Vassar, Wellesley, Smith, Harvard, MIT, Chicago, Northwestern, California, Howard and Minnesota. It was certainly the case in the late thirties and middle forties that Communist groups were active in the city colleges of New York, where red teachers issued "shop papers" like *Teacher-Worker* at CCNY and *Staff* at Brooklyn (as well as *Spark* at Columbia). Elsewhere, however, the numbers involved were minuscule; at Harvard, where a CP unit was organized in 1937 by William T. Parry and Louis Harap, and joined by Granville Hicks, Daniel Boorstin, Robert Gorham Davis and Wendell Furry, there were never more than twelve or fourteen avowed Communists out of a faculty of some two thousand. What is more, these incendiaries made no effort to influence Harvard students; they confined their militant teaching to the classes they conducted at the Central Labor School and the Samuel Adams School, Boston.[5]

## CASUALTIES OF 1948

The Progressive Party campaign in 1948 precipitated collisions and a crop of academic casualties. Activity on behalf of the party or its presidential candidate, Henry A. Wallace, in a climate of mounting Cold War tension, brought about a considerable number of dismissals.[6] One of the most interesting cases occurred at Evansville College, Indiana, whose board of trustees was dominated by the Methodist church and the local Chamber of Commerce. These dignitaries were greatly scandalized when a young teacher, George F. Parker, not only emerged as chairman of the Vandenberg County organization for Wallace, but was even photographed with Wallace in Evansville. So high did local feeling run that when Dr. Lincoln B. Hale, president of the college, next called in at the Rotary Club, he felt as if he had contracted smallpox (as he put it). Deluged with protests and forgetting that he had recently distributed to his faculty an admirable address stressing the right, indeed the duty, of professors to participate in civic affairs, Hale dismissed Parker on April 7 for "political activity both on and off the campus." Although the college did honor its contract and paid Parker in full for the rest of the year, the AAUP investigated the affair and felt compelled to condemn Evansville College for "failure to understand and support the principles of academic freedom." [7]

At Oregon State College, both Dr. L. R. LaVallee, assistant professor of economics, and Dr. Ralph W. Spitzer, associate professor of chemistry, were vigorous Wallace supporters. In February 1949 the college's president, Dr. A. L. Strand, announced that their contracts would not be renewed. He complained that Spitzer had published a letter in the *Chemical and Engineering News* (January 1949) in which, Strand claimed, he had supported the theories of Trofim D. Lysenko—"he goes right down the party line without any noticeable deviation." When Dr. Linus Pauling, president of the American Chemical Society, wrote protesting Spitzer's dismissal, Strand said in reply, "how much impudence do we have to stand for to please the pundits of dialectical materialism? . . . academic freedom entails some discipline in regard to truth." [8] As for LaVallee, he continued to lead a politically turbulent career; in 1956 following his appearance before HCUA, he was dismissed from Dickinson College.

## THE UNIVERSITY OF WASHINGTON

In the State of Washington the Joint Legislative Fact-Finding Committee on Un-American Activities under Senator Albert F. Canwell began hearings on the University of Washington in July 1948,[9] inspired by the claim of State Senator Bienz that "probably not less than 150 on the University of Washington faculty are Communists or sympathizers." The university's Board of Regents hastened to welcome the Canwell investigation and promised to dismiss any subversives uncovered. In preparation for the open hearings, the Committee staff grilled some forty members of the faculty in private, searching out possible informers and inviting students to denounce their teachers. In the end, ten members of the faculty were named; five agreed that they had been Communists in the past, two denied any association with the CP, and three refused to testify. In September 1948 the university's Board of Regents filed charges against the latter three (Herbert J. Phillips, Joseph Butterworth and Ralph Gundlach) and also against three who, while admitting past membership, had declined to discuss their colleagues (Garland Ethel, Harold Eby and Melville Jacobs). An Academic Tenure Committee then conducted hearings to consider the administration's charge that CP membership violated the university's Administrative Code, because it involved (a) incompetency, (b) neglect of duty and (c) dishonesty or immorality.

Herbert J. Phillips, a fifty-seven-year-old member of the philosophy department, told the Tenure Committee quite frankly that he had been a loyal member of the Party since 1935, though he insisted that every man had a "sacred obligation" to reach his own independent conclusions which, in his own case, included a belief in God and a sympathy for the "platonic theory of universals"—both strictly deviationary in Marxist terms. "He had an inexhaustible fund of witty stories, a shrewd capacity to penetrate into another person's mind, a superb skill in philosophical argument . . . the contemporary philosopher he admired most was Alfred North Whitehead . . ." Not only did five of his former students testify that, far from indoctrinating his class, he warned it of his Marxist bias, but six of his colleagues came forward to describe him as able, objective and candid.

Joseph Butterworth, a fifty-one-year-old associate professor of English who had joined the department in 1929 and was writing about "The Textual Tradition of Chaucer's Minor Poems," also admitted current Party membership. Five graduate students attested to his qualities as a teacher. A colleague, Melvin Rader, has recently recalled of Butterworth: "I thought of him as a tragic figure—a crippled and lonely man, whose wife had committed suicide and whose only child had been committed to an institution." Although Ralph H. Gundlach, associate professor of psychology and a member of the psychology department since 1927, denied ever having joined the CP, the university administration imported four Canwell Committee witnesses to try to prove the contrary. Gundlach's record was certainly a radical one: his associations included the Seattle Labor School, the Medical Bureau to Aid Spanish Democracy and the JAFRC. When Melville Jacobs, associate professor of anthropology and an admitted former Communist, was asked at his faculty trial whether he was likely to participate in radical politics again, he replied: "In my present frame of mind, something would have to happen to some of the cells in my cerebrum before anybody could persuade me even to touch politics with a ten-foot pole after what I have been through." [10]

When the Tenure Committee reported to President Raymond Allen in January 1949, eight of its eleven members recommended that all those on trial be retained, none of them having violated the Administrative Code. The minority recommended that Gundlach be dismissed for "neglect of duty." The next move belonged to President Allen, a fighting Cold Warrior who had warned the faculty in the fall of 1947 that if Commies were masquerading as liberals they had better get out before they were "smoked out." Now, in his report to the Regents, Allen disregarded the majority report of the Committee on Tenure (though he argued elsewhere that he had done no such thing) [11] and recommended the dismissal of Phillips and Butterworth, on the ground that they had been guilty of "jeopardizing the academic freedom of the University of Washington by becoming secret members of a clandestine party dedicated to the overthrow of American institutions of freedom."

It was this kind of prose that earned Allen the support of the Seattle Real Estate Board, the Amvets, the Legion, the Central Labor Council and the Chamber of Commerce—and of the Regents themselves, who decided to dismiss Phillips, Butterworth and Gundlach without severance pay. Eby, Ethel and Jacobs were put on probation for two years on condition that they formally renounce all sympathy or connection with the CP. Although one hundred members of the faculty filed a protest, Allen cried loudly that the classroom must be the "chapel of democracy," that teachers must be "the priests of the temple" and that it was those whom he had fired who had violated academic freedom. A year earlier the Canwell Committee's chief counsel, William J. Houston, had prophesied: "Teachers are going to get fired at the University . . . They will be unable to find new teaching posts elsewhere." He was right; neither Phillips, Butterworth nor

Gundlach was ever able to return to academic life. In fact Phillips spent three months in jail before being acquitted of contempt before the State Superior Court in 1949. Four years later he was a defense witness in the Seattle Smith Act trial.

In May 1948, two months before the Committee opened its hearings, a pair of investigators knocked on the office door of Professor Melvin Rader: "Our information puts you in the center of the Communist conspiracy." When Rader demurred, the Committee imported from New York the black professional informer George Hewitt, who swore that Rader had in 1939 attended a secret CP summer school in New York State at which Hewitt had served as an instructor. Certainly Rader had been on the Left—a member of the League against War and Fascism, a sponsor of the JAFRC in Seattle and the author of a book published in 1939 that treated the new Soviet constitution as widening the traditional liberal notions of human rights. Houston asked Rader, "Do you believe in the capitalist form of government [sic] as it exists in the United States today?"

At home the Rader family began to receive hostile phone calls— "Communist rat," et cetera. When Rader applied for a loan at the National Bank of Commerce, an embarrassed official explained that his tenure now appeared insufficiently secure. In order to refute Hewitt and document his actual movements during the summers of 1938, 1939 and 1940, he was obliged to cancel his summer teaching at UCLA and a sabbatical at the Hoover Library, Stanford, for which he had a Rockefeller grant. When Hewitt fled, vested interests ensured that he was not extradited from New York to stand trial for perjury. In May 1950 State Attorney General Troy announced that the Canwell Committee had actually had in its possession clear documentary evidence of Rader's innocence when it officially accused him of lying. It was a dirty business.

At the University of Colorado the Regents brought in two former FBI bloodhounds to sniff out campus subversives. Morris Judd, a philosophy instructor who in 1947 had blotted his copybook by opposing the ban on the campus chapter of the AYD, and who now refused to talk with the bloodhounds, was given a terminal contract. The second victim was a confessed former Communist, Irving Goodman, whose contract as assistant professor of chemistry was not renewed.

## MIT AND HARVARD

Meanwhile, the center of the storm at the Massachusetts Institute of Technology was the Dutch-born professor of mathematics Dirk Struik, a devoted Stalinist, coeditor of *Science and Society*, a cofounder of the Jefferson School and an obvious target for the Massachusetts Special Commission on Communism under the chairmanship of State Senator Philip Bowker. When Herbert Philbrick broke cover in 1949 to testify at the Foley Square trial, he alleged that Struik, a member of a "top-secret Pro-4 group," had lectured in December 1947 to the Communists of Cambridge and had described the revolution in Indonesia as a model. In September 1951 Struik was indicted under a Massachusetts criminal-anarchy statute for conspiracy to advocate and incite the violent overthrow of the Commonwealth of Massachusetts and of the United States. MIT suspended him on full pay. Proceedings dragged slowly. In April 1953 three of Struik's colleagues turned informer against him; appearing before HCUA, Professors William T. Martin, Norman Levinson and Isador Amdur testified that he had attended the same meetings as they when they were Party members.[12] Struik invoked the Fifth. For five years Struik remained in limbo, forbidden to teach yet receiving full pay until the indictment against him was dismissed in May 1956 following the Supreme Court's ruling in the Steve Nelson case. On his retirement in July 1960 Struik became professor emeritus. Less fortunate was Professor Lawrence B. Arguimbau, also of MIT, who confessed before the SISS in April 1953 that he had been a Party member from 1937 to 1950, but declined to name others on moral grounds. He was forced to resign. After finding work with a New York manufacturer, he was some time later able to secure industrial employment in New England and so be reunited with his family. He never went back to teaching.

MIT's Cambridge neighbor, Harvard, came under attack in 1953 from both McCarthy's Permanent Subcommittee on Investigations and the SISS. Helen Deane Markham, assistant professor of anatomy in the Harvard Medical School since 1944, took the Fifth Amendment on a wide range of political questions, including CP membership, when she appeared before the SISS on March 27. Privately she confided to the five-man Harvard Corporation that she had never belonged to the Party, although she had been active in the Progressive Party and had taught at the Samuel Adams School, Boston, in 1948. In June she was informed that she would not be reappointed a year hence, in June 1954. At this juncture, Herbert Philbrick testified before the SISS that Helen Deane Markham and her husband had been CP members in 1947; another witness swore that he had paid dues to her while she was treasurer of the Harvard branch of the CP. The Corporation thereupon suspended her with pay, pending the outcome of a new investigation. On August 31, Harvard announced that, while not entirely convinced by Dr. Markham's version, it intended to reinstate her for the remainder of the academic year.

The challenge from McCarthy forced the Corporation into several general positions of principle. It declined to adopt a blanket rule about faculty members who invoked the Fifth Amendment; Provost Paul H. Buck stressed that each such case would be judged on its merits. Yet on May 20 the Corporation announced that the use of the Fifth was not consistent with the candor to be expected of someone devoted to the pursuit of truth. "We will not shut our eyes to the inferences of guilt which the use of the Fifth Amendment creates as a matter of common sense."

The day before Helen Deane Markham faced the Jenner Committee, Leon J. Kamin took the Fifth Amendment on past membership, although he denied present membership. Kamin had entered Harvard in 1944 at the age of sixteen and joined the CP a year later. By 1949 he was writing for the *Daily Worker* under the name of Leo Soft. New England editor of the paper and a regular Party employee, he dropped out without a formal resignation about July 1950, and in September 1951 he began part-time teaching at Harvard. His confrontation with the SISS in March 1953 was followed by one with McCarthy ten months later, by which time he was prepared to admit past membership but refused to discuss his associates. Having taken refuge as a research assistant at Queen's University, Ontario, he returned to face trial for contempt in October 1955. After a boisterous appearance in court by McCarthy had led the liberal Judge Bailey Aldrich to declare a mistrial, the same judge acquitted Kamin at a second trial on the ground that the Senator's questions had exceeded his Subcommittee's authority. Kamin, who is now professor of psychology at Princeton, later recalled having received "very great personal support and sympathy" from his Harvard colleagues.[13]

In February 1953, following confessional testimony from three distinguished scholars, Granville Hicks, Robert Gorham Davis and Daniel Boorstin (appointed Librarian of Congress in 1975), who recalled not only their Communist days but also, on a more sensitive ethical point, their Communist colleagues at Harvard, HCUA subpoenaed one of those they named, the physicist Professor Wendell Furry. But Furry could not or would not do what they had done. A member of the Harvard physics department for twenty years (and now for over forty), he invoked the Fifth, but argued strongly that the Soviet Union had not started the Korean war. To the Harvard Corporation he explained that he had been a Party member from 1938 to 1947. On May 20, the Corporation announced:

> We think membership in the Communist Party by a Faculty member today, with its usual concomitant of secret domination by the Party, goes beyond the realm of his political beliefs and

associations . . . By the same token it is beyond the scope of academic freedom . . . We think membership in the Communist Party . . . today . . . cuts to the core of his ability to perform his duties with independence of thought and judgment.

Then, dealing directly with Furry:

Dr. Furry's teaching is of high quality and has reflected no Communist slant, nor has he ever engaged in recruiting students for the Communist Party or in attempting to influence their political thinking . . . He has at no time permitted his connection with the Party to affect his teaching . . .

These statements are logically compatible only if a particular historical myth is accepted—that at some time the Party decided to impose rigorous discipline and thought control on its members, having provisionally licensed them to honor their role as objective teachers. But Harvard Corporation launched no such historical notion, nor indeed did Sidney Hook. Furthermore, in virtually every case about which we know, the evidence conforms to the same pattern as Furry's—"He has at no time permitted his connection with the Party to affect his teaching." Furry was not the exception, he was the rule. Yet in 1948–49 both Conant of Harvard and Charles Seymour of Yale had promised legislators and alumni they would not appoint a Communist, and in October 1957 Conant's successor, Dr. Nathan Pusey, declared that a Communist had no right to belong to any university faculty. In short, Harvard's liberal leadership wobbled under the force of the primary superstition of the day.

When Furry faced McCarthy in November 1953, he took the Fifth. It was now that McCarthy referred to the "smelly mess" at Harvard, describing Furry as one of "Pusey's Fifth Amendment Communists" and proposing that federal tax exemptions be withdrawn from the university. Evidently Harvard too was unhappy about Furry's testimony, and in January 1954 he made a second appearance before McCarthy during which he abandoned the Fifth in order to avoid "undue harm to me and the great institution with which I am connected." He now agreed that he and five of his co-workers had been Communists while employed by the Signal Corps, but he refused to name them, "to secure the innocent from persecution." Indicted for contempt, he never came to trial, his counsel having wisely played for time; in June 1956 the government dropped its charges following the Kamin decision.

Cases involving Congressional committees provoked publicity, but there were others—we do not know how many—where a man or woman was shut out by discreet administrative means in a climate where the institution and the victim shared a common interest in silence. In late March or early April 1954, McGeorge Bundy, Dean of the Faculty of Arts and Sciences at Harvard, offered Sigmund Diamond an appointment as Counselor for Foreign Students and Dean of Special Students, with some teaching in the history department. On April 21, Diamond was visited by two FBI agents inquiring about his previous membership in the CP. Diamond declined to discuss the matter. Four or five days later (as Diamond has recently recalled), Dean Bundy also questioned him. Diamond explained that he had joined the Party in 1941, at the age of twenty-one, and had left it "several years after World War II." Bundy wanted to know what he would do if called upon to discuss his past with "civic authority." Diamond replied that he would, like Furry, talk fully about himself but not about others, who, to his knowledge, had committed no crimes and whose jobs would be in jeopardy. Bundy refused to accept this: either Diamond would declare his willingness to name names or Bundy would not recommend his appointment to the Corporation. President Pusey was in full agreement.

In a letter published in May 1977, Bundy explained that he reached his decision on two grounds: Diamond should have confessed his past membership in the Party when the job was offered to him, and an ex-Communist with such attitudes was unacceptable to Harvard in any administrative post. (Indeed Bundy insists that "academic freedom" was not involved because the job offered to Diamond was not an academic one.) He adds: "I think I did tell him that if he changed his position I would try to persuade the Corporation to overlook his earlier failure to tell me of his problem . . ." This can mean only that in Bundy's opinion Diamond would have been an acceptable administrator if he had been prepared to name names to the FBI or a Congressional committee.[14]

## Fifth Amendment Dismissals: Professors

The Senate Internal Security Subcommittee staged a series of hearings from September 1952 until June 1953 which amputated the careers of many teachers. According to the *Harvard Crimson*, by June 1953 over one hundred university professors had taken the Fifth, fifty-four of whom had been dismissed or suspended, and the others put on probation or under censure.[15]

The first Fifth Amendment dismissals took place at Rutgers, the State University of New Jersey. Two days after Professor Simon W. Heimlich, of the College of Pharmacy, took the Fifth Amendment in September 1952 before the SISS, the president of Rutgers, Dr. Lewis

Webster Jones, declared how shocked he was. Heimlich then explained to Jones that he had never been in the CP and had never recruited for the AYD, but he opposed all public investigations of political opinions. Heimlich later told the faculty committee set up to consider his case that a discussion group with which he had been associated in 1946 examined Communism from a strictly scientific, methodological viewpoint. As for his connection with the National Committee to Win the Peace, it had been designed to prevent the rebirth of anti-Semitism and Nazism in Germany. A second Rutgers professor, the classical historian Moses I. Finley of the Newark College of Arts and Sciences, had appeared before the SISS in March, denied present Party membership, but took the Fifth as to the past. (He also invoked the First Amendment.) Finley, who in August of the previous year had been accused by Professor Karl A. Wittfogel and William M. Canning of having been a Communist in or about 1939, assured the faculty committee that he had not been a Communist since 1941, but would not commit himself as to earlier years.

The Special Trustee Faculty Committee set up to consider the basic principles involved reported on October 14, 1952: "Such doubt as to the loyalty of any of its teachers also tends to affect the confidence which the public is entitled to feel in a university . . . In the case of a state university, such a situation may also tend to impair the confidence of state officials and the legislature . . ." Reporting on December 3, a Special Faculty Committee of Review stressed the exemplary academic and teaching record of both men and the absence of any recorded bias in their approach to students, and recommended no charges and no further action. But on December 12 the Board of Trustees brushed this advice aside on the ground that taking the Fifth Amendment was "incompatible with the standards required" of the academic profession. Dismissing both Heimlich and Finley, President Jones stressed the university's absolute obligation to clear up any doubt as to Party membership. Yet no real doubt prevailed: public relations was the sole issue.

Dr. Gene Weltfish, an anthropologist on the staff of Columbia University since 1947 and vice-president of the pro-Communist International Federation of Democratic Women, came before the SISS in September 1952 and took the Fifth Amendment as to past and present membership. Asked why she had charged the United States with practicing germ warfare in Korea, she explained that she had received the information from the Reverend Dr. Endicott of the Canadian Peace Congress. In April 1953 Columbia announced that her contract would not be renewed, but denied (most unconvincingly) that the decision was in any way politically motivated.[16]

Professor Edwin B. Burgum, associate professor of English at

New York University, took the Fifth before the SISS in October 1952. The administration at NYU then set up a twelve-man faculty committee of inquiry, to which it submitted two charges: that Burgum's use of the constitutional privilege amounted to conduct unbecoming a professor; and that he had employed the privilege to avoid disclosing his own and other people's relations to the CP. Manning Johnson and Herbert Philbrick were called in as witnesses. When Burgum did not attempt to refute the record but merely protested the propriety of the whole proceeding and refused to testify, the faculty committee recommended dismissal. The AAUP blacklisted NYU for refusing him severance pay despite his eighteen years' service. According to Burgum, the ACLU turned down his case.[17] Also at NYU, Lyman Bradley, a veteran of the First World War and an associate professor of German, was dismissed in June 1951 following hearings before the University Senate. The direct cause of his dismissal was the fact that a year earlier he had been sentenced to three months' imprisonment and a $500 fine for contempt of Congress, after he and other directors of the Joint Anti-Fascist Refugee Committee had refused to hand over lists of Spanish Republican sympathizers to HCUA.

Invoking the Fifth was normally fatal.[18] After Dr. Horace Bancroft Davis, associate professor of economics at the University of Kansas City, had done so before the SISS in June 1953, subsequently refusing to tell the university's tribunal of inquiry whether he had been in the CP, he was dismissed on the pretext that he had not revealed relevant biographical details to the university. The AAUP's report on this episode, published in April 1957,[19] was somewhat tortured in its conclusions:

> A refusal to answer questions about possible Communist affiliations is ill considered; but, standing alone, it does not merit dismissal . . . The refusal . . . to answer the Board's questions . . . raised serious doubts about him, however . . . he was teaching labor economics and comparative economic systems . . . There was, however, impressive testimony that he had not abused his position . . . In the Davis case, both sides were at fault.

But in fact Davis had simply refused to answer questions which no one had the right to ask him in circumstances of duress.

Byron T. Darling, professor of theoretical physics at Ohio State University, took the Fifth before HCUA in March 1953 and was promptly suspended. During hearings before President Howard Bevis, Darling denied that he had ever belonged to the CP or any affiliated organization, and he contended that had he said as much before

HCUA he would have run the risk of a perjury charge. It now emerged that one of his own graduate students had been appointed by the Air Force—for whom Darling had been conducting nonclassified research—to spy on him. In April 1953 Darling was dismissed by the Board of Trustees for "lack of candor and moral integrity" and for damaging Ohio State University's good reputation in the public mind.[20]

Dr. Alex B. Novikoff, a biochemist working at the University of Vermont, was suspended without pay in July 1953 after he had taken the Fifth before the SISS as to whether he had been a Party member eight years previously. He explained to a trustee-faculty committee that he had not wished to implicate past friends; the committee, which described him as "an excellent teacher and scientist," voted 5 to 1 to retain him, but late in August the Board of Trustees voted 14 to 8 to dismiss him. Like Ohio State, the University of Vermont was sensitive to political pressures.

Meanwhile Professor Barrows Dunham of Temple University declined to provide more than his name and date of birth when subpoenaed by HCUA in 1953. A faculty-administrative committee had then to decide whether Dunham was subversive as defined by Pennsylvania's Pechan Act. (Temple was in receipt of state funds and had to comply with the certification provisions of the Act.) Although the committee's conclusions were not published, the Board of Trustees dismissed him and refused to reinstate him, even after he had been acquitted of contempt in October 1955. Dunham believed that the local chapter of the AAUP had betrayed him. In March 1953, Dr. Maurice Halperin, head of Latin-American regional studies at Boston University, took the Fifth before the SISS, having been named by J. Edgar Hoover as a source of information for the Soviet Union. Nathanael Weyl told the SISS that Halperin had been identified to him as a Communist in 1936. Halperin was fired in January 1954.

Trouble came to the University of Michigan when three members of the faculty took the First and Fifth Amendments before HCUA. Mark Nickerson, a thirty-five-year-old associate professor of medicine (without tenure), told the university's committee of inquiry that he had been in the CP but had drifted out and away. After the committee voted merely to censure him, President Harlan H. Hatcher argued that Nickerson had not disavowed his Communist commitments and had withdrawn only because he lacked the time for Party work; on the recommendation of the president, the Board of Regents in August 1954 dismissed the man who in 1949 had won the John Abel award for the "most outstanding work in the United States" in the field of pharmacology.[21] Chandler Davis, a math instructor aged twenty-eight, having taken the First Amendment before HCUA, refused to answer any of the university committee's questions about CP membership or political attitudes and was dismissed.[22] The third member of the University of Michigan to be dismissed, having taken both the First and Fifth Amendments before HCUA, was an assistant professor of zoology who remains unnamed in the record but who, according to the AAUP, was able to demonstrate a clean break with the CP.

Dr. Lee Lorch, professor of mathematics at Fisk University, Nashville, Tennessee, appeared before HCUA in September 1954, criticized its procedure, challenged its right to ask him political questions, and testified that he had not been a Party member since 1950, when he came to Fisk—he had wished to guard Fisk against unfavorable publicity. As for alleged membership in 1941 and later, Lorch resorted to the First Amendment. In some constitutional confusion, Dr. Charles S. Johnson, president of Fisk, immediately released a statement to the press—". . . invoking the Fifth [sic] Amendment . . . is for all practical purposes tantamount to admission of membership."

A radical with a stormy civil-rights record, Lorch had in 1949, amid heavy controversy, been one of twenty-eight teachers whose appointments had not been renewed by City College of New York. In September 1954, the month HCUA summoned him, he had caused a furore in Nashville by attempting to enroll his daughter in a segregated school for Negroes. When he came before the University Board on October 28, he declined to discuss his beliefs and associations prior to the time he joined Fisk. Forty-seven of the seventy eligible faculty members at Fisk urged that he be retained, as did twenty-two student leaders, 150 alumni and 157 citizens. Nevertheless, the executive committee of the Board of Trustees voted not to renew his contract when it expired in June 1955. For this action a two-man AAUP Committee condemned the Trustees and President Johnson.[23]

If we take all categories of teacher together, both college [24] and school, we find that in the course of 1952–53 seventy-seven of them took the Fifth before the SISS on past and present membership, and twelve on past membership alone. This blacklist of eighty-nine names was of course widely circulated.

## FIFTH AMENDMENT DISMISSALS: TEACHERS

Turning now to schoolteachers, of apparently thirty-one of those who refused to cooperate with the SISS, and possibly four more, only five kept their jobs.[25] In July 1953 the *Harvard Crimson* estimated that over one hundred schoolteachers had been suspended or fired for noncooperation with Congressional committees.

Late in 1953 a hurricane struck the teaching profession in Philadelphia, where the Communist Party had in the late thirties accumulated more support among teachers than in any other East Coast city
except New York. In November HCUA came to town and achieved
what school Superintendent Louis P. Hoyer had failed to accomplish
earlier in the year, when he summoned twenty-nine teachers who
refused to discuss their past affiliations on the ground that it was not
required by the state's Loyalty (Pechan) Act. Hoyer was now able to
suspend thirty-two teachers for taking the Fifth, or for refusing to
answer his questions, or both. Trials before the Board of Education
followed, with the result that twenty-six teachers who had appeared
before the Velde Committee were fired for "incompetence," although
none of them had ever been rated unsatisfactory. In total HCUA,
which visited the city in 1952, 1953 and again in 1954, called forty-one
teachers, thirty-six of whom took the Fifth Amendment and two of
whom turned informer, admitted past membership and described
Communist attempts to control the Teachers Union.

A particularly sad case was that of Dr. Wilbur Lee Mahaney, Jr.,
a high-school teacher who discussed his own record in February 1954
but declined to talk about others. Cited for contempt and suspended
from his job, he later collapsed and appealed to the Committee to
allow him to rectify his "false sense of loyalty." HCUA instructed him
first to tell everything to the FBI; he did; HCUA then consented in
July to hear his confession and allow him to purge himself by identifying sixteen colleagues as having been Party members.[26]

Herman A. Beilan had in October 1952 declined to answer the
Superintendent's questions, yet nevertheless kept his job. In November 1953, during a televised HCUA hearing, Beilan denied present
membership, took the Fifth as to the past and swore he had never
advocated the violent overthrow of the government. In January 1954
the Philadelphia Board of Education dismissed him. At the age of
forty-three he was not only out of a job, he was out of a career. (Four
years later his lawsuit failed in the Supreme Court.) Along with Beilan, Samuel M. Kaplan, aged forty-four, and Solomon Haas, aged
forty-eight, were the first of twenty-seven teachers to be heard on
charges brought by Superintendent Hoyer. Both were fired. A week
later Abraham Egnal, Louis Ivens and Joseph Ehrenreich, all schoolteachers, were also fired. By February 20, Hoyer had suspended
thirty-two. By May 5, he had fired fourteen. More dismissals followed,[27] including that of Mrs. Goldie Watson, the first witness since
the Hollywood Ten to confront HCUA on the frail but principled
basis of the First Amendment alone, and, after her dismissal, an activist in the ECLC. The Philadelphia Board of Education was trans-
parently eager to fire teachers with exceptionally long records of de-

voted service; for example, four teachers [28] dismissed on May 3 had an average teaching service of twenty-two years. (All four had refused to tell Hoyer whether they were Communists.) [29]

Three Newark, New Jersey, teachers who took the Fifth before HCUA in May 1955 were immediately suspended and a month later dismissed, even though they offered to swear on oath before the Board of Education that they were not Communists. After the anti-Communist Teachers Guild had decided to underwrite their legal expenses, the State Commissioner of Education ruled, a year after their suspension, that the three—Estelle Laba, of the Central High School; Dr. Robert Lowenstein, of Barringer High School; and Perry Zimmerman, of Dayton High School—had been fired on insufficient evidence.

But the decisions of school boards were not always the only salient factor; "public opinion," as expressed by vigilantes and pressure groups, also had its effect. When Mrs. Margaret Schudakopf, a Tacoma, Washington, school counselor, explained to the Board that she had taken the Fifth before HCUA only in order to avoid naming others, and that she had not been a Party member since signing the state loyalty oath, they voted to retain her by 3 to 2. Whereupon the local Legion whipped up a Citizens for America group and produced 23,000 signatures calling for Mrs. Schudakopf's dismissal. Soon afterward the Pierce County School Superintendent conveniently stumbled upon an old statute that enabled him to fire her without a hearing on the ground that the public had "lost confidence in her." [30]

## OTHER VICTIMS

To Fairmont, West Virginia, came in September 1949 Dr. Luella Raab Mundel, described by William Manchester as "a frail, bespectacled, somewhat nervous Iowan in her late thirties," to head Fairmont State College's art department.[31] On one occasion, while arguing for an across-the-board salary raise at a faculty meeting, she was heard to remark casually, "I guess I'm a Socialist." This was forgiven but not forgotten. In March 1951 she attended a Legion "Americanism seminar" at which she challenged a patriot to prove that Lattimore was a Communist and contentiously took issue with the prevailing view that liberals were no different from Communists. Mrs. Thelma Loudin, a member of the State Board of Education, then suggested to President George Hand of Fairmont State College that he check Luella Mundel's record with the FBI. He did, and drew a blank. Nevertheless, Mrs. Loudin persuaded the Board to vote her dismissal as an "atheist" in July 1951. Luella Mundel appealed to the Board for a hearing, sup-

ported by 125 students, the AAUP, the ACLU and two other education associations. The Board met and grilled President Hand on his
failure to suppress her supporters. A hearing was refused.

On September 27, Mundel filed a $100,000 suit charging Mrs.
Loudin with slander. The case came up in Marion County Courthouse, where Mrs. Loudin was defended by State Senator Matthew
M. Neely, who orated to the jury about "atheists, Communists, horse
thieves, murderers . . ." and called for teachers "without any highfa-
lutin ideas about not being able to prove there is a God," for teachers
untainted "by foreign isms." How dare she criticize the Legion,
"those boys . . . [who] fought to the death in the Argonne Forest and
the Belleau Wood." Later, when Miss Mundel's abstract-Cubist paint-
ings were exhibited in court, the jurors twisted the frames at various
angles and nudged one another. Although he permitted Senator
Neely to orate at will, Judge Meredith would not allow entered as
evidence Article 3, Section 11, and Section 15, of the West Virginia
Constitution: ". . . no religious or political test oath shall be required
as a prerequisite or qualification to . . . pursue any profession or employment . . . all men shall be free to . . . maintain their opinion in
matters of religion." Finally, on a defense motion, the judge declared
a mistrial. In March 1952 the Board dismissed without a hearing President Hand, Mundel's chief witness, and librarian Harold D. Jones.
Nine members of the faculty resigned in protest.

A bitter experience was that of Forest O. Wiggins, a black Ph.D.
and a popular philosophy instructor at the University of Minnesota.
Vice-chairman of the Minnesota Progressive Party—"I told my students always to keep in mind that I was a Socialist. Since there were
only two of us out of a faculty of more than two thousand . . . I
thought the other view could take care of itself adequately"—Wiggins
was dogged by the FBI, harassed by rumors ranging from homosexuality to having had relations with white female students and finally
dismissed, without a hearing, for "lack of scholarly promise." He appealed in vain to the local chapter of the AAUP. His wife, one of the
first blacks to get a job in her social agency, felt that her marriage
would now jeopardize her career, and she divorced him. Some of the
students who rallied to his defense were subsequently rejected for
state employment.

In 1956 a fifty-three-year-old professor of economics at Kansas
State Teachers College, Emporia, was dismissed after signing a petition urging that certain Communists jailed under the Smith Act be
pardoned. The AAUP, according to the victim, Professor W. Tandy,
"did what it could in a rather weak way, but accomplished nothing."

A peculiar case of reverse discrimination was that of Professor
Herbert Fuchs, who came before HCUA in executive session in June

1955 and admitted having once belonged to Communist units operating within the staffs of the Wheeler Committee on Interstate Commerce and the NLRB. A CP member from 1934 to 1946, Fuchs admitted having perjured himself in this regard in the past, but nevertheless refused to identify former Communist colleagues. President Hurst R. Anderson of the American University, where Fuchs taught law, promptly described him as "a loyal and devoted teacher" who had made "a serious mistake in the past" but redeemed himself by recognizing it. However, when Fuchs went a step further in July and named names to HCUA's staff, Anderson promptly requested him to ask for temporary leave of absence; a month later the Executive Committee of the Board of Trustees recommended that Fuchs's contract not be renewed. When L. Brent Bozell, of the right-wing *National Review*, pressed President Anderson to explain his turnabout, Anderson replied that Fuchs was a perjurer as well as an atheist or agnostic, and that it was unwise to employ even ex-Communists.[32] Nevertheless, the impression remained that this Methodist university had upended the logic of the era by firing a teacher because he named names.

## THE UNIVERSITY OF CALIFORNIA OATH CALAMITY

California was a world, and to some extent a law, unto itself. A decade of political persecution that began with the oath controversy at Berkeley climaxed in January 1961 when John Harrison Farmer, having read in a hate pamphlet that Thomas Parkinson, poet and Yeats scholar, was both a Communist and a homosexual, burst into Parkinson's Berkeley office, shot him in the face at close range and killed his teaching assistant, Stephen Thomas.

The most damaging of the confrontations began when the University of California's twenty-four Regents voted in 1949 to impose a private oath on the faculty.[33] The idea was apparently put up to President Robert Gordon Sproul by James H. Corley, vice-president, comptroller and business manager of UC, with the aim of buying off a Tenney bill then pending in the state legislature. This was the innoculation principle—a small dose of the germ to avoid the disease. On February 24, 1950, the Regents voted by 12 to 6 that those who had not signed the non-Communist oath by the last day of April would automatically sever their connection with UC as of June 30. This position was enthusiastically supported by the *Los Angeles Times*, the Chamber of Commerce, the Realty Board, the Republican Association and the majority of women's clubs. On March 7, the northern Senate of UC, meeting at Berkeley with 900 academics in attendance and 8,000 students jammed into the Greek Theater in support, voted to reject the special oath (in fact, some 300 of Senate rank had so far refused to sign it). As a shoddy compromise the faculty voted (by 724 to 203 in the north, by 301 to 65 in the south) a resolution to placate the Regents, declaring that Communists should not be allowed to teach at UC.

In several leading universities the California oath controversy was regarded as one of crucial importance. Moral support and money arrived in April 1950 from 245 faculty members at Stanford, from Chicago, where the faculty voted a 2 percent voluntary contribution from salaries, and, in September, from the Institute for Advanced Study at Princeton, where Einstein, Oppenheimer and others wrote to the UC academic Senate urging resistance to the oath.[34] By April 21, when the Regents met again, about 280 had refused to sign the special oath. The Regents now voted 21 to 1 to rescind the special oath requirement, and to transfer its burden to the annual contract, requiring every faculty member to sign a statement that "I am not a member of the Communist Party or any other organization which advocates the overthrow of the Government . . . ." Hearings would be available to those who refused to sign.

At Berkeley, where some 20 percent had refused to sign, there was widespread depression, insomnia, inability to work. In June President Sproul announced that sixty-two Senate members who had refused to sign had all received hearings before the Committee on Privilege and Tenure. Of these, Sproul had recommended for retention thirty-nine, all of whom had given assurances they were not Communists and were refusing to sign on principle. By only 10 to 9 the Regents voted to accept Sproul's recommendation. Six faculty members were dismissed on the recommendation of the Committee on Tenure for lack of cooperation in refusing to answer questions. (In essence, you either stood by your principles at stage one, the contract, then abandoned them at stage two, the Committee, in which case you were retained; or you were consistent with your principles and were fired.) The six dismissed, who included the historian Professor John W. Caughey of UCLA, were known by the university not to be Communists. On August 25, the Regents reversed themselves by 12 to 10 and decided not to issue contracts to the thirty-nine. The legality of this decision was to be tested in the courts. By September, capitulations and resignations had reduced the number of nonsigners to about twenty-five.[35]

The general effect of the crisis on the University of California was catastrophic. By March 1951 it had lost 110 scholars—twenty-six dismissed, thirty-seven who had resigned in protest and forty-seven outsiders, including leading scholars, who refused offers of appointment. During a year of bitterness and failure, no fewer than fifty-five regular courses had had to be dropped. In September 1950 the American Psychological Association "blacked" the university and urged its members not to teach or do research there. The Dean of the College of Chemistry commented: "No conceivable damage to the university at the hands of the hypothetical Communists among us could have equaled the damage resulting from the unrest, ill-will and suspicion engendered by this series of events." Twenty litigants from Berkeley claimed that the Constitution of California forbade test oaths. In October 1952 the California Supreme Court agreed and declared the Regents' oath to be unconstitutional, but the Court said nothing about back salaries. As a result, although the Regents allowed those dismissed to return in the spring semester of 1953, they refused to pay the salaries withheld during thirty months of unlawful exclusion. Nor would they award severance pay to those who had chosen to resign. The professors therefore sued again, finally winning their point in March 1956.[36] Later some wounds were healed: David Saxon, dismissed as assistant professor of physics at UCLA after refusing the oath, was vice-chancellor there twenty years later.

## THE PURGE IN CALIFORNIA

It was in California that a state legislative committee undertook the severest measures against the academic profession and succeeded in transforming the periodic harassment characteristic of such committees into a permanent, quasi-legal purge machine. In June 1952, twenty-eight private and public colleges, including Stanford and UC, agreed to collaborate with the state's Un-American Activities (Burns) Committee and to install on each campus a contact man formerly employed by the FBI or military intelligence, and responsible to Richard E. Combs, the Burns Committee's chief counsel. In March 1953 Combs told the SISS that this system had resulted in more than one hundred dismissals or resignations in less than a year, and in the prevention of about two hundred appointments. In May 1954 President Sproul claimed that William Waldman, the university's security officer at Berkeley, was keeping files only on those faculty members engaged in federally classified research, but an ACLU investigation revealed that on June 7 Waldman admitted to Berkeley's Chancellor, Clark Kerr, that despite earlier denials he was receiving and filing reports on the whole faculty on behalf of the Burns Committee.[37]

Both loyalty oaths and legislative committees [38] exacted a particularly heavy toll among professors and teachers in California. For example, in November 1950 seven faculty members of San Francisco

State College were dismissed for refusing to sign the Levering Act oath ("gross unprofessional conduct").[39] An academic who was caught both ways (oath and committee) was John W. Mass, an instructor in English at San Francisco City College; he invoked the Fifth before HCUA in 1953, at the same time admitting that he had belonged to the CP when he signed the Levering Act oath in October 1950. He was dismissed under the Dilworth Act of 1953, which specified dismissal of public employees for refusing to testify about Communist Party membership during the period since September 1948. In February 1957 the California Supreme Court, basing itself on the Slochower (1956) decision, ruled that Mass had been improperly dismissed and referred the case back to the San Francisco Superior Court. In 1954 Dr. Henry C. Steinmetz, a fifty-four-year-old associate professor of psychology at San Diego State College, who had served in both world wars, was dismissed after refusing to say whether he was a Party member. At least 250 students signed petitions on his behalf, and the ACLU helped, but, so Steinmetz claimed, the AAUP "passed the buck back and forth between local and national."

Metropolitan California, together with New York and Philadelphia, constituted the three largest pockets of political radicalism in the teaching profession. In the 1950s the schoolteachers of California, no less than their East Coast colleagues, suffered for their heresies (or, as Sidney Hook would insist, for their conspiracies). The Los Angeles Board of Education, for example, operated under the same rule as its counterpart in New York: automatic dismissal for any teacher invoking the Fifth Amendment.

In 1946 the Tenney Committee fired a blast at two Canoga Park High School teachers, Mrs. Frances R. Eisenberg and Mrs. Blanche Bettington, on the ground that Mrs. Eisenberg was a member of Local 430 of the AFT, "a thoroughly Communist-dominated union" (in fact, Local 430 was expelled by the AFT after HCUA had investigated it), and that "she has followed *the Communist Party line* in ranting at such publications as the *Reader's Digest.*" What was worse, she had taught "disrespect for the capitalist system of the government of the United States." As a result, the Los Angeles Board of Education staged a four-day inquiry in October and exonerated the two women after witnesses testified that they encouraged pupils to express themselves, to dig out facts, and to see all sides of a question. Tenney denounced the verdict as a whitewash. However, fate finally caught up with Mrs. Eisenberg in the shape of the Burns Committee, before which she declined to answer questions in October 1952. In January 1954 a Superior Court judge upheld her dismissal by the Los Angeles Board of Education.

In 1947 the Tenney Committee introduced eight bills to prevent the teaching of controversial subjects in elementary schools and to increase legislative control over textbooks. Although only one of these bills became law, in the same year the legislature created the Senate Investigating Committee on Education under the chairmanship of Senator Nelson S. Dilworth, himself a member of the Tenney Committee. Working in close collaboration with the Sons of the American Revolution, and focusing its attention on the Los Angeles area, the Dilworth Committee so alarmed Los Angeles's Superintendent of Schools, Alexander J. Stoddard, that he announced that every teacher would have to read a pamphlet on Americanism and sign an oath. Stoddard also called upon citizens and parents to report instances of subversive teaching [40]—reputedly a Soviet practice. In January 1949 he loudly announced his intention to dismiss all Communists.

Most teachers instinctively sought to conceal rather than publicize the allegations against them. From 1952 to 1958, Los Angeles teachers and school librarians worked in a state of constant anxiety lest something they said, or the teaching materials they used, be construed as subversive or pro-UNESCO by civic and business groups or by such papers as the *Los Angeles Times*. Across their careers lay the shadow of the Dilworth Act of 1953, which stipulated that all teachers must take a non-Communist oath and that any who refused to testify would be dismissed. To stave off further attacks, and in an ecstasy of capitulation, the Los Angeles Board of Education submitted its entire list of 30,000 educational personnel to counsel Richard Combs of the Burns Committee. It was Combs who now held every schoolteacher and a large number of college teachers by the throat. In March he announced that more than 100 teachers had been dismissed since June 1952 and a similar number had been refused appointments.

The year 1953 brought the Luckel Act, which conferred investigating authority on the State Board of Education, and the Dilworth Act, which endowed every school board with similar powers. To make matters worse, the Velde Committee convened in March, with the result that five teachers lost their jobs and a sixth resigned. The Committee returned in December, and in the same month the Los Angeles Board of Education opened an inquiry, with Superintendent Stoddard publicly naming 171 teachers as suspects. Seven who were summoned in mid-December refused to answer about CP membership. Two substitute teachers among them were dismissed and five regular teachers suspended. Eventually ten or twelve were dismissed for insubordination.

In 1959 HCUA scheduled hearings in California on teachers and finally, after a long controversy and after no fewer than 110 teachers had been subpoenaed, canceled them. The Committee did, however, release the teachers' names to the press and turned over their files to the State Attorney General and the various school boards for "necessary action." Six were fired. Then HCUA returned and subpoenaed forty-eight teachers for May 1960, the final outcome being that a total of about twenty-five teachers were forced out of the profession by nonrenewal of contracts or teaching credentials, or by forced resignation.[41]

### THE TILLETT SURVEY: PREDICAMENT OF THE DISCHARGED TEACHER

In the early sixties Professor Paul Tillett, of the Eagleton Institute of Politics, Rutgers University, sent out a questionnaire to 140 professors and schoolteachers who had been dismissed on account of their political beliefs. Forty-three replied. I was able to examine the replies Tillett received, by courtesy of the late Professor H. H. Wilson, into whose custody the Tillett Survey passed after Tillett's death. These replies provide a unique insight into the impact of the purge on the lives of individual teachers. Did professors and teachers who lost their jobs generally receive moral and financial support from their colleagues? What were the legal costs of a defense? How many were later able to find their way back into teaching and how many were compelled to change their careers and undergo retraining? What kind of work did they settle for? And what was the effect on their families and on their own health? The answers offered by the victims themselves are discussed and correlated in Appendix B, below.

### THE FBI ON CAMPUS

Writing in *The New York Times* in May 1951, Kalman Siegel described the long shadow of the FBI that had fallen across American campuses. Whenever a student applied for federal employment, an agent would question his professors and check his name against the membership lists of the more liberal university clubs. Dean Carl W Ackerman, of the Columbia University School of Journalism, complained that investigators from the FBI, CIA and Civil Service were interrogating college and public-school teachers and generally "following up leads like prosecuting attorneys." Professor H. H. Wilson, of the Princeton political science department, a dedicated civil libertarian who sent the agents packing whenever they requested to see his students' course papers, recalls how a student in the English department, Sanford Coleman Nemitz, visited the famous Communist intellectual Mike Gold while preparing a thesis on the proletarian writers of the thirties, only to be grabbed and thoroughly grilled by the FBI.

A national organization was set up, staffed largely by ex-FBI men, with chapters in the colleges, specifically to report to the FBI. In California, as we have seen, a legislative committee established on campus an intelligence network whose agents regularly reported on the affiliations and teaching record of the faculty. The University of Colorado called in two former G-men to investigate the faculty, following the example set in 1949 by the president of the University of Idaho, who enlisted FBI cooperation in a survey of subversive influences in the state's educational system.

Roger Burlingame reported an incident at the State University, Brockport, New York, where thirty professors led by Dr. Edward R. Cain, associate professor of government, sent a petition in 1961 to Congressman Harold C. Ostertag, calling for the abolition of HCUA as a standing committee. Back came not only a polite reply expressing Ostertag's disagreement, but also two officers of the New York State Bureau of Criminal Intelligence, one of whom interrogated the president for two hours and swore him to secrecy, while the other roamed the campus and questioned students about the faculty members who had signed the petition. Before they left the agents demanded the files of all thirty signatories; State University officials in Albany instructed the president to comply.[42]

The activities of an organization such as the FBI are difficult to document comprehensively. The historian must therefore be grateful for the audacity of a radical group that on March 8, 1971, raided the FBI office in Media, Pennsylvania, and "ripped off" a haul of documents that shed a good deal of light on the Bureau's methods of political surveillance. Now, it is true that methods employed in the early seventies were not necessarily identical with those used fifteen or twenty years earlier; yet the continuity of Hoover's leadership and obsessions throughout that period is only one of several factors suggesting consistency. The Media papers [43] confirm the general belief that the campus police have usually worked hand-in-glove with the FBI. Administrative and faculty personnel also figured high on the list of informants and "sources" whom agents contacted regularly.

In view of the physical violence, not stopping short of bombings, to which American universities were subjected in the late sixties and early seventies, a case could be made out in defense of such contacts. And yet, even though universities were generally calm, stable and even politically miasmic during the fifties, there is evidence that administrations collaborated with the FBI and local police agencies. It was in 1955, for example, that the chairman of the Detroit Loyalty

Investigating Committee, Alfred A. May, wrote Professor Alfred H. Kelly of Wayne University, thanking him for assistance in checking the political backgrounds of city employees who had attended Wayne. In 1959 the FBI launched an inquiry into who was responsible for inviting a Polish lawyer to lecture at the University of Wyoming Law School.[44] This aspect of our subject would certainly reward further research.

## FEAR IN THE SCHOOLS

As Robert M. Hutchins was to put it, "The question is not how many teachers have been fired, but how many think they might be, and for what reasons . . . The entire teaching profession of the U.S. is now intimidated." Despite a 5 to 1 protest by the faculty, the University of Wyoming went ahead with an examination of hundreds of its textbooks for subversive or un-American material. Surveying seventy-two major colleges in the early part of 1951, Kalman Siegel reported "a subtle, creeping paralysis of freedom of thought and speech" and "a narrowing of the area of tolerance." Two years later *Time* magazine, somewhat tardily noticing "The Danger Signals," cited a wide variety of distinguished academics whose alarm could not be attributed to camouflaged radicalism. Robert Bolwell, professor of American literature at George Washington University, commented: "I confess that after finishing a lecture, I sometimes wonder if somebody is going to take it to Papa or to some reporter . . . One lecture could damn anybody." Dean Carl W. Ackerman, of the Columbia University Graduate School of Journalism, said, "Today the vast majority of teachers . . . have learned that promotion and security depend upon conformity to the prevailing . . . concept of devotion to the public welfare." [45]

The Lazarsfeld study,[46] based on 2,451 interviews conducted in 165 colleges in 1955, revealed that 63 percent of the social scientists interviewed believed the threat to intellectual activity was greater than a generation before. Only 16 percent of the incidents recorded by the respondents had to do with anything so specific as Party membership or invocation of the Fifth Amendment; the great majority—84 percent—reflected the nebulous, pervasive concern with "sympathizers," "subversives," "un-Americans." No fewer than 365 respondents had been offered advice by colleagues on how to avoid political trouble on campus. Courses on Soviet economics, et cetera, were liable to cause comment, to be vetted by administration officials, to be toned down, to be canceled. Fear of recommending radical reading material paralleled fear of student informers; more than half reported

that one colleague or another had been accused of subversive sympathies. The effect of this climate on the content and tone of American
sociological writing lies beyond the scope of this study; yet it is surely
no coincidence that it was at this time that the "discovery" was made
that "left" and "right" were no longer political terms of any relevance;
and that the productive, quantitative triumphs of managerial-capital-
ist society had rendered the whole concept of ideology obsolete. The
fifties were coated in chromium.

# 23

## New York Teachers on Trial

The New York schools were no strangers to politically inspired purges. In 1919 Superintendent of Schools John L. Tildsley issued instructions forbidding the employment of teachers who belonged to the Marxist wing of the Socialist Party. About fifty teachers were summoned to account for their beliefs and a few were fired on charges of having propagandized their pupils. Bolshevism and, later, the League of Nations were banned subjects. Twenty years later, in 1939, the Devaney Act proscribed teachers belonging to organizations that advocated violent overthrow of the government—but without naming the CP as such an organization. Perhaps for this reason the act was not invoked when State Senator Frederic Coudert brought a wave of terror to the city's radical teachers in the course of a legislative investigation staged in 1941–42.

The Teachers Union and the CP organized the defense: Bella Dodd, legislative representative of the Union, burned the membership lists in her possession. Over 600 subpoenas were issued. The general line recommended by the union, and almost universally followed, was for non-Party teachers to deny membership and for Party members to do likewise. The Committee, for its part, was sufficiently well briefed by informers like former Party treasurer William Canning, previously a member of the CP unit at CCNY, who named fifty-four teachers as Communists, to identify the teachers who had falsely denied Party membership, almost fifty of whom were suspended and later dismissed for "conduct unbecoming." No attempt was made either to contest their high qualities as teachers or to argue that they had introduced propaganda into the classroom.

How great, in fact, was Communist influence among New York teachers at that time? Of the city's 35,000 public schoolteachers, some 4,000 were members of the Teachers Union in 1941. According to Bella Dodd, writing after her renunciation of Communism, and therefore perhaps prone to exaggerate, about 1,000 were CP members.[1] Five hundred would seem a more plausible estimate; when John Lautner was expelled from the Party in 1950, he claimed that of "about 500" CP teachers, 300 had regrouped into cells of three for security reasons.

Stampeded by Coudert's investigation, the Board of Higher Education resolved in March 1941 that CP membership was ground for dismissal. When a three-man committee of the Board opened hearings, the subpoenaed college teachers, like their public-school colleagues, uniformly denied Party membership, while the union and its shrill organ, New York Teacher, hurled bitter recriminations against the Coudert Committee and its "puppet," the Board. Twenty-four college teachers were dismissed in the upshot, eleven resigned, and a number of others were later not reappointed.[2]

But until the SISS arrived to hold hearings in September 1952, the political tensions within the higher-education system of New York City were kept under control, although in 1949 twenty-eight untenured teachers at CCNY were refused reappointment without charges, hearings or explanations. There is no doubt that some of them, like the mathematician Lee Lorch, had given political offense, but it is not certain whether such considerations applied to all of them. What was certain was that a showdown between the Board of Education and the Teachers Union became inevitable once the Cold War seized New York by the throat during the summer of 1949.

## THE TEACHERS UNION AND THE BOARD OF EDUCATION

Founded in 1916, the Teachers Union of New York, which had fallen increasingly under Communist influence in the 1930s, constituted Local 5 of the American Federation of Teachers, AFL, until its expulsion from the AFT in 1941. Following its expulsion (together with that of the Philadelphia local), the TU moved across into the CIO, merging with other CIO public-employees unions in 1946 to form the United Public Workers of America, of which the New York TU became Local 555. At this stage the Union's membership reached a peak of about 7,000; by 1963 the purges had withered it to 2,000. The TU's influence was increasingly resented after it decided by referendum vote to endorse the candidacy of Henry Wallace, but local issues were equally important; not only did the Union agitate for better salaries and working conditions, it ceaselessly criticized the Board of Education for its failure to racially integrate the city's schools, and for its tolerance of racially prejudiced teachers and textbooks. Nor was there any love lost between the TU and the anti-Communist Teachers Guild (Local 2 of the AFT). Indeed the Delegate Assembly of the Teachers Guild voted by 27 to 19 to oppose the employment of Communists in schools. (This position was adopted by the parent AFT in 1952.)

The Board of Education, for its part, began to gird its loins for a trial of strength against the TU in mid-1948. It is interesting to recall that two years earlier, in September 1946, the Board's president, Andrew G. Clauson, Jr., and the Superintendent of Schools, William Jansen, had assured a Senate committee that there was no evidence of Communist influence among the city's teachers. By the time that the House Committee on Education and Labor turned its attention in September to the UPWA and its subsidiary, the TU, a split was apparent within the Board, a split not on fundamentals, not on policy, but on tactics and public relations. While Clauson and Jansen judged it expedient to commend Local 555 of the UPWA (i.e., the TU) as a most responsible organization, and its president, Abraham Lederman, as a "very good teacher," another member of the Board loudly insisted before the House Committee that the TU followed the Party line. Here we encounter the vigilante who was to become the leading spirit behind the purge, George A. Timone, a right-wing Catholic appointed in 1946 by Mayor O'Dwyer from a list (one dismissed teacher claimed) "submitted by Cardinal Spellman." [3] It was Timone who was rapidly to prevail—so rapidly that on December 22 Jansen and the Board's legal secretary, Nicholas Bucci, summoned Lederman and asked him whether he had ever collected money for the CP. On January 12 Jansen summoned the TU's president yet again, and again he refused to answer on First Amendment grounds. Clearly the Board wanted a showdown.

The same month Jansen also dispatched Assistant Superintendent John F. Conroy, together with legal counsel Nicholas Bucci and a stenographer, to a school in Staten Island where, without prior notice to her, they questioned Mrs. Minnie Gutride about political meetings she might have attended in 1940 and 1941. When she asked for time to consult a lawyer they threatened her with a charge of conduct unbecoming a teacher. That afternoon she called in at the TU office for comfort and advice; that night she committed suicide. She had lived alone since the death of her husband in the Spanish Civil War.

On April 15, 1949, Celia Zitron, secretary of the Union, and six other teachers took the First Amendment when Jansen summoned them for questioning.

Meanwhile, the burning issue of 1949 in New York educational circles was the Feinberg Law, which went into effect on July 1. Henceforward a special official in each school district would submit an annual report on the political health of each teacher. Membership in subversive organizations would count as *prima facie* evidence of disqualification, while past membership would be taken as presumptive evidence of present membership unless proved otherwise. The burden of proving his innocence would reside with the teacher.[4] When the purge of teachers was finally launched, however, the Feinberg Law proved to be a paper tiger, so cumbersome and slow-moving were its procedures. In fact, New York's teachers were about to be purged for refusal to answer questions posed by the employing authority. In January 1950 New York Supreme Court Justice Ferdinand Pecora oiled the gearbox of the impending purge by ruling that the Board of Education could dismiss teachers under Section 903 of the City Charter of 1936 if they refused to answer questions posed by Congressional committees.

## THE PURGE BEGINS

It was not until 1950 that the terror fully returned among New York teachers with radical backgrounds. Defended by the redoubtable Rose Russell, who had taught French at Thomas Jefferson High School until she took over as legislative representative of the TU from Bella Dodd in 1944, a succession of teachers went to the block. At a stormy meeting on March 16, with 300 protesters parading outside, the Board of Education voted on the motion of Superintendent William Jansen to dismiss Mrs. Sylvia Schneiderman, an elementary teacher in her late thirties working at PS 3, Brooklyn, on the ground that she had lied about her political affiliation.

Six weeks later, on May 3, Alice Citron, a teacher with eighteen years' experience, was congratulating herself on having chosen such a fine day to take her eleven-year-olds to the Botanical Gardens, when she received a summons to the school office. There she was handed a note from Jansen, suspending her without pay. On the same day seven other teachers were suspended, including such pivotal figures in the struggle as the president and secretary of the TU, Abraham Lederman and Celia Zitron. Lederman, a teacher for twenty-three years, had helped to devise the math syllabus for the Junior High School, while Zitron, a teacher for twenty-seven years, had been responsible for introducing Hebrew into the city school system. Another notable casualty was Isidore Rubin, editor of *Teacher News* and the author of a book, *Schools in Crisis*, which purported to expose collusion between the School Board officials and the Catholic Church over land deals.[5] Against these eight teachers Section 903 of the City Charter was invoked. All eight had refused to answer the Superintendent's political interrogatory; all eight were Jews.

In June a test-case charge of CP membership (a very rare charge) was brought against David L. Friedman, whom Corporation Counsel John P. McGrath described as a "fifth columnist" and a "potential Quisling on our payroll," although under cross-examination Jansen agreed that there was not the slightest evidence that Friedman had ever advocated violent overthrow. The usual professional ex-Communist witnesses—Kornfeder, Budenz—were wheeled out to testify that the Party advocated violent overthrow of the government and that the CPUSA was counting on Red Army help in seizing America for Socialism, but it was the testimony of Detective Stephanie Horvath that revealed the city administration's most valuable source of information about Communists in its employ. A member of the New York City Red Squad, Horvath had joined the Communist Political Association in 1944 and subsequently recruited for the Party at a May Day rally in 1945 and at a meeting in April 1947. (If there were also informers among the teachers themselves, as there may have been, their identity was not known to the defendants and their counsel, Nathan Witt and Harold I. Cammer.) [6]

Of the eight teachers against whom charges were brought, only Feingold, a veteran of the First World War, opted to testify, but he refused to divulge whether or not he was in the CP. In December, Trial Examiner Theodore Kiendl recommended the dismissal of all eight, even though he admitted in each case: "I have heard no proof of any conduct unbecoming a teacher on the part of [him, her] in the classroom or in [his, her] extracurricular activity." In February, the Board unanimously resolved to dismiss them. It was only a beginning.

In January 1951, City Corporation Counsel Saul Moskoff was assigned to the Board of Education to head Jansen's investigating team. In May, Jansen announced that he intended to take action against Norman London, a teacher at Junior High School 52, Manhattan, and a veteran of the First World War, who had been reported by his principal for refusing to collaborate in an enterprise launched by Jansen himself—special celebrations in all schools to honor the return home of General Douglas MacArthur. (Jansen was also extremely keen on defense drill and identification tags for pupils; the pro-Communist or "peace" teachers hated to take part, since it suggested the slanderous and inconceivable—that the USSR might one day rain fire on America's little children.) On January 23, 1952, it was reported that Moskoff had hitherto interrogated twenty-five teachers, of whom six had resigned.

A week later eight more teachers [7] were suspended without pay for conduct unbecoming and insubordination. Cyril Graze, of the math department at Forest Hills High School, was described by his department chairman as "one of the finest teachers I had occasion to meet," and indeed two hundred parents wrote to Jansen describing Graze as "the kind of teacher we want for our children." However, Graze was known for his outspoken criticisms of the Board for its tolerance of teachers and textbooks hostile to Jews, blacks and the foreign-born. Another who had given offense was Arthur Newman, chairman of the Better Schools Committee in the southeast Bronx, where some 75 percent of families were on home relief and certain schools had to work on a double- or triple-session system. It emerged that Newman's principal at the Gompers Vocational High School had kept a secret dossier on his outside activities and speeches and had sent it to Moskoff.

At the trial of seven of the eight, which began on October 1, Colonel Arthur Levitt served as Trial Examiner even though himself a member of the Board of Education. When a defense attorney argued that Article 5, Section 6 of the State Constitution made merit and fitness the sole tests for the civil service, and that Section 26 (a) of the Civil Rights Law prohibited political interrogations of civil service employees, Levitt remained unmoved. These, he concluded, were "teachers of long service with records of conspicuously fine achievement, frequently under adverse conditions." Yet he recommended to the Board that they be fired forthwith.[8]

Between the trial and the dismissal of these seven teachers the Superintendent struck again in November 1953, suspending without pay Irving Adler, of Straubenmuller Textile High School; Philip Horowitz, of Seward Park High School, Manhattan; Morris H. Lipschitz, of PS 253, Brooklyn; and Ruth Finkelstein, a school clerk at PS 155, Brooklyn; and some others. Six of those suspended brought suit challenging the Board of Education's right to dismiss them for refusing to answer political questions. Adler had already been associated with a suit against the Feinberg Law.

Meanwhile, the war against the Teachers Union itself intensified. One of its reports, *Bias and Prejudice in Textbooks in Use in New York City Schools*, demanding that twenty-seven books be "scrapped or corrected," angered the Board of Education into voting, on the motion of George A. Timone, to bar the TU from all dealings with the city's school system. Thus, on June 1, 1950, the Board, by a vote of 7 to 1, withdrew recognition from the union. This move was supported by the American Jewish League Against Communism, the Catholic War Veterans, the Legion, the Teachers Alliance and the Coordinating Committee of the Archdiocese of New York. A Timone resolution banning the use of school buildings to organizations listed by the Attorney General was extended in the summer of 1952 to the TU, although the Attorney General had never listed it.

Relying not only on the dues of $18 per year that member teachers paid in, but also on the fund-raising activities of its Freedom Fund Committee, the TU was able to subsidize the legal defense costs of suspended teachers and even to provide loans of $100 or $250 to help dismissed teachers find their feet or retrain. Nevertheless, the impact of the purge was such that TU membership fell from 7,000 to 4,000 in February 1953. When the SISS arrived in New York in September 1952, it took care to subpoena the whole TU leadership; [9] most took the Fifth, and not one of those kept his or her job.

## CATHOLICISM AND ANTI-SEMITISM

The Board of Education, chief adversary of the TU, represented certain specific social and religious forces. There is ample evidence that the Catholic Church—and particularly the Brooklyn diocese—was extremely active throughout the purge. (The Feinberg Law can be regarded as the joint achievement of the Church and the Republican Party.) The unofficial voice of the Brooklyn diocese, the *Tablet*, articulated the anti-Marxist traditions of the Church, and more particularly its Irish wing, in the crude, rabble-rousing phraseology of Coughlinite fascism. Timone's leading role we have already emphasized; both Corporation Counsel John P. McGrath and his successor, Adrian Burke, were Catholics, as was assistant prosecutor Daniel Scannell. Mary Riley, assistant to the Superintendent in charge of personnel, dispatched Catholic books and magazines to Bella Dodd, the ex-Communist former legislative representative of the TU, now returned to the faith by way of the good offices of Monsignor Fulton J. Sheen. A lawyer who defended many of the suspended teachers, Harold I. Cammer, regards the whole witch hunt as having been precipitated by a conscious decision of the Catholic hierarchy working through Timone and McGrath, to promote a climate favorable to parochial schools.

The Catholic factor and the anti-Semitic factor were closely interwoven. The *Tablet* constantly excited not only anti-Communist but also anti-Semitic emotions. Catholic and Jewish teachers competed for jobs. One particular Catholic teacher, Mae Quinn, notorious for her outburts against Jews, blacks and aliens, was finally brought to trial behind closed doors by a fellow Catholic, Nicholas Bucci (legal secretary of the Board), and gently reprimanded. The great majority of New York teachers purged in the fifties were Jews; all thirty-three of those who had their pension benefits restored in 1972 were Jews. In 1952 a group of about three hundred mothers asked the Board of Education why it invariably suspended Jewish teachers. A research student who has recently investigated the subject reports: "As for anti-Semitism, 80 percent of the dismissed teachers that I interviewed cited anti-Semitism as a cause for dismissal." [10]

## DEGRADATIONS AND REWARDS

The inquisition was conducted at the most degrading level. In February 1952 Harvey Matusow received a letter from Jansen inviting his cooperation as a consultant for at least ten days at $25 a day. Matusow duly made his way to 131 Livingston Street, Brooklyn, where Moskoff maintained his filing cabinets, his two investigators and what Matusow describes as "an interrogation room" with a "dual-purpose mirror." It was here that teachers were asked what books they read, what people they knew, what feelings they harbored about Spain, whether they voted for the ALP and about the nomination petitions they had signed. According to (the unreliable) Matusow, who in 1955 confessed to the TU that he had named thirteen or fourteen teachers, Corporation Counsel Moskoff wrote a memo boasting how he, calling himself Nat Moss, had phoned the sister and mother of one of the named teachers, to obtain information.

In October 1955 Moskoff defended the use of anonymous informers against teachers. Harold Cammer recalls taking him to see Arthur Miller's play, *The Crucible*, but to no effect: Moskoff could discern no relationship between the Salem witch hunt and what had recently happened to the New York teachers. As for his boss Jansen, Cammer describes the Superintendent who wrought such destruction as merely a wheel horse who had come up through the ranks, a gentle, affable man who "hated to do this" and who could on occasion be genuinely helpful, allowing a doomed teacher a disability retirement instead of a dismissal, thus avoiding loss of pension rights. Cammer estimates that he was able to arrange such deals with Jansen on about twenty occasions.

Those who served the inquisition were in their turn well served. As of July 1974, Arthur Levitt was the long-serving Comptroller of the State of New York; Saul Moskoff was a judge of the New York Family Court; Michael Castaldi, a prosecutor in the teachers' trials, was a justice of the State Supreme Court; and Daniel Scannell, an assistant prosecutor, was executive director of the Metropolitan Transportation Authority. According to Cammer, Scannell respected some of the purged teachers but believed that their exemplary records as teachers made them doubly dangerous—like Socrates? [11]

By October 3, 1952, Moskoff was able to report having interrogated forty-five teachers, seventeen of whom subsequently resigned. By the end of November, sixty-nine had been interrogated and 193 were considered to be under investigation. On June 18, 1953, eleven teachers were suspended or dismissed under Section 903 of the City Charter, including Norman London, who, it will be recalled, had earlier aroused Jansen's wrath by refusing to celebrate the homecoming of General MacArthur. [12]

## THE SISS COMES TO TOWN

Twenty-five of the thirty-one public-school teachers whom the one-man SISS (Homer Ferguson accompanied by counsel Robert Morris) subpoenaed in 1952–53, worked in New York City. Thirteen of them were fired without a hearing under Section 903 of the City Charter after invoking the Fifth. [13] (Astonishingly, the Supreme Court's Slochower decision in 1956 was destined to have no effect whatsoever in rescinding these dismissals.) Notable among this crop of casualties was Louis Relin, who had been awarded a certificate of merit for helping to build morale in East Harlem and who had received three fellowships from the Rockefeller Foundation in conjunction with the Board of Education and Teachers College. But perhaps the most distinguished victim of all was Dr. Julius H. Hlavaty, chairman of the mathematics department of the Bronx High School of Science, who was dismissed in April 1953, having invoked the Fifth before McCarthy during the Voice of America investigation. The only non-Jew caught up in this purge (although married to a Jew), Hlavaty was regarded by many as the most brilliant math teacher in the United States. (The Board of Education had proudly dispatched him across America to lecture.) His dismissal caused Jansen considerable embarrassment, and eventually he was reinstated. [14]

## PRESSURE TO INFORM

Yet the Board of Education was determined to dream up new avenues of dismissal. Accordingly, in March 1955, the Board voted, 7 to 1, that teachers must inform on their colleagues when commanded to do so by the Superintendent. This measure was recommended by the

Board's law committee, as chairman of which William O'Shea had recently replaced Timone. The new policy was opposed by the ADA and the anti-Communist Teachers Guild, but was supported by the Queens and Kings County American Legion, the AJLAC, the *Tablet* and the Catholic Teachers Association of Brooklyn. Forty teachers who had refused to inform on others were summoned again and warned: thirty-five capitulated. But five who did not, Harry Adler, Julius Nash, Irving Mauer, Minerva T. Feinstein and Samuel S. Cohen (principal of PS 103, Manhattan), all of them admitted former Communists, were suspended without pay in September by Jansen. The five appealed to State Commissioner of Education James E. Allen, who ruled in August 1956 that such inquisitions had no place in any school system. But the Board did not respond to this ruling by reinstating the teachers; on the contrary, it launched a dogged struggle to challenge the ruling in the courts, under the leadership of the strongly anti-Communist City Corporation Counsel Peter Campbell Brown, formerly a member of the federal Subversive Activities Control Board. Encouraged by the rulings of the New York Supreme Court and the Court of Appeals that Allen's decision must stand, the five teachers brought suit against the Board of Education in the Brooklyn Supreme Court in November 1959. A month later the Board announced that it would reinstate Adler and Feinstein but would charge the other three with "false swearing under oath." In January 1960 the Board brought this same new charge against four more teachers. What was it all about? Some indication was provided when, in April 1960, Samuel S. Cohen pleaded guilty to having falsely denied past membership in the CP on two application forms in 1949.[15]

Let us consider Mr. Cohen's case, as it appears from these bare facts. In 1949 he twice applies for a new post; he is no longer in the CP, but he fears that past membership, if he admits to it, will be construed as present membership (and therefore cause for dismissal) if he does not renounce his past and denounce certain colleagues. This he cannot bring himself to do. About five years later, when the purge is at its height and the Board's information system is much improved, Mr. Cohen, now principal of PS 103, Manhattan, is again questioned. He no longer dares to deny past membership; he confesses it and is immediately asked to name former colleagues. He refuses. Later he is summoned again and given an ultimatum; again he refuses, and this time he is suspended. The State Commissioner of Education rules that he should not be suspended; the Board ignores the Commissioner. The state courts uphold the Commissioner; the Board ignores the courts. Finally cornered, the Board snarls: "OK, Wise Guy, we gonna fix ya for perjury back in forty-nine!"

## THE BALANCE SHEET AND REHABILITATION

The impact of it all on the 58,000 employees of the Board of Education (1955 figure) and on their "sense of freedom" was, as the ACLU lamented, serious. Fear, of course, is contagious, particularly among the children of immigrants who feel themselves to be ethnically or economically insecure. Many teachers came from upwardly mobile ethnic backgrounds, with fathers who were unskilled immigrant laborers, and grew up in cowed, silent communities where the English language and literacy and the filling-in of forms were problems.

Fear was all the more acute insofar as the generation of teachers that came under fire in the fifties had learned its radicalism during the Depression of the thirties. These were teachers who, as often as not, had graduated straight into the dole line, as with one college graduate who received a notice to report to a regimental armory to sign on for a job worth $27 a week, only to find on arrival half her graduating class competing for the same job. This same teacher qualified in four license examinations but did not find a job in teaching until the late thirties. Who, having heaved neck and shoulders out of that predicament, would wish to jeopardize it on behalf of some abstract political principle?

By the end of the 1950s, 38 New York City teachers had been dismissed after trials, and a further 283 had resigned or retired before or after being interrogated. A further 126 managed to convince the Board of Education that their break with Communism was both complete and genuine. This makes a total of 447 teachers who directly and at first hand experienced the inquisition.

What happened to the teachers who were suspended and later dismissed? Some experienced gratifying acts of kindness in their local communities, as when a neighborhood laundry and shoemaker put TU protest posters in their windows. On the other hand the unfriendly superintendent of an apartment block might warn other tenants that they had a dangerous Communist in their midst; he could hardly be blamed, since the FBI had called on him and asked to examine the suspended teacher's garbage. Because the Board of Education published their addresses, almost all the suspended teachers and their families suffered the miseries of obscene or threatening phone calls in the middle of the night. The impact of these experiences has left some of the victims in a state of residual nervousness or suspicion, which lingered ten or twenty years later. Leonard Buder of *The New York Times* summed it up:

Some became teachers in private schools, often at salaries one-half or two-thirds of the city school rate. Two opened a school for retarded and emotionally disturbed children. Some got jobs at colleges . . . A few became psychologists. But first many experienced periods of unemployment or working at nonprofessional jobs, such as clerking in an office or being a salesman in a store.

The shock to the teacher and his family, the trauma and the bitterness, can be imagined when one considers the case of Eugene Jackson, a veteran of the First World War, who had been teaching for forty years, and stood only five years short of retirement and a pension, when he was told to clear out of his high school overnight. Fortunately he was able to write and publish five language books in the evening of his working life.[16]

It was not until August 1961 that the old Board of Education, rigidly wedded to the Cold War mentality to the very last, was thrown out by the state legislature. The only teacher the Board had dismissed under Section 903 of the City Charter and later reinstated was Dr. Julius Hlavaty, to whose mathematical brilliance we have already referred. After twenty-four years' service, Hlavaty had taken the Fifth before McCarthy in March 1953; in October 1956 an order for his reinstatement was signed by Justice Philip M. Kleinfeld in the State Supreme Court. With the old Board gone, the Teachers Union achieved, in effect, new recognition in August 1962. In November of the following year the TU voted to disband itself as of January 1964 and to merge with the United Federation of Teachers. Slowly, very slowly, a movement for the reinstatement of the dismissed teachers was set in motion. After the U.S. Supreme Court, in 1967–68, struck down the laws and statutes under which the teachers had been dismissed, the Board of Education paved the way for rehabilitation by amending its bylaws in September 1972: "Some brushed tears from their eyes as the board, by a unanimous vote, approved the amendments. Several kissed their long-time lawyer, Benjamin M. Zelman, on the cheek." In November 1973 thirty-one teachers, waiving any claim to back pay, had their pension rights restored, but on the basis of the lower salaries prevailing in the early 1950s.

## PURGE OF THE MUNICIPAL COLLEGES

We turn back, now, to the situation prevailing in New York's five city colleges (controlled by the Board of Higher Education), whose presidents tended to be vehement anti-Communists of the more flamboyant variety. Harry Gideonse, a charter member of the Committee for

Cultural Freedom, became president of Brooklyn College in June 1939 and pursued anti-Communist policies with vigor and passion. By November 1947 Brooklyn, along with Queens College, had revoked the campus charter of the American Youth for Democracy, although the Board of Higher Education at that stage rejected a proposal to ban subversive groups from the municipal colleges.[17] Brooklyn and CCNY, of which Dr. Buell G. Gallagher was then president, demonstrated the scope of their prejudice by refusing to charter on campus the Young Progressive Citizens of America.

Not the least fanatical of the red-baiting college presidents was Dr. John Jacob Theobald, of Queens, who eventually succeeded Jansen as Superintendent of Schools. When in May 1950 Queens students defied his ruling and invited Mrs. Celia Zitron, secretary of the TU and one of the suspended teachers, to speak, Theobald promptly suspended the Student Council and three other organizations, putting twenty-one students on probation, with the threat of instant rustication if such impiety should ever recur. Theobald even turned up in the cold-water apartment of Harvey Matusow to solicit the informer's help in "cleansing" Queens. Indeed the city colleges were very much on their knees to the professional vigilantes; the Matusow files, for instance, contain a letter addressed to *Counterattack* by Lawrence D. Weiner, assistant director of public relations at CCNY, and dated July 4, 1952, virtually pleading that a recent student strike at CCNY had *not* been Communist-inspired. In February 1955 Gallagher declared: "Let it be recognized that CCNY is actually the college which won the Purple Heart for its front-rank and continuing battle against Communism." [18]

It is therefore not surprising that faculty members of the city colleges who ran afoul of legislative committees and of the Board of Higher Education received no sympathy or protection from their principals.[19] For example, Frederic Ewen, professor of English literature at Brooklyn College, and a distinguished biographer of Brecht, was fired soon after taking the Fifth before the SISS in September 1952. A crucial case was set in motion when on April 16, 1950, Harry Slochower, associate professor of German at Brooklyn College, invoked the Fifth Amendment as regards past membership and denied present membership of the Party. In November 1940 he had been "identified" to the Coudert Committee as a member of a Party cell at Brooklyn College, but a month later he had submitted a sworn statement that he had never belonged. Now, in 1953, several witnesses identified him as a former Communist, leading him to liken his lot to that of K in *The Trial*. He was dismissed without a hearing. Supported by the Teachers Union (the AAUP let him down), he set in motion a legal suit demanding a hearing and a trial, which culminated in the

Supreme Court's ruling in 1956 that he was indeed entitled to these elements of due process. The Court ordered his reinstatement with more than $4,000 in back pay and court costs. The president of Brooklyn College, Dr. Harry Gideonse, then announced that he would comply with the order only as a prelude to suspending Slochower again on charges of "untruthfulness and perjury" relating to denial of CP membership in December 1940! When the Board of Higher Education met on February 27, 1957, five witnesses were on hand to swear that he had been a Communist. According to Gideonse's ardent supporter Professor Sidney Hook, Party membership book No. 689 was also revealed to complete Slochower's disgrace. On that day Slochower chose to resign. He was reappointed to Brooklyn College in 1974, by which time he was in his seventies and Gideonse was teaching at the New School.

By June 1953 fourteen teachers in the municipal colleges had been dismissed under Section 903 of the City Charter for refusing to testify, mainly before the SISS. The Board of Higher Education was now, albeit belatedly, beginning to recognize the political dividends accruing from a witch hunt; in June it requested $35,000 to investigate subversion in the municipal colleges; in September the Board empowered a special committee headed by a trial lawyer, Gustave G. Rosenberg, assisted by Michael Castaldi, the "Saul Moskoff" of higher education, to interrogate all 1,900 staff members of the city colleges, with dire warnings to those who failed to cooperate. The level of intellectual life represented by Gustave G. Rosenberg was demonstrated a few months earlier, in March, when in the course of a Board of Higher Education meeting at which four professors were dismissed, a young woman from Brooklyn College pleaded: "If you fire the teachers, academic freedom becomes a myth." Rosenberg, himself a member of the Board, then warned her: "Some day you may want to apply for admission to the bar and to some other place. Why don't you watch what you say? Your names are being taken down. Some of the remarks you make today may be misrepresented."

But the popular hero of the new purge was Joseph B. Cavallaro, elected chairman of the Board in May 1953, a Catholic as dear to the Church hierarchy in New York as was George Timone of the Board of Education. Following a series of flamboyant speeches, Cavallaro stepped forward on October 18 to receive seven Americanism awards presented to him at an Astor Hotel luncheon attended by 1,300 persons; plaques and medals were bestowed on him by Rabbi Schultz of the American Jewish League Against Communism and by Mayor Vincent Impellitteri, who was lavish in his praises.[20]

As a result of the investigations that the Board of Higher Education set in motion in June 1953, three professors were suspended from

Hunter College in April 1954. They were Louise Weisner, professor of mathematics, Charles W. Hughes, professor of music (both of whom had served on the faculty since 1927), and V. Jerauld McGill, professor of psychology (on the faculty since 1929). What was primarily held against them was not that they had been Communists for short periods of time in the late thirties (as they confessed), but that they refused to purge themselves by naming others. The Board adopted the position that without such a ritual of purification they must be assumed to remain secret Party members. In October all three were fired when in 1956 State Commissioner of Education Allen invalidated the dismissal of Charles W. Hughes, and a new trial was ordered. But not until Hughes finally bent under pressure in June 1959 and named eleven others who once belonged to the same Hunter College cell that he had been in, was he reinstated with back salary.

In the meantime other heads continued to roll.[21] Henry Steele Commager commented in June 1959 that the Board of Higher Education—and in this respect it differed not at all from the Board of Education—did not know that the McCarthy period was over. Among others who did not know were the victims of the purge—

*fourteen* college teachers dismissed under the City Charter after refusing to answer questions put by Congressional committees;

*four* dismissed after Board trials;

*twenty-two* who anticipated adverse verdicts and resigned or retired after being questioned;

*eighteen* who quit before they were questioned;

122 who had come under investigation.[22]

Thus, in summary, we must ask how many teachers in New York lost their jobs and, usually, their careers, as a result of the political purges of the 1950s. Our calculations indicate a total expulsion of approximately 321 school teachers and 58 college teachers.

# 24

## Newspapermen and Librarians

### THE PURGE AND THE PRESS

An adequate account of the role of the press during the great fear
would fill a book in itself. The point must, however, be made that,
without the assistance of the right-wing press, red-baiting would have
yielded much lower dividends for the politicians and prosecutors, just
as a more principled resistance by supposedly liberal newspapers
might have stiffened the spine of the Jeffersonian tradition. Even in
the new television age it was mainly the printed word that gave wing
to hysteria.

Pride of place for witch-hunting histrionics undoubtedly belonged to the Hearst chain, with its eighteen daily papers (in 1952),
nine magazines and three radio stations. In New York, the *Journal-
American* and the *Daily Mirror* perennially screamed about reds in
the White House, about spies and plots and sabotage, about pink
perverts in the State Department and pederastic professors enthralled
by the Kremlin. On the West Coast the *Los Angeles Examiner*, the
*San Francisco Examiner*, the *Oakland Post-Enquirer* and other Hearst
papers egged the Tenney Committee on to even more heroic feats of
investigation and exposure:

PROBERS FEAR PORT MENACED
DEFENSE AREA DECLARED INFILTRATED
SECRET FBI MAN REVEALS: 3,500 STUDENTS RECRUITED HERE
FOR RED FIFTH COLUMN
POST EDITOR ADMITS HE WAS YOUNG RED; WECHSLER TIES
BARED

Few could compete in venom and vindictiveness with the Hearst columnists George Sokolsky, Howard Rushmore, Westbrook Pegler, Victor Riesel and J. B. Matthews, though the columnists of the Patterson-McCormick *New York Daily News*, *Chicago Tribune* and *Washington Times-Herald* offered genuine competition. For these journalists every McCarthy belch was Holy Writ, every allegation instant reality.

Hundreds of local papers across the nation were committed to this furore, clutching at circulation by feeding their dazed readers ever stronger doses of panic and hatred, while sniffing at the portals of rival papers in search of a staff member who might have been a Young Communist in 1934. In Detroit, the *News* and the *Free Press* leap-frogged one another in a series of extravagant exposés. The *Miami Daily News* discovered that the Red Army was planning to make Florida its first port of call—any day now. COMMUNISTS MARK 12 CITY PLANTS FOR SABOTAGE! yelled the *Cincinnati Enquirer;* then it resorted to the tested tactic of persuading HCUA to listen to the ravings of its own informant, so that the long list of names he spewed out could be printed in the paper without fear of libel. But such cases could be catalogued almost indefinitely, and these few must suffice to establish the tenor of the time.

But what of the avowedly liberal press, of the "quality" papers whose reach and influence, one can assume, extended into the heartland of the professions? The record of *The New York Times* throughout these years can be summarized in a sentence: sensitive to the rights and liberties of certifiable anti-Communist liberals, insensitive to the rights and liberties of the Left, of those who questioned the rectitude of the Truman Doctrine. (But McCarthy rammed home the lesson that liberty is not easily divisible.) Having accepted a full-page advertisement by the Communist Party in March 1947, the *NYT* subsequently refused to carry ads by organizations listed as subversive by the Attorney General. Increasingly the paper prefaced its reports with headlines far from objective: COMMUNIST INFLUX SEEN IN ALL FIELDS. When, in April 1948, the State Department refused to issue a passport to Congressman Leo Isaacson, who had just won a startling pro-Wallace victory on behalf of the ALP in New York's Twenty-fourth Congressional District, the *NYT* editorialized its support for the State Department's attitude. Backing Dewey, the paper played down its distaste for HCUA's ungentlemanly style—during the five months from May 1 to September 30, at least 171 items concerning domestic Communism appeared, not counting reports of the Chambers-Bentley espionage hearings. Increasingly *NYT* headlines embraced HCUA's assumptions:

*September 2:* HOUSE BODY TO SIFT SPYING FOR RUSSIA BY ATOM SCIENTISTS

Insensitivity to civil liberties (and to the facts) was apparent in the *NYT*'s warm endorsement on June 18, 1950, of the Westchester County grand jury's whitewashed presentment of the Peekskill riots of the previous summer. The *Times* agreed that no racial prejudice had been involved and agreed also that the whole affair had been "a calculated display of Communist organizational strength."

Between 1945 and 1950, specialists connected with the IPR reviewed 22 out of 30 books about China in the *NYT*'s book pages; but after McCarthy and McCarran launched their attacks on the IPR, not one of those reviewers made an appearance in the book pages until 1955.

Though calling for more due process, the *Times* raised no objections to the sweeping purge of municipal employees and teachers in the city; the Board of Education, according to an editorial published on February 10, 1951, had adopted "the only course legally or morally supportable." Over twenty years later the paper lauded the reinstatement of the same teachers.

What did arouse the paper's ire were McCarthyite attacks on liberals of impeccably anti-Communist credentials, like Wolf Ladejinsky and the editor of the *New York Post*, James Wechsler. All the victims whose cases were taken up in the middle fifties by Anthony Lewis and other reporters were "innocent" casualties of slander and malice, but when a pro-Communist editor like Cedric Belfrage was harassed and deported the event was reported on page nine (August 16, 1955), and the freedom of the press was not called into question.

McCarthy and his followers, complained an editorial on September 13, 1953, claimed the right "to cheat, misrepresent, bully their neighbors and ignore the laws of the land." But Communism remained the mortal sin and as soon as the Senator claimed to have trodden on a nest of genuine leftists the *NYT* abandoned all caution, presenting allegations as facts:

*October 15:* FIVE MORE ARMY RADAR AIDES SUSPENDED FOR RED ACTIVITIES

*October 27:* MONMOUTH FIGURE LINKED TO HISS RING

*November 7:* TOP RED AGENT TIED TO FORT MONMOUTH

But when it all began to look like pie in the sky, an editorial complained on November 16 that closed hearings had given the Senator "an opportunity to present his own version of things, without any possibility of verification." Feeble indeed was the paper's plea (January 14, 1954) that "it is difficult, if not impossible, to ignore charges by Senator McCarthy just because they are usually proved exaggerated or false. The remedy lies with the reader." The issue, of course, was not whether to take note or to "ignore" charges; the issue was how to present them. When McCarthy attacked *bona fide* anti-Communist liberals, the NYT invariably applied the remedy en route to the reader.

Of that other respectable daily, the *New York Herald Tribune*, much the same can be written. After 1950, however, the *NYHT* ran neck and neck with the popular press in scandalous sensationalism, offering its readers a steady supply of red villains who, "by various spiderlike ruses" garrotted defense wardens and shot down patriots. On November 29, 1949, for example, one could read:

THE THREAT OF RED SABOTAGE: SARDINE CANS USED TO IMPORT COMMUNIST MANUALS OF DESTRUCTION

These manuals turned out to be Spanish-language pamphlets purporting to explain the rules of various sports from soccer to table tennis, but in reality blueprints for sabotage. So it went on, a regular "The Red Underground" column full of patent nonsense and written, after May 1952, by the former FBI agent and Foley Square witness, Herbert A. Philbrick. Indeed it was J. Edgar Hoover and his G-men who remained the best-loved heroes of the *Herald Tribune*.

Such papers did indeed intermittently raise their voices against excesses and on behalf of due process. But their double standards reflected, and presumably intensified, the temporary moral collapse of American liberalism.

## NEWSPAPERMEN WHO WERE FIRED

The casualty rate in the newspaper industry was not particularly high, but it was high enough, and it was also spread quite evenly across the political spectrum, from the Hearst press to *The New York Times*. When it came to firing Communists or, more commonly, invokers of the Fifth Amendment, liberal proprietors and editors were just as trigger-happy as conservative and reactionary ones. Drew Pearson, the liberal syndicated columnist, came under attack in 1951 for having employed Andrew Older, whom a HCUA witness, a woman undercover agent, described as having been a Party member. McCarthy seized on this stick with which to beat his enemy Pearson. On July 6, 1951, Pearson noted in his diary:

Of course, it is always difficult when you have to explain things, but the fact was that I fired Older when I learned that he was a member of the Communist party. I confess that at the time I felt I was a little unfair because I was convinced Andy was trying to force himself from his Communist surroundings . . . In view of what has happened since, however, I am certainly glad that I did fire him.

The *Detroit News*, a right-wing paper, fired the artist Joseph Bernstein in February 1952, after he had been accused before HCUA of having once been membership director of the Michigan CP. In July 1953 the *Knickerbocker News*, of Albany, New York, dismissed Janet Scott after twenty-five years' service for her "gross misconduct" in refusing to tell HCUA whether she had ever been a Communist. In the same year *Collier's* magazine dismissed a fiction editor, Bucklin Moon, after a pressure group had complained that he had Communist-front connections. Moon's immediate superior, who protested his dismissal, was subsequently discharged.[1]

A middle-of-the-road paper, the Erie, Pennsylvania, *Dispatch*, fired Stanley Hancock as public-relations director in December 1949 after the rival *Erie Times* had drawn attention to his erstwhile Communist activities. One of the three major press agencies, UP, dismissed the writer Theodore S. Polumbaum after he invoked the Fifth before HCUA in April 1953. Although an arbitrator ruled in his favor, his discharge was sustained in court in March 1956. Precisely the same pattern of events was repeated after UP dismissed Negley Farson in 1954, also for taking the Fifth. The *Long Island Star-Journal* fired a couple of linotypists, one of whom admitted former Party membership and who had also mis-set some copy, substituting the phrase "American system of fascism" for "American system of government." The International Typographical Union supported both men, lost the cases in arbitration and later decided to introduce a loyalty oath while excluding Communists from membership. The *Los Angeles Daily News*, which had in the late forties insisted that "Reds should be smoked out—not persecuted that is, but simply exposed," decided in 1952 to smoke out two of its own editorial staff after they had been named as Communists before HCUA and had resorted to the Fifth. The American Newspaper Guild took their cases to an arbitration board which voted, 3 to 2, that their dismissal was justified on the ground of damage to business.[2]

## THE AMERICAN NEWSPAPER GUILD

The American Newspaper Guild found itself in a rather anomalous position, having recently decided to dismiss Communists from paid jobs on its own staff. A major putsch had occurred within the New York Guild in 1948 when, after fourteen years of Communist domination of the elected Assembly, the Communists and their supporters were beaten in the Guild elections.

Although the ANG's constitution forbade political bars to membership, the annual convention, meeting in August 1954 and representing 27,157 members in the United States and Canada, voted to bar Communists from membership as from August 1955. The minutes of an ACLU Labor Committee meeting held in New York on February 16, 1955, record that the ANG asked the ACLU to suggest fair procedures for excluding Communists. The ACLU declined to do so on the ground that such discrimination violated ACLU policy—although the ACLU itself had closed its doors to Communists since 1941! However, in June 1955, the ANG resolved to fully protect their members' constitutional rights, and the move to amend the constitution to exclude Communists was rejected. Writers for the *Daily Worker* and the *Morning Freiheit* remained members of the Guild.

## THE EASTLAND PURGE

At this juncture the Senate Internal Security Subcommittee (James O. Eastland and committee counsel J. G. Sourwine) arrived in New York and subpoenaed a number of newspapermen, some of whom, like Clayton Knowles of *The New York Times*, named names. The most spectacular friendly witness was the CBS commentator Winston Burdett, who claimed not only that he had been a Communist from 1937 to 1942, but had been used as a spy by the Soviet Union in seven countries. The Russians, he said, had instigated the "assassination" of his first wife, the Italian journalist Lea Schiavi, after he quit the CP. "She knew too much." Burdett named as Communists thirteen former colleagues, some of whom had worked with him on the Brooklyn *Daily Eagle*, including Alvah Bessie, David Gordon and two who now worked for the *Times*, Melvin Barnet and Charles Grutzner. Bessie, Gordon and Barnet invoked the Fifth while Grutzner told of having been in the Party from 1937 to 1940.[3] The *Times* promptly fired Barnet and later the *Daily News* fired Gordon.

In December Eastland and Sourwine returned to New York and issued thirty-eight subpoenas, thirty of them to past or present staff members of the *Times*, for closed hearings. Public hearings followed in Washington early in January 1956. Benjamin Fine, education editor of the *Times*, testified to having been a Party member in the thirties, and named one associate. Daniel Mahoney, who denied current membership but took the Fifth on the past, was fired by the Hearst *Daily Mirror* in January 1956. (A year later another Hearst paper, the *San Francisco Examiner*, dismissed Jack Eshelman after he invoked the Fifth before HCUA.) [4] William A. Price of the *New York Daily News* invoked the First Amendment and was dismissed, also in January 1956.

But it was the situation at the *Times* that deserves particular attention. This paper had angered Eastland by "hassling" him about the status of blacks in the South and about his opposition to the integrationist philosophy of the Supreme Court's historic ruling in *Brown v. Board of Education* (1954). On June 15, 1953, Arthur Hays Sulzberger, publisher of the *Times*, had delivered a speech at John Carroll University, Cleveland, in which he suggested that anyone who had parted company with the CP or its fronts no later than the time of the Berlin airlift (1948–49) should benefit from a moratorium and be accorded the benefit of the doubt. Sulzberger complained of "a smoke screen of intimidation that dims essential thought and essential talk and begets a fog through which we wander uncertainly. Nor is it the super-zealots who bother me so much in all of this—it is the lack of plain, old-fashioned guts on the part of those who capitulate to them." He added that although he would not employ a Communist on the *Times*, he was determined to allow no witch hunt to take place on that paper. Yet when in 1955 the SISS distributed about thirty subpoenas to the *Times*'s staff, each recipient was interviewed by the paper's counsel, Louis M. Loeb, and warned that he would be fired if he invoked the Fifth Amendment. Copyreader Melvin Barnet was duly fired in July 1955, and copyreader Jack Schafer in November. Schafer, who had taken the Fifth before the SISS, later told an arbitrator that he had been a Party member in 1940–41 and 1946–49, before he joined the *Times*. But the *Times* kept two craftsmen who made a clean breast of their record to the paper but intended to invoke the Fifth before the SISS.[5] The *Times* explained that their work did not affect the reporting or editing of news.

The grievance committees of the New York Guild at the *Times* and the *Daily News* decided not to contest the dismissal of staff members who invoked the Fifth. At the *Times* the Guild members voted by 337 to 235 not to carry Melvin Barnet's case to arbitration on the ground that "every loyal American is obliged to waive the use of the Fifth Amendment in dealing with Congressional Committees." Of those eligible to vote, 766 did not do so. In December the New York Guild voted by 3,185 to 2,064 not to defend the contracts of those who took the Fifth. It was the ANG's executive board that overruled these votes and decided to carry all the cases to arbitration.

As Alden Whitman recalls, the Guild vote at the *Times* was

"pretty shaming"—the issue was discussed very little, each kept his own thoughts to himself on "the world's greatest liberal newspaper." In an editorial printed on January 9, 1956, the *Wall Street Journal* commented that "honest men need not fear exposure." Meanwhile the ANG, the American National Publishers Association and the American Society of Newspaper Editors held their tongues. The *New York Post* (which protested the SISS hearings vigorously, and supported its subpoenaed staff) polled 190 daily papers in the 100 largest cities, and discovered that 112 had maintained editorial silence on the whole SISS investigation, thirty-five had criticized it and thirty-three had justified it.

The *Times* and the *Daily Mirror* were upheld by arbitrators, who ruled that the dismissals had been justified on the ground of potential damage to business. Ruling on the case of the *Mirror*'s man, Daniel Mahoney, who denied current membership and had worked on the paper for twenty-one years, arbitrator Burton B. Turkus declared that Mahoney was in a position "to do incalculable harm if he is so inclined" because he was on the rewrite desk.

Several senior *Times* men adopted the course of openly confessing their Communist records before the SISS, while risking a contempt citation by declining to name others. This option, which the management accepted as legitimate, was adopted by Seymour Peck, a Party member from 1937 to 1949, the music critic Robert Shelton and Alden Whitman, a Party member from 1935 to 1948. All three had left the Party before joining the *Times*. Whitman, who had worked for both the *Tribune* and the *Times* as a copyreader, would have preferred to rely on the Fifth, but the *Times*'s counsel, Louis M. Loeb, made it plain to him that dismissal would ensue. On November 26, 1956, a federal grand jury in Washington indicted Whitman, Shelton and Peck for contempt of Congress. William A. Price, of the *Daily News*, who had invoked the First Amendment, was also indicted, and by April 1957 he, Peck, Whitman and Shelton had all been convicted. Shelton was sentenced to six months' imprisonment and a $500 fine. Price received a suspended sentence, which was eventually reversed. In July Peck's conviction was reversed as a result of the Watkins decision. At a later date Whitman won his appeal in the Supreme Court, by 6 to 2, on the ground that the indictment had been too vaguely phrased. But subsequently Attorney General Robert F. Kennedy had all those who benefited from this decision reindicted, with the result that in the middle sixties they were all convicted again. When Shelton appealed, however, the District Court ruled that the subpoena had been invalidly voted (only Eastland had been present), and the cases were then dropped. Thus these newspapermen lived with the consequences of the SISS subpoena from 1955 to 1966.[6]

## LIBRARIANS

In May 1952 *The New York Times* reported intimidation of librarians across the nation, by Legionnaires, by Sons and Daughters of the American Revolution, by Minutewomen in Texas and California. School textbooks became the subjects of hysterical debate. "That book is communistic. It advocates medical-aid and hot-lunch programs." Or "Why do they show these pictures of city slums? That's what makes Communists out of people." From 1952 all UNESCO material was purged from school libraries and school curricula by the Los Angeles Board of Education; henceforward school librarians and administrators in California frequently cleared new programs with the Legion. *The Nation* was removed from school libraries in New York City and Newark; what hope, then, for the *National Guardian* or the *Daily Worker?* Out went the books of Howard Fast, including his popular biography of Tom Paine.

A few librarians were dismissed as a by-product of political tensions. A month after the outbreak of the Korean war, Ruth Brown lost her job as librarian of Bartlesville, Oklahoma, although she had never been a Communist. A citizens committee complained that she accorded shelf space to the *New Republic* (which was removed from the Champaign, Illinois, public library in 1948), *The Nation, Soviet Russia Today,* and similar magazines. She was also accused of having taken part in group discussions on race relations. Later, when the City Commission recommended her discharge, it added *Consumers' Research* and *Negro Digest* to the list of objectionable periodicals that she had tolerated. Although the library board in Oklahoma, an autonomous body, supported her, the City Commission invoked the home-rule charter to repeal the relevant ordinance, pass a new one and take control of the library. Two years later the Oklahoma Supreme Court ruled against Ruth Brown.

In November 1954 the Directors of the Oakland, California, branch library dismissed Rebecca Wolstenholme for refusing to talk about alleged Communist affiliations before 1948. (She swore she had not been in the CP since that time.) In 1959 the District Court of Appeals ordered her restored as senior librarian in the Oakland Free Library.

The most heated and protracted case of a dismissed librarian was that of Mrs. Mary Knowles. Subpoenaed by the SISS in 1953 after Herbert Philbrick testified that she had been a Communist in 1947, she took the Fifth Amendment. The DAR thereupon demanded her dismissal from Norwood, Massachusetts, public library, Community

Chests threatened to cut off support, and she was quickly fired. The sympathetic Quakers who ran the Jeanes Library of Plymouth Meeting, Pennsylvania, gave her a job, a gesture rewarded by the Fund for the Republic with a grant of $5,000 to the Jeanes Library. This infuriated those who wished to exercise absolute control over whether a person should eat or not; when in September 1955 Mrs. Knowles was subpoenaed by the SISS for a *third* time, she abandoned the Fifth Amendment but refused to answer questions about her political past, although she said she was not now a Communist. Two months later Philbrick wrote in his *Tribune* column that she had once been secretary of the Samuel Adams School in Boston, but he avoided any explicit claim that she had ever been a Communist. In November 1956 a federal grand jury indicted her for contempt of Congress; in the following January she was convicted on fifty-two counts and sentenced to 120 days in jail and a fine of $500. The Society of Friends promptly raised her salary. In June 1960 the Court of Appeals for the District of Columbia reversed her conviction.[7]

# 25

## Science: Sanity or "Security"?

The loyalty-security program applied to three groups of scientists. First, the more than 12,000 civilians employed by the Armed Services; secondly, the many government scientists who, while technically employed by civilian agencies, were working on military projects, as in the National Bureau of Standards, the Bureau of Mines and the TVA; finally, the scientists employed by universities or industrial corporations who were subject to loyalty-security checks by the Industrial Employment Review Board.

According to the President's Scientific Research Board, by 1947 the federal government was financing 54 percent of all American scientific research (excluding atomic research); more sinister, the War and Navy Departments accounted for four-fifths of all government research spending. *Business Week* commented in September 1946, "The odds are getting better all the time that pure scientific research will become, permanently, a branch of the military establishment." By 1954 about one out of every five American natural and physical scientists worked for the government *directly*. Nearly three thousand scientists were involved in research under the supervision of the Office of Naval Research, which was operating more than twelve hundred projects in over two hundred institutions.[1]

Until late 1949, the Industrial Employment Review Board was staffed entirely by military men and operated under the office of the Provost Marshal General of the Army. Following criticism of this system by the American Association for the Advancement of Science, the ACLU and other organizations committed to the defense of civil liberties, the IERB became in 1949 a joint board of all three services, composed of both military men and civilians. The IERB loomed large in the life of all scientists engaged in classified work; against its verdicts there was no appeal.

During the year July 1, 1946, to June 30, 1947, when the investigatory emphasis was on subversive *activities*, the IERB considered the cases of only three scientists. But the year 1949, taken as a whole, reflected the shift to the criterion of "subversive associations"; 110 cases came before the IERB, virtually all of them arising from associations rather than activities. It would, therefore, be tempting to conclude that not until 1949 did scientists feel the full heat of the witch hunt, but IERB statistics by no means tell the whole story. Some cases did not reach the Board and others were in the pipeline long before it adjudicated them.[2]

A considerable number of scientists were suspended although not ultimately dismissed. The *Bulletin of the Atomic Scientists* reported in September 1948 the case of Dr. A. Offered a post as Physiologist P-6 in an Army laboratory, and informed that he had been cleared by Military Intelligence, he moved to the East Coast from California. Two months after his arrival he was informed that he had not, after all, been cleared; he must either "resign without prejudice" or be suspended. If suspended, he would—they told him—later be dismissed "with cause," and this would be entered on his record. Although there was no formal charge against Dr. A., he did glean that he was regarded as a potential risk because of his parents' birthplace, because he belonged to the Federation of Atomic Scientists and to the IC-CASP, and because he knew too many left-wingers. Five months after his suspension the Secretary of the Army ordered his reinstatement with back pay and an apology. Dr. A. then resigned to accept a civilian job.

Dr. X., who joined the staff of Edgewood Arsenal in 1946, and who had taken part in wartime studies on motion sickness and related subjects, had published some forty papers in physiology and biochemistry. His clearance was withdrawn two months after he started at the Arsenal, the choice offered him being one of resignation "without prejudice" or suspension followed by dismissal "with cause." Although there were no formal charges, a security officer reminded him off the record that: (a) his parents were born abroad (Dr. X. himself was born in New York City in 1905); (b) he was a member of two non-scientific organizations (neither of which had been listed by the Attorney General or even HCUA); (c) he had had contact with the late Brigadier General Evans Carlson, during his wartime work on motion sickness; and (d) in 1940 he had attended a lecture in a university hall given by a "fellow traveler." Dr. X. submitted a statement in his own defense and an impressive array of supporting affidavits. Five months later he was reinstated with full arrears of pay, and on November 12, 1946, he was recalled to duty. Two days later he resigned.

An academic scientist agreed to work for six months for one of the armed services but was soon charged with disloyalty because he had said that HCUA was a greater threat to civil liberties than the CP. David Feinberg, an orthodox Jew from Philadelphia, was suspended for a year as a Navy chemist because: (a) before his marriage he had courted a girl alleged to have been a Communist; (b) he had signed a petition attesting to the good character of a non-Communist leftist; and (c) he was allegedly on the mailing list of a front. After a year he was reinstated.[3]

We can now turn to cases where scientists were actually dismissed. Dr. C., a biologist with nineteen years' experience, the author of more than sixty published papers, was in 1946 appointed chief of a section at an Army laboratory. Despite the fact that he had already been cleared during the war, his work was terminated after several months because he had not been granted access to classified documents. He refused to resign. The next day "a GI entered my bedroom at 6:20 A.M. without knocking and ordered me to report to the kitchen . . . said . . . that a civilian on a military reservation had no civil rights. . . . [The officer in charge] said that if I did not follow his orders, he would send over some soldiers and throw the stuff out." At C-2 (military intelligence) in Washington, a colonel refused to inform Dr. C. of the charges against him, even though he was required to do so by the Civilian Personnel Regulations. (Although Dr. C. was never a member of the CP, he was born in Lithuania and had subscribed to *PM, In Fact* and the *New Republic*.) He was dismissed. After five months of unemployment, he got a job in another laboratory working on unclassified material, but after six months in this new job the Army's Central Intelligence Bureau sent agents along to hound him out yet again.

Mr. E. had worked in the research laboratory of an electrical manufacturing company for seven-and-a-half years, including the war, when suddenly he was denied clearance. The security officer would reveal nothing except that "they knew who my friends were." No appeal was possible. Even his qualification to engage in nonsecret work for the company was challenged, and when he turned to another firm he discovered that the withdrawal of his clearance now lay across his career like a curse.

Dr. F., according to his own account, by and large subscribed to "the editorial policies expressed in the *Wall Street Journal, Fortune,* and *Time* magazine." A physicist and mechanical engineer employed by an aircraft manufacturer, he had been cleared during the war by Navy and Army Intelligence and by the FBI. After the war his company took on an Army-Air Force project, and application for Dr. E.'s clearance was made early in 1946. Having heard nothing in reply, the company notified him late in 1947 that it could no longer find work for him. He discussed a new job with the head of the mechanical engineering department of a university but discovered that 99 percent of its funds were supplied by the Navy.[4]

"A.," a scientist with a good wartime record of work at MIT's radar laboratory, turned down four university offers in 1946 in order to take a job as section chief in an Army research station. Three months later he was dismissed without any reason being given—but he assessed his own crimes as past membership of the ICCASP, occasional contributions to the CIO-PAC and the JAFRC and a subscription to the *Soviet Information Bulletin*. It took him thirteen months to get another job. A woman mechanical engineer, hired in May 1946 by an educational institution to work on an Army-financed research project, was dismissed a year later at the request of the local Army security officer; there had been no charge or hearing.

A scientist in the field of medicine applied for a job on a research project having no relation to military security. The chairman of the Loyalty Review Board panel said to him:

> The point that I'm disturbed about is that while you neither advocate Communism nor do anything consciously to implement it, nevertheless you would go to the limit in defending the right of other people . . . to advocate Communism . . . and the only limitation . . . was that you would limit it, or forbid it, if the conditions at the time happened to be such that a political upheaval of some kind might result.

These remarks mirrored the establishment's intense preoccupation with the "clear and present danger" doctrine—even if the present danger was a future one. Although accused only of such thoughts, the scientist was found ineligible for the job.

A young scientist working at the Berkeley Radiation Laboratory was reported to the FBI by his neighbor, a San Francisco teacher and youth counselor, not because he believed the scientist was a member of a subversive organization, but because his views and friends disturbed him: "I was very much perturbed about the young fellow getting involved in the wrong kind of situations . . ." As a result it took two-and-a-half years for the scientist to gain access to classified military material.[5]

Dr. B. emigrated from Britain to the United States before the Second World War and taught at West Coast colleges. In 1952 he was appointed as a high-grade physicist at an Army research installation. During the following year the Loyalty Board sent notice of charges against him. Statements expressing admiration for Communism had been attributed to him. (He replied that, on the contrary, he had spoken out strongly against Communism.) He was said to have tried to convert an associate to Communism. (This victim turned out to be an hysterical female colleague with whom he had had a FDR-versus-Dewey dispute, and who was later committed to a mental home.) He was also accused of having made a trip to Russia. (He had gone sight-seeing between the wars.) At the hearing, new charges were produced: that he opposed American aid to Greece; that he had said that at some time he had been secretary of a Fascist group in England, therefore he might be a Communist (!); that he favored socialized medicine in England; and that he belonged to a group that held political discussions. A year after his hearing he was informed that he was not suitable for government employment, an added reason being that in the 1930s "he was very active in the British Labor Party, at a time when Communists were attempting to infiltrate the Party." Dr. B. returned to England in disgust.

Mr. D., a physicist in his forties, was hired by a Midwestern industrial company in 1953. In May 1954 its request for his clearance was refused by the Security Board's Screening Division on the ground that the *Daily Worker* had been seen in his home "on numerous occasions." Mr. D. strenuously denied this and produced supporting affidavits from those who visited his home and from his mailman. When he appealed, he was additionally charged with having attended a campus meeting against lynching sponsored by a subversive organization, and with having changed his name in the 1930s. Finally he was cleared. However, his company had already forced him to resign by threatening to blacklist him throughout the profession if he did not; consequently the Industrial Security Board did not compensate him. He became an associate professor at an Eastern university.

Mr. E. accepted a one-year appointment as chief physicist in a military laboratory, and then, in November 1952, agreed to stay on for a further year as a consultant. He was, however, denied clearance by a military officer, who refused to see him; his request for a review was denied. Mr. E. suspected that the root of the matter was that he had once supported the employment application at a nonclassified laboratory of a person sympathetic to labor causes and called a Communist by some people in his small town.

Dr. F., a physical chemist employed at a government laboratory, was removed from his "sensitive" work in September 1952, pending investigation of his security status. In April 1953 he received a loyalty interrogatory alleging that he admitted having a Communist friend, that he had criticized American Far Eastern policy and the Korean war, and that he had been critical of the administration of the loyalty program. In May he received a letter from the Board finding "no reasonable doubt" as to his loyalty, yet clearance never came and he decided to resign. Such instances—where the scientist himself virtually dismissed himself to escape from an impossible impasse or atmosphere of suspicion—were not uncommon. Mr. G. was working in a large industrial-research department as a chemical engineer when, in July 1952, his employer requested "secret" clearance for him. Over a year later clearance was tentatively denied; then it was denied; and finally, in January 1954, he was granted clearance for *top*-secret work!

For many scientists, final clearance could not mitigate the shock and disgust they had already experienced during their suspension. In April 1954, Fred A. Karpoff, Jr., a thirty-two-year-old Cleveland aeronautical scientist, was dismissed from his $7,000-a-year job at the Cleveland-Hopkins Airport's aeronautical laboratory, for close and continuing association with his parents. In October 1955, he was offered reinstatement; he rejected it.[6]

## THE EFFECT ON RESEARCH

According to an official of the Federation of American Scientists, by the middle fifties about one thousand scientists had encountered security difficulties. *The New York Times* reported that, in any single year, between 20,000 and 50,000 technicians, engineers and scientists were not working or were marking time pending security clearance.[7] The results, as leading scientists constantly tried to impress on the politicians and the public, inevitably made America less, not more, secure from attack. Working directly or indirectly for the government became something that young scientists strove to avoid: in 1957 a survey of 209 young physicists who had registered with the placement service of the American Institute of Physics revealed that government jobs ranked bottom in popularity, even though salaries were comparable. Fields like radiochemistry and radiobiology were increasingly avoided by young graduates because they were so hedged about by secrecy rules. Karl T. Compton, chairman of the Research and Development Board of the National Military Establishment, remarked that "this great furor about possible leaks of secrets" resulted in investigation procedures that "seriously impeded our progress towards security through scientific advancement." (Yet, for expressing just such opinions many scientists found their jobs jeopardized.) Dr. Leland T.

Haworth, Director of Brookhaven National Laboratory, said, "When we bring up these flimsy 'association' charges, we're likely to lose more than we gain. We lose the talents of the suspects and we scare hell out of the rest." In December 1954 the Board of Directors of the AAAS emphasized that there were no permanent secrets in science. The question should be: What risk of delayed progress is there in *not* hiring or retaining this scientist? When the Sputnik went up, sensible Americans recognized that the United States had been jealously guarding secrets that only the Russians possessed.

## LEADING SCIENTISTS PROTEST

Soon after Truman signed his loyalty order in March 1947 leading scientists began to raise their voices in warning against the climate of rising suspicion and conformity. Many of them had been closely associated with the advance of nuclear research or the creation of the atomic bomb, notably Albert Einstein, of the Princeton Institute for Advanced Study, Leo Szilard, professor of biophysics at the University of Chicago, Edward U. Condon, director of the National Bureau of Standards from 1945 to 1951, and Eugene Rabinowitch, professor of biophysics at the University of Illinois. Professor Hans Bethe commented: "Perhaps the greatest impediment to the scientist . . . is the political climate of the country." Lee A. DuBridge, of Caltech, stressing that good brains and curious political ideas often coexisted, warned against "police-state methods." Dr. Enrico Fermi could see nothing wrong in a young person experimenting with Communism, while J. Robert Oppenheimer, in a letter to Senator Brien McMahon, boldly pointed out that Communists had made important contributions to atomic science. Dr. Arthur H. Compton told Rotary International in June 1949 that the current American terror of radical political thought led many scientists to ask whether the German situation was repeating itself in the United States. Vannevar Bush, president of the Carnegie Institution and head of the Office of Scientific Research during the Second World War, said in January 1955:

> We have a system of security clearance . . . which seems almost calculated to destroy . . . reputations by innuendo and charges based on spite . . . worst of all, we have the evil practice of ruthless, ambitious men, who use our loyalty program for political purposes.

The Engineers and Scientists of America adopted a liberal position as regards loyalty and security, as did the AAAS, which by August 1949 represented 24,000 members in 211 affiliated organizations. The AAAS consistently raised its voice against the probing of mere beliefs and the notion of guilt by association, while protesting against the effect of the passport and visa regulations on the international exchange of ideas and information. The AAAS's presidents during the crucial years of rising hysteria, Kirtley F. Mather, professor of geology at Harvard, and (from December 1952) Edward U. Condon, were themselves both the victims of perpetual political harassment. The *Christian Science Monitor* reported a symposium held by the AAAS in Boston in December 1953 on the subject of security and loyalty investigations: "Then came the question period and the pent-up feelings of the audience broke loose." [8]

## THE ATOMIC ENERGY ACT AND AFTER

Soon after the war the issue was raised whether the further development of atomic energy should fall under civilian or military control. With the support of local atomic scientists' committees, and of the Federation of Atomic Scientists, formed in November 1945 from nuclei at Columbia, Chicago, Los Alamos and Oak Ridge, the civilian cause triumphed and the Atomic Energy Act of 1946 transferred control of nuclear research and development from the Army-run Manhattan Engineer District to a new civilian Atomic Energy Commission. The defeated opponents of civilian control now launched a rearguard action by impugning the loyalty of the AEC's five members and of the atomic scientists themselves. In June 1947 J. Parnell Thomas alleged that fellow travelers were working in the AEC's laboratory at Oak Ridge. Senator Bourke B. Hickenlooper quoted FBI dossiers to denounce twenty-four AEC employees for disloyalty and subversive associations. Three were fired or forced to resign, three others were reassigned to nonsecret work, and although the rest were temporarily retained, some of them later fell by the roadside, including J. Robert Oppenheimer. The Federation of Atomic Scientists was so alarmed that in October 1948 it set up a committee to deal with loyalty problems and to provide legal advice to members. This followed an exploitation of the loyalty issue during the presidential election campaign so inflammatory that on September 7, 1948, eight leading atomic scientists telegrammed both Truman and Dewey with a plea that issues of national security be removed from partisan politics. Such was the growing fear of any sort of association that membership of the Federation of Atomic Scientists had by 1950 fallen to half its postwar peak of 3,000. [9]

The AEC's loyalty-security program extended to about 200,000 employees in all, including those working on classified contracts for private corporations like Westinghouse Electric and the Bethlehem Steel Company. The Atomic Energy Act generated a system of scrutiny that, as an Atomic Scientists of Chicago poll conducted in March 1948 showed, antagonized the majority of scientists working on government projects. Five times as many respondents criticized the AEC's security methods as praised them—the complaints raised most frequently were of lack of due process, concealment of the nature and source of the charges, the use of hearsay, assumptions of guilt by association, and the tendency to regard liberalism as tantamount to disloyalty.

In January 1949 the AEC confirmed the justice of these criticisms when it introduced new criteria for "determining eligibility." Proscribed were the following: membership in organizations listed by the Attorney General; advocacy of violent revolution; "sympathetic interest" in Fascist, Communist or subversive ideologies; "sympathy" for front organizations; visiting or communicating with people with subversive interests or associations. Such broad notions as these, of course, legitimize a full-scale witch hunt.

The tension in the atomic atmosphere was sharply raised in May 1949 when it was disclosed that a young Communist had been granted a $1,600 AEC fellowship at the University of North Carolina. Uproar ensued in Congress. The villain of the piece was Hans Freistadt, twenty-three years old, Jewish, born in Vienna, a refugee who arrived in the United States in 1941, was naturalized three years later, and joined the CP in 1946. Appearing voluntarily before the Joint Committee on Atomic Energy, Freistadt (who had formed a Karl Marx Study Group at the University of North Carolina), insisted that he would resign from the CPUSA if he thought it was an agent of a foreign power, but quoted President Adams: "I disclaim any patriotism incompatible with justice." The University fired him on May 24, 1949, the AEC withdrew its fellowship before it was due to take effect, and then announced that all future fellowships would be issued conditional upon a loyalty oath and a non-Communist affidavit. This step was passionately opposed by Alfred N. Richardson, president of the National Academy of Sciences, and by such eminent establishment scientists as Detlev W. Bronk, James B. Conant, Oppenheimer, and Lee A. DuBridge, as well as the executive committee of the American Institute of Physics.

Leo Szilard recalled how German learned societies had declined to protest against the Nazi purge of Jews in order to protect the universities from greater purges. "Once we give up this stand and retreat, there is no second line of defense behind which we can unite." The result of this furor (Senator O'Mahoney, chairman of the Senate Appropriations Committee, called for a full FBI investigation of all AEC fellowship applicants) was that in the period which followed the fellowship program yielded only seventy-five postdoctoral awards and 140 predoctoral, instead of an anticipated 500.[10]

We will now consider some typical AEC loyalty-security cases. Dr. B. and Dr. D., husband and wife, had worked as physicists for General Electric for five and ten years respectively when in October 1946 they were persuaded to accept nonsecret work at the new Brookhaven National Laboratory of the AEC. In January 1947, on the day they were due to move, they heard that their clearances were held up. In March the FBI called on them and asked about Dr. Israel Halpern, a college friend whom they had not seen for six years but who had been arrested during the Canadian spy crisis, then exonerated and reinstated at Queen's University; about their membership in the United Electrical Workers; about their opinions on Communism, the international control of atomic energy, and the treatment of spies and saboteurs. In July they were invited to visit Washington at their own expense for a hearing. Early in August the Federation of American Scientists wrote to the AEC about the case, whereupon clearance was promptly given, but without compensation for the half year both were unemployed. It transpired that the husband had given offense by displaying sympathy for the UE during its 1946 strike against General Electric, his erstwhile employer.

Dr. D., a young physicist, was employed at a company research laboratory when clearance was denied. He spent eighteen months trying to obtain the charges against him and a hearing, first from the Manhattan Engineer District and then from its successor, the AEC. He had no luck.[11]

In July 1947 J. Parnell Thomas launched blistering charges against the scientific personnel working at Oak Ridge. A witch hunt followed. Interrogations at Oak Ridge began in August 1947. The impact was devastating; according to one source, during the first six months of 1948, 20 to 30 percent of research scientists employed there departed to take jobs elsewhere. According to another, by the end of May more than one third of sixty senior physicists and chemists had left—and morale among the remainder was extremely low.

By the end of 1952, about 400,000 personnel had been investigated by the AEC. Of these, we can estimate that scientists and technicians working on the staffs of the AEC's national laboratories, or working on the AEC's research projects in nongovernmental laboratories, numbered at any one time about *nine to ten thousand*. (The AEC also maintained five hundred fellowships in the physical and biological sciences.) By 1956 about five hundred AEC scientists had been either dismissed or denied clearance when applying for promotion.[12]

## SPY MANIA: ENTER HCUA

Since Hiroshima the popular image of the scientist had been that of the Man Who Knows the Secret of the Bomb. What he knew, he could divulge or sell—the fear has always been widespread that men of superintelligence are likely to scorn moral constraints; hence, perhaps, the popular tendency to equate the name Frankenstein with the monster, not his stunned creator. The first Soviet atomic test in August 1949, quickly followed as it was by the arrest of Klaus Fuchs, a top-ranking British nuclear physicist who confessed to having passed information to the Russians, provoked a wave of spy hysteria, which was fanned and exploited by right-wing elements in Congress. In May 1958, for example, the SISS reported that the launching of the Sputnik "more sharply highlighted the value of Soviet espionage than any recent happening." [13] (What it should have highlighted was the disastrous impact of witch-hunting Congressional committees on American science.)

It was HCUA that led the way in generating a climate of alarm and despondency within the scientific community. Fired by an ambition to uncover the Alger Hiss of science, the committee began to interrogate a talented group of young physicists who had flirted with Communism in the late thirties and early forties. In September 1948 HCUA issued a 20,000-word report, *Soviet Espionage Activities in Connection with the Atom Bomb*, accusing the Truman administration of "inexcusable" lack of action in tracking down atom spies, and of attempting to frustrate the Committee's own inquiries. In the spring of 1949, loudly alleging that Communists had penetrated the Berkeley Radiation Laboratory early in the war, HCUA proceeded to subpoena the physicists David Bohm, Giovanni Rossi Lomanitz, Joseph Weinberg and Max Friedman, all former students of J. Robert Oppenheimer, and all the subjects of FBI and Army Intelligence reports. They invoked the Fifth Amendment.

HCUA pinned its hopes on a few cases, notably that of Joseph Weinberg, to whom the Committee (and its handmaiden, the press) for some time referred as "Scientist X." Three times Weinberg testified before HCUA, and each time he swore he had never known the CP leader and "master spy" Steve Nelson. Accused of having passed information to the Russians while under FBI surveillance, Weinberg was indicted on three counts of perjury. The government, however, dropped one count, the judge dismissed the second and the jury acquitted him of the third. So much for the Hiss of American science: Chairman Harold Velde is said to have wept when he heard the news.[14]

Weinberg, meanwhile, had been suspended by the University of Minnesota in May 1951; he worked for a while in private industry and only later got back into teaching. The Harvard physicist Wendell Furry recalls meeting him at a convention: Weinberg extended his hand and announced, "I'm Scientist X."

Irving David Fox had worked at the Berkeley Radiation Laboratory from 1942 to 1945, spent a year in the Navy, and then, in 1946, became a teaching assistant in the physics department at Berkeley. Subpoenaed by HCUA, he refused in September 1948 to answer certain questions, taking the Fifth Amendment on Party membership, on having been a member of a Communist cell at the Radiation Laboratory and on whether his father was in the Party. In December he explained to the Regents of the University of California that he had belonged to front organizations in the thirties and had attended Party meetings until 1942 or 1943, although never strictly a member. Fox spoke freely to the Regents about himself but not about others. The Regents promptly dismissed him, paying $840 in lieu of salary for the remainder of the academic year.

The Congressional investigation of subversion among scientists accelerated as the public imagination became increasingly inflamed. Of the thirty or more intellectuals who either admitted past membership before HCUA and the SISS, or were identified by at least two former Communists, more than half were physicists and mathematicians who had joined the CP in those seminal years, 1936 to 1938. One such was David Hawkins, who had moved from Stanford to the University of California at Berkeley in 1941 and who, as he admitted before HCUA in December 1950, had been a Party member from 1938 to 1943, motivated by the victory of Fascism in Spain, the danger of war, the policy of appeasement, by the Depression and labor strife in the valleys and on the waterfront. Subsequently he had felt antagonized by the behavior of American Communists when Norway and France were invaded, but it was not until 1943 that he finally made the break.

When HCUA demanded evidence that he really had resigned, all Hawkins could offer as proof was "my life since then." Both Hawkins and his wife refused to discuss their colleagues, relying on the First and Fourth Amendments. At the direction of the Regents, President Robert C. Stearns of the University of Colorado drew up allegations against Hawkins (who had tenure as a full professor) as a basis for an investigation by a Committee on Faculty Privilege and Tenure. After two months the Committee concluded that there was no evidence of subversion or disloyalty and in a remarkable decision the Regents voted by 4 to 1 to accept the report and to retain him. In 1953 he was appointed to a Carnegie Fellowship at Harvard.

Another physicist who admitted former membership in the Party but declined to identify his comrades was J. Robert Oppenheimer's younger brother, Frank. Appearing before HCUA in June 1949, he admitted what he had previously denied, that both he and his wife Jacquenette had been Party members from 1937 to 1941. After the war he had been associated with the California Labor School. An hour after he testified he was dismissed by the University of Minnesota as assistant professor of physics (without tenure). The fact that he had falsely denied previous Party membership to university officials in 1947 became the formal basis for his dismissal, which was conducted summarily and despite the recommendation of his department chairman that he be retained.

Having turned down an industrial job in 1949, he made repeated attempts during the following ten years to return to university teaching and research, but always without success. It was only after seven years of working as a rancher in Colorado that he at last found a job in a high school. In 1959 he was hired by the physics department of the University of Colorado, and two years later he was appointed to the faculty. "The circumstance of blacklist," he later recalled, "and the continued harassment through visits to my home and the homes of my neighbors by the FBI must have been extremely disconcerting to my children." Describing himself as a Democrat and a Socialist in the sixties, Frank Oppenheimer added: "I have not felt that I could be effective in any political movements." [15] In 1960, after repeated refusals, he was granted a passport.

Giovanni Rossi Lomanitz, born in Oklahoma, was only nineteen years old when J. Robert Oppenheimer arranged a job for him at the Berkeley Radiation Laboratory. Soon afterward he was drafted into the Army at the insistence of security officers who were apparently convinced that he was not only a lively Party member, active in the Federation of Architects, Engineers, Chemists and Technicians, but also in contact with Steve Nelson. Lomanitz came out of the Army in 1946, returned to Berkeley, moved on to Cornell and had taken up a job at Fisk University, Nashville, Tennessee, when he was subpoenaed by HCUA in the spring of 1949. He took the Fifth Amendment on Party membership and whether he had known Nelson. The next day he was fired as assistant professor by Fisk, without any semblance of due process. Having appealed fruitlessly to the AAUP and the ACLU, and comforted only by the protests of his department chairman, faculty colleagues and students, he returned to his native Oklahoma City.

With only $50 unemployment compensation, Lomanitz built himself a shack outside Oklahoma City, cooked on a wood stove, pumped his own water and read by a kerosene lamp. In June 1951 he was tried and acquitted for contempt of Congress; for the next two years he repaired railroad tracks. From 1950 until 1954 he had to accept menial jobs worth between 75 cents and $1.35 an hour, working as a laborer for the Oklahoma Gas and Electric Company, tarring roofs, loading burlap bags for the Arrow Bag Company, placing bearings in boxes for the L & S Bearing Company, trimming trees for a tree-trimming company and bottling hair oil for Rossman Products. The FBI pursued him doggedly, scaring one employer after another. For six years he found work as a self-employed private tutor, then in 1960 he got his break when he was taken on by the department of mineral technology at Berkeley. Only in 1962 was he able to resume his research. "They have put me ten years or more behind in my field."

Another of J. Robert Oppenheimer's protégés, David Bohm, followed Oppenheimer to Princeton from Berkeley in 1949. Subpoenaed by HCUA in the spring of that year, he invoked the Fifth, was indicated for contempt, tried and acquitted. Despite a plea for tolerance from a group of physicists, the president of Princeton allowed Bohm's contract to lapse. Unable to find work in his own country (even though he possessed a letter of recommendation from Einstein), he eventually found a job in São Paulo, Brazil. The American Consulate promptly removed his passport and stamped it valid only for return to the United States; Bohm thereupon adopted Brazilian citizenship. After a spell at the University of Haifa he accepted a chair at the University of London. When Brandeis offered him a post in 1961, Bohm provided the State Department with a statement of nonsympathy with Communism, but a fuller recantation was demanded by the bureaucrats and he declined to make it.[16]

Among physicists harassed by Congressional committees, a few survived in their employment, most notably Philip Morrison, whose distinction it was to have assembled the first atom bomb on Tinian Island, but who had subsequently issued a passionate appeal for American-Soviet friendship much publicized by the American Peace Crusade and *Soviet Russia Today*. Subpoenaed by the SISS in May 1953, he spoke frankly about himself but declined to discuss others; Cornell nevertheless retained him.

Less happy was the fate of Sidney Weinbaum, a fifty-year-old physicist who was brought to trial in Los Angeles in 1950 on a charge of perjury arising out of his denial of CP membership before an Army appeal hearing officer. The government claimed that the Russian-born Weinbaum also operated as a Party member under the name of

Sidney Empson. In 1946 he had been dismissed from Caltech's jet propulsion laboratory after denial of security clearance by the Army. The Los Angeles jury found him guilty, and the judge sentenced him to four years' imprisonment. By the middle fifties HCUA's interest in scientific espionage, real or imagined, was on the wane: the political rewards had proved disappointing. But the Committee's capacity to cause men to lose their jobs continued to apply to scientists. In March 1958, for example, Dr. Elias Snitzer and David M. Fine were dismissed from the Lowell Technological Institute, Massachusetts, after appearing before HCUA.[17]

## CONDON AND PAULING

Three scientists of great distinction suffered grievously for their political beliefs or past associations during the Truman-Eisenhower era. Two were harassed relentlessly; the third was subjected to a sudden, crushing blow.

Edward U. Condon, an authority on quantum mechanics, microwave electronics and radioactivity, was called to serve on the National Defense Research Committee in 1940 and, a year later, on the Roosevelt Committee on Uranium Research. He was then thirty-nine years old. After directing work on an atom-smasher and in the general field of uranium fission, he served in 1943 as Oppenheimer's deputy at Los Alamos, but after ten weeks he resigned, apparently because he found the strict security onerous. The head of the Manhattan Project, General Leslie Groves, made a mental note of this; it was on Groves's instructions that Condon's passport was withdrawn in June 1945 when the physicist was about to attend a conference in Moscow.

Soon afterward Condon was appointed Director of the National Bureau of Standards by Secretary of Commerce Henry A. Wallace. Elected president of the American Physical Society, Condon impudently issued an "Appeal to Reason," calling for closer working relations with Russia.

> What is going on? Prominent scientists are denied the privilege of traveling abroad. Physicists are not allowed to discuss certain areas of their science with each other . . . Let us cast this isolationist, chauvinist poison from our minds before we corrode our hearts.

This message was badly received by a number of Congressmen, notably J. Parnell Thomas, a dedicated proponent of military control of atomic energy. After Condon had invited a delegation of Russians to visit the Bureau of Standards, the *Washington Times-Herald* launched in March 1947 a series of Thomas-inspired leaks linking Condon to a number of organizations with subversive names, like the American-Soviet Science Society. At Condon's request the new Secretary of Commerce, W. Averell Harriman, had his loyalty thoroughly investigated. Yet only six days after the Department's Loyalty Board had unanimously cleared him, HCUA issued a report on March 1, 1948, describing him as "one of the weakest links in our atomic security" and claiming that he had rubbed shoulders with Soviet agents.[18]

Soon after Representative Richard B. Vail, a veteran of HCUA, renewed the onslaught in April 1951 by calling for Condon's suspension, the physicist quit government employment to become research director with Corning Glass Works. But HCUA kept after him, demanding an explanation for his friendships with left-wing physicists at the Berkeley Radiation Laboratory during the war. When he appeared before the Committee in Chicago in September 1952, fellow scientists from the Midwest were waiting in line an hour early in a striking demonstration of sympathy. He informed the Committee that he had never been a Communist and knew nothing about espionage. Yes, he knew Joseph Weinberg, Frank Oppenheimer, Rossi Lomanitz, Martin Kamen and David Bohm—why not?

Addressing the AAAS in Boston in December 1953 as retiring president, he urged: "Be true to your friends. If they are in trouble, stand behind them . . ." For those whose inquiring minds had led them to associate with Communism in the thirties and later to reject it, he had only respect. But Vice-President Richard M. Nixon did not; in October 1954 he rekindled the fire of his HCUA days by calling for the revocation of Condon's security clearance pending yet another investigation. (The Corning Glass Company was working on classified contracts, thus Condon required clearance.) In what essentially emerged as a crude tribal maneuver designed to thwart the New York gubernatorial campaign of W. Averell Harriman, Condon's erstwhile chief and protector, Nixon and Brownell intervened with Secretary of the Navy Charles S. Thomas, who dutifully suspended the clearance he had issued three months earlier. Condon stoically announced that he was ready to be cleared "a fifth time," but then depression set in and in December he resigned from Corning Glass with a statement that no fair and independent judgment was any longer available. His successor as president of the AAAS, Warren Weaver, described Condon as a victim of "a present sickness in our country" and of the "pathological arrogance of demagogues with small and nasty minds."

In 1948 the eminent chemist Linus C. Pauling, chairman of the division of chemistry at Caltech, was awarded the Medal of Merit for wartime contributions to rocket research. Pauling's opinions on the major political issues of the day were certainly radical: he opposed the Smith and McCarran Acts, he opposed the introduction of the Attorney General's list and the treatment of the Hollywood Ten, he agitated for world peace and publicly doubted whether justice was done in the case of the Rosenbergs and Morton Sobell. He was active in the American Peace Crusade. In the spring of 1951 an invitation to him to dedicate the new chemistry building of the University of Hawaii was withdrawn, although, in point of fact, his most important theoretical contribution, the theory of resonance, had for two years been under attack in the Soviet Union as bourgeois, anti-Marxist and vicious.

In 1952 Pauling was invited to take part in a discussion of the structure of proteins by the Royal Society, London. He applied for a passport on January 24, and, through the efforts of Senator Wayne Morse, finally got it on July 15—ten weeks after the conference. To get it Pauling signed a statement that he had never been a Communist. In 1953 and 1954 he again encountered passport difficulties; not until he won the Nobel Prize in 1954 did the State Department allow him to leave the country.

Among his other research projects, Pauling was working on a synthesis of a suitable blood substitute, with the aid of a grant from the Department of Health, Education and Welfare. One need not be a scientist to recognize the benefit to the nation, particularly in time of war, should such research prove fruitful. Nevertheless it came to light in 1954 that Pauling was among a number of scholars whose research grants had been withheld by the Department, without charges or hearings, on the instructions of the Secretary, Mrs. Oveta Culp Hobby. In the period from June 1952 to April 1954, nearly thirty such grants to scientists were canceled for "security" reasons. In April 1956 the Department announced that it had modified its policies, yet in October 1969 it was disclosed that the DHEW had blacklisted certain scientists for fifteen years, barring presidents of learned societies, graduate-school deans and figures of comparable distinction from advisory panels.

In June 1960 Pauling was subpoenaed by the SISS and interrogated about his international petition against nuclear testing and about who had paid for it. When Pauling declined to turn over his correspondence or to say how many signatories to the petition each respondent had supplied, Senator Norris Cotton of New Hampshire asked him whether he knew that Willard Uphaus was in jail for such a refusal. Subpoenaed again in October, Pauling again stuck to his position. Chairman Thomas Dodd (D., Connecticut), who referred to "Dr. Pauling's long record of services to Communist causes and objectives," nevertheless did not order him to answer or force the contempt issue. During the October hearing Pauling was interrogated by counsel Sourwine about thirty-four organizations and twenty-five individuals he had had the temerity to be associated with.[19]

## THE DOWNFALL OF J. ROBERT OPPENHEIMER

The downfall of J. Robert Oppenheimer, perhaps the most intellectually distinguished victim of the Great Fear, was staged in Euripidean form. Blessed with the early advantages of wealth and native brilliance, achieving by a relatively young age almost every ambition except a fundamental theoretical discovery in the field of physics, celebrated in the courts of commissars as well as venerated in the quieter quadrangles inhabited by yogis, Oppenheimer was finally offered up as a sacrifice on the altar of the Pax Americana that he, in his own liberal style, had helped to decorate.

Oppenheimer had taken up a teaching position at the University of California in 1929, and there he remained for thirteen years, embracing almost all the left-wing causes of the Popular Front era, joining Local 349 of the Teachers Union, the Friends of the Chinese People and, as he later remarked to General Leslie Groves, "probably . . . every Communist-front organization on the West Coast." Oppenheimer is known to have given cash to the CP through a Dr. Thomas Addis, and later directly to the Party through one of its officials, Isaac Folkoff. Although, according to his own account, his contributions to Party causes—he described himself as having been a "fellow traveler"—had ended by 1942, before severing his emotional ties he had been instrumental in obtaining appointments at Ernest Lawrence's Berkeley Radiation Laboratory for many of the young Communist physicists whose postwar misfortunes we have already discussed, including his brother Frank (who apparently told him he had left the CP in the spring of 1941), Rossi Lomanitz and David Hawkins.

Oppenheimer began full-time work at Los Alamos in May 1942, following a decision by Vannevar Bush, James B. Conant and General Leslie R. Groves that he was the right man to direct the laboratory there. It was a bold decision in view of Oppenheimer's youth and radicalism, reflecting a kind of scientific pragmatism or shrewdness which was obliterated after the war by ideological hysteria. But the new director, whom the security agencies quite understandably refused to clear, was placed under total surveillance by Colonel John Lansdale; finally in July 1943 Groves ordered that Oppenheimer be cleared.

After the war, honors were heaped upon Oppenheimer. In December 1947 Truman appointed him a member of the nine-man General Advisory Committee to the AEC, and in January the other members elected him chairman. Under Acheson he was also appointed State Department adviser on atomic energy, rendering him, in effect, the most politically influential scientist in the nation; he picked up a Presidential Citation and the Medal of Merit, besides being appointed Director of the prestigious Institute for Advanced Study at Princeton. His political opinions had by now changed from a pro-Marxist radicalism to a tolerant liberalism sympathetic toward the international objectives of the Truman administration. As one of the authors of the Acheson-Lilienthal Report of March 1946, the basis of the so-called Baruch Plan, Oppenheimer now believed that Russia's aim was to deprive the United States of the atomic superiority that alone kept Russia out of Western Europe, although he remained hostile to the spirit of revanchism increasingly pervading official policy toward science and scientists.

Following the Hans Freistadt fiasco, described above, Oppenheimer wrote in May 1949 to Senator Brien McMahon, chairman of the Joint Congressional Committee on Atomic Energy, urging that AEC fellowships be granted without regard to the political affiliations of qualified recipients.

> There are many examples of discoveries basic to the present work of the [AEC] which were in fact made by Communists or . . . sympathizers . . . It would be foolish to suppose that a young man sympathetic to . . . Communists in his student days would by that fact alone become disloyal . . . these intrinsically repugnant security measures [should] be confined to situations where real issues of security do in fact exist. . . .[20]

In view of his record of youthful fellow-traveling, and of his continued tolerance for such indiscretions in others, it may seem surprising that his own security status survived the postwar age of suspicion. It did, but only precariously. In March 1947 J. Edgar Hoover urged AEC chairman David E. Lilienthal to study Oppenheimer's file, and particularly the "Chevalier incident" (to which we shall return), but the AEC cleared him without dissent. Even the members of HCUA were so charmed by Oppenheimer when he appeared in closed session on June 7, 1949, that when he declined to discuss his brother Frank, counsel Tavenner, with uncharacteristic indulgence, passed on to the next question. Oppenheimer was also allowed to give answers protective of Weinberg and Lomanitz.

On the other hand, his testimony about the young German-born physicist Bernard Peters, of the University of Rochester, was certainly very strange. Peters, he said, had fought street battles as a Communist and had escaped from a concentration camp by "guile," all "past incidents not pointing to temperance." Oppenheimer was here testifying to a notoriously reactionary group of politicians about a colleague who was a refugee from Nazism, whom he had known for eleven years, and who had worked for his Ph.D. under his supervision; Peters's wife Hannah, moreover, had served as his doctor when he had pneumonia. Edward U. Condon wrote to him that he was "shocked beyond description"; why should one talk of "guile" in a man who had got away from Dachau? "One is tempted to think," wrote Condon, "you [hope you] can buy immunity for yourself by turning informer." No doubt such a rebuke from such a colleague stung Oppenheimer to the quick; in any event, a letter carrying his signature soon appeared in the Rochester *Democrat-Chronicle* emphasizing that he had never known Peters to commit "a dishonest act, nor a disloyal one," and warning: "We have seen in other countries criteria of political orthodoxy applied to ruin scientists, and to put an end to their work." As H. Stuart Hughes later wrote: ". . . public and personal loyalty gave contrary promptings. For more than a decade Oppenheimer had tried to keep the two in uneasy balance, protecting his old friends as best he could while giving his government the minimum of information he thought he could get away with." [21]

It is doubtful whether Oppenheimer's radical past would ever have brought him down had he not in the late forties and early fifties made new and powerful enemies, including the vain Lewis L. Strauss, a conservative member of the AEC who regarded himself as Oppenheimer's patron at the Princeton Institute but who suffered the patrician scientist's withering verbal scorn during a dispute. An even more formidable opponent was the U.S. Air Force, whose ire was aroused by Oppenheimer's eloquently expressed opposition to the Big Bang philosophy of national security. Proponents of the H-bomb like Air Force General Roscoe C. Wilson, Air Force Secretary Thomas K. Finletter (to whom Oppenheimer had been contemptuous at a luncheon) and David Griggs, chief scientist of the Air Force since September 1951, blamed Oppenheimer for influencing many leading scientists to oppose it. When Oppenheimer was appointed a State Department disarmament adviser in the spring of 1952, Air Force suspicions were deepened. In fact his conflict with the Air Force and its supporters was not simply about the H-bomb, to which he himself announced his conversion after Edward Teller made the practical breakthrough in 1951[22]—"technically so sweet that you could not argue," Oppenheimer commented—but about the whole Big Weapons fetish. Oppenheimer recommended a diversified armory and flexibility of defense based on a ring of early-warning stations and guided missiles. He criticized the Air Force for being indifferent to the fate of American civilians.

Following his resignation from the AEC's Advisory Committee, Oppenheimer's classified documents were removed from his custody at Princeton in December 1952. Although he was retained as an AEC consultant, from the summer of 1953 all restricted data was kept from his gaze by order of the President. This semidisgrace coincided with the rapid rise of Oppenheimer's vindictive critic, Lewis L. Strauss, who was appointed special assistant to the President on atomic energy, and then, in July 1953, the AEC's third chairman. In and through the person of Strauss all the vested interests dedicated to Oppenheimer's downfall, not only as an individual but as an attitude, coalesced. In December, when Oppenheimer's clearance for any sort of government work was lifted, he was offered the opportunity to resign as an AEC consultant, and so avoid a hearing. He declined to do so; from that moment his phone was tapped, his home and office bugged, his mail opened and even his conversations with his attorney recorded.

On December 23, 1953, General K. D. Nichols, General Manager of the AEC, sent him a letter of accusations; the front organizations to which he had belonged before the war, the causes to which he had subscribed, the Communists with whom he had associated in his private and professional life, the young Communist scientists whom he had employed on the A-bomb project—all this was hurled at him. Viewed from the perspective of the McCarthy era, the record certainly looked grim: his wife, his wife's first husband, his brother, his brother's wife and his woman friend Dr. Jean Tatlock had all been Party members. According to Nichols's letter, Oppenheimer himself had been contributing $150 a month to the CP until April 1942. The letter also claimed that between 1942 and 1945 various officials of the CP had said he was a secret member. Vulturelike, smelling an impending death, the politicians now descended on him; his suspension, said McCarthy, was "long overdue—it should have been taken years ago." Nixon told a press conference that while Oppenheimer *might* be loyal, he might also be a security risk. Representative Sterling Cole, chairman of the Joint Committee on Atomic Energy, announced that if the AEC cleared Oppenheimer, "then we may hold hearings"; if not, not.

Oppenheimer sent his reply to the AEC on March 4, 1954. It was a long and intimate document, stressing its author's unworldliness, ignorance of economics, politics and the media. The AEC appointed a three-man board, chaired by Gordon Gray, president of the University of North Carolina and former Secretary of the Army, to conduct hearings. Strauss, a man who needed to be agreed with and admired, directed not only that the charges against Oppenheimer should be couched in the harshest possible terms, but also that the AEC's counsel at the hearings should be Roger Robb, a tough, right-wing attorney who acted for Fulton Lewis, Jr. Oppenheimer's attorney, Lloyd K. Garrison, was not granted clearance, with the intended result that when certain matters were discussed he was obliged to leave the hearing. Most of his requests to inspect documents relevant to the defense were denied. Furthermore, the three "judges" had not only studied the record privately, but in the highly partisan company of AEC counsel Roger Robb. So little regard did the board have for due process that in its final verdict it raised points never alluded to during the hearings, thus giving Garrison no opportunity to reply.[23]

Continually the scientist apologized for his past: "I am not defending the wisdom of these views. I think they were idiotic." He now agreed that fellow travelers should not be employed on a secret project because to be one "manifestly means sympathy for the enemy." As for the important Chevalier incident, he said, simply: "I was an idiot"—words that reverberated in many languages across the headlines of the world's press. What was the Chevalier incident? It was something about which Roger Robb cornered Oppenheimer into admitting his own version had been a "tissue of lies."

In January or February 1943 Oppenheimer was entertaining guests in his Berkeley home, among them a professor of French at the University of California named Haakon Chevalier, well known for his translations of André Malraux's novels. Chevalier was an intellectual very far to the Left; almost all official versions described him as a Party member—which he neither confirmed nor denied in his memoirs. According to the quasi-official version of what happened, summed up in investigator Louis J. Russell's testimony before HCUA on October 30, 1947, Chevalier had been approached by a pro-Communist British petroleum engineer, George Eltenton, who was employed by the Shell Development Corporation at Emoryville, California, and who had earlier worked in the Soviet Union. Eltenton had been approached by Peter Ivanov, Soviet vice-consul in San Francisco, and asked to find out more about the work of the Berkeley Radiation Laboratory. Eltenton went to Chevalier, knowing of his friendship with Oppenheimer, and Chevalier chose his moment to speak to Oppenheimer when they were alone in the kitchen. But what did he say to Oppenheimer? In his own memoirs, which are fired by moral indignation against Oppenheimer, Chevalier insisted that he merely conveyed Eltenton's plea for better scientific cooperation between America and Russia. In the HCUA version, he passed on Eltenton's request for specific information—thus himself making an espionage overture to Oppenheimer—and was turned down in a shocked manner by the scientist. (Eltenton was no longer available for subpoena, having returned to England in October 1947.)

In August 1943, some time after this kitchen meeting with Chevalier, Oppenheimer did something rather odd: he told a security officer that an "intermediary" had approached *three* scientists, requesting information that would be conveyed on microfilm to Russia through the Soviet consulate. But Oppenheimer did not divulge the intermediary's name. During a subsequent interview he apparently altered the number of scientists approached from three to two. Still later, when General Groves, his superior on the Manhattan Project, ordered him to supply the name of the intermediary, he produced Chevalier's. In 1954 Oppenheimer told the Gray Board that he had at the same time confessed to Groves that his earlier tales of espionage had been cock and bull: "I was an idiot." But the harassments and interrogations that Chevalier endured after the war indicated that the intelligence services were convinced that Oppenheimer had first told the truth and then retracted it to protect his friend Chevalier.[24] The Gray Board was inclined to view the affair in the same light, concluding that Oppenheimer's temperament and associations made him a genuine security risk.

Among the witnesses who now rallied to help Oppenheimer were two former AEC chairmen, three former AEC commissioners, establishment scientists like James B. Conant and Vannevar Bush, both of whom had been responsible for Oppenheimer's appointment as director at Los Alamos in 1942. Bush commented that the inclusion of charges of having frustrated development of the H-bomb in the AEC's indictment was "placing a man on trial because he held opinions." Nobel laureates Enrico Fermi, Isidor I. Rabi and Hans Bethe spoke up for Oppenheimer, as did Lee DuBridge, John von Neumann and Robert F. Bacher. But not so David Griggs, chief scientist of the Air Force, and not so the genius of the American H-bomb, Edward Teller. When he came before the Gray Board, Teller generously assumed Oppenheimer's loyalty only to thrust the knife into the gut: "If it is a question of wisdom and judgment, as demonstrated by actions since 1945, then I would say we would be wiser not to grant clearance." The prototype refugee who becomes *plus Américain que les Américains*, and not adverse to polluting the global atmosphere with ever-increasing quantities of strontium 90, Teller later campaigned against the nuclear-test-ban treaty. As a result of his testimony to the Gray Board, he was for years afterwards ostracized by liberal scientists.

On June 1, 1954, the Gray Board concluded, by 2 to 1, that Oppenheimer was a security risk and should not be granted access to classified material. His "susceptibility to influence" was emphasized, and he was taken to task for not having made known his abandonment of opposition to the H-bomb. But the only scientist on the Board, Ward Evans of Loyola University, Chicago, had to dissent: Oppenheimer's defenders, he noted, were the "scientific backbone of the nation . . ."; and so, "to damn him now and ruin his career and his service, I cannot do it." [25] Meanwhile General Manager Nichols of the AEC reached his own conclusions, namely that Oppenheimer had been guilty of lying six times. In the AEC report published on June 29, from which only the physicist Henry D. Smythe dissented, Strauss wrote of "falsehoods, evasions, misrepresentations," and of social relations with Communists "far beyond the tolerable limits of prudence and self-restraint." And so the American inquisition claimed its most distinguished victim in typical style: by diagnosing the cancerous, Communistic core of liberalism as personified in the conversion of a radical too superficial for credibility.

In 1962 Oppenheimer declined the offer of a new hearing by the AEC. On November 22 of the following year the White House announced that President Kennedy would present him with the Fermi Award. The ceremony, in which President Lyndon B. Johnson replaced his assassinated predecessor, was boycotted by the Republican members of the Congressional Joint Committee on Atomic Energy. Senator Hickenlooper found the proceedings "revolting."

## HAVOC AT FORT MONMOUTH

In the Army Signal Corps Engineering Laboratories at Fort Monmouth, New Jersey, and at two similar establishments, 1,300 scientists and engineers were engaged in work on a 75-million-dollar budget to develop radar, fire control and communications equipment, as well as guided missiles and defenses against aerial attack. Into this china shop charged a bull claiming an intense concern for national security—so intense that within ten days of his raucous intervention key men, working on defense against aerial attack were suspended. McCarthy had long since recognized the high yield to be gained from farming the pastures of putative scientific treachery. In October 1950 he had alleged that more than 500 of the 50,000 listed in *American Men of Science* had been "openly associated" with Communist fronts, and that the AAAS was "dominated" by a clique of fellow travelers.[26]

McCarthy's aides, Roy Cohn and Frank Carr, their noses into the wind, were aware that a new personnel security review under E.O. 10450 was imminent in the Signal Corps laboratories. When they also learned that the Army had suspended several civilians working at Fort Monmouth, they tipped off their chief, who on October 8, 1953, launched what was to become his fatal confrontation with the Army, although Secretary of the Army Robert T. Stevens tried to appease him by taking him on a tour of security measures at Monmouth on October 20. "All the earmarks of extremely dangerous espionage," he announced on October 12, adding darkly that the "Rosenberg spy ring" might well still be operating within the Monmouth laboratory complex. McCarthy asked one witness: "Do you feel you should be walking the streets free—or have the same fate as the Rosenbergs?" To another he remarked: "We had 140,000 casualties because of the treason of sleazy characters like you."

McCarthy cast his net widely among former Monmouth scientists, employees of private electronics companies and even relatives. The Subcommittee's report, published in January 1954, claimed that "over 20 witnesses connected in various ways with the radar establishments invoked the Fifth Amendment as to Communist, and in a number of cases, espionage activities." The report omitted to mention that not one of the twenty was then employed at Monmouth. A witness who was supposed to have "cracked" during closed session, a thirty-seven-year-old electronics engineer named Carl Greenblum, had been a classmate of Julius Rosenberg at City College and had known Morton Sobell very slightly, but apparently he himself had never been sympathetic to Communism. Major General Kirke B. Lawton promptly suspended him at the Evans Radar Laboratory, twelve miles from Fort Monmouth's headquarters. His wife received abusive phone calls, threatening notes were pinned to the door and a hammer-and-sickle appeared on the back of the house. Other children were instructed not to play with their three-year-old son. After Greenblum had defended himself in a press interview, Lawton suspended him a second time.[27] He was later dismissed.

The Army panicked. By February it had suspended forty-two scientists and engineers, mostly without charges. One hundred and twenty charges were leveled against nineteen of them. Only six of the charges involved Communist membership or affiliation, and five of these were immediately denied under oath. The sixth man agreed that he had attended Communist meetings in the company of his mother at the age of twelve or thirteen. About 85 percent of the charges concerned past activities or present associations with individuals who were allegedly members of undesirable groups. Of approximately one hundred such associational charges, some sixty-nine concerned individuals (seventeen of them being blood relatives), and thirty-one, organizations, including the Federation of American Scientists and the American Veterans Committee.

What was the Julius Rosenberg connection? Not much. A number of young Jewish electrical engineers had trained at CCNY in the late thirties and casually known each other; Rosenberg was one of them. From 1940 to 1945 he had worked for the Army Signal Corps as a civilian employee; he was said to have visited Monmouth or to have attended a course there. The wartime Rosenberg "spy ring" was always mere supposition; its connection with Monmouth, sheer fantasy. Yet even a liberal writer like Michael Straight, editor of the *New Republic*, could claim as if self-evident that Monmouth had been subjected "to an organized espionage drive led by Julius Rosenberg during World War II" [28]—in the course of a book debunking McCarthy.

The Federation of American Scientists sponsored a report by its Scientists' Committee on Loyalty and Security, the majority of whose members taught at Yale. It is to this calm, rational but unpublished document [29] that we owe much of our information. The average age of those suspended was thirty-seven; the average grade, GS-11, at a salary of $7,400. On average they had fourteen years' professional experience (eleven with the Signal Corps laboratories) and supervised the work of fourteen subordinates. Fifteen of those suspended had supervisory responsibility at the level of section chief or above. Not one of them was ever accused of espionage. By February 25, 1954, the "leper colony" (working without clearance) included Fred B. Daniels, Alan Sterling Gross, Kenton Garoff, Benjamin Fox, Louis Le Kaplan, Alan J. Lovenstein, Joe Bert, Frank Utrianitka, Sol Lasky and Al Lopato. Lovenstein (GS-12), an electrical engineer in radar, was subpoenaed by McCarthy and remained "uncleared" for over twenty weeks. His wife, also employed at the Evans Laboratory, was moved to a post where no clearance was required. Lovenstein attributed his trouble to rumors spread by two discontented subordinates.

But what of those against whom charges were brought?

Hans E. Inslerman had been employed at Fort Monmouth since 1935. On October 27, 1953, he was suspended without charges, reinstated as of November 19 and then suspended with charges on January 5. The charges against Inslerman were exceptionally serious, although they all referred to associations rather than actions. It was alleged that he had: (1) registered as an affiliate of the CP in New York City in 1933 (reply: false; registered only once, as a Socialist, in 1931); (2) maintained a close and continuous relation with his brother, Felix A. Inslerman, who was said to have registered as a CP affiliate in 1933 and who was identified by Whittaker Chambers as having been a photographer for a Party underground apparatus in 1937–38 (reply: from 1936 to 1948 the brothers met only half a dozen times, and since 1949 there had been only a single contact between them). Apparently Hans Inslerman had been questioned by a grand jury in February 1949, returned to work with full clearance, and then been approached by the FBI in the hope he could persuade his brother to cooperate during the Hiss trial as a prosecution witness. Hans swore that neither he nor his wife had ever been members of the Party or of front organizations.[30] He was dismissed.

Melvin H. Morris (born 1907, grade GS-13) had been employed as a physicist in the Office of the Director of Research since 1942. He was accused of activity in the pro-Communist United Public Workers of America. It was also charged that his wife, Rose, had been reported to have been sympathetic to Communism in the early 1930s, and that as late as 1950 she was reported to have made pro-Russian and pro-Communist remarks. Morris was dismissed. Harold Ducore (born 1919, grade GS-14) had been working at Monmouth since 1941 and was currently a section chief in the Radar Equipment Section of the Evans Laboratory. He was charged with activity in the UPWA, with having uttered pro-Russian remarks and with having married a Communist sympathizer. Ducore was dismissed.

Aaron H. Coleman, a radar expert, had a record which could only quicken the pulse and activate the saliva glands of a security officer or a Senator. For one thing, he had known Julius Rosenberg at City College; for another, he admitted that after persistent persuasion by Rosenberg he had gone along with him to attend a YCL meeting in 1937. (Coleman said he never again attended any Communist meeting.) To make matters worse, he had been listed as a reference and acquaintance of twelve years' duration by none other than Morton Sobell, sentenced in 1951 to thirty years' imprisonment for conspiracy to commit espionage. To top it all, Coleman had been found guilty in 1946 of having forty-eight classified documents from the Evans Signal Laboratory in his home. Although it had been agreed that this was due to a combination of carelessness and zeal, it has to be remembered that so rarely in security proceedings was it possible to accuse an employee of having *done* something, that such explanations were liable to be brushed aside.[31] Coleman was dismissed.

Two brothers were each accused of knowing the other. Paul M. Leeds (born in 1920) had been since 1950 chief of the unit servicing procurement contracts for meteorological equipment. Among the charges leveled against him was: "You favored the 'leftist' policies of Max Lerner." He was also said to have listed as a reference someone reported to have been in the YCL and suspended on security grounds in 1951. Leeds wrote of his experiences since suspension: "My wife, who has been our chief bread-winner for the past 4½ months, has taken the stresses and strains admirably . . . I worked in New York City during the Christmas rush in a humiliating job for little pay . . . I answered the ad of a local company for an engineering job that I could easily have filled. There was no response. . . ." He began working as an assistant to a surveyor, at a salary half his normal one. His brother, Sherwood Leeds, a chemical engineer, was suspended and charged with having told a colleague in 1949 that during the Second World War he "fell for the Communist Party propaganda." He was also said to have attended a rally at Yankee Stadium in 1948 at which Paul Robeson spoke, and to have signed a Workers Party petition in 1940 on behalf of Max Schachtman. And just as Paul M. Leeds had associated with a suspended employee, Sherwood Leeds, so had Sherwood Leeds associated with a suspended employee, Paul M. Leeds.[32]

The charges against Harold Stein were typical of the era:

1. You maintained a friendly association with Albert Socol, who is reported to have been known as a member of the Communist Party.
2. You are reported to have said that Albert Socol was unjustly persecuted and that Socol's discharge from employment at Ft. Monmouth on security grounds was unwarranted.
3. You are reported to have said that the alarm over Communists in the Gov't. and loyalty checks were "witch hunts" and an opportunity for "boondogglers" to find easy work and, further, that the cold war talk was a lot of propaganda.
4. You have admitted membership in the Monmouth Chapter of the American Veterans Committee which is reported to have been infiltrated and controlled by Communists and Communist sympathizers.

Then why had the Attorney General not listed it? But what is most clearly brought out here is an underlying theme of the whole inquisition: only absolute, discreet, unquestioning acceptance of the orthodoxy of the day, and of the rectitude of the government machine, stood between a man and a potential accusation of disloyalty.

A scientist to whom the Scientists' Committee in their report referred to as Case A. had been working on a top-secret project until 1951, when his clearance was reduced to "Restricted." Following suspension, a hearing and reinstatement, his clearance was again raised to "secret" in 1952. Case A. was suspended on October 20, 1953, reinstated on November 19 and suspended again the following day. "Having now," the Committee wrote, "been suspended three times on the same charges, he intends to resign when and if his name is cleared." The charges of which he was cleared in 1952 were virtually identical with those on which he was suspended in 1953—that he had lived with and maintained a continuing association with his father until June 1947. His father was accused of active CP membership since the late 1930s and of nine other charges relating to pro-Communist activity. Case A. declared himself strongly opposed to both Communism and Marxism, adding, "Although many characteristics are inherited from parents by their offspring, political opinion is certainly not one of them."

Case B. worked at Fort Monmouth from May 1942 until his suspension in October 1953. In his answering affidavit he said that he had "made and disclosed about 100 inventions to the Signal Corps Patent Agency. I hold seven patents . . . in radar, electronics . . . available to the government without royalties." He was charged with having attended the "Shore Conference on Atomic Energy" in May 1947; being active in the Association of Monmouth Scientists and the Federation of American Scientists, "reported to have been infiltrated by Communists or Communist sympathizers;" having attended a social function for the benefit of Russian War Relief with alleged Communists present; and having attempted to transmit a technical article he had written to a professor in Czechoslovakia. (Case B., in reply, pointed out that the article was unclassified and appeared in *Physical Review*, which circulated even behind the Iron Curtain.) Case B. insisted that he was anti-Communist and pro-democratic.

The result of the suspensions at Fort Monmouth was a sharp drop in morale. When Personnel Officer Robert Aldinger visited the Air Force missile installation at Banana River, Florida, which was about to close down, in the hope of persuading engineers to transfer to Fort Monmouth, not a single one agreed to do so.[33] For the victims, several years were to pass before the shadow of McCarthyism was to be lifted from their lives. As of February 1955, eight had been dismissed after charges and hearings (one opened a small shop, three found technical jobs with the help of friends). Eleven against whom no charges had been leveled had been reinstated; fifteen had been reinstated after charges and hearings; two were still awaiting decisions. About a dozen were working without clearance in the "leper colony." Only three or four of those reinstated chose to remain in government service in an era when clearance was merely a prelude to a new suspension. Within a year of McCarthy's attack, about thirty-six men of GS-11 rank or above had left the Evans Signal Laboratory without being replaced—this meant the loss of about one quarter of the upper civil-service grades.

In November 1957 six of those who had been dismissed, including Aaron H. Coleman, Harold Ducore, Melvin H. Morris and Carl Greenblum, lost the first round of their legal fight for reinstatement. But in June 1958 the Court of Appeals voided their dismissals on the ground that the Army had failed to give reasons, and in October the federal District Court reinstated them.[34]

# PART SEVEN

---

# Show Business:
# The Blacklists

# 26

## Hollywood

The obvious reason for the extent of Communist influence in Hollywood was the relative weakness of alternative Socialist movements. Almost any committed "liberal"—any partisan of the Spanish Republic or the unemployed—sooner or later found himself drawn into the Communist orbit. Here, on the West Coast in the sunshine of California, the *nouveaux riches* purchased a good conscience by writing checks just as the wealthy men of pre-Reformation Europe had paid for indulgences issued in Rome. John Howard Lawson recalls "a desire . . . [for] an eventual change in the whole social structure of the United States." But did that "eventual change" entail, however "eventually," the redistribution of the $200,000 a year that Dalton Trumbo, as a successful screenwriter, was earning before the catastrophe of 1947 struck?

From the middle thirties to the middle fifties, some three hundred film directors, actors, writers and designers joined the CP. By 1950 fewer than one hundred remained loyal or could stand the heat. Max Silver, organizational secretary of the Southern California CP from 1938 to 1945, later testified that the Los Angeles County CP had reached a wartime peak of 4,000.[1] But Communist influence, of course, extended beyond the Party itself and into such fronts as the Hollywood Anti-Nazi League (founded in 1936), which doggedly followed the Party line to the point of liquidating itself after the Nazi-Soviet Pact, and the Hollywood Writers' Mobilization, which attracted many New Deal liberals during its wartime ultrapatriotic

487

phase, but lost most of them after the war, when it echoed the Soviet line with regard to the Popular Democracies and international relations. And all the time the fires of West Coast Communism were fueled and refueled by incoming New York radicals (like Lawson and Clifford Odets) hungry both for money and for the overthrow of the system that secreted it.[2]

To understand the background of the anti-red purge of Hollywood launched by the House Committee on Un-American Activities in 1947, and resumed even more furiously in 1951, we must also take into account industrial relations during the early forties. In May 1947 HCUA's counsel, Robert Stripling, asked Jack Warner of Warner Brothers: "Doesn't it kind of provoke you to pay them $1,000 or $2,000 a week and see them on the picket lines and joining all of those organizations and taking your money and trying to tear down a system that provides the money?" Reflecting on this Dos Passos-like stream of social articulation, Warner concluded: "That is absolutely correct."

## LABOR AND THE STUDIOS

The issue that had come to the boil in 1945–46 was whether the Hollywood labor force should be represented by a militant, independent and left-wing trade-union coalition called the Conference of Studio Unions, or by a racket-dominated setup known as the International Alliance of Theatrical Stage Employees. In the golden years (1935–41) of the IATSE, its president, George E. Browne, and his Hollywood representative, Willie Bioff, pursued the classic "shakedown" policy of extracting money from the studio executives in return for limiting the union's demands. According to sworn statements made by studio executives in later years, Louis B. Mayer (of MGM), Joe Schenck (of Fox), Nick Schenck (of Loew's, Inc.) and Leo Spitz (of Universal-International) saved about fifteen million dollars in wages by paying off Browne and Bioff. Following the conviction of Browne and Bioff (who were controlled by Frank Nitti, Al Capone's successor as head of the Chicago crime syndicate) for extortion, Bioff was succeeded by Roy M. Brewer, a pudgy Nebraskan who took over IATSE's affairs in Hollywood in March 1945. The change was not radical; all seven who had sat on Browne's executive board in 1940 were still seated in 1946. Like his predecessors, Brewer had one answer to any rival labor leader aspiring to structure genuinely independent unions in Hollywood: that answer was "Communist!"

The "Communist" whom Brewer and the studio executives most strongly deplored and decided to crush was Herbert K. Sorrell, whose

Conference of Studio Unions, AFL, founded in 1941, by 1945 embraced some nine unions, representing nine or ten thousand workers in the film industry. Whether or not he was actually a Communist, Sorrell was certainly affiliated with a number of left-wing fronts; in 1945 he condemned the AFL for not joining the World Federation of Trade Unions. In March of that year the CSU launched a strike in Hollywood, the immediate cause of which was a jurisdictional conflict with Brewer's IATSE. An AFL arbitration committee ruled in favor of the CSU's United Brotherhood of Carpenters against the IATSE's new union of "set-erectors," but both the IATSE and the producers ignored this ruling. The producers also refused to pay up when the War Labor Board arbitrators ruled in favor of the CSU's interior decorators' wage claim, resulting in a strike by Local 1421 (Decorators) and a further weakening of the CSU's treasury.

Violent scenes took place. On October 5, 1945, a picket line of more than one thousand men formed outside Warner's studio gates at Burbank. Before noon tear gas bombs had been thrown from inside the gates. Later the fire department turned its hoses on the pickets while police reserves clubbed them off the streets. Walt Disney venomously red-baited his CSU Screen Cartoonists when they dared to strike, while other studio bosses, disguising a lockout as a strike, managed by September 1946 to clean out some nine or ten thousand CSU members, particularly painters and carpenters who were never again able to return to the film industry. When Brewer and the Teamster leader Joe Tuohy transported busloads of strikebreakers through picket lines, the police fell upon the pickets and dragged them off to court, where summary injustice was handed down to them in batches of twenty to forty. Tuohy was rewarded in January 1947, when he was put on the payroll of Joe Schenck's National Theaters at a salary of $400 a week (his union salary was $175).

Ready to admit defeat after a two-year struggle, Sorrell was hunted by a succession of committees, including the Tenney Committee and the House Committee on Education and Labor. HCUA heard its favorite witness, Roy Brewer, describe how Sorrell and John Howard Lawson were in cahoots to tie up all the jobs in the film industry for reds and fellow travelers. Sorrell was expelled from the Los Angeles Central Labor Union as a Communist (a charge that he continued to deny) and the CSU fell apart. Brewer was king now.[3]

## THE POLITICIANS SET THE PACE

From all this we are not, however, entitled to conclude that the studio bosses prompted the HCUA hearings of October 1947, the "exposure" of the Hollywood Ten, as a maneuver to crush the CSU. It was Brewer and the politicians who emphasized the sentimental links between the CSU and the left-wing film artists, transmogrifying them into conspiratorial links. For their part, the studio executives feared adverse publicity above all else, and would gladly have employed Lawson, Trumbo and their colleagues to the end of time so long as their talents yielded a profit. But once "cornered into the open" by the anti-New Deal HCUA, the film bosses stampeded to disown their own directors and screenwriters. Here again it was the politicians, and notably Martin Dies, Jack Tenney, John Rankin and J. Parnell Thomas, who made the running—not the capitalists. Tenney regularly assailed the Hollywood Writers Mobilization, the Screenwriters Guild and Dore Schary, the head of production at RKO, as well as such actors as Chaplin, Fredric March, John Garfield and Edward G. Robinson as aiders and abetters of Communism. One of his most frequent targets was the actor-dancer Gene Kelly, who became national chairman of the Young Progressives in 1948. A year later Kelly resigned from the Progressive Citizens of America and took cover.[4]

## Pro-Soviet War Films

What most enraged the conservatives in Congress was Hollywood's unabashed love affair with Russia during the war. To the film moguls, such wartime productions as *Mission to Moscow* (1943), *Song of Russia* (1943) and *Days of Glory* (1944) constituted a form of spiritual lend-lease; for J. Parnell Thomas, they constituted the logical extension of the New Deal ethos into fellow-traveling. This was an accusation that the film bosses became desperate to rebut once the Cold War had reversed the norms of patriotic orthodoxy. Louis B. Mayer, of MGM, boasted that he had personally ordered the excision of a collective-farm sequence from *Song of Russia*: "I will not preach any ideology except American and I don't even treat that."

Most of these pro-Soviet wartime films were ideologically harmless: RKO's *Days of Glory*, for example, showed Gregory Peck leading a group of stock characters dressed up as Soviet partisans repelling the Hun invaders by means of stock clichés, clinches and a dialogue so inexorably mechanical that the Nazi war machine could not withstand it.[5] On the other hand, Warner Brothers' version of *Mission to Moscow* (written by Howard Koch, later one of the Hollywood Nineteen, and based on the memoirs of former Ambassador Joseph E. Davies) did devote spectacular resources of showmanship to blatant political propaganda; even J. Edgar Hoover spoke the truth when he described the film as "a prostitution of historical fact." The film depicted the Moscow trials straight down the Party line—the sallow, vituperative prosecutor, Andrei Vishinsky, glowed from the screen like a handsome god. Jack Warner later pleaded before HCUA that the film had been made "only to help a desperate war effort and not for posterity."[6]

Most of those who in October 1947 came to be known as the Hollywood Ten had war-film credits. There was little evidence of Communist propaganda in such films, though in John Howard Lawson's *Action in the North Atlantic* the heavily weighted patriotism was spliced by unsubtle glimpses of the hammer-and-sickle. (As the Liberty ship reaches Murmansk, among the crowd of joyful Russians waiting on the quayside is a beautiful woman who calls out, "Tovarich! Tovarich!" An American sailor explains to his less linguistically gifted colleague: "That means 'comrade'—that's good.") In general, however, directors like Edward Dmytryk preferred to limit themselves to the general popular-front ideology of the anti-Fascist era, and in particular to attacks on racism, as in Dmytryk's films *Hitler's Children* (1943) and *Crossfire* (1947). A study by Dorothy B. Jones of 159 movies released between 1929 and 1949, in which the Hollywood Ten had credits, indicated that about 31 percent of these films dealt with themes of "social significance," a proportion high in comparison to the industry's output as a whole. But Dorothy Jones could find no trace of Communist propaganda.[7]

One should not, however, conclude that Hollywood Communists were inevitably tame Communists; it was merely that they understood the ground rules of the industry. Dalton Trumbo lashed out in the *Daily Worker* against renegades like John Dos Passos, Arthur Koestler and James T. Farrell, and snarled that the "non-Communist Left" had become the non-anti-Fascist Left. He also claimed that 3.5 million Jews lived in the Soviet Union "under the protection of laws which ban discrimination of any kind."[8] When Albert Maltz, another of the Ten, dared to suggest in print that a politically committed work of art ought to be first and foremost a work of art, he was torn limb from limb for his heresy by Dalton Trumbo, Herbert Biberman, Howard Fast and John Howard Lawson: Maltz duly recanted.

## HCUA AND THE HOLLYWOOD TEN

In March 1947 Representative John Rankin of HCUA called for a cleansing of the film industry. Two months later a HCUA subcommittee report alleged that "some of the most flagrant Communist propaganda films were produced as a result of White House pressure" during the war, and that the NLRB had infiltrated Commies into the film industry. In September the Committee set history on fire by sub-poenaing forty-one witnesses, nineteen of whom (the Nineteen) were expected to be "unfriendly"; of these, thirteen were Jews. The Nine-teen included, besides the Ten eventually summoned to the wit-ness stand and questioned: Richard Collins, scriptwriter of *Song of Russia*, and a Party member from 1937 to 1947; Howard Koch, scriptwriter of the propagandistic *Mission to Moscow;* Gordon Kahn, Robert Rossen, Waldo Salt, Lewis Milestone, Irving Pichel and Larry Parks. Thirteen were writers, four were directors, one was a writer-producer and one (Parks) was an actor. According to Trumbo, they spent some $70,000 on publicizing their defense and on legal costs.[9] The Nineteen were mostly represented by two distinguished, non-Communist lawyers, Bartley Crum and Robert W. Kenny; whether these two lawyers knew the real political affiliations of *all* their clients is open to doubt.

On the first day, October 20, J. Parnell Thomas promised to present the records of seventy-nine people who were both prominent in motion pictures and members of the CP, or closely sympathetic to it. Reuter reported: "Autograph hunters thronged the corridors . . . an active black market was being orgánized for seating. Newsreel, broadcasting, televisión paraphernalia cluttered the floor . . . Com-mittee members and witnesses were dazzled by the glaring lights." When Robert Taylor and Gary Cooper appeared as "friendly" wit-nesses, a thousand women mobbed the caucus room and clothes were torn. Taylor, who spoke of Party-liners within the Screen Actors Guild and explained that he had "objected strenuously" to taking part in *Song of Russia,* promised he would never again work with anyone suspected of being a Communist or fellow traveler: ". . . I would love nothing better than to fire every last one of them and never let them work in a studio or in Hollywood again." Cooper said he had "turned down quite a few scripts because I thought they were tinged with Communistic ideas." However, he couldn't recall any of them.

Other leading anti-Communist actors who testified included Ronald Reagan, then president of the Screen Actors Guild, George Murphy, Robert Montgomery and Adolphe Menjou. *Time* reported Menjou's appearance, dapper and graying, in a double-breasted, pin-stripe suit and heavy, shell-rimmed glasses. "As the applause quick-ened, he turned bowing and smiling to his expectant audience, ma-neuvering his profile skillfully into the fusillades of exploding flash bulbs." Stressing his close friendship with Senator Rober A. Taft and J. Edgar Hoover, Menjou praised the Motion Picture Alliance for the Preservation of American Ideals, for having detected and prevented "an enormous amount of sly, subtle, un-American class-struggle prop-aganda from going into pictures." Calling on America to "arm to the

teeth" and to introduce universal military training, Menjou announced: "I am a witch-hunter if the witches are Communists. I am a
Red-baiter. I would like to see them all back in Russia." The bulbs
again flashed when Mrs. Lela Rogers announced that she had turned
down a part for Ginger Rogers in *Sister Carrie*, because Dreiser's
novel was "open propaganda" for Communism.[10]

The general drift of these witnesses' testimony was that reds and
fellow travelers habitually purchased the film rights of books written
by other reds, then hired their fellow reds as scriptwriters, actors and
directors. Roy M. Brewer testified for two hours. Anti-Communist
witnesses were permitted to testify at inordinate length, even slapping
down members of the Committee: thus Ayn Rand, a writer who had
emigrated from Russia in 1926, dealt sharply with Representative
Wood when he dared to intervene after she had remarked that *Song
of Russia* "made me sick":

> MR. WOOD: Do you think that it was to our advantage . . . to
> keep Russia in this war, at the time this picture was made?
> MISS RAND: That has absolutely nothing to do with what we are
> discussing.
> MR. WOOD: Well—

But there were also witnesses of greater weight and influence whose
posture was ominously conducive to a purge: Walt Disney, who testified that the Screen Cartoonists Guild was Communist-dominated
and had tried to take over his studio with a view to having Mickey
Mouse follow the Party line; the severe, cautious Louis B. Mayer; and
Jack L. Warner.

It has been said that Crum and Kenny, the principal attorneys
for the Nineteen, advised them on legal grounds to resort to the Fifth
Amendment. But the Nineteen decided that resort to the Fifth would
appear to imply guilt, whereas the First Amendment symbolized the
fundamental liberties enshrined in the Bill of Rights. There was, of
course, a third alternative, favored by the writer Samuel Ornitz, one
of the Ten—to tell the truth: "Comrades," he is reported to have
urged, "let us be as brave as the people we write about." In the event,
Kenny attempted to argue before the Committee that the whole investigation was unconstitutional because it was in violation of the
First Amendment.[11]

The atmosphere during the testimony of the "unfriendly" witnesses was very different. While each side attempted to shout the
other one down, Chairman Thomas had one crucial advantage—
armed guards at his command to drag from the hearing room witnesses who got his goat. And Thomas was very like a goat, puffing

and blustering and charging. Here, for example, he confronted the screenwriter Alvah Bessie:

> MR. THOMAS: Any real American would be proud to answer that question.
> MR. BESSIE: Well—it depends.
> MR. THOMAS: Any real American.
> MR. BESSIE: . . . See, I could answer it but if I did I'd . . .
> MR. THOMAS: Leave the witness stand. Leave the witness stand. Leave the witness stand . . . take him away. . . .

Dalton Trumbo, who was then commanding $4,000 a week from MGM—"I never felt the slightest guilt about making what I earned. The pictures were making millions, if I got a small part, fine, I enjoyed it"—emphasized in a statement he was not allowed to read, the sacred right to secret membership of trade unions; the workers must defend such rights against the encroachments of the corporate state. "You have produced a capital city on the eve of its Reichstag fire! This is the beginning of concentration camps in America!" [12] Lawson, too, was not allowed to read his prepared statement. "It is absolutely beyond the power of this Committee," insisted Hollywood's top literary Communist, "to inquire into my association in any organization." To which Thomas replied: "And if you are just trying to force me to put you in contempt, you won't have to try much harder." When Thomas asked him whether he was a Party member, the following colloquy ensued:

> MR. LAWSON: You are using the old technique, which was used in Hitler Germany in order to create a scare here—
> THE CHAIRMAN: (*pounding his gavel*) Oh—
> MR. LAWSON: —in order to create an entirely false atmosphere in which this hearing is conducted—
> (*The chairman pounding gavel*)
> MR. LAWSON: —in order that you can smear the motion picture industry, and you can proceed to the press, to any form of communication in this country.
> THE CHAIRMAN: You have learned—
> MR. LAWSON: The Bill of Rights was established precisely to prevent the operation of any committee which could invade the basic rights of Americans. Now, if you want to know—
> MR. STRIPLING: Mr. Chairman, the witness is not answering the question.
> MR. LAWSON: If you want to know
> (*The chairman pounding gavel*)
> MR. LAWSON: —about the perjury that has been committed here and the perjury that is planned—
> THE CHAIRMAN: Mr. Lawson—

Ring Lardner, Jr., a descendant of a member of the Governor's Council in Colonial Pennsylvania, was also informed by Thomas that if he had been "a real American" he would have been proud to answer the question put to him. Lardner, then on a salary of $2,000 a week following his Oscar-winning film, *Woman of the Year*, later explained to the press why he refused to respond to the question, Are you a Communist? If he were, he would expose himself to inspired hysteria and banish himself from the film industry; but if he were not, he would contribute to the precedent that non-Communists answered such questions in order to isolate the Communists and to please their employers. In Edward Dmytryk's opinion the whole strategy was designed to split the film guilds at a time when they were achieving unity of purpose. Samuel Ornitz and Adrian Scott stressed the racial theme. In a statement that he was not allowed to read, Ornitz pointed out that he was a Jew and that Rankin was an anti-Semite, like Hitler. Scott, producer of *Crossfire*, also accused HCUA of being prejudiced against Jews and Negroes. Albert Maltz, who by some quirk of fate was allowed to read his prepared statement, drew attention to the fact that both Thomas and Rankin, whom he likened to Goebbels and Hitler, had opposed an anti-lynching bill. Emphasizing that his film, *The Pride of the Marines*, had been premiered in twenty-eight cities at Guadalcanal Day banquets sponsored by the Marine Corps, Maltz concluded: "I will take my philosophy from Thomas Paine, Thomas Jefferson, Abraham Lincoln . . ."

The Ten did themselves little credit, rolling in the mud with the Committee, kicking and biting. They shouted and railed and visualized themselves as Dimitrov confronting a rising American Fascism. But Dimitrov was proud to call himself a Communist. As each witness was dismissed or hustled away by J. Parnell Thomas's guards, the Committee produced the last card: a Party registration card. Trumbo's number was 47187; Maltz's was 47196; Lawson's was 47275. None of the Ten dared to call these cards forgeries; Trumbo merely quibbled when he argued that HCUA had not produced membership cards, only alleged office records of alleged membership cards. In fact it would seem that Scott and Dmytryk were no longer members at the time of the hearings, and it is known that Trumbo, Lardner and Lawson left the Party soon afterward, probably for tactical reasons. Trumbo is said to have joined again from 1954 to 1957.[13]

Very different in style was the testimony of two German émigrés peripherally connected with Hollywood. Hanns Eisler, composer, collaborator with Bertolt Brecht and brother of the notorious Gerhart Eisler, had supplemented his income by writing one or two film scores a year since his entry to the United States in 1940. Denounced by his sister, Ruth Fischer, a German ex-Communist then living in

New York, as no less a GPU agent then brother Gerhart, Hanns stood up for his Communist principles where Brecht ducked and weaved with the wind. Unrepentant about having composed "The Comintern March," when Committee counsel Stripling called him "the Karl Marx of Communism in the music field," Eisler commented, "I would be flattered." He added: "The Communist underground workers in every country have proven that they are heroes. I am not a hero. I am a composer." Three days after the hearing, on September 27 (his appearance preceded that of the Ten), HCUA recommended that he be prosecuted for perjury and illegal entry, then deported. Eisler departed on March 20, 1948.

Brecht too was not a hero. Subpoenaed with the Nineteen, he arrived at the House Office Building carrying a passport and plane ticket in his pocket. He denied Party membership at any time, even in Germany, and explained his collaboration with Hanns Eisler on such songs as "In Praise of Learning" in terms of the democratic popular-front spirit of the thirties. When Stripling read aloud in English one of Brecht's revolutionary poems, then asked him whether he had written it, Brecht replied: "No, I wrote a German poem, but that is very different from this." (*Laughter.*) Although Chairman J. Parnell Thomas congratulated him on his frankness and held him up as a "good example" to the Ten, Brecht was taking no chances and left America immediately after the hearing. In an article published in Germany in 1950, he conveyed the erroneous impression that most of the Nineteen had never been Communists.[14]

The hearings ended abruptly, inexplicably, when only eleven of the nineteen promised unfriendly witnesses had been heard. The Committee came to no conclusions; the *Annual Report* issued on December 31 allocated only one sentence to Hollywood; exposure was enough. But for the Ten the story had several sequences yet to run. In November, the House cited them for contempt; in December, they were indicted by a grand jury. Eight were charged with refusing to answer about membership of the CP and the Screen Writers Guild; two, about the CP alone. They toured the country and made a film to publicize their defense.

To begin with—that requires some emphasis—they were not without friends. A Gallup poll taken after the hearings on November 29 showed that only 14 percent believed they should be punished for contempt, whereas 39 percent were definitely against such action. On October 15, a mass rally had been staged in Los Angeles by the Progressive Citizens of America, with Gene Kelly as master of ceremonies, in support of the Nineteen. Early in October the Committee for the First Amendment was founded by John Huston, William Wyler and others, with the support of four Senators.[15] A number of famous film people, including Huston, Humphrey Bogart, Kelly and Wyler, chartered a plane and flew to Washington where, with the support of the Authors League of America, they arranged two broadcasts on the ABC network entitled "Hollywood Fights Back." Said Judy Garland on the radio: "It's always been your right to read or see anything you wanted to. But now it seems to be getting kind of complicated." The impressive concentration of talent among the CFA's five hundred members [16] reflected the commitment of Hollywood's finest writers, directors and actors to liberal values and the New Deal before the Great Fear descended. The CFA soon broadened into the Committee of One Thousand, with the support of prominent liberals and progressives outside Hollywood. Meanwhile, the Nineteen launched an appeal for money and support through the Freedom from Fear Committee. [17]

Most of those who vigorously and confidently lent their names to petitions and advertisements on behalf of the Nineteen, or the First Amendment, or against HCUA, did not foresee how they would later suffer for their rashness. MGM received so many letters denouncing Katharine Hepburn that Louis B. Mayer finally informed her he could not use her again until she became publicly acceptable. Of 313 who signed the CFA advertisement in *Variety* on October 28, 1947, twenty-one were later black or gray listed. Of the 204 who later signed the *amici curiae* brief to the Supreme Court on behalf of the Ten, no fewer than eighty-four were blacklisted. (Eight gained a reprieve by naming names and others managed to "clear" themselves.) Indeed some were already having second thoughts by early 1948, when Lillian Ross interviewed Humphrey Bogart on the set of *Key Largo*:

> "Roosevelt was a good politician," he said. "He could handle those babies in Washington, but they're too smart for guys like me. Hell, I'm no politician. That's what I meant when I said our Washington trip was a mistake."

At which John Huston intervened: "Bogie owns a fifty-four-foot yawl. When you own a fifty-four-foot yawl, you've got to provide for her upkeep." Edward G. Robinson grunted: "The Great Chief died and everybody's guts died with him."

> "How would you like to see *your* picture in the front page of the Communist paper in Italy?" asked Bogart.
> "Nijah," Robinson said, sneeringly.
> "The *Daily Worker* runs Bogie's picture and right away, he's a dangerous Communist," said Miss Bacall.
> "Let's eat," said Huston.

For the Ten, eating was soon to become a problem. Within a month of the HCUA hearings, five of the Ten who were at that time still under contract were summarily fired: Trumbo and Cole by MGM, Dmytryk and Scott by RKO and Lardner by Twentieth Century-Fox. In April 1948 Lawson and Trumbo, whom the others agreed to regard as test cases, were found guilty of contempt of Congress. The decision was upheld on appeal and in April 1950—following the deaths of two liberal justices, Murphy and Rutledge—the Supreme Court denied *certiorari*, with Black and Douglas dissenting. And so the Ten, who had twenty-three children among them, went to prison: two to Danbury, Connecticut; two to Texarkana, Texas; three to Ashland, Kentucky; two to Millpoint, West Virginia; while Samuel Ornitz, for health reasons, served in the Federal Medical Center, Springfield, Massachusetts. Trumbo began to write poems to his wife and children for publication in *Masses and Mainstream*:

> *Say then but this of me:*
> *Preferring not to crawl on his knees*
> *In freedom to a bowl of buttered slops*
> *Set out for him by some contemptuous clown,*
> *He walked to jail on his feet.*[18]

The most bizarre episode in the imprisonment of the Ten occurred when Ring Lardner, Jr., taking exercise in the yard of Danbury prison, came across the short, tubby, red-faced J. Parnell Thomas, whose career in politics had been cut short by the discovery of certain financial irregularities known as payroll padding. No word was exchanged between them.

## THE FILM BOSSES PANIC

But what of the film bosses? When two HCUA staffmen, H. A. Smith and A. B. Leckie, called on Louis B. Mayer, head of MGM and from 1941 to 1945 the highest-salaried executive in the United States, and urged him to clean house before forced to do so by Congress or public opinion, he handed over a couple of token names and urged Congress to pass legislation that would enable private employers to dismiss Communists. He didn't mean it, of course: as his general manager, F. J. Mannix, told the same two investigators: "I don't give a damn whether they are Communists or not. All I am looking for is getting people to write scripts for me." Only Jack L. Warner, vice-president in charge of production at Warner Brothers, displayed any real enthusiasm for the purge, yet he too was caught in confusion.

Testifying in executive session in May 1947, he named sixteen writers as reds and claimed he had fired or "let go" most of them, although he hadn't; testifying before HCUA in October, he apologized: "I was naturally carried away . . . I was rather emotional, being in a very emotional business, to a degree." Of Elia Kazan he remarked: "This fellow is also one of the mob. I pass him by and won't talk to him." He pledged that he and his brothers would contribute to a fund to "ship to Russia the people who don't like our American system of government." [19]

The film bosses were at first cautioned by legal advice that to eliminate proven Communists from the industry might amount to a conspiracy. Eric A. Johnston, head of the Motion Picture Association and the Association of Motion Picture Producers, had suggested such an agreement to a meeting of top executives on June 2, 1947, but the lawyers had vetoed it. Johnston, a former president of the U.S. Chamber of Commerce, assured the Nineteen and their lawyers in the Shoreham Hotel that the MPA would never be a party to a blacklist. On October 27, he announced: "We are not going to be pushovers for outside regulation. We are going to fight back at the threat of official censorship wherever it exists"; but he also told HCUA he would not employ any *proven* Communists. He thought there was an obligation to expose them. [20]

On November 24, after the HCUA hearings, a crucial meeting of the MPA and of the AMPP took place in the Waldorf-Astoria, New York, attended by some fifty executives and the long shadow of the New York financiers. Paramount, Columbia, MGM, RKO, Twentieth Century-Fox, Warner Brothers and Universal were all tied up with banking and industrial interests. A statement was issued that "nothing subversive or un-American has appeared on the screen," and that the studios intended to discharge or suspend without compensation those (five) of the Ten still in their employ. However, the tone remained bold and liberal: "In pursuing this policy, we are not going to be swamped by hysteria or intimidated from any source . . . There is the danger of hurting innocent people. There is the risk of creating an atmosphere of fear."

Although Sam Goldwyn, producer of Lewis Milestone's *North Star*, had taken a skeptical view of the HCUA hearings and opposed the blacklist, he now went along with the majority. But it was Dore Schary, head of production at RKO, and in his time widely criticized as a leftist, who epitomized the abject capitulation of the producers. Before HCUA he had boldly insisted that until it was proved that a Communist was a man dedicated to the overthrow of the government by force or violence, he would judge him by his personal capabilities alone. After the November 24 meeting of the MPA, Schary had to change his approach or change his profession. He now explained to the SWG that in order to protect the freedom of the industry it would henceforward be necessary to fire and blacklist the Ten, and to reject anyone thought to be a Communist. In mid-November this became RKO's policy.[21]

About that time Lillian Ross visited the Hollywood home of N. Peter Rathvon, president of RKO and former New York attorney and investment banker. Someone reminded him that *Crossfire* had cost only $595,000 and had grossed $3,000,000. Yet he had fired Scott and Dmytryk, producer and director of the film.

> "I sure hated to lose those boys," Rathvon said miserably. "Brilliant craftsmen, both of them. It's just that their usefulness to the studio is at an end. Would you like to go out on the terrace and look down on the lights of Hollywood?"

Eric Johnston, who had the impudence to receive an award given to *Crossfire* in Philadelphia, delivered a speech in which he promised that Hollywood would be vigilant against all forms of intolerance.[22] Ahead of Johnston and the MPA lay a deal with HCUA that was destined to endure throughout the 1950s: the producers would sacrifice individuals, while HCUA would never again attack films and the studios that made them.

As the studios prepared to impose their new policy, the Screen Writers Guild (founded in 1937 and with some 937 voting members by the late forties) became the center of the storm. There is no doubt that within the Guild the Communists and their friends exercised an influence disproportionate to their numbers by means of militant trade-union negotiating and by shouldering the donkey work around the office. Feelings now ran high; at a packed meeting Dalton Trumbo described Dore Schary as a thief, to say the least. The right-wing *Hollywood Reporter* now characterized the archetypal screenwriter as the "Molotov of our industry" and screamed: "SOMETHING MUST BE DONE ABOUT THESE PEOPLE." [23] The SWG decided by a large majority to oppose any blacklist, and in 1949 it brought suit against the producers to restrain them from blacklisting on political grounds.

## 1951: HCUA RETURNS

The political and psychological groundwork for the Hollywood purge was laid in 1947. During the four years that followed, however, there was an uneasy lull; those film people who had rashly committed themselves to a liberal position in 1947 were able—in most, but not all cases—to find work. It was in 1951 that the gorgon's eye focused once more, fatally this time, on Hollywood. The blacklist was born.

HCUA's second investigation began on March 8, 1951. On this occasion all the accusations were against individuals; no films were censured. The sole preoccupation of the Wood Committee, which subpoenaed forty-five unfriendly witnesses, was naming names— names, names, more names. HCUA already knew the names, of course, either from the researches of its investigators or from executive-session testimony; but only through the humiliating ritual of informing on former colleagues could the penitent ex-Communist purge and purify himself and so regain the confidence of the inquisition. Consequently the friendly witnesses were now no longer vigilantes of crackpot disposition like Adolphe Menjou or frightened executives like Jack L. Warner, but ex-Communists scrambling to save their own careers. In 1951 some thirty Hollywood ex-Communists named some three hundred colleagues. A new kind of talkie was born.

A new generation of defiant witnesses, some taking the First Amendment but all taking the Fifth to protect themselves from the fate of the Ten, now faced the ruination of their careers. The actor Howard Da Silva, who accused the Committee of trying to equate peace with subversion, not only became unemployable after some forty films, he was actually excised from the RKO film *Slaughter Trial*, which he had just shot, at a cost of $100,000. The actress Gale Sondergaard, whose 1945 Party registration card HCUA claimed to possess, the actor Will Geer, and the screenwriters Robert Lees, Waldo Salt (who wrote *Midnight Cowboy*, 1969) and Paul Jarrico were all blacklisted. Taking the Fifth, Jarrico defended his "dear friends," the Ten. Representative Clyde Doyle of HCUA assured him that "we are not interested in blacklisting anyone."

The studios were thrown into panic. This new onslaught came at a time when the film industry was beginning to experience a financial crisis brought on by new patterns of leisure-spending and by television.[24] In this climate the industry was bound to avoid all political and social subjects of a possibly "controversial" nature. In 1950 a studio even shelved a film about Hiawatha after six months' work, because it was feared that the message for peace might be misconstrued. At the same time Hollywood attempted to appease the gods, or the Legionnaires, by churning out anti-Communist films of dubious artistic quality.[25] Fifty such feature films, besides many documentaries and shorts, had been released or were in production by 1951. The fictional American reds of Hollywood's imagining were mostly gangsters in fast get-away cars who machine-gunned all opposition. As for the films set in Eastern Europe, the Communist world was henceforward populated by somber bureaucrats and dedicated robots. Most of these films were commercial failures—protection money paid to the *Zeitgeist*.

## VIGILANTES AND PRESSURE GROUPS

Foremost among the pressure groups baying for blood were the Legion, representing Middle America outside the industry, and the Motion Picture Alliance for the Preservation of American Ideals, founded in 1944, whose president in 1951 was John Wayne and whose executive committee included the union boss Roy M. Brewer, Gary Cooper, John Ford, Clark Gable, James K. McGuinness, Adolphe Menjou and Robert Tuohy. It was the Alliance that published Ayn Rand's *Screen Guide for Americans*—"Don't smear the free enterprise system . . . don't glorify the collective." At a meeting on March 22, Wayne declared, "The bankers and stockholders must recognize that their investments are imperiled as long as we have these elements in our midst." Professional hate-columnists like Victor Riesel and Hedda Hopper (she was an MPAPAI vice-president) castigated as insincere the lukewarm repentances of actors such as José Ferrer (whose film *Cyrano de Bergerac* was put in jeopardy) and Larry Parks. Here is Hopper in action before an enthusiastic Alliance audience: "And I'm wondering if the mothers and fathers of those who've died and the wounded who are still living will be happy to know their money at the box office has supported and may continue to support those who have been so late in the defense of their country." [26] Columbia responded by canceling the contract of Larry Parks, who was hounded by the vigilantes until he begged forgiveness before HCUA in 1953.

Without doubt the politically most powerful figure in the MPAPAI was Roy M. Brewer, labor boss of the IATSE, a friend of the studios, and strikebreaker extraordinary—qualities for which he was duly rewarded in 1955 when appointed a New York studio executive for Allied Artists. Closely associated as he was with leading practitioners of the "clearance business," like Vincent Hartnett and George Sokolsky, Brewer negotiated the repentance, confession and final clearance of Dmytryk, Ferrer, Kelly and Huston. Like J. Edgar Hoover, he constantly referred to "our Judeo-Christian heritage."

Trailing the wolves and darting for the limelight were the jackals of the exposure racket: Myron C. Fagan, author of *Documentation of the Red Stars in Hollywood*, et cetera, and Ed Gibbons, editor of *Alert*, a West Coast magazine whose general style can be judged from the following headlines taken from the February 1952 issue:

Stalinist Aroma Is Heavy Over Radio Writers Guild Voting/Red Current in Grid Film/Demos' Reds Spotlighted/Tenney Probe On/Commie Campaign Hits U.S. Law and Order/Global Peace Agitation Order by Reds/Film Cleanup Stymied/Stalin's Stooges in Hollywoodland/Capitalism for the Millions.

Also involved was the union-busting, blacklisting group called the Wage Earners Committee, which in 1951 listed ninety-three films "which employ commies and fellow travelers and contain subversive matter designed to defame America throughout the world." Such a film, in the eyes of these defenders of "our boys in Korea," was *Death of a Salesman*, based on Arthur Miller's play, starring Fredric March and produced by Stanley Kramer. The WEC threw up yet another of its picket lines outside the cinemas.[27]

But no pressure group could begin to compete in influence with the American Legion, with its 2.5 million members and its million "auxiliaries" (wives, etc.). In May 1949 the *American Legion Magazine* ran an article by Richard E. Combs, counsel to the Tenney Committee, about "How Communists Make Stooges out of Movie Stars." Two years later the Legion's national convention called for the launching of a "public information program" on this subject, and the *Legion Magazine* unleashed a blow that brought the film industry, already groggy from HCUA's jabs, to its knees. The veteran Hearst expert on Communist subversion, J. B. "Doc" Matthews, had been hired to answer the question "Did the Movies Really Clean House?" with a resounding—and menacing—No.

Matthews estimated that HCUA had by that time exposed two hundred of the roughly three hundred Hollywood personalities who had at one period or another held Party cards. But, he warned, powerful fellow travelers remained undetected and unpunished, notably those who, like Ferrer and Judy Holliday, had sponsored the Waldorf Conference in 1949, or those who, like Chaplin, Garfield, Huston, Burt Lancaster, Arthur Miller, Clifford Odets, Sam Wanamaker and William Tyler, had signed the *amici curiae* brief to the Supreme Court on behalf of the Ten. Matthews raised blood pressures among studio executives by listing the films recently made and released with the collaboration of "Communists" or their "collaborators."[28]

March 31 was the first of two occasions in 1952 when studio executives met Legion officials, including the national commander, Donald R. Wilson. In May, Legion representatives inspected the West Coast studios. Promising not to employ anyone who resorted to the Fifth Amendment, the producers begged the Legion to provide information about suspects and to set up a machinery by which the innocent could clear themselves. The Legion agreed to send the studio its dossiers on two or three hundred characters in the film industry. By the summer of 1952 the Legion's offices were swamped with desperate appeals for clearance from actors and their agents, but the Legion, like the FBI, delighted in the claim that it passed judgment on nobody—merely information. Yet James P. O'Neill, head of the Legion's blacklisting operations, was regarded, along with Sokolsky, Brewer and Riesel, as one of the Big Four in the clearance business.

The studios, meanwhile, instructed some three hundred of their employees to write long letters to the Legion explaining their past political heresies and stressing their repentance. "The spirit of the Legion in this matter is one of friendly cooperation," said Y. Frank Freeman, vice-president of Paramount. Apparently all but about twenty-five of those who followed this groveling procedure—Why did you write anti-loyalty-oath editorials in your college magazine? Why did the *Daily People's World* review a movie in which you worked? Why are you so active in your trade union?—gave satisfaction.[29]

In December 1952 the Legion began picketing *Moulin Rouge*, whose star and director, Ferrer and Huston, were both in disgrace. Evidently these two hastened to make their peace, for the Legion announced on January 15, 1953, that "they are displaying the type of cooperation we have requested in the past." Yet the Legion also warned that some left-wing producers were now working in collaboration with French and Italian Communists. United Artists had promised to scrutinize more carefully the foreign films it distributed; the loophole must be closed.

## THE BLACKLIST IN OPERATION

HCUA, meanwhile, kept the studios on their toes, returning to the subject of screen subversion in 1953, 1955, 1956 and 1958, by which time seventy-two "friendly" witnesses had named about 325 film people as past or present Communists. Every studio now had a Mr. X who acted as "clearer," the man who would call you in and tell you what you had to do. He might be a lawyer, a labor-relations specialist, or a vice-president; at MGM the job was performed by L. K. Sidney, and at Columbia by B. B. Kahane. New contracts tended now to specify suspension if the employee refused to testify or was cited for contempt. The atmosphere was fraught. One actor who had worked in cinema and theater since 1925 was summoned by an MGM executive during the 1952 production of *Julius Caesar*. Still wearing a toga, he was fired on the spot for refusing to say whether he was a Party member. All doors were then closed to him.[30]

The will of the Screen Writers Guild to resist the blacklist was gradually eroded. After Paul Jarrico took the Fifth in 1951, Howard Hughes's RKO announced that he had thereby breached the morals clause of his contract and that the studio would therefore excise his name as writer of *The Las Vegas Story*. The SWG brought suit against RKO, lost, appealed and lost again. The trial judge found that the Legion, *ergo* the general public, bore ill will toward Jarrico. The SWG now capitulated. In April 1953 it signed an amendment to its agreement with the Association of Motion Picture Producers that left blacklisted writers without any protection. In August 1954 the SWG voted by 325 to 12 in favor of an amendment barring Communists from membership. Not until June 1960, following a six-month strike by the Guild, was Article 6 of the Minimum Basic Agreement, covering credits, revised to its original status. Meanwhile the Screen Actors Guild, under the presidency of Ronald Reagan, introduced a loyalty oath for new members in 1953, and required its officials to sign non-Communist affidavits. In July 1953 the SAG voted by 3,769 to 152 to ban Communists from membership. But the really crucial capitulation had come two years earlier, in March 1951, when the SAG had announced it would not force the employment of any actor whose "actions outside of union activities have so offended American public opinion that he has made himself unsaleable at the box office."

The operation of the blacklist and graylist was something the studios did not want to talk about and, in the case of the graylist, something the victim too did not wish to advertise, lest he further jeopardize his job chances. In films, as in radio and television, profiteers fed off the blacklist and worked to perpetuate it. Spyros Skouras of Fox, who asked several people working on Kazan's *Viva Zapata!* to write him letters explaining their front associations, joined with Nate Spingold, vice-president of Columbia, in contacting the Hearst journalist George Sokolsky as to how people might clear themselves. Sokolsky wrote to HCUA that he had undertaken "the burdens of a private citizen judging the political trustworthiness of other private citizens." He claimed that about three hundred members of the film industry had been rehabilitated with his help. The actor Edward G. Robinson recalled that when his career was threatened he one day received a visit from the journalist Victor Lasky, who had prepared a twenty-six-page confession for him to sign. (He didn't.) John Garfield got in touch with Arnold Forster, of the Anti-Defamation League, who in turn put him in touch with Victor Riesel. Forster on several occasions acted as an intermediary between Jews who repented of their erstwhile Communist connections and the right-wing clearance racketeers.[31]

There were also lawyers and psychoanalysts who profited from the blacklist. One Beverly Hills psychoanalyst eased the pangs of conscience of eight witnesses before HCUA, all of them cooperative. The moral angle was simple: "Hell, they've all been named already . . . they can't be killed twice." The technical angle was less simple: to compose a plausible *mea culpa* in which the penitent depicted himself as a duped, naïve artist. The actor Sterling Hayden later recalled sardonically the energy and enthusiasm that his lawyer and his psychoanalyst, not to mention his studio executives, had devoted to his confession.[32]

## Those Who Named Names

With their careers threatened by HCUA, by the Legion, by the MPAPAI, many actors, writers and directors swallowed their pride, suppressed their sense of honor and licked the boots of their tormentors. In general the big stars capitulated most completely; those with the most to lose were the most reluctant to lose it.

Larry Parks was the only actor among the Nineteen subpoenaed in 1947. He had recently made his name in *The Al Jolson Story* when, in 1951, HCUA subpoenaed him again; this time he was called upon to testify. Admitting that he had been a CP member from 1941 to 1945, he begged the Committee not to force him to name others: "Don't present me with the choice of either being in contempt of this Committee and going to jail or forcing me to really crawl through the mud to be an informer." Threatened with a contempt citation, Parks named one writer and eleven actors and actresses in executive session as former Communists, including Lee J. Cobb, Morris Carnovsky, Ann Revere, Karen Morley and Gale Sondergaard. But Parks, who had some twenty-six film credits from 1941 to 1950, managed to find only two film parts during the fifties.

John Garfield was the star and part owner of a new film, somewhat cruelly entitled *He Ran All the Way*, when HCUA subpoenaed him. Active in the Group Theater in the late thirties, and a member of the Young People's Socialist League, Garfield had endorsed the Moscow trials in 1938, supported Henry Wallace in 1948 and associated himself with the JAFRC and the CFA. Possibly he had never joined the CP. Certainly he insisted before HCUA that he couldn't give the names of any Communists because he didn't know any. The Committee sent his testimony to the Justice Department for a possible perjury prosecution; Garfield went to pieces under the strain and died of a heart attack in May 1952.

"I am not arguing the point. I was just offering one more weak excuse." This was the tone adopted by José Ferrer when he testified before HCUA in May 1951 and urged that the CP be outlawed. The star of *Othello* and of Stanley Kramer's *Cyrano de Bergerac*, which was due for release, Ferrer took out paid advertisements in the press in a desperate attempt to dissociate himself from his own past. Admitting that he had supported Benjamin Davis, Jr., for the New York City Council, he pleaded naïveté and bad memory: "You know, it was only the other day that I discovered that May Day is a Communist celebration." Why had he helped to raise money for the Spanish Refugee Appeal and other Spanish Republican causes? Well, he was from Puerto Rico. Why had he sponsored a host of Communist-front activities since the war? Why had he criticized HCUA and the Tenney Committee? Why had he sent anniversary greetings to the Moscow Art Theater in November 1948? Well, "When I see something endorsed by the AF of L, of which I am a member, and the CIO, when I see Mrs. Eleanor Roosevelt's name, or Fiorello LaGuardia's name, or Mayor O'Dwyer's name, I drop my guard and say 'Yes, I think it is safe to go along with those people.' I have been wrong time and again." He now believed that HCUA was "fulfilling an extremely important function" in a fair and decent way.[33]

"I was duped and used. I was lied to. But, I repeat, I acted from good motives and I have never knowingly aided Communists or any Communist cause." Thus spake Edward G. Robinson, when he appeared for the third time before HCUA in April 1952. Born in Rumania as Emanuel Goldenberg, and made famous as a screen gangster by his role in the film *Little Caesar*, Robinson had never joined the CP but had come too close to it for comfort in Cold War America. Letting it be known that he possessed letters of commendation not only from the California Legion but also from J. Edgar Hoover, for his performance as an FBI agent in a radio play, he decided to prepare a list of every organization he had ever belonged to, and of every check he had ever paid to a good cause, and send the lot to Hoover. Came back only a chillingly impassive routine reply card. Attacks on him multiplied. His passport expired and he could not get a new one. When an invitation to speak in Chicago at an "I am an American" event sponsored by Hearst was abruptly withdrawn, Robinson wrote a long and distressed letter to William Randolph Hearst—"I served in the Navy in World War I. I went to England in World War II and spent several weeks there during the 'Blitz' as an accredited officer of OWI. I was the first Hollywood actor to follow the troops into Normandy." The letter had its effect; Robinson's invitation to speak was cordially renewed.

From prison Dalton Trumbo wrote asking him for a $2,500 loan to help his family out. Robinson sent Mrs. Trumbo a check. This became known and the harassment intensified. He could get no film work now, yet HCUA refused to call him until Mayor Sam Yorty of

Los Angeles successfully interceded on his behalf. In executive session Robinson was questioned by HCUA's staff investigator Louis Russell (to whom he had lent $300), but the actor failed to prostrate himself as a duped tool of the Communist conspiracy. He had thought it would be enough to prove that he had never joined the Party, but he was wrong. In 1952 Yorty again fixed a hearing for him, and again he testified in closed session, naming names (but none as Party members), apologizing for having supported the ACPFB and the CFA, and silently taking it in the groin when Representative Francis Walter commented: "I think you are number one on the sucker list in this country." Afterward Yorty took him to lunch with Sokolsky and Riesel; he was cleared, he got a passport, he got work too. In October he published in the *American Legion Magazine* an article "How the Reds Made a Sucker Out of Me," ghost-written by either Sokolsky or Riesel, men whom Robinson feared and despised: "My defenses were down and I said it. My judgment was warped and I said it. My heart was sick and I said it."

In May 1953 the bandleader Artie Shaw groveled before HCUA and tried to explain how the Communists had duped him into joining numerous front organizations, like the World Peace Congress. He wept with remorse.[34] It was an era of demeaning collapse which to this day haunts the participants.

The director Elia Kazan, after refusing to name names, changed his mind on the pretext that the American people needed to know the facts. Having been heard in executive session in January 1952, he appeared before HCUA in public session in April to name eleven former Communists, including Clifford Odets and the actors J. Edward Bromberg and Morris Carnovsky. On April 12 he inserted a full-length, quarter-page "Statement" in *The New York Times*, stressing his "abiding hatred of Communist philosophy and methods." Kazan had been a Party member back in the days of the Group Theater, in 1934–35: "I was taken in by the Hard Times version of what might be called the Communists' advertising or recruiting technique." Yes, he had supported the Ten until he became "disgusted" by their "silence" and "their contemptuous attitude."

For the benefit of the Committee, he itemized his many productions, pleading that they were neither political nor propagandistic, even including Miller's *All My Sons*. Passionately he described his recent *Viva Zapata!* as an "anti-Communist picture." At a later date Kazan collaborated with another informer, Budd Schulberg, on the film *On the Waterfront*, which specifically explored the morality of informing through a young hero who eventually squeals on a corrupt union boss to keep his self-respect. Without doubt Kazan's performance before HCUA aroused a greater hostility, a more biting contempt, than that of any other Hollywood informer. His extraordinary talent as a director may have had something to do with this, and particularly the callous renunciation of his calling as an intensely committed artist. To Lillian Hellman he said: "All right, I earned over $400,000 last year from theater. But Skouras says I'll never make another movie. You've spent your money, haven't you? It's easy for you. But I've got a stake . . ."

When the writer Abe Burrows appeared before HCUA in November 1952, his name had been listed in *Red Channels*, and the American Tobacco Company, sponsors of "This Is Show Business," had received about six thousand letters a week protesting his presence as a panel member. Even more ominous, Paramount had dropped its film option on his hit musical, *Guys and Dolls*. Thoroughly alarmed, Burrows hired the expert clearance lawyer Martin Gang, hastily made his peace with the Catholic War Veterans, and groveled before HCUA:

> MR. BURROWS: . . . this whole point of my Americanism being under suspicion is very painful to me, not just painful economically but painful as it is to a guy who loves his country.
>
> . . .
>
> MR. VELDE: I must say, Mr. Burrows, you were pretty naïve.
> MR. BURROWS: Well, I would go stronger than that. I would say I was stupid.[35]

His wife, Karin Kinzel Burrows, who had left the CP after the war, also went "stronger than that" by naming more than twenty names. Burrows himself went on to greater things as author, television celebrity and Broadway play doctor.

The writer Richard Collins, one of the Nineteen subpoenaed by HCUA in 1947, appeared before HCUA on April 12, 1951, to confess that he had been a member of the CP from 1938 to 1948 and to name Lawson, Lardner, Maltz, Samuel Sillen, Lester Cole, Robert Rossen, Samuel Ornitz, Waldo Salt, Gordon Kahn, Budd Schulberg and others as his comrades in crime.

Clifford Odets, famous as a radical New York playwright in the middle thirties, author of *Waiting for Lefty*, had joined in a rally on behalf of the Ten as late as June 1950. He still regarded himself as a man of the Left, but when he came before HCUA in May 1952 and admitted having been a Party member from 1934 to 1935 (he reported that the actor J. Edward Bromberg had recruited him), the release and success of his film *Clash By Night* was at stake. So he named Kazan just as Kazan had named him. He complained how the Party had pressured him, how he had been duped, and how "the lines of leftism, liberalism, in all their shades and degrees, are constantly crossing like a jangled chord on a piano." [36] Expressing the wish that an American liberal-labor party would soon come into existence— "We have no party to join"—he proceeded to name six colleagues.

When Robert Rossen, director, writer and one of the Nineteen, testified before HCUA in June 1951, he denied current Party membership but invoked the First and Fifth Amendments with regard to the past. This devotion to the Bill of Rights is said to have cost him $100,000 in lost contracts. In 1953 he came forward to report that he had been a Party member from 1937 to 1947, and that he had contributed no less than $40,000 to CP causes. He named fifty-seven names. "I don't think, after two years of thinking, that any one individual can indulge himself in the luxury of individual morality or pit it against . . . the security and safety of this nation." The director Frank Tuttle, an ex-Communist who named seven fellow directors and twenty-nine others, pleaded that, although all decent people detested an informer, it was now a man's duty to inform in view of the ruthless aggression America was suffering from abroad. Nevertheless, Tuttle's career temporarily foundered; money for two new films was withdrawn, and producers refused to distribute any more of his pictures. Later he came back.

The choreographer Jerome Robbins, then thirty-five years old and enjoying a dazzling success, appeared before the Committee in May 1953 to confess that he had joined the Communist Political Association in 1944 and had left the CP in 1947. To save his career, the choreographer of *Call Me Madam* and *West Side Story* named names, including Lloyd Gough, Elliott Sullivan and Jerome Chodorov.

MR. ROBBINS: Sir, all my works have been acclaimed for its [*sic*] American quality particularly.
MR. DOYLE: I realize that, but let me urge you to even put more of that in it, where you can appropriately.

*Variety* announced: "Hayden Washes Out Past Red Taint." An ex-marine and heavily decorated war hero, the rugged actor Sterling Hayden came forward in April 1951 to explain how he had picked up his Communism from the Yugoslav partisans alongside whom he fought as a special commando, how he had briefly joined the CP in 1946, and how the actress Karen Morley had tried to persuade him to rejoin it in 1947, or at least to contribute money. Although Hayden had already confessed to the FBI in 1950, after the Korean war started, his HCUA subpoena arrived in the middle of his expensive film, *Skid Row*, causing panic in the studio. HCUA investigator William A. Wheeler made one of his many trips from Washington to

California to prearrange Hayden's public performance, which finally took place before three hundred excited fans and apparently went down well where it counted—"Reagan, As SAG Prez, Kudos Hayden's Honesty," announced *Variety* (April 11, 1951). In later years Hayden disparaged his own action and regretted that most of the two thousand-odd press clippings he had received in 1951 had praised his "one-shot stoolie show." [37]

Like his fellow actor Edward G. Robinson, Lee J. Cobb carried to the screen a creased, rugged countenance, suggesting a certain resolve; and, like Robinson, he collapsed before HCUA under severe strain, confessing to having joined the CP in 1940 or 1941 for less than a year, and to having rejoined from 1945 to 1946. Of the twenty actors and writers Cobb named in private testimony to Committee investigator William A. Wheeler, at least one, the actor Ludwig Donath, did not find a new Hollywood part until 1966. "I would like to thank you," Cobb said before the Committee, "for the privilege of setting the record straight . . . if belatedly this information can be of any value in the further strengthening of our Government . . ."

A month earlier Chairman Velde received a desperate letter from the blacklisted Hungarian-born writer and director Nicholas Bela, pleading for an opportunity to clear himself and mentioning that Harvey Matusow had contacted the FBI, the SISS and HCUA on his behalf. In December 1954 Bela finally got his hour with HCUA, confessed to Party membership from 1938 to 1943, and named Waldo Salt among others. "I have to humbly apologize for the grave error which I have committed, and beg of you to forgive me." [38]

But it was the screenwriter Martin Berkeley who broke all records by naming 162 Hollywood artists as past or present Communists. Himself a Party member from 1936 to 1943, he had been named by Richard Collins, promptly sent HCUA an indignant telegram of denial and then reversed himself into the role of professional informer.

Imprisoned for contempt, the director Edward Dmytryk had continued to collaborate with his comrades of the Ten to the point of signing the Stockholm Pledge on the steps of the District Court the day he went for trial. From prison, however, he issued a statement that he had left the Party in 1945 after only one year, no longer felt sympathy for it and was loyal to the United States. At his own request Dmytryk met with the MPAPAI in February 1951 and asked for help in rehabilitating himself. He got it, and quickly. Appearing before HCUA on April 25, he named seven members of the Screen Directors Guild including Biberman, Tuttle and Jules Dassin as Communists, and also fifteen members of the SWG as past or present Communists. He described Lawson as the "high lama" of the Hollywood CP.

> An informer . . . informs against colleagues . . . who are en-
> gaged in criminal activity. I think the Communists, by using this
> word . . . are in effect admitting they are engaged in criminal
> activity. I never heard of anyone informing on the Boy Scouts.

Many years later Dmytryk was asked whether he had experienced
some revulsion at turning informer. His reply makes a curious contrast with the remarks quoted above:

> Not necessarily—not necessarily. Now the Communist Party was
> a legal party and actually the officers . . . except during a short
> time when the Smith Act was involved and even then it didn't
> work because it was declared unconstitutional very quickly, they
> weren't being thrown in jail—nothing was done to them.

This, of course, was not accurate history. But had not those he
named suffered as a consequence?

> Not necessarily. For instance, not a single person that I named
> hadn't already been named at least half a dozen times . . .

To complete the process of self-purgation, Dmytryk repeated his
story, "What Makes a Hollywood Communist," under the pseudonym
Richard English, in the *Saturday Evening Post*, May 10, 1951. Albert
Maltz commented bitterly: "The truth about Dmytryk is simple and
ugly. He believed in certain principles, no doubt very sincerely, until
the consequences of those beliefs became painful. He has not now
made a peace with his conscience, he has made it with his pocket
book and his career." According to Maltz, in September 1950 Dmytryk had told him in prison that his views had not changed but he
wanted to work again. Work he did. In 1954 he directed *The Caine
Mutiny* and in 1958 *The Young Lions*.[39]
   The career benefits for people in the film industry of confessing,
repenting and informing can be simply illustrated by listing the
credits, during the 1950s, of those who confessed, repented and informed.[40]
   Others defied HCUA and the pressure groups, gravely damaging
their careers. Subpoenaed, Lillian Hellman proposed to the chairman
a deal: she would speak freely about herself, "but to hurt innocent
people whom I knew many years ago in order to save myself is, to
me, inhuman and indecent and dishonorable." Wood rejected any
deals. Thus when Lillian Hellman faced the Committee in May 1952,
she resorted to the diminished Fifth on the advice of her lawyer Joseph L. Rauh, Jr., and her friend Dashiel Hammett, who had recently been in prison.

Sidney Buchman who, as both writer and executive (he was trusted assistant to Columbia's boss, Harry Cohn), had been responsible for some twenty films, explained that he himself had been a Party member from 1938 to 1945, but firmly declined to divulge in whose company he had shared those years of youthful idealism—"First, because these persons never planned an illegal act. Secondly, the names of such a person or persons already have been made public to you and I therefore do not see how it will aid you if I repeat it. Thirdly, it is repugnant to an American to inform upon his fellow citizens." Buchman was again subpoenaed in January 1952, failed to appear because of poor health and was sentenced to one year in prison (suspended) and a $150 fine. Harry Cohn fired him, appalled, as he put it, by the Committee's revelations.

Tragic was the fate of the actor J. Edward Bromberg, who refused to answer most of the questions put to him in June 1951, and then, desperate for work, went to London, where he died a year later, at the age of forty-seven and in great loneliness, while rehearsing Trumbo's play, *The Biggest Thief in Town*. Seventeen years later, in December 1969, his son Conrad's play, *Dream of a Blacklisted Actor*, was produced at the Theater DeLys, New York. Conrad Bromberg recalls: "I remember a sense of silence that pervaded that apartment for those two years . . . very few people came to see us . . . he would be sitting at his desk waiting for the phone to ring . . . he would literally sit for hours and hours."

Among those who made no secret of the scorn they felt for HCUA and the whole inquisitorial process was the actor Elliott Sullivan. The tall, gaunt, forty-eight-year-old Texan, a veteran of stage and screen best known for his gangster roles, had been "identified" by four ex-Communists including Lee J. Cobb and Jerome Robbins. Sullivan, who scorned to take the Fifth Amendment, commented: "They sold their honor for a mess of pottage." He and the actor George Tyne, who adopted the same attitude, were convicted of contempt, but the conviction was later reversed.

But by far the most flamboyantly and wittily defiant performance was the one staged by the gravel-voiced actor Lionel Stander. Subpoenaed by the Dies Committee in 1940, Stander had at that time denied Party membership, but in April 1951 the actor Marc Lawrence had named him. So now, in May 1953, he came before the Committee armed with the First, Fifth and Ninth Amendments and a voice like a saw. When counsel Frank Tavenner suggested that Stander and his wife had belonged to a Hollywood Communist cell in the thirties, he rasped: "Which wife?" And he added, "I figured I needed $1,250 a week to break even, so I went to work on Wall Street, where there is no blacklist." One of the biggest TV agencies had told him that if he would go in front of the Committee and swear that he was not a Communist he could have his own television program worth $150,000 a year. So here he was, not a Communist. But was it true that he had been a Party member from 1935 to 1948? As regards that he declined to answer, not wishing to become part of "a whole stable of informers, stoolpigeons, and psychopaths and ex-political heretics, who come in here beating their breast and say, 'I'm awfully sorry, I didn't know what I was doing. Please, I want absolution, get me back into pictures . . .' " [41]

A more creative form of defiance inspired the film *Salt of the Earth*, produced by Paul Jarrico, directed by Herbert J. Biberman (one of the Ten) and written by Michael Wilson, all three of whom had been blacklisted. This excellent film, so completely estranged from the dominant aesthetic style of chromium Hollywood in the early fifties, was based on a strike of the Mine, Mill and Smelter Workers Union against the copper corporations in 1951–52. Strong, direct and simple, *Salt of the Earth* depicts the heroic role of the union in defending the underpaid Mexican workers against the sneering, superior, racist company representatives and the thuggish deputy sheriffs who serve them during a strike. When the Taft-Hartley Act is invoked to prevent the strikers from picketing, their wives take over, thus conquering the male-chauvinist prejudices of their otherwise progressive menfolk.

Upon this one heterodox protest film converged the concerted rage of the American Celebration. Howard Hughes, head of RKO, wanted its export forbidden; Representative Donald Jackson of HCUA denounced it; Roy M. Brewer urged theaters and projectionists across the country to boycott it; during shooting, locals were incited to make trouble, and the leading Mexican actress Rosaura Revueltas was deported before shooting was complete; Biberman even discovered that his cutter had been reporting regularly to the FBI. In March 1953 HCUA subpoenaed the film's principal backer, Simon M. Lazarus, but he took the Fifth Amendment and refused to discuss others involved. Although some ten thousand people saw *Salt of the Earth* at a drive-in cinema in Silver City, and although the film later won a prize at the Karlovy Vary film festival in Czechoslovakia, it finally landed the producers $250,000 in debt or, as the saying goes, in the red. [42]

## LAWSUITS

A number of dismissed or blacklisted artists brought suit against their former employers. Five of the Ten, Trumbo, Maltz, Cole, Lardner and Dmytryk (before his apostasy), sued for wrongful dismissal. In March 1948, the month the Ten brought a collective suit against all the studios for damages resulting from the blacklist, Lester Cole received a favorable verdict against MGM from Judge Leon Yankwich in the federal District Court, Los Angeles; in December a jury ordered MGM to restore Cole to the payroll at $1,350 a week, plus back salary of $74,250. Ring Lardner, Jr. also won a case in the lower court and was awarded $25,788 damages against Fox, but both cases were lost on appeal. The studios adopted the position that by refusing to say whether they were members of the Communist Party, the writers had breached the "morals clause" in their contracts and made themselves objects of public scorn or hatred. In *Cole v. Loew's Inc.* (1949), the California Supreme Court ruled that it was detrimental to business when an employee refused to deny being a Communist, which was *per se* defamatory in California, because a person who refused to make such a denial was publicly regarded as a Communist. This justified dismissal even before the contract expired. But in three other cases juries refused to accept the studios' contention, and in June 1952 four of the "majors," MGM, Universal, Columbia and Warners', made out-of-court settlements to the sum of $107,500. Adrian Scott brought an action against RKO but lost it on appeal. When Paul Jarrico sued RKO for removing his credit from *The Las Vegas Story* after he took the Fifth Amendment, RKO cited as evidence an opinion poll taken in Muncie, Indiana, which found that 68 percent of those questioned believed that people who took the Fifth Amendment were Communists, and that 61 percent harbored ill-will toward such a person.[43] In November 1952 the judge upheld RKO.

In *Wilson et al. v. Loew's Inc.*, filed in the California State Court in March 1953, twenty-three plaintiffs brought suit against nineteen production companies and twenty executives, together with the members and investigators of HCUA, alleging conspiracy to blacklist those who used their constitutional rights, and demanding 52 million dollars for damages. In the Nedrick Young case, a suit for 20 million dollars was brought against the Motion Picture Producers Association under the Sherman Anti-Trust Act, but the case was lost in the Supreme Court.

## THE CASUALTY COUNT

What was the casualty list? About 250 were blacklisted and about 100 graylisted, including some of the most talented directors, writers and actors in Hollywood. Among HCUA's unfriendly witnesses, about sixty or seventy were blacklisted,[44] while more than 120 others who were named but not subpoenaed also fell into the underworld. Those graylisted were normally the victims of rumors or remote guilt-by-association.

## EXILES

Among the refugees from the American Century who hotfooted it to Europe, the most distinguished heretic was Charlie Chaplin, whose troubles began, he believed, in 1942, when he delivered a speech in San Francisco calling for a second front and describing the Russians as fighting for "our way of life" as well as theirs. In July he followed this up with a telephoned message to a second-front rally at Madison Square Garden. Chaplin remained friendly with the wrong kind of artists and intellectuals: Picasso, Hanns Eisler, Clifford Odets, Brecht, Dreiser, Thomas Mann. After the war, for example, he cabled Picasso urging a demonstration in Paris against the deportation of Hanns Eisler. He also protested on behalf of the Communists Eugene Dennis and Leon Josephson when they were imprisoned for contempt of Congress. Chaplin had been a resident in America for forty-one years but he had never applied for citizenship and this fact in itself caused resentment; Senator Harry Cain, of Washington, complained that Chaplin "has sat out in luxurious comfort two wars in which his native Britain and his hospitable United States were involved . . ." Chaplin, said Cain, had come "perilously close to treason" and should be deported. The clown vainly protested that two of his sons had fought in Patton's army. In New Jersey the Catholic War Veterans picketed *Monsieur Verdoux* with banners: "Kick the Alien Out of the Country" and "Send Chaplin to Russia." In Denver the Legion managed to close the film.

In 1952 Chaplin was planning a six-month visit to Europe, but his reentry permit was indefinitely delayed while the Immigration Department sent teams of investigators to interview him:

"You say you've never been a Communist?"
"*Never. I have never joined a political organization in my life.*"
"You made a speech in which you said 'comrades'—what did you mean by that?"
"Have you ever committed adultery?"
"If this country were invaded, would you fight for it?"
"But you have never become a citizen."
"But why did you follow the Party line?"

Finally he got his reentry permit; but while abroad he learned that before being allowed back into the United States he would have to appear before an Immigration Board of Inquiry to answer charges not only of a political nature but also of moral turpitude. Wisely opting to stay abroad, he sent his American wife back to bring out his fortune. Not until April 1972 did he return, briefly, to receive a special Academy Award.

Among the original Ten, Lester Cole found an audience in the European theater; his plays were produced in Prague, London and Germany. Dmytryk produced two films in England in 1948. Adrian Scott worked in London as a production executive, until the State Department refused to renew his passport and he had to return to America. Howard Koch, one of the Nineteen and scriptwriter of *Mission to Moscow*, who had reportedly earned $50,000 a script, also emigrated to Europe in search of work. So, too, did Donald Ogden Stewart, screenwriter of the Oscar-winning *The Philadelphia Story* (1941), who was at one time earning $4,600 a week and who became in the late thirties president of the pro-Soviet Hollywood Anti-Nazi League.[45] After Stewart and his wife, Ella Winter, had fellow-traveled to the Wroclaw Peace Congress in 1947, MGM's legal department informed him that he should clear himself before HCUA: "I couldn't do it, so I pulled out." He pulled out to England, whose desperate struggle against Hitler he and his friends had turned their back on until the Soviet Union was attacked in 1941.

Carl Foreman moved to England in 1951 after he had been "identified" by friendly witnesses before HCUA and had invoked the Fifth Amendment. The scenarist of *Home of the Brave* and *High Noon*, he now worked mainly under pseudonyms; with eleven credits gained between 1941 and 1951, he had none from 1951 until 1957. But in 1956 he apparently made his peace with HCUA at a meeting in closed session with Chairman Walter, who inexplicably absolved him from naming names, enabling Columbia to announce in March 1957 that, having testified "without recourse to the Fifth Amendment," Foreman would be making four films for it in England. Pressure groups like the VFW, the Legion and Aware, Inc. agitated excitedly, conscious that a dangerous precedent had been set, but Walter explained: "I wasn't interested in getting names from Foreman of people who had already been identified as Communists. I wanted someone who could get up and tell what a sucker he'd been."

Abraham L. Polonsky was employed by Fox until April 1951, when he took the Fifth. He had served in the OSS during the war, directing a clandestine radio broadcasting to Germany from England and France. Before his subpoena he had enjoyed a considerable success with *Body and Soul*, directed by Rossen and starring Garfield. But soon after Representative Velde of HCUA called him a "very dangerous citizen," Polonsky departed from America.

Jules Dassin, sometimes mistaken for a Frenchman, but born in Connecticut, found himself blacklisted from 1947 until at least 1960 after several HCUA witnesses had "identified" him as a Communist. He worked in Europe. When his film *Rififi* won a Cannes film festival award in 1956 as a French entry, a Frenchman remarked to him: "*Quelle belle revanche.*" But, "the truth is it made me sad." After *Rififi* and *He Who Must Die* became popular in America, Dassin asked theater managers whether they ever received protests or threats of a boycott. He heard of none.

Despite seven Hollywood credits as a director in the period 1948 to 1951, Joseph Losey had to decamp to Europe after two witnesses "identified" him before HCUA in 1951 (and again in 1953). While directing *Stranger on the Prowl* in Italy, his name was removed from the credits, and that of "Andrea Forzano" was substituted. In Britain he directed *The Sleeping Tiger* (1954) under the name of "Victor Hanbury," but he was able to direct two films under his own name in 1956 and 1957. His international success in the 1960s, of course, was considerable.[46]

Others were not so lucky. They drove trucks, set up typing agencies, worked as gardeners or in humble clerical jobs. Some of the blacklisted used two social security numbers to preserve their anonymity.

## THE FATE OF BLACKLISTED ACTORS

Although there was a black market for writers' scripts, there could be none for actors' faces or voices. Once blacklisted, actors and actresses found themselves exiled from the screens for a very long time indeed (and time—growing old—is more expensive to an actor than to a writer). John Randolph and his wife Sarah Cunningham were out of films for more than fifteen years. Howard Da Silva managed to support himself on Broadway (in 1969 he starred as Benjamin Franklin in a musical called *1776*). Gale Sondergaard did not return to films until 1969, Will Geer not until his part in *The Reivers* in 1970. Morris Carnovsky made a living in the New York theater, the actor Jeff Corey became a drama teacher and later made a comeback as a film and television actor. Zero Mostel, who was out of films for many years after Martin Berkeley accused him of Communist affiliations, proved to be a singularly uncooperative yet witty witness before HCUA in October 1955. Directors were sometimes able to take refuge in the legitimate theater: Michael Gordon directed ten theater productions between 1951 and 1958 before returning to films.

## The Black Market Breaks the Blacklist

None of the major studios would touch black-market scripts. King Brothers Productions, Inc., the leading consumer of black-market scripts, distributed most of its films through United Artists, at that time a nonestablishment company belonging neither to the MPA or the AMPP. It was King Brothers who constantly employed the most successful of black-market writers, Dalton Trumbo. In February 1948 he took on his first assignment, a week's work that brought him five thousand dollars.[47] When Trumbo's script for *The Brave One* won an Oscar in 1957, he naturally could not be present to accept it, so King Brothers announced that the screenwriter, "Robert Rich," was a young man who had served in the Army in Germany but could not now be traced! Suspicious, the Academy refused to hand over the Oscar until the truant "Robert Rich" presented himself. Inundated with plagiarism suits by people claiming to have written the script, King Brothers wearily asked Trumbo to reveal himself. It was now 1959.

The blacklisted screenwriters included the best: Sidney Buchman, Donald Ogden Stewart, Ring Lardner, Jr., Lillian Hellman, Guy Endore, Albert Maltz, Dorothy Parker, Abe Polonsky, Carl Foreman and Michael Wilson had all been awarded, or nominated for, Academy Awards during the years 1941–51. A number of them won awards in the fifties, but not under their own names. Abe Polonsky wrote fifteen scripts pseudonymously and contributed secretly to the television series, *You Are There*, directed by Sidney Lumet. In 1958 Pierre Boule, author of the novel *Bridge on the River Kwai*, received the "Best Screenplay" award for the film version although it was really the work of the blacklisted Foreman and Wilson. Lardner recalled how a prominent star hired him to write a script, met him at the bank and paid him in cash. Before he went to prison, Lardner had to sell his house and rent modest quarters for his wife and five children. Once out of jail, he wrote pseudonymously for television, constantly changing his name to avoid attention. Whenever he visited Hollywood he registered in hotels under a false name so that producers could telephone him through their studio switchboard.[48]

The blacklist disintegrated in the late fifties—though not entirely. It was in 1959 that the Academy rescinded its bylaw prohibiting awards to those who refused to cooperate with Congressional committees. It was Trumbo, more than any other writer, who broke the blacklist by exposing its absurdity, its unworkability in the face of an unpatriotic industry's insatiable appetite for money-spinning talent. After more than a year's hesitation, Universal announced in August 1960 that he would be credited as the writer of *Spartacus*. Although picketed, the film was nevertheless an immense commercial success. In 1960 the California Legion found itself compelled to launch a last-ditch "war of information" to combat the return of "Soviet-indoctrinated" artists, and indeed to condemn every major company except Disney and Allied Artists for lending comfort to the "Communist conspiracy." This rearguard action was not totally without effect: Frank Sinatra, for example, backed down under fire from the Legion, the Catholic War Veterans and the Hearst press, having announced in March 1960 that he would be hiring one of the Ten, the writer Albert Maltz. Yet two months later MGM embraced Dassin and Fox hired Sidney Buchman—henceforward, it would be at least three steps forward for every one step back.

Nevertheless, for every one who came back (Waldo Salt later wrote *Midnight Cowboy*, Lardner wrote *M.A.S.H.*) ten or twenty did not.[49] These were the fatalities: the majority. Just how they died, how work dried up, after they had been "named," "identified" or subpoenaed, is charted in Appendix A.

# 27

## Radio, Television and Theater

### RADIO, TELEVISION AND RED CHANNELS

In the year 1950 radio was still the dominant medium of communication, penetrating directly into the American home. Radio still commanded the lion's share of advertising revenue, and the amounts of money invested in sponsorship of radio programs by certain large companies was, by the standards of the time, considerable. Commercial fixations (ratings, profits) dominated the outlook of networks, sponsors and advertising agencies. And when television began to boom—the number of sets shot up from 9.8 million in 1950 to 40 million in 1956—the lowest common denominator quickly established sovereignty in this realm too.[1] It was in 1958 that Edward R. Murrow referred to the "decadence, escapism and insulation from the realities of the world" as characteristic of American television.[2]

In radio and television private blacklisters played an even more destructive role than in the film industry. In May 1947 three ex-FBI agents set up at 240 Madison Avenue in an office that was small, dark and attainable only by the freight elevator. A year earlier these three, Ted Kirkpatrick, Jack Keenan, and Ken Bierly, had met the China Lobby businessman Alfred Kohlberg, who agreed to put up the money for American Business Consultants, as this new blacklisting unit called itself, and for a regular newsletter called *Counterattack* (edited by Frank McNamara, later director of anti-Communist activities for the Veterans of Foreign Wars). A network of useful contacts was built up; the key liaison man between the four-page *Counterattack* and the advertising agencies that controlled the casting of radio and television shows was Jack Wren, formerly of Naval Intelligence, who handled "security" for the huge advertising agency of Batten, Barton, Durstine and Osborn. Frequent visitors to the American Business Consultants office included such anti-Communist professionals as Victor Riesel, Victor Lasky, Howard Rushmore, and Rabbi Benjamin Schultz.

Lists were compiled with the help of HCUA's copious but scarce *Appendix IX*, the records of the Tenney Committee and by a certain amount of beavering in back copies of the *Daily Worker*. A series of mimeographed "Confidential Communications" was issued—No. 447, of April 2, 1951, for example, detailed the political record of José Ferrer; No. 478, of May 25, that of the actress Mary Virginia Farmer; No. 514, of July 18, that of the singer Josephine Baker. The style of *Counterattack* is well illustrated in the issue of February 29, 1952:

> WHAT DO YOU THINK OF THESE CELANESE STARS? . . . KIM HUNTER and LLOYD GOUGH had leading roles . . . KIM HUNTER'S *Communist front record* was given in COUNTER-ATTACK . . . after she appeared on Johnson Wax program . . . GOUGH refused to say if he is now, or ever was . . . WHAT CAN YOU DO TO HELP DEFEAT THE COMMUNISTS? *Write to:* HAROLD BLANCKE, President, Celanese Corporation of America, 180 Madison Avenue, New York City, NY.

Basically, American Business Consultants was in business to sell and withhold protection, having first created the economic violence against which protection was necessary. A company that sponsored programs and was eager above all to project a healthy image would, once publicly accused of foisting reds and un-Americans on its audience, quickly come to heel and pay up consultancy fees. Emerson P. Schmidt, of the U.S. Chamber of Commerce, praised *Counterattack* as "an indispensable source of knowledge"; at $24 a year, most producers and many sponsors found it worth the price.[3]

In 1952 one of the three partners, Kenneth M. Bierly, split away with the pious intention of rehabilitating the innocent artists—Judy Holliday, for example—whom the group had ruined. (When the light-headed comedienne came before the SISS in 1952 she called herself a "sucker" for having backed the ALP and Henry Wallace: "I don't say 'yes' now to anything except cancer, polio, and cerebral palsy, and things like that.")[4] American Business Consultants, of course, did not neglect to rehabilitate a proportion of its own victims—the singer Lena Horne was a case in point—for a fee. And no doubt there was more to the clearance racket than money, for blacklisters and Congressmen alike; for small-town credit salesmen (Ted Kirkpatrick had once been credit manager for the Personal Finance Company of Arizona), who would not normally have gotten nearer a star than her autograph, the pleasure of make-or-break power over the famous and the sexually glamorous must have been appreciable.

The group's master stroke was the publication, three days before the outbreak of the Korean war, of a 213-page booklet called *Red Channels*, subtitled "The Report of Communist Influence in Radio and Television." Although calling no one a Communist (a lawsuit brought by the actors Fredric and Florence Eldridge March had taught them *that* lesson),[5] *Red Channels* listed 151 people of prominence in alphabetical order under a front cover depicting a microphone entrapped by a red hand. Each name was followed by a professional description, the phrase "reported as" and then a list of damaging citations.[6]

The actors, directors and writers listed soon discovered the astonishing influence of this shabby booklet.[7] Millard Lampell, a blacklisted radio writer, wrote: "By 1951, standard equipment for every Madison Avenue and Hollywood producer's desk, included along with the onyx ashtray and penholder and the gold cigarette lighter, was a copy of *Red Channels* in the bottom drawer." Although twenty of the listed organizations had been defunct since the late thirties, and although one actor's most recent listing was 1938, another's 1941 and a sizable minority's 1945, the sponsors, advertising agencies and network companies were interested in ratings, not history. When the playwright Elmer Rice suggested in 1951 five actors who might fill the leading role in his television play, *Counsellor-at-Law*, the attorney for the Ellington Advertising Agency ruled out all five—Lee J. Cobb, Edward G. Robinson, Sam Wanamaker, José Ferrer and John Garfield—as having been listed in *Red Channels*. The sponsors, the Celanese Corporation of America, had to be protected. When Rice blasted this "crass commercial cowardice," and the Authors League of America launched an inquiry into blacklisting, *Counterattack* hit back, claiming that Rice had supported eleven fronts in the late thirties and early forties, and recently four more. (In fact, Rice had supported the successful motion to exclude Communists from the ACLU in 1941.) Nor did the impact of *Red Channels* quickly wane. When one of the listed actors, Joe Julian, brought suit in 1954, Charles E. Martin, a producer-director, testified: "We quarantine everybody in the book. We cannot take any chances." [8]

## BLACKLISTERS, SPONSORS, ADVERTISERS

It was in 1952 that two blacklisters, Vincent Hartnett and Paul Milton, set up Aware, Inc., whose membership had reached 600 by 1956.

Milton, a tireless witness before Congressional committees and an equally tireless exploiter of Congressional immunity (if you merely reported what you had told a committee you could not be sued for libel), served as the main link between the anti-Communist Aware and a red-baiting faction within the Radio Writers Guild which called itself "We, the Undersigned." [9] It was, however, Hartnett who emerged as the most ruthless blacklister of the decade. A Catholic graduate of the University of Notre Dame, a former Naval Intelligence officer and a former $60-a-week hack in a radio script department, Hartnett launched his own *Confidential Notebook* in mimeographed form at $5 a copy. The newssheet *Aware* was also his doing. To promote himself in so competitive a field as blacklisting he not only advertised ($50 a lecture) in the Brooklyn *Tablet*, et cetera, he even wrote an article under a pseudonym in the Catholic magazine *Sign*, praising himself (i.e., Hartnett) for his "firsthand knowledge of certain Communist activities in program production."

In 1962 another expert clearance specialist to whom we have referred briefly, the advertising agent Jack Wren, jumped off the sinking ship and testified against Hartnett in court: "I had to treat with him as a merchant treats with a racketeer who sells protection." A racketeer, nevertheless, with impressive collaborators; in May 1955 J. Edgar Hoover wrote to Hartnett thanking him for the cooperation he had given to FBI agents. Hartnett's earnings rose to $26,000 a year. He cleared names—actors, directors, producers, technicians, assistant stage directors, the lot—for Young & Rubicam at $5 per head. David Levy of Young & Rubicam told the producer David Susskind: "I deplore this practice as much as you do. We're caught in a trap. I have no alternative." Hartnett made his own files available "to a few qualified persons," as he put it, at fees of about $500 a time. Following classic protection-racket tactics, he wrote an article for the *American Legion Magazine* criticizing the Borden Milk Company for being careless about sponsoring reds; by a miracle, before the article could be printed, Hartnett had been hired by Borden (for $6,095 in 1954 and for $10,000 in 1955) and the article had transformed itself into one of congratulation. [10] Testifying in court in 1962, Hartnett listed among his past or present clients Lever Brothers, the American Broadcasting Company and the Kudner Agency.

Hartnett was utterly methodical; very probably his rigor was sustained by a genuine fanaticism—"the typical spoiled-priest type." Each year he photographed the May Day parade, then scanned his prints for victims. In 1952 he thought he spotted someone resembling the actor Leslie Barrett and wrote to him: "If I do not hear from you, I must conclude that your marching . . . is still an accurate index of your position and sympathies. . . ." A stamped, addressed envelope was politely enclosed. He was wrong about Barrett, but the actor suffered. Hartnett later explained: "Admittedly it's a trick. It's a strategy in interrogation procedure." On another occasion, when the anti-Communist faction of the American Federation of Television and Radio Artists (AFTRA) was under challenge, Hartnett attended an informal meeting of members in the Blue Ribbon Restaurant, carrying a hidden tape recorder.

Kim Hunter, Olive Deering, James Thurber and Franchot Tone were among those he tried to blacklist, warning the networks of the risk of "adverse public opinion." Hartnett's harassment of Kim Hunter was not fully exposed until John Henry Faulk sued him for damages in 1962. A little research on Hartnett's part brought to light that Kim Hunter had attended a meeting in support of the Hollywood Ten, had signed the call for the Waldorf Conference and had supported a CRC petition to the Supreme Court calling for a new trial for Willie McGee, a Negro later executed in Mississippi. For the three years after she won an Academy Award in 1952, the blacklisted actress was offered no movie parts and only one or two a year on television. In 1953 her press agent wrote to Hartnett asking what she must do to clear herself. The answer was simple: she must review and regret her entire record. Hartnett would do the reviewing, for a fee of $200, and Miss Hunter would do the regretting. During the Faulk court case in 1962 the attorney Louis Nizer described how Roy Brewer collaborated with Hartnett on such clearances, and how in 1953 Brewer offered to tutor Miss Hunter in the kind of affidavit that would satisfy Hartnett. In 1955 the affidavit was ready: "It was only after I had made several errors in judgment," Kim Hunter was forced to declare, "that I was finally alerted to a clearer and more intelligent understanding of the insidious workings of the Communist conspiracy." But the ventriloquist was not quite satisfied; one small practical service was still called for; he urged her to speak at an AFTRA meeting in defense of his own pressure group, Aware. Instead she compromised and sent AFTRA a telegram warning against any steps which might aid and abet the Communist conspiracy.[11] It was enough; she got work.

The professional blacklisters traded on the climate of the times, a climate stimulated by their friends in the press like Westbrook Pegler, Walter Winchell, Howard Rushmore, George Sokolsky and Victor Riesel, by the Legion, the Catholic War Veterans and the Veterans of Foreign Wars, by Catholic journals like the *Tablet* and *Sign*. But not the least important were those inspired amateurs, the Republican matrons, who could whip up letterwriting or telephone campaigns such as the one that greeted the appearance in January 1950 of the dancer Paul Draper on CBS's "Toast of the Town" television show. As a result, CBS received 350 protest calls and over sixty telegrams. This was no coincidence, since Draper and the harmonica player Larry Adler had brought a libel suit against one of these amateur vigilantes, Mrs. Hester McCullough, after she called them "pro-Communist." (In May 1950 a jury in Hartford, Connecticut, was unable to reach a verdict; Draper and Adler did not request a retrial.)

The most persistent and influential amateur blacklister of the fifties, a genuine fanatic, was the Syracuse, New York, supermarket proprietor and ex-farmer, Laurence (Larry) Johnson. Then in his sixties and a keen American folklorist, who recreated nineteenth-century stores as exhibits in his supermarkets, Johnson made much of the fact that his son-in-law was a reservist serving in Korea, as a result of which Johnson's daughter, Eleanor Buchanan, became an energetic crusader against reds on TV. Johnson himself was forever hurrying up and down Madison Avenue, handing out lists of actors and directors who had signed the *amici curiae* brief on behalf of the Hollywood Ten. Although he failed to intimidate the Metropolitan Opera, his attacks usually had their effect. When he accused the advertising agency of Lennen & Mitchell of employing alleged Communist-fronters in the "Schlitz Playhouse of the Stars," sponsored by the Schlitz Brewing Company, a number of actors did not receive credits for their parts in films already made. In 1952 Johnson's Veterans Action Committee of Syracuse Supermarkets collaborated with *Counterattack* to deter CBS and other companies from issuing statements denouncing blacklistings.

In the same year Johnson warned the Block Drug Company, producers of Ammident toothpaste, against advertising on the TV program "Danger," which, according to Johnson, employed many of "Stalin's little creatures." Likewise he complained to Seabrook Farms that they had been sponsoring the actor Joseph Cotten. Although Cotten arranged to meet and appease Johnson, bringing with him proof that he had entertained the armed forces and engaged in warbond drives, the series in which he appeared was later canceled when Seabrook timidly withdrew its sponsorship. The advertising agency of Hilton & Riggio lost the Seabrook account. After Johnson wrote in December 1953 to C. A. Swanson & Company, sponsor of a TV panel show called "The Name's the Same," protesting against the appearance on the show of Judy Holliday as a guest celebrity, she was not used again on the show. Two years later he toured Madison Avenue demanding that the sponsors of John Henry Faulk's radio programs (see below) withdraw, and he warned the Grey advertising agency that unless it removed the Hoffman Beverage account from Faulk's show he would boycott Hoffman in his supermarkets and enlist the support of the Legion.[12] Out of this came Faulk's suit for damages. At the end of the trial, just before the jury retired, the seventy-three-year-old Johnson was found dead in a Bronx motel. Judgment was given against his estate.

The great props of the blacklisters, of course, were the Congressional committees, particularly HCUA, whose staff maintained close, cooperative relations with the more professional blacklisters. When a major assault on blacklisting was launched by liberals, HCUA hurried to the defense. Following the publication of John Cogley's two-volume *Report on Blacklisting*, sponsored by the Fund for the Republic, the Committee opened an investigation of "So-Called Blacklisting in the Entertainment Industry" in July 1956.[13] Harnett accused Cogley, former executive editor of the liberal Catholic weekly *Commonweal*, of "McCarthyism in reverse," and Roy M. Brewer stoutly denied that he was involved in clearing artists. "I did not want, I did not seek, I do not want, any power over anyone." Chairman Walter called Cogley's *Report* a "partisan, biased attack on all persons and organizations who are sincerely and patriotically concerned" to purge the entertainment industry of Communists and sympathizers. Pressed to hand over his notebooks and reveal his frightened anonymous sources of information, Cogley firmly refused and then, on second thought, burned all his notes.[14]

The record of the large commercial enterprises that sponsored radio and television programs in the 1950s, of the advertising agencies that served them and of the network corporations themselves, reminds us what havoc the profit motive can wreak on human values. General Foods, which sold Jell-O through the television serial "The Aldrich Family," announced in 1950 that it was the policy of the company to avoid "material and personalities which, in its judgment, are controversial." Accordingly, the actress Jean Muir was dropped from the show because she had been listed in *Red Channels*. Even the pretext of public opinion was weak here: General Foods received 3,300 letters protesting her firing, and only 2,065 in favor of it; most editorials condemned the action. But General Foods had a record that the Legion had already commended, and the voice of the Legion could not be ignored.

The fear of "controversy" became universal. An oil company sponsoring the NBC quiz broadcast "Who Said That?" dictated its own blacklist, banning Norman Thomas, Al Capp and several Congressmen and Senators because "they might just say something." In 1952 James Wechsler, the liberal anti-Communist editor of the *New York Post*, but in distant days a member of the YCL, appeared on the television program "Starring the Editors." As soon as the Hearst *Journal-American* muckraked Wechsler's political past, the Grand Union grocery chain ordered the advertising agency to drop him. Jack Gould wrote in *The New York Times:* "How many people objected to Mr. Wechsler? No one knows. Who did the objecting? No one knows." [15]

The advertising agencies learned to forestall controversy by prophylactic measures. The producer David Susskind recalled how he had to submit the name of every artist he intended to use to Young & Rubicam, acting for the sponsor, Lorillard cigarettes. From April 1955 to March 1956, he submitted five hundred names, about one third of which were rejected. Disturbed by the cost of this clearance operation, Young & Rubicam offered Susskind the program "Justice"—half an hour per week on behalf of the Borden Milk Company—on condition that he would confine himself to a "whitelist" of 150 politically irreproachable actors. The president of the Block Drug Company, Melvin A. Block, apologized for the presence of the actor John Randolph in the TV program "Danger," promised that it would not happen again and emphasized that CBS had given assurances that "they will be meticulous in their screening." Paul M. Hahn, president of the American Tobacco Company, reported to Laurence Johnson that he had purged his company's program, "The Big Story," of subversives. Procter & Gamble's Howard J. Morgens hastened to Syracuse to pay his respects to Johnson and promised that "our operating methods . . . will be tightened wherever possible." [16]

## NETWORKS AND UNIONS UNDER PRESSURE

The network companies and local stations soon abandoned all thought of resistance. In December 1950, Station WPIX, New York, canceled a series of Chaplin movies dating from 1916 and 1917, after protests from the Hudson County, New Jersey, Catholic War Veterans. Most serious was the rapid capitulation of the Columbia Broadcasting System under the leadership of William S. Paley and Frank Stanton. CBS hired American Business Consultants to investigate its employees soon after *Counterattack* charged: "All networks let some Communists and Communist fronters get on their programs, but CBS is the worst of all." CBS appointed a vice-president to handle policy on blacklisting, while a spokesman of NBC, which delegated the problem to its legal department, referred to blacklisting as "a business safeguard." In December 1950 Joseph H. Ream, executive vice-president of CBS, announced that the network's 2,500 employees would be required to sign a loyalty statement based on the Attorney General's list as of October 30, 1950. A few dismissals followed as a result of refusals to sign, but signing could not save an individual listed in *Red Channels*. Matusow reproduced in facsimile form a letter from J. L. Van Volenburg, president of CBS television, to the irate Laurence Johnson, apologizing for having hired the comedian Jack Gilford on the program "Arthur Godfrey and His Friends." Under pressure, CBS rejected Oscar Hammerstein, Richard Rodgers, Moss Hart and Jerome Robbins. It was painful, of course, since the best talent seemed almost by definition "controversial"; a CBS executive confided to Merle Miller that "we're relying on mediocrities now, and the three boys on the flying trapeze are responsible. My God, it's straight out of Kafka, isn't it?" [17]

With five VHF stations owned and operated in extremely rich markets, and with 71 percent of its profits deriving from television, CBS was able in 1957 to announce an annual net profit of twenty-two million dollars. Despite these figures, or perhaps because of them, the safety-first policy was sustained. In June 1958, CBS dismissed the highly talented Joseph Papirofsky (Joe Papp), a director of the New York Shakespeare Festival who worked as a floor manager for the network, after he had taken the Fifth Amendment before HCUA as regards past CP membership since February 1955. (He denied membership since June 1955.) The same day, NBC fired Charles S. Dubin, director of a TV quiz show, who had likewise resorted to the Fifth. After the Radio and Directors Guild challenged Papp's dismissal an arbitrator ordered his reinstatement, and in a similar case brought by the American Federation of Technical Engineers, Local 241, the arbitrator ordered RCA to reinstate Herschel Baron, who had invoked the First and Fifth Amendments before the SISS.[18] The line, at last, was being drawn.

Among the unions representing artists employed in radio and television, the most determined resistance to blacklisting came from the leadership of the Radio Writers Guild, upon whom a fierce and coordinated assault, from both within the Guild and without, was accordingly launched. An SISS subcommittee chaired by Eastland subpoenaed the Guild's leaders and referred darkly to a tiny band of "pro-Communists" who "indirectly controlled" 90 percent of scripts broadcast. In October 1952 the anti-Communist faction within the Guild actually issued a blacklist to record the alleged Communist-front records of their colleagues.[19]

But in general the trade unions panicked pitifully. In September 1950 the council of the American Federation of Radio Artists even proposed an industry loyalty board (on the pretext that victims would at least receive a hearing). In August 1951 AFRA voted to bar anyone proven in court to have been a Communist since 1945 or, much more elastically, "identified" as such by the Justice Department or the FBI. Of AFRA's 7,000 members, 2,118 voted in favor of this ban and only 457 against. Soon afterward AFRA merged with the television wing to become AFTRA, to which all performers were obliged to belong, and the policy of the leadership became even more repressive—suspension of members who failed to satisfy legislative committees.

By 1955 the membership of AFTRA was torn between hatred of Aware and the blacklisters on the one hand, and fear that open opposition could be construed as aiding and abetting Communism. These mixed emotions were reflected in two apparently contradictory motions passed by the membership in July and August. In the first mail referendum the members voted 982 to 514 to condemn Aware; in the second, they voted by 3,967 to 914 to authorize local boards to discipline by fine, suspension or expulsion, members who refused to answer Congressional questions. In December a liberal "middle of the road" slate won twenty-seven of the thirty-five seats on the Board, and the following summer the New York local warned networks and sponsors that if a member was denied employment because of misleading statements by Aware or similar pressure groups, then action would follow against the employer.[20] But the pro-Aware faction within AFTRA, led by the *Daily News* columnist and television compere Ed Sullivan, launched a vicious campaign of innuendo against the leaders of the "Middle of the Road" slate, the result being that in June 1957 the right wing returned to power.

## THE CASUALTY COUNT

The ACLU estimated that by 1953 the blacklist in radio extended to about 250 people. Some years later, *The New York Times* calculated the number affected in radio and television in 1954 at 1,500. Most of the victims were never explicitly informed why they could no longer find work, and it would certainly have been difficult to explain to the eight-year-old actress who, as Susskind recalled, was rejected because her father was considered suspect. Particularly bewildered were the quite numerous victims whose names or faces were confused with those on the list. The actor Everett Sloan suffered because his name resembled that of the scriptwriter and self-professed former Communist Allen E. Sloane; when the actress Madeline Lee, a specialist in radio baby noises, was blacklisted, three other actresses, innocent of all political activity, faced ruin—one because she was called Madeline Lee, one (Camilla Ashland) because she resembled Madeline Lee and one (Madeline Pierce) because she too was a proven baby-gurgler. John Cogley cited the case of an actor who spent four years trying to prove that he could not have served in the Abraham Lincoln Brigade.

Among actors, the first major casualty of the era was Jean Muir. Listed with nine alleged affiliations in *Red Channels*, she publicly denied any association with four of them, insisted she was anti-Communist, but proudly stood by her association with the Southern Conference for Human Welfare. Although she was paid in full for the period of her contract, she was quickly dropped from "The Aldrich Family," sponsored by General Foods, and was subsequently so reduced by unemployment that she voluntarily appeared before HCUA in June 1953 to compliment the Committee on its "fine and educational work." Gypsy Rose Lee, a versatile dancer, wit and writer, also listed in *Red Channels* and normally a guest artist on radio or television three times a week, became virtually unemployable. Hazel Scott, pianist, singer and wife of Representative Adam Clayton Powell, lost her place on DuMont Television. Nor were these misfortunes merely temporary; when in January 1961 the actor Jeff Corey, blacklisted ten years earlier, resumed work in a television series appropriately called "The Untouchables," *The New York Times* commented that he was perhaps the first thoroughly blacklisted television actor to have found his way back.[21]

Among black actors who fell victim to American Business Consultants were William Marshall, star of CR-TV's dramatic show, "Harlem Detective," whose career was amputated by a blast in *Counterattack*, and the exceptionally gifted Canada Lee, famous as Bigger Thomas in the Broadway production of Richard Wright's *Native Son*. Active in antiracist organizations listed by the Attorney General, Lee was rolled in the mud (FBI files packed with gossip) of the Judith Coplon trial, listed in *Red Channels* and let drop by his television sponsor, the American Tobacco Company. The ban was soon total. Stefan Kanfer describes the actor's last days:

> At last, destitute, he delivered an attack upon Paul Robeson. The film industry thereupon relented and granted him one final role, as the Reverend Stephen Kumalo in *Cry, the Beloved Country*, filmed on location near Johannesburg, South Africa . . . He returned to New York . . . afflicted by failing health, unable to work in his own country. Four TV sponsors offered roles, then withdrew . . . he died penniless and alone.

Also befouled by *Red Channels* was the actress Mady Christians, a veteran of more than sixty films, lecturer in drama at Columbia and a dedicated supporter of refugees. Blacklisted as a member of the ACPFB, she began to suffer from high blood pressure and died of a cerebral hemorrhage. Before her death she referred to what had hit her as "something unbelievable."

Particularly terrible was the fate of the tragicomic actor Philip Loeb, who had signed an apology for the Moscow trials in the *New*

*Masses* in 1936, and had gained a reputation in Actors' Equity of being a political troublemaker. First attacked in the *Tablet*, then listed in *Red Channels* with seventeen affiliations, Loeb was prospering in CBS's *The Goldbergs* as the suffering Jewish father, when General Foods decided to drop the whole show. Angrily rejecting a payoff of $85,000, he was later reduced to accepting a sum which had fallen to $40,000. He told HCUA that he had never been a Communist but intended to go on collaborating with anyone he admired. NBC took over *The Goldbergs*, but without Philip Loeb. His financial difficulties became acute; his wife had died, and it cost him $12,000 a year to keep his schizoid son in a private institution. By the time Loeb took his last acting job, downtown in *The Three Sisters*, at $87.50 a week, his son had been moved to a state institution, where he wrote him an agonized letter; at the age of sixty-one Loeb could bear it no more and committed suicide in the Hotel Taft.

In the aftermath of their unsuccessful libel suit against Mrs. Hester McCullough, Paul Draper and Larry Adler had to work abroad. In December 1950, Adler, then thirty-six, wrote to Arthur Garfield Hays from London, complaining of pressure from the Hearst press, the Legion and the Catholic War Veterans. His contract with a harmonica manufacturer had been withdrawn and twelve concerts at the Hilton Hotels in Chicago and New York had been canceled. "Is there any chance," he wrote, "that the ACLU would do anything active in this matter?" There was not. Twenty-three years later, firmly settled in England, he still regarded himself as being on the American television blacklist because, as he put it, sponsored shows are run by Republican grandmothers with long memories.[22]

Folk singers, too, were frequent targets. Burl Ives was listed in *Red Channels*. Tom Glazer was listed and suffered for it, even though, as an opponent of the Communists within the American Veterans Committee, he had been one of the first members of ADA and had supported Truman against Henry Wallace. Another listed in *Red Channels* was Pete Seeger. Having entertained the armed forces in the Pacific during the war, he returned home to combine Communist-front politics—he was the bard of the Wallace movement—with making records for Folkways. He joined with others in People's Artists and, in 1949, formed the Weavers, a group that sold four million records in its first year and was scheduled for "prime time" on television. All this collapsed in 1950. Subpoenaed by HCUA in 1955, he disdained to take the Fifth Amendment:

CHAIRMAN WALTER: Did you sing that song?
MR. SEEGER: I can sing it. I don't know how well I can do it without my banjo.

CHAIRMAN WALTER: I said, Did you sing it on that occasion?

MR. SEEGER: . . . I am not going to go into where I have sung it . . .

In 1957 Seeger was indicted for contempt and convicted four years later but the verdict was reversed on the ground that the Committee had not proven its authority to ask the questions he had refused to answer. After seventeen years on the blacklist, he returned to television in 1967, and to "prime time" two years later.

Many writers, like Dorothy Parker and Arthur Miller, while still acceptable on Broadway, were banned from television or radio. For a while writers whose livelihood depended on these media were able to work anonymously, attributing their work to "fronts" who took the public credit and tended to demand an increasing share of the fee.

One of the most talented of the blacklisted writers, Millard Lampell, formerly a speech writer for Henry Wallace and later named as a Communist by Allen E. Sloane, recalled how his income suddenly fell from "a comfortable five figures to $2,000 a year." An old friend, a producer, told him: "Pal, you're dead. I submitted your name for a show and they told me I couldn't touch you with a barge pole." Then he patted Lampell on the cheek: "Don't quote me, pal, because I'll deny I said it." [23] Friends passed him on the street with a furtive nod. Lampell sold his car, moved his family to a small apartment in a cheap area and lived off loans from friends, plus a few pseudonymous scripts for the government of Israel and other irregular clients. Subpoenaed in 1952 by the SISS, he took the Fifth Amendment. A very conservative actor who had starred in one of his radio plays sent him a check for five hundred dollars, which Lampell returned with thanks. Frequently his path crossed that of other casualties—for example, the television writer whom fear had inspired to hire a professional investigator to clear him, who was duly cleared, but who then discovered that all doors were closed simply because the investigator had been going around inquiring about him. It was not until 1962 that Lampell received his first credit from a major Hollywood studio, and not until 1964 that he was accepted in television. His play *No Hiding Place* promptly won half a dozen awards.

## A TEXAN CALLED JOHN HENRY FAULK

The victim whose stubborn and courageous fight against those who had vindictively destroyed his career called down the curtain on the blacklisters was an utterly non-red Texan called John Henry Faulk, who normally talked, spun yarns and commented on the news of the day every afternoon on WCBS in New York. It had been Faulk's fool-hardy gesture to tackle the Hartnett, pro-Aware faction within AFTRA and, during the short period in 1955–57 when the "middle of the road" slate was in control, to have been elected 2nd vice-president of the New York local. While Hartnett warned Young & Rubi-cam in December 1955 that Faulk had "a significant Communist-front record," Johnson called Rheingold Brewery with the news that Faulk was a Communist, and also persuaded Libby's Frozen Foods to cancel its sponsorship of his program. In August 1957 Faulk was fired by WCBS.

Faulk filed suit for conspiracy against Aware, Hartnett and John-son in the New York State Supreme Court, an action which, he soon discovered, made him even more controversial and therefore less em-ployable than ever. (This was the factor, plus the cost, that deterred so many from going to law.) The flamboyant and successful attorney Louis Nizer agreed to take on the case for a mere $10,000 retainer, to cover expenses, but money like that was not negligible to a man with-out work. Although Ed Murrow generously contributed $7,500, Faulk was soon in debt; the few jobs he was offered were invariably with-drawn—those he had sued were keeping close to his tail even in Aus-tin, Texas. He tried to work as a salesman of stocks and bonds, but failed.

When the case finally came to trial in April 1962, Faulk desper-ately searched New York for witnesses, but so great was the fear still prevailing that several directors and advertising executives who, he knew, detested blacklisting refused to help him. Even so, Nizer was so confident that he could destroy the defense witnesses that he raised the claim for damages to one million dollars.

Nizer's confidence was not misplaced. Paul Milton, of Aware, admitted in court that he did not know whether any of the allegations against Faulk were true. As for Hartnett, during pretrial examination he conceded that he had no evidence to show that Faulk had been pro-Communist: "I was sold a barrel of false information." Now, dur-ing the trial itself, he confessed that in framing Faulk he had taken a report from the *Herald Tribune* and deliberately attributed it to the *Daily Worker*.

The most telling moment of the trial occurred when Nizer, ob-serving that Hartnett was busily noting down the names of actors and actresses in the audience, suddenly asked him whether he could iden-tify Faulk's wife among those present. Hartnett hesitated, then identi-fied a woman who was not Mrs. Faulk. Pandemonium broke out as Nizer thundered: "Sir, is that an example of the accuracy with which you have identified your victims for the past ten years?" Evidently the jury regarded this question as a good one; Faulk was awarded compensatory damages of one million dollars against Aware, Inc., Hartnett and the estate of the recently deceased Laurence Johnson, plus $1,250,000 punitive damages against Aware, and the same amount against Hartnett. In November 1963 the Appellate Division cut the total damages from $3.5 million to $550,000, and in July 1964 the New York State Court of Appeals upheld this. When the defendants petitioned the Supreme Court for *certiorari*, pleading, ironically, First Amendment freedoms, only Justices Black and Douglas, the archlibertarians, voted to grant it. The blacklist was thus broken, the blacklisters too; Hartnett withdrew to teach in a Westchester suburb and to send small checks to John Henry Faulk. The networks now capitalized on indignation. In a bold gesture, CBS presented in 1963 a drama by Ernest Kinoy about an actor blacklisted in the fifties, even though the actor John Randolph was still blacklisted by CBS.[24]

## ON BROADWAY

Throughout the fifties, Broadway remained the thorn in the flesh of the professional show-business blacklisters operating in New York. Occasionally pressure proved effective, as when Ed Sullivan, *Daily News* columnist and television personality, raised a fuss about three hundred seats purchased by the *National Guardian* for a benefit performance of the musical *Wonderful Town*. The producer canceled the performance, refunded the money and refused to sell the *National Guardian* tickets for any future performance. Otherwise, Broadway remained, if not exactly as Vincent Hartnett described it, "New York's Great Red Way," a haven for performers with left-wing backgrounds. An article by Hartnett in June 1953 attacking this state of affairs revealed how great was the concentration of money-coining talent on the Left. Spewing out names from his filing cards in a venomous stream of insinuation, Hartnett asked helplessly, "When will the theatergoing public get wise to the con game being operated in New York's Great Red Way?" [25]

In August 1955, when HCUA came to New York to investigate an unregenerate Broadway, it met with considerable defiance. Of twenty-seven artists subpoenaed, eighteen took the Fifth Amendment, including the actor Zero Mostel. But the Committee enjoyed no success in blacklisting such actors on Broadway. It was in the electronic media, on which most of them relied to supplement their income, that they were vulnerable.

Actors' Equity Association generally adopted a policy more liberal than the unions representing performers in films, radio and television. In 1952 the SISS, angered by the joint statement issued by

Equity and the League of New York Theaters against blacklisting—the League was perhaps the first employers' group to adopt such a stand—reported that Equity had been dominated by pro-Communists from 1937 to 1950. Equity actually set up an antiblacklist committee whose job it was to reveal and rectify any cases in the legitimate theater. But not even Equity was immune to the intense pressures of the time: in June 1953 it was reported that the actors' union, with a membership of 6,700, had voted to expel anyone proven by due process of law to be a Communist or a member of an affiliated organization. As regards the American Federation of Musicians, AFL, its bylaws excluded Communists and Fascists from membership.[26]

## ARTHUR MILLER AND THE WITCHES OF SALEM

In 1956 HCUA subpoenaed the playwright Arthur Miller, who had long since been blacklisted by the film, television and radio companies. Although acceptable on Broadway, his work had frequently come under attack during provincial tours, as when Hartnett arrived in Peoria, Illinois, in October 1950 to attend a Conference to Combat Communism, and described *Death of a Salesman* as a "Communist-dominated play." The Peoria Junior Chamber of Commerce and the local Legion Post put pressure on the city manager of the Publix-Grand States Theaters to cancel the production. He refused, but the boycott soon brought down the curtain. In 1955 Miller contracted to write a screenplay on the subject of juvenile delinquency; the New York City Youth Board was to lend him its cooperation in return for "5 percent of the monies of this picture." He had been winning the confidence of rival Brooklyn gangs, the Viceroys and the Dragons, when the *Journal-American*, the *World-Telegram* and Aware began throwing political stuff at him; after the Legion and the Catholic War Veterans joined in, the Youth Board backed out by 11 to 9, and the film was stillborn.

According to Miller himself, Chairman Walter of HCUA actually offered to call off the hearing in 1956 if Miller would permit a photograph of him standing with Miller and his fiancée, Marilyn Monroe. Up to a point Miller was a cooperative witness, wordy rather than eloquent, less at home with the spoken than the written word. The charges against him were numerous: signing CRC statements against anti-Communist legislation and against HCUA itself; appealing on behalf of Gerhart Eisler and Howard Fast; attending five or six meetings of Communist writers in 1947. Miller firmly denied that he had ever applied to join the Party. Committee counsel Arens insisted,". . . you did make application for membership . . . and . . . the number of your application is 23345." Miller said no. He felt now that it had been a "great error" not to have come to the aid of those persecuted by Communists in other countries, and he regretted that he had supported organizations dominated by Communists.

His play *You're Next* was an attack on HCUA, complained Arens. Furthermore, the Communist press had drawn parallels between the New England witch hunt depicted in *The Crucible* and contemporary Congressional investigations. Miller nodded: "The comparison is inevitable, sir."

He would talk about himself but, like his seventeenth-century hero John Proctor, he drew the line at others. "I could not use the name of another person and bring trouble on him . . . I will protect my sense of myself." [27] He was cited for contempt. When the case came to trial in May 1957, Arens, the leading prosecution witness, claimed that Miller had been a Party member from 1943 to 1947 at least; but he declined to reveal the source of the allegation. The court did not convict Arens of contempt, but it did convict Miller. In August 1958 this was reversed on a technicality.

## PROVINCIAL THEATERS

Perhaps the most lethal attack on a provincial theater was the one launched in 1948 against Mrs. Florence Bean James's Seattle Repertory Playhouse by the Canwell Committee. Although Mrs. James and her husband were Wallace supporters with left-wing records (the perjurious government informer George Hewitt swore he had run into her in the Soviet Union not once, not twice, but three times), they were also the victims of local enmities, as in Miller's Salem. Director also of the University of Washington Theater Workshop, Mrs. James believed that she was the victim of a plot engineered by the director of the university's drama department; was it a coincidence that when the Playhouse finally collapsed in 1950 it was purchased by the drama department? The Playhouse collapsed because the adverse publicity of the Canwell hearings, followed by her trial for contempt, resulted in the mass cancellation of bookings and a fall in gross revenue from $40,000 in 1946–47 to $14,000 in 1948–49. [28]

By the middle fifties there were signs of a recovery of nerve among provincial theater managements. At the city-owned Playhouse in the Park, Philadelphia, rehearsals were due to begin on July 9, 1956, for the play *Anastasia*, starring Gale Sondergaard as the Dowager Empress. Miss Sondergaard had taken the Fifth Amendment before HCUA in 1951, inevitably a red rag to the Legion bull. Nevertheless, the battering-ram assaults of the Legion and VFW failed to knock a hole in the walls of the Playhouse—the first night duly took place on July 17, with a packed auditorium and prolonged applause for Miss Sondergaard. Even though HCUA, mesmerized by the smell of grease paint, arrived in town to subpoena the actress (she took the Fifth again), the play grossed $14,000 during its first week, the best return of the season.[29]

A milder season lay ahead; the worst was past.

# Conclusion

In the course of this book we have pointed to the social, economic, ethnic, cultural and religious factors that rendered America vulnerable to a fear, and a purge, of the kind that took place under Truman and Eisenhower. In this brief conclusion we will attempt to indicate why the purge occurred when it did, and why it died away when it did. One must, of course, remember that throughout the twentieth century America has suffered a succession of "red scares," and that the one we have described was only the most far-reaching and corrosive (if not the most explosive and violent).

Let us first consider the international scene: America's place in the postwar world.

The Second World War had just ended. For certain nationality groups and right-wing elements it had always been the wrong war against the wrong enemy—the desire for retribution remained strong. These groups were joined after 1944 by others initially favorable to the war but subsequently appalled by the spread of Soviet Communism in Eastern Europe and by the reduction of Poland, Hungary and other East European nations to satellite status. Here Catholic indignation ran high.

For others, the majority, it had been the right war and the right outcome (victory over the Axis). Then elation turned to alarm; Stalin was intractable; a shattered Western Europe lay at the mercy of the Red Army. Had such sacrifices been made, so many lives lost, that one expansionist totalitarianism might supplant another? Among the Cold War liberals there soon developed a determination to halt Soviet encroachment by every available means and to deal roughly with elements at home—Communists, fellow travelers, Progressives—who foolishly or wickedly adopted the Soviet point of view.

The knowledge that America alone possessed the resources, economic and military, to "defend democracy" opened the door wide to a sentiment that had long been brewing in the consciousness of American internationalists: that America alone possessed the will, the spiritual resources, the psychic energy to do so. Hence the sense of destiny, of a mission, of a fundamental rectitude—of the Pax Americana, an ideology both idealistic and imperialistic. The Second World War lent wings to the mission; henceforward it would be the American Century; the Bear and his domestic acolytes would be slapped down.

Let us turn now from international to internal factors, and particularly to the varied consequences of the New Deal, the bloodless revolution achieved by Roosevelt.

The Democrats had, by 1948, occupied the White House for fifteen years. After Truman's victory over Dewey the Republicans became embittered, desperate, anarchic in their bid for power. At the same time conservative elements in Congress (of both parties) fought to restore the power of the legislature against the significant advances made by the executive and the burgeoning bureaucracy under the New Deal. Congressional investigations of red influence, particularly in government, were adopted as the most punishing available weapon.

Business too regarded the New Deal with less than enthusiasm (though to speak of "business" as a homogeneous unit in this context is misleading); the graduated income tax, the wealth tax, the welfare spending, the powers of the NLRB, the sudden growth in the power and militancy of trade unions. Fearing another postwar recession, business elements sought (a) to make the world safe for American investment and exports; and (b) to curb the power of government and unions. Both campaigns coalesced in a common hostility toward Russia (then China) and their American friends. The fear of Communism within the New Deal was both genuine and fabricated, a rhetorical extension of the fear of Socialism in any form.

Out of the war there emerged yet another salient factor or threat, though full consciousness of it was delayed, perhaps, until the early fifties. As the European empires collapsed so a vast horde of poor "natives," hitherto securely ruled by the white man or politically dormant, began to stir, to speak. The fear that they would be "subverted" by Moscow or Peking was the corollary of that aggressive guilt that the privileged "haves" ubiquitously focus on the "have nots." The world threatened to close in and grab America's pie: Communism was seen as the catalyst, and the pernicious new doctrine of neutralism (Nehru, Nasser) as the agent.

This horror of the envious advance of the Asian and African millions coincided with a lively anxiety about the encroachments of the poor and underprivileged at home. Millions of beneficiaries of the New Deal, slum children in their time, were rapidly putting behind them memories of the Depression and the bread line, ironing out their hyphenated traits, staking out their plot in the property-owning democracy. The census of 1950 showed a 50 percent increase in home owners since 1940; the median family income had risen from $1,325 to $3,240. Though often benefiting from the GI Bill of Rights, the new middle class began to call for a halt to taxation and government spending, and to barricade their neighborhoods and schools against Negroes migrating from the South or Puerto Ricans flooding in from the island. Thus a vast social backlash offered itself to anti-Communist politicians and pressure groups.

Despite rapid material progress, this was a time of universal shocks and traumas. The Celebration remained haunted by the war itself, the loss of life; by the coming of air power, shrinking the world; by the atomic bomb, an agent of mass destruction; then by Korea—the return of the ghost at high noon. Though science, technology and centralization lent wings to material progress, these alien, remote powers and mysteries also frightened people into a state of largely incoherent resentment, generating a need for scapegoats—spies, treacherous scientists, pederastic State Department officials with an allegiance elsewhere. In short—Communism!

Why did it slow down and die in the late fifties? Such things do slow down by a process of inertia and revulsion. People shook their heads as if they had been sleepwalking through the underworld, amazed to discover where it had all led. McCarthy's role was historically healthy because he dramatized intolerance, lent it crude, villainous features, personalized it, stole it away from the low-profiled bureaucrats. Once he had turned their own weapon against themselves, writ large, the leadership cadres concluded that enough was enough, that liberty was, after all, not easily divisible.

Gradually, too, the slow, soporific, conservative tempo of the Eisenhower regime deflated anxiety, bringing reassurance. For a while the blacks kept their place. The Russians were still there, but no nearer. Ike said that one had to live with them. People shrugged: why not invite those collective farmers over here to see how we grow corn in Iowa?

When Kennedy took office there was both a joyous confirmation of the new liberalism and, in certain quarters, a sharp reaction, a paranoid scare campaign. Despite the Birch Society and other vigilante groups of the New Right, and despite Goldwater's success in capturing the Republican Party, the liberal establishment easily disposed of the challenge until the Vietnam war and the rise of the militant New Left completely changed the face of the political landscape. But that is another story.

# Abbreviations
## used in the text

| | |
|---|---|
| AAA | Agricultural Adjustment Administration |
| AAAS | American Association for the Advancement of Science |
| AAUP | American Association of University Professors |
| ABA | American Bar Association |
| ABC | American Broadcasting Company |
| ABMAC | American Bureau for Medical Aid to China |
| ACLU | American Civil Liberties Union |
| ACPFB | American Committee for the Protection of the Foreign Born |
| ACTU | Association of Catholic Trade Unionists |
| ADA | Americans for Democratic Action |
| AEC | Atomic Energy Commission |
| AFL | American Federation of Labor |
| AFM | American Federation of Musicians |
| AFRA | American Federation of Radio Artists |
| AFT | American Federation of Teachers |
| AFTRA | American Federation of Television and Radio Artists |
| AIPR | American Council, Institute of Pacific Relations |
| AJLAC | American Jewish League Against Communism |
| ALP | American Labor Party |
| ALPD | American League for Peace and Democracy |
| AMPP | American Motion Picture Producers |
| ANG | American Newspaper Guild |
| AP | Associated Press |
| ASC | American Security Council |
| AT&T | American Telephone & Telegraph Company |
| AYD | American Youth for Democracy |
| BIA | Board of Immigration Appeals |
| CBS | Columbia Broadcasting System |
| CCNY | City College of New York |
| CFA | Committee for the First Amendment |

| | |
|---|---|
| CIA | Central Intelligence Agency |
| CIO | Congress of Industrial Organizations |
| CPUSA (CP) | Communist Party of the United States of America |
| CRC | Civil Rights Congress |
| CSC | Civil Service Commission |
| CSU | Conference of Studio Unions |
| CWV | Catholic War Veterans |
| DAR | Daughters of the American Revolution |
| DHEW | Department of Health, Education and Welfare |
| DPOWU | Distributive, Processing and Office Workers Union |
| ECLC | Emergency Civil Liberties Committee |
| ERP | European Recovery Program |
| FBI | Federal Bureau of Investigation |
| FCC | Federal Communications Commission |
| GE | General Electric Company |
| GM | General Motors |
| GPU | Soviet Political Police |
| HCUA | House Committee on Un-American Activities |
| HISC | House Internal Security Committee |
| IATSE | International Alliance of Theatrical Stage Employees |
| IBEW | International Brotherhood of Electrical Workers |
| ICCASP | Independent Citizens Committee for the Arts, Sciences and Professions |
| IERB | Industrial Employment Review Board |
| IIA | International Information Agency |
| ILWU | International Longshoremen & Warehousemen's Union |
| IOELB | International Organizations Employees Loyalty Board |
| IPR | Institute of Pacific Relations |
| ISL | Independent Socialist League |
| IUE | International Union of Electrical Workers |
| IWO | International Workers Order |
| IWW | International Workers of the World |
| JAFRC | Joint Anti-Fascist Refugee Committee |
| LRB | Loyalty Review Board |
| LYL | Labor Youth League |
| MCS | Marine Cooks and Stewards |
| MGM | Metro-Goldwyn-Mayer |
| MIT | Massachusetts Institute of Technology |
| MPA | Motion Picture Association |
| MPAPAI | Motion Picture Alliance for the Preservation of American Ideals |
| NAACP | National Association for the Advancement of Colored People |
| NATO | North Atlantic Treaty Organization |
| NBC | National Broadcasting Company |
| NCASF | National Council for American-Soviet Friendship |
| NKVD | Soviet Political Police |
| NLG | National Lawyers Guild |
| NLRB | National Labor Relations Board |
| NMU | National Maritime Union |
| NYU | New York University |
| OSS | Office of Strategic Services |

| | |
|---|---|
| OWI | Office of War Information |
| PAC-CIO | Political Action Committee-CIO |
| PCA | Progressive Citizens of America |
| PEC | People's Educational Center |
| PIC | Peace Information Center |
| PP | Progressive Party |
| RCA | Radio Corporation of America |
| SACB | Subversive Activities Control Board |
| SAG | Screen Actors Guild |
| SCHW | Southern Conference for Human Welfare |
| SIM | Military Investigation Service (Spanish Republic) |
| SISS | Senate Internal Security Subcommittee |
| SWG | Screen Writers Guild |
| SWP | Socialist Workers Party |
| TU | Teachers Union |
| TVA | Tennessee Valley Authority |
| UAW | United Automobile Workers |
| UC | University of California |
| UCLA | University of California at Los Angeles |
| UCR | United China Relief |
| UERMWA (UE) | United Electrical, Radio and Machine Workers of America |
| UN | United Nations |
| UNESCO | United Nations Educational, Scientific, and Cultural Organization |
| UNRRA | United Nations Relief and Rehabilitation Administration |
| UP | United Press |
| UPWA | United Public Workers of America |
| USIA | United States Information Agency |
| USSR | Union of Soviet Socialist Republics |
| VFW | Veterans of Foreign Wars |
| WEC | Wage Earners Committee |
| WPA | Works Progress Administration |
| WPU | Washington Pension Union |
| YCL | Young Communist League |

# Appendix A

# Undercover Agents

Females of the species were numerous. They included Mrs. Noiselle Clinger, Mrs. Albert Ahearn, Rowena Paumi, Mrs. Daisy Van Dorn, Mrs. Edith Macia, Lola Bella Holmes and Mrs. Ann Ruth Steinberg. Clinger testified before HCUA in 1959, describing how she had worked for the FBI within the CP for fifteen years, mingling with workers at the Douglas Aircraft plant at Santa Monica, California, and noting the names of technicians whom she considered "liberal." Ahearn appeared as a prosecution witness in 1956 at the Kentucky sedition trial of Carl Braden, who, she swore, had originally inducted her into the Party. Paumi joined the Party for the Bureau and later testified before HCUA. Van Dorn worked for the FBI as an elevator operator in the San Francisco building housing the Party's headquarters and earned over $4,000 from the FBI between 1945 and 1951. Macia, a sixty-eight-year-old Los Angeles grandmother, provided HCUA with 120 names in March 1953, explaining that she had acted as an FBI agent within the Party from 1943 to 1948—for expenses only. Holmes, a black woman from Chicago and an FBI informer, testified at the Smith Act trial of Claude Lightfoot and later became an itinerant speaker for the Birch Society.[1] Steinberg, a twenty-one-year-old freshman at Boston University, testified before the SACB in December 1953 that she had been an FBI agent for the past two years within the Labor Youth League, whose subversive nature the Board was then considering. Other FBI witnesses against the LYL included: George Christopher, of Albany, New York, who had joined the League in 1950 at the request of the FBI, and quit in 1951 after serving as a delegate to the first national convention; Dennis L. James, who joined in January 1950 after contacting the Bureau, and who became financial secretary of the LYL in New Jersey; and Jacqueline Wilson, of the Bronx, who joined in March 1952 after discussions with the Bureau. James, an accountant for the New York Port Authority, later testified before HCUA in September 1958.[2]

547

William A. Wallace joined the Party in 1949 and reported regularly to the FBI from 1952 to 1955. In April 1956 he testified before the SACB against the American Peace Crusade. Clifford Miller, Jr., a graduate of the University of West Virginia, went to work for the Bethlehem Steel Corporation in 1945, became an active Communist in 1948, was disillusioned a year later, agreed to rejoin the Party in 1952 on behalf of the FBI, and broke cover in May 1957. Karl Prussion, until recently an FBI informer, gave HCUA forty names when he testified in San Francisco in May 1960. A father and his son, Worden C. Mosher and Harold W. Mosher, testified before HCUA in New Haven in September 1956 as to how they had operated as FBI "plants" within the CP. Harold Mosher, a TV repairman who joined the Party for the FBI in 1947, became chairman of the New Haven youth branch. Harold Kent had a similar story to tell. Emanuel Ross Richardson had served as coordinator of the CP Club at Cornell University while informing for the FBI. Regularly he drove students to meetings at which he himself presided. Later he remarked before HCUA: "Whenever you do that kind of work, you have some sort of qualms." [3]

John J. Huber, of New York City, was working for the WPA in 1937 when the Bureau recruited him. He served in the Party as an informer for the next nine years, during which time he kept a meticulous diary. In September 1949 he provided the Senate Subcommittee on Immigration with a long list of names and addresses of members of the CP's James Connolly Branch, in the Eleventh Assembly District. He also spoke of free liquor and immoral women, warned that the police of most American cities could not cope with real red riots, and hinted darkly that up in Harlem the blacks were being subverted by Negro Communists such as Benjamin Davis, Jr., and Henry Winston. The Subcommittee duly released his testimony to the press. [4]

Blames Hidalgo, Jr., the government's thirteenth witness at the Foley Square trial in May 1949, attended a Party meeting the night before he testified. Other FBI agents who revealed themselves at the same trial included Thomas A. Younglove, of St. Louis (who also appeared at the Baltimore Smith Act trial in 1952), and Garfield Herron. Government witnesses at the Baltimore trial included Ralph V. Long, of Durham, North Carolina, who joined the Party in 1946 at the age of twenty-two, and who, between 1949 and 1954, was tried twenty times for public drunkenness and twice for assault and battery; Harry Bartlett, a timber cutter from West Virginia, who served the FBI inside the CP from 1940 until 1948; Charles M. Craig, a maintenance supervisor who worked for the Bureau from 1943 until 1948; and Robert A. Benner, formerly a steelworker and undercover agent for the FBI.

Meanwhile, on the West Coast the Smith Act trial of the California Communist leaders produced another crop of FBI undercover agents as witnesses: Lloyd N. Hamlin, a photographer, joined the Party in 1945 on behalf of Naval Intelligence and later reported to the Bureau. (In order to maintain his cover he had refused to testify before a California investigating committee and had been sentenced for contempt, but the U.S. Attorney's office had kept him out of jail.) Hamlin earned $13,182 from the FBI between 1946 and 1952. Timothy Evans, Jr., a Negro former football star at Xavier University, New Orleans, who joined the Oakland CP in 1948 as an FBI agent, also testified, as did Stephen A. Wereb, an FBI plant inside the Party from 1944 to 1947. Jessica Mitford recalls how an FBI informer, Dickson Hill, camouflaged his role by applying himself dourly and diligently to his duties as membership director of the Oakland CP club to which she belonged. A small business-man, Hill had been visited by Party workers and recruited after filling in a postcard requesting a trial subscription to the *People's World*. Taking the wit-ness stand before HCUA in San Francisco in 1953, he recalled having nagged laggardly Communists to improve their attendance record at Party meetings. During the Detroit Smith Act trial in 1953, testimony was heard from Berry Cody, a fifty-six-year-old Negro who had worked for the FBI inside the CP since 1944, and who said the Bureau had paid him about $8,000 in ten years. A former machine operator, foundry worker and laundry hand, Cody had contrived, while serving the FBI, to penetrate the executive board of the Amalgamated Garment Workers Union and to become a trusted officer of the National Negro Labor Council. At the Philadelphia Smith Act trial, evidence was heard from Ralph K. Keltzinger, who had joined the Party in 1944 at the FBI's request and had remained a member till July 1954. Appearing before the SISS in October, he named seventy-two names. At the Pittsburgh Smith Act trial the prosecution produced Dewey C. Price, who started undercover work for the FBI in 1935, joined the CP in November 1948, became one of the West Virginia's six top Party members, and quit only in March 1953. Price, a turbine repairman in a chemical plant, testified in January 1954 dur-ing the SACB's investigation of the Jefferson School of Social Sciences.[5]

Some informers adopted the dual role of FBI employee and company labor spy. The Ford Motor Company, famous for its anti-red Service Depart-ment, was in 1953 employing at least two FBI undercover agents, Stephen Schemanske and Milton J. Santwire, to spy on their fellow workers within the United Automobile Workers (UAW). Santwire, who was receiving $90 a month from the Bureau and $75 from Ford, had received a total of $4,800 from Ford when his true identity came to light at the Detroit Smith Act trial. Schemanske's undercover employment by Ford dated back to 1940 and had brought him $70,000. The Detroit automobile industry was honeycombed with agents. Richard F. O'Hair, an FBI agent within the CP from 1943 to 1947, testified before HCUA in February 1952 about Communist penetration of the UAW, naming eighty-two Michigan workers as Communists. Another agent operating in the Detroit area, Glenn M. Irving, testified in 1950 to a city loyalty committee.[6]

Other agents who managed to penetrate radical unions included Jan Jan-owitz, a Cleveland organizer for the pro-Communist United Electrical Work-ers (UE), who testified before the SACB in February 1952 that he had been an FBI agent since 1943, and William H. Feto, an upholstery-supply dealer, who had worked since 1941 as an undercover operator in the General Electric plants at Lynn, Fitchburg, Everett and Schenectady. Herman E. Thomas, who worked as an FBI agent at the Bethlehem Steel Company for ten years, and who testified before the McCarthy Subcommittee in December 1954 dur-ing the inquiry into "defense plant risks," [7] was probably known to the com-pany in his true colors. FBI informers were also much in demand at the trials of labor leaders accused of having falsely sworn Taft-Hartley non-Communist affidavits. In January 1958 the government's case in the Cleveland trial of eight defendants rested mainly on the evidence of eight experienced informers, David Garfield, Arthur Strunk, William G. Cummings, Frank Peoples, John Nello Anidei, John E. Janowitz, Halbert Baxter, and Fred E. Gardner.[8]

Second only to the labor unions as FBI targets were the foreign-born. During the SACB's hearings on the American Committee for the Protection of the Foreign Born, a large number of former undercover agents surfaced as government witnesses, including James W. Glatis, who had worked inside the CP for the Bureau from 1949 to 1954, and who helped to cause a Wayland, Massachusetts, school teacher to lose her job in August 1954,[9] and Clark M. Harper, whose ten-year stint in the CP ended in 1953. The prosecution relied heavily on informers during deportation and denaturalization proceedings. Thaddeus Zygmont, frequently employed as a witness in such cases, testified at the trial of Stanley Nowak in 1954 in flat contradiction of a pamphlet he had written in 1938. Cornered about this, Zygmont explained that he had lied in the pamphlet. Forgetful about most things, he nevertheless "remembered" Nowak preaching violent revolution thirty years earlier; Nowak, he said, definitely joined the CP in 1924. Another witness, William O. Nowell, swore Nowak joined in 1935. Nowak said he never joined. Earl Reno, formerly organization secretary of the Michigan CP, had first contacted the FBI in 1947 and later worked as an informer for the Immigration Service; he named Nowak as a "secret Communist." Dr. William F. Hewitt, Jr., who was a professor of physiology at Still College of Osteopathy, Des Moines, Iowa, and formerly an employee of the Wilmark Detective Agency, Chicago (a colorful career), claimed to have paid his CP dues to Nowak in 1938 and to have received from him orders about establishing a Party unit in Michigan State College. Apart from this, Hewitt could remember little else under cross-examination.[10]

# Appendix B

## *The Tillett Survey: The Predicament of the Discharged Teacher*

Did college and school teachers who lost their jobs on account of their political beliefs generally receive moral and financial support from their colleagues? And what was the average legal cost of a defense? Obviously no two individuals underwent identical experiences, but the evidence that follows, drawn mainly from the Tillett files, suggests some tentative generalizations.

Quite a few professors fought protracted legal battles, incurring high costs but receiving adequate legal aid. Dirk J. Struik, of MIT, ran up expenses of $18,000 partly payable to the Boston lawyers Oliver S. Allen and Lawrence Shubow, but the burden was carried mainly by an *ad hoc* Struik Defense Committee and by the Emergency Defense Committee of Massachusetts. Moses I. Finley, of Rutgers, reported that his legal costs were carried by the university itself, while Professor Bernard Riess, of Hunter College, had his expenses paid by the New York Teachers Union, a benefit that also accrued to Professors D. Straus and Oscar Schaftel, of Queens College, Harry Slochower, of Brooklyn College, and Philip S. Foner, of CCNY. Lyman Bradley, of NYU, received legal support from the Joint Anti-Fascist Refugee Committee, while his colleague Edmund Burgum incurred legal costs of about $2,000 but received adequate aid. Marcus Singer, who ultimately retained his job at Cornell, estimated his costs at about $10,000, of which $3,000 was raised by sympathetic colleagues and $2,000 by the Quaker Legal Group. Since Singer was suspended on full pay, he was presumably able to find the balance out of his own pocket. Henry C. Steinmetz, of San Diego State College, reported adequate legal aid, even though his costs were $3,000; so also did Barrows Dunham, of Temple University, who ran up costs of $5,700. Most of the $10,000 required by Leon J. Kamin, of Harvard, was raised by the sympathetic Cambridge intellectual community.

Others were fortunate enough to incur only minor expenses or to be served free of charge by idealistic attorneys. Dr. Horace B. Davis, dismissed by the University of Kansas City, found such a lawyer in Fyke Farmer. The ECLC took up the Davis case and by May 1955 had raised $662 to help defray court costs.¹ Herbert J. Phillips, dismissed by the University of Washington, was advised by an attorney specializing in civil-liberties cases, John Caughlan, and had to find only about $500, which was contributed by university colleagues. Professor Leonard Marsak, of Reed College, received free legal assistance, while Mark Nickerson, of the University of Michigan, paid only $200; apparently his attorney donated most of his time. Professor Frank Oppenheimer, of the University of Minnesota, did not receive aid, but his costs were insubstantial. Professor Richard Reichard, of George Washington University, paid out $200 and received adequate legal aid. Thomas M. McGrath, of Los Angeles State College, reported costs of "a few hundred dollars."

A few complained. Professor Chandler Davis, of the University of Michigan, and Professor Giovanni Rossi Lomanitz, of Fisk College, regretted the lack of help. Among school teachers, a few felt aggrieved: Max Weitzman, a Boston public-school teacher, paid $300, which he described as "a substantial sum," to a lawyer "who lacked civil-liberties experience." Estelle T. Lishinsky, a Philadelphia elementary-school teacher, reported having paid $400 in legal fees—her first lawyer had to abandon her case because he was threatened with loss of position by an organization he belonged to. But the majority of schoolteachers had no complaints about this aspect of their personal tragedies. The members of the New York and Philadelphia Teachers Unions were particularly well served. Abraham Egnal, of Philadelphia, paid out $500, but received adequate support; his colleague Solomon Haas got legal advice gratis "due to professional courtesy"; one Philadelphia high-school teacher wishing to remain anonymous reported costs of $11,000, yet good legal aid. Samuel Kaplan, a Philadelphia high-school teacher, reported that his attorney worked for him free of charge and did a good job, while Lillian Lowenfels, also of Philadelphia, received help from a committee towards covering her expenses of $500. Teachers who, like Eugene Jackson, belonged to the New York Teachers Union were fully satisfied with the union's financial support. Robert Lowenstein, one of the Newark "Fifth Amendment" teachers dismissed in 1954, reported having spent about $15,000 during six years of litigation, yet the aid he received from the ACLU and the AAUP was, again, adequate. Sadder was the case of an isolated Massachusetts woman teacher who not only lost her job but also about $1,000 in legal expenses.²

Replies to Professor Paul Tillett's questionnaire to 140 academics who had been dismissed on account of their political beliefs, indicated that the majority had subsequently been compelled to change their careers and undergo extensive retraining. A few prospered: Bernard F. Riess, of Hunter College, became a self-employed analytical psychotherapist and research director of a large mental-health clinic, earning approximately $30,000 a year. Another academic psychologist, Ralph H. Gundlach, dismissed by the University of Washington in 1949, trained as a practicing psychologist in New York, paying his passage with a part-time research job at the American Jewish Congress. The certificate to practice in New York State, which he received after four years' training, was presumably a license to prosper.³

After "a great deal of re-education," Ed Burgum, once of NYU, became a psychoanalyst with annual earnings of $22,000, more than double his salary at the university. With some retraining, Harry Slochower, of Brooklyn College, was able to practice psychotherapy at a salary equal to that of his associate professorship. Professor Simon W. Heimlich, dismissed from the Rutgers College of Pharmacology in 1952, wrote to Paul Tillett in August 1964 under the letterhead: "Simon W. Heimlich, Inc.—A Personalized Investment Service." Those who moved of necessity from academic life into profit-making companies tended to experience greater personal freedom there; this was the case with Irving Stein, dismissed by Wayne State University, who worked as a laborer for six months before falling on his feet in the field of industrial research. But, prudently steering clear of classified projects, he lost touch with the work of most interest to him.

Many made the effort to get back into teaching. Gene Weltfish, of Columbia, was unemployed for many years; Lyman Bradley tried but failed; Chandler Davis made futile attempts for eight years; Leonard Marsak, of Reed College, was denied fourteen academic positions during the two years following his dismissal; Herbert J. Phillips applied to some 2,000 colleges, of which only 10 percent replied and only one offered a summer job; John Reynolds, of the University of Florida, tried without avail to find a new teaching post; after ten years Oscar Shaftel was hired for an evening course in writing by a department head who was a former colleague; Henry C. Steinmetz found himself blacklisted in California, and even Cornell withdrew a summer teaching engagement, but after several years he got a temporary post in Michigan, followed by one in Morehouse College, a Negro institution in Atlanta. Philip S. Foner, of CCNY, applied widely in the New York vicinity, but received no response. Forest O. Wiggins sent "about a hundred" letters of application, but no school would hire him, until he was accepted by a Negro college in Georgia. Barrows Dunham, of Temple University, was also turned down; he recalled that Temple circulated the Trustees' pejorative statement about his dismissal even after he was acquitted in court of contempt; he had to threaten legal action.

But some made it back into teaching. Others could remain in their profession only by working abroad. After three years of part-time employment on research projects at Columbia, Moses I. Finley moved to Cambridge, England, where he remained. In 1962 Chandler Davis concluded a frustrating period of working in advertising research by taking a post as associate professor at Toronto University. When his University of Michigan colleague Mark Nickerson became a professor and then department head in the University of Manitoba, this initially involved a drop in salary of some $4,000, but later his salary increased to $16,600. With some bitterness, he regarded his emigration as permanent: ". . . our eldest son, who was seven at the time of my dismissal . . . was subjected to a considerable amount of both verbal and physical abuse, and has never forgotten it . . . One can speak more freely here [in Canada], and it is a better place to raise and educate children." [4] Maurice Halperin, of Boston University, also took himself abroad: in 1967 he was working as an economic expert for "juseplan" in Cuba. Leon J. Kamin taught at McGill and Queen's Universities in Canada before accepting a chair at Princeton.

Others just stumbled along uncategorizable paths of survival: Lyman Bradley arranged convention exhibits of books; John Reynolds, of the University of Florida, worked as a $400-per-year tutor to a football team, then managed a bookstore for $3,000 a year. Oscar Shaftel free-lanced for two years, worked in trade journalism and public relations—"all of it somewhat distasteful"—before becoming an editor in book publishing. D. Straus, of Queens College, got $45 a week for his first job, "but there's no way of conveying those first five years." Philip S. Foner, of CCNY, worked as educational director for a trade union and edited the writings of Tom Paine for the Citadel Press, of which he later became a member. Thomas M. McGrath, of Los Angeles State College, had skills as a machinist up his sleeve but could not get a job, because all such work in the Los Angeles area was defense-connected. No fate was more painful than that of Herbert J. Phillips, dismissed in his late fifties by the University of Washington for admitted membership of the CP. He reported in 1964:

> Two [years] were spent lecturing in defense of academic freedom, when I earned no more than traveling expenses. Mrs. Phillips kept up the domestic establishment (two children still in school) by boarding babies, doing housework, dress making, and using up our savings. Two more years were spent as a building laborer earning around $2,000 a year. The next 2½ years were spent doing odd jobs and unpaid political work . . . For the next three years I worked on the assembly line of a furniture factory, and the family income was around $7,000 a year. For the last six years I have been a recipient of social security, as well as a $30 teacher's annuity . . . For eight years after my dismissal I was active in the Communist Party at a more or less rank-and-file level . . . The loss of academic association which had constituted my milieu for thirty years was the most negative effect of my dismissal. Teaching was the only outlet of expression I knew, and I felt that I was effective in that vocation—especially after I was able to orientate philosophy with practical social concerns.

So wrote the seventy-three-year-old Herbert J. Phillips, who had served in U.S. Naval Aviation as far back as 1917.[5]

The families of these men were also liable to suffer more than financial insecurity. Nickerson mentioned the mental and physical assaults on his seven-year-old son; Phillips spoke of "severe handicaps" in the careers of his three children; John Reynolds wrote that "both my family and I have suffered varying degrees of unpleasantness . . . I had a severe emotional breakdown." Bernard Riess reported "family anxiety due to front-page publicity" and that "there is still residual anxiety about participating in social-action organizations and causes." Oscar Shaftel described "the obscene letters and phone calls, the puzzlement of the children." According to W. Tandy, the "extent of worry . . . disruption . . . can never be measured nor described. It has distorted our children's lives." D. Straus wrote, "To be unfrocked at age forty-two after an academic lifetime is an absolutely terrifying experience, particularly when there are children, and newspaper publicity, and ugly phone calls." Thomas M. McGrath wrote: "largely responsible for destroying a marriage and a family because of lack of money to live on, lack of security, the resultant anxieties . . . Times have changed, people say. But I know I will *never* have the security of a 'good American.' But I have learned not to need it." Forest O. Wiggins commented: "At fifty-seven I feel that my life is behind me."

Of the sixteen schoolteachers who responded to Paul Tillett's questionnaire, all had BA degrees, five of them being MA's and two, PhD's. They all received adequate legal aid, but only six were able to ultimately to return to teaching. Of the others, one became an author, one a draftsman, one an accountant, one a clerk, one a researcher, one a salesman, three went into private business, one retired. Five of the sixteen reported subsequent harassment by the FBI; six mentioned traumatic effects on their families.

Among the casualties of the purge that struck the Philadelphia school system in 1953–54, Abraham Egnal, then in his early fifties, found some part-time teaching on the side, tried his hand at business, and later got work as a substitute teacher, by concealing his record. For himself and his family the experience was traumatic. Solomon Haas was in his middle thirties when the ax fell; he was then able to devote himself full-time to a business that he had prudently begun in anticipation of such a purge. Samuel Kaplan, an Air Force veteran in his early forties, attempted for five years to get back into teaching, but without avail, and went to work in the office of a manufacturer, starting at $75 a week later rising to $6,200 a year. A few years after his dismissal he was visited by precisely the same FBI agent who had pursued him before HCUA issued its fatal subpoena. Kaplan's conclusion was a bitter one: "The teachers of America are pretty low on the totem pole, and they deserve it. They have allowed themselves to be pushed around by ignora-muses, by self-seekers, and they deserve it."

Estelle Lishinsky lost her job in a Philadelphia elementary school when she was in her early forties, even though a week before the Velde Committee arrived in town she had received a letter of commendation from the Board of Education. Harassed by the FBI and by notoriety, she and her husband left Philadelphia. After an abortive attempt to work as a craftswoman in New York, she was unemployed for a year, her health deteriorated, she suffered stomach disorders. In applying for teaching jobs, she was never able to refer to her service in Philadelphia; even so, she got a post working with cerebral-palsy children, and then in a private nursery. Lillian Lowenfels, who taught French in a veterans' program in Philadelphia, was the wife of Walter Lowenfels, one of the CP leaders awaiting trial under the Smith Act. When told of her dismissal in the anteroom of the principal's office, she was forbidden to return to the classroom to collect her personal effects—she would never forget this insult. After her dismissal she could obtain no employment, lost her insurance and pension benefits and began to suffer from high blood pressure.

Max Weitzman was teaching the fifth grade in Boston public schools when he invoked the Fifth Amendment before HCUA. After the School Committee granted him a public hearing on charges of insubordination and unfitness to teach, he was dismissed. He experienced what he called "a sharp drop in social and community status to a position of second-class citizenship," finding himself reduced to menial jobs at 90 cents or $1.25 an hour, but even these jobs inevitably came to an end when the FBI contacted his employer; as late as 1960 he had a confrontation with agents. "When an employer asks, 'Where were you working in such and such a year and why did you leave?' what kind of answer can you give him? One becomes immediately defensive, and the feeling communicates itself to the interviewer. The result is easily imaginable." Finally Weitzman found secure employment in a Hasidic denomination school—"the Jewish community was primarily responsible for my rehabilitation."

"In trying to get back into teaching, or even child care, I was turned down at every place that knew my history . . . I learned to keep quiet." Thus wrote a schoolteacher ten years after her dismissal in August 1954 by the Wayland (Massachusetts) School Committee. (It was alleged that she had not told the truth about CP connections during the years 1938 to 1954. The Committee heard evidence against her from an FBI agent who had penetrated the Party; the teacher herself relied on the First Amendment.) Her troubles did not end with discharge; in January 1955 she was hauled forth to an open hearing of the State Commission investigating Communism. She found work in a SPCA hospital, lost it when her past was revealed, resorted to a bench job in a shoe factory, then to domestic work, became director of a home for disturbed girls, and then found teaching jobs out of state. A long period of low income left her in debt—"I can only be at home on weekends, I live in the basement, and rent the upstairs part of the house."[6] Even ten years later she insisted on anonymity.

# Appendix C

# The Hollywood Blacklist

What follows is a representative sample of actors, directors and writers whose careers were blighted by the blacklist. The list is by no means complete. Other victims are referred to in Chapter 26; still others are merely presented as statistics.

The term "identified" refers only to an allegation by a witness and in no way implies that the allegation was correct. The term "credit" refers only to credits in American films under the artist's normal professional name.

Sources: Leslie Halliwell, *The Filmgoer's Companion*, 5th Edition, London, Paladin, 1976; John T. Weaver, *Forty Years of Screen Credits*, 1929–1969, Metuchen, N.J., The Scarecrow Press, 1970; *Who Wrote the Movie and What Else Did He Write? An Index of Screen Writers and their Film Works*, 1936–1969, Los Angeles, The Academy of Motion Picture Arts and Sciences and the Writers Guild of America, West, 1970; Cogley, Vol. 1 (see Bibliography); *International Motion Picture Almanac*, 1968, New York, Quigley Publications, 1968; British Film Institute Library Personalities Index, London.

BEN BARZMAN, writer: identified as a Communist by witnesses, 1951–1954; eight credits, 1943–1952, then none in the United States until 1959.

CONNIE LEE BENNETT, writer: identified by a witness in 1953; twenty-four credits, 1937–1953, then none.

LEONARDO BERCOVICI, writer: took the Fifth Amendment in May 1951; six credits, 1939–1953, then none until 1963.

JOHN BERRY, director: identified by witnesses, 1951–1952; six credits, 1945–1951, then none in the United States until 1959.

ALVAH BESSIE, writer: one of the Hollywood Ten; five credits, 1943–1948 (completed, November 1947), then none.

HERBERT BIBERMAN, writer and director: one of the Ten; seven credits, 1935–1947, then none in Hollywood until 1968.

ALLEN BORETZ, writer: identified by witnesses, 1951 and 1953; twelve credits, 1936–1948, then none.

JOHN BRIGHT, writer: identified by witnesses, 1951–1953; twelve credits, 1937–1951, then two abroad, none in the United States.

HAROLD BUCHMAN, writer: took the Fifth Amendment, April 1951; twenty-five credits, 1936–1947, then none until 1965.

SIDNEY BUCHMAN, writer: convicted of contempt of Congress, 1952; twelve credits, 1936–1951, then none in the United States until 1962.

HUGO BUTLER, writer: identified by witnesses, 1951–1953; twenty-two credits, 1936–1952, then none until 1963.

MORRIS CARNOVSKY, actor: took the Fifth Amendment, April 1951; eighteen credits, 1937–1951, then none until 1962.

HOWLAND CHAMBERLAIN, actor: took the Fifth Amendment, September 1951; sixteen credits, 1947–1953, then none.

EDWARD CHODOROV, writer and producer: identified by witnesses, 1951–1953; nine writing credits, 1936–1951, then none.

ANGELA CLARKE, actress: in June 1955 she discussed her own CP membership from 1942 to 1949, but refused to testify about other people; seventeen credits, 1949–1955, then none until 1962.

LESTER COLE, writer: one of the Ten; thirty-six credits, 1932–1948 (completed, August 1947), then none until the 1970s.

JEFF COREY, actor: took the Fifth Amendment, September 1951; thirty-six credits, 1941–1951, then none until 1963.

HOWARD DA SILVA, actor: took the Fifth Amendment, March 1951; thirty-seven credits, 1936–1951, then none until 1963.

HOWARD DIMSDALE, writer: identified by witnesses, 1951–1953; thirteen credits, 1942–1953, then none.

LUDWIG DONATH, actor: identified by Lee J. Cobb, June 1953; thirty-four credits, 1942–1953, then none until 1966.

EDWARD ELISCU, writer: identified by witnesses, 1951–1953; thirteen credits, 1936–1951, then none.

CYRIL ENDFIELD, writer and director: identified by witnesses, 1951–1953; eight writing credits, 1946–1950, then none in the United States until 1965.

GUY ENDORE, writer: identified by witnesses, 1951–1953; eleven credits, 1937–1951, then none in the United States until 1963.

MARY VIRGINIA FARMER, actress: took the Fifth Amendment, September 1951; fifteen credits, 1943–1952, then none.

WILL GEER, actor: took the Fifth Amendment, April 1951; eighteen credits, 1932–1951, then none until 1962.

JODY GILBERT, actress: took the Fifth Amendment, March 1953; twenty-six credits, 1939–1952, one credit in 1959, one in 1969.

MICHAEL GORDON, director: took the Fifth Amendment, September 1951; twelve credits, 1942–1952, then none until 1958.

LLOYD GOUGH, actor: took the Fifth Amendment, May 1951; thirteen credits, 1948–1951, then none until 1967.

MORTON GRANT, writer: identified by witnesses, 1951–1953; thirty-one credits, 1937–1949, then none.

DASHIELL HAMMETT, writer: identified by witnesses and imprisoned for contempt of court, 1951; eight credits, 1937–1947, then none.

LILLIAN HELLMAN, writer: took the Fifth Amendment, February 1952; eight credits, 1936–1946, then none in the United States until 1961.

EDWARD HUEBSCH, writer: took the Fifth Amendment, March 1953; seven credits, 1946–1951, then none.

IAN MCLELLAN HUNTER, writer: identified by witnesses, 1951–1953; fifteen credits, 1939–1953, then none until 1969.

PAUL JARRICO, writer: took the Fifth Amendment, April 1951; twelve credits, 1937–1949, one in 1958, then none.

GORDON KAHN, writer: one of the Hollywood Nineteen in 1947; identified by witnesses, 1951–1953; twenty-eight credits, 1937–1949, then none.

VICTOR KILIAN, actor: took the Fifth Amendment, April 1951; eighty-four credits, 1929–1951, then none.

RING LARDNER, JR., writer: one of the Ten; ten credits, 1939–1948, then none until 1965.

JOHN HOWARD LAWSON, writer: one of the Ten; sixteen credits, 1929–1947, then none.

ROBERT LEES, writer: took the Fifth Amendment, April 1951; sixteen credits, 1940–1952, then none.

ALFRED LEWIS LEVITT, writer: took the Fifth Amendment, September 1951; five credits, 1948–1953, then none.

PAUL MCVEY, actor: identified by witnesses, 1953; thirty-two credits, 1936–1953, then none.

BEN MADDOW, writer: took the Fifth Amendment, March 1953; six credits, 1947–1952, then none until 1960.

ALBERT MALTZ, writer: one of the Ten; seven credits, 1932–1948 (completed, September 1947), then none until 1969.

EDWIN MILLER MAX, actor: took the Fifth Amendment, October 1952; twenty credits, 1946–1954, then none.

KAREN MORLEY (MRS. LLOYD GOUGH), actress: took the Fifth Amendment, November 1952; forty-four credits, 1931–1951, then none.

ZERO MOSTEL, actor: denied current membership but refused to discuss the past, October 1955; seven credits, 1943–1951, one in 1959, the next in 1966.

SAMUEL ORNITZ, writer: one of the Ten; twenty-six credits, 1929–1945, then none.

DOROTHY PARKER, writer: identified by witnesses, 1951; eleven credits, 1936–1951, one listed in 1954, then none.

ABRAHAM LINCOLN POLONSKY, director and writer: took the Fifth Amendment, April 1951; four credits, 1947–1951, then none until 1968.

ANNE REVERE, actress: took the Fifth Amendment, April 1951; thirty-nine credits, 1934–1951, then none until 1969.

ROBERT L. RICHARDS, writer: took the Fifth Amendment, September 1951; eight credits, 1945–1951, then none.

FREDERIC I. RINALDO, writer: identified by witnesses, 1951–1954; sixteen credits, 1940–1952, then none.

MARGUERITE ROBERTS, writer: took the Fifth Amendment, September 1951; twenty credits, 1936–1951, then none until 1962.

LOUISE ROUSSEAU, writer: took the Fifth Amendment, September 1951; sixteen credits, 1944–1949, then none.

WALDO SALT, writer: one of the Nineteen; took the Fifth Amendment, April 1951; nine credits, 1938–1951, then none until 1962.

ADRIAN SCOTT, writer and producer: one of the Ten; eleven credits, 1940–1947, then none.

ART SMITH, actor: identified by witnesses, 1951; twenty-six credits, 1943–1952, then none.

GALE SONDERGAARD (MRS. HERBERT BIBERMAN), actress: took the Fifth Amendment, March 1951; thirty-nine credits, 1936–1949, then none until 1969.

LIONEL STANDER, actor: denied current membership but took the Fifth Amendment on the past, March 1953; forty-one credits, 1935–1951, then none until 1963.

DONALD OGDEN STEWART, writer: identified by witnesses, 1951; eighteen credits, 1937–1949, then none.

ARTHUR STRAWN, writer: took the Fifth Amendment, May 1951; nine credits, 1941–1953, then none.

ELLIOTT SULLIVAN, actor: identified by witnesses, 1951–1954, and himself an uncooperative witness, August 1955; eighteen credits, 1938–1953, one listed in 1956, then none until 1969.

DOROTHY TREE (MRS. MICHAEL URIS), actress: identified by witnesses, 1951–1953; sixteen credits, 1939–1953, then none.

DALTON TRUMBO, writer: one of the Ten; twenty-seven credits, 1936–1945, then none officially acknowledged until 1959.

GEORGE TYNE, actor: identified by witnesses, 1951–1953, and himself an uncooperative witness, August 1955; eight credits, 1946–1951, then none until 1966.

BERNARD VORHAUS, director: identified by witnesses, 1951–1953; nineteen credits, 1933–1951, then none.

RICHARD WEIL, writer: identified by witnesses, 1951; fourteen credits, 1942–1952, then none.

CRANE WHITLEY, actor: took the Fifth Amendment, April 1953; eighteen credits, 1942–1954, then none.

MICHAEL WILSON, writer: took the Fifth Amendment, September 1951; seven credits, 1941–1952, then none officially acknowledged until 1962.

# Notes and References

(Full publication details of the works cited below are given in the Bibliography.)

## Abbreviations Used in the Notes and References

AAUP       American Association of University Professors
ACLU       American Civil Liberties Union
BAS        *Bulletin of the Atomic Scientists*
Besig Files   Ernest Besig Files (see Bibliography)
CSM        *Christian Science Monitor*
DAMP       Detroit Archives, Mayor's Papers (see Bibliography)
Donner Files   Frank J. Donner Files (see Bibliography)
DT         *Daily Telegraph* (London)
DW         *Daily Worker* (New York or London, as indicated)
Duran Papers   Gustavo Duran Papers (see Bibliography)
MG         *Manchester Guardian*
Matusow Papers   Harvey Matusow Collection (see Bibliography)
NYHT       *New York Herald Tribune*
NYRB       *New York Review of Books*
NYT        *New York Times*
Stamler    In the Supreme Court of the United States. October Term 1968. *Jeremiah Stamler* . . .(see Bibliography, Legal Documents, for full reference)
Tillett Papers   Paul Tillett Papers (see Bibliography)
TLS        *Times Literary Supplement*
UE Files   United Electrical, Radio & Machine Workers of America Personnel Security Files (see Bibliography)
USNWR      *U.S. News & World Report*
WRL        Walter Reuther Library, Labor History Archives (see Bibliography)

CHAPTER 1: THE TRUMAN DOCTRINE

1. It was this Congress that reduced tax by 3 percent on incomes of $2,400 or less; by 8 percent on incomes up to $10,000; by 15 percent on incomes up to $20,000; and by 48–65 percent on incomes over $100,000.

2. William F. Buckley, Jr., and L. Brent Bozell, *McCarthy and His Enemies*, p. 22; William R. Tanner and Robert Griffith, "The Internal Security Act of 1950," p. 175.

3. John Steinke and James Weinstein, "McCarthy and the Liberals," p. 43; *New York Sun*, Oct. 2, 1946; Gordon W. Allport, *The Nature of Prejudice*, p. 186; Jack Anderson and Ronald W. May, *McCarthy: The Man, the Senator, the "Ism,"* p. 110; Earl Mazo, *Richard Nixon*, pp. 39–40; Vern Countryman, "Washington: The Canwell Committee," p. 284.

4. Karl M. Schmidt, *Henry A. Wallace: Quixotic Crusade*, 1948, p. 27; Joseph Starobin, *American Communism in Crisis, 1943–1957*, p. 276; Thomas I. Emerson and David M. Helfeld, "Loyalty Among Government Employees," p. 20.

5. Fred J. Cook, *The Nightmare Decade: The Life and Times of Senator Joe McCarthy*, p. 64; *NYT*, March 12, 1947; ACLU, *In Times of Challenge: U.S. Liberties, 1946–47*, p. 4.

6. Harry S. Truman, born in 1884 on a Missouri farm, did not enter politics until the age of thirty-eight, when Boss Thomas Pendergast arranged for his election as county judge of Kansas City. Twelve years later, in 1934, Pendergast chose him to be Democratic candidate for the Senate. During the war this reliable but somewhat obscure New Dealer made his name by presiding over a Senate committee to investigate waste in national-defense industries. In 1944 he was nominated vice-presidential candidate as a compromise between the incumbent Henry Wallace and James Byrnes. On April 12, 1945, Roosevelt died, and Truman became president.

7. *NYHT*, June 22, 1946; Richard Freeland, *The Truman Doctrine and the Origins of McCarthyism*, pp. 219, 359–60; *NYT*, Feb. 11, 1947.

8. Allen Yarnell, *Democrats and Progressives: The 1948 Presidential Election as a Test of Postwar Liberalism*, p. 17.

9. Simone de Beauvoir, *America Day by Day*, p. 37; Alonzo L. Hamby, *Beyond the New Deal*, p. 401.

10. Athan Theoharis, *Seeds of Repression*, p. 58; Freeland, pp. 101, 41; Harry S. Truman, *Years of Trial and Hope, 1946–1953*, p. 113.

11. Freeland, pp. 5, 10; Henry A. Wallace, *Soviet Asia Mission*, *passim*; Eric Goldman, *The Crucial Decade—and After*, pp. 39–40.

12. Dwight MacDonald, *Henry Wallace: The Man and the Myth*, pp. 148, 59; *NYHT*, May 30, 1948; *NYT*, June 3, 1948.

13. David A. Shannon, *The Decline of American Communism*, p. 175; Starobin, pp. 182–83, 185.

14. Wallace remained at the head, but not the helm, of the PP until the Korean war ruptured his last remaining ties with the Communists. The extent of the CP's control of the PP was exposed at the PP's Chicago congress in

1950, when a resolution that "it is not our intention to give blanket endorsement to the foreign policy of any nation" was actually voted down. I. F. Stone called this "sectarian idiocy." Wallace now deplored "the force, deceit and intrigue for which Communism stands." In 1952 the PP ticket of Vincent Hallinan and Mrs. Charlotta Bass picked up only 140,023 votes, a figure that must cast some doubt on J. Edgar Hoover's claim that for every CP member there were ten sympathizers willing to undertake the direst and dirtiest work. Voting Progressive was the least this fifth column could have done! I. F. Stone, *The Truman Era*, p. 161; Sidney Hook, *Political Power and Personal Freedom*, p. 193.

15. Yarnell, pp. 40, 51; *MG*, May 31, 1948.

16. Mundt (R., South Dakota) was, with Richard M. Nixon, coauthor of a bill that attempted to outlaw the CP without naming it, by making it unlawful to remain a member of any organization that failed to register as a Communist political organization within 120 days after the Attorney General had issued a final order that it do so. Penalties, even for native-born citizens, included loss of citizenship. Registered organizations would be obliged to divulge their membership lists. In May 1948 the House voted by 295 to 40 to take up the bill, indicating how far the majority of liberals had stampeded. On May 19, the House passed the Communist Control Bill, as it was known, by 319 to 58, but in June the Senate Judiciary Committee put off action on it until the bill died with the 80th Congress, although it was destined to be revived.

17. Alan D. Harper, *The Politics of Loyalty*, pp. 72–76; *NYT*, Oct. 20, 1948; Theoharis, *Seeds of Repression*, pp. 134–35.

18. *NYHT*, June 17, 1949.

19. Max Lowenthal, *The Federal Bureau of Investigation*, p. 450; Hamby, p. 394.

20. *NYT*, Sept. 21, 1950; Richard P. Longaker, *The Presidency and Individual Liberties*, p. 61; Merle Miller, *The Judges and the Judged*, p. 62.

21. See pp. 261–63.

22. Hamby, pp. 396–468.

23. Carey McWilliams, *Witch Hunt: The Revival of Heresy*, pp. 8–10; H. S. Truman, p. 286; *NYT*, April 19, 20, 1960.

24. David B. Truman, *The Congressional Party*, pp. 107, 17, 111.

25. Walter and Miriam Schneir, *Invitation to an Inquest*, p. 69; *NYT*, Sept. 29, 1950; Richard M. Fried, "Electoral Politics and McCarthyism," pp. 216, 194–96.

26. Mazo, pp. 70–73; Fried, pp. 206, 210; Theoharis, *Seeds of Repression*, p. 166.

27. As regards the registration clauses, the act defined three types of subversive Communist organization: "Communist-action"; "Communist-front"; and "Communist-infiltrated." Communist-action organizations would be obliged when registering to list their members as well as their officers and funds. Members would be ineligible for nonelective federal employment and for work on defense contracts in private industry. All literature or airwave material put out by registered organizations would have to be stamped "Dissemi-

nated by————, a Communist organization." Section 6 made it illegal for members of registered organizations to apply for a new passport or for renewal of an old one.

28. Not until January 1955 did the Court of Appeals for the District of Columbia vote, 2 to 1, to uphold the act as constitutional, and therefore to uphold the SACB's right to order the CP to register. After protracted litigational maneuvers, in 1961 the Supreme Court voted, 5 to 4, that the SACB's order to the CP to register was substantively justified. Dissenting, Justices Warren, Black and Douglas argued that the act violated the Fifth Amendment. Frankfurter disagreed: "Merely potential impairment of constitutional rights under a statute does not of itself create a justifiable controversy . . . It is wholly speculative now to foreshadow whether . . . a member of the Party may in future apply for a passport, or seek government or defense-facility or labor-union employment." On December 1, 1961, the CP was indicted for refusal to register and later was fined $120,000 in the District Court. In December 1963 the Court of Appeals, and in November 1965 the Supreme Court, found the registration provision to be in violation of the Fifth Amendment.

29. *Rights*, Vol. 6, No. 2 (Dec. 1958), p. 14; Tanner and Griffith, p. 186; Robert Griffith, *The Politics of Fear*, pp. 222–23, 195.

### CHAPTER 2: THE REPUBLICAN CATHARSIS

1. Samuel Lubell, *The Future of American Politics*, pp. 154, 230; Samuel Lubell, *Revolt of the Moderates*, pp. 85, 98; Michael Paul Rogin, *The Intellectuals and McCarthy*, pp. 84, 129–30; Nelson Polsby, "McCarthyism at the Grass Roots," p. 101.

2. Selig Adler, *The Isolationist Impulse*, p. 337; Angus Campbell and Homer C. Cooper, *Group Differences in Attitudes and Votes*, p. 74.

3. Goldman, *The Crucial Decade*, pp. 127–28, 125; Joseph R. McCarthy, *America's Retreat from Victory*, pp. 161, 132; René A. Wormser, "Foundations: Their Power and Influence," pp. 105–12.

4. *NYHT*, July 25, 1949; *NYT*, Aug. 19, 1949; Sheppard Marley, "Trygve Lie: Stalin's Tool in the UN?" pp. 5–6.

5. Robert K. Carr, *The House Committee on Un-American Activities, 1945–1950*, p. 99; Selig Adler, pp. 383, 452–53; *I. F. Stone's Weekly*, Vol. 1, No. 30 (Aug. 15, 1953); McCarthy, *America's Retreat from Victory*, p. 163; McCarthy, *McCarthyism: The Fight for America*, p. 50.

6. Walter F. Murphy, *Congress and the Court*, p. 155; Edward N. Chester, *Radio, Television and American Politics*, p. 84; James Rorty and Moshe Decter, *McCarthy and the Communists*, p. 69.

7. Mazo, *Richard Nixon*, pp. 119, 59–60; Matusow Papers.

8. Steinke and Weinstein, "McCarthy and the Liberals," pp. 45–50; James A. Wechsler, *The Age of Suspicion*, p. 205; Michael O'Brien, "The Cedric Parker Case, November 1949," pp. 236–37.

9. This speech came only three months after the Appleton State Bank had warned him that unless he paid his loans in full, his collateral would be sold.

With his lecture fee hiked up to $500 as a result of Wheeling, he was able to pay off his bank debt by September 1951.

10. Anderson and May, *McCarthy*, pp. 206–7; Polsby, p. 101.

11. It was Taft who, as Senate Majority Leader, endowed McCarthy with a license to print subpoenas and harry the Eisenhower administration by appointing him chairman of the Committee on Government Operations.

12. *Rights*, Vol. 6, No. 2 (Dec. 1958), p. 14; Irving Howe, "The Shame of U.S. Liberalism," p. 308.

13. Lionel Trilling, *The Liberal Imagination*, p. 98.

14. *Commentary*, Vol. 44, No. 3 (Sept. 1967), p. 69.

15. *Ibid.*, p. 39.

16. Max Ascoli, "The American Politburo," pp. 4–5.

17. Sidney Hook, *Political Power and Personal Freedom*, pp. 293–94.

18. *New Leader*, Aug. 25, 1952; Hook, p. 238; Rebecca West, "As a Briton Looks at 'McCarthyism,' " *USNWR*, Vol. 34, No. 22 (May 22, 1953), p. 60.

19. Quoted in Michael Harrington, "The American Committee for Cultural Freedom," p. 118.


### CHAPTER 3: ESPIONAGE FEVER

1. Drew Pearson, *Diaries*, 1949–59, p. 277; Theodore Draper, *American Communism and Soviet Russia*, p. 213.

2. The Report of the Canadian Royal Commission, a cautious, calm and judiciously researched document, inevitably reinforced American prejudices about the link between the USSR, the CP, the intellectuals, and the Jews. Involved in the Canadian espionage ring were two leading Communists, Sam Carr, national organizer of the Labor-Progressive Party, and Fred Rose, organizer of the Party in Quebec. The Party was in fact the main base from which the Military Attaché, Colonel Zabotin, operated his network. Scientists and intellectuals were also heavily involved, many of them Jews—"a number of documents from the Russian Embassy specifically note 'Jew' or 'Jewess' in entries on their relevant Canadian agents"; *Canada: Report of the Royal Commission to Investigate . . . the Communication, by Public Officials and Other Persons . . . of Secret and Confidential Information to Agents of a Foreign Power.*

3. David J. Dallin, *Soviet Espionage*, p. 460; Earl Latham, *The Communist Controversy in Washington*, p. 204; Fred J. Cook, *The FBI Nobody Knows*, p. 281.

4. Including Victor Perlo, Nathan Witt, John Abt, Charles Kramer, Lee Pressman, Henry H. Collins, Alger Hiss and Harold Ware as having been members of a Communist study group within the AAA in 1934–35.

5. She alleged that Nathan·G. Silvermaster, his wife, and William Ullman, government employees, gave her microfilmed documents containing classified information during the war. She also named Solomon Adler, Frank Coe, William H. Taylor, Irving Kaplan, A. G. Silverman, Victor Perlo, John Abt, Edward Fitzgerald, Harold Glasser and Charles Kramer.

6. Schneir, *Invitation to an Inquest*, p. 311.

7. Elizabeth Bentley, *Out of Bondage*, p. 146.

8. Including Silvermaster, Ullman, Perlo, Glasser, Harry Magdoff, Fitzgerald, Maurice Halperin, Kramer, Abt, Coe, Allen Rosenberg, Silverman.

9. *NYT*, May 24, 1956, Nov. 4, 1953; Norman Redlich, "Spies in Government: The Bentley Story," pp. 85–86.

10. When White moved to the IMF, he took with him two economists also named by Bentley and Chambers, Harold Glasser and Frank Coe. Coe was able to retain his $15,000-a-year job with the IMF until December 1952, when he resigned after taking the Fifth before the SISS on CP membership and wartime espionage. In May 1956 he testified before the SISS that he had never been a spy, but he adhered to the Fifth on past Party membership. *NYT*, Dec. 4, 1952, May 16, 1956.

11. FBI reports were widely discounted under Roosevelt and Truman. White's subordinate Harold Glasser attended the Moscow meeting of the Council of Foreign Ministers as adviser to Secretary of State Marshall two years after the FBI had first suggested to the White House that he was a spy. Duncan Lee retained the confidence of Major General William Donovan, head of the OSS, despite an adverse FBI report. Despite the warnings about Nathan Gregory Silvermaster, Under Secretary of War Robert P. Patterson examined the case and concluded that "the facts do not show anything derogatory to Mr. Silvermaster's character or loyalty to the United States." Alan Barth, "How Good is an FBI Report?", pp. 25–26.

12. Carr, *The House Committee on Un-American Activities, 1945–1950*, p. 96; *Millhouse*, a film directed by Emile de Antonio.

13. In February 1954, Felix A. Inslerman testified before the McCarthy Subcommittee that he had belonged to a Soviet espionage ring, had visited Moscow in 1935 on false papers, and had photographed the documents produced by Chambers from the pumpkin. *NYT*, Feb. 21, 1954.

14. Chambers, *Witness*, pp. 9, 566.

15. A. J. Liebling, "The Wayward Press: Spotlight on the Jury," p. 61.

16. Released from Lewisburg prison on November 27, 1954, Hiss had to face his own virtual unemployability, although he spent the first year of his release writing his book, *In the Court of Public Opinion*, assisted by $5,000 advances from Alfred Knopf in New York and John Calder in London. Later he found work as assistant to a manufacturer of women's hair restrainers at a salary of $6,000, rising to $12,000 when he became in effect general manager. Following a disagreement with the owner he left, was unemployed for six months, and then in 1960 found the job he still holds, as salesman for Davison-Bluth, stationers and printers.

A gentle, inquisitive, quasi-encyclopedic gentleman in his early seventies, Alger Hiss remains today earnestly and industriously committed to one thing—his own vindication with the help of the Freedom of Information Act. Interestingly, his attitudes now appear much less anti-Communist than at the time of his trial; he no longer feels obliged to prove his innocence by emphasizing his conservatism, a tribute, no doubt, to the changing *Zeitgeist*. His exact contemporary, the lawyer Nathan Witt, described by Chambers as a Communist colleague of Hiss in New Deal Washington, and a man who has frequently taken the Fifth Amendment, still declines to say whether Hiss was a Communist, or even to say whether he knows whether Hiss was, or say whether he, Witt, ever met Chambers. "If I did know, I would not want to involve others." Asked why Witt, of whom he speaks warmly, should adopt this attitude, Hiss expresses puzzlement. Alger Hiss, Interview; Nathan Witt, Interview.

17. On December 20, 1948, five days after Hiss's indictment, forty-three-year-old Lawrence Duggan fell—or threw himself, it is not certain—from the fourth-floor window of his New York office. Duggan, whose career paralleled that of Hiss, had served in the State Department for fourteen years. Ten days earlier he had been questioned by the FBI. Four days after his death, Attorney General Clark said the investigation had produced no evidence linking Duggan with espionage or the CP. On the other hand, Whittaker Chambers alleged that he had given Duggan's name, together with those of Hiss and others, to Adolphe Berle in 1939; at the Hiss trial, a Berle memo that Duggan had been in the CP was produced. In *Witness*, Chambers named him as an espionage agent. The columnist Drew Pearson, a friend of Duggan, noted that he had been "eased out" of the State Department and into UNRRA, concluded speculatively that Duggan had joined the Party during the Depression but had latterly become a farsighted public servant "under whom our Good Neighbor policy reached a genuine peak of success."

In June 1948, Morton Kent, a former State Department employee pursued by the FBI and accused of seeking to contact a Soviet agent, killed himself by cutting his own throat. Carr, p. 159; Pearson, pp. 11–12.

18. Gold was also the apparent recipient of classified information about high explosives passed to him by a Syracuse chemist, Alfred Dean Slack, in 1943–44. Slack pleaded guilty at his trial in September 1950 and was sentenced to a savage fifteen years' imprisonment.

We also know that Gold had testified before a grand jury in 1947 and was well known to the FBI. Too well known perhaps? Too malleable in the Bureau's hands? Certainly he constantly changed his testimony; in 1950 he confessed to having lied before the grand jury in 1947 and implicated his former employer, Abraham Brothman, and Miriam Moskowitz, who were duly arrested and charged with having conspired to impede the grand jury's investigation. They pleaded not guilty but were convicted. Passing sentence, Judge Irving Kaufman gave warning of the intemperance, the commitment to the American Century, which later colored his notorious remarks at the conclusion of the Rosenberg trial. He congratulated the U.S. attorney for his "ingenuity in searching the statute books and finding the obstruction of justice statute . . ." He called the work of "Mr. Hoover and the Bureau" nothing short of "just amazing," and he added: "I have no sympathy or mercy for the defendants in my heart, none whatsoever." Regretting that he could not be more severe, he sentenced Brothman to seven years' imprisonment and a $15,000 fine; Moskowitz to two years in prison and a $10,000 fine. On appeal, Brothman's sentence was reduced to match Moskowitz's.

The principal witness against this unhappy pair was Harry Gold. A twisted, lonely bachelor, he was on his own frequent admission a habitual liar. At the Brothman trial he admitted that he had invented for himself a wife, home and children for the benefit of his co-workers. Phonograph records of his consultations with a court-appointed attorney, John D. M. Hamilton, show, according to writers who have heard them, that he constantly changed his confession and frequently admitted that he had lied. Having assured Hamilton that he had never taken money from the Russians, he later told him that he had taken money from the beginning. At the Brothman trial he claimed that he had been engaged in espionage until February 1946; at the Rosenberg trial he extended the period until the time of his arrest in March 1950. Schneir, pp. 105, 420, 424.

19. Malcolm P. Sharp, *Was Justice Done? The Rosenberg-Sobell Case*, p. 91; Leonard Boudin, Interview.

20. *The Rosenberg Letters*, p. 177; Sharp, p. 4; John Wexley, *The Judgment of Julius and Ethel Rosenberg*, pp. 591–92, 599; Jonathan Root, *The Betrayers*, p. 219.

21. *Libération* (Paris), June 22, 1953; *Rosenberg Letters*, pp. 26, 30.

22. Kim Philby, *My Silent War*, pp. 25, 135; E. L. Doctorow, *The Book of Daniel*, pp. 213–14.

## CHAPTER 4: THE STATES AND SUBVERSION

1. The Ober Act was imitated in various forms by Florida, Georgia, Mississippi, New Hampshire, Ohio, Pennsylvania and Washington. Cross-breeds of the Ober Act and the Massachusetts Anti-Communism Act appeared in Alabama, Louisiana, Michigan and Texas.

2. William B. Prendergast, "Maryland: The Ober Anti-Communist Law," pp. 140–81.

3. Thomas I. Emerson and David Haber, *Political and Civil Rights in the United States*, p. 429.

4. The guardians of counties and cities were equally eager to prove their vigilance in combatting the Peril. By 1951 about 150 municipalities had passed antisubversion ordinances; some thirty cities and three counties did so in 1950 alone. Actions ranged from arrests in Providence, Rhode Island, for placing Communist handbills on the windshields of parked cars, to the refusal of permits to Communists wishing to fish in New York City's reservoirs. But a lack of information about their operation has always made it difficult to assess the actual impact of these local ordinances. *Open Forum*, March 17, 1951; AP Report, *Daily Express*, April 18, 1948.

5. Walter Gellhorn, "A General View," p. 365; Robert J. Mowitz, "Michigan: State and Local Attack on Subversion," p. 195; William Albertson, *The Trucks Act: Michigan's Blueprint for a Fascist State, passim*.

6. Towns and cities, notably Cambridge, Massachusetts, eagerly adopted the registration gambit, including New Rochelle, New York, Jersey City and Hoboken, New Jersey, Erie and McKeesport, Pennsylvania, Miami, Florida, Cumberland, Maryland, and Weirton, West Virginia. Whereas in some cases the provision applied only to CP members, and in others to members of Communist-front organizations as well, in Jacksonville, Florida, the edict applied to anyone who communicated with a present or former Communist. A few cities adopted a "get out of town or else" ordinance; both Birmingham, Alabama, and Macon, Georgia, gave Communists forty-eight hours to leave

town, with a fine of $100 and 180 days in prison awaiting those who failed to comply. (This and similar ordinances were declared unconstitutional by federal and state courts.) Birmingham threatened to jail anyone found guilty of "voluntary association" with a Communist, and indeed the city did arrest some Communists in 1950 and prosecute them for vagrancy.

In August 1950 Los Angeles County ordered that all subversives living in or traveling regularly through the jurisdiction must register with the sheriff. George B. Kelly, assistant county counsel, explained that after the County's purge of its public employees, civic organizations were demanding that the subversives thus let loose should be identified. But the ordinance was declared unconstitutional by the Appellate Division of the Superior Court in the spring of 1951. Carey McWilliams, "The Case of David Hawkins."

7. NYT, Sept. 9, 17, Oct. 8, Nov. 29, 1950; Rights, Vol. 3, No. 1 (Sept. 1955), pp. 11–13; William B. Prendergast, "State Legislatures and Communism," p. 572.

8. Including Alaska, Florida, Georgia, Hawaii, Kansas, Maryland, Massachusetts, New Jersey, New York, Oklahoma, Texas.

9. James M. Patton, "The Pennsylvania Loyalty Act," p. 100.

10. Arkansas, California, Delaware, Illinois, Florida, Indiana, Maryland, New Jersey, Oklahoma, Oregon, Pennsylvania, Tennessee, Texas, Wisconsin, Wyoming and Alabama denied to the CP the status of a political party.

11. New York Post, April 1, 1966.

12. See pp. 149–50.

13. Milton Konvitz, First Amendment Freedoms, p. 692; Emerson and Haber, p. 1056; Leo Huberman, "The Daggett-Sweezy Case," passim.

14. Edward L. Barrett, Jr., The Tenney Committee. Legislative Investigation of Subversive Activities in California, passim; ACLU News, Vol. 13, No. 4 (April 1948) and No. 6 (June 1948).

15. After his defeat in 1946, DeLacy became state organizer for the PP. In 1954 he took the Fifth on CP membership before HCUA.

16. Vern Countryman, Un-American Activities in the State of Washington, passim.

17. E. Houston Harsha, "Illinois: The Broyles Commission," pp. 65–66; Frank W. Fetter, "Witch Hunt in the Lincoln Country," pp. 349–52.

18. Arizona, California, Florida, Illinois, Maryland, Massachusetts, Michigan, New Jersey, New Hampshire, Ohio, Oklahoma, Tennessee, Washington.

19. Frank T. Bow, "Ohio Fights Communism," pp. 1–2; Warren P. Hill, "A Critique of Recent Ohio Anti-Subversion Legislation," pp. 445–79.

## CHAPTER 5: THE CONGRESSIONAL INQUISITION

1. Walter Gellhorn, American Rights, The Constitution in Action, p. 117; Robert Griffith's Introduction in The Specter, p. 13.

2. Edward Shils, The Torment of Secrecy, pp. 105–12; Shils, "The Legislator and his Environment," p. 575.

3. In 1935 more social legislation was passed than in any other year in American history, notably the "wealth tax," the (Wagner) Labor Relations Act, the

Social Security Law, the creation of the WPA, the Public Utilities Holding Law, the start of the Rural Electrification Administration.

4. *MG*, Jan. 28, 1947; *CSM*, Jan. 31, 1947.

5. It would be historically inaccurate to assume that Congressional investigations were traditionally favored by the Right and deplored by the Left. The wheel has come full circle more than once. Major investigations of bankers, trusts and monopolies had been popular on the Left, from the time of Taft to F.D.R. It was the young liberal lawyer Felix Frankfurter who published an article in 1924 entitled "Hands off the Investigations," and it was another future liberal Supreme Court Justice, Hugo Black, who in February 1936 praised the powers of Congressional exposure, argued that special privileges should be "destroyed by the rays of pitiless publicity," and quoted Woodrow Wilson to the effect that, "If there is nothing to conceal, then why conceal it?" Yet Black became after the war the strongest defender of civil liberties, particularly those protected by the First Amendment, against the encroachments of fact-hungry committees. In the thirties it was the liberals who disingenuously asked how an elected Congress could possibly flaunt the will of the people. Indeed the Roosevelt administration capitalized on Congressional investigations. Harry S. Truman, *Years of Trial and Hope*, pp. 297–98; "A Symposium on Congressional Hearings and Investigations," pp. 74, 84–86; William F. Buckley, Jr., *The Committee and Its Critics*, p. 234.

6. Martin Dies, *The Trojan Horse In America*, pp. 302, 354, 360–61, 364; Raymond A. Ogden, *The Dies Committee*, 1938–44, p. 110. On the Dies Committee's campaign against the PAC-CIO in 1944, see Robert Stripling, *The Red Plot Against America*, p. 48.

7. By 337–37 in 1948; by 353–29 in 1949; by 348–12 in 1950; by 352–1 in 1953 (there was no vote in 1951 and 1952); by 363–1 in 1954; by 385–1 in 1956 (there was no vote in 1955).

8. Robert E. Cushman, *Civil Liberties in the United States*, p. 199; O. John Rogge, *Our Vanishing Civil Liberties*, p. 65; Carr, *The House Committee*, pp. 223, 56, 51; *CSM*, Sept. 26, 1945.

9. *NYT*, April 2, 24, 1947; Alan D. Harper, *Politics of Loyalty*, p. 46; Cook, *The FBI Nobody Knows*, p. 287; Pearson, *Diaries*, pp. 5–6.

10. *Thirty Years of Treason: Excerpts from Hearings Before the House Committee on Un-American Activities*, 1938–1968, pp. 267ff.

11. Carr, pp. 29, 294.

12. *CSM*, Sept. 26, 1945; *NYT* and *NYHT*, Dec. 27, 1946.

13. Much of the pre-hearing field work in Hollywood was performed by William A. Wheeler, the Committee's West Coast investigator from 1947 to 1960, and by Louis J. Russell, whose ten years' service with the FBI probably accounted for HCUA's possession of the CP registration card numbers of the Ten. Appointed by HCUA in May 1945, Russell lost his $11,600-a-year post in January 1954 after reports of improper financial relations with a witness. It later came out that he had borrowed $300 from the actor Edward G. Robinson, who was browbeaten into saving his career by abasing himself before the Committee. *NYT*, July 4, 1973; Edward G. Robinson, *All My Yesterdays*, pp. 262–63.

14. In 1950 Russell, Mandel and Tavenner were earning $10,846, while six of the subordinate investigators were paid between $8,000 and $10,000 each.

15. Murray Kempton, *America Comes of Middle Age*, p. 18; Frank J. Donner, *The Un-Americans*, p. 51; *Thirty Years of Treason*, pp. 952–53.

16. Behind the scenes, HCUA's investigating, research and filing staff played an important role. Nixon's "legman" in the Chambers-Hiss operation was investigator Donald T. Appell, but the preliminary research and liaison with the FBI, Chambers and Isaac Don Levine was the work of the Committee's director of research and *Hintermann*, Benjamin Mandel. A former Communist and business manager of the *Daily Worker*, Mandel had also strengthened his apprenticeship for the role of witch hunter by a brief stint in the State Department's security staff. (*If* Hiss was framed, *if* the documents which Chambers produced were forgeries, then Mandel was most probably at the dark heart of the plot.) In any case it was he who had supplied HCUA material to Father John Cronin for his November 1945 report on Communism to the Catholic bishops.

It was on the advice of Stripling, Russell, Wheeler, Appell, Raphael I. Nixon (appointed director of research in 1952), Earl Fuoss (an investigator who had worked for the FBI), Tavenner and Arens that the Committee chose its friendly witnesses and put some of them under contract. An enclosure was customarily reserved in the hearing rooms for friendly witnesses, FBI men, local employers, local red-squad men, and so forth. Professional ex-Communists and former undercover agents for the FBI were highly prized as witnesses.

Elizabeth Bentley testified in three separate public sessions; Matt Cvetic in four; John Lautner in ten; Barbara Hartle in four; Armando Penha in five; and Berenice Baldwin in five. In the course of five years, Irving Fischman of the New York Customs Bureau testified before HCUA no fewer than ten times on the subversive printed matter that, but for his vigilance and incinerators, would have been pumped, fatally no doubt, into the national artery. Intermittently such witnesses were put under contract: Maurice Malkin for $400, John Lautner for $1,000, and John Santo for $2,500. Santo's career was a remarkable one: expelled from the U.S. as a Communist leader of the Transport Workers Union in 1949, he settled in Hungary, where he became an official in the government. At the time of the Hungarian revolution in 1956 he escaped to Vienna and eventually returned to America, where an alcove as a professional informer awaited him. Peter H. Irons, "The Cold War Crusade of the United States Chamber of Commerce," p. 83; Stamler, pp. 4–5, 7.

17. A *Quarter-Century of Un-Americana*, p. 81; Gordon Kahn, *Hollywood on Trial*, p. 190.

18. *Thirty Years of Treason*, p. 636; Bishop G. Bromley Oxnam, *I Protest*, p. 22; Carr, p. 224; Rogge, p. 47; *NYT*, June 30, 1955.

19. Stamler, p. 45; *Thirty Years of Treason*, p. 740.

20. Carl Beck, *Contempt of Congress*, p. 110; Oxnam, p. 148.

21. Not until August 1950 did the Committee decide to test the Fifth Amendment in the courts; of the seventy or more witnesses who had pleaded this

amendment in 1949–50, fifty-six were cited. From 1951 to 1957, twenty-two people were indicted for invoking the Fifth where not applicable. The Velde Committee broke all records: 350 of its 650 witnesses resorted to the Fifth. Of twenty-six witnesses it cited for contempt, eighteen were on the ground of improper use of the privilege.

Taking the period 1946–67, 91 percent of a sample of seventy-five un-cooperative witnesses who refused to answer HCUA's questions invoked the Fifth Amendment; 51 percent invoked both the Fifth and the First Amendments; and 2 percent took the First alone. Gellhorn, *American Rights*, p. 117; Beck, pp. 186, viii, 17, 65, 100; *NYT*, Aug. 12, 1950; *Congressional Record*, Vol. 117, No. 61 (April 29, 1971).

22. Stamler, p. 26.

23. Among unfriendly witnesses before HCUA who went to prison for contempt were Lloyd Barenblatt, college lecturer (6 months); Chandler Davis, professor of mathematics (6 months); Carl Braden, Kentucky newspaperman (1 year); Frank Wilkinson, social worker and political activist (1 year); Arthur McPhaul, black car worker and civil-rights leader from Detroit (9 months); Paul Rosenkrantz, former seaman and electrical worker (3 months); Donald Wheeldin, black journalist from Pasadena (1 month).

24. Carr, pp. 295, 300, 298, 303.

25. *A Symposium on Congressional Hearings*, p. 10; Stamler, pp. 78–82; *NYT*, Dec. 22, 1955, Nov. 15, 1956; *Thirty Years of Treason*, p. 730.

26. *Communist Activities Among Aliens and National Groups*, pp. 182, 203.

27. *NYT*, May 21, 1953; *Thirty Years of Treason*, pp. 425–26, 429, 817–18.

28. Stamler, p. 119; In the Supreme Court of the United States. October Term, 1960. No. 37. *Frank Wilkinson v. United States of America*. Brief of *amicus curiae* National Lawyers Guild, p. 2.

29. *Thirty Years of Treason*, p. 322; Ogden, p. 44; Stamler, pp. 98–102; Donner, *The Un-Americans*, p. 296.

30. *100 Things You Should Know About Communism in the U.S.A.*, Prepared by the Committee on Un-American Activities, U.S. House of Representatives, 82nd Congress, 1st Session, House Doc. No. 136, pp. 16, 13.

31. The seventh volume of the Dies Committee's celebrated *Appendix ix* (1944), containing the names of 22,000 radicals, became a bible for intelligence and security officers. In December 1948 HCUA published a handbook listing 563 organizations and 190 publications "which have been declared to be outright Communist or Communist-front enterprises." In 1951 the Committee published a list of 624 subversive organizations.

32. By December 1948 the files contained 300,000 card references on individuals, as well as a list of 363,119 people who had at one time or another signed CP election petitions. By April 1971 HCUA's successor, the House Internal Security Committee, possessed 754,000 names on 3″-x-5″ cards. When HISC was finally abolished by the House on January 14, 1975, the fate of these files remained in doubt. Carr, pp. 358, 259–60; *Congressional Record*, Vol. 117, No. 61 (April 29, 1971); *Rights*, Vol. 21, Nos. 1, 2 (April, May 1975), pp. 13–14.

33. *Bishop Oxnam and the Un-American Activities Committee*, pp. 5–17; Oxnam, p. 116.

34. Stamler, pp. 59, 64, 145.

35. *Anatomy of Anti-Communism*, p. 37; Donner, p. 67; Alan Barth, *The Loyalty of Free Men*, p. 68.

36. *Thirty Years of Treason*, pp. 865, 871.

37. Jane De Hart Mathews, *The Federal Theatre, 1935–1939*; Alan Barth, "McCarran's Monopoly," p. 27.

38. The quality of Jenner's mind was given full expression during a speech that he delivered in Springfield, Ohio, in April 1954—"There is no place even for innocents who scatter the Soviet word mines because the Soviet agents say they aren't loaded . . . If they are foreigners, let us deprive them of the rights they despise. Let them earn their living as dishwashers or ditch diggers, but not in places where they can poison our minds." *NYT*, July 27, 1953; Willard S. Elsbree and E. Edmund Reutter, Jr., *Staff Personnel in the Public Schools*, p. 323; Alan Barth, *Government by Investigation*, p. 82.

39. *USNWR*, Vol. 36 (April 9, 1954), p. 31; Harry Kalven, Jr., "Congressional Testing of Linus Pauling," pp. 490–91.

40. Alan Harper, p. 220; *NYT*, April 21, 1958.

41. The Democrats were John C. McClellan (Arkansas), who succeeded McCarthy as chairman in January 1955, Stuart Symington (Missouri) and Henry M. Jackson (Washington). The record shows Jackson and Symington hectoring witness who took the Fifth Amendment in May 1953. From January to July 1954 counsel for the Democratic minority was Robert F. Kennedy, whose father, the Boston millionaire Joseph P. Kennedy, was a strong supporter of McCarthy.

42. Martin Merson, *The Private Diary of a Public Servant*, p. 85; Straight, pp. 80, 177; *Point of Order*, a film directed by Emile de Antonio, *passim*.

43. After the fall of his patron, Cohn returned to private law practice, and later became President of the American Jewish League Against Communism (whose director, Rabbi Benjamin Schultz, together with the Hearst columnist George Sokolsky, had originally introduced Cohn to Schine). Cohn was also a captain in the National Guard and a recipient of the New York State Legion's Americanism Award in 1956. The Catholic War Veterans' Patriotism Award came to him in 1970.

44. William V. Shannon, *The American Irish*, p. 388.

45. S. M. Lipset, "Opinion Formation in a Crisis Situation," p. 27.

46. Joseph Stocker, "Father Dunne: A Study in Faith," *passim*.

CHAPTER 6: THE FBI AND THE INFORMERS

1. Frank Donner to the author, July 9, 1974; Harold M. Hyman, *To Try Men's Souls*, p. 322; Frank J. Donner, "Hoover's Legacy."

2. Emerson and Helfeld, "Loyalty Among Government Employees," p. 55; Eleanor Bontecou, *The Federal Loyalty-Security Program*, pp. 33–34; Don Whitehead, *The FBI Story*, pp. 345–46.

3. Whitehead, p. 276; *Washington Post*, July 5, 1957.

4. *Sunday Times* (London), March 2, 1975. On the FBI's political surveillance methods, see also Donner, "Hoover's Legacy," p. 697; *Times* (London),

Nov. 19, 1974; *NYRB*, Oct. 17, 1974, pp. 35–37. In 1975 Congress also turned its attention to the CIA's surveillance of domestic radicalism.

5. Cook, *The FBI*, pp. 29, 289; Lowenthal, *The Federal Bureau of Investigation*, pp. 353, 359; J. Edgar Hoover, "Loyalty Among Government Employees," pp. 404–11; Bert Andrews, *Washington Witch Hunt*, p. 100; Carr, *The House Committee* . . . , p. 203; Pearson, *Diaries*, pp. 58–59.

6. For example, with regard to the physicist Frank Oppenheimer. See Philip M. Stern, *The Oppenheimer Case*, p. 107.

7. Lowenthal, pp. 357; Roger Burlingame, *The Sixth Column*, pp. 156–57; *New York Journal-American*, Oct. 1, 1946.

8. *NYHT*, May 6, 1947; J. Edgar Hoover, *Masters of Deceit*, pp. 289–335; Cook, *The FBI*, p. 422; *J. Edgar Hoover Speaks Concerning Communism*, p. 75.

9. Alan Harper, *Politics of Loyalty*, p. 35; Hoover, *Masters*, p. 406; Emerson and Helfeld, p. 70; "J. Edgar Hoover Tells How Communists Operate," *USNWR*, Vol. 29, No. 6, Aug. 11, 1950, p. 30; Andrews, p. 92; Whitehead, p. 282; Athan Theoharis, "The Threat to Civil Liberties," p. 280.

10. Lowenthal, p. 383; Kempton, *America*, pp. 27–28.

11. Cook, *The FBI*, p. 33; Frank Donner to the author, Sept. 6, 1976; Aubrey Grossman, Interview; Sam Kushner, Interview; Simon Gerson, Interview; George Blake Charney, *A Long Journey*, p. 207.

12. Nat Ganley Collection, 13/10, WRL.

13. For example, Armand Penha, who served as an FBI agent within the Party's national textile commission from 1950 to 1958, later testified before HCUA in public session on no less than five occasions.

14. At the age of thirty-four Herbert Philbrick embarked on a lucrative career as a professional ex-Communist. His dreary autobiography, *I Led Three Lives*, became the basis for a television series. As a syndicated "Red Underground" columnist for the *New York Herald Tribune*, Philbrick resorted to melodramatic speculation whenever his hard information ran out, which was often enough. Thus, in pointing out that three presidents of a right-wing pressure group had died in office, ostensibly of heart attacks, he added: ". . . ostensibly, I say, because it is well known that the MVD knows how to destroy enemies by means totally impossible to detect." His stock-in-trade was mumbo jumbo—"Selected CP members received orders by courier early this month to prepare to receive espionage instructions from behind the Iron Curtain by shortwave radio." The Legion sponsored a dinner, and Massachusetts named a day, in his honor. Herbert Philbrick, *I Led Three Lives, passim*; Cedric Belfrage, *The American Inquisition, 1945–1960*, p. 235; *NYHT*, March 22, 1953.

15. Angela Calomiris, *Red Masquerade*, p. 30.

16. Reuben J. Hardin of Large, Pennsylvania, was also identified as a CP organizer by Cvetic while testifying before HCUA in March 1950; subsequently Hardin had stones hurled through his windows, was fired from his job as a miner and was evicted by his landlord. It later emerged that he was an FBI agent with a high sense of duty. So, too, was Hamp Golden, who was removed as president of Canning Workers Local 325 at the Heinz Company, Pittsburgh, blackballed by a veterans' organization and twice forced to move

home with his family, after Cvetic named him. In March 1959 Golden and his wife testified before HCUA in Pittsburgh, revealing their true identity as FBI undercover agents. An old fellow called Joseph Schoemehl testified during the St. Louis Smith Act trial in 1954 that he had been unaware that the previous witness, the Reverend Obadiah Jones, also had been working for the FBI. Charles B. Childs and Odis R. Reavis, both agents within the North Carolina CP, reported on one another for several years. Joseph A. Poskonka complained before HCUA in 1959 that after he had been named as a Communist in 1952 by another agent, Roy Thompson, "my family and myself have been discriminated very badly and hurt, cut up to pieces because people pointed and throw bricks and slapped me in the face . . ." Cook, *The FBI*, p. 42; Stamler, p. 60; Richard Rovere, *The American Establishment*, p. 69; *NYT*, March 15, 1953, Dec. 10, 1954; Donner, *The Un-Americans*, p. 95.

17. This process, whereby police indefinitely defer prosecution of a potential informer, is known as "hooking"; the FBI has constantly sifted radicals in search of those who were indictable, or deportable, and could therefore be "hooked." (Alternatively the agent, on unearthing an angry or disaffected radical, persuades him to perform one, very minor, initial service; thereafter the informer is hooked in the sense that the agent can blackmail him with the threat of exposure to other radicals.) One regular Immigration Service informer, Ernest Courey, a man of Syrian origins, had been convicted of murder in 1925 and was living under the constant threat of deportation. Another, Claudius M. Russell of Toledo, Ohio, admitted that he had been arrested five or six times for illegal gambling and took the Fifth Amendment when asked about sex crimes. Clearly he was hooked.

18. *NYT*, March 11, 1952; *NYHT*, April 1, 1952; *NYT*, June 7, 1954; Edward Lamb, *No Lamb For Slaughter*, pp. 143, 145.

19. Hyman Lumer, *The Professional Informer*, pp. 13–14; Herbert Aptheker, *Dare We Be Free?* pp. 18–21; *NYT*, Jan. 13, 1954.

20. Donner Files; *DW*, May 3, 1955; *NYHT*, May 18, 1949.

21. *NYT*, Nov. 24, 1950; Samuel A. Stouffer, *Communism, Conformity and Civil Liberties*, p. 45; *J. Edgar Hoover Speaks*, p. 147; Lewis Coser, "The Age of the Informer," pp. 248–49; William O. Douglas, *Go East, Young Man* (1974), quoted in *The Nation*, Vol. 218, No. 17 (April 27, 1974), p. 515; *J. Edgar Hoover Speaks*, p. 98.

22. *NYT*, July 28, 1948, April 28, 1960, June 10, 1954; Stamler, p. 4; John Henry Faulk, *Fear on Trial*, p. 327.

23. "Effectiveness of State Anti-Subversive Legislation," pp. 512–13; Albert E. Kahn, *High Treason*, p. 293; William Allan, *Toy Must Go!* pp. 8, 11 (in Stanley Nowak Collection, box 2, WRL); DAMP, 1951, box 6, Loyalty Committee.

It should be made clear that the red squads were, by comparison with the FBI, much less influential in countersubversion operations in the 1940s and 1950s than they were before the New Deal. They became influential again in the 1960s. It was on the local red squads and private detectives that employers had once relied to monitor strikes and picket lines, and to expel militants. New Deal legislation put a certain check on this activity; then the war brought heavy industry under federal surveillance; after the war the Taft-Hartley Act and the industrial personnel security program provided the FBI with full scope for penetration of the labor field. Only when ghetto unrest and local anarchism displaced the CP as the main focus of official concern in the sixties did the local red squads once more come into their own. *NYT*, Nov. 10, 1955; Frank Donner, Interview.

24. Isaac Deutscher, *Heretics and Renegades*, p. 14; see also Hannah Arendt, "The Ex-Communists"; and Bernard De Voto, "The Ex-Communists."

25. Including *Men Without Faces; The Cry is Peace; The Technique of Communism; The Bolshevik Invasion of the West*; Packer, *Ex-Communist Witnesses*, p. 124; Rovere, *American Establishment*, p. 67; *NYHT*, April 5, 1949.

26. Joseph Alsop, "The Strange Case of Louis Budenz," p. 29; *NYT*, Sept. 26, 1950; Packer, pp. 154, 146; Louis Budenz, *The Techniques of Communism*, p. 107.

27. The event which particularly provoked this remark was Budenz's shifting testimony in the matter of the Far East expert Owen Lattimore. When the Tydings Subcommittee was looking into McCarthy's allegations against Lattimore in 1950, Budenz had said that Harrison Forman, a left-wing writer on Chinese affairs, "was not, so far as I know, a Communist." But later he told the SISS that he "knew Forman was a Communist from official reports." A day later he described Forman as a close fellow traveler. Budenz had (he said) testified to the FBI for three thousand hours between 1946 and 1949. Yet never during this gargantuan debriefing had he mentioned the names of John Carter Vincent and Owen Lattimore, both influential in the formulation of American Far East policy. He told the Tydings Subcommittee that he was not sure about Vincent, a State Department official; later he told the SISS that he knew Vincent had been in the CP, "from official reports I have received." About Lattimore's possible membership of the CP, Budenz was completely agnostic when testifying before Tydings and completely certain when testifying before McCarran. Ralph Lord Roy, *Communism and the Churches*, p. 355; Lowenthal, p. 459; Burlingame, p. 321; Joseph Alsop, "The Strange Case . . ." p. 30.

28. *DT*, Oct. 8, 1953; *NYT*, Dec. 24, 25, 31, 1952.

29. A year later, when Joseph Starobin, foreign correspondent for the *Daily Worker*, visited Budapest and interviewed Matyas Rakosi, general secretary of the Hungarian Party, he realized how little evidence the Hungarians had against Lautner; his wartime service for the OSS (an organization popular among American Communists) was mistrusted in Budapest, but so endemic was Hungarian suspicion that Rakosi informed Starobin that he also regarded Louis Weinstock as an American government agent! Charney, p. 220; Starobin, *American Communism in Crisis*, pp. 218–19; Frank Donner, Interview; Simon Gerson, Interview.

30. Packer, pp. 213, 217; Al Richmond, *A Long View From the Left*, p. 334; *NYT*, May 9, 1956.

31. Kornfeder had been trade-union secretary of the Party and also attended the Lenin School in Moscow. Known as Joseph Zack, he was appointed a member of the CP's national committee and of the Comintern secretariat before he quit in 1934. He was damned as a Trotskyist. In September 1948 he was principal witness at the deportation trial of the New York CP leader

Alexander Bittelman. He also "identified" James Matles and James Lustig, leading officials of UE, as having been Party members in 1931–32. He drew the normal government witness fee of $25 a day plus expenses.

32. *NYT*, Aug. 10, 1949; *NYHT*, Sept. 21, 1950.

33. David L. Weissman, "The Proceedings to Disbar Leo Sheiner," p. 137; Joseph and Stewart Alsop, in *NYHT*, Jan. 18, 1953; Willard Shelton, "Paul Crouch, Informer," *passim*.

34. Rovere, p. 67; Mrs. Sylvia Crouch to Harvey Matusow, July 23, 1952, Matusow Papers.

35. Rovere, pp. 63, 67–68; *Communist Activities*, pp. 144, 474–503.

36. Jacob Spolansky, *The Communist Trail in America*, p. 39; Conrad Komorowski, *The Strange Trial of Stanley Nowak*, *passim*; *NYHT*, July 4, 1954; Rovere, p. 70.

37. *NYT*, Sept. 16, 1948; McWilliams, *Witch Hunt*, p. 151; Melvin Rader, *False Witness*, p. 98; Vern Countryman, "Washington: The Canwell Committee," pp. 328–38; Countryman, *Un-American Activities*, p. 131. Hewitt fell on hard times. Although he did odd jobs for the anti-Communist businessman Alfred Kohlberg, the informer found it increasingly hard to earn enough to support his family and his own alcoholism. Drink had been his problem: "The Russians tried to get me to taste that vile thing called vodka but I saw what it did to Nazula, the South African secretary, who drank a little bit of it. They picked him up in the snow dead the following morning." Hewitt died of a stroke in July 1952, destitute. In 1956 his three young children were temporarily refused social-security benefits on the ground that their father had once been a Communist. *NYT*, May 4, 1956.

38. *NYT*, Jan. 18, 1953; see Bella Dodd, *School of Darkness*, *passim*; *NYT*, Jan. 7, 1956; *NYT*, April 23, 1949.

39. Warren Olney, III, "The Use of Former Communists as Witnesses"; Rovere, p. 60.

40. *Rights*, Vol. 2, Nos. 4, 5, December 1954, January 1955; Lamb, pp. 141–88; Donner Files.

41. Matusow Papers; Martha Edmiston to Harvey Matusow, May 16, 1952, and H. M. to M. E., Feb. 11, 1954, Matusow Papers.

42. The Bartoline correspondence is in the Matusow Papers.

43. Affidavit, Matusow Papers; Harvey Matusow to Henry R. Luce, April 23, 1954, Matusow Papers; Warren Olney III to Harvey Matusow, June 28, 1954, and William F. Tompkins to Harvey Matusow, Sept. 15, 1954, Matusow Papers.

44. Charles F. Herring to Harvey Matusow, Feb. 5, 1954, Matusow Papers.

45. District Court for the Western District of Texas at El Paso, *U.S.A. v. Clinton E. Jencks*, Criminal No. 54013, Affidavit of Harvey Matusow, Matusow Papers; *Strategy and Tactics of World Communism (Significance of the Matusow Case)*, p. 14.

46. *NYHT*, Feb. 6, 28, 1955; for the reaction of the Alsop brothers, see *NYHT*, Feb. 27, 1955.

47. Whitehead, p. 346; *NYT*, March 22, 1955; "The Nation and Mr. Brownell's Justice"; Finis Farr, "To the Aid of the Party," pp. 517–19.

48. Harvey Matusow, *False Witness*, pp. 133–34; *NYT*, May 1, 1955.

49. NYT, June 28, 1957; Murray Kempton, "The Achievement of Harvey Matusow," pp. 7–10.


CHAPTER 7: THE CONSTITUTION CONCUSSED IN THE COURTS

1. Robert W. Iversen, The Communists and the Schools, p. 306; NYT, Aug. 12, 1948; Richmond, A Long View, pp. 315–18.

2. Charles E. Wyzanski, Jr., "The Communist Party and the Law," pp. 28–29; Nathan Witt, Interview; Nat Ganley Collection, 14/5, WRL.

3. Vern Countryman, "The Canwell Committee," p. 338; David I. Ashe, "Expulsion of Communists Upheld," p. 22; New York Law Journal, May 22, 1950 (reprint); A. Krchmarek, "The Ohio Smith Act Trial," p. 62.

4. Weissman, "Proceedings to Disbar Leo Sheiner," p. 139; Royal W. France, "Miami Miasma," pp. 4–5; Belfrage, The American Inquisition, p. 223.

5. The odd man out in many of this court's political rulings was Henry W. Edgerton, a "First Amendment liberal" in the style of Supreme Court Justice Hugo Black. Edgerton was Chief Judge of the Court of Appeals from 1955 until October 1958.

6. NYT, June 4, 1952; E. L. Barrett, The Tenney Committee, p. 246; Countryman, "The Bigots and the Professionals," p. 642; Barth, Government by Investigation, p. 24.

7. These nine men of the Supreme Court can be viewed in two, apparently conflicting, theoretical perspectives: as reflecting the consensus, the central nerve system, of ruling-class opinion; and as an aggregate of highly principled philosopher-lawyers always liable to confound the expectations of the President who appointed them and of the Congress that confirmed them. At first sight, the Vinson Court fits one theoretical glove, the Warren Court the other. It is also the case that the life of the Vinson Court coincided with the creation of an almost monolithic Cold War consensus within the United States; whereas the Warren Court reflected the ruling class's reappraisal of its own purge strategy following Bandit McCarthy's anarchic guerrilla warfare against the establishment.

8. Pearson, Diaries, pp. 131–32; Merle Miller, Plain Speaking, p. 225; Barth, Government by Investigation, p. 24.

9. The Court upheld the Attorney General's list (JAFRC v. McGrath, 1951); sanctioned the lack of due process, the absence of specific charges, and the use of anonymous informers, a practice characteristic of the loyalty program (Bailey v. Richardson, 1950); sustained as constitutional the imposition of a non-Communist oath on all candidates for state and municipal office in Maryland (Gerende v. Board of Supervisors, 1951); upheld as "a reasonable regulation to protect the municipal service" a local Los Angeles ordinance obliging all city employees to swear that they did not advocate violent overthrow of the government or belong to any organization that did (Garner v. Board of Public Works, 1951); sustained the anti-Communist oath of the Taft-Hartley Act (American Communications Association v. Douds and Osman v. Douds, both 1950); and upheld the Smith Act, which sent the leaders of the Communist Party to jail (United States v. Dennis, 1951). Justices Hugo Black

and William O. Douglas, in almost perpetual dissent, were powerless to stem the tide.

10. *NYT*, Oct. 9, 1956; Murphy, *Congress and the Court*, pp. 246, 251, 284.

11. Telford Taylor, *Grand Inquest*, p. 151; *NYT*, Nov. 23, 1957.

12. Corliss Lamont, noted author, Columbia philosopher and inveterate fellow traveler, faced the Senator on September 23, 1953, during McCarthy's supposed probe of Communist infiltration of the Army. Lamont told McCarthy that he was never in the CP, but refused to answer twenty-one other questions.

13. Court of Appeals of Kentucky, *Carl Braden v. Commonwealth of Kentucky*, Brief of National Lawyers Guild as *amicus curiae*, p. 6; Supreme Court of United States No. 34, Oct. Term 1958, *Uphaus v. Wyman* (June 8, 1959), Mr. Justice Clark, pp. 5, 8–9; *ibid.*, Mr. Justice Brennan, p. 1.

14. *NYT*, June 20, 1951; Willard Uphaus, *Commitment*, *passim*.

15. In the case of the Vassar psychology instructor, Lloyd Barenblatt, the Supreme Court ruled, 5 to 4, that HCUA was entitled to investigate Communist infiltration of universities, because the CP was not an ordinary party (whereas the PP was—hence the Sweezy ruling).

16. Robert E. Cushman, *Civil Liberties in the United States*, p. 142; Sidney Hook, *Political Power and Personal Freedom*, p. 265.

17. Among those jailed were three Los Angeles officials of the CP, Ben Dobbs, Harry Steinberg and Harry Kasinovitz, as well as Robert Blair, Merle Brodsky, Irving Caress, Frank Spector, Philip Bock and Lillian Doran, sister of Rose Chernin.

18. *NYT*, Dec. 15, 1948, March 29, 1949, Sept. 1, 1950; *NYHT*, Nov. 27, 1948; Carl Beck, *Contempt of Congress*, pp. 116–17.

19. "Symposium on Congressional Hearings and Investigations," p. 99; In the Supreme Court of the United States, October Term 1955, No. 58, *William Ludwig Ullman v. United States of America*, Brief of NLG as *amicus curiae*, pp. 1–15.

20. To his credit, Frankfurter joined Black and Douglas in dissenting from this cynical ruling. But it was not until 1967 that the Supreme Court struck down the Feinberg Law as too vague and sweeping.

21. *The Supreme Court and Education*, pp. 99–103; Henry Mayer, "How the Loyalty-Security Program Affects Private Employment," p. 126.

22. Kenneth Culp Davis, "The Requirement of a Trial-Type Hearing," p. 230.

23. United States Court of Appeals for the District of Columbia Circuit, No. 12,628, *John W. Nelson v. General Electric Company*, Petition for a Writ of Certiorari to the Court of Appeals for the District of Columbia Circuit, *passim*; *NYT*, March 2, Jan. 22, 1960.

24. Favoring impeachment in Congress were Senators J. Strom Thurmond (D., South Carolina), George Andrews (D., Alabama), Clare Hoffman (R., Michigan) and Noah Mason (R., Illinois).

25. Murphy, pp. 97, 103; Benjamin Ginzburg, *Rededication to Freedom*, p. 7.

26. This bill, which emerged from the SISS early in 1958, carried the endorsement of the Veterans of Foreign Wars, the Dames of the Loyal Legion,

and the American Coalition of Patriotic Societies, but was opposed by the ACLU, the ADA, the NAACP, the American Jewish Congress and Attorney General William Rogers (infuriated though his predecessor Brownell had been—"a grave emergency in law enforcement"—by the Jencks decision).

27. This bill attracted the support of the National Association of Manufacturers, the Chamber of Commerce, and the American Farm Bureau Federation, while the AFL-CIO opposed it, bearing heavily as it did on "right to work" laws.

28. Certain liberals in the Congress fought a rearguard action on behalf of the Court, notably Paul Douglas, Thomas Hennings, Frank Church, William Proxmire, Tom Carroll, Jacob Javits, Joseph Clark, Wayne Morse, Hubert Humphrey, Pat McNamara, Richard Neuberger and John F. Kennedy in the Senate, and Emanuel Celler in the House.

### CHAPTER 8: BUREAUCRATIC PERSECUTION

1. *CSM*, Aug. 12, 1947; DAMP, box 6, Loyalty Committee, 1951; *ACLU News*, Vol. 14, No. 4 (April 1949), Vol. 18, No. 1 (Jan. 1953).

2. *NYT*, July 20, 1951.

3. *NYHT*, May 30, 1950; *Rights*, Vol. 3, No. 6 (March 1956), pp. 2, 7, Vol. 14, No. 5 (March 1957), p. 4.

4. Bontecou, *The Federal Loyalty-Security Program*, p. 178; *NYT*, Aug. 3, 1950, April 25, May 2, 1953.

5. Albert Kahn, *High Treason*, pp. 286–88; *NYT*, Nov. 2, 1947.

6. Albert Kahn, p. 289.

7. Rogge, *Our Vanishing Civil Liberties*, pp. 242–43; Calomiris, *Red Masquerade*, p. 246.

8. Paul Robeson, the focal point of the Peekskill riots, was born in 1888, the son of a Methodist minister who had once been a slave. Robeson had emerged from Rutgers with a Phi Beta Kappa key and from Columbia Law School with an LL.B. degree, only to commit his fine voice and splendid physical presence to a career as actor and singer. He developed a deep friendship for Britain, a passion for Soviet Russia—in time he was awarded a Stalin Peace Prize.

9. This account of the Peekskill riots is derived mainly from two divergent accounts: ACLU, "Violence in Peekskill," and James Rorty and Winifred Raushenbush, "The Lessons of the Peekskill Riots."

10. *NYT*, Sept. 21, 1949, June 17, 1950, Jan. 24, 1952; *NYHT*, Sept. 15, 1949.

11. *Thirty Years of Treason*, p. 773.

12. David Brion Davis, *The Fear of Conspiracy*, p. 316; Murphy, *Congress and the Court*, pp. 86, 89.

13. Thomas A. Bledoe, "Daymare in Louisville," pp. 2–5; In the Supreme Court of the United States, October Term 1960, No. 54, *Carl Braden, Petitioner v. United States*, p. 6.

14. Harsha, "Illinois: The Broyles Commission," pp. 72–73; McWilliams, *Witch Hunt*, p. 141.

15. Alan Harper, *The Politics of Loyalty*, pp. 48–49.

16. Milton Konvitz, *First Amendment Freedoms*, p. 588; Gellhorn, *Security, Loyalty and Science*, p. 152.

17. (a) Communist or Communist-front, (b) Totalitarian, (c) Fascist, (d) Subversive, (e) advocating the use of force and violence to deny others their rights, (f) aiming to alter the form of government by unconstitutional means. A particular organization could be listed under more than one heading.

18. In May 1948, a further thirty-two were added. By November 16, 1950, the list had grown to 197, of which only 132 were designated Communist or Communist-front, compared with HCUA's list of 624 organizations similarly designated. In 1953, when the list was unified and the six categories were eliminated, Attorney General Brownell announced that he intended to list a further sixty-two organizations, bringing the total up to 254.

19. In other cases the struggle was more protracted; not until 1972 were the Veterans of the Abraham Lincoln Brigade removed from the list.

20. Bontecou, *The Federal Loyalty-Security Program*, p. 177; Freeland, *The Truman Doctrine*, p. 208.

21. When on June 4, 1974, Attorney General Saxbe announced the abolition of the list by E.O. 11785, of the 300 organizations listed approximately 30 remained alive. Most of the 52 groups the FBI regarded as subversive in 1974 had been born after 1955, when the list was frozen.

22. The SACB's five members were appointed by the President with the consent of the Senate. In October 1950 Truman appointed Seth W. Richardson chairman, and Charles M. LaFollette, David Coddaire, Peter Campbell Brown and Dr. Kathryn McHale as members. In 1955 a former chairman of HCUA, John Wood, of Georgia, was appointed. One apparently "safe" appointment, that of former Washington Senator Harry P. Cain in 1953, misfired when this conservative Republican told the Anti-Defamation League in 1955 that the Attorney General's list was "vastly misleading" and creative of "distrust, suspicion and misgivings." Cain resigned from the SACB in August 1956.

23. The IWO, the American Slav Congress, the Committee for a Democratic Far Eastern Policy, the JAFRC, the Council on African Affairs.

24. The LYL, the Jefferson School, Veterans of the Abraham Lincoln Brigade, the NCASF, the United May Day Committee, the California Labor School, the American Peace Crusade, the CRC, the WPU, the ACPFB.

25. See SACB Docket No. 102-53, *Herbert Brownell, Jr. v. Labor Youth League*. Decided February 15, 1955, Report of the Board.

26. This effectively put the SACB out of business, although a bill inspired by HCUA and Senator Everett M. Dirksen was passed in 1968 empowering the SACB to decide which organizations were Communist fronts and to publish the names of their members. Nixon's Executive Order 11605 of July 2, 1971, gave the moribund SACB the task of advising the Attorney General whether a particular organization was subversive and should be listed. But the SACB was abolished on March 27, 1973, when Congress dropped it from the budget. The Justice Department's Internal Security Division perished at the same time by order of the Attorney General.

27. E. Merrill Root, *Collectivism on the Campus*, p. 142.

28. Bontecou, *The Federal Loyalty-Security Program*, p. 187; David A. Shannon, *The Decline of American Communism*, p. 85.

29. David Saposs, *Communism in American Politics*, p. 28.

30. Including the Seattle Labor School, the Pacific Northwest Labor School, Seattle, the Samuel Adams School, Boston, the Tom Paine School of Social Science, Philadelphia, the Abraham Lincoln School, Chicago, the Joseph Wedmeyer School of Social Science, St. Louis, the Michigan School of Social Science, Detroit, and the Ohio School of Social Science, Cleveland. The People's Educational Center, Los Angeles, had been founded in 1943 with AFL and CIO support to provide workers with a broad education. Although John Howard Lawson and the (Marxist) Los Angeles Workers School took an interest in the PEC, Professor Dean H. McHenry told the Tenney Committee in January 1946 that the PEC was not Communist-dominated. But the Attorney General listed the PEC.

31. In October 1956 the trustees of the Jefferson School included Herbert Aptheker, William Alphaeus Hunton, William L. Patterson, Dr. Howard Selsam, Alexander Trachtenberg and Doxey Wilkerson; *NYT*, April 14, 1954; *NYHT*, Oct. 6, 1956.

32. Louis Nemzer, "The Soviet Friendship Societies," *passim*. George Marshall, chairman of the National Federation for Constitutional Liberties, was also convicted of contempt.

33. Witnesses on behalf of the NCASF included Robert Morss Lovett, Corliss Lamont, Arthur Upham Pope, Ralph Barton Perry and Benjamin Spofford. See also SACB Docket No. 104-53, *Herbert Brownell, Jr. v. National Council of American-Soviet Friendship, Inc.*, Hearing, June 3, 1954; *MG*, Sept. 30, 1954.

34. *NYHT*, March 3, 1951; W. E. B. Du Bois, *Autobiography*, pp. 368, 375.

35. Howard Fast, "We Have Kept Faith," p. 23. Among the directors of the JAFRC were Ruth Leider, an immigration lawyer, James Lustig, of UE, Charlotte Stern, of the Hotel and Restaurant Workers, Professor Lyman R. Bradley, of NYU, Harry Justis, a lawyer, and two physicians, Louis Miller and Jacob Auslander. According to Sidney Hook, the publication of photostatic copies of checks issued by the JAFRC to Gerhart Eisler led to the demand that the books be inspected.

36. Hamby, *Beyond the New Deal*, p. 389.

37. Including the Benjamin Davis, Jr., Freedom Committee, the Citizens Committee for Harry Bridges, the California Emergency Defense Committee and the Hollywood Writers Mobilization. Later the Families of the Smith Act Victims was listed.

38. Aubrey Grossman, Interview; Sidney Hook, "Academic Integrity and Academic Freedom," p. 333.

39. *NYHT*, July 16, 1948; Belfrage, *The American Inquisition*, p. 143; *NYT*, July 17, 1951; *NYHT*, July 12, 1951. Judge Ryan ordered fourteen of the defendants to post $165,000 substitute bail.

40. Lillian Hellman, *An Unfinished Woman*, pp. 261–62; Simon Gerson, Interview; Aubrey Grossman, Interview; *NYHT*, Aug. 9, 1951.

41. *NYT*, May 6, 1952; *NYHT*, July 1, 1952; *NYT*, April 24, 1953, Jan. 8, 1956; Jessica Mitford, *A Fine Old Conflict*, p. 202.

42. NYT, Jan. 30, 1948; Emerson and Haber, *Political and Civil Rights*, p. 546.

43. "Denial of Federally Aided Housing to Members of Organizations on the Attorney General's List," pp. 551–58; *ACLU News*, Vol. 18, No. 3 (March 1953); Gustave Jurist was the victim of a housing eviction in Detroit in 1952, as was Alexander Staber in Pittsburgh in 1959.

44. NYT, April 4, 1956; *Rights*, Vol. 3, No. 6 (March 1956), p. 6; NYT, June 19, 1947, May 29, 1956; *Rights*, Vol. 3, No. 6 (March 1956), pp. 5–6.

45. NYT, June 18, 1959; New York Supreme Court, Appellate Division, Third Judicial Department. Decision handed down June 17, 1959. Nat Ganley Collection, 14/39, WRL.

46. *ACLU News*, Vol. 17, No. 4 (April 1952); Ralph S. Brown, Jr., *Loyalty and Security*, p. 173; *Rights*, Vol. 6, No. 1 (September 1958), p. 11.


CHAPTER 9: THE COMMUNIST PARTY GOES UNDER

1. Nathan Glazer, *The Social Basis of American Communism*, pp. 116–17; *Chicago Daily News*, April 16, 1946; Morris Ernst and David Loth, *Report on the American Communist*, p. 221; David A. Shannon, *The Decline of American Communism*, pp. 362, 88, 219.

2. W. Z. Foster was later severed from the case on the ground of ill health.

3. In January 1950, Attorney General McGrath reported that the trial had cost the government $128,000. Defense attorneys' fees were said to cost $2,275 a week; by April 1949 the CRC had raised $74,095 for the defense.

4. Bruce Bliven, "Two Worlds at Foley Square," *passim*; Andrews, *Washington Witch Hunt*, p. 169; John Lord O'Brian, "Loyalty Tests and Guilt by Association," p. 592.

5. NYT, Feb. 1, 10, 1949; NYHT, Feb. 17, 1949; Abraham J. Isserman, Interview; Thomas I. Emerson, Interview; Robert Bendiner, "Communists on Trial," p. 118.

6. CSM, March 17, 1949; Isserman, Interview.

7. NYT, March 24, 1949; on Younglove, see NYT, May 4, 1949; on Cummings, see NYT, May 10, 1949; Bliven, p. 13; Calomiris, *Red Masquerade*, pp. 249, 247.

8. "From the Court Testimony of the Communist Leaders," pp. 28, 31–32; Eugene Dennis, *American Communists on Trial*, pp. 15–28; Bliven, p. 13; Albert E. Kahn, *High Treason*, p. 340.

9. NYT, April 4, 1949; David Shannon, p. 199; "Judge Medina's Charge to the Jury," p. 301.

10. Elliot L. Richardson, "Freedom of Expression and the Function of the Courts," pp. 11, 29; John Sommerville, *The Communist Trials and the American Tradition*, p. 141; Bernard A. Petrie, "Reformulation of the Clear and Present Danger Doctrine," pp. 452–60; Gellhorn, *American Rights*, p. 78.

11. Frank Donner, Interview.

12. It was a peculiar feature of the Smith Act trials that the Supreme Court's finding that the CP advocated violent overthrow of the government carried no weight in subsequent trials and had to be argued afresh on each occasion. Hence the value of John Lautner, who, following his expulsion from the CP

in 1950, served as the government's principal witness at all the post-Foley Square trials and testified that within the Party's inner circle the elite understood that revolutionary action was imminent. Lautner also described the underground or clandestine structure of the Party as it developed after 1949, with its seven "vertical" levels, from the base unit to the state leadership, each unit composed of three militants appointed by the unit above. This structure, he testified, was supplemented by a "horizontal" reserve leadership, communications and propaganda system equipped with photo-offset machines, shortwave radios and mimeographs. Although not directly probative in terms of the indictment, this testimony was certainly immensely suggestive to juries.

13. Herbert L. Packer, *Ex-Communist Witnesses*, pp. 190, 192; Somerville, p. 52.

14. Henry Steele Commager, *Freedom, Loyalty, Dissent*, p. 20; NYT, August 9, 1951; In the Supreme Court of Pennsylvania, No. 208, March Term 1960, *In the Matter of Hymen Schlesinger*, Brief of NLG, *amicus curiae*, p. 20.

15. Twenty-one were indicted. Two of those arrested, Israel Amter and Marion Bachrach, were severed from the trial on the ground of ill health. Four others fled to avoid trial. Of the accused, two were black and nine had been born in Russia or Eastern Europe.

16. Simon Gerson, Interview.

17. Elizabeth Gurley Flynn, *The Alderson Story*, p. 14; NYT, Nov. 20, 1952; NYHT, Dec. 4, 1952; Flynn and Others, *Thirteen Communists Speak to the Court*, pp. 7–94; NYT, Feb. 3, 1952, April 23, 1955; Matusow, *False Witness*, pp. 131–34.

18. The fourteen were: William Schneiderman, West Coast leader, Al Richmond, executive editor of the *Daily People's World*, Carl Lambert, Albert Lima, Loretta Stack, Ernest Fox, Bernadette Doyle, Philip Connelly, Dorothy Healey, Rose Chernin, Harry Steinberg, Ben Dobbs, Frank Carlson and Frank Spector.

19. DW (London), Aug. 7, 1951; Richmond, *A Long View from the Left*, pp. 302, 323, 325.

20. In the United States Court of Appeals for the Fourth Circuit, No. 6437, *Philip Frankfeld (et alia) v. United States of America*, Appendix to Appellant's Brief, pp. 2–4, 11.

21. The Hawaiian group consisted of Jack W. Hall, John E. Reinecke, Charles E. Fujimoto, his wife Eileen Fujimoto, Kojo Airyoshi, Jack D. Kimoto (both newspapermen) and Dwight Freeman, a construction worker.

22. The Seattle group consisted of Henry P. Huff, state chairman of the CP, William J. Pennock, Karly Larsen, Terry Pettus, Barbara Hartle, John S. Daschbach and Paul M. Bowen.

23. Starobin, *American Communism in Crisis*, pp. 208 and 302; A. L. Wirin and Sam Rosenwein, "The Smith Act Prosecutions," p. 489. Pettus, born in Wisconsin, had joined the CP in 1938. Active as a reporter in the Newspaper Guild, he had been North West editor of the *Daily People's World* since 1948.

24. William Allan, editor of the *Michigan Worker*; Nat Ganley, born in New York, business agent of UAW Local 155 from 1937 to 1947, a member of the Party's national committee, and from 1947 until 1950 publisher of the *Michi-*

*gan Herald* as well as Michigan editor of the *Daily Worker*; Thomas Dennis, Jr., CP organizing secretary for the Ford Motor Company; Mrs. Helen Winter, a state organizing secretary and wife of Carl Winter, one of the eleven national leaders tried in 1949.

25. William Sentner, Robert Manewitz, Marcus Murphy, James F. Forest, chairman of the Missouri CP, and Dorothy Forest.

26. *NYT*, Oct. 11, 1953; *Spotlight* (Committee to Keep McCarthyism Out of Michigan); *NYT*, April 3, 1954.

27. *Let Freedom Ring* (Pennsylvania Civil Rights Congress); Somerville, pp. 174, 53, 61.

28. Davis was the veteran organizer for Local 155, UE. Klonsky had fought with the Abraham Lincoln Brigade and, like Labovitz, was a veteran of the Second World War. Lowenfels, labor journalist and poet, had served as editor of the *Pennsylvania Worker*. Nabried, a worker in the building trades, was a noted black Communist. Weiss, a Jewish veteran of the Second World War, was then Party leader in Philadelphia.

29. *NYT*, April 16, 1959.

30. Professor Broadus Mitchell, of Rutgers (economic conditions), Professor H. H. Wilson, of Princeton (political and social conditions), Professor Ralph S. Brown, Jr., of Yale Law School (security problems), Professor Stringfellow Barr, of Rutgers (international law).

31. "The Communist Control Act of 1954," *Yale Law Journal*, Vol. 64 (April 1955), p. 751; *NYT*, Feb. 11, 1956.

32. Whitehead, *The FBI Story*, pp. 24, 241; Starobin, p. 290; Royal W. France, *My Native Grounds*, p. 244.

33. Robert Elkins, Sid Taylor, Joseph Dimow, James S. Tate, Joseph Goldring and Martha Asher.

34. Inevitably, the Communist press had suffered various forms of harassment. In 1950 the Newsdealers' Association of Greater New York voted to ban the *Daily Worker* from its 500 stands, but later reversed the decision. In August of that year news vendors in Los Angeles voted not to handle the *Daily People's World*, whose reporters were barred from meetings of the City Council in September 1953. In Detroit, the Common Council banned the sale on street newsstands of the *Daily Worker* and its affiliate, the *Michigan Herald*.

35. *Rights*, Vol. 3, No. 6 (March 1956), pp. 6–7; *NYT*, March 28, 1956.

36. Eugene Dennis, *Letters from Prison*, p. 65; William T. Baird, "The Lightfoot Case," p. 16; *NYT*, Oct. 1, 1954; Somerville, pp. 210–11; Belfrage, *The American Inquisition*, p. 250.

37. Emerson and Haber, p. 391; *Communism, the Courts and the Constitution*, p. 395; Telford Taylor, Interview.

38. Carl Marzani, "Thoughts Behind Bars," p. 53; DW (London), Dec. 16, 1955. In London Claudia Jones edited the *West Indian Gazette*. Starobin, pp. 241, 280. Winston was released in 1961, recuperated in the Soviet Union and was elected Party Chairman in 1964 on the death of Elizabeth Gurley Flynn.

39. NYHT, Oct. 24, 1953; DW (London), June 27, 1956; John Gates, *The Story of an American Communist*, p. 148.

40. Dennis, *Letters*, pp. 181, 36, 64; Flynn, *Alderson Story*, p. 21; George Charney, *A Long Journey*, p. 15; Rose Chernin, Interview.

41. Exiles living in Mexico included Frederick V. Field and his wife, Maurice Halperin, Albert Maltz, Samuel J. Novick, Asa Zatz and Max Schlafrock (Bert Quint in *NYHT*, Sept. 2, 1957).

42. Starobin, p. 306; Hoover, *Masters of Deceit*, pp. 276–81.

43. Starobin, pp. 221–22; *NYT* and *NYHT*, Nov. 2, 1954; David Englestein, Interview.

44. Sam Kushner, Interview; Simon Gerson, Interview; Aubrey Grossman, Interview.

45. *Public Opinion*, 1935–1946, p. 131.

46. S. A. Stouffer, *Communism, Conformity and Civil Liberties*, pp. 43, 177–78.

### CHAPTER 10: HELL IN PITTSBURGH

1. *NYT*, June 23, 1950; Joseph L. Rauh, Jr., "Informers, G-Men, and Free Men," p. 11; Donner, *The Un-Americans*, p. 143.

2. Stamler, p. 60; Donner, *The Un-Americans*, p. 143; David Englestein, Interview; Emerson and Haber, *Political and Civil Rights*, p. 486; *NYT*, March 8, 1950.

3. Steve Nelson, *The 13th Juror*, pp. 161, 146, 151, 157; *NYT*, Oct. 4, 1950. It was no coincidence that in a part of the world where Democrats smeared their Republican rivals as "red fellow travelers," Musmanno launched his crusade against Nelson when he was running for governor. Musmanno didn't make it, but, like his colleague Gunther, he did later secure election by popular vote to the State Supreme Court, at an initial salary of $22,000.

4. Nelson, pp. 115, 122–23, 182; *The Times* (London), Nov. 3, 1953; Donner Files.

5. Belfrage, *The American Inquisition*, p. 152; Nelson, pp. 49, 78; Donner Files, press clippings.

6. William Albertson, born in 1910, grew up in Pittsburgh, where he served as an officer of the Hotel and Restaurant Workers Union, AFL, from 1935 to 1943. He then became labor secretary to New York's ALP Councilman Peter V. Cacchione. He returned to Pittsburgh, then moved to Detroit and became executive secretary of the Michigan CP.

7. *NYT*, Aug. 21, 1953; *Spotlight*; Weissman, "Proceedings to Disbar Leo Sheiner," pp. 140–41.

8. Weissman, "Sheiner," pp. 146–47; *NYT*, Sept. 26, 1956, Nov. 10, 1953, Jan. 4, 1955; Kempton, *America* . . . , p. 12.

9. In the Supreme Court of Pennsylvania, *Hymen Schlesinger*, pp. 4, 13; *In re Schlesinger*, 404 Pa. 584 172A 2d 835 (1961); Belfrage, *The American Inquisition*, p. 284.

### CHAPTER 11: THE DEPORTATION TERROR

1. *Communist Activities Among Aliens and National Groups*, pp. 394–401.

2. Among those listed by Clark were the American Committee for Yugoslav

Relief, the American Croatian Congress, the American Poles for Peace, the American Polish Labor Council, the American Polish League, the American Slav Congress, the Bulgarian-American People's League, the Hungarian-American Council for Democracy, the Polonia Section of the IWO, the Serbian American Fraternal Society, the Slovak Workers Society and the Ukrainian-American Fraternal Union.

3. The Act stipulated that citizenship could be canceled up to ten years after naturalization if at any time during those ten years the offender was convicted of contempt of Congress for refusal to testify about subversion or joined any subversive organization as defined by the Internal Security Act within five years of naturalization, or could be proved to have concealed such membership at the time of naturalization.

4. Louise Pettibone Smith, *Torch of Liberty*, p. 209; Belfrage, *The American Inquisition*, p. 257; Rose Chernin, Interview; *New York Journal-American*, April 11, 1953; Simon Gerson, Interview.

5. John Abt to Stanley Nowak, June 9, 1950, Stanley Nowak Collection, box 2, 1950 Congressional Election, and Nowak Collection generally, WRL: see also *Detroit News*, July 23, 1950; In the Supreme Court of the United States, October Term 1957, No. 729, *Stanislaw Nowak v. United States*, Brief of NLG as *amicus curiae, passim*.

6. Robert K. Murray, *Red Scare*, pp. 207, 251.

7. Will Maslow, "Recasting Our Deportation Law," p. 334; Smith, pp. 291, 353–54; USNWR, vol. 38 (April 1, 1955), p. 69; Rose Chernin, Interview.

8. NYT, Oct. 24, 1950; ACLU News, Vol. 16, No. 12 (Dec. 1951); Alan Harper, *Politics of Loyalty*, pp. 224–26.

9. *Harisiades v. Shaughnessy*, 1952, *Carlson v. Landon*, 1952, and *Galvan v. Press*, 1954.

10. Rose Chernin, Interview; Lena L. Orlow, "The Immigration and Nationality Act in Operation," pp. 156–60; J. Campbell Bruce, *The Golden Door*, p. 219; *New York Post*, March 28, 1967.

11. Graded CS-12, their average pay was $7,570 a year compared with 123 hearing officers in other agencies who were earning $11,610 in June 1954, and fifty-four who were earning $10,320.

12. ACLU News, Vol. 16, No. 10 (Oct. 1951); Ginzburg, *Rededication to Freedom*, p. 51.

13. The eight were: Harry Yaris, 44, of New York, born in Russia; Jack Schneider, 55, of the Bronx, born in Rumania; Frank Borich, 51, of Brooklyn, born in Yugoslavia; Samuel Milgrom, 47, of New York, born in Minsk; Paul Juditz, 64, of the Bronx, born in Kiev; Joseph Simonoff, 53, of Brooklyn, born in Russia; Andrew Dmytryshyn, 60, of New York, born in the Ukraine; and Michael Nukk, 45, of Tuckahoe, New York, born in Estonia. NYT, October 23, 1952.

14. NYT, May 6, Aug. 4, 1948, Feb. 22, Nov. 1, 1950, March 11, 1952; K. C. Davis, "Requirement of a Trial-Type Hearing," p. 232; *Rights*, Vol. 3, No. 2 (Oct. 1956), p. 14; Maslow, p. 321; Marion Bachrach, "Bail Granted!" pp. 315–18; *Open Forum*, Jan. 20, 1951; Abner Green, *The Deportation Terror*, p. 15; Milton Konvitz, *Civil Rights in Immigration*, pp. 124, 130; Abner Green, *The Walter-McCarran Law*, p. 46.

15. Smith, p. 207; Freeland, *The Truman Doctrine* . . . , p. 219; *NYT*, Oct. 20, 1948.

16. Chambers, *Witness*, p. 29; Ruth Fischer was author of *Stalin and the German Communist Party*.

17. *Thirty Years of Treason*, pp. 63, 67; *CSM*, May 31, 1949; Starobin, *American Communism in Crisis*, p. 304; *NYHT*, June 6, 1949; *NYT*, March 2, 1948, Jan. 5, 1957.

18. Steve Tandaric, who came to America as an infant from what is now Yugoslavia, a veteran of the Abraham Lincoln Brigade, was deported after fifty-two years' residence. Expelled by Yugoslavia because he insisted he had not come there voluntarily, he found himself in a camp in northern Italy.

The following cases occurred in California. Dr. Nydia Barkau Luthy, a biochemist and formerly of Stanford University, born in the Ukraine but resident in the United States for thirty-three of her thirty-eight years, was charged with having been a member of the YCL from 1928 to 1937, and of the CP from 1933 to 1934. Although she denied ever having joined the CP, she was ordered deported in March 1951 and decided to leave for Israel at her own expense. (*NYT*, Aug. 17, 1950, March 3, 1951.) In May 1953 Philip Cherner, a Russian-born resident of Los Angeles who had come to America in 1948 and who was alleged to be a Communist, was arrested for deportation. The Korean-born architect and ILWU activist David Hyun was arrested in October 1950. Only after he had spent a year in prison did the Supreme Court reduce his bail to $5,000. Arguing that he faced death if he returned to South Korea, Hyun survived two adverse decisions in the U.S. Supreme Court, and finally won a reprieve when the government dropped its charges against him in 1964. (Rose Chernin, Interview.) Less fortunate was the British-born film writer Harry Carlisle, who had lived in America for some thirty years, then found himself blacklisted. After his appeals against deportation had failed, he departed for London in 1962. Reuben Ship, thirty-six, a Canadian-born radio writer, was deported in August 1953.

19. *NYT*, Feb. 19, 1948, Nov. 18, 1949, Nov. 11, 1950.

20. In September 1948 the following were arrested: Wilhelm Weber (who came from Germany in 1937), Charles Kratochvil (from what was later Czechoslovakia, in 1906), Abraham Mallin (from Poland in 1920), William Weiner, alias Welwel Warszower, a former CP treasurer, Morris E. Taft (from Lithuania in 1906), Michael Salerno (from Italy in 1923), Charles Bidien (from Indonesia in 1930), Sol and Anna Taffler (from Russia in 1918 and 1914 respectively), Dora Lipschitz (from Russia in 1906). Mallin broke into tears at his hearing and pleaded that he had left the CP soon after joining it in 1937. He was married to an American citizen and had a son who had enlisted in the Army. (*NYT*, Sept. 25, 1948.) In April 1950 a deportation order was served on David Balint, a Czech-born resident of America since 1920, who became a Communist labor leader in Cleveland. (*MG*, April 13, 1950.) In October 1952 Allen and Agnes Edgar, British Communists, were deported. In July 1953 a deportation order was made against a New York CP official, Felix Kusman, and in December against José Angel Ocon, a resident of America since 1918, but alleged to be the Communist leader among Mexicans living in the Los Angeles area.

21. By 1953, 41 of the 135 people facing deportation as subversives were officials or active members of trade unions.

22. NYT, Jan. 22, 1948, Jan. 1, 1947; Komorowski, *Strange Trial of Stanley Novak*, p. 22; CSM, Feb. 17, 1948; NYT April 8, 1948, Nov. 2, 1947, Dec. 11, 1952.

23. NYT, Aug. 17, 1950; Green, *The Deportation Terror*, pp. 17–18; UE Files; Green, *The Walter-McCarran Law*, p. 33.

24. Kempton, *America* . . . , p. 13; A *Quarter-Century of Un-Americana*, p. 21; Fowler Harper, "The Crusade Against Bridges," *passim*; Paul Jacobs, "The Due Processing of Harry Bridges," pp. 36–39.

25. NYT, Dec. 2, 1949; Albert Kahn, *High Treason*, p. 282; ACLU News, Vol. 17, No. 1 (Jan. 1952) and No. 8 (Aug. 1952).

26. Luigi Mascitti and Mrs. Dora Coleman pleaded that they had no longer been CP members when the Alien Registration Act was passed in 1940. Each of them had lived in America for over thirty-two years. Mascitti, a resident of Philadelphia, had been a member of the Party from 1923 to 1929. Mrs. Coleman, from the same city and a native of Russia, had a husband and three children who were American citizens.

27. Deportation proceedings were launched against Anthony P. Minerich, owner of a Croatian-language paper in Chicago; Paul Novick, editor of the *Morning Freiheit*; John Steuben, editor of *March of Labor*; Katsu Asano, editor of the Japanese-language *Chicago Shimpo*; and Boris Sklar, 68, editor of *Russky Golos*, a charter member of the CPUSA and an American resident since 1913.

28. A near-casualty from the field of journalism was the Chicago *Sun-Times* cartoonist, Jacob Burck, formerly a contributor to the *Daily Worker* but subsequently an anti-Communist and Pulitzer Prize-winner. Only after a five-year legal battle did a special Congressional resolution rescue him from a deportation order.

29. Elizabeth Bentley, *Out of Bondage*, p. 167; Cedric Belfrage, *The Frightened Giant*, pp. 112, 146, 175; MG, Aug. 18, 1953; NYT, May 10, July 7, 1950; NYHT, Feb. 26, 1953; NYT, Nov. 26, 1959.

30. By 1956, Bulgaria, Czechoslovakia, Hungary, Latvia, the Soviet Baltic States, Poland and Rumania among them had permitted the return of only twenty-three nationals. According to Commissioner Swing, there were in 1954 as many as 228 subversive aliens who had been ordered deported but whom no country would accept.

31. Maslow, pp. 335, 362–63, 365; Harold W. Chase, *Security and Liberty*, p. 74.

32. Maslow, p. 362. The fourteen were Michael Nukk, Frank Borich, Joseph Siminoff, Felix Kusman, Rose Nelson Lightcap, Ida Gottesman, Anna Taffler, Benny Saltzmann, Bessie Geiser, Martin Young, Boris Sklar, Betty Gannett, Alexander Bittelman, Claudia Jones (NYT, Oct. 20, 1955).

33. Edith Lowenstein, *The Alien and the Immigration Law*, Case No. 1533; Smith, p. 355; *End Exile* (pamphlet), pp. 4–6; Zechariah Chafee, Jr., *The Blessings of Liberty*, p. 34; Konvitz, *Civil Rights in Immigration*, p. 99; Detroit Free Press, Oct. 14, 1951; *We Need a Statute of Limitations* (ACPFB pamphlet), n.d., p. 2.

34. Bernice Polites, *In Memory of My Father; We Need . . .* , pp. 5–8.

35. *NYT*, May 8, Jan. 13, 1953; I. F. Stone, *The Best of I. F. Stone's Weekly*, p. 37; Smith, p. 34.

36. Rose Chernin, Interview; Subversive Activities Control Board Docket No. 109–53, *William P. Rogers v. ACPFB*, June 27, 1950, pp. 1–43, 45; Green, *The Walter-McCarran Law*, p. 45; Smith, p. 374; *NYT*, March 12, 1958.

### CHAPTER 12: THE GOLDEN CURTAIN

1. Emerson and Haber, *Political and Civil Rights*, p. 504–5.

2. Cushman, *Civil Liberties*, p. 115; *National Guardian*, April 25, 1955; *ACLU News*, Vol. 19, No. 5 (May 1954), p. 1; Longaker, *The Presidency and Individual Liberties*, p. 91.

3. Walter Bergman, "State Department 'McCarthyism'," *passim*.

4. Paul Robeson, *Here I Stand*, pp. 63, 72; "The Case of Paul Robeson," pp. 79–80.

5. Tillett Papers, Universities.

6. *ACLU News*, Vol. 20, No. 7 (July 1955), Vol. 20, No. 10 (Oct. 1955).

7. For the cases of Mrs. Jane Zlatovski, an American painter resident in Paris, and Gordon McIntire, dismissed from the UN's Food and Agricultural Organization under State Department pressure, see *Rights*, Vol. 3, No. 2 (Nov. 1955), p. 9.

8. "The Passport Puzzle," pp. 262–89; Rockwell Kent, *This Is My Own*, pp. 361, 371.

9. *Freedom in the Balance*, pp. 160–61.

10. Murphy, *Congress and the Court*, p. 192.

11. "Passports for U.S. Reds," pp. 103–4.

12. *NYT*, May 26, 1948.

13. *CSM*, Jan. 17, 1948.

14. *Sunday Express* (London), Oct. 30, 1949; *NYT*, Dec. 11, 1949.

15. Ellen Knauff, *The Ellen Knauff Story*, pp. 166, 163.

16. *MG*, Dec. 23, 1950; Belfrage, *American Inquisition*, pp. 100–101; Lowenstein, *The Alien and the Immigration Law*, p. 7. In Arthur Miller's play, *After the Fall*, the character Holga declares: "In fact, when I first visited America after the war I was three days under questioning before they let me in. . . . In fact, it was only when I told them that I had blood relatives in several Nazi ministries that they were reassured." (p. 13.)

17. Frank L. Auerbach, *Immigration Laws of the United States*, p. 294; *NYT*, March 23, 1952.

18. *CSM*, Aug. 13, 1952; *NYT*, Feb. 2, 1952; *Daily Herald* (London), Feb. 20, 1952.

19. *NYHT*, April 21, 1951; *NYT*, April 26, 1951; *BAS*, Vol. 8, No. 7 (Oct. 1952), p. 246.

20. Michael Polanyi, "Securing a Visa," *passim*.

21. "Some British Experiences," p. 232; Shils, *The Torment of Secrecy*, p. 187; Victor Weisskopf, "Report on the Visa Situation," p. 221.

22. "Some British Experiences," pp. 239, 237, 240.

23. *Ibid.*, pp. 236, 243; "American Visa Policy," p. 369; Kirtley F. Mather, "Scientists in the Doghouse," p. 640.

24. Weisskopf, p. 221; "Some British Experiences," pp. 238, 231, 248; *NYT*, March 6, 1951.

25. Leonard Engel, "Science Notebook," pp. 238–39; Edward Shils, "America's Paper Curtain," pp. 416–17; *BAS*, Vol. 8, No. 7, (Oct. 1952), p. 230.

26. "Some British Experiences," pp. 230, 244–45, 232, 250.

27. "American Visa Policy," p. 369.

28. This account is based mainly on Milton Viorst, "The Bitter Tea of Dr. Tsien"; see also *NYT*, Sept. 8, Nov. 16, 1950, Dec. 3, 1952.

29. For example: Mezei, Rumanian-born and resident in the U.S. for twenty-five years but still an alien, traveled in 1948 to visit his dying mother. Arriving back in America with a valid visa, he was interned on Ellis Island for no stated reason and twice shipped to Europe, where a dozen countries refused to accept him. In 1953 the Supreme Court ruled that he had no right to due process. He was eventually allowed to stay. (Konvitz, *Civil Rights in Immigration*, p. 51; K. C. Davis, "Requirement of a Trial-Type Hearing," p. 25.) Alexander Lobanov, a Soviet defector, worked on American ships from 1944 to 1951 but was periodically detained by the Immigration Service. Not until the ACLU intervened in 1951 did he get a hearing. Mrs. Valentina Gardner, Russian-born wife of a GI, was detained and was denied entry in 1948 for thirteen months. (*ACLU News*, Vol. 16, No. 9 [Sept. 1951], Vol. 17, No. 3 [March 1952], Vol. 18, No. 9 [Sept. 1950].) The Austrian-born wife of an American citizen was denied a visa because she could show no evidence of anti-Communist activity since she dropped out of the Austrian CP in 1947. (Lowenstein, p. 67.) Celia Pomeroy, the Filipino wife of the American journalist William Pomeroy, had been imprisoned with her husband in the Philippines as a HUK activist. They were released in 1962 but had to settle in England after she was refused a visa to enter the U.S. Pomeroy had joined the CP in 1937, later left it, but remained sympathetic. (William Pomeroy, Interview.)

30. Knauff, *passim*.

## CHAPTER 13: THE FEDERAL CIVIL SERVICE

1. Harold M. Hyman, *To Try Men's Souls*, p. 269.

2. Francis Biddle, *The Fear of Freedom*, p. 115; Bontecou, *The Federal Loyalty-Security Program*, pp. 10, 14–15.

3. H. Stuart Hughes, "Why We Had No Dreyfus Case," pp. 473–78. Two sources provide basically compatible statistics concerning the impact of the wartime loyalty program. According to one, from 1940 to March 21, 1947, 6,296 cases were considered under the Hatch Act, resulting in 114 dismissals and 46 resignations during investigation. According to the other, from July 1942 to June 1946 some 6,193 cases were referred to the FBI for investigation, resulting in 101 discharges and 21 resignations during investigation. Meanwhile, the President's Interdepartmental Committee had considered 729 cases by December 1946, 24 of whom were dismissed. (Some of these discharges overlap with those mentioned above.)

4. As regards applicants for the federal service, from July 1, 1940, to March 31, 1947, 395,000 were subjected to a loyalty investigation, of whom 1,313 were held ineligible on loyalty grounds; 714 of these were described as Communists or "followers of the Party line"—about 0.01 percent of all appointees. Slightly fewer, about 500, were barred for being pro-Axis. Whitehead, *The FBI Story*, p. 345; Emerson and Helfeld, p. 55; Bontecou, p. 15.

5. Murray Kempton, "Truman and the Beast," p. 6; Alan Harper, *The Politics of Loyalty*, p. 35.

6. Bontecou, p. 28.

7. *Ibid.*, p. 32; Harry Truman, *Years of Trial and Hope*, p. 297.

8. NYHT, March 30, 1952.

9. Andrews, *Washington Witch Hunt*, pp. 58, 99.

10. S.A. Goudsmit, "The Task of the Security Officer," p. 145; Elmer Davis, *But We Were Born Free*, p. 22.

11. *Congressional Record*, Vol. 117, No. 61 (April 29, 1971); NYT, Nov. 29, 1955; Joseph and Stewart Alsop, *We Accuse!* p. 76.

12. Bontecou, p. 63; Kempton, "Truman and the Beast," p. 8.

13. Bontecou, p. 33; Buckley and Bozell, *McCarthy and His Enemies*, p. 219; NYHT, May 5, 1950; MG, May 19, 1951; Athan Theoharis, "The Escalation of the Loyalty Program," pp. 255–59.

14. R.W. Scott McLeod, *American Political Democracy and the Problem of Personnel Security*, p. 12; Ralph S. Brown, *Loyalty and Security*, p. 491; Mayer, *How the Loyalty-Security Program Affects Private Employment*, p. 122; John H. Schaar, *Loyalty in America*, p. 126; Alan Barth, *The Loyalty of Free Men*, p. 126.

15. The first stage was to check all employees' names against the files of the FBI and other agencies. In June 1949 J. Edgar Hoover announced that 99.6 percent of 2,251,717 loyalty forms processed by the FBI had been returned to the CSC stamped "No disloyal data." On May 5, 1950, the FBI stated that 11,813 cases had merited full field investigations for loyalty. By March 1952 this figure was up to 20,733, according to one source, and 18,424 according to another. By May 1953 it was 27,326. As regards security-risk field investigations, there had been 10,415 by March 1952.

From these figures we can conclude that by the end of the Truman era, over 40,000 federal employees had come under sufficient suspicion to merit a full-scale investigation. Very few of them can have been unaware of their predicament, since denial of access to classified material and sometimes suspension confirmed the threatening situation already indicated by the questions of security officers.

How many were dismissed? It should be borne in mind that while figures up to 1950 represent loyalty dismissals alone, figures after that date cover both loyalty and security discharges.

The CSC reported 83 dismissals by the end of June 1949. By November the figure was 123. As of March 31, 1950, the CSC reported 202 dismissals on grounds of disloyalty. By May it was 225. In October, the CSC reported 280. In April 1951 the LRB reported that 308 had been dismissed since March 1947. The available figures for March 1952 are 384 for loyalty and 141 for security. Professor Ralph S. Brown, Jr., concluded that by May 1953 there had been 560 loyalty dismissals, a further 150 discharged under the military departments' security programs prior to 1950, and a further 500 discharged from 1950 to 1953 under P.L. 733 combined with summary dismissals in the State and Commerce Departments.

This gives a grand total of 1,210 dismissals during a period of six years, *not including* military personnel. Brown's estimate for all federal personnel, civilian and military, is 3,900 dismissals (not including industrial and transport workers in private employment but subject to the federal Industrial Security Program).

Yet dismissals represented only the tip of the iceberg. When a man resigns under investigation it may mean that he recognizes his own "guilt" and inevitable detection, or that, believing himself innocent he nevertheless sees no hope of reprieve. A resignation looks better on the record. On the whole, we should regard those who resigned under investigation, or before final adjudication of their cases, as no less victims of the system than those formally discharged. By November 1949 there had been 2,214 such resignations. In November 1951 it was reported that 3,645, or 22 percent of those subjected to full field investigation, had resigned. According to one source, resignations had reached 6,382 by May 1953.

By June 1954, 6,926 employees had been dismissed or had resigned as a result of adverse information, but only 1,743 of them were apparently related to subversive activities or associations. Of these, between four and five hundred were dismissals. Brown estimated 1,500 security dismissals, associated with political activity or associations, from 1953 to 1956. Bearing in mind a report of 5,447 resignations by July 1955, and if we calculate the dismissal-resignation ratio as at least 1:4, we can hypothesize at least 6,000 resignations during that period. The Eisenhower program, as we have noted, made no distinction between sensitive and nonsensitive positions, and the departmental figures reinforce the impression that the swing of the ax was not so much correlated with national security as with the hysteria or vindictiveness prevailing in certain departments. Thus, up to January 1955 the Veterans Administration reported 353 dismissals and 1,112 resignations, and the Post Office 324 and 519. *NYT*, June 6, 1945; *NYHT*, March 30, 1952, June 24, Nov. 28, 1949; Schaar, p. 142; Barth, p. 125; Theoharis, "The Threat to Civil Liberties," p. 266; *NYHT*, March 30, 1952; Brown, *Loyalty and Security*, p. 487, *NYHT*, Nov. 28, 1949; Schaar, p. 142; *NYT*, Oct. 30, 1950; *NYHT*, Nov. 28, 1951; *Joseph R. McCarthy*, ed. Allen J. Matusow, p. 5; Norman A. Graebner, *The New Isolationism*, p. 136; Schaar, p. 142; *MG*, July 30, 1955; *NYHT*, Jan. 4, 1955.

16. Paul Tillett, Interview with Joseph Fanelli, March 1, 1962, Tillett Papers; *NYHT*, April 13, 1953; Paul Tillett, "The Social Costs of the Loyalty Program" (preliminary draft, unpublished), Tillett Papers, pp. 8, 13–14; Marie Jahoda and Stuart W. Cook, "Security Measures and Freedom of Thought," *passim*.

17. Jahoda and Cook, pp. 307–8; Marie Jahoda, "Morale in the Federal Civil Service," p. 110.

18. What was it like to be accused? Robert T. Bower concluded that approximately 14 percent continued on work of the same classification, 7 percent were relegated to work of lower classification, 6 percent were instantly dismissed, and 60 percent were suspended, 98 percent of them without pay. The period between suspension or receipt of charges and the final decision was less than six months in 38 percent of cases, from six to twelve months in 40 percent, from twelve to eighteen months in 17 percent, and over eighteen months in 10 percent of cases. A civilian employee of an armed-services department with fifteen years' service was suspended under P.L. 733 a month before he received charges. Four months later he was granted a hearing. Four months after that he received an adverse decision. Four months later he came before the Loyalty-Security Appeal Board, which—two years later—upheld the adverse decision. He was thus dismissed three years after being suspended. Of 326 cases tabulated by Professor Bower, 12 percent had hearings lasting less than four hours, 12 percent lasted from four to seven hours, 24 percent lasted from eight to fifteen hours, and 12 percent lasted more than fifteen hours (20 percent had no hearing at all). Brown, *Loyalty and Security*, pp. 493, 492; Adam Yarmolinsky, *Case Studies in Personnel Security*, p. 27.

19. Bontecou, pp. 131–32, 226–34.

20. Harry S. Truman, p. 296; K.C. Davis, p. 212; Brown, *Loyalty and Security*, p. 491; Barth, p. 113; "An Informer's Tale," pp. 217–24.

21. Mayer, p. 121; Bontecou, p. 132; Alsop, p. 61; Tillett, *The Social Costs . . .* , pp. 9–10; Paul Tillett, Interview with Milton Mandell, June 13, 1962, Tillett Papers.

22. *ACLU News*, Vol. 16, No. 11 (Nov. 1951); Bontecou, p. 129.

23. *ACLU News*, Vol. 14, No. 5 (May 1949); "An Informer's Tale," p. 231; K.C. Davis, p. 212; Joseph Fanelli, Letter to Paul Tillett, Nov. 12, 1964, Tillett Papers; Emerson and Haber, *Political and Civil Rights*, p. 609.

24. *ACLU News*, Vol. 14, No. 1 (Jan. 1949), Vol. 20, No. 11 (Nov. 1955); Besig Files, L.M. Laurenti.

25. *NYT*, Dec. 17, 1953; *ACLU News*, Vol. 14, No. 1 (Jan. 1949), Vol. 15, No. 3 (March 1950); Bontecou, p. 110; *ACLU News*, Vol. 16, No. 4 (April 1951); Yarmolinsky, *Case Studies*, p. 21; Chafee, p. 25.

26. Yarmolinsky, *Case Studies*, pp. 32, 152–57; Bontecou, p. 142.

27. *ACLU News*, Vol. 15, No. 9 (Sept. 1950); Konvitz, *First Amendment Freedoms*, p. 590; Yarmolinsky, *Case Studies*, pp. 206–13, 51, 12, 89; Andrews, p. 35; Bontecou, pp. 138, 142, 141, 108.

28. One of the possible exceptions to this rule was Edward Rothschild, a bookbinder working in the Assembly Room of the Government Printing Office, with access to top-secret documents. He took the Fifth on CP membership before the McCarthy Subcommittee. He was discharged. See *The Meaning of McCarthyism*, pp. 354, 212.

29. Yarmolinsky, *Case Studies*, p. 80; *ACLU News*, Vol. 14, No. 2 (Feb. 1949) and Vol. 14, No. 1 (Jan. 1949); see also Besig Files, Rita Cravanas Ross; Tillett Papers, Fort Monmouth, Bernice Levine; *ACLU News*, Vol. 14, No. 5 (May 1949); Yarmolinsky, *Case Studies*, p. 99; Bontecou, pp. 108–11.

30. *ACLU News*, Vol. 16, No. 4 (April 1951); Konvitz, *First Amendment Freedoms*, p. 585; *NYT*, June 22, 1959; Besig Files, L. M. Laurenti.

31. Yarmolinsky, *Case Studies*, p. 50; *NYT*, Aug. 19, 1955, June 6, 1957; Yarmolinsky, *Case Studies*, pp. 112–14 (this case is recorded anonymously); Tillett Papers, Fort Monmouth, Bernice Levine.

32. Yarmolinsky, *Case Studies*, pp. 171–76, 206–14, 29–31, 13, 189–93.

33. On the Remington case, see Carr, *The House Committee* . . . , pp. 196–197; Barth, *The Loyalty of Free Men*, pp. 68–70; Packer, pp. 76–79; Cook, *The FBI Nobody Knows*, pp. 327–45; Kempton, *Part of Our Time*, p. 225.

34. *NYHT*, Oct. 26, 1951, Jan. 14, 1953; *NYT*, Nov. 25, 1953.

35. Packer, p. 116; Brown, *Loyalty and Security*, p. 59; Schneir, *Invitation to an Inquest*, pp. 318–19; *NYHT*, Jan. 12, 1956; Paul Tillett, Interview with Ralph Russell, April 12, 1962, Tillett Papers.

36. Paul Tillett, Interview with Joseph Borkin, Tillett Papers; Adam Yarmolinsky, "How a Lawyer Conducts a Security Case"; Paul Tillett, Interview with Joseph Fanelli, March 1, 1962, and Joseph Fanelli to Paul Tillett, Nov. 12, 1964, Tillett Papers.

37. Of 326 cases checked by Yarmolinsky and others, and tabulated by Robert T. Bower, in 3 percent the cost to the client was under $100, in 11 percent it ranged from $100 to $199, in 25 percent from $200 to $499, in 11 percent from $500 to $749, and in 11 percent of cases the cost was over $1,000. One survey estimated the average lawyer's fee for an appeal at about $1,000. Brown, *Loyalty and Security*, p. 494.

38. "The Role of Employer Practices in the Federal Industrial Personnel Security Program—a Field Study," p. 257 n; Paul Tillett, Interview with Milton I. Sacks, March 28, 1962; Interview with Fanelli; both in Tillett Papers.

39. The figures indicate a general average of about $10 an hour, and the most expensive rate-per-hour cited in the *Case Studies* compiled by Yarmolinsky from a wide range of attorneys was only $750 for thirty-five hours' work, charged to a labor-relations consultant with one of the armed forces who could doubtless afford it out of his $10,000-a-year salary. Case No. 4, who faced fifteen charges and brought to his hearing four witnesses and thirty supporting affidavits, paid $1,200 for ninety-five hours of his attorney's time. Other lawyers charged even less: counsel for a Post Office clerk charged $125 for thirty hours, one third of his normal rate. In some instances the rate was merely nominal: a clerk-typist earning $3,360 a year was charged $200 for sixty hours' work, and one lawyer made a habit of charging all loyalty-security clients $100, which he sent to a charity.

40. Bontecou, pp. 65–66; Andrews, pp. 60 ff.; Tillett, Interview with Russell, Tillett Papers; Tillett, Interview with Harry Magdoff, June 20, 1962, Tillett Papers.

41. C. Herman Pritchett, *Congress versus the Supreme Court*, 1957–1960, p. 106; Sidney Lens, *The Futile Crusade. p.* 159.

## CHAPTER 14: THE ARMED FORCES

1. Of these, Dondero named ten (most of whom had already resigned), including Abraham L. Pomerantz, former war-crimes prosecutor, Josiah Dubois, deputy chief counsel at the Nuremberg trials, Richard Sasuly, whose

book I.G. *Farben* offended Dondero by drawing attention to links between American and German business, George Shaw Wheeler, former chief of the de-Nazification branch of the Army manpower division, and Max Lowenthal, former legal adviser in the American zone of Germany.

2. These civilians included Dr. George S. Counts of Columbia University, Professor Louis Wirth of the University of Chicago, Roger Baldwin, head of the ACLU, Dr. Theresa Wolfson, Professor Kimball Young of Northwestern University and Professor John M. McConnell of Cornell.

3. *NYT*, July 10, Sept. 9, 1947; *NYHT*, Sept. 25, 1947; *NYT*, March 11, Aug. 3, June 10, 1949; *NYHT*, June 15, 1949.

4. Brown, *Loyalty and Security*, p. 56; Bontecou, *The Federal Loyalty-Security Program*, p. 14; Rorty and Decter, p. 7; Brown, p. 59; ACLU, *Liberty Is Always Unfinished Business*, p. 20.

5. I. F. Stone, "The Army and the 'Reds,' " p. 238.

6. *NYT*, March 9, 1946; *NYHT*, July 21, 1947; Brown, *Loyalty and Security*, pp. 48, 487; *NYHT*, Dec. 29, 1957.

7. *NYT*, Aug. 6, 1953.

8. *NYT*, June 12, 15, 1955.

9. Stanley Faulkner, "Security Program in the Armed Forces," p. 147; Rowland Watts, *The Draftee and Internal Security*, pp. 20–21, 42.

10. Watts, pp. 20–21, 42; *Rights*, Vol, 3, Nos. 8–9 (May-June 1956), p. 19; *NYT*, April 28, June 21, 1956; Faulkner, p. 61; *Rights*, Vol. 2, No. 2 (Oct. 1954), p. 12; *NYHT*, Dec. 29, 1957; Faulkner, p. 151.

11. Such charges included corresponding with the Four Continents Book Corporation; parading on behalf of the American Peace Crusade; applying for membership in the IWO. There were also numerous accusations of having sold or subscribed to Communist newspapers. An inductee at Fort Ord was— again, typically—accused of "sympathetic association" with his mother, who had been involved with the Southern Negro Youth Congress. Another Fort Ord soldier was charged with associating with members of the Architects Committee of the NCASF. Faulkner, p. 146; Watts, pp. 56, 42, 28–40.

12. *ACLU News*, Vol. 20, No. 10 (Oct. 1955), p. 3; Watts, p. 19.

13. *Rights*, Vol. 2, No. 8 (April 1955), p. 5, Vol. 3, No. 2 (Nov. 1955), p. 11; *ACLU News*, Vol. 21, No. 12 (Dec. 1956); Watts, pp. 40–41; *NYT*, Nov. 2, Aug. 23, 1955.

14. *NYT*, Jan. 31, 1951; Harry P. Cain, "Security of the Republic," p. 8; Faulkner, p. 151.

15. *ACLU News*, Vol. 21, No. 1 (Jan. 1956), Vol. 21, No. 5 (May 1956).

16. The other seven soldiers were: Stanley Hauser, Bertram Lassuck, David Lubell, Jonathan Lubell, Bernard Radoff, Samuel Suckow and Rudolph Thomas.

17. Faulkner, p. 148; *Rights*, Vol. 3, No. 2 (Nov. 1955), pp. 10–11, Vol. 4, No. 2 (Nov. 1956), pp. 4–5; *NYT*, Nov. 22, 1955, Oct. 26, 1956.

18. United States Court of Appeals for the District of Columbia, No. 13587, *Howard D. Abramowitz, Appellant, v. Wilbur M. Brucker, Appellee*, Brief for the Appellee, pp. 1–7; *Rights*, Vol. 4, No. 6 (April 1957), p. 13; *NYT*, Jan. 16, March 4, 1958; *Rights*, Vol. 6, No. 3 (March 1959), p. 9.

CHAPTER 15: THE STATE DEPARTMENT AND THE
CHINA EXPERTS

1. Buckley and Bozell, *McCarthy and His Enemies*, pp. 9–12, 16–17, 215.
2. *NYT*, May 21, 23, 1947. There were a number of subsequent prosecutions of government employees for falsely denying past or present CP membership. Among those convicted were William Remington, Sidney Weinbaum and Wallace Spradling, an Army Reserve major sentenced to five years' imprisonment. Franklin V. Reno and Sidney Galloway pleaded guilty. Thomas B. Bennett was acquitted.
3. Marzani, "Thoughts Behind Bars," p. 54.
4. Andrews, *Washington Witch Hunt*, pp. 1–77.
5. Cook, *Nightmare Decade*, pp. 149, 153, 166; Anderson and May, *McCarthy: The Man, the Senator, the "Ism,"* p. 352.
6. Anderson and May, pp. 226, 412; Buckley and Bozell, pp. 273, 166.
7. Buckley and Bozell, p. 205; Anderson and May, p. 210; Bontecou, *The Federal Loyalty-Security Program*, pp. 49–50.
8. Paul Tillett, Interview with Val Lorwin, Sept. 15, 1962, Tillett Papers; Shils, *The Torment of Secrecy*, p. 167.
9. Tillett, "Social Costs" (unpublished), p. 36; McLeod, *American Political Democracy*, pp. 13–18.
10. Hans J. Morgenthau, "The Impact of the Loyalty-Security Measures on the State Department," p. 138.
11. James Rorty, "The Dossier of Wolf Ladejinsky"; Harry P. Cain, "Security of the Republic," p. 8; *The Times* (London), July 4, 1955.
12. Henry Wriston, chairman of the bipartisan committee appointed in 1954 to study the Foreign Service, reported in March 1954 that 7,752 candidates had taken the written examination since 1946; of those who passed, 1,168 underwent a security investigation at a cost of $204,225, and of these only 355 were adjudged loyal or "secure" enough to appoint. The statistics for these appointments reflected the graph of anxiety: 110 in 1947, 77 in 1948, 65 in 1949, 47 in 1950, 56 in 1951, and *none at all* from April 1952 until May 1954. Theodore H. White, *Fire in the Ashes*, p. 354; Morgenthau, p. 140; Rorty and Decter, *McCarthy and the Communists*, p. 105; Cook, *Nightmare Decade*, p. 551; Tillett, "Social Costs," pp. 38–43.
13. White, pp. 354 ff; Tillett, "Social Costs," pp. 56, 9; *NYT*, Jan. 17, 1954; McCarthy, *America's Retreat, passim*; H. S. Truman, pp. 423–34.
14. As General Douglas MacArthur put it on May 3, 1951, following his dismissal by Truman: "I believe that from our standpoint we practically lose the Pacific Ocean if we give up or lose Formosa."
15. John N. Thomas, *The Institute of Pacific Relations*, pp. 39, 46; White, p. 356.
16. O. Edmund Clubb, *The Witness and I, passim*; Latham, *The Communist Controversy*, p. 222 n.
17. Alsop, "Budenz," pp. 29–33; Buckley and Bozell, p. 88. After McCarthy's attack a petition had been circulated in that part of Virginia where the Han-

sons had a farm, asking them to leave the area, but apparently most neighbors refused to sign it. Cook, *Nightmare Decade*, p. 270.

18. Cook, p. 270; Brown, *Loyalty and Security*, p. 46; Packer, *Ex-Communist Witnesses*, p. 170; Emerson and Haber, *Political and Civil Rights*, p. 598; Latham, *The Communist Controversy*, p. 222 n; Thomas, p. 51.

19. Buckley and Bozell, p. 152; Bontecou, pp. 70–71; Latham, *The Communist Controversy*, p. 204; *NYHT*, Aug. 1, 1957; Clubb, p. 268. A luncheon was given in the State Department on Jan. 30, 1975 for Service, Clubb, Robert W. Barnett and others. Vincent had died.

20. McCarthy, *McCarthyism*, pp. 53–54; Buckley and Bozell, pp. 101, 105; Cook, *Nightmare Decade*, pp. 195–99, 202, 205, 243; Anderson and May, p. 193.

21. To take an example: in 1948 Milton I. Sacks was a junior employee of the State Department specializing in South-East Asian Communism. Soon after taking leave of absence to work on a thesis at Yale, he faced loyalty charges relating to prewar activity with the SWP. A hearing cleared him for loyalty but not for security. But when he was awarded a fellowship for travel to Vietnam, his particular field of interest, he could not obtain the necessary passport validation. Thus a potential expert on Vietnam remained a potential. Paul Tillett, Interview with Milton I. Sacks, Tillett Papers.

22. Dean Acheson, *A Democrat Looks at His Party*, pp. 126–32.

23. McCarthy, *McCarthyism*, p. 55; Latham, *The Communist Controversy*, p. 367; Buckley *et al.*, *The Committee . . .* , p. 73; Thomas, p. 24; Elizabeth Bentley, *Out of Bondage*, p. 159.

24. Thomas, p. 110; John K. Fairbank and James Peck, "An Exchange," pp. 56–57.

25. Thomas, pp. 148, 111, 110; Tillett, *Social Costs*, p. 94; Nathaniel Peffer, "IPR: A Probe in Perspective," p. 14.

26. Lattimore's books include *The Desert Road to Turkestan; The Mongols of Manchuria; Inner Asian Frontiers of China; Solution in Asia; The Situation in Asia*.

27. McCarthy, *McCarthyism*, p. 20; Packer, pp. 143, 140, 153–55, 142, 139, 135; Thomas, p. 72.

28. Sidney Hook, "Lattimore on the Moscow Trials," p. 16; Cook, *Nightmare Decade*, pp. 370–71; Anderson and May, p. 218; Owen Lattimore, *Ordeal by Slander*, pp. 27, 89, 210; Lattimore, *The Situation in Asia*, pp. 58, 63, 96–97.

29. Bontecou, *Freedom in the Balance*, p. 63; United States Court of Appeals for the District of Columbia Circuit, No. 11849, *U.S.A., Appellant, v. Owen Lattimore, Appellee, passim*; "The Lattimore Case: Congressional Investigations and the Constitution," *passim*; Iversen, *The Communists and the Schools*, p. 354.

30. Merson, *Private Diary*, p. 14; Rorty and Decter, p. 43; Latham, *The Communist Controversy*, p. 338; Merson, pp. 42, 101, 9, 26, 59.

31. Philip Horton, "Voices Within the Voice"; Merson, pp. 92–93, 143, 147, 46; Seymour M. Lipset and Earl Raab, *The Politics of Unreason*, p. 222; *NYT*, April 22, 1957.

32. Arthur Webb in *Daily Herald* (London), March 10, 1954; Brown, *Loyalty*

*and Security*, p. 30 n; Latham, *The Communist Controversy*, p. 344; *Rights*, Vol. 2, No. 6 (Feb. 1955), p. 4; Telford Taylor, *Grand Inquest*, p. 270.

## CHAPTER 16: THE UN, BRIEF REFUGE

1. *NYT*, Aug. 9, 19, 1949; Shirley Hazzard, *Defeat of an Ideal*, pp. 15, 28, 33.

2. On January 9, 1953, Canada's Secretary of State for External Affairs, Lester Pearson, pointed out that Canadians were appointed to the staff of the UN without the knowledge or consent of their government—a procedure that he termed "quite proper."

3. Brown, *Loyalty and Security*, p. 78; Hazzard, *Defeat of an Ideal*, pp. 23, 31; Buckley and Bozell, *McCarthy and His Enemies*, p. 33; Dallin, *Soviet Espionage*, p. 478; "What Grand Jury Found in UN," pp. 88–92.

4. American employees of the UN known to have been dismissed by Lie after taking the Fifth Amendment before the SISS or the grand jury were: Alfreda Abell, Frank D. Bancroft, Leo M. Drozdoff, Sidney Glassman, Joel Gordon, Jacob Grauman, Stanley Graze, Sonia Gruen, Jack S. Harris, Jerome A. Oberwager, Irving P. Schiller, Herbert Schimmel, Eugene Wallach, Benjamin Wermiel. Those known to have been dismissed between 1950 and 1953 for general loyalty-security reasons included: Benedict S. Alper, Jack Becker, Madeline Gaims, William F. Gilbert, Andrew Grad, Mary Jane Keeney, Abraham Nadel, William Pogorelsky, Theodor Rosebury, Adele Rotkin, Ursula Wasserman, Victor Yakhontoff. After "adverse comment" David Zablodowsky resigned. Other employees dismissed are listed in note 7, below.

5. Ruth Elizabeth Crawford, "I Have a Thing to Tell You," *passim*.

6. Belfrage, *American Inquisition*, pp. 22, 61; Bontecou, *Freedom in the Balance*, p. 75; *NYT*, June 10, 1949; UN: *Statement by the Staff Council on Personnel Policy* (mimeographed), pp. 3, 9, 11.

7. Those whose dismissals were sustained by the Tribunal were: Helen Pozner Kagen, Irving Kaplan, Alfred J. Van Tassel, Herman Zap and Marjorie L. Zap, all of whom had invoked the Fifth. Mary Middleton, Martin Rubin, Celia Saperstein and Sonya D. Sokolow had been dismissed on loyalty-security charges.

Among those reinstated by the Tribunal were Ruth Elizabeth Crawford, Dorothy H. Eldridge, Eda H. Glaser and Alexander H. Svenchansky, all of whom had taken the Fifth.

Frank Carter was awarded $12,000, plus $300 costs; Leon Elverson, $7,000, plus $300 costs; and Jane Reed, $10,000, plus $300 costs. All three had taken the Fifth.

8. Hazzard, p. 70; Shils, *The Torment of Secrecy*, p. 170.

9. *NYT*, April 11, 1954.

10. Edwin H. Fedder, "United States Loyalty Procedures and the Recruitment of UN Personnel," p. 706.

11. *NYHT*, Oct. 17, 1954; *NYT*, Sept. 21, Dec. 20, 1954.

12. The author was permitted access to the files of the late Gustavo Duran by courtesy of Mrs. Bonté Duran and her family, and of Mr. Geoffrey Ryan, in whose keeping they are held.

13. Duran Papers: *Interrogatory*, April 7, 1954, p. 37; Duran, *Affidavit*, Jan. 7, 1955, pp. 2–5.

14. *Ibid.*, pp. 7–8.

15. *Ibid.*, pp. 11–12, 14.

16. Duran Papers: G. Duran to Hiram C. Todd, May 28, 1954; Baldwin, Todd and Lefferts to Joseph McCarthy, March 17, 1950; *Statement* by G. Duran, March 15, 1950.

17. Duran Papers: S. Braden to H.R. Norweb, May 28, 1946; I. Prieto to G. Duran, April 3, 1946.

18. *New York World-Telegram*, March 14, 1950.

19. Duran Papers: Mrs. Bonté Duran to Styles Bridges, March 14, 1950.

20. Duran Papers: G. Duran to Edward P. Morgan, May 10, 1950; G. Duran, *Memorandum to Senator Tydings, passim*, and pp. 8–9.

21. Duran Papers: *Memorandum* from Duran's superior, Julia Henderson, to Trygve Lie, Sept. 5, 1951; Mrs. H.C. Ramsdell to G. Duran, June 18, 1953.

22. Duran Papers: *Memorandum* from G. Duran to Hiram C. Todd, Dec. 13, 1954; I. Prieto to DeWitt Marshall, March 3, 1954.

23. Duran Papers: *Memorandum for the File*, May 18, 1954; *Hearing* Before the International Organizations Employees Loyalty Board, pp. 6, 19–20; G. Duran, *Trial Memorandum*, n.d., pp. 3, 5, 7–8, 21, 23, 34, 42.

## CHAPTER 17: STATE AND CITY EMPLOYEES

1. Prendergast, "State Legislatures," p. 556; Scott Keyes, "Round Two of the Pechan Bill," p. 235; Clark Byse, "A Report on the Pennsylvania Loyalty Act," pp. 482–84.

2. For cases of victimization, see: Edmund E. Reutter, *The School Administrator and Subversive Activities*, p. 57; Stamler, pp. 62, 72; Jay G. Sykes, "The Investigated," p. 28; *NYT*, Oct. 6, 1953.

3. *Detroit News*, July 4, 1949; *Detroit Free Press*, July 3, 1949; *Detroit Times*, July 6, 1949; Yale Stuart Collection, WRL: box 1, circulars, late 1940s, box 2, loyalty oath controversy July-Aug. 1949, box 1, correspondence July-Dec. 1949.

4. DAMP: Harry S. Toy and others to Mayor, July 11, 1949, box 7, Loyalty Investigation Commission, 1950.

5. Robert J. Mowitz, "Michigan: State and Local Attacks on Subversion," pp. 206–7, 229; DAMP, box 6, Loyalty Committee, 1951; box 6, Loyalty Committee, 1955; box 6, Loyalty Committee, 1956; box 4, Loyalty Committee, 1956.

6. An equipment operator, two maintenance laborers, a construction helper, a civil-engineering associate, an electrical mechanic, a tree trimmer, a junior mechanical engineer, 2 nurses, 5 clerks, a librarian, a photographer.

7. Emerson and Haber, *Political and Civil Rights*, pp. 656–57; Saposs, *Communism in American Politics*, p. 98; *NYT*, Nov. 3, 1950, Jan. 28, 1948; Raymond M. Hilliard, "We Threw the Commies Out," pp. 20–21, 114–17.

8. Brown, *Loyalty and Security*, p. 102 n; *NYT*, May 12, 19, July 25, 1951; *NYHT*, Feb. 17, 1953.

9. *NYT*, Nov. 11, July 24, 1953, Nov. 18, 1954, Feb. 15, 16, 1956; *Rights*, Vol. 3, Nos. 8–9 (May, June 1956), p. 15.

10. *New York Post*, March 7, 1957; NYT, July 8, 1960; Brown, *Loyalty and Security*, p. 488.

## CHAPTER 18: HOW TO BREAK A UNION

1. D. A. Hulcy, "Management Sees Red," p. 534.
2. Max Kampelman, *The Communist Party vs. the CIO*, p. 186; Philip Taft, *Organized Labor in American History*, p. 613; William Paschell and Rose Theodore, "Anti-Communist Provisions in Union Constitutions," pp. 1097–1099.
3. NYT, Oct. 18, 1953; Doris Lissaman, "The Taft-Hartley Non-Communist Affidavit Provision," *passim*; John A. Morgan, Jr., "The Supreme Court and the Communist Affidavit," *passim*; Joe Hill, "Anti-Red or Anti-Union? The Boston Labor Probe," p. 33; NYT, March 27, Aug. 10, Oct. 22, 1955; on the Travis case see David J. Saposs, *Communism in American Unions*, p. 126; NYT, June 1, 1960.
4. *National Guardian*, April 28, 1958; Taft-Hartley Newsletter, Nat Ganley Collection, box 14/40, WRL.
5. Alfred Long Scanlan, "The Communist-Dominated Union Problem," p. 48; Laurent B. Frantz, "H-Bomb for Unions: The Butler Bill," pp. 442–44; NYT, Sept. 1, 1953; "The Communist Control Act of 1954," pp. 751–61; Paul Jacobs, "Communists in the Unions."
6. NYT, April 14, 26, 1950; Stamler, p. 70; Committee on Un-American Activities, U.S. House of Representatives, *Colonization of America's Basic Industries by the CPUSA*, Sept. 3, 1954, pp. 15–17; NYT, June 6, 1956, Oct. 17, 1953, May 17, 18, 1955.

## CHAPTER 19: HOW TO FIRE A WORKER

1. Among those workers who were dismissed after being mentioned unfavorably before committees were: Esther Tice, of the Formica Plant, Cincinnati, 1950; John Cherveny, American Metal Products Company, Detroit, 1952; Russell J. Kitto, Cadillac plant, Detroit, 1952; Herman Burt, Midland Steel Products Company, Detroit, 1952; Jean L. Asselin, Fisher Body Plant 1, G.M., Flint, 1954.

Among workers who had been subpoenaed and whom the companies fired on the *expectation* that they would take the Fifth were: James F. Wood and Van Frederick, of the Bechtel Corporation, San Francisco, 1953; Tom Ellis, of the Motor Carrier Central Freight Association, Detroit, 1954; William Evans, of the White Furniture Company, Hillsboro, North Carolina, 1956; James Zarichny, of Chevrolet Manufacturing Plant 5, Flint, 1954; Charles Schinn, of Fisher Body Plant 2, Flint, 1954. Court of Appeals, *John W. Nelson v. General Electric*, pp. 243a–244a; Stamler, p. 68; Sykes, "The Investigated," p. 27; Stamler, pp. 60–64.
2. NYHT, Dec. 8, 1954; Brown, p. 145 n; Bruno Stein, "Loyalty and Security Cases in Arbitration," p. 106; NYT, Dec. 11, 1954; Walter L. Daykin, "The Operation of the Taft-Hartley Act's Non-Communist Provisions," *passim*.

3. Jacob Moscou, Mervin Engle and Murray Borod, of the Chevrolet Manufacturing plant, Howard Falk and Martin Flint, of Buick, William Van De Does, of Fisher Body Plant 1; Stamler, pp. 70–71.

4. On the same pretext GM also fired Jacob Moscou, Murray Borod (both of Chevrolet), Martin Flint (Buick), and William Van De Does (Fisher Body Plant 1).

5. Some examples of "Fifth Amendment" discharges: Maurice K. Slater, of UE, who worked for the Ingersoll Rand Company, New Jersey; Herbert Slater and Frank Parker, both of the Worthington Corporation, Holyoke, Mass.; Vincent Pacile and James Annaccone, of Westinghouse Electric, New York; Stanley Michalowi, of Pratt and Whitney Company, New Haven.

6. Stein, p. 106; Tillett Papers: Singer Manufacturing Co., Statement, Oct. 9, 1956.

7. Benjamin Fino, Joseph P. Henderson, Levi Williamson, William H. Wood, Aaron Ostrofsky, Milton Seif, Irving Spector.

8. Julian Chazin, Everett S. Jones, Sam Brook, Miroslaw Zelman, Edward A. Wolkenstein.

9. The Detroit workers were: Van A. Brooks, of the Chrysler Jefferson plant; Leon England, of the Kercheval plant; George Burt, of Midland Steel Products; and Fred Fische, of the GM Transmission Division.

10. Mary Englestein, Interview; NYT, Aug. 17, 1, 1950; "Communists on the Job," p. 47; ACLU News, Vol. 15, No. 8, Aug. 1950; Open Forum, Aug. 5, 1950; Stamler, p. 62; NYT, Feb. 28, 29, 1952; Court of Appeals, Nelson, pp. 492a, 469a–472a; Stamler, pp. 70–71; NYT, May 15, 1954; Donner, The Un-Americans, p. 41.

11. Brown, Loyalty and Security, p. 488; Harry Fleischman, Joyce L. Kornbluh and Benjamin D. Segal, Security, Civil Liberties and Unions, p. 21, provides statistics for the period July 1953–March 1955.

12. Yarmolinsky, Case Studies, p. 280; Cook, Nightmare Decade, pp. 562–64, 568; Benjamin D. Segal and Joyce L. Kornbluh, "The Insecurities of our Security Program," p. 16; Fleischman et al., p. 28; Charles Lam Markmann, The Noblest Cry, p. 185.

13. R. S. Brown, Loyalty and Security, p. 244; John Warner, "Labor Unions and 'Security Risks,' " p. 16; "The Role of Employer Practices," p. 257; Segal and Kornbluh, p. 16.

14. Tillett Papers: Memo from "Dr. X" (name supplied) to Rowland Watts, of the ACLU, June 30, 1960.

15. This case is discussed in detail in Cook, Nightmare Decade, pp. 554–56, from which the present account is derived.

16. Arbitrators took this view in the Bell Aircraft (1951), Rudolph Wurlitzer Company (1952), Liquid Carbonic Corporation (1954), Wisconsin Telephone Company (1956), and M & M Restaurants (1957) cases. The opposite view was taken by arbitrators in three cases (1947, 1954 and 1955).

17. Bontecou, Freedom in the Balance, pp. 148–49; Brown, Loyalty and Security, p. 488; "Loyalty and Private Employment," p. 966; Stein, p. 99; Walter L. Daykin, "The Communist Employee: What Grounds for Discharge?," pp. 65–66; Rose Chernin, Interview.

18. "Loyalty and Private Employment," pp. 959–61; Stein, p. 101; Corliss Lamont, "Conform or Lose Your Job," p. 406.

19. Francis Downing, "Substitute for Debate"; Mayer, "How the Loyalty-Security Program Affects Private Employment," p. 123; John C. Cort, "The Hearn's Strike"; Joe Hill, "Anti-Red or Anti-Union?" p. 33.

20. Saposs, *Communism in American Unions*, pp. 227–30; Brown, *Loyalty and Security*, p. 180; Alan F. Westin, "Anti-Communism and the Corporations," p. 486; Brown, *Loyalty and Security*, pp. 140, 173; Fleischman *et al.*, p. 35.

21. *NYT*, Dec. 23, 1953; *Detroit News*, Feb. 7, 1954; Allan, *Toy Must Go!*, p. 6.

22. "Loyalty and Private Employment," p. 995; "Role of Employer Practices," p. 247; Myron Brenton, *The Privacy Invaders*, pp. 187–98.

23. Frank Donner, Interview; H. Matusow, *False Witness*, p. 77; Stein, p. 113; "Loyalty and Private Employment," pp. 976, 965.

24. *Rights*, Vol. 2, No. 6 (Feb. 1955), p. 14; Stein, p. 97.

25. *Rights*, Vol. 6, No. 1 (Sept. 1958), p. 11; *ACLU News*, Vol. 21, No. 11 (Nov. 1956); Stamler, pp. 73–74; *Rights*, Vol. 4, Nos. 9, 10 (Aug., Sept. 1957), p. 9; Yarmolinsky, p. 222.

26. Yarmolinsky, p. 222; UE Files, Allan R. Rosenberg to David Scribner, April 23, 1951.

### CHAPTER 20: UNITED ELECTRICAL WORKERS

1. Robert Z. Lewis, Interview; Kampelman, *The Communist Party vs. the CIO*, p. 132; David Oshinsky, "The CIO and the Communists," p. 136; D. A. Shannon, *Decline of American Communism*, p. 215.

2. James J. Matles and James Higgins, *Them and Us*, pp. 200–202; Oshinsky, pp. 138–39; Frank Donner, Interview; Delco Local 755 IUE-CIO *News*, Feb. 1950, Donner Files, p. 4.

3. Mary Englestein, Interview; Matles and Higgins, pp. 193–94.

4. Scanlan, "The Communist-Dominated Union Problem," p. 466; Carey's article is reprinted in *The Communist Problem in America*, pp. 361–62; *NYT*, Dec. 11, 1953; UE Files; Joe Hill, "Anti-Red or Anti-Union?" p. 32; Matles and Higgins, p. 231.

5. Saposs, *Communism in American Unions*, p. 235; Arthur Eggleston, "Labor and Civil Liberties," p. 650; Matles and Higgins, pp. 198, 255.

6. UE Files, Frank Carner and Herb Lewin; UE Files, Irving R. M. Panzer, Memo, Sept. 1948; UE Files, IERB, Hearing, Sept. 1, 1948; UE Files, J.M.

7. UE Files, Case of E.L.; UE Files, Memo from Bruce Waybur to Russ Nixon, April 17, 1950; UE Files, Memo by Frank Cohen, March 13, 1951; UE Files, J. Tenney Mason, chairman IERB, Letter to F.P., April 27, 1951.

8. UE Files, Memo, March 12, 1948; UE Files, Panzer, Memo, Sept. 1948.

9. UE Files; Yarmolinsky, *Case Studies*, p. 244.

10. UE Files, Memo from Bruce Waybur to Russ Nixon.

11. UE Files.

12. UE Files, Statement by Opal V. Cline, Sept. 30, 1948; UE Files, Opal Cline to editor of *Evansville Courier*, n.d.; UE Files, William Sentner to Lt. Col. E. H. Farr, Oct. 5, 1948; UE Files, Memo from Bruce Waybur.

13. UE Files, Helen A. Sage, Memo; UE Files, Marshall Perlin to Basil Pollitt, Nov. 1949.

14. UE Files, Memo from Bruce Waybur; Harry Fleischman, Joyce L. Kornbluh and Benjamin D. Segal, *Security, Civil Liberties and Unions*, pp. 7–10.

15. UE Files, John T. Gojak to David Scribner, Aug. 8, 1952, and David Scribner to John T. Gojak, n.d.; UE Files, LeRoy Williams to C. J. VanDerhaegen, Nov. 22, 1954, and William A. Ives to C. J. VanDerhaegen, Jan. 23, 1954.

16. Matles and Higgins, p. 202; Stamler, p. 111; Donner, *The Un-Americans*, p. 65.

17. U.S. Court of Appeals, *John W. Nelson*, pp. 378a–379a, 382a, 374a, 375a; *NYT*, Dec. 10, 1953, March 4, 1954.

18. Nelson, *The 13th Juror*, pp. 41a–46a, 262a, 18a, 621a–625a.

19. John Nelson, of Erie, and Alexander Staber, suspended December 11, 1953, discharged March 11, 1954; Victor Bolys, Alexander Gregory and Theodore Pappas, of Lynn, suspended January 22, 1954, discharged April 22; Robert F. Goodwin, Henry C. Archdeacon, Nathaniel Mills, Donald H. Morrill and Witulad Piekarski, all of Lynn, all suspended December 11, 1953, discharged March 11, 1954; Gordon Belgrave, Dewey F. Brashear, Emmanuel Fernandez, Sidney Friedlander, Joseph Gebhardt, Robert Northrop and Arthur Lee Owens, all of Schenectady, all suspended February 26, 1954, discharged May 27; Louis Passikoff, of Schenectady, suspended August 17, 1954, discharged November 15; James I. Jones, Jr., and Edwin R. Wagner, of Syracuse, suspended April 4, 1954, discharged July 12; Joseph O. Mattson, Waino S. Nisula and Waino E. Suokko, all of Fitchburg, suspended August 18, 1954, discharged November 16; Lewis Lubka, of Louisville, suspended October 15, 1954.

20. Gordon Belgrave, thirty-seven, had worked for GE for seventeen years and was earning $5,158 when dismissed; Dewey F. Brashear, forty-four, had thirteen years' service with the company and was earning $3,868; Robert Northrop, thirty-three, had worked for GE for four years and was earning $4,781; Sidney Friedlander, fifty, had worked for thirteen years with GE and was earning $4,659; Emmanuel Fernandez, thirty-seven, was earning $4,492 and had also worked for GE for thirteen years.

21. U.S.A.: Before the National Labor Relations Board, Case No. 5-RC-2929, In the Matter of Westinghouse Electric Corporation, Air Arm Division, Employer, and United Electrical, Radio and Machine Workers of America (UE), Petitioner:

(1) Petitioner's Exceptions to Regional Director's Report on Objections (signed by Frank J. Donner and Robert Z. Lewis, attorneys for Petitioner).

(2) Affidavit signed by Clarence E. Wallace, July 27, 1960.

22. Matles and Higgins, p. 225.

23. Frank Donner to the author, Sept. 1976.

CHAPTER 21: ON THE WATERFRONT

1. Rogge, *Our Vanishing Civil Liberties*, pp. 125–31, 140–49, 42–43; *NYHT*, Dec. 25, 1947. These officers had developed an obsession not only about the

Book Find Club but also about Feuchtwanger, a liberal German novelist who had taken refuge in the United States.

2. *NYT*, Dec. 28, Sept. 6, 1950; *NYHT*, Sept. 28, 1950; Ralph S. Brown, Jr., and John D. Fassett, "Security Tests for Maritime Workers," p. 1207.

3. *NYT*, July 31, Aug. 20, 1950; *NYHT*, Aug. 21, 1950; Brown and Fassett, p. 1170; Starobin, *American Communism in Crisis*, p. 300.

4. *ACLU News*, Vol. 16, No. 4 (April 1951); Brown and Fassett, p. 118.

5. Besig Files, Case of James D. Tucker.

6. Besig Files, Case of James L. Kendall.

7. Besig Files, Case of Frank C. Drum; for other cases, see also *ACLU News*, Vol. 20, No. 7 (July 1955); *NYT*, Aug. 19, 1955; *Rights*, Vol. 2, No. 10 (July 1955), p. 3.

8. Tillett Papers, Norval Welch to Herbert Aptheker, Jan. 17, 1964; see also *ACLU News*, Vol. 18, No. 12 (Dec. 1953), Vol. 19, No. 2 (Feb. 1954).

9. Walter Millis, *Individual Freedom and the Common Defense*, p. 53; Brown, *Loyalty and Security*, p. 73.

10. Early in 1953 the Coast Guard announced that it had completed the screening of 90 percent of the total work force: 250,000 waterfront men and 336,000 seamen. Of the waterfront men, 1,481 had been initially denied clearance; of these, 1,072 appealed to local boards; 547 were cleared. Eighty-two persisted and appealed to the National Board; nineteen were cleared. In the case of fifty-six favorable recommendations by local boards, the Coast Guard commandant overruled. Thus, about 971 waterfront men lost their jobs by the end of 1952—0.38 percent.

Among the seamen, 2,918 were initially denied clearance; 1,603 appealed to local boards; 887 were cleared. Of the remainder, 387 appealed to the National Board; 199 were cleared. In eleven cases, favorable recommendations by the local board were overruled by the Coast Guard commandant. Thus, about 1,821 seamen lost their jobs by the end of 1952—0.54 percent.

11. Brown, pp. 179, 485; Brown and Fassett, "Security Tests for Maritime Workers," pp. 1185–86; *ACLU News*, Vol. 23, No. 4 (April 1958).

CHAPTER 22: PURGE OF THE "REDUCATORS"

1. Dorothy Kahn, "Abe Goff, Our Chief Censor," p. 7. At least 215,000 pieces of mail were opened during an illegal CIA project that lasted from 1953 to 1973. The CIA put into its computers 1,500,000 names derived from its mail-opening project, *The Times* (London), August 20, 1977.

2. Robert M. MacIver, *Academic Freedom in Our Time, passim;* David Riesman, *Constraint and Variety in American Education, passim.*

3. George R. Stewart, *The Year of the Oath*, p. 97; *NYT*, March 20, 1953.

4. Paul F. Lazarsfeld and Wagner Thielens, *The Academic Mind*, p. 70.

5. Iversen, *The Communists and the Schools*, p. 165; Daniel Bell, "Interpretations of American Politics," p. 22.

6. Including Professor Don West, of Oglethorpe College; Dr. Clarence R. Athearn, of Lycoming College, Pennsylvania; Professor Luther K. McNair, Dean of Lydon State Teachers College, Vermont; and three instructors at the University of Miami, Leonard Cohen, Charles C. Davis and Daniel D. Ash-

kenes. Professor Clyde Miller, of Columbia, was dropped after he was listed as a member of the PP's national committee. The University of Georgia fired Professor James Barfoot when he emerged as a PP gubernatorial candidate. At the University of New Hampshire, Professor John E. Rideout was forced to resign when he became state chairman of the PP. Albert Kahn, *High Treason*, p. 239; Dalton Trumbo, *The Time of the Toad*, p. 53; Schmidt, *Henry A. Wallace*, p. 87.

7. "Academic Freedom and Tenure: Evansville College," *passim*.

8. Carey McWilliams, *Witch Hunt*, p. 217.

9. This account of events at the University of Washington draws heavily on Countryman, *Un-American Activities in the State of Washington*. See also McWilliams, *Witch Hunt, passim*.

10. Rader, *False Witness*, pp. 109–10; *American Scholar*, Vol. 18 (1949), p. 33; Countryman, *Un-American Activities*, p. 232; Tillett, *Social Costs* . . . , p. 76.

11. Raymond B. Allen, "Communists Should Not Teach in American Colleges," p. 438.

12. *NYHT*, April 9, 1949; Iversen, pp. 170, 389.

13. "It Also Happened at Harvard," pp. 368–70, 366; Tillett Papers, Universities, Leon J. Kamin.

14. "It Also Happened," pp. 365–66; *NYT*, Oct. 7, 1957; Telford Taylor, *Grand Inquest*, p. 2; Wendell Furry, Interview; Sigmund Diamond, "Veritas at Harvard," *NYRB*, April 28, 1977, pp. 13–17; letters from McGeorge Bundy and Sigmund Diamond, *NYRB*, May 26, 1977; letters from Seymour Martin Lipset and Sigmund Diamond, *NYRB*, June 9, 1977; letters from Robert N. Bellah and McGeorge Bundy, *NYRB*, July 14, 1977.

15. In the course of his survey, Lazarsfeld found that of twenty-five sample instances involving CP membership or resort to the Fifth, 64 percent resulted in dismissal or forced resignation. In July 1953 Robert M. Hallett examined the cases of forty-five professors and students who since September 8, 1952, had taken the Fifth before the SISS or HCUA; 14 had been dismissed, 4 had resigned, 4 had been suspended, 3 were retained, 4 were special cases, 14 were still pending. In fact, those who invoked the amendment and yet ultimately retained their positions, like Professor Abe Gelbart of Syracuse University, and Professor Marcus Singer of Cornell, constituted a fortunate but very small minority, which included Irvin Isenberg, a physicist, and Sidney J. Socolar, a chemistry instructor, both of the University of Chicago, and Professor Robert Metcalf of Antioch College. Brown, *Loyalty and Security*, pp. 126–27; *NYT*, April 22, July 29, 1953; Tillett Papers, Universities, Metcalf, also Singer; Iversen, p. 353.

16. "It Did Happen at Rutgers," pp. 154–78; *NYT*, April 1, 1953.

17. Tillett Papers, Universities, Burgum; Budenz, *Techniques of Communism*, p. 168; Emerson and Haber, *Political and Civil Rights*, p. 1093.

18. Two Ohio State University employees, George D. Pappas and Harston A. Hamlin, lost their jobs after refusing to cooperate with the Ohio Un-American Activities Commission in May 1952. John Reynolds, assistant professor of sociology (with tenure) at the University of Florida, took the Fifth before HCUA, then abandoned hope and resigned after the local chapter of the

AAUP voted by 58 to 53 not to support his case. In September 1953 Rensselaer College dismissed Dr. Arthur Levy, an assistant professor, after he had declined to tell HCUA whether he had belonged to a Communist student group at Yale. Warren P. Hill, A *Critique* . . . , p. 446.

19. "Academic Freedom and Tenure: Three Reports."

20. Iversen, p. 343; "Academic Freedom: Some Recent Instances," p. 82.

21. Harold Taylor, "The Dismissal of Fifth Amendment Professors," pp. 83–84; *NYT*, Aug. 30, Nov. 20, 1953; Tillett Papers, Universities, Dunham; Emerson and Haber, p. 1094; *NYT*, Aug. 27, 1954; Tillett Papers, Universities, Nickerson.

22. Horace Chandler Davis actually went to prison in 1960 after the Supreme Court had refused to review his sentence of six months' imprisonment and a $250 fine.

23. "Academic Freedom and Tenure: Fisk University"; "Academic Freedom: Some Recent Instances," p. 88.

24. Further Fifth Amendment casualties: Dr. Gerald Harrison, a mathematician, and Dr. Irving Stein, a physicist, both of Wayne State University; Stanley William Moore of Reed College; Laurent R. LaVallee of Dickinson College; John V. Myers of Campbell College, N.C.; and Richard W. Reichard, an associate professor of history at George Washington University, dismissed in December 1959 despite support from both the ACLU and the AAUP. His was apparently a stand of pure principle: "I could have answered all the questions asked me by those Congressmen in the negative." Tillett Papers, Universities, Reichard.

25. Three cases, representative of many others: William W. Hinchley, a teacher in a Montgomery County, Maine, high school was dismissed under the Ober Act after taking the Fifth before HCUA in 1950; Mrs. Elinor Maki, an art teacher, was suspended then fired by the Detroit Board of Education after invoking the Fifth before HCUA; in the same year, 1953, Miss Elizabeth Guarnaccia, a Somerville, Massachusetts, high-school teacher, was suspended without pay and subsequently dismissed, after refusing to tell the SISS whether she had once been in the CP. Prendergast, "Maryland," p. 169; *NYT*, April 1, 1953.

26. *NYHT*, July 31, 1954; Iversen, p. 329.

27. Sadie T. Atkinson, Thomas Deason, William G. Solar, Angela Intille.

28. Mrs. Caroline K. Perloff, Mrs. Eleanor Fleet, Samuel Drasin, Mrs. Sofie Elfont.

29. *NYT*, May 4, 1954; Byse, "Report," pp. 482–83; Tillett Papers, Bessie K. Stensky to Paul Tillett, July 10, 1964.

30. Jay Sykes, "Post-McCarthy Delusions of Liberty," p. 397; Sykes, "The Investigated," p. 29. Margaret Gustafson, of Bremerton, Washington, was fired in 1953, the same day she took the Fifth.

31. This account is drawn mainly from William Manchester, "The Case of Luella Mundel"; see also "Academic Freedom Survey."

32. Tillett Papers, Universities, Wiggins; *ibid*, Tandy; *National Review*, Vol. 1, No. 10 (Jan. 25, 1956), pp. 13–15.

33. See George R. Stewart, *The Year of the Oath*, *passim*; Jean Begeman, "The California Loyalty Oath," *passim*.

34. *NYT*, Sept. 22, 1950.

35. John Caughey, "A University in Jeopardy," pp. 213–23.

36. *NYT*, March 11, June 12, 1951; *Open Forum*, Sept. 30, 1950; Barth, *Loyalty*, p. xxix; John Caughey, Interview.

37. *ACLU News*, Vol. 19, No. 5 (May 1954), No. 8 (Aug. 1954); see also Walter Gerstel, "G-Men on the Campus," *passim*.

38. Examples of legislative committee casualties: Thomas M. McGrath, of Los Angeles State College, was not rehired (no hearing granted) after he had taken the Fifth before HCUA; he later described the vice-president of the college as the local representative of the FBI. At the University of Southern California, Andries Deinum and Janet Stevenson, a cinema instructor and a lecturer in drama respectively, lost their jobs as a result of refusing to answer political questions. Tillett Papers, Universities, McGrath.

Among schoolteachers, a few examples: in 1954 John and Inez Schnigten, of Richmond, were dismissed under the Dilworth Act after taking the First and Fifth before the Burns Committee; Charlotte Appel, of Los Angeles, suffered the same fate for the same offense, as did Jack Armand Chassen, also of Los Angeles, and Jean Wilkinson, whose husband Frank had been fired by the Los Angeles Housing Authority for refusing to testify before the same Committee. In 1957 the Dixie School District at San Rafael voted 3 to 2 to dismiss Edward Hanchett, after he had refused to tell HCUA whether he had once been in the CP. *ACLU News*, Vol. 19, No. 7 (July 1954), Vol. 22, No. 10 (Nov. 1957); Tillett Papers, Public Schools.

39. The seven fired at SF State College were: Professor Albert Eason Monroe, chairman of the language arts division, and later executive director of the Southern California ACLU; Dr. Leonard Peckman, assistant professor of social science; Dr. Jack Patten, instructor; Herbert Bisno, instructor; Miss Phiz Mezey and Frank A. Rowe, both assistants. The poet and teacher John Beecher lost his job at San Francisco State University in 1950 because he refused to sign the Levering Act oath. Although the oath was declared unconstitutional in 1967 by the California Supreme Court, his application for reinstatement was not granted until 1977, *Authors Guild Bulletin*, June–August, 1977.

40. Edward L. Barrett, Jr., *The Tenney Committee*, p. 166; *NYT*, Jan. 8, 1954; Reutter, *The School Administrator*, p. 44.

41. *NYT*, March 20, Dec. 17, 1953; John Caughey, *In Clear and Present Danger*, p. 154; Donner, *The Un-Americans*, pp. 195–200.

42. *NYT*, April 4, 1953; H. H. Wilson, Interview; Robert E. Cushman, *Civil Liberties in the United States*, p. 83; Reutter, p. 72; Burlingame, *The Sixth Column*, p. 102.

43. See *WIN*, Vol. 8, Nos. 4 and 5 (March 1972), pp. 48, 36, 37, 71, 72, 38–39.

44. DAMP, box 6, Loyalty Committee, 1955; William O. Douglas, *America Challenged*, p. 13.

45. *NYHT*, Dec. 24, 1947; "The Danger Signals," *Time*, Vol. 61, No. 15 (April 13, 1953), p. 86.

46. Sponsored by the Fund for the Republic. Interviews conducted by Elmo Roper and Associates and by the NORC of the University of Chicago.

CHAPTER 23: NEW YORK TEACHERS

1. Lawrence H. Chamberlain, *Loyalty and Legislative Action*, pp. 67, 125, 132, 147–48; Dodd, *School of Darkness*, p. 130; Nathan Glazer, *The Social Basis of American Communism*, p. 227.

2. Dodd, pp. 128–29; the case of Morris U. Schappes and his later career is documented in Tillett Papers, Public Schools, Schappes.

3. Celia L. Zitron, *The New York City Teachers Union, 1916–1964*, p. 220; NYT, Sept. 28, 1948; Zitron, "Teachers Under Fire," p. 29.

4. Zitron, *Teachers Union*, pp. 206–10; Chamberlain, p. 197; Judith Crist, "A Blow for Freedom." Catholic members of the Board included Andrew G. Clausen, Jr., president, George A. Timone (Brooklyn), Anthony Campagna (Bronx), Harold C. Dean and Vito F. Lanza (both of Queens). Maximilian Moss, although Jewish, was a member of the largest Catholic law firm in Brooklyn. Charles Silver, who succeeded him on the Board, was also Jewish, but a close friend of Cardinal Spellman. Harold I. Cammer to the author, July 26, 1976.

5. The other four were: Louis Jaffee, David L. Friedman, Abraham Feingold and Mark Friedlander.

6. Alice Citron, "Teachers in Battle," pp. 64–66; NYT, Sept. 19, 1950; Harold I. Cammer, Interview.

7. Of whom the others were Hyman Koppelman of Prospect Heights High School (Spanish), Mrs. Dorothy Rand, who fostered the study of Negro history in Harlem grade schools, Samuel Wallach, former president of the TU, Mildred Flacks of PS 35, Brooklyn, and Julius Lemansky and Dorothy Bloch of George Washington Vocational High School (English).

8. Zitron, *Teachers Union*, p. 233; NYT, May 13, 1951; Zitron, "Teachers Under Fire," pp. 28–34; *Conformists, Informers or Free Teachers*, pp. 3–7, 16, 26, 27.

9. NYT, Feb. 14, 1953, Sept. 24, 1952.

10. Harold I. Cammer, Interview; Zitron, "Teachers Under Fire," p. 34; Yaffa Schlesinger to the author, July 19, 1974.

11. H. Matusow, *False Witness*, p. 90; *New York Teachers News*, Vol. 15, No. 23 (March 5, 1955); NYT, Oct. 31, 1955; Harold I. Cammer, Interview.

12. Others included Leo Auerbach, Benjamin H. Baronofsky, Henry Danielowitz, and Charles Eckstat. Dismissed were: William Frauenglass, who received a letter from Einstein supporting his refusal to answer political questions; Harold Blau; Robert Cohen; David Flacks (whose wife, Mildred, as we have seen, had already been dismissed); Julius G. Jacobs; and Florence Jacobs. NYT, Oct. 4, Nov. 27, 1952, June 19, 1953.

13. Including Henry F. Mins, Louis Cohen, Mrs. Mary I. Daniman, Meyer Case, Louis Spindell, Tima Ludins. Mrs. Diana Wolman was dismissed in January 1954 after taking the Fifth before the McCarthy Subcommittee during the Fort Monmouth investigation.

All the above teachers were employed in high schools and grade schools in Brooklyn and the Bronx, most notably the Brooklyn Technical High School, the Franklin Lane High School, the Abraham Lincoln High School and the Jefferson High School.

14. Zitron, *Teachers Union*, p. 244; *NYT*, April 10, 1953; Harold I. Cammer, Interview; *NYHT*, Jan. 7, 1954. To sum up: before the visit of the SISS to New York in September 1952, 24 teachers had been dismissed, and a further 49 had resigned or retired while under investigation. As of September 15, 1953, 31 had been dismissed, 36 had resigned and 28 had retired when called for questioning. *Fourteen* had resigned or retired while under investigation. Early in January 1954 it was reported that 156 had been "removed" since 1950, 84 of them during the year ending November 30, 1953, and that a further 189 investigations were pending. Iversen, *The Communists and the Schools*, p. 267; *NYT*, Sept. 15, 1953; *NYHT*, Jan. 7, 1954.

15. *New York Teachers News*, Vol. 15, No. 23 (March 5, 1955); *NYT*, Sept. 10, 1955, Aug. 9, 1956, Nov. 17, Dec. 10, 1959, April 23, 1960.

16. *NYT*, Dec. 1, 1971; see also Tillett Papers, Public Schools, L. Relin, E. Jackson.

17. *Rights*, Vol. 4, No. 2 (Nov. 1956), p. 13; Chamberlain, pp. 168–69; *NYHT*, Nov. 21, 1947.

18. *ACLU News*, Vol, 15, No. 7 (July 1950); H. Matusow, *False Witness*, pp. 95–96; Lawrence D. Weiner to Mr. Matt, July 4, 1952, Matusow Papers; *NYT*, Feb. 15, 1955.

19. Victims included Bernard F. Riess, associate professor of psychology at Hunter College, who took the Fifth, was suspended and appealed to the local chapter of the AAUP in vain; Vera Shalakman of Queens College; Joseph Bressler of Brooklyn College; and Oscar H. Shaftel, professor of English at Queens, who received AAUP support. Two instructors at Brooklyn College, Elton T. Gustafson and Murray Young, were dismissed. Tillett Papers, Universities, Riess; *NYHT*, March 4, 1953.

20. Sidney Hook, *Common Sense and the Fifth Amendment*, p. 20; *NYT*, July 1, Sept. 29, March 17, Oct. 19, 1953; *Rights*, Vol. 2 (Oct. 1954), p. 13.

21. Dudley D. Straus, of Queens, was dismissed for refusing to answer the Board's interrogatory. Dr. Warren B. Austin, of CCNY, was suspended then dismissed on a charge of falsely denying past membership of the CP.

22. *NYT*, June 23, 25, July 24, 1959; May 22, 1957; March 18, 1958.

CHAPTER 24: NEWSPAPERMEN AND LIBRARIANS

1. Pearson, *Diaries*, p. 173; *NYT*, Feb. 28, 1952; Barth, *Government by Investigation*, p. 125; Brown, *Loyalty and Security*, p. 148.

2. Brown, pp. 174 n, 150, 146, Stein, "Loyalty and Security Cases," p. 108; "Loyalty and Private Employment," p. 977.

3. *NYT*, Aug. 7, 1954; *Rights*, Vol. 3, No. 1 (Sept. 1955), p. 9; *NYHT*, June 30, 1955; *USNWR*, Vol. 39 (July 8, 1955), p. 71.

4. James Aronson, *The Press and the Cold War*, p. 141; Stamler, p. 74.

5. *NYT*, July 22, 1955, June 20, 1956; *I. F. Stone's Weekly*, Vol. 3, No. 46 (Dec. 5, 1955); Alden Whitman, Interview: M. L. Barnet, "Probers and the Press," p. 554.

6. Mayer, "How the Loyalty-Security Program Affects . . . ," p. 128; Barnet, p. 554; Aronson, p. 137; James Wechsler, *Reflections of an Angry Middle-Aged Editor*, p. 134; Stein, p. 107; Alden Whitman, Interview.

7. *The First Freedom*, pp. 303–4; *ACLU News*, Vol. 19, No. 12 (Dec. 1954), Vol. 24, No. 10 (Oct. 1959); *NYHT*, Nov. 6, 1955; *NYT*, Jan. 25, 1957.

CHAPTER 25: SCIENCE AND SANITY

1. James S. Allen, *Atomic Imperialism*, pp. 116, 118, 133; Gellhorn, *Security, Loyalty and Science*, pp. 98–99, 102–3.
2. In September 1948 the Federation of American Scientists' Committee on Secrecy and Clearance reported that it had learned of fifty-six cases of loyalty-security difficulties during the previous ten months and concluded that these probably represented only "a small fraction of the total number of cases." In January 1948 Leonard Engel reported that "hundreds" of federal research posts stood vacant because scientists recoiled from the new climate of suspicion. "Some Individual Cases of Clearance Procedures," p. 281; Leonard Engel, "Fear in Our Laboratories," *passim*.
3. "Some Individual Cases," p. 281; Gellhorn, *Security, Loyalty and Science*, pp. 98–99, 151; Markmann, *The Noblest Cry*, p. 185.
4. "Some Individual Cases," pp. 282–83.
5. Engel, "Fear"; Barth, *Loyalty of Free Men*, p. 122; *ACLU News*, Vol. 19, No. 9 (Sept. 1954).
6. "Some Individual Cases," pp. 152–53, 158; *NYT*, Oct. 27, 1955.
7. Shils, *Torment*, p. 183; Stern, *The Oppenheimer Case*, p. 467. The extent of the devastation was summed up by Henry Mayer in 1955: "The number of scientists, engineers and production workers disqualified for security reasons is still unknown, but it is certainly much larger than the four thousand who have been dismissed from government jobs as 'security risks.' Today, in the Eastern region alone, there are more than 1100 such cases before security boards." (Note that Mayer includes "production workers"; there is no suggestion that four thousand scientists and engineers had been dismissed.) Mayer, "How the Loyalty-Security Program Affects . . . ," p. 119.
8. Tillett, "Social Costs" (unpublished), p. 60; Chafee, *The Blessings of Liberty*, p. 26; Gellhorn, *Security, Loyalty and Science*, pp. 56, 112; *NYT*, Dec. 10, 1954, Oct. 18, 1948; Eugene Rabinowitch, "The 'Cleansing' of AEC Fellowships"; Shils, *The Torment of Secrecy*, p. 188; *CSM*, Jan. 1, 1955, Dec. 30, 1953; Mather, "Scientists in the Doghouse," p. 639.
9. Sumner T. Pike, "Witch-Hunting Then and Now," pp. 93–94; Nuel Pharr Davis, *Lawrence and Oppenheimer*, p. 286 n. An illustration of the impact of the fear on scientists: before E.O. 9835 the American-Soviet Medical Society had about six hundred members in Washington, D.C. Two years after the executive order, there were only thirty. Subscribers in Bethesda, Maryland, to the *American Review of Soviet Medicine* fell from 150 to none. The *Review* ceased publication.
10. Shirley A. Star, "Loyalty Investigations—A Poll of Atomic Scientists," p. 218; Leo Szilard, "The AEC Fellowships"; Gellhorn, *Security, Loyalty and Science*, p. 199.
11. "Some Individual Cases," pp. 282–83; Engel, "Fear in Our Laboratories."
12. Emerson and Helfeld, "Loyalty Among Government Employees," pp. 72–73; Richard B. Gehman, "Oak Ridge Witch Hunt," p. 14; *NYHT*, May 28,

1948; Gellhorn, *Security, Loyalty and Science*, p. 220. For AEC dismissals, see *NYT*, March 30, 1952 (up to Dec. 1951, 425 were denied clearance, while 1,800 either resigned, were transferred or were terminated); see also Lewis Strauss, *Men and Decisions*, p. 259 (according to whom 3,910 were denied clearance, were dismissed or resigned during the AEC's first seven years); see also Brown, *Loyalty and Security*, pp. 63, 488 (according to whom 494 were dismissed or denied clearance up to March 1955).

13. Whitehead, *The FBI Story*, p. 302; Burlingame, *The Sixth Column*, p. 106; *NYT*, May 11, 1958.

14. Dallin, *Soviet Espionage*, p. 470; Countryman, *Un-American Activities*, pp. 94-95; *NYHT*, Oct. 16, 1952; Carr, *The House Committee*, pp. 175-79.

15. MacIver, *Academic Freedom in Our Time*, pp. 290-94; McWilliams, "Hawkins," p. 228; Tillett Papers, Universities, Frank Oppenheimer.

16. Tillett Papers, Universities, G. R. Lomanitz; Stern, pp. 437-38; Iversen, *Communists and the Schools*, p. 304; James Allen, p. 116; *NYT*, May 20, 1953.

17. Stern, pp. 123, 439; *NYT*, Aug. 30, 1950; Stamler, p. 65.

18. *NYHT*, Sept. 6, 1952; E. U. Condon, "An Appeal to Reason," pp. 357-60; *Rights*, Vol. 1, No. 8 (March 1954), p. 9.

19. *NYT*, Sept. 6, 1952; *NYHT*, Sept 6, 1952; *CSM*, Dec. 30, 1953; *Rights*, Vol. 1 No. 8 (March 1954), p. 9; Drew Pearson in *Nippon Times*, Nov. 7, 1954; *NYT*, Dec. 29, 1954; *NYT*, Sept. 2, 1951; L. V. Berkner, "Secrecy and Scientific Progress," p. 785; Kalven, in *The Atomic Age, passim*.

20. Stern, pp. 21, 99; P.M.S. Blackett, *Military and Political Consequences of Atomic Energy*, pp. 139, 172; J. Robert Oppenheimer, "A Letter to Senator McMahon," pp. 163-78.

21. Stern, pp. 103, 125, 127; Riesman, *Constraint and Variety in American Education*, p. 90; H. Stuart Hughes, "Closing the Oppenheimer Case," p. 20.

22. The U.S. exploded its first H-bomb at Eniwetok in November 1952, and the Russians tested their own version in August of the following year.

23. Charles P. Curtis, *The Oppenheimer Case*, pp. 21-25; Alsop, *We Accuse*, pp. 15, 30-31; see Stern's excellent account, *passim*.

24. *Thirty Years of Treason*, pp. 242-44; Haakon Chevalier, *Oppenheimer*, pp. 90-112; Philip Rieff, "The Case of Dr. Oppenheimer," *passim*.

25. Strauss, p. 228; Stern, p. 339; Nuel Pharr Davis, p. 348.

26. *NYHT*, Oct. 24, 1950.

27. T. Taylor, *Grand Inquest*, p. 96; *NYHT*, Dec. 11, 1953; *NYT*, Dec. 16, 1953; Scientists' Committee on Loyalty and Security, New Haven, *The Fort Monmouth Security Investigation*, August 1953-April 1954 (mimeographed, issued April 25, 1954), p. 4/11; *NYT*, Nov. 17, 1953; Cook, *Nightmare Decade*, p. 449.

28. Scientists' Committee on Loyalty and Security, New Haven, *The Fort Monmouth Security Investigation*, p. 148; *Fort Monmouth Security Investigation*, p. 4/30; Straight, p. 166.

29. See *Fort Monmouth Security Investigation*, note 27 above.

30. Tillett Papers, Fort Monmouth: Memo from Ira Katchen to Harry Green, Feb. 10, 1954; *ibid.*, Lovenstein; *Fort Monmouth Security Investigation*, pp. 4/17 to 4/20.

31. Tillett Papers, Fort Monmouth, Melvin Morris; *ibid.*, H. Ducore; *Fort Monmouth Security Investigation*, pp. 4/19 to 4/22.

32. Tillett Papers, Fort Monmouth, Paul M. Leeds; *Fort Monmouth Security Investigation*, pp. 4/24 to 4/28; the Sherwood case is given as "Case C," unnamed, in this source.

33. Tillett Papers, Fort Monmouth, Harold Stein; *Fort Monmouth Security Investigation*, pp. 4/22 to 4/24; *ibid.*, pp. 4/24 to 4/27; Tillett Papers, Fort Monmouth, Ira Katchen to Harold Green, Feb. 8, 1954.

34. The lawyers Harry Green and Ira J. Katchen represented many of the scientists and technicians suspended at the Army Signal Laboratory at Fort Monmouth. The two partners accepted from each client a note for $500, of which $100 was paid down and the rest was payable when and if the client gained clearance. They finally won $280,000 in back pay for their clients, and sent out bills in March 1956 ranging from $50 to $580. The one big bill, for $1,733.24, went to Hans E. Inslerman. Considering that these cases had been fought for nearly three years, the fees charged were indeed modest. Tillett Papers, Fort Monmouth, Paul Tillett, Interview with Harry Green and Ira Katchen, Dec. 9, 1962.

### CHAPTER 26: HOLLYWOOD

1. *Hollywood on Trial*, BBC TV film, first shown Nov. 4, 1973; Harold W. Horowitz, "Loyalty Tests for Employment in the Motion Picture Industry," p. 439; Howard Suber, "Hollywood's Political Blacklist," in *The American Cinema*, p. 294.

2. Including Albert Maltz, John Wexley, George Sklar, J. Edward Bromberg, Hester Sondergaard, John Garfield.

3. Elizabeth Poe, "The Hollywood Story," p. 20; Father George H. Dunne, *Hollywood Labor Dispute*, pp. 4, 37; Saposs, *Communism in American Unions*, p. 47; Gordon Kahn, p. 31; NYT, March 13, 1948.

4. Ogden, *The Dies Committee*, p. 13; Dies, *The Trojan Horse*, pp. 41–42; Barrett, *The Tenney Committee*, pp. 128, 208, 366; *Hollywood Reporter*, Nov. 4, 1947.

5. See Melvin Small, "How We Learned to Love the Russians"; Melvin Small, "Buffoons and Brave Hearts"; Gordon Kahn, p. 31; *Days of Glory* (film).

6. *Mission to Moscow* (film); Gordon Kahn, p. 24; Carr, *The House Committee . . .* , p. 61.

7. John Cogley, *Report on Blacklisting*, Vol. 1: *Movies*, pp. 203–4; Saposs, *Unions*, p. 21; Kempton, *Part of Our Time*, p. 195; *Hitler's Children* (film); *Crossfire* (film); *Action in the North Atlantic* (film); see John Howard Lawson, "Can Anything Be Done About Hollywood?", *passim*.

8. Trumbo, *Time of the Toad*, p. 39; Philip Selznick, *The Organizational Weapon*, p. 235.

9. NYT, March 28, May 29, 1947; Alvah Bessie, *Inquisition in Eden*, p. 213; Trumbo, *Time of the Toad*, p. 22.

10. MG, Oct. 21, 1947; *Thirty Years of Treason*, pp. 140, 148, 122, 128; Burlingame, *The Sixth Column*, p. 127; Bessie, p. 226.

11. Andrews, *Washington Witch Hunt*, p. 111; *Thirty Years of Treason*, p. 116; Lester Cole, Interview, in *Hollywood on Trial* (film); Frank Donner, Interview; Kempton, *Part of Our Time*, p. 205.

12. *Hollywood on Trial* (film); Dalton Trumbo, Interview, in *Hollywood on Trial*; Gordon Kahn, pp. 84, 133.

13. *Thirty Years of Treason*, pp. 157–58, 167; Gordon Kahn, p. 89; Trumbo, *Time of the Toad*, p. 29; Stefan Kanfer, *A Journal of the Plague Years, passim*.

14. *Thirty Years of Treason*, pp. 75, 220; *NYHT*, Sept. 27, 1947; Stripling, *The Red Plot*, p. 75.

15. Harvey Kilgore, W. Va., Claude Pepper, Fla., Elbert Thomas, Utah, Glen Taylor, Idaho.

16. *Hollywood on Trial* (film). Signatories of the CFA petition included Cornel Wilde, Gregory Peck, Bennett Cerf, Lucille Ball, Burt Lancaster, Robert Ryan, John Garfield, Myrna Loy, Frank Sinatra, Edward G. Robinson, Robert Young, Joseph Cotten, Clifton Fadiman, Van Heflin, Paulette Goddard, Henry Fonda, Irwin Shaw, Katharine Hepburn, Richard Brooks, Sidney Buchman, Joan Bennett, Pete Seeger, Leonard Bernstein, Ethel Barrymore, Eddie Cantor, Louis Calhern, Jerome Chodorov, Kirk Douglas, Jules Dassin, Howard Da Silva, Agnes DeMille, Deanna Durbin, Melvyn Douglas, Ava Gardner, Benny Goodman, Moss Hart, Uta Hagen, Harold Hecht, Ben Hecht, Walter Huston, William Holden, Canada Lee, Fritz Lang, Peter Lorre, Groucho Marx, Abe Polonsky, Ann Revere, Artie Shaw, Franchot Tone, Orson Welles, Billy Wilder.

17. *NYT*, Dec. 5, 1947. The Freedom from Fear Committee was sponsored by Richard Collins, Gordon Kahn, Howard Koch, Lewis Milestone, Irving Pichel, Larry Parks, Robert Rossen and Waldo Salt. It issued a publicity questionnaire:

> Tired? Jittery? Sleeping Badly? Find Out The Reason. Test Yourself!
>
> Here are 10 Questions. Score 5 for YES answer. If You Score 25 You're in the Danger Zone!
>
> Are you disturbed because you are a Jew? A Catholic? A Union or Guild member?
>
> Are you haunted by your past? Remember? Your fourth vote for Roosevelt? The ambulance you helped send to Republican Spain? Your signature to a protest against lynchings in the South?
>
> Are you thinking you'd better drop your subscriptions to [a list of periodicals]?
>
> Do you experience mixed feelings at the news that England has offered sanctuary to political refugees from the American motion picture industry?
>
> Do you think YOU are safe from blacklists?

18. Poe, p. 12; Lillian Ross, "Onward and Upward with the Arts," p. 40; Dalton Trumbo, "Poems on Parting," pp. 20–22.

19. *NYT*, Dec. 9, 1948; Poe, p. 9; Gordon Kahn, pp. 14, 17; Carr, p. 61.

20. Gordon Kahn, p. 21; Bessie, p. 216; Barth, *Loyalty of Free Men*, p. 66.

21. In a recent interview Schary has argued that if the Ten had taken the First Amendment on principle, then immediately announced to journalists that they were CP members, he would have supported them. Lester Cole

ridicules this; ". . . he was a frightened man . . . He was already part of management and on the other side." Dore Schary, Interview, and Lester Cole, Interview, in *Hollywood on Trial* (film).

22. Ross, p. 35; Gordon Kahn, pp. 188, 192.

23. Philip Dunne, Interview, in *Hollywood on Trial* (film); Edmund North, Interview; *Hollywood Reporter*, Dec. 17, 1947.

24. Fox's profits had fallen from $12.5 million in 1949 to $9.5 million in 1950. By 1951 film attendance in Los Angeles had fallen by 30 percent; in that year more than three thousand movie theaters closed across the country. Ticket sales fell from 90 million a week in 1944 to 35 million in 1953.

25. Lawson, p. 41; Kanfer, p. 128; *NYT*, Nov. 30, 1947, Sept. 13, 1950. Among the anti-Communist films deserving mention were: *The Iron Curtain* (1948); *I Was a Communist for the FBI* (1951), which showed a real Communist, Steve Nelson, committing a fictitious murder; *Guilty of Treason; Walk East on Beacon; High Treason; The Woman on Pier 13; The Red Danube; I Married a Communist; My Son John; Big John McLain; The Conspirator; Red Planet Mars.*

26. *Thirty Years of Treason*, p. 300; *Hollywood Reporter*, March 23, 1951; Kanfer, p. 89.

27. Poe, p. 23; *Thirty Years of Treason*, p. 197; *Alert*, Vol. 6, No. 2 (Feb. 1952); Cogley, p. 181; *Hollywood Reporter*, May 18, 1951.

28. These included the comedy *On the Riviera*, starring Danny Kaye, at one time treasurer of the Hollywood Independent Citizens Committee and a member of the CPA; *Death of a Salesman*, produced by Stanley Kramer, who, said Matthews "taught at the Los Angeles Communist training school in 1947"; *Sirocco*, starring Lee J. Cobb and Zero Mostel; *Singin' in the Rain* and *An American in Paris*, both of which starred the versatile Gene Kelly; *The Red Badge of Courage*, directed by John Huston; *High Noon*, produced by Kramer with associate production by Carl Foreman, "a named Communist," and directed by Fred Zinneman, who had signed the *amici curiae* brief, as had Joseph Losey, director, and Van Heflin, leading actor, of *The Prowler; A Streetcar Named Desire*, directed by Elia Kazan and starring Marlon Brando, a sponsor of the Waldorf Conference; *A Place in the Sun*, starring both Shelley Winters, who had signed the *amici curiae* brief, and Ann Revere, "identified in testimony as a Communist Party member."

29. J. B. Matthews, "Did the Movies Really Clean House?", pp. 13–56; Phil Kerby, "The Legion Blacklist," pp. 14–15; Poe, p. 12; Horowitz, "Loyalty Tests," p. 461.

30. R. S. Brown, *Loyalty and Security*, p. 154; Robert B. Pitkin, "The Movies and the American Legion," p. 14; Edmund North, Interview; Cogley, Vol. 1, pp. 138–39.

31. *NYT*, Aug. 27, 1954, July 28, 1953; Matusow, *False Witness*, p. 118; Thomas C. Reeves, *Freedom and the Foundation*, p. 221; Murray Kempton, Interview.

32. Hayden's lawyer was in fact Martin Gang, of Gang, Kopp and Tyre, who also represented Abe Burrows, Richard Collins and about fifty HCUA witnesses, twenty of them from the film industry. Gang perfected the formula of frequently flying to Washington to probe HCUA's attitudes; he also pleaded

cases with Roy Brewer and studio executives. Gang claimed that, far from making money out of clearances, he had lost about $50,000 in terms of the time he would otherwise have invested as a highly paid theater lawyer. In any case, the racketeers sprang up like mushrooms, causing even the Legion to complain about the shark lawyers who claimed they could "fix" matters and swamped its New York office with requests for clearance. Poe, p. 15; Sterling Hayden, *Wanderer, passim; Thirty Years of Treason,* p. 706; Cogley, Vol. 1, pp. 87–88; Pitkin, p. 14.

33. *Thirty Years of Treason,* pp. 333, 322, 346, 431, 422–23, 429; William V. Shannon, "Hollywood Returns to the Stand," *passim.*

34. Robert Vaughn, *Only Victims,* p. 165. Robinson's previous appearances before HCUA had been in 1950 and 1951. Robinson, *All My Yesterdays,* pp. 249, 251, 263; *NYT,* May 5, 1953.

35. Howard Da Silva, Interview, in *Hollywood on Trial* (film); *Thirty Years of Treason,* pp. 483, 546, 566; Kanfer, p. 173.

36. Richard Collins, "Confessions of a Red Screenwriter," pp. 7–10; Vaughn, p. 161.

37. *Thirty Years of Treason,* p. 576–634; Kanfer, p. 134; Hayden, p. 389.

38. See Matusow Papers, Harvey Matusow to Nicholas Bela, Feb. 9, 1953 and May 21, 1953, Nicholas Bela to Harvey Matusow, May 1, 1953; Vaughn, p. 196.

39. *NYT,* Sept. 11, 1950; *Thirty Years of Treason,* pp. 400, 401, 404; Edward Dmytryk, Interview, in *Hollywood on Trial* (film).

40. *Martin Berkeley,* writer: eleven credits, 1953–1957.
 *Lee J. Cobb,* actor: twenty-three credits, 1950–1959.
 *Richard Collins,* writer: eleven credits, 1953–1960.
 *Edward Dmytryk,* director, one of the Hollywood Ten, but repented in 1951: no credits, 1949–1951, then fourteen credits, 1952–1959.
 *Sterling Hayden,* actor: thirty-four credits, 1951–1958.
 *Harold Hecht,* producer: produced seventeen films, 1950–1961.
 *Roy Huggins,* writer: eight credits, 1951–1961.
 *Elia Kazan,* director: seven credits, 1952–1960.
 *Clifford Odets,* writer: six credits, 1952–1961.
 *Edward G. Robinson,* actor: fourteen credits, 1952–1959.
 *Robert Rossen,* writer and director: eight credits, 1951–1961.
 *Budd Schulberg,* writer: four credits, 1954–1958.
(*Sources are given in the introductory paragraphs in Appendix C.*)

 Others who continued to enjoy professional success after cooperating and naming names included the cartoonist and writer David A. Lang, the writer Isobel Lennart, the actor Paul Marion, the composer David Raksin, and the writers Irving Ravetch and Leo Townsend.

41. Hellman's letter to Wood was read into the hearing transcript. For her own version of these events, see Lillian Hellman, *Scoundrel Time, passim.* Kanfer, p. 138–39; Conrad Bromberg, Interview, in *Hollywood on Trial* (film); *Thirty Years of Treason,* pp. 634–35, 641, 648–49.

42. *Salt of the Earth* (film); *NYT,* March 27, 1953.

43. Bessie, p. 254; Horowitz, p. 449.

44. Including Carl Foreman, Howard Da Silva, Lillian Hellman, Paul Jar-

rico, Karen Morley, Abe Polonsky, Ann Revere, Waldo Salt, Gale Sonder-gaard, Michael Wilson. See Suber, "HPBL," p. 297. One authority calculated that of 324 film-connected people who were named before HCUA in a hostile context between 1951 and 1954, 212 were blacklisted. Of those who were named as Communists or ex-Communists, 50 percent were writers; 17 percent, actors; 5 percent, directors; and 2 percent were producers. Those gray-listed were normally the victims of rumor or remote guilt-by-association. Poe, p. 9; Horowitz, p. 444 n; Suber, p. 290.

45. *Communist Activities*, p. 103; Charles Chaplin, *My Autobiography*, pp. 441–506; Kenneth Hurren, "20 Years After the Blacklist," pp. 73–74.

46. Paul Jacobs, "Good Guys, Bad Guys, and Congressman Walter," pp. 30–31; *NYT*, Oct. 16, 1960, Section II, p. 9; National Film Theatre (London) program note, July-Aug. 1973, p. 7.

47. Hurren, p. 79; Dalton Trumbo, Interview, in *Hollywood on Trial* (film).

48. National Film Theatre (London) program note, April-May 1972, p. 14; Ring Lardner, Jr., "My Life on the Blacklist."

49. *The Times* (London), Dec. 12, 1972; Tillett Papers, John Howard Lawson to Paul Tillett, Jan. 23, 1965; Hurren, p. 79.

## CHAPTER 27: RADIO, TELEVISION AND THEATER

1. Merle Miller, *The Judges and the Judged*, pp. 210, 12; Fred Friendly, *Due to Circumstances Beyond Our Control*, p. 99.

2. Total radio advertising revenue was $415 million. In the last six months of 1950, Procter & Gamble spent $997,752 on radio advertising; General Mills, $886,848; and General Foods, $394,158. By the late 1950s a program like "The $64,000 Question" could command $80,000 in advertising revenue for a single show.

3. H. Matusow, *False Witness*, pp. 110–11; Miller, *The Judges*, pp. 88, 93.

4. F. Woltman in *New York World Telegram & Sun*, Sept. 24, 1952; Stefan Kanfer, *A Journal of the Plague Years*, pp. 186–87.

5. Fredric and Florence March had been under attack since the Dies Committee subpoenaed them in 1940. The couple were prodigious joiners and money-givers. After they had been named as CP members in *Counterattack*, work dried up. They sued, and American Business Consultants settled out of court, withdrawing the allegation.

6. Sample listings from *Red Channels*:
   LILLIAN HELLMAN:
   Harlem Women for Wallace. Speaker, September 6, 1948; gave a forceful tribute to Wallace. *Daily Worker*, October 6, 1948, p. 6.
   Moscow Art Theatre. Sent greetings to directors and members. Celebration of MAT's 50th anniversary. *Daily Worker*, January 11, 1948, p. 13.
   HOWARD DA SILVA:
   Council on African Affairs. Participant. Rally, June 6, 1946. Handbill.
   Jefferson School of Social Science. Instructor. Catalog, Spring 1946.
   Faculty member 1946–47. Pamphlet.

7. Including the performers José Ferrer, Edward G. Robinson, Orson Welles, Gypsy Rose Lee, Hazel Scott, William Redfield, Joe Julian, Judy Hol-

liday, Burl Ives, Lee J. Cobb, Pete Seeger, Sam Wanamaker and John Garfield; the commentators William L. Shirer and Howard K. Smith; the writers Lillian Hellman, Irwin Shaw, Abe Burrows, Dorothy Parker, Arthur Miller, Millard Lampell; the music critic Olin Downes, the conductor Leonard Bernstein, the composer Aaron Copland and the director Hiram Brown. One of those listed in *Red Channels*, the novelist Irwin Shaw, soon afterward earned the praise of *Counterattack* by writing to the *NYT* to announce that he would allow no further productions of his antiwar play, *Bury the Dead*, in order to "balk those double-tongued gentlemen [i.e., the Soviet leaders] with whatever small means at my disposal . . ." In 1951 Shaw published a novel, *The Troubled Air*, which provides a vivid account of the social attitudes and vested interests involved in radio blacklisting.

8. *Thirty Years of Treason*, p. 702; Elmer Rice, *Minority Report*, p. 430; Cogley, *Report on Blacklisting*, Vol. 2, *Radio–Television*, p. 52.

9. Faulk, *Fear on Trial*, p. 51; Miller, *The Judges*, p. 169; Tillett Papers, Norman Ober to Paul R. Milton, Oct. 24, 1952; *Facts about the Blacklist*, No. 2 (May 1954), p. 4 (Matusow papers); J. Gould in *NYT*, June 26, 1955.

10. Faulk, pp. 364, 176; J. Edgar Hoover to Vincent Hartnett, May 10, 1955, Matusow Papers; M. Miller, "Trouble on Madison Avenue, N.Y.," pp. 632–634; Faulk, p. 330.

11. *Rights*, Vol. 4, No. 2 (Nov. 1956), p. 15; Faulk, pp. 334, 227, 225; Kempton, *America Comes of Middle Age*, pp. 343–44.

12. Miller, *The Judges*, p. 151; H. Matusow, pp. 123–25; *Counterattack*, Vol. 6, No. 4 (Oct. 10, 1952); Faulk, pp. 264–65, 234, 230, 43.

13. *Rights*, Vol. 3, Nos. 8, 9 (May, June 1956), pp. 6–7. Cogley's *Report* followed four years after Miller's, which was sponsored by the ACLU and based on interviews with 14 advertising executives, 8 writers' and actors' agents, executives of ABC, CBS, NBC and MBS, sponsors, union officials and others.

14. Vaughn, *Only Victims*, pp. 205, 210; Kanfer, p. 272; *NYHT*, June 15, 1955.

15. Saul Carson, "On the Air: Trial by Sponsor," p. 23; M. Miller, *The Judges*, p. 40; Friendly, p. 25; Wechsler, *The Age of Suspicion*, pp. 253–55.

16. Faulk, pp. 174–77; *NYHT*, May 15, 1955; Kanfer, p. 165; O. Pilat, "Blacklist."

17. Cogley, Vol. 2, p. 23; Matusow, p. 115; Faulk, p. 249; Miller, *The Judges*, p. 149.

18. *NYT*, Nov. 13, 1958; *Rights*, Vol. 6, No. 2 (Dec. 1958), p. 19.

19. Martin Berkeley, "Reds in Your Living Room," pp. 56–59; Bulletin of "We, the Undersigned," Radio Writers Guild, Oct. 1952, Matusow Papers; C. P. Trussell in the *NYT*, Aug. 28, 1952.

20. Poe, "The Hollywood Story," p. 19; *NYT*, July 4, 1955; *NYHT*, Aug. 11, 1955; *Rights*, Vol. 3, Nos. 8–9 (May-June 1956), pp. 4–5.

21. *NYT*, April 28, 1962; Cook, *Nightmare Decade*, p. 14; *NYT*, Jan. 10, 1961.

22. Kanfer, pp. 116–18, 154–55, 4–6; Kempton, *America* . . . , p. 21; Tillett Papers, Memorandum; *The Times* (London), Sept. 19, 1973.

23. Millard Lampell, in *Thirty Years of Treason*, pp. 690, 70.

24. Faulk, *passim*; Kanfer, pp. 282–84, 287.

25. Markmann, *The Noblest Cry*, pp. 290–91; Vincent Hartnett, "New York's Great Red Way," pp. 66–72.

26. Max Mandel, of the Pittsburgh Symphony Orchestra, was expelled from the AFM and the Pittsburgh Musical Society in March 1950 after an unfriendly appearance before HCUA. Two years later, Jules Yanover, of the Detroit Symphony Orchestra, was questioned by the AFM about Communist affiliations, then fired by the Orchestra. In March 1956, HCUA dispatched a subcommittee to Los Angeles with the aim of discrediting a left-wing group within Local 47 of the AFM. Thirty-five were subpoenaed. On March 9, the Hearst *Los Angeles Examiner* listed the names and employers of twenty-two musicians, as a result of which at least three were barred from a tour by the Los Angeles Philharmonic. *NYT*, Feb. 28, 1952; Stamler, *Appendix*, p. 62; Donner, *The Un-Americans*, p. 65.

27. Merle Miller, *The Judges*, pp. 119–20; Kanfer, pp. 250–52; Arthur Miller, Interview, in *Hollywood on Trial* (film); *Thirty Years of Treason*, pp. 823, 820.

28. Countryman, "Washington: The Canwell Committee," pp. 316–17; Countryman, *Un-American Activities*, p. 147; *NYT*, Feb. 28, 1953; *DT*, May 27, 1959; *NYT*, Sept. 15, 1958.

29. "Courage in Action: Philadelphia Theater," pp. 234–37.

## Appendix A:

1. *NYHT*, Feb. 13, 1952; *NYT*, March 1, 1952; *DT*, Oct. 22, 1959; Frank Donner, "The Informer," p. 307; *NYT*, March 29, 1953; Frank Donner to the author, July 9, 1974.

2. *NYT*, Dec. 10, 1953; SACB Docket No. 102–53, *Herbert Brownell, Jr. v. Labor Youth League*, Feb. 15, 1955. Report of the Board; *NYT*, Sept. 5, 1958.

3. *NYT*, April 12, 1956; *The Times* (London), May 8, 1957; *NYT*, Dec. 12, 1953; Donner, *The Un-Americans*, p. 125.

4. *Communist Activities*, pp. 517–18; *NYHT*, Dec. 18, 1949.

5. *NYT*, Feb. 16, 1952; Donner, "The Informer," p. 307; *NYHT*, Dec. 10, 1953; *NYT*, Oct. 29, Jan. 15, 1954; Mitford, *A Fine Old Conflict*, p. 202.

6. Jacob Spolansky, *The Communist Trail in America, passim*; *Detroit News*, Feb. 7, 1954; *NYT*, Dec. 23, 1953; *NYHT*, Feb. 26, 1952.

7. *NYT*, Feb. 28, 1952, Nov. 20, 1953, Dec. 8, 1954.

8. Taft-Hartley Case Newsletter, Nat Ganley Collection, box 14, folder 14-40, WRL.

9. Tillett Papers. The teacher's name is withheld at her request.

10. Conrad Komorowski, *The Strange Trial of Stanley Nowak*, pp. 56, 69, 38.

## Appendix B:

1. *Rights*, Vol. 2, No. 9 (May 1955), p. 7.

2. Tillett Papers, Public Schools.

3. Tillett Papers, Paul Tillett interview with Dr. Ralph Gundlach, June 20, 1962.

4. Tillett Papers, Universities, Nickerson.

5. *Ibid.*, Phillips.

6. Tillett Papers, Public Schools, name supplied.

# Bibliography

## I: UNPUBLISHED SOURCES

### Manuscript Collections

*Ernest Besig Files*. Private files relating to personnel security cases represented by the San Francisco attorney Ernest Besig, formerly chairman of the Northern California ACLU.

*Detroit Archives, Mayor's Papers*, Burton Historical Collection, Detroit Public Library: (1) Loyalty Committee Files; (2) Loyalty Investigation Commission Files.

*Frank J. Donner Files*. A useful collection of published and unpublished material, much of it relating to the activities of the FBI, its informers, and the red squads, in the possession of Frank J. Donner.

*Gustavo Duran Papers*. The personal papers of the late Gustavo Duran, now in the custody of Mrs. Bonté Duran and her family, and in the care of Mr. Geoffrey C. Ryan, of New York City.

*Harvey Matusow Collection*, Department of Documents and Manuscripts, Sussex University Library, England. This very large collection of private papers and public documents was assembled by Harvey Matusow.

*Walter Reuther Library, Labor History Archives*, Wayne State University, Detroit: (1) Nat Ganley Collection; (2) Stanley Nowak Collection; (3) Yale Stuart Collection.

*Paul Tillett Papers*, Department of Politics, Princeton University. Now in the custody of Mrs. H. H. Wilson. In the early 1960s Professor Paul Tillett sent out questionnaires to many people who had been involved in the political purges of the 1940s and 1950s. The result of his investigations, and the documents he assembled, are of considerable interest, notably in the fields of education and science.

*United Electrical, Radio & Machine Workers of America Personnel Security Files*, 11 East 51st Street, New York, N.Y. 10022.

## Interviews with the Author

Ernest Besig, May 25, 1974
Leonard Boudin, June 10, 1974
Ralph S. Brown, Jr., June 21, 1974
Harold I. Cammer, June 12, 1974
John Caughey, May 21, 1974
Rose Chernin, May 22, 1974
Vern Countryman, June 3, 1974
Frank J. Donner, June 16, 1974
Thomas I. Emerson, June 21, 1974
Mary and David Englestein, May 25, 1974
Wendell Furry, June 5, 1974
Simon Gerson, June 13, 1974
Aubrey Grossman, May 23, 1974
Alger Hiss, June 15, 1974
Berenice Hoffman, June 10, 1974
Abraham J. Isserman, June 17, 1974
Murray Kempton, June 14, 1974
Sam Kushner, May 28, 1974
Robert Z. Lewis, June 24, 1974
Carey McWilliams, June 14, 1974
James B. Mauro, Jr., June 20, 1974
Edmund H. North, May 19, 1974
William Pomeroy, July 10, 1974
Telford Taylor, June 6, 1974
Edith Tiger, June 12, 1974
Robert E. Treuhaft, November 28, 1974
Alden Whitman, June 11, 1974
H. H. Wilson, June 18, 1974
Nathan Witt, June 11, 1974

(Note: A number of other interviewees wished to remain anonymous.)

## Letters to the Author from:

Ralph S. Brown, Jr., August 2, 1974
Harold I. Cammer, July 26, 1976
Rose Chernin, July 19 and August 20, 1976
Frank J. Donner, July 9, 1974, July 14, September 6, 1976
Bonté Duran, September 6, 1976
Alger Hiss, July 9, 1974
Murray Kempton, October 5, 1974
Carey McWilliams, July 15, 1974
Will Maslow, September 16, 1974
Edmund H. North, July 26, 1976

William Pomeroy, July 15, 1974
Geoffrey C. Ryan, August 4, 1976
Yaffa Schlesinger, July 19, 1974
Oliver Walston, September 10, 1974
Alden Whitman, July 2, 1974, July 22, 1976
H. H. Wilson, August 9, 1976

### Other Unpublished Documents

ACLU Academic Freedom Committee, New York, *Minutes*, February 2, 1950
ACLU Committee on Civil Rights in Labor Relations, New York, *Minutes*, August 17, 1950
ACLU Labor Committee, New York, *Minutes*, November 2, 1951
ACLU Labor Committee Meeting, New York, *Minutes*, February 16, 1955
Scientists' Committee on Loyalty and Security, New Haven, *The Fort Monmouth Security Investigation, August 1953–April 1954* (mimeographed, issued April 25, 1954).
Tillett, Paul, "The Social Costs of the Loyalty Programs: A Preliminary Draft" (unpublished typescript: Tillett Papers).
United Nations, *Statement by the Staff Council on Personnel Policy*, February 25, 1953 (mimeographed).
U.S.A.: Before the National Labor Relations Board, Case No. 5-RC-2929, In the Matter of Westinghouse Electric Corporation, Air Arm Division, Employer, and United Electrical, Radio and Machine Workers of America (UE), Petitioner:

(1) *Petitioner's Exceptions* to Regional Director's Report on Objections (signed by Frank J. Donner and Robert Z. Lewis, attorneys for Petitioner).

(2) *Affidavit* signed by Clarence E. Wallace, July 27, 1960.
(UE Files.)

## II: Published Sources

### Newspapers and Periodicals

The names and dates of issue of newspapers and periodicals consulted are given in the Notes and References.
*ACLU News* is the organ of the Northern California Civil Liberties Union.
*The Open Forum* is the organ of the Southern California Branch of the ACLU.
*Rights* is the organ of the Emergency Civil Liberties Committee.

### Legal Documents and Court Cases

Court of Appeals of Kentucky. *Carl Braden v. Commonwealth of Kentucky*. Brief of National Lawyers Guild as *amicus curiae*.
District Court for the Western District of Texas at El Paso, *U.S.A. v. Clinton E. Jencks*, Criminal No. 54013, Affidavit of Harvey Matusow.

*Maurice Braverman v. Bar Association of Baltimore City.* Court of Appeals of Maryland (121 A. 2d 473) March 13, 1956, and (352 U.S. 830) No. 151, October 8, 1956.

*In re* Schlesinger, 404 Pa. 584 172A 2d 835 (1961).

In the Supreme Court of Pennsylvania. No. 208. March Term 1960. *In the Matter of Hymen Schlesinger.* Brief of the National Lawyers Guild as *amicus curiae.*

In the Supreme Court of the United States. October Term 1955. No. 58. *William Ludwig Ullmann v. United States of America.* Brief of National Lawyers Guild as *amicus curiae.*

In the Supreme Court of the United States. October Term 1955. *John W. Nelson v. General Electric Company,* Petition for a Writ of Certiorari to the Court of Appeals for the District of Columbia Circuit.

In the Supreme Court of the United States. October Term 1957. No. 729. *Stanislaw Novak v. United States of America.* Brief of National Lawyers Guild as *amicus curiae.*

Supreme Court of the United States. October Term 1958. No. 34. *Willard Uphaus v. Louis C. Wyman* (June 8, 1959.)

In the Supreme Court of the United States. October Term 1960. No. 12. *Communist Party v. Subversive Activities Control Board.* Brief of National Lawyers Guild as *amicus curiae* on Petition for Rehearing.

In the Supreme Court of the United States. October Term 1960. No. 37. *Frank Wilkinson v. United States of America.* Brief of National Lawyers Guild as *amicus curiae.*

In the Supreme Court of the United States. October Term 1960. No. 54. *Carl Braden, Petitioner v. United States of America.* Brief for the United States.

In the Supreme Court of the United States. October Term 1960. No. 58. *In re George Anastalpo, Petitioner* (April 24, 1961).

In the Supreme Court of the United States. October Term 1968. *Jeremiah Stamler, M.D. and Yolanda F. Hall, Plaintiffs-Appellants v. Hon. Edwin E. Willis et al., Defendants-Appellees.* Jurisdictional Statement and Appendices 4 and 5 to Jurisdictional Statement.

United States Court of Appeals for the District of Columbia Circuit No. 11845. *United States of America, Appellant v. Owen Lattimore, Appellee.*

In the United States Court of Appeals for the District of Columbia Circuit No. 12,027. *Abram Flaxer, Appellant v. United States of America, Appellee.*

United States Court of Appeals for the District of Columbia Circuit No. 12,628. *John W. Nelson v. General Electric Company.*

United States Court of Appeals for the District of Columbia No. 13587. *Howard D. Abramowitz, Appellant v. Wilber M. Brucker, Appellee.* Brief for the Appellee.

In the United States Court of Appeals for the Fourth Circuit. No. 6437. *Philip Frankfeld (et alia) v. United States of America.* Appendix to Appellants' Brief.

In the United States Court of Appeals for the Seventh Circuit. No. 11470. *United States of America v. Claude Mack Lightfoot*.

## Books, Articles and Congressional Publications

"Academic Freedom and Tenure: Evansville College," *AAUP Bulletin*, Vol. 35, No. 1 (Spring 1949).

"Academic Freedom and Tenure: Fisk University," *AAUP Bulletin*, Vol. 45, No. 1 (March 1959).

"Academic Freedom and Tenure in the Quest for National Security: Report of a Special Committee of the American Association of University Professors," *AAUP Bulletin*, Vol. 42, No. 1 (Spring 1956).

"Academic Freedom and Tenure: Report of Committee A for 1947," *AAUP Bulletin*, Vol. 34, No. 1 (Spring 1948).

"Academic Freedom and Tenure: Report of Committee A for 1948," *AAUP Bulletin*, Vol. 35, No. 1 (Spring 1949).

"Academic Freedom and Tenure: Three Reports," *AAUP Bulletin*, Vol. 43, No. 1A (April 1957).

"Academic Freedom in a Climate of Insecurity," *Journal of Social Issues*, Vol. 9, No. 3 (1953).

"Academic Freedom: Some Recent Instances," *AAUP Bulletin*, Vol. 42, No. 4 (Winter 1956).

"Academic Freedom Survey," *The Harvard Crimson*, June 17, 1952.

Acheson, Dean G., *A Democrat Looks at His Party*. New York: Harper & Brothers, 1955.

———, *Present at the Creation: My Years in the State Department*. London: Hamish Hamilton, 1970.

Adler, Les K., "Hollywood and the Cold War," in *The Specter* (q.v.).

Adler, Selig, *The Isolationist Impulse*. New York: Abelard-Schuman, 1957.

Albertson, William, *The Trucks Act: Michigan's Blueprint for a Fascist State*. New York: New Century, 1952.

Allan, William, *Toy Must Go!* Detroit: Michigan State CP, April 1948.

Allen, James S., *Atomic Imperialism*. New York: International Publishers, 1952.

Allen, Raymond B., "Communists Should Not Teach in American Colleges," *Educational Forum*, Vol. 13, No. 4 (May 1949).

Allport, Gordon W., *The Nature of Prejudice*. Boston: Beacon Press, 1955.

Alsop, Joseph, "The Strange Case of Louis Budenz," *The Atlantic Monthly*, Vol. 189 (April 1952).

———, and Alsop, Stewart, *We Accuse! The Story of the Miscarriage of American Justice in the Case of J. Robert Oppenheimer*. London: Gollancz, 1955.

*American Cinema, The*, ed. Donald E. Staples. Voice of America Forum Series, n.d. (1973?).

American Civil Liberties Union, *In Times of Challenge, U.S. Liberties, 1946–1947*. New York: ACLU, August 1947.

————, *Liberty Is Always Unfinished Business*, 36th Annual Report of the ACLU, July 1, 1955–June 30, 1956. New York: ACLU, 1956.

————, *The Smith Act and the Supreme Court*. New York: ACLU, 1952.

————, *Violence in Peekskill*. New York: ACLU, 1950.

"American Visa Policy," *Bulletin of the Atomic Scientists*, Vol. 11, No. 10 (December 1955).

*Anatomy of Anti-Communism*, a report prepared for the Peace Education Division of the American Friends Service Committee. New York: Hill and Wang, 1959.

Anderson, Jack, and May, Ronald W., *McCarthy: The Man, the Senator, the "Ism,"* Boston: Beacon Press, 1952.

Andrews, Bert, *Washington Witch Hunt*. New York: Random House, 1948.

"Anti-Intellectualism in the United States," *Journal of Social Issues*, Vol. 11, No. 3 (1955).

Appel, M., "Academic Freedom: Its Second Front," *AAUP Bulletin*, Vol. 41, No. 3 (Autumn 1955).

Aptheker, Herbert, "Communism and Truth," *Masses and Mainstream*, Vol. 6, No. 2 (February 1953).

————, *Dare We Be Free? The Meaning of the Attempt to Outlaw the Communist Party*. New York: New Century, 1961.

Arendt, Hannah, "The Ex-Communists," *Commonweal*, Vol. 57, No. 24 (March 20, 1953).

Aronson, James, *The Press and the Cold War*. Indianapolis, Ind.: Bobbs-Merrill, 1970.

Ascoli, Max, "The American Politburo," *The Reporter*, Vol. 5, No. 1 (July 10, 1951).

Ashe, David I., "Expulsion of Communists Upheld," *The American Federationist*, Vol. 57 (July 1950).

*Atomic Age, The: Scientists in National and World Affairs; Articles from the Bulletin of the Atomic Scientists, 1945–62*, eds. Morton Grodzins and Eugene Rabinowitch. New York: Basic Books, 1963.

Auerbach, Frank L., *Immigration Laws of the United States*. Indianapolis, Ind.: Bobbs-Merrill, 1955.

Bachrach, Marion, "Bail Granted!" *Political Affairs*, Vol. 27, No. 4 (April 1948).

————, "This Obvious Violence," *Political Affairs*, Vol. 28, No. 1 (January 1949).

Baird, William T., "The Lightfoot Case," *The American Socialist*, Vol. 2, No. 4 (April 1955).

Baker, Roscoe, *The American Legion and American Foreign Policy*. New York: Bookman, 1954.

Baldinger, Wilbur H., "The Endless Chase," *The Progressive*, Vol. 19, No. 6 (June 1955).

Bales, James D., ed., *J. Edgar Hoover Speaks Concerning Communism*. Nutley, N.J.: Craig Press, 1970.

Barnet, M. L., "Probers and the Press," *The Nation*, Vol. 181, No. 26 (December 24, 1955).

Barrett, Edward L., Jr., *The Tenney Committee: Legislative Investigation of Subversive Activities in California*. Ithaca, N.Y.: Cornell University Press, 1951.

Barrett, William, "Cultural Conference at the Waldorf," *Commentary*, Vol. 7, No. 5 (May 1949).

Barth, Alan, *Government by Investigation*. New York: Viking, 1955.

————, "How Good Is an FBI Report?" *Harper's Magazine*, Vol. 208 (March 1954).

————, *The Loyalty of Free Men*. London: Gollancz, 1951.

————, "McCarran's Monopoly," *The Reporter*, Vol. 5, No. 4 (August 21, 1951).

Beauvoir, Simone de, *America Day by Day*, trans. Patrick Dudley. London: Duckworth, 1952.

Beck, Carl, *Contempt of Congress: A Study of the Prosecutions Initiated by the Committee on Un-American Activities, 1945–1957*. New Orleans: Hauser Press, 1959.

Beck, Hubert P., *Men Who Control Our Universities*. New York: King's Crown Press, 1947.

Beecher, John, "California: There She Goes!" *The Nation*, Vol. 172 (June 30, 1951).

Begeman, Jean, "The California Loyalty Oath," *New Republic*, Vol. 122, No. 13 (March 27, 1950).

Belfrage, Cedric, *The American Inquisition, 1945–1960*. Indianapolis, Ind.: Bobbs-Merrill, 1973.

————, *The Frightened Giant*. London: Secker & Warburg, 1957.

Bell, Daniel, "The Dispossessed," in *The Radical Right* (q.v.).

————, "Interpretations of American Politics," in *The Radical Right* (q.v.).

————, ed., *The New American Right*. New York: Criterion Books, 1955.

————, ed., *The Radical Right*. New York: Doubleday Anchor, 1964.

Bendiner, Robert, "Communists on Trial," *The Nation*, Vol. 168, No. 5 (January 29, 1949).

————, "Surgery in the C.I.O.," *The Nation*, Vol. 169, No. 20 (November 12, 1949).

Bentley, Elizabeth, *Out of Bondage*. London: Hart-Davis, 1952.

Bentley, Eric, ed., *Thirty Years of Treason: Excerpts from Hearings Before the House Committee on Un-American Activities, 1938–1968*. New York: Viking, 1971.

Bergman, Walter G., "State Department 'McCarthyism,'" *The Socialist Call*, Vol. 22, No. 1 (January 1954).

Berkeley, Martin, "Reds in Your Living Room," *American Mercury*, Vol. 77 (August 1953).

Berkner, L. V., "Secrecy and Scientific Progress," *Science*, Vol. 123 (May 4, 1956).

Bernstein, Barton, "American Foreign Policy and the Origins of the Cold War," *Politics and Policies of the Truman Administration* (q.v.).

————, *Politics and Policies of the Truman Administration*. Chicago: Quadrangle, 1970.

Bessie, Alvah, *Inquisition in Eden*. Berlin: Seven Seas, 1967.

Biddle, Francis, *The Fear of Freedom*. Garden City, N.Y.: Doubleday, 1951.
———, "Subversives in Government," *Annals of the American Academy of Political and Social Science*, Vol. 300 (July 1955).
*Bishop Oxnam and the Un-American Activities Committee*. Boston: Beacon Press, 1953.
Blackett, P. M. S., *Military and Political Consequences of Atomic Energy*. London: Turnstile Press, 1948.
Bledoe, Thomas A., "Daymare in Louisville," *Rights*, Vol. 2, Nos. 4, 5 (December 1954, January 1955).
Bliven, Bruce, "Two Worlds at Foley Square," *New Republic*, Vol. 120, No. 19 (May 9, 1949).
Bontecou, Eleanor, *The Federal Loyalty-Security Program*. Ithaca, N.Y.: Cornell University Press, 1953.
———, ed., *Freedom in the Balance: Opinions of Judge Henry W. Edgerton Relating to Civil Liberties*. Ithaca, N.Y.: Cornell University Press, 1960.
Bow, Frank T., "Ohio Fights Communism," *National Republic*, Vol. 41, No. 1 (May 1953).
Braden, Anne, *House Un-American Activities Committee: Bulwark of Segregation*. Louisville, Ky.: Southern Conference Educational Fund, n.d.
Brenton, Myron, *The Privacy Invaders*. New York: Coward-McCann, 1964.
Brown, Joseph M., "Labor Out of the Red," *Plain Talk*, Vol. 2, No. 5 (February 1948).
Brown, Ralph S., Jr., "Lawyers and the Fifth Amendment," *American Bar Association Journal*, Vol. 40 (May 1954).
———, *Loyalty and Security: Employment Tests in the United States*. New Haven: Yale University Press, 1958.
———, and Fassett, John D., "Security Tests for Maritime Workers: Due Process under the Port Security Program," *Yale Law Journal*, Vol. 62 (July 1953).
Brownell, Herbert, Jr., "Reds Are Trying to Wreck Informant System of FBI," *U.S. News & World Report*, Vol. 38 (April 1, 1955).
———, "Shall Doors Be Opened to Spies and Subversives?" *U.S. News & World Report*, Vol. 38 (April 29, 1955).
Bruce, J. Campbell, *The Golden Door—The Irony of Immigration Policy*. New York: Random House, 1954.
Buckley, William F., Jr., and Bozell, L. Brent, *McCarthy and His Enemies*. Chicago: Henry Regnery, 1954.
———, and the Editors of National Review, *The Committee and Its Critics: A Calm Review of the House Un-American Activities Committee*. New York: Putnam, 1962.
Budenz, Louis F., *The Techniques of Communism*. Chicago: Henry Regnery, 1954.
Burlingame, Roger, *The Sixth Column*. Philadelphia: Lippincott, 1962.
Byse, Clark, "A Report on the Pennsylvania Loyalty Act," *University of Pennsylvania Law Review*, Vol. 101 (January 1953).
———, "Teachers and the Fifth Amendment," *University of Pennsylvania Law Review*, Vol. 102 (1954).

Cain, Harry P., "Security of the Republic," *New Republic*, Vol. 132, No. 5 (January 31, 1955).

Calomiris, Angela, *Red Masquerade: Undercover for the FBI*. Philadelphia: Lippincott, 1950.

Campbell, Angus, and Cooper, Homer C., *Group Differences in Attitudes and Votes: A Study of the 1954 Congressional Election*. Ann Arbor: University of Michigan Press, 1956.

"Can Atom Secrets Be Kept?" *U.S. News & World Report*, Vol. 24, No. 21 (November 24, 1950).

Cantril, Hadley, ed., *Public Opinion, 1935–46*. Princeton, N.J.: Princeton University Press, 1951.

Carey, James B., "We've Got the Reds on the Run," *The American Magazine*, Vol. 146, No. 3 (September 1948).

Carr, Robert K., *The House Committee on Un-American Activities, 1945–1950*. Ithaca, N.Y.: Cornell University Press, 1952.

Carson, Saul, "On the Air: Trial by Sponsor," *New Republic*, Vol. 123, No. 11 (September 11, 1950).

"Case of Paul Robeson, The—Why Some Americans Can't Get Passports," *U.S. News & World Report*, Vol. 39, No. 9 (August 26, 1955).

Cater, Douglas, "The Great Attack on Fort Monmouth," *The Reporter*, Vol. 10, No. 1 (January 5, 1954).

Caughey, John, *In Clear and Present Danger: The Crucial State of Our Freedoms*. Chicago: University of Chicago Press, 1958.

———, "A University in Jeopardy," in *The Communist Problem in America: A Book of Readings* (q.v.).

Chafee, Zechariah, Jr., *The Blessings of Liberty*. Philadelphia: Lippincott, 1956.

Chamber of Commerce of the United States, *Communist Infiltration in the United States*. Washington: 1946.

Chamberlain, Lawrence H., *Loyalty and Legislative Action: A Survey of Activity by the New York State Legislature, 1919–49*. Ithaca, N.Y.: Cornell University Press, 1951.

Chambers, Whittaker, *Witness*. London: André Deutsch, 1953.

Chaplin, Charles, "All Is Forgiven," *Sunday Times* (London), April 9, 1972.

———, *My Autobiography*. London: Bodley Head, 1964.

Charney, George Blake, *A Long Journey*. Chicago: Quadrangle, 1968.

Chase, Harold W., *Security and Liberty: The Problem of Native Communists, 1947–1955*. Garden City, N.Y.: Doubleday, 1955.

Chester, Edward W., *Radio, Television and American Politics*. New York: Sheed and Ward, 1969.

Chevalier, Haakon, *Oppenheimer: The Story of a Friendship*. London: André Deutsch, 1966.

Citron, Alice, "Teachers in Battle," *Masses and Mainstream*, Vol. 3, No. 7 (July 1950).

*Civil Liberties under Attack*, ed. Clair Wilcox. Philadelphia: University of Pennsylvania Press, 1951.

Clubb, O. Edmund, *The Witness and I*. New York: Columbia University Press, 1974.

Cogley, John, *Report on Blacklisting*, 2 vols. New York: Fund for the Republic, 1956.

Cohen, Murray, and Fuchs, Robert F., "Communism's Challenge and the
Constitution," *Cornell Law Quarterly*, Vol. 34, No. 3 (Spring 1949).

*Cold War Critics: Alternatives to American Foreign Policy in the Truman
Years*, ed. Thomas G. Paterson. Chicago: Quadrangle, 1971.

Collins, Richard, "Confessions of a Red Screenwriter," *The New Leader*, Vol.
35 (October 6, 1952).

Commager, Henry Steele, *Freedom, Loyalty, Dissent*. New York: Oxford
University Press, 1954.

———, "Red-Baiting in the Colleges," *New Republic*, Vol. 121, No. 4 (July
25, 1949).

———, "Who Is Loyal to America?" in *Primer of Intellectual Freedom* (q.v.).

Committee on Un-American Activities, U.S. House of Representatives, *Colonization of America's Basic Industries by the CPUSA*, September 3,
1954, Washington, D.C.

———, 82nd Congress, 1st Session, House Document No. 136, 100 *Things
You Should Know About Communism*.

"Communication, A," *New Republic*, Vol. 132, No. 7 (February 14, 1955).

*Communism, the Courts and the Constitution*, eds. Allen Guttmann and
Benjamin Ziegler. Boston: D. C. Heath, 1964.

*Communist Activities Among Aliens and National Groups*, Hearings Before
the Subcommittee on the Judiciary, U.S. Senate, 81st Congress, 1st Session.

"Communist Control Act of 1954, The," *Yale Law Journal*, Vol. 64 (April
1955).

*Communist Domination of Certain Unions*, Report of the Subcommittee on
Labor and Public Welfare, U.S. Senate, 82nd Congress, 1st Session.
Washington, D.C.: Government Printing Office, 1951.

*Communist Problem in America, The: A Book of Readings*, ed. Edward E.
Palmer. New York: Thomas Y. Crowell, 1951.

"Communists in the New Deal?" *U.S. News & World Report*, Vol. 24, No. 11
(September 15, 1950).

"Communists on the Job," *Fortune*, September 1950.

Condon, Edward U., "An Appeal to Reason," in *The Atomic Age* (q.v.).

*Conformists, Informers or Free Teachers*. New York: Teachers Union, 1953.

"Congressional Investigations: Defamation Immunity," *University of Chicago
Law Review*, Vol. 18 (1950–51).

*Congressional Record*, Vol. 117, No. 61 (April 29, 1971).

Cook, Fred J., *The FBI Nobody Knows*. London: Jonathan Cape, 1965.

———, *The Nightmare Decade: The Life and Times of Senator Joe McCarthy*.
New York: Random House, 1971.

———, *The Unfinished Story of Alger Hiss*. New York: William Morrow,
1958.

Cook, Thomas I., *Democratic Rights Versus Communist Activity*. Garden
City, N.Y.: Doubleday, 1954.

Cooke, Alistair, *A Generation on Trial, U.S.A. v. Alger Hiss*. London: Hart-
Davis, 1950.

Cort, John C., "The Hearn's Strike," *Commonweal*, Vol. 58, No. 15 (July 15, 1953).

Coser, Lewis, "The Age of the Informer," *Dissent*, Vol. 1, No. 3 (Summer 1954).

Countryman, Vern, "The Bigots and the Professionals," *The Nation*, Vol. 174, No. 26 (June 28, 1952).

——, *Un-American Activities in the State of Washington*. Ithaca, N.Y.: Cornell University Press, 1951.

——, "Washington: The Canwell Committee," in *The States and Subversion* (q.v.).

"Courage in Action: Philadelphia Theatre," *The Nation*, Vol. 183, No. 12 (September 22, 1956).

Crawford, Ruth Elizabeth, "I Have a Thing to Tell You," *The Nation*, Vol. 176, No. 4 (January 24, 1953).

Crist, Judith, "A Blow for Freedom," *The Nation*, Vol. 169, No. 24 (December 10, 1949).

Crosby, Donald F., S.J., "American Catholics and the Anti-Communist Impulse," in *The Specter* (q.v.).

Cruse, Harold, *The Crisis of the Negro Intellectual*. London: W. H. Allen, 1969.

Curtis, Charles P., *The Oppenheimer Case: The Trial of a Security System*. New York: Simon and Schuster, 1955.

Cushman, Robert E., *Civil Liberties in the United States*. Ithaca, N.Y.: Cornell University Press, 1956.


Dallin, David J., *Soviet Espionage*. New Haven: Yale University Press, 1955.

Davis, David Brion, *The Fear of Conspiracy: Images of Un-American Subversion from the Revolution to the Present*. Ithaca, N.Y.: Cornell University Press, 1971.

Davis, Elmer, *But We Were Born Free*. London: André Deutsch, 1955.

Davis, Kenneth Culp, "The Requirement of a Trial-Type Hearing," *Harvard Law Review*, Vol. 70 (December 1956).

Davis, Nuel Pharr, *Lawrence and Oppenheimer*. New York: Fawcett, 1969.

Daykin, Walter L., "The Communist Employee: What Grounds for Discharge?" *Personnel*, Vol. 36, No. 1 (January-February 1959).

——, "The Operation of the Taft-Hartley Act's Non-Communist Provisions," *Iowa Law Review*, Vol. 36, No. 4 (Summer 1951).

De Caux, Len, *Labor Radical: From the Wobblies to the C.I.O.* Boston: Beacon Press, 1970.

"Denial of Federally Aided Housing to Members of Organizations on the Attorney General's List," *Harvard Law Review*, Vol. 69 (January 1956).

Dennis, Eugene, *American Communists on Trial: The Opening Speech to the Jury*. London: Communist Party of Great Britain, 1949.

——, *Letters from Prison*. New York: International Publishers, 1956.

Deutscher, Isaac, *Heretics and Renegades*. London: Jonathan Cape, 1955.

De Voto, Bernard, "The Ex-Communists," *The Atlantic Monthly*, Vol. 187, No. 2 (February 1951).

Diamond, Sigmund, "Veritas at Harvard," *New York Review of Books*, Vol. 24, No. 7 (April 28, 1977).

Dies, Martin, *The Trojan Horse in America*. New York: Dodd, Mead, 1940.

Diggins, John P., *The American Left in the Twentieth Century*. New York: Harcourt Brace Jovanovich, 1973.

Doctorow, E. L., *The Book of Daniel*. London: Macmillan, 1972.

Dodd, Bella V., *School of Darkness*. New York: Kenedy, 1954.

Donner, Frank J., "Hoover's Legacy," *The Nation*, Vol. 218, No. 22 (June 1, 1974).

———, "The Informer," *The Nation*, Vol. 178, No. 15 (April 10, 1954).

———, "The Theory and Practice of American Political Intelligence," *New York Review of Books*, April 22, 1971.

———, *The Un-Americans*. New York: Ballantine, 1961.

Downing, Francis, "Loyalty Affidavits," *Commonweal*, Vol. 50, No. 20 (August 26, 1949).

———, "Stockholm and Detroit," *Commonweal*, Vol. 52, No. 19 (August 18, 1950).

———, "Substitute for Debate," *Commonweal*, Vol. 54, No. 16 (July 27, 1951).

Downs, Robert B., ed., *The First Freedom*. Chicago: American Library Association, 1960.

Draper, Theodore, *American Communism and Soviet Russia*. New York: Viking, 1960.

Dubinsky, David, "How I Handled the Reds in My Union," *Saturday Evening Post*, Vol. 225, No. 45 (May 9, 1953).

Du Bois, W. E. B., *Autobiography*. New York: International Publishers, 1968.

Dunne, Father George H., *Hollywood Labor Dispute: A Study in Immorality*. Los Angeles: Conference Publishing Company, n.d.

"Effectiveness of State Anti-Subversive Legislation," *Indiana Law Journal*, Vol. 28 (Summer 1953).

Eggleston, Arthur, "Labor and Civil Liberties," *The Nation*, Vol. 174, No. 26 (June 28, 1952).

Elsbree, Willard S., and Reutter, E. Edmund, Jr., *Staff Personnel in the Public Schools*. New York: Prentice-Hall, 1954.

Emerson, Thomas I., and Haber, David, *Political and Civil Rights in the United States*, 2 vols. Buffalo, N.Y.: Dennis & Co., 1958.

——— and Helfeld, David M., "Loyalty Among Government Employees," *Yale Law Journal*, Vol. 58 (December 1948).

*End Exile*. New York: ACPFB, n.d.

Engel, Leonard, "Fear in Our Laboratories," *The Nation*, Vol. 166, No. 3 (January 17, 1948).

———, "Science Notebook," *The Nation*, Vol. 173, No. 12 (September 22, 1951).

English, Richard, "We Almost Lost Hawaii to the Reds," *Saturday Evening Post*, Vol. 224, No. 31 (February 2, 1952).

Ernst, Morris L., and Loth, David, *Report on the American Communist*. New York: Henry Holt, 1952.

Fairbank, John K., and Peck, James, "An Exchange," *Bulletin of Concerned Asian Scholars*, Vol. 2, No. 3 (April-July 1970).

Farber, Maurice L., "The Communist Trial, College Student Opinion and Democratic Institutions," *The Public Opinion Quarterly*, Vol. 14 (1950).

Farr, Finis, "To the Aid of the Party," *The National Review*, Vol. 5 (May 31, 1958).

Fast, Howard, *The Naked God*. London: Bodley Head, 1958.

———, "We Have Kept Faith," *Masses and Mainstream*, Vol. 3, No. 7 (July 1950).

Faulk, John Henry, *Fear on Trial*. New York: Simon and Schuster, 1964.

Faulkner, Stanley, "Security Program in the Armed Forces," *Lawyers Guild Review*, Vol. 15 (Winter 1955-56).

"FBI Director Hoover Tells How Communists Work in U.S.," *U. S. News & World Report*, Vol. 23, No. 25 (June 23, 1950).

Fedder, Edwin H., "United States Loyalty Procedures and the Recruitment of UN Personnel," *Western Political Quarterly*, Vol. 15, No. 4 (December 1962).

Fellman, David, ed., *The Supreme Court and Education*. New York: Bureau of Publications, Teachers College, 1960.

Fetter, Frank W., "Witch Hunt in the Lincoln Country," *The South Atlantic Quarterly*, Vol. 53, No. 3 (July 1954).

*First Freedom, The*, ed. Robert B. Downs. Chicago: American Library Association, 1960.

Fischer, Stephen, "Notes on the C.I.O. Convention," *Monthly Review*, Vol. 1, No. 8 (December 1949).

Fleischman, Harry, Kornbluh, Joyce L., and Segal, Benjamin D., *Security, Civil Liberties and Unions*. AFL-CIO, 1956.

Flynn, Elizabeth Gurley, *The Alderson Story: My Life as a Political Prisoner*. New York: International Publishers, 1963.

———, and others, *Thirteen Communists Speak to the Court*. New York: New Century, 1953.

Fortas, Abe, "Outside the Law," *The Atlantic Monthly*, Vol. 192, No. 2 (August 1953).

*Foundations Under Fire*, ed. Thomas C. Reeves. Ithaca, N.Y.: Cornell University Press, 1970.

France, Royal W., *My Native Grounds*. New York: Cameron, 1957.

———, "Miami Miasma," *Rights*, Vol. 2, No. 3 (November 1954).

Frantz, Laurent B., "H-Bomb for Unions—The Butler Bill," *The Nation*, Vol. 177, No. 22 (November 28, 1953).

Freedman, Blanch L., "The Loyalty-Security Program—Its Effect in Immigration and Deportation," *Lawyers Guild Review*, Vol. 15 (Winter 1955-56).

*Freedom at Harvard*. An Exchange of Letters by Frank B. Ober, of Baltimore, President Conant, and Grenville Clark, Fellow of Harvard College. Reprinted from *Harvard Alumni Bulletin*, June 25, 1949.

*Freedom in the Balance: Opinions of Judge Henry W. Edgerton Relating to Civil Liberties*, ed. Eleanor Bontecou. Ithaca, N.Y.: Cornell University Press, 1960.

Freeland, Richard M., *The Truman Doctrine and the Origins of Mc-Carthyism*. New York: Knopf, 1972.

Fried, Richard M., "Electoral Politics and McCarthyism: The 1950 Campaign," in *The Specter* (q.v.).

Friendly, Fred W., *Due to Circumstances Beyond Our Control*. New York: Vintage Books, 1968.

"From the Court Testimony of the Communist Leaders," *Political Affairs*, Vol. 28, No. 9 (September 1949).

Fuchs, Ralph F., "Administration Defense of Academic Freedom: Some Recent Instances," *AAUP Bulletin*, Vol. 42, No. 4 (Winter 1956).

Gaddis, John Lewis, *The United States and the Origins of the Cold War, 1941–1947*. New York: Columbia University Press, 1972.

Gardner, Lloyd, *Architects of Illusion: Men and Ideas in American Foreign Policy, 1941–49*. Chicago: Quadrangle, 1970.

Gates, John, *The Story of an American Communist*. New York: Thomas Nelson, 1958.

Gehman, Richard B., "Oak Ridge Witch-Hunt," *New Republic*, Vol. 119, No. 1 (July 5, 1948).

Gellhorn, Walter, *American Rights: The Constitution in Action*. New York: Macmillan, 1960.

——, "General View, A," in *The States and Subversion* (q.v.).

——, "Report on a Report of the House Committee on Un-American Activities," *Harvard Law Review*, Vol. 60, No. 8 (October 1947).

——, *Security, Loyalty and Science*. Ithaca, N.Y.: Cornell University Press, 1950.

——, ed., *The States and Subversion*. Ithaca, N.Y.: Cornell University Press, 1952.

Gerstel, Walter, "G-Men on the Campus," *The Nation*, Vol. 178, No. 5 (January 30, 1954).

Gilbert, Brian, "The Irony of the Peters Case," *New Republic*, Vol. 132, No. 24 (June 13, 1955).

Ginzburg, Benjamin, *Rededication to Freedom*. New York: Simon and Schuster, 1959.

Glazer, Nathan, *The Social Basis of American Communism*. New York: Harcourt, Brace & World, 1961.

——, and Lipset, Seymour Martin, "The Polls on Communism and Conformity," in *The New American Right* (q.v.).

Goldbloom, Maurice, *American Security and Freedom*. Boston: Beacon Press, 1954.

Goldman, Eric, *The Crucial Decade—and After: America 1945–60*. New York: Vintage, 1960.

Goodman, Walter, *The Committee: The Extraordinary Career of the House Committee on Un-American Activities*. London: Secker & Warburg, 1969.

Goudsmit, S. A., "The Task of the Security Officer," *Bulletin of the Atomic Scientists*, Vol. 11, No. 4 (April 1955).

Graebner, Norman A., *The New Isolationism: A Study in Politics and Foreign Policy Since 1950*. New York: Ronald Press, 1956.

Green, Abner, *The Deportation Drive vs. the Bill of Rights*. New York: ACPFB, 1951.

———, *The Deportation Terror*. New York: ACPFB, 1950.

———, *The Walter-McCarran Law: Police-State Terror Against Foreign-Born Americans*. New York: New Century, 1953.

Griffith, Robert, "American Politics and the Origins of McCarthyism," in *The Specter* (q.v.).

———, *The Politics of Fear: Joseph R. McCarthy and the Senate*. Lexington, Ky.: University of Kentucky Press, 1970.

———, and Theoharis, Athan, eds., *The Specter*. New York: Franklin Watts, 1974.

Griswold, Erwin N., *The 5th Amendment Today*. Cambridge, Mass.: Harvard University Press, 1955.

Grodzins, Morton, *The Loyal and the Disloyal: Social Boundaries of Patriotism and Treason*. Chicago: University of Chicago Press, 1956.

———, and Rabinowitch, Eugene, eds., *The Atomic Age: Scientists in National and World Affairs*; articles from the *Bulletin of the Atomic Scientists*, 1945–62. New York: Basic Books, 1963.

"Guilt by Association—Three Words in Search of a Meaning," *University of Chicago Law Review*, Vol. 17 (1949–50).

Guttmann, Allen, and Ziegler, Benjamin, eds., *Communism, the Courts and the Constitution*. Boston: D. C. Heath, 1964.

Haerle, Paul R., "The Communist Control Act of 1954," *Michigan Law Review*, Vol. 53, No. 8 (June 1955).

Hamby, Alonzo L., *Beyond the New Deal: Harry S Truman and American Liberalism*. New York: Columbia University Press, 1973.

*Happy Endings!* (leaflet). New York: ACPFB, n.d.

Harper, Alan D., *The Politics of Loyalty: The White House and the Communist Issue, 1946–1952*. Westport, Conn.: Greenwood, 1969.

Harper, Fowler, "The Crusade Against Bridges," *The Nation*, Vol. 174, No. 14 (April 5, 1952).

———, and Haber, David, "Lawyer Troubles in Political Trials," *Yale Law Review*, Vol. 60 (1951).

Harrington, Michael, "The American Committee for Cultural Freedom," *Dissent*, Vol. 2, No. 2 (Spring 1953).

Harris, Robert J., "The Impact of the Cold War upon Civil Liberties," *Journal of Politics*, Vol. 18, No. 4 (November 1956).

Harsha, E. Houston, "Illinois: The Broyles Commission," in *The States and Subversion* (q.v.).

Hartman, Hershl, "The Trial on Columbus Avenue," *Jewish Life*, Vol. 4 (September 1950).

Hartnett, Vincent, "New York's Great Red Way," *American Mercury*, Vol. 76 (June 1953).

Hayden, Sterling, *Wanderer*. London: Longmans, 1964.

Hazzard, Shirley, *Defeat of an Ideal: A Study of the Self-Destruction of the United Nations*. London: Macmillan, 1973.

*Hearings Regarding Communist Infiltration of Minority Groups* before the Committee on Un-American Activities, House of Representatives, 81st Congress, 1st Session, July 1949. Washington, D.C.: Government Printing Office, 1949.

Hellman, Lillian, *An Unfinished Woman*. London: Macmillan, 1969.

———, *Scoundrel Time*. Boston: Atlantic-Little, Brown, 1976.

Hicks, Granville, *Where We Came Out*. London: Gollancz, 1954.

Hill, Joe, "Anti-Red or Anti-Union? The Boston Labor Probe," *The Nation*, Vol. 180. No. 2 (January 8, 1955).

Hill, Warren P., "A Critique of Recent Ohio Anti-Subversion Legislation," *Ohio State Law Journal*, Vol. 14, No. 4 (Autumn 1953).

Hilliard, Raymond M., "We Threw the Commies Out," *Saturday Evening Post*, Vol. 223 (June 30, 1951).

Hiss, Alger, *In the Court of Public Opinion*. New York: Knopf, 1957.

Hofstadter, Richard, *The Paranoid Style in American Politics and Other Essays*. London: Jonathan Cape, 1966.

———, and Metzger, Walter P., *The Development of Academic Freedom in the United States*. New York: Columbia University Press, 1955.

Hook, Sidney, "Academic Integrity and Academic Freedom," *Commentary*, Vol. 8, No. 4 (October 1949).

———, *Common Sense and the Fifth Amendment*. New York: Criterion, 1957.

———, "The Fifth Amendment: A Crucial Case," *The New Leader*, Vol. 40 (April 22, 1957).

———, *Heresy, Yes—Conspiracy, No*. New York: John Day, 1953.

———, "Justice Black's Illogic," *The New Leader*, Vol. 40 (December 2, 1957).

———, "Lattimore on the Moscow Trials," *The New Leader*, Vol. 35 (November 10, 1952).

———, *Political Power and Personal Freedom*. New York: Criterion, 1959.

———, and Fuchs, Ralph F., "A Joint Statement in a Matter of Importance," *AAUP Bulletin*, Vol. 42, No. 4 (Winter 1956).

Hoover, J. Edgar, "Loyalty Among Government Employees," *Yale Law Journal*, Vol. 58 (1948–49).

———, *Masters of Deceit: The Story of Communism in America*. London: Dent, 1958.

Horowitz, Harold W., "Loyalty Tests for Employment in the Motion Picture Industry," *Stanford Law Review*, Vol. 6, No. 3 (May 1954).

———, "Report on the Los Angeles City and County Loyalty Programs," *Stanford Law Review*, Vol. 5 (February 1953).

Horton, Philip, "Voices Within the Voice," *The Reporter*, Vol. 9, No. 2 (July 21, 1953).

Howe, Irving, "The Shame of U.S. Liberalism," *Dissent*, Vol. 1, No. 4 (Autumn 1954).

———, "This Age of Conformity" (1954), *The Partisan Review Anthology*, eds. William Phillips and Philip Rahv. London: Macmillan, 1962.

————, and Coser, Lewis, *The American Communist Party: A Critical History*. New York: Praeger, 1962.

Huberman, Leo, "The Daggett-Sweezy Case," *Monthly Review*, Vol. 6, No. 4 (August 1954).

Hudson, G. F., "The Dexter White Case," *The Twentieth Century*, Vol. 155, No. 923 (January 1954).

Hughes, H. Stuart, "Closing the Oppenheimer Case," *New York Review of Books*, July 2, 1970.

————, "Why We Had No Dreyfus Case," *The American Scholar*, Vol. 30, No. 4 (Autumn 1961).

Hulcy, D. A., "Management Sees Red," *Education*, Vol. 72 (April 1952).

Humphrey, Hubert, "Should the Government Control Communist Unions?" *The New Leader*, Vol. 35 (June 2, 1952).

Hurren, Kenneth, "20 Years After the Blacklist," *Nova*, July 1971.

Hyman, Harold M., *To Try Men's Souls*. Berkeley, Calif.: University of California Press, 1959.

Hyman, Herbert H., and Sheatsley, Paul B., "Trends in Public Opinion on Civil Liberties," *Journal of Social Issues*, Vol. 9, No. 3 (1953).


*Immigration and Naturalization Systems of the United States, The*. Report of the Committee on the Judiciary, Pursuant to S. Res. 137 (80th Congress, 1st Session). Washington, D.C.: Government Printing Office, 1950.

"Informer's Tale, An: Its Use in Judicial and Administrative Proceedings," *Yale Law Journal*, Vol. 63, No. 2 (1953).

" 'I Refuse to Answer'—and U.N. Pays Him Off With $40,000," *U.S. News & World Report*, Vol. 35, No. 16 (October 16, 1953).

Irons, Peter H., "The Cold War Crusade of the United States Chamber of Commerce," in *The Specter* (q.v.).

"It Also Happened at Harvard," *The Educational Record*, Vol. 34, No. 4 (October 1953).

"It Did Happen at Rutgers," *The Educational Record*, Vol. 34, No. 2 (April 1953).

Iversen, Robert W., *The Communists and the Schools*. New York: Harcourt, Brace, 1959.

"I Was in a Communist Unit with Hiss," *U.S. News & World Report*, Vol. 34, No. 2 (January 9, 1953).


Jacobs, Paul, "Communists in Unions," *Commonweal*, Vol. 63, No. 16 (January 20, 1956).

————, "The Due Processing of Harry Bridges," *The Reporter*, Vol. 14, No. 5 (March 8, 1956).

————, "Good Guys, Bad Guys, and Congressman Walter," *The Reporter*, Vol. 18, No. 10 (May 15, 1958).

Jahoda, Marie, "Morale in the Federal Civil Service," *Annals of the American Academy of Political and Social Science*, Vol. 300 (July 1955).

————, and Cook, Stuart W., "Security Measures and Freedom of Thought:

An Exploratory Study of the Loyalty and Security Programs," *Yale Law Journal*, Vol. 61, No. 3 (March 1952).

*J. Edgar Hoover Speaks Concerning Communism*, ed. James D. Bales. Nutley, N.J.: Craig Press, 1951.

"J. Edgar Hoover Tells How Communists Operate," *U.S. News & World Report*, Vol. 24, No. 6 (August 11, 1950).

Johnson, Robert N., "The Eisenhower Personnel Security Program," *Journal of Politics*, Vol. 18, No. 4 (November 1956).

Jones, Howard Mumford, ed., *Primer of Intellectual Freedom*. Cambridge, Mass.: Harvard University Press, 1949.

*Joseph R. McCarthy*, ed. Allen J. Matusow. Englewood Cliffs, N.J.: Prentice-Hall, 1970.

"Judge Medina's Charge to the Jury," *Current History*, Vol. 17, No. 99 (November 1949).


Kahn, Albert E., *High Treason: The Plot Against the People*. New York: Lear, 1950.

Kahn, Dorothy, "Abe Goff, Our Chief Censor," *The Reporter*, Vol. 12, No. 10 (May 19, 1955).

Kahn, Gordon, *Hollywood on Trial*. New York: Boni & Gaer, 1948.

Kalven, Harry, Jr., "Congressional Testing of Linus Pauling: The Legal Framework," in *The Atomic Age* (q.v.).

———, "Congressional Testing of Linus Pauling: Sourwine in an Old Bottle," in *The Atomic Age* (q.v.).

Kampelman, Max, *The Communist Party vs. the C.I.O.* New York: Praeger, 1957.

Kanfer, Stefan, *A Journal of the Plague Years*. New York: Atheneum, 1973.

Kempton, Murray, "The Achievement of Harvey Matusow," *The Progressive*, Vol. 19, No. 4 (April 1955).

———, *America Comes of Middle Age, Columns 1950–62*. Boston: Little, Brown, 1963.

———, *Part of Our Time: Some Monuments and Ruins of the Thirties*. New York: Delta, 1967.

———, "Son of Pinkerton," *New York Review of Books*, May 20, 1971.

———, "Truman and the Beast," *New York Review of Books*, March 11, 1971.

Kent, Rockwell, *This Is My Own*. New York: Duell, Sloan & Pearce, 1940.

Kerby, Phil, "The Legion Blacklist," *New Republic*, Vol. 126, No. 24 (June 16, 1952).

Keyes, Scott, "Round Two of the Pechan Bill," *The Nation*, Vol. 173, No. 12 (September 22, 1951).

Knauff, Ellen, *The Ellen Knauff Story*. New York: Norton, 1952.

Komorowski, Conrad, *The Strange Trial of Stanley Novak*. Detroit: Novak Defense Committee, 1954.

Konvitz, Milton, *Bill of Rights Reader: Leading Constitutional Cases*. Ithaca, N.Y.: Cornell University Press, 1965.

———, *Civil Rights in Immigration*. Ithaca, N.Y.: Cornell University Press, 1953.

————, *First Amendment Freedoms: Selected Cases*. Ithaca, N.Y.: Cornell University Press, 1963.

Krchmarek, A., "The Ohio Smith Act Trial," *Political Affairs*, Vol. 35, No. 6 (June 1956).


Lamb, Edward, *No Lamb for Slaughter*. New York: Harcourt, Brace & World, 1963.

*Lamont Case, The: History of a Congressional Investigation*, ed. Philip Wittenberg. New York: Horizon Press, 1957.

Lamont, Corliss, "Conform—Or Lose Your Job," *Monthly Review*, Vol. 7, No. 10 (February 1956).

Lardner, Ring, Jr., "My Life on the Blacklist," *Saturday Evening Post*, Vol. 234, No. 41 (October 14, 1961).

Lasch, Christopher, *The Agony of the American Left*. London: André Deutsch, 1970.

————, *The New Radicalism in America, 1889–1963*. New York: Vintage, 1965.

Latham, Earl, *The Communist Controversy in Washington*. Cambridge, Mass.: Harvard University Press, 1966.

————, ed., *The Meaning of McCarthyism*. Boston: D. C. Heath, 1965.

Lattimore, Owen, *Ordeal by Slander*. London: Macgibbon & Kee, 1952.

————, *The Situation in Asia*. Boston: Little, Brown, 1950.

"Lattimore Case, The: Congressional Investigations and the Constitution," *Northwestern University Law Review*, Vol. 9, No. 1 (March-April 1954).

Lawson, John Howard, "Can Anything Be Done About Hollywood?" *Masses and Mainstream*, Vol. 5, No. 11 (November 1952).

Lazarsfeld, Paul F., and Thielens, Wagner, Jr., *The Academic Mind: Social Scientists in a Time of Crisis*. New York: Free Press of Glencoe, 1958.

"Legislative Control of Loyalty in the School System," *Nebraska Law Review*, Vol. 29 (1950).

Lens, Sidney, *The Crisis of American Labor*. New York: Sagamore Press, 1959.

————, *The Futile Crusade: Anti-Communism as an American Credo*. Chicago: Quadrangle, 1964.

————, *Left, Right & Center: Conflicting Forces in American Labor*. Hinsdale, Ill.: Henry Regnery, 1949.

Lerner, Max, "The Mandarins and the Pariahs," *The American Scholar* (Summer 1949).

*Let Freedom Ring* (Pennsylvania Civil Rights Congress), Vol. 1, No. 1 (November 1953).

Lewis, Sinclair, *Babbitt*. London: Jonathan Cape, 1922.

Liebling, A. J., "The Wayward Press: Spotlight on the Jury," *The New Yorker*, July 23, 1969.

Lipset, Seymour M., "Opinion Formation in a Crisis Situation," *Public Opinion Quarterly*, Vol. 17 (Spring 1953).

————, and Raab, Earl, *The Politics of Unreason: Right-Wing Extremism in America, 1790–1970*. London: Heinemann, 1971.

Lissaman, Doris, "The Taft-Hartley Non-Communist Affidavit Provision," *Labor Law Journal*, Vol. 5 (October 1954).

Longaker, Richard P., *The Presidency and Individual Liberties*. Ithaca, N.Y.: Cornell University Press, 1961.

Lowenstein, Edith, *The Alien and the Immigration Law*. New York: Oceana Publications, 1958.

Lowenthal, Max, *The Federal Bureau of Investigation*. London: Turnstile Press, 1951.

"Loyalty and Private Employment: The Right of Employers to Discharge Suspected Subversives," *Yale Law Journal*, Vol. 62 (1953).

Lubell, Samuel, *The Future of American Politics*. London: Hamish Hamilton, 1952.

——, *Revolt of the Moderates*. New York: Harper, 1956.

Lumer, Hyman, *The Professional Informer*. New York: New Century, 1955.

Lynd, Helen M., "Truth at the University of Washington," *The American Scholar* (Summer 1949).

MacDonald, Dwight, *Henry Wallace: The Man and the Myth*. New York: Vanguard Press, 1948.

MacIver, Robert M., *Academic Freedom in Our Time*. New York: Columbia University Press, 1955.

Manchester, William, "The Case of Luella Mundel," *Harper's Magazine*, Vol. 204 (May 1952).

Markmann, Charles Lam, *The Noblest Cry: A History of the American Civil Liberties Union*. New York: St. Martin's Press, 1965.

Marley, Sheppard, "Trygve Lie: Stalin's Tool in the UN?" *Plain Talk*, Vol. 2, No. 1 (October 1947).

Marzani, Carl, "Thoughts Behind Bars," *Masses and Mainstream*, Vol. 3, No. 7 (July 1950).

Maslow, Will, "Recasting Our Deportation Law: Proposals for Reform," *Columbia Law Review*, Vol. 56, No. 3 (March 1956).

Mather, Kirtley F., "Scientists in the Doghouse," *The Nation*, Vol. 174, No. 26 (June 28, 1952).

Mathews, Jane De Hart, *The Federal Theatre, 1935–1939*. Princeton, N.J.: Princeton University Press, 1967.

Matles, James J., and Higgins, James, *Them and Us: Struggles of a Rank and File Union*. Englewood Cliffs. N.J.: Prentice-Hall, 1974.

Matthews, J. B., "Communism and the Colleges," *American Mercury*, Vol. 76 (May 1953).

——, "Did the Movies Really Clean House?" *American Legion Magazine*, December 1951.

Matusow, Allen J., ed., *Joseph R. McCarthy*. Englewood Cliffs, N.J.: Prentice-Hall, 1970.

Matusow, Harvey, *False Witness*. New York: Cameron & Kahn, 1955.

Maxwell, James A., "Cincinnati's Phantom Reds," *The Reporter*, Vol. 15, No. 7 (September 26, 1956).

Mayer, Henry, "How the Loyalty-Security Program Affects Private Employment," *Lawyers Guild Review*, Vol. 15 (Winter 1955–56).

Mazo, Earl, *Richard Nixon*. New York: Harper & Brothers, 1959.

McCarthy, Joseph R., *America's Retreat from Victory: The Story of George Catlett Marshall*. New York: Devin-Adair, 1952.

———, *McCarthyism: The Fight for America*. New York: Devin-Adair, 1952.

McGrath, Earl James, "Communism and the Schools: The Real Dangers," *School Life*, Vol. 32, No. 5 (February 1950).

McLeod, R. W. Scott, *American Political Democracy and the Problem of Personnel Security*, Publication 6106. Washington, D.C.: Department of State, 1958.

McWilliams, Carey, "The Case of David Hawkins," *The Nation*, Vol. 172, No. 10 (March 10, 1951).

———, "No Reds in Mill Valley," *The Nation*, Vol. 173, No. 1 (July 7, 1951).

———, *Witch Hunt—The Revival of Heresy*. Boston: Little, Brown, 1950.

*Meaning of McCarthyism, The*, ed. Earl Latham. Boston: D. C. Heath, 1965.

Merson, Martin, *The Private Diary of a Public Servant*. New York: Macmillan, 1955.

Miller, Arthur, *After the Fall* (drama). New York: Viking, 1964.

———, *The Crucible* (drama). London: Penguin, 1971.

———, "It Could Happen Here—and Did," *New York Times*, April 30, 1967, Part 2, p. 17.

Miller, Merle, *The Judges and the Judged*. Garden City, N.Y.: Doubleday, 1952.

———, *Plain Speaking: An Oral Biography of Harry S. Truman*. London: Gollancz, 1974.

———, "Trouble on Madison Avenue, N.Y.," *The Nation*, Vol. 174, No. 26 (June 28, 1952).

Millis, Walter, *Individual Freedom and the Common Defense*. New York: The Fund for the Republic, 1957.

Mitchell, Broadus, "How to Traduce Teachers," *The Nation*, Vol. 175, No. 26 (December 27, 1952).

Mitford, Jessica, *A Fine Old Conflict*. London: Michael Joseph, 1977.

Morgan, John A., Jr., "The Supreme Court and the Communist Affidavit," *Labor Law Journal*, Vol. 10 (January 1959).

Morgenthau, Hans J., "The Impact of the Loyalty-Security Measures on the State Department," *Bulletin of the Atomic Scientists*, Vol. 11, No. 4 (April 1955).

Mowitz, Robert J., "Michigan: State and Local Attack on Subversion," in *The States and Subversion* (q.v.).

Murphy, Walter F., *Congress and the Court*. Chicago: University of Chicago Press, 1965.

Murray, Robert K., *Red Scare: A Study in National Hysteria, 1919–1920*. Minneapolis: University of Minnesota Press, 1955.

"Nation and Mr. Brownell's 'Justice,' The," *The Nation*, Vol. 181, No. 4 (July 23, 1955).

Nelson, Steve, *The 13th Juror: The Inside Story of My Trial*, 2nd ed. New York: Masses and Mainstream, 1955.

Nemzer, Louis, "The Soviet Friendship Societies," *Public Opinion Quarterly*, Vol. 13, No. 2 (Summer 1949).
*New American Right, The*, ed. Daniel Bell. New York: Criterion Books, 1955.

O'Brian, John Lord, "Loyalty Tests and Guilt by Association," *Harvard Law Review*, Vol. 61 (1947–48).
——, *National Security and Individual Freedom*. Cambridge, Mass.: Harvard University Press, 1955.
O'Brien, Michael, "The Cedric Parker Case, November 1949," in *The Specter* (q.v.).
Ogden, Raymond A., *The Dies Committee: A Study of the Special House Committee for the Investigation of Un-American Activities, 1938–1944*. Washington, D.C.: Catholic University of America Press, 1945.
Olney, Warren, III, "The Use of Former Communists as Witnesses," *Vital Speeches of the Day*, Vol. 20, No. 21 (August 15, 1954).
*On Intellectuals*, ed. Philip Rieff. New York: Doubleday, 1969.
Oppenheimer, J. Robert, "A Letter to Senator McMahon," *Bulletin of the Atomic Scientists*, Vol. 5, Nos. 6, 7 (June, July 1949).
Orlow, Lena L., "The Immigration and Nationality Act in Operation," *Temple Law Quarterly*, Vol. 29 (Winter 1956).
Oshinsky, David M., "The C.I.O and the Communists," in *The Specter* (q.v.).
Oxnam, G. Bromley, *I Protest*. New York: Harper, 1954.

Packer, Herbert L., *Ex-Communist Witnesses*. Stanford, Calif.: Stanford University Press, 1962.
Palmer, Edward E., ed., *The Communist Problem in America: A Book of Readings*. New York: Thomas Y. Crowell, 1951.
Parsons, Talcott, "Social Strains in America," in *The New American Right* (q.v.).
——, "Social Strains in America: A Postscript," in *The New Radical Right* (q.v.).
Paschell, William, and Theodore, Rose, "Anti-Communist Provisions in Union Constitutions," *Monthly Labor Review*, Vol. 77, No. 10 (October 1954).
" 'Passport Denied.' State Department Practice and Due Process," *Stanford Law Review*, Vol. 3 (February 1951).
"Passport Puzzle, The," *Chicago Law Review*, Vol. 23, No. 2 (Winter 1956).
"Passports for U. S. Reds—Both Sides of Growing Debates," *U. S. News & World Report*, Vol. 45, No. 23 (December 5, 1958).
Paterson, Thomas G., ed., *Cold War Critics: Alternatives to American Foreign Policy in the Truman Years*. Chicago: Quadrangle, 1971.
Patton, James M., "The Pennsylvania Loyalty Act," *University of Pittsburgh Law Review*, Vol. 14, No. 1 (Fall 1952).
Pearson, Drew, *Diaries, 1949–1950*. London: Jonathan Cape, 1974.
Peffer, Nathaniel, "IPR: A Probe in Perspective," *New Republic*, Vol. 127, No. 5 (August 4, 1952).

Petrie, Bernard A., "Reformulation of the Clear and Present Danger," *Michigan Law Review*, Vol. 50 (1952).

Philbrick, Herbert, *I Led 3 Lives*. New York: McGraw-Hill, 1953.

Philby, Kim, *My Silent War*. London: Macgibbon & Kee, 1968.

Pike, Sumner T., "Witch-Hunting Then and Now," *The Atlantic Monthly*, Vol. 180, No. 5 (November 1947).

Pilat, Oliver, "Blacklist," *New York Post*, January 26–31, 1953.

Pitkin, Robert B., "The Movies and the American Legion," *American Legion Magazine*, Vol. 54, No. 5 (May 1953).

Poe, Elizabeth, "The Hollywood Story," *Frontier*, May 1954.

Polanyi, Michael, "Securing a Visa," in *The Atomic Age* (q.v.).

"Policy of Colleges Toward Communist Teachers," *U. S. News & World Report*, Vol. 34, No. 15 (April 10, 1953).

Polites, Bernice, *In Memory of My Father* (leaflet). New York: ACPFB, 1967.

*Politics and Policies of the Truman Administration*, ed. Barton Bernstein. Chicago: Quadrangle, 1970.

Polsby, Nelson, "McCarthyism at the Grass Roots," in *The Meaning of McCarthyism* (q.v.).

Pomerantz, Charlotte, ed., *A Quarter-Century of Un-Americana*. New York: Marzani & Munsell, 1963.

Prendergast, William B., "Maryland: The Ober Anti-Communist Law," in *The States and Subversion* (q.v.).

———, "State Legislatures and Communism: The Current Scene," *American Political Science Review*, Vol. 44, No. 3 (September 1950).

Preston, William, Jr., *Aliens and Dissenters: Federal Suppression of Radicals, 1903–1933*. Cambridge, Mass.: Harvard University Press, 1963.

*Primer of Intellectual Freedom*, ed. Howard Mumford Jones. Cambridge, Mass.: Harvard University Press, 1949.

Pritchett, C. Herman, *Congress versus the Supreme Court, 1957–1960*. Minneapolis: University of Minnesota Press, 1961.

*Public Opinion, 1935–46*, ed. Hadley Cantril. Princeton, N.J.: Princeton University Press, 1951.

*Quarter-Century of Un-Americana, A*, ed. Charlotte Pomerantz. New York: Marzani & Munsell, 1963.

Rabinowitch, Eugene, "The 'Cleansing' of the AEC Fellowships," *Bulletin of the Atomic Scientists*, Vol. 5, Nos. 6, 7 (June, July 1949).

Rader, Melvin, *False Witness*. Seattle: University of Washington Press, 1969.

*Radical Right, The*, ed. Daniel Bell. New York: Doubleday Anchor, 1964.

Rauh, Joseph L., "Informers, G-Men and Free Men," *The Progressive*, Vol. 14, No. 5 (May 1950).

Record, Wilson, *The Negro and the Communist Party*. Chapel Hill, N.C.: University of North Carolina Press, 1951.

*Red Channels: The Report of Communist Influence in Radio and Television*. New York: Counterattack, n.d. (1950).

Redlich, Norman, "Spies in Government: The Bentley Story," *The Nation*, Vol. 178, No. 5 (January 30, 1954).

————, "Spies in Government: The Jenner Report," *The Nation*, Vol. 178, No. 6 (February 6, 1954).

Reeves, Thomas C., *Freedom and the Foundation: The Fund for the Republic in the Era of McCarthyism*. New York, Knopf, 1969.

————, ed., *Foundations under Fire*. Ithaca, N.Y.: Cornell University Press, 1970.

*Report of the Royal Commission to Investigate . . . the Communication, by Public Officials and Other Persons . . . of Secret and Confidential Information to Agents of a Foreign Power*. Ottawa: June 1946.

Reutter, Edmund E., *The School Administrator and Subversive Activities*. New York: Teachers College, Bureau of Publications, 1951.

Rice, Elmer, *Minority Report: An Autobiography*. London: Heinemann, 1963.

Richardson, Elliot L., "Freedom of Expression and the Function of the Courts," *Harvard Law Review*, Vol. 65 (1951).

Richmond, Al, *A Long View from the Left*. Boston: Houghton Mifflin, 1973.

Rieff, Philip, "The Case of Dr. Oppenheimer," in *On Intellectuals* (q.v.).

Riesman, David, *Constraint and Variety in American Education*. Lincoln, Neb.: University of Nebraska Press, 1956.

————, "The Intellectuals and the Discontented Classes: Some Further Reflections," in *The Radical Right* (q.v.).

————, and Glazer, Nathan, "The Intellectuals and the Discontented Classes," in *The New American Right* (q.v.).

*Rights of the Foreign Born* (leaflet). New York: ACPFB, n.d.

Robeson, Paul, *Here I Stand*. London: Dennis Dobson, 1958.

Robinson, Edward G., with Leonard Spigelgass, *All My Yesterdays: An Autobiography*. London: W. H. Allen, 1974.

Rogge, O. John, *Our Vanishing Civil Liberties*. New York: Gaer Associates, 1949.

Rogin, Michael Paul, *The Intellectuals and McCarthy: The Radical Specter*. Cambridge, Mass.: M.I.T. Press, 1967.

"Role of Employer Practices in the Federal Industrial Personnel Security Program, The—A Field Study," *Stanford Law Review*, Vol. 8 (March 1956).

Root, E. Merrill, *Collectivism on the Campus*. New York: Devin-Adair, 1956.

Root, Jonathan, *The Betrayers: The Rosenberg Case*. London: Secker & Warburg, 1963.

Rorty, James, "The Dossier of Wolf Ladejinsky," *Commentary*, Vol. 19, No. 4 (April 1955).

————, and Decter, Moshe, *McCarthy and the Communists*. Boston: Beacon Press, 1954.

————, and Raushenbush, Winifred, "The Lessons of the Peekskill Riots," *Commentary*, Vol. 10, No. 4 (October 1950).

*Rosenberg Letters, The*. London: Dennis Dobson, 1953.

Ross, Lillian, "Onward and Upward with the Arts," *The New Yorker*, February 21, 1948.

Rovere, Richard H., *The American Establishment* (including "The Kept Witnesses"). London: Hart-Davis, 1963.

————, *Senator Joe McCarthy*. New York: Harcourt, Brace, 1959.

Roy, Ralph Lord, *Communism and the Churches*. New York: Harcourt, Brace, 1960.

Rushmore, Howard, "Robert Morris," *American Mercury*, Vol. 76 (March-April 1953).

Saposs, David J., *Communism in American Politics*. Washington, D.C.: Public Affairs Press, 1960.

———, *Communism in American Unions*. New York: McGraw-Hill, 1959.

Scanlan, Alfred Long, "The Communist-Dominated Union Problem," *Notre Dame Lawyer*, Vol. 28, No. 4 (Summer 1953).

Schaar, John H., *Loyalty in America*. Berkeley and Los Angeles: University of California Press, 1957.

Schlesinger, Arthur M., Jr., *The Vital Center: The Politics of Freedom*. London: André Deutsch, 1970.

Schmidt, Karl M., *Henry A. Wallace: Quixotic Crusade, 1948*. Syracuse, N.Y.: Syracuse University Press, 1960.

Schneir, Walter and Miriam, *Invitation to an Inquest*. London: W. H. Allen, 1966.

Scientists Committee on Loyalty and Security, "Fort Monmouth One Year Later," *Bulletin of the Atomic Scientists*, Vol. 11, No. 4 (April 1955).

Scobie, Ingrid W., "Jack B. Tenney and the 'Parasitic Menace': Anti-Communist Legislation in California, 1940–49," *Pacific Historical Review*, Vol. 43, No. 2 (May 1974).

Segal, Benjamin D., and Kornbluh, Joyce L., "The Insecurities of Our Security Program," *The Progressive*, Vol. 21, No. 8 (August 1957).

Seidman, Joel, *Communism in the United States. A Bibliography*. Ithaca, N.Y.: Cornell University Press, 1969.

Seldes, George, *Never Tire of Protesting*. New York: Lyle Stuart, 1968.

Selznick, Philip, *The Organizational Weapon: A Study of Bolshevik Strategy and Tactics*. New York: McGraw-Hill, 1952.

Shannon, David A., *The Decline of American Communism: A History of the Communist Party of the United States Since 1945*. London: Atlantic Books, 1959.

Shannon, William V., *The American Irish*. New York: Macmillan, 1963.

———, "Hollywood Returns to the Stand," *New Republic*, Vol. 124, No. 26 (June 25, 1951).

Sharp, Malcolm P., *Was Justice Done? The Rosenberg-Sobell Case*. New York: Monthly Review Press, 1956.

Shaw, Irwin, *The Troubled Air*. London: Jonathan Cape, 1951.

Shelton, Willard, "Paul Crouch, Informer," *New Republic*, Vol. 131, No. 3 (July 19, 1954).

Shils, Edward, "America's Paper Curtain," in *The Atomic Age* (q.v.).

———, "The Legislator and His Environment," *University of Chicago Law Review*, Vol. 18 (1950–51).

———, *The Torment of Secrecy*. London: Heinemann, 1956.

Small, Melvin, "Buffoons and Brave Hearts: Hollywood Portrays the Russians, 1939–44," *California Historical Quarterly*, Vol. 52 (Winter 1973).

————, "How We Learned to Love the Russians," *The Historian*, Vol. 36 (May 1974).

Smith, Louise Pettibone, *Torch of Liberty: Twenty-five Years in the Life of the Foreign Born in the U.S.* New York: Dwight-King, 1959.

"Some British Experiences," *Bulletin of the Atomic Scientists*, Vol. 8, No. 7 (October 1952).

"Some Individual Cases," *Bulletin of the Atomic Scientists*, Vol. 11, No. 4 (April 1955).

"Some Individual Cases of Clearance Procedures," *Bulletin of the Atomic Scientists*, Vol. 4, No. 9 (September 1948).

Somerville, John, *The Communist Trials and the American Tradition*. New York: Cameron, 1956.

*Specter, The*, Robert Griffith and Athan Theoharis, eds. New York: Franklin Watts, 1974.

Spolansky, Jacob, *The Communist Trail in America*. New York: Macmillan, 1951.

*Spotlight* (Committee to Keep McCarthyism out of Michigan), Vol. 2, No. 1 (March 1955).

Star, Shirley A., "Loyalty Investigations—A Poll of Atomic Scientists," *Bulletin of the Atomic Scientists*, Vol. 14, No. 7 (July 1948).

Starobin, Joseph, *American Communism in Crisis, 1943–1957*. Cambridge, Mass.: Harvard University Press, 1972.

*States and Subversion, The*, ed. Walter Gellhorn. Ithaca, N.Y.: Cornell University Press, 1952.

Stein, Bruno, "Loyalty and Security Cases in Arbitration," *Industrial and Labor Relations Review*, Vol. 17, No. 1 (October 1953).

Steinke, John, and Weinstein, James, "McCarthy and the Liberals," *Studies on the Left*, Vol. 2, No. 3 (1962).

Stern, Philip M., *The Oppenheimer Case: Security on Trial*. London: Hart-Davis, 1971.

Stewart, George R., *The Year of the Oath: The Fight for Academic Freedom at the University of California*. Garden City, N.Y.: Doubleday, 1950.

Stillmans, Edmund, and Pfaff, William, *The Politics of Hysteria*. London: Gollancz, 1964.

Stocker, Joseph, "Father Dunne: A Study in Faith," *The Nation*, Vol. 173, No. 12 (September 22, 1951).

Stone, I. F., "The Army and the 'Reds,' " *The Nation*, Vol. 160, No. 9 (March 3, 1945).

————, *The Best of I. F. Stone's Weekly*. London: Penguin, 1973.

————, *The Truman Era*. London: Turnstile Press, 1953.

Stouffer, Samuel A., *Communism, Conformity and Civil Liberties*. Garden City, N.Y.: Doubleday, 1955.

Straight, Michael, *Trial by Television*. Boston: Beacon Press, 1954.

*Strategy and Tactics of World Communism (Significance of the Matusow Case)*, Report of the Subcommittee to Investigate the Administration of the Internal Security Act and Other Internal Security Laws, 84th Congress, 1st Session, April 6, 1955. Washington, D.C.: Government Printing Office, 1955.

Strauss, Lewis L., *Men and Decisions*. London: Macmillan, 1963.

Stripling, Robert, *The Red Plot Against America*. New York: Bell, 1949.

Suber, Howard, "Hollywood's Political Blacklist," in *The American Cinema* (q.v.).

Subversive Activities Control Board Docket No. 102–53, *Herbert Brownell, Jr., v. Labor Youth League*. Decided February 15, 1955. Report of the Board.

Subversive Activities Control Board Docket No. 104–53, *Herbert Brownell, Jr., v. National Council of American-Soviet Friendship, Inc.*, Hearing, June 3, 1954.

Subversive Activities Control Board Docket No. 109–53, *William P. Rogers v. American Committee for Protection of Foreign Born*, June 27, 1960.

*Supreme Court and Education, The*, ed. David Fellman. New York: Bureau of Publications, Teachers College, 1960.

Sutherland, Arthur E., "British Trials for Disloyal Association During the French Revolution," *Cornell Law Quarterly*, Vol. 34, No. 3 (Spring 1949).

———, "Freedom and Internal Security," *Harvard Law Review*, Vol. 64 (1950–51).

Sykes, Jay G., "The Investigated," *The Progressive*, Vol. 19, No. 4 (April 1955).

———, "Post-McCarthy Delusions of Liberty," *Monthly Review*, Vol. 7, No. 10 (February 1956).

"Symposium on Congressional Hearings and Investigations, A," *Federal Bar Journal*, Vol. 14, Nos. 1, 2 (January-March, 1954; April-June, 1954).

Szilard, Leo, "The AEC Fellowships: Shall We Yield or Fight?" *Bulletin of the Atomic Scientists*, Vol. 5, Nos. 6, 7 (June, July 1949).

Taft, Philip, *Organized Labor in American History*. New York: Harper & Row, 1964.

Tanner, William R., and Griffith, Robert, "The Internal Security Act of 1950," in *The Specter* (q.v.).

Taylor, Harold, "The Dismissal of Fifth Amendment Professors," *The Annals of the American Academy of Political and Social Science*, Vol. 300 (July 1955).

Taylor, Telford, *Grand Inquest: The Story of Congressional Investigations*. New York: Simon and Schuster, 1955.

Theoharis, Athan, "The Escalation of the Loyalty Program," in *Politics and Policies of the Truman Administration* (q.v.).

———, *Seeds of Repression: Harry S. Truman and the Origins of McCarthyism*. Chicago: Quadrangle, 1971.

———, "The Threat to Civil Liberties," in *Cold War Critics: Alternatives to American Foreign Policy in the Truman Years* (q.v.).

*Thirty Years of Treason: Excerpts from Hearings Before the House Committee on Un-American Activities 1938–1968*, ed. Eric Bentley. New York: Viking, 1971.

Thomas, John N., *The Institute of Pacific Relations: Asian Scholars and American Politics*. Seattle: University of Washington Press, 1974.

Trilling, Lionel, *The Liberal Imagination*. London: Secker & Warburg, 1951.

Trow, Martin, "Small Businessmen, Political Tolerance, and Support for McCarthy," *American Journal of Sociology*, Vol. 64 (November 1958).

Truman, David B., *The Congressional Party: A Case Study*. New York: John Wiley, 1959.

Truman, Harry S., *Years of Trial and Hope, 1946–53*. London: Hodder & Stoughton, 1956.

Trumbo, Dalton, "Poems on Parting," *Masses and Mainstream*, Vol. 3, No. 7 (July 1950).

————, *The Time of the Toad: A Study of Inquisition in America*. New York: Harper & Row, 1972.

United States Congress, House of Representatives, 79th Congress, 1st Session, Committee on Immigration and Naturalization, *Hearings*, Washington, D.C., 1945.

United States Congress, Senate, 84th Congress, 2nd Session, Document No. 148, Committee on Government Operations, *Congressional Investigations of Communism and Subversive Activities. Summary Index*, July 25, 1956.

University of Texas Oath or Affirmation required by House Bill No. 21, 53rd Legislature.

Uphaus, Willard, *Commitment*. New York: McGraw-Hill, 1963.

Vaughn, Robert, *Only Victims: A Study of Show Business Blacklisting*. New York: Putnam, 1972.

Viorst, Milton, "The Bitter Tea of Dr. Tsien," *Esquire*, Vol. 78, No. 3 (September 1967).

Wallace, Henry A., *Soviet Asia Mission*. New York: Reynal & Hitchcock, 1946.

Warner, John, "Labor Unions and 'Security Risks,' " *The Reporter*, Vol. 11, No. 1 (July 6, 1954).

Watts, Rowland, *The Draftee and Internal Security*. New York: Workers Defense League, 1955.

Wechsler, James A., *The Age of Suspicion*. New York: Random House, 1953.

————, *Reflections of an Angry Middle-Aged Editor*. New York: Random House, 1960.

Weinstein, Allen, "Agit-Prop and the Rosenbergs," *Commentary*, Vol. 50, No. 1 (July 1970).

————, "The Alger Hiss Case Revisited," *American Scholar*, Winter 1971–72.

Weinstein, Sandra, *Personnel Security Programs of the Federal Government*. New York: Fund for the Republic, 1954.

Weisskopf, Victor, "Report on the Visa Situation," *Bulletin of the Atomic Scientists*, Vol. 8, No. 7 (October 1952).

Weissman, David L., "Sacher and Isserman in the Courts: Note II," *Lawyers Guild Review*, Vol. 14 (1954).

————, "The Proceedings to Disbar Leo Sheiner," *Lawyers Guild Review*, Vol. 16 (Winter 1956).

*We Need a Statute of Limitations*. New York: ACPFB, n.d.

Westin, Alan F., "Anti-Communism & the Corporations," *Commentary*, Vol. 36 (December 1963).

———, *The Constitution and Loyalty Programs*. New York: Carrie Chapman Catt Memorial Fund, 1954.

Wexley, John, *The Judgment of Julius and Ethel Rosenberg*. London: Bookville, 1956.

Weyl, Nathaniel, *Treason: The Story of Disloyalty and Betrayal in American History*. Washington, D.C.: Public Affairs Press, 1950.

"What Grand Jury Found in U.N.: Text of Presentment," *U.S News & World Report*, Vol. 33, No. 24 (December 12, 1952).

White, Nathan I., *Harry D. White—Loyal American*. Waban, Mass.: Bessie (White) Bloom, 1956.

White, Theodore H., *Fire in the Ashes: Europe in Mid-Century*. London: Cassell, 1954.

Whitehead, Don, *The FBI Story*. London: Muller, 1957.

"Who Will Stand Up to McCarthy?" *New Republic*, Vol. 128, No. 2 (January 12, 1953).

Wilcox, Clair, ed., *Civil Liberties under Attack*. Philadelphia: University of Pennsylvania Press, 1951.

*WIN*, Vol. 8, Nos. 4, 5 (March 1972), Box 547, Rifton, N.Y. 12471.

Winter, Ella, *And Not to Yield*. New York: Harcourt, Brace & World, 1963.

Wirin, A. L., and Rosenwein, Sam, "The Smith Act Prosecutions," *The Nation*, Vol. 177, No. 24 (December 12, 1953).

Wittenberg, Philip, ed., *The Lamont Case: History of a Congressional Investigation*. New York; Horizon Press, 1957.

Wormser, René A., "Foundations: Their Power and Influence," in *Foundations Under Fire* (q.v.).

Wrong, Dennis H., "Theories of McCarthyism—A Survey," *Dissent*, Vol. 1, No. 4 (Autumn 1954).

Wyzanski, Charles E., Jr., "The Communist Party and the Law," *The Atlantic Monthly*, Vol. 187, No. 5 (May 1951).


Yarmolinsky, Adam, *Case Studies in Personnel Security*. Washington, D.C.: Bureau of Internal Affairs, 1955.

———, "How a Lawyer Conducts a Security Case," *The Reporter*, Vol. 10, No. 5 (March 2, 1954).

Yarnell, Allen, *Democrats and Progressives: The 1948 Presidential Election as a Test of Postwar Liberalism*. Los Angeles: University of California Press, 1974.

Younger, Irving, "Was Alger Hiss Guilty?" *Commentary*, Vol. 60, No. 2 (August 1975).


Zitron, Celia L., *The New York City Teachers Union, 1916–1964*. New York: Humanities Press, 1968.

———, "Teachers Under Fire," *Masses and Mainstream*, Vol. 5, No. 4 (April 1952).

## Motion Pictures

*Action in the North Atlantic*. Directed by Lloyd Bacon, script by John Howard Lawson, 1943.

*Crossfire*. Directed by Edward Dmytryk, script by John Paxton, produced by Adrian Scott, RKO/Dore Schary, 1947.

*Days of Glory*. Directed by Jacques Tourneur, script by Casey Robinson, produced by Casey Robinson, RKO, 1944.

*Hitler's Children*. Directed by Edward Dmytryk, script by Emmet Lavery, produced by Edward A. Golden, RKO Radio, 1943.

*Hollywood on Trial*. BBC TV film, November 4, 1973, written and directed by Tristram Powell, research by Ann Bluber, executive producer Mike Wooler.

*Millhouse*. Directed by Emile de Antonio.

*Mission to Moscow*. Directed by Michael Curtiz, script by Howard Koch, Warner Brothers, 1943.

*Point of Order*. Directed by Emile de Antonio, 1971.

*Salt of the Earth*. Directed by Herbert J. Biberman, script by Michael Wilson, produced by Paul Jarrico, Independent Productions Corporation, 1954.

# Index

## About the Author

David Caute's books include *The Fellow-Travellers, Communism and the French Intellectuals, Frantz Fanon* and *The Left in Europe Since 1789*. He also writes novels, plays and criticism. From 1959 to 1965 he was a Fellow of All Souls College, Oxford, subsequently was appointed Visiting Professor at New York and Columbia universities, and then Reader in Political Theory at Brunel University. Since 1970 he has devoted himself full time to writing. He is a member of the executive council of the Writers' Guild of Great Britain. He lives in London.